A. L. Campbell.
Paisley
11/2/43

THE LIFE AND TIMES OF ST. LEO THE GREAT

THE LIFE AND TIMES OF ST. LEO THE GREAT

BY

TREVOR JALLAND, M.A., B.D.

Published for the Church Historical Society

LONDON
SOCIETY FOR PROMOTING
CHRISTIAN KNOWLEDGE
NORTHUMBERLAND AVENUE, W.C. 2
NEW YORK: THE MACMILLAN COMPANY
1941

Made in Great Britain

CONTENTS

INTRODUCTION

AMONG the many distinguished occupants of the Roman See few are better known to English students of Christian Doctrine and Church History than Leo I, commonly called "the Great." Yet hitherto, apart from a number of French and German monographs, they have been largely dependent on incidental notices and references contained in works of a more general character. Dr. Bright has provided us with a selection of Leo's *Sermons on the Incarnation,* and Dr. Gore has given us a sketch of his life in the series *The Fathers for English Readers,* but neither of these is sufficient to do justice to his importance in relation to the history of the Church as a whole.

The Vatican Constitution of 1870, *De Ecclesia Christi,* assigns a twofold Primacy to the Roman See, one of Jurisdiction and one of Doctrine. It may perhaps be admitted that it is not till the appearance of the Fourth Tractate of Gelasius I that we find a clear and unequivocal assertion of the former. Yet it is beyond any possibility of doubt that we owe to Leo I the earliest affirmation of the Doctrinal Primacy, an affirmation which was widely accepted or conceded by churches in the East as well as in the West. The fact that certain subsequent occupants of the Roman See did much to undermine the grandeur of Leo's conception of the office of the Papacy affects in no way this simple fact of history.

It is hoped that the present study may be useful, not only to the student of Papal History in particular, but to the more general reader, and by making use of much recent investigation of the problems involved in the consideration of this period, may give not only a more accurate picture than has hitherto been available of the life and work of this great Christian bishop against the background of contemporary history, but may serve to bring into clearer relief the outstanding features of a noble character.

In the preparation of this work, which has been much delayed by preoccupation with pastoral duty, the present writer has been under considerable obligation to a number of distinguished scholars and authorities, among whom he would particularly wish to thank Dr. Darwell Stone, formerly Principal of Pusey House, for his goodness in finding time to read the work in manuscript, and for supplying a number of valuable suggestions; Fr. Thornton, C.R., author of *The Incarnate Lord,* for his help with the chapter on St. Leo's Theology, and Dr. Lowther Clarke, Editorial Secretary to the S.P.C.K., for his patience in difficulties connected with the manuscript. Among current works he has been specially indebted to Erich Caspar's monumental *Geschichte des Papsttums,* invaluable for its detailed accuracy and copious references to modern works and articles, and in more than one respect to the Master of Pembroke's recent life of *St. Ambrose,* a debt which he desires to acknowledge with real gratitude. Finally he would wish to express his deep appreciation of the kindness shown by Miss B. M. Hamilton Thompson, Vice-Principal of St. Mary's College, Durham, in making opportunity amid the special distractions of war to construct a comprehensive and exhaustive index, and of the help given by Mr. J. E. Taylor of St. Stephen's House, Oxford, in checking a large number of references.

At a time when the world is distracted by strife, it is of the utmost importance that those who have a vocation to theological study should devote themselves to whatever may serve to promote the peace and unity of the Catholic Church. The present writer ventures to hope that by throwing new light on a significant period of Church History and by delineating afresh the portrait of a great pastor, teacher and administrator, to whom that ideal was dear above all else, he may have contributed something to its realization.

TREVOR JALLAND

Oxford

Vigil of St. Thomas the Apostle, 1940

CHAPTER I

THE ROMAN EMPIRE IN THE FIFTH CENTURY

THE earlier half of the fifth century of our era, which coincides with the lifetime of Leo, may be characterized pre-eminently as an age of transition. In some respects it is true that the process had already begun long before the fourth century had come to an end, yet in the century which followed, its pace was accelerated with amazing rapidity. It was a transition so far as the West was concerned from a world state, the *Imperium Romanum,* to separate national polities, from a civilization in which Graeco-Roman culture was predominant to one in which the ideas and outlook of the Teutonic tribes took the first place. Yet however much we may regret the passing of an order, for which we may claim with justice that it upheld an ideal and a system of law and organization without parallel elsewhere, it is impossible to regard the consequences of its disappearance as altogether disastrous. Even men who were witnesses of those changes were able to appreciate the possibility that they might effect some general moral improvement, and some, like Salvian, went so far as to suggest that the new masters of Western Europe provided better examples of the natural virtues than the Romans themselves:

"(In the Empire)," he writes, "the poor were plundered, the widows in misery, the orphans trampled under foot, so that many of them, and those of high birth and liberal education, fled to the enemy, lest they should fall victims of imperial persecution. Among the barbarians they sought Roman humanity, because they could not endure barbarian inhumanity among the Romans. And though they differed from those, to whom they fled, in manners and speech, and were repelled, so to speak, by the smell of the barbarians' bodies and of their clothes, yet they preferred to put up with different ways among the barbarians than with the injustice which is in fashion among the Romans." [1]

[1] *De gubernatione Dei,* V, 5. *P.L.* 53, 99.

But from Leo's point of view the Roman Empire, like the Roman see, was a divine institution, formed by the providence of God for the express purpose of promoting the spread of the Christian Gospel. Hence in speaking of the condescension of God in the Incarnation of His Son he says: "That the consequences of this unspeakable generosity might be made known throughout the whole world, divine providence fashioned the Roman Empire; the growth of which was extended to boundaries so wide that all races everywhere became next-door neighbours. For it was particularly germane to the divine scheme that many kingdoms should be bound together under a single government, and the world-wide preaching should have a swift means of access to all peoples, over whom the rule of a single state held sway."[2]

To him it must have seemed almost unthinkable that the Empire, as he knew it, should ever cease to exist. Yet by the time of his election the sands were fast running out and within two decades of his death the last ruler of the West, who might be regarded as a legitimate successor of Augustus, had passed into oblivion.[3]

At the time of Leo's birth it is possible that Theodosius I was still alive.[4] Theodosius had done much to restore to the prestige of the Roman name the losses which it had suffered as a consequence of the defeat and death of the Emperor Valens on the field of Adrianople [5] at the hands of the Goths. Following this defeat he reformed the diminished Roman forces, largely by means of recruits drawn from among the Goths themselves, and after establishing his base of operations at Thessalonica inflicted a number of comparatively severe defeats on the enemy. The presence of native or even of

[2] *Serm.* 82, 2. *P.L.* 54, 423. "Ut autem huius inerrabilis gratiae per totum mundum effunderentur effectus, Romanum regnum divina providentia praeparavit; cuius ad eos limites incrementa producta sunt, quibus cunctarum undique gentium vicina et contigua esset universitas."

[3] Julius Nepos, the last legitimate Emperor of the West, who died A.D. 480. *Consularia Italica.* *M.G.H.*, Auct. antiqu., Vol. IX, *Chron. min.*, Vol. I, pp. 310ff.

[4] The date of Leo's birth cannot be determined with certainty, but it is likely that it took place in the last decade of the fourth century. See Chap. II.

[5] A.D. 378. *Consularia Constantinopolitana,* sub ann. *M.G.H.*, Auct. antiqu., Vol. IX, *Chron. min.*, Vol. I, p. 243.

barbarian elements in the Roman armies was not in itself a novelty. The chief innovation for which Theodosius was responsible lay in the assignment of the highest positions, both in the military and in the civil service of the empire, to men whose names alone were enough to betray their barbarian origin. Such men were Arbogast and Stilicho. From this time on Gothic or other barbarian commanders played an increasingly important part in imperial politics. Stilicho, who was a Vandal by origin, enjoyed a peculiarly high place in the Emperor's confidence and it was said that it was to him that Theodosius had commended his two youthful sons, Honorius and Arcadius, on his death-bed.†

Honorius had been proclaimed Augustus by his father two years previously, so that when Theodosius died on January 17th, A.D. 395,[6] no difficulty arose regarding the question of succession.[7] Equally Arcadius had already reigned for the past twelve years as co-regent at Constantinople.[8] Arcadius was now in his seventeenth or eighteenth year, while his brother was but a child of ten years. But in any case neither of them had shown any promise that he would be fit to govern an empire.

The effective masters of the Roman world at this time were, in the West Stilicho, in the East Rufinus. Rufinus had ruled at Constantinople as Theodosius' vicegerent since A.D. 394[9] and was probably aiming at sharing the principate with the new Emperor. The first blow to his ambition was the marriage of Arcadius, not to his own daughter, but to Eudoxia, who had been selected as the imperial bride by the court Chamberlain, the eunuch Eutropius.[10]

Presently, however, Rufinus came into collision with Stilicho. While it is highly probable that his character has been blackened by the admirers of his rival, it is clear that

† Zosimus, *Historia nova,* 5, 34, 6.

[6] *Consularia Constantinopolitana. M.G.H.,* Auct. antiqu., Vol. IX, *Chron. min.,* Vol. I, p. 298. Socrates, *H.E.,* 5, 26. *Consularia Italica, M.G.H., ibid.,* p. 298 gives January 1st, A.D. 396.

[7] Ambrose, *De obitu Theod.* 5.

[8] *Consularia Constantinopolitana,* sub ann. 383, *ibid.,* p. 244.

[9] Rufinus had been appointed Prefect of the East in the later part of A.D. 392. *Cod. Theod.,* XII, i, 129, ed. Mommsen-Meyer, Vol. I, p. 694.

[10] Marcellinus, *Chronicon. M.G.H.,* Auct. antiqu., Vol. XI. *Chron. min.,* Vol. II, p. 64. Zosimus, *Historia nova,* 5, 3.

he was ambitious and not highly scrupulous as to the means by which he accomplished his purposes. Stilicho, on the other hand, though equally ambitious, appears to have been devoted to the cause of the Empire as a whole, and it is this devotion which goes far to account for the attitude which he adopted towards the government of Constantinople, to whose policy he was vigorously opposed. The immediate cause of the collision between these two statesmen was a rebellion of the Visigoths.[11] They had been settled in the province of Lower Moesia by Theodosius, and found in Alaric, who now appears on the stage of history for the first time, a competent leader both in diplomacy and war. Alaric at once marched on Constantinople, but was persuaded by Rufinus to withdraw. He then turned aside to ravage the prefecture of Eastern Illyricum. Meanwhile Stilicho was hastening eastwards in command not only of the western legions but also of the eastern forces, who had been taking part in Theodosius' campaigns against the usurper Eugenius.[12] Possibly it was Stilicho's intention to claim for Honorius authority over the prefecture, and thus restore the boundaries of western jurisdiction as they had been before A.D. 379, when the dioceses of Dacia and Macedonia had been entrusted by Gratian to Theodosius.[13] Rufinus, however, succeeded in persuading Arcadius peremptorily to order the withdrawal of the western armies by Stilicho and to insist on the restoration of his own troops.[14] Resigning the command of the eastern section of his army to the Goth Gaïnas, Stilicho obeyed, thereby leaving Illyricum to the mercy of Alaric.[15] Gaïnas pushed on to Constantinople and on his arrival procured the assassination of Rufinus.[16] Probability suggests that this deed was perpetrated in fulfilment of a compact made on the eve of Stilicho's departure from the East.[17]

[11] This and subsequent events are described by Claudian, *In Rufin.*, II, 7–100. Zosimus, *op. cit.*, 5, 5. Jordanes, *De Rebus Geticis*, 29. *M.G.H.*, Auct. antiqu., Vol. V, 1, pp. 96f. Marcellinus, *Chronicon*, sub ann., 395. *M.G.H.*, Auct. antiqu., Vol. XI. *Chron. min.*, Vol. II, p. 64.
[12] Claudian, *op. cit.*, II, 101–6.
[13] Sozomen, *H.E.*, 7, 4.
[14] Claudian, *op. cit.*, II, 195ff.
[15] Id. *op. cit.*, II, 130–70.
[16] Id. *op. cit.*, II, 366–439.
[17] Zosimus, *op. cit.*, 5, 7. Philostorgius, *H.E.*, 11, 3.

The eunuch Eutropius now became the effective ruler of the East. Meanwhile, after a second expedition against Alaric, of which little is known except that it left him at liberty to accept an offer from Arcadius of the office of *Magister militum* in Illyricum,[18] Stilicho returned to deal with the revolt of Gildo in Africa. The campaign, which occupied the latter part of the year A.D. 397 and most of A.D. 398, was entirely successful,[19] and as a result his influence in imperial politics now reached its zenith. His former lieutenant, Gaïnas, was appointed *Magister militum* at Constantinople and, after procuring the fall of Eutropius,[20] made himself master of the city. This was in the year A.D. 400, a year which is notable for the fact that at least for a short time the whole empire was at the disposal of a Vandal and a Goth. Gaïnas' triumph, however, was short-lived and towards the end of the year he was killed in a campaign against the Huns north of the Danube.[21]

With the first year of the new century began a period of invasion of the western provinces, such as the East had suffered for the past quarter of a century. It seems that Alaric, after taking every advantage of his position as *Magister militum* in Illyricum during recent years, thought the moment had now come to attack the dominions of Honorius. Towards the end of A.D. 401 Alaric crossed the Alps and took by storm the city of Aquileia.[22] Stilicho was occupied at the time in repelling an attack launched by the Vandals on Noricum and Rhaetia. After checking the invaders he returned to Italy and, following an indecisive battle at Pollentia (Pollenzo), persuaded the Goths to withdraw.[23] In spite of this, however, Alaric carried out a fresh invasion in the early summer of A.D. 403. Once more he was obliged to abandon his project. Yet the fact that no steps were taken to inflict a decisive defeat on the invaders

[18] Claudian, *De Bello Goth.*, 535–9; *In Eutrop.* II, 216.
[19] Id., *De Bello Gildon.*; *De cons. Stilich.*, I.
[20] The tyranny of the Goths at Constantinople is described by Synesius, *De Providentia*; Zosimus, *op. cit.*, 5, 19; Philostorgius, *H.E.*, 11, 8; Socrates, *H.E.*, 6, 6; Sozomen, *H.E.*, 8, 4.
[21] Marcellinus, *Chronicon*. *M.G.H.*, Vol. XI. *Chron. min.*, Vol. II, p. 66.
[22] *Consularia Italica*. *M.G.H.*, Auct. antiqu., Vol. IX. *Chron. min.*, Vol. I, p. 299.
[23] Orosius, *Adv. pagan.*, 7, 37, 2. *C.S.E.L.*, Vol. V, p. 537.

unmistakably suggests that Stilicho was temporizing with them, and ready to make use of them to serve his own ends. Towards the end of the previous year the Emperor Honorius had transferred his residence from Milan to Ravenna, which henceforth, apart from some short intervals spent in Rome, became his permanent residence.

A short period of respite followed, which lasted till the latter part of A.D. 405. In that year a large body of Ostrogoths overran the northern provinces of Italy, only to be defeated in the following year by Stilicho near Florence. Their leader Radagaisus was captured in this battle and put to death immediately.[24] In the following year Alaric once again led out his troops, but this time instead of crossing the Alps he encamped in the province of Noricum and demanded payment from Rome for his support of Honorius. At Stilicho's suggestion the payment was made, a huge sum amounting to £180,000 according to modern values.[25] It was the beginning of the Vandal's undoing. He was already heartily detested by the old Roman nobility, and Honorius was beginning to suspect that the loyalty of his Gothic army was open to doubt. While the Emperor was on his way back to Ravenna the news was brought that his brother Arcadius was dead.[26] Stilicho now proposed that in order to protect the interests of the new Emperor Theodosius II, still but a child, he should be commissioned to proceed to Constantinople. This was too much for his enemies. After poisoning the ears of Honorius by leading him to suppose that Stilicho was plotting treason on his own account, as soon as the Vandal reached Ravenna they caused him to be arrested and summarily put to death.[27] Stilicho's temporizing policy in regard to Alaric and his provocative attitude towards the

[24] (August 23rd, A.D. 406.) *Consularia Italica. M.G.H.*, Auct. antiqu., Vol. IX. *Chron. min.*, Vol. I, p. 299. Cf. Seeck, *Gesch. des Unterg. d. ant. Welt.*, Vol. V, p. 587.

[25] This estimate is the one supplied by Bury, *History of the Later Roman Empire*, Vol. I, p. 170.

[26] Zosimus, *Historia nova*, 5, 31, 1.

[27] His execution took place on August 22nd, A.D. 408. *Consularia Italica. M.G.H.*, Auct. antiqu., Vol. IX. *Chron. min.*, Vol. I, p. 300. Zosimus, *op. cit.*, 5, 34, 7. For the "nationalist" revolution which brought about his fall, cf. *Chron. min.*, Vol. I, *ibid.*; Zosimus, *op. cit.*, 5, 32.

government at Constantinople may perhaps justify some doubt as to his inner loyalty to the Roman State; nevertheless his character as a whole compares favourably with that of his imperial master. With his death co-operation between the two halves of the Empire was resumed, but already the mischief arising from the mutual hostility engendered by Stilicho's behaviour had been done. The path of Alaric to Rome lay open at last.

The king of the Visigoths now entered Italy for the third time.[28] His march was in an almost direct line towards Rome, to which he at once laid siege. Hard pressed by hunger and plague the Senate found itself obliged to accept the humiliating terms imposed on the city by the invader.[29] The conditions included the delivery into the hands of the enemy of a vast treasure and the giving of an assurance that pressure would be brought to bear on Honorius to conclude with their leader a favourable agreement. By the beginning of the year A.D. 409 nothing had been done and a further embassy was despatched to Ravenna, which included among its members the reigning pope, Innocent I.[30] It was suggested by others that the Emperor should create Alaric *Magister utriusque militiae,* and when this proposal was indignantly rejected the Goths prepared once more to march on Rome.[31] A second time the Gothic army invested the city. This time resistance was brief and, after making himself master of the Portus, Alaric proclaimed Attalus, hitherto *Praefectus urbi,* as Augustus.[32] The news caused considerable consternation in Ravenna and it seemed likely that Honorius would take to flight. But before long a rift appeared in the relations between the Goth and his newly created Emperor,[33] and by arrangement with Honorius Attalus was deposed.[34]

On approaching Ravenna Alaric found himself attacked,

[28] Seeck, *op. cit.,* Vol. V, p. 391.

[29] Zosimus, *op. cit.,* 5, 44 mentions an embassy to Ravenna on this affair.

[30] Id. *ibid.,* 5, 45.

[31] We learn from Orosius, *Historia,* 7, 39, that Innocent remained at Ravenna till after the death of Alaric.

[32] Seeck, *op. cit.,* Vol. V, p. 596.

[33] The cause of dissension between Attalus and Alaric arose concerning the policy to be adopted in regard to the usurpation of Heraclian in Africa. Seeck, *op. cit.,* Vol. V, p. 410.

[34] *Ibid.,* p. 412.

in spite of a truce, by a substantial force under the command of Sarus the Visigoth, who had been a friend of Stilicho. The king withdrew at once and for the third time marched on Rome. After effecting an entry into the city on August 24th, A.D. 410 he allowed his soldiers to plunder it at will. A number of important buildings were destroyed by fire but most of the churches were spared.[35] Among the numerous captives taken was Galla Placidia, the sister of Honorius. After the sack Alaric marched southwards, intending to seize the rich provinces of Africa, but while his fleet was being prepared in the latter part of the year he was overtaken by death.[36] He was succeeded as king by his brother-in-law, Athaulf, who withdrew the Gothic army from Italy, plundering the Italian provinces on his way, and entered Gaul.[37]

In the same year (A.D. 406) that Radagaisus invaded Italy, the Vandals, Suevians and Alans crossed the Rhine near Moguntiacum (Mainz) and poured into Gaul.[38] They encountered little resistance, for in that year many of the western legions had been withdrawn by Stilicho for the defence of Italy. The only forces now opposed to them were those of the Franks, but their numbers were inadequate to stem the onrush and within a few months northern and western Gaul were in the power of the invaders. A temporary diversion was caused in the following year by the arrival of Roman legions from Britain, under the leadership of Constantine, whom the soldiers had recently proclaimed Emperor there.[39] By skilful leadership and diplomacy the new rival to Honorius obtained control of eastern Gaul, including the imperial city of Trêves. Presently Arles and the southern provinces fell into his hands. Honorius was powerless to resist the usurper, and in the year A.D. 408 Constantine obtained in addition control of the greater part of Spain.[40] His next move was to obtain recognition from Ravenna as Augustus, a

[35] Prosper, *Chronicon*, sub ann. 410. *M.G.H.*, Auct. antiqu., Vol. IX, *Chron. min.*, Vol. I, p. 466. Theophanes, *Chronog.*, 5903. *P.G.* 108, 224. Seeck, *op. cit.*, Vol. V, pp. 413f., 599.

[36] Jordanes, *De Rebus Geticis*, 30.

[37] *Chron. Gall.*, 67. *M.G.H.*, Auct. antiqu., Vol. IX, p. 654.

[38] *Consularia Italica*. *M.G.H.*, Auct. antiqu., Vol. IX. *Chron. min.*, Vol. I, p. 299. Prosper, *Chronicon*. *M.G.H.*, Vol. IX, p. 465.

[39] Seeck, *op. cit.*, Vol. V, pp. 378, 590.

[40] Zosimus, *op. cit.*, 6, 4.

request which was granted with some reluctance and repudiated soon afterwards. It was even agreed that he should assist Honorius to destroy Alaric. Meanwhile the German tribes who had been harassing western Gaul crossed the Pyrenees into Spain.[41] Now that Alaric was dead, however, the Emperor was able to attend to the task of recovering the provinces which had been seized by Constantine, and for this purpose an army under the Illyrian general Constantius, who had recently been raised to the position of *Magister utriusque militiae,* was sent over from Italy into Gaul.[42] The supporters of the legitimate Emperor had little difficulty in overcoming the troops of various rivals and laid siege to Arles. Constantine surrendered and, in spite of the promises which had been made that his life would be spared, was put to death near Ravenna (September, A.D. 411).[43]

The Goths who had elected Athaulf as their king, and had now entered Gaul, came to terms with Honorius and, as his supporters, defeated and put to death Jovinus, a recently elevated usurper.[44] Meanwhile Constantius was engaged in protecting Italy from an invasion threatened by Heraclian, another tyrant who had arisen in Africa. But the support given by Athaulf to Honorius was short-lived, and in the course of A.D. 415 Constantius marched against him and succeeded in driving him into Spain.[45] A few months later the king of the Visigoths fell a victim to an assassin's dagger and Wallia was elected to fill his place.[46]

At the beginning of A.D. 417 Honorius entered on his eleventh consulship and celebrated his triumph in Rome.[47] By agreement with Wallia the Empress Placidia, who for some years had been the wife of Athaulf, was now sent back to Italy and thus became the wife of Constantius.[48] In the

[41] Idatius, *Chronicon. M.G.H.,* Auct. antiqu., Vol. XI. *Chron. min.,* Vol. II, p. 17.

[42] Prosper, *Chronicon,* sub ann. 411. *M.G.H.,* Auct. antiqu., Vol. IX. *Chron. min.,* Vol. I, p. 466.

[43] *Consularia Italica. M.G.H.,* Vol. IX. *Chron. min.,* Vol. I, p. 246.

[44] Bury, *op. cit.,* Vol. I, p. 195.

[45] Athaulf had compelled Placidia to marry him shortly before this. Olympiodorus, *Fragm.* 24. *Fragm. Hist. Graec.,* Vol. IV, p. 62.

[46] Marcellinus, *Chronicon. M.G.H.,* Vol. XI. *Chron. min.,* Vol. II, p. 72. Prosper, *Chronicon, M.G.H.,* Vol. IX. *Chron. min.,* Vol. I, p. 467.

[47] Seeck, *Regesten,* p. 334.

[48] Olympiodorus, *Fragm.* 34. *Ibid.,* p. 65.

same year Wallia subdued various German tribes who had invaded Spain and in return was given a permanent home for his Visigothic followers in the province of *Aquitania Secunda*.[49] His successor Theoderic I who took his place in the following year[50] occupied the early years of his reign in adjusting the relation between his followers and the settled Roman population in regard to the ownership of property. The frequent changes which had taken place in Gaul during the past decade had made some political reorganization of those provinces which still remained in Roman hands urgently necessary. Trêves, since its capture by the Franks in A.D. 412, had already ceased to be a centre of administration, and now its replacement by Arles was officially recognized.[51]

A son was born to Constantius and Placidia on July 2nd, A.D. 419, to whom the name Valentinian was given.[52] Two years later his father was acknowledged as a colleague in the principate by Honorius,[53] but he only lived eight months longer to enjoy the honour.[54] Meanwhile a new divergence of policy had taken place between the western and eastern governments; this time it concerned the authority of the see of Constantinople in Eastern Illyricum.[55] At the request of the reigning pope, Boniface I, a protest was addressed by Honorius to his imperial nephew,[56] and an assurance was received that the offending edict would be withdrawn.[57] Two years later Honorius died a natural death at Ravenna.[58]

The obvious successor to the vacant western throne was the child Valentinian, but as for the past few months he and his mother Placidia had been residing at Constantinople,[59] the death of his uncle provided an obvious opportunity for the advancement of a rival claimant. Possibly Theodosius II who,

[49] Bury, *op. cit.*, Vol. I, p. 204.
[50] Id. *ibid.*, p. 205.
[51] *M.G.H.*, *Epp.*, Vol. III, *Epp. Merov.*, Vol. I, p. 13.
[52] Seeck, *op. cit.*, Vol. VI, p. 64.
[53] Theophanes, *Chronog.*, 5913. *P.G.* 108, 229.
[54] *Ibid.*
[55] *Cod. Theod.*, XVI, 2, 45, ed. Mommsen-Meyer, Vol. I, p. 852.
[56] *P.L.*, 20, 769.
[57] *Inter Bonif. Epp.*, No. 11. *P.L.* 20, 770.
[58] Socrates, *H.E.*, 7, 22, 20; Theophanes, *Chronog.*, 5915; *Chron. Gall.* *M.G.H.*, Vol. IX. *Chron. min.*, Vol. I, p. 658.
[59] Prosper, *Chronicon*, sub ann. 423. *M.G.H.*, *Chron. min.*, Vol. I, p. 470.

as we have seen, had succeeded his father Arcadius at Constantinople, was contemplating the possibility of asserting his authority over the western provinces and thus uniting in his hands the whole of the Empire. But his plans were forestalled by the elevation of John, the head of the governmental secretariat, to the principate.[60]

It is at this juncture that a new figure in imperial politics, in the person of Aetius comes to the fore. Aetius at this time was about thirty-three years of age and had spent a considerable part of his earlier years as a hostage with the Huns.[61] The latter formed a loose federation of Asiatic tribes living to the north of the Danube, and had hitherto only indirectly caused trouble to the Empire by reason of the pressure which they exercised on their Gothic neighbours. Yet it had had the effect of causing the Teutonic migrations already mentioned.[62] The Huns were also a fertile source from which the Roman armies since the time of Stilicho had been recruited. No sooner had John been proclaimed at Ravenna than an unexpected contestant of his claim arose in Africa. The challenge was presented by Count Boniface, who declared himself a supporter of Valentinian and his mother.[63] So while John's forces were engaged in dealing with this sudden *démarche*, the usurper fell an easy victim to the army despatched by Theodosius to the support of his nephew, and was put to death by Placidia's order at Aquileia.[64] The opening of the new reign was marked by the abandonment of that hostility which had characterized the relations between the two imperial governments, both in the days of Stilicho and in those of Constantius.

It was fortunate for the young Emperor that his government was successful in coming to terms with Aetius. It awarded him the title of *Comes* and after appointing him to a military command in Gaul persuaded him to leave

[60] *Ibid.*
[61] Bury, *op. cit.*, Vol. I, p. 223.
[62] For details regarding the Huns see Bury, *History of the Later Roman Empire*, Vol. I, Chap IX. *Cambridge Mediæval History*, Vol. I, pp. 360–6.
[63] Bury, *op. cit.*, Vol. I, p. 223.
[64] Seeck, *op. cit.*, Vol. VI, p. 95.

Placidia and her son to enjoy the fruits of their success.[65] Meanwhile a new crisis was approaching in Africa. Count Boniface on being called to account for misgovernment prepared to resist, and invited to his aid the Vandal tribes who, under Gaiseric, had succeeded in establishing themselves in Spain.[66] In the spring of A.D. 429 Gaiseric crossed the sea and proceeded to occupy the Roman province of Mauretania.[67] But it soon became clear that the Vandals had come not as allies but as conquerors, and the imperial and rebel forces united to repel their attacks. Unfortunately the mischief was already done, and Gaiseric, after defeating the attempts to dislodge him made by Boniface and later by the troops sent from Constantinople under Aspar, had little difficulty in making himself master of the rich province of *Africa proconsularis*.[68]

Meanwhile Boniface was recalled by Placidia to Italy in order to counteract the growing influence of Aetius.[69] The latter, since his departure from Italy, had restored Roman authority in a considerable part of Gaul and had even vindicated it in Rhaetia and Noricum as well.[70] After procuring the murder of the Patrician, Felix, his chief opponent at Ravenna, he became *Magister utriusque militiae* and consul for the year A.D. 432.[71]

Alarmed by the rapid success of her commander, Placidia dismissed him from office and appointed Boniface in his place. In the struggle which followed it is probable that, at least for the time being, Boniface was the victor. A decisive battle was fought near Ariminum (Rimini), but Boniface did not long survive his success.[72] In the following year Aetius

[65] Prosper, *Chronicon,* sub ann. 425. *M.G.H., Chron. min.,* Vol. I, pp. 470f.

[66] Idatius, *Chronicon,* sub ann. 429. *M.G.H., Chron. min.,* Vol. II, p. 21.

[67] Prosper, *Chronicon,* sub ann. 427. *M.G.H.,* Vol. IX, p. 472. Idatius, *Chronicon,* sub ann. 425, 429. *M.G.H.,* Vol. XI, *Chron. min.,* Vol. II, p. 21, merely mentions his attacks on Mauretania.

[68] Prosper, *Chronicon,* sub ann. 439. *M.G.H., Chron. min.,* Vol. I, p. 477.

[69] Prosper, *Chronicon,* sub ann. 432. *M.G.H., Chron. min.,* Vol. I, 90, p. 476.

[70] Id. *ibid.,* sub ann. 428, p. 472.

[71] Id. *ibid.,* sub ann. 430, p. 473. *Chron. Gall.,* sub ann. 432, p. 659; Idatius, *Chronicon,* sub ann. 434, *M.G.H.,* Vol. XI, p. 22.

[72] *Chron. Gall.,* sub ann. 432. *M.G.H.,* Vol. IX. *Chron. min.,* Vol. I, p. 658.

returned at the head of a formidable army of Huns, and Placidia found herself obliged, not only to restore him to office, but to appoint him Patrician.[73] From now till A.D. 454, the year of his death, Aetius remained undisputed master of the West, and enjoyed the singular distinction for a private citizen of the Empire of holding the consulship three times.

In consequence of the attention which Aetius paid to the pacification of Gaul, Africa was abandoned step by step to the power of the Vandals, and nothing that the eastern government could do was able to prevent their arms and diplomacy from gradually exterminating imperial authority in those provinces.[74] That authority was already practically extinct in Spain, and since, by a treaty concluded with Theodosius in A.D. 437, Western Illyricum had been assigned to the jurisdiction of Constantinople,[75] nothing now remained of the western provinces but Italy and certain parts of eastern and southern Gaul.

We shall follow the story of the later misfortunes of these provinces and of the final disappearance of Roman control there in later chapters, when we shall resume the story of the inglorious reigns of Valentinian and his successors.

I. THE DIVISIONS OF THE EMPIRE

Among the changes effected by the government of Diocletian at the beginning of the fourth century had been the abolition of the somewhat cumbersome and haphazard organization of the imperial provinces, which up to that time had remained to a great extent as they had been under the Republic and in the early days of the Principate. Of the original provinces, some were modified in area and others subdivided, each being placed under the control of a civil governor. The new provinces were then agglomerated as parts of a larger circumscription known as a "Diocese," and the "Dioceses" in turn formed part of a "Prefecture." At the beginning of the fifth century the whole Empire was

[73] *Nov. Valent. III*, 9, ed. P. Meyer, p. 90.
[74] See below. Chap. VI, pp. 105f.
[75] See below. Chap. VIII, p. 201.

divided into four prefectures, two of which belonged to the western sphere of jurisdiction and two to the eastern. These were the *Praefectura Galliarum*, embracing Britain, Gaul proper, Spain and the north western province of Africa; *Italiae*, including besides Italy, Africa, Western Illyricum and the Alpine provinces; *Illyrici*, the provinces of which had only been formed into a distinct prefecture since they had been transferred to the control of the eastern government towards the end of the fourth century,[76] and embraced Dacia, Macedonia and Achaia; and finally the *Praefectura Orientis*, which included Egypt and extended from Thrace to Mesopotamia.

Each prefecture was governed by a Praetorian Prefect, who normally at least delegated his immediate authority in relation to the provinces subject to his jurisdiction to a subordinate officer, known as the *Vicarius*. Over each of the provinces there was placed a rector or governor. It is remarkable that each of these officials possessed civil authority without any military control.† As will appear, the importance of this imperial organization for ecclesiastical history is the influence which it exercised on the nature and circumscriptions of ecclesiastical authority.

2. THE CONSTITUTION OF THE EMPIRE

It is a plain fact of history that the effect of the constitutional changes, introduced by Diocletian and developed by Constantine I, was to transform the nominally republican constitution of the Roman State into an autocracy. Nevertheless the autocracy so created was not in a strict sense a monarchy, since, apart from short periods during which the Empire was under the control of a single ruler, for the greater part of the fourth and fifth centuries the supreme power was vested in two or more Emperors, who recognized one another as colleagues and nominally at least governed the Roman world as co-regents. Yet it frequently came about that so far as imperial policy was concerned it was the senior colleague who had the decisive voice, and although, at least, as late as

[76] Sozomen, *H.E.*, 7, 4.

† It should be appreciated that there were direct relations between the local governor and the Prefect, and that every officer of whatever rank was considered to be personally responsible to the Emperor.

the middle of the fifth century edicts promulgated by either Emperor were issued in the name of both, such edicts by no means always represented an agreed decision. In fact, as we have seen, the policy adopted by the Government, with its seat of administration in Italy, that is to say, usually at Rome, Milan or Ravenna, and the one chosen by the Constantinopolitan Government were not seldom diametrically opposed. Nevertheless the theory that the *Imperium Romanum* was but a single political entity was carefully maintained down to the time of Justinian I and even later.

Among the titles bestowed upon the holder of a partnership in the Roman Principate, the most distinctive was that of Augustus, the possession of which was essential if he was to exercise the prerogatives of an *Imperator*. Originally conferred by proclamation by the army, and acknowledged by the Senate with the acquiescence of the populace, the office, though in theory elective, was usually conveyed, during the fourth and fifth centuries, to a prospective successor in the lifetime of the holder by an application of the principle of heredity. Thus it became usual for the reigning emperor to nominate his eldest son as his colleague, so that on the father's death the son automatically took his place. And if, as at the decease of Theodosius II, there was no male issue, the problem of succession was occasionally solved by the marriage of a near female relative and the election of her husband to the Principate. It was thus that the Empress Pulcheria, sister of the deceased Emperor, secured the maintenance of the Theodosian dynasty in A.D. 450.

In the fifth century the Emperors alone enjoyed the right of legislation. Constitutionally it was derived from the practice in vogue since the time of Augustus of issuing edicts and rescripts, documents which expressed the mind or the will of the *Princeps* regarding a particular question, and as such automatically possessed of legal validity. But in practice legislation was often a consequence of joint action between the Emperor and the Senate. Nevertheless the Emperor retained the sole right to interpret the laws and, where necessary, to dispense from their application.

Since the refoundation of Byzantium by Constantine I as Constantinople, a second Senate had come into existence.

Both this body and the original Roman Senate were recruited from the sons of senators and from those who had held magisterial office The consulship was filled only by those who already held senatorial rank and was shared between the western and eastern governments; that is to say, normally each Emperor nominated one of the consuls for the ensuing year. But this and other magistracies, which like it had survived from republican times, had long ceased to possess any executive power; in fact the sole privilege remaining to the consul, apart from certain honorific rights, was that of giving his name to his year of office. The functions of the Senate included the nomination of praetors and the exercise of some measure of control over the funds expended by them on public and social services. Its advice was normally sought by the Emperor in the promulgation of laws, and on occasion it might be required to sit in a judicial capacity.

For the most part the ancient magistracies, which had existed under the Republic and early Principate, now survived only in name. In their place a new executive bureaucracy had arisen. The characteristic feature of the Diocletianic autocracy was that public administration was regarded, at least in theory, as personal service on the *Imperator* or commander of the army. Thus every department of it was designated *militia,* and all officers of state from the Emperor downwards, with the exception of the *Praefectus urbi,* wore military uniform. Chief among those in personal attendance on him was the *Praepositus sacri cubiculi,* or Great Chamberlain, who as in the case of Eutropius and Chrysaphius at Constantinople, was often a eunuch and held the reins of government far more effectively than his master.

Apart from the high officials of the imperial court, the most important civil officer was the *Praefectus Praetorio.* His functions covered every department of state except the purely military ones and his responsibilities included the supervision of taxation and the all-important corn supply for the capitals in East and West. Subordinate to him and having the supervision of a subdivision of the prefecture, yet personally and directly responsible to the Emperor, was the *Vicarius,* while as we have seen each province was under the direct control of a *Rector,* who was principally concerned with the maintenance of public order within the area subject to his jurisdiction.

Side by side with the normal hierarchy of provincial administration was a vast and elaborate secretariat, the chief officer of which was known as the *Magister officiorum,* whose subordinates were distributed throughout the province and exercised an embarrassing control over the administration. In fact the whole organization formed a kind of governmental secret service.

Far-reaching changes had been carried out in the organization of the army. Their general effect was to render the military forces of the Empire more mobile and to complete the severance of civil from military duties. New military offices came into existence, such as a *Magister equitum* and a *Magister peditum,* created by Constantius as his principal officers. But as time went on the division of duties broke down in practice, and a *Magister utriusque militiae* was frequently appointed. The sphere of authority possessed by such an official was usually coextensive with the "Diocese" within which war occurred or was being threatened, and since in the fifth century the Emperor rarely took the field in person, the *Magister* himself often became the effective ruler of the Empire. He frequently bore the title of *comes* or Patrician, which, being at the Emperor's disposal, were occasionally extorted from the latter even against his better judgment.

The centre of this elaborate and complicated structure of imperial administration was the Imperial *Consistorium,* a body which was so designated because its members stood in the Emperor's presence. It was composed of the *Praepositus sacri cubiculi,* the *Praefectus Praetorio praesens* and of other high officers of state, but its functions remained, in theory at least, strictly advisory.

3. SOCIAL CONDITIONS

During the fourth century Roman society had gradually become demarcated into social classes, the limits of which were so rigid that it was difficult if not impossible for anyone to escape from the condition of life into which he had been born.[77] Apart from the general tendency to stagnation produced by these divisions, serious injustice was inflicted on certain members of society. In the cities and towns the whole burden of the maintenance of public services fell on the upper classes, from whom the civil magistrates, known as *decuriones,* were wholly recruited,[78] and so irksome was it, that measures had to be taken by the Government to prevent evasion of this duty by voluntary resignation of magisterial status, or even by flight.[79] Similarly each trade or profession tended to form a *collegium* from which there was in effect no means of escape. The labouring class [80] fared worst of all. Forbidden to abandon the cultivation of the land in the place of their birth, they were slowly reduced to a condition of serfdom, which differed little from a state of actual slavery. The slaves themselves were certainly not less numerous now than for some centuries past; if anything, their condition of life was improving,[81] so that paradoxically in the declining years of the Empire a slave might well find himself more fortunate than his nominally free master.

4. THE ORGANIZATION OF THE CHRISTIAN CHURCH

By the beginning of the fifth century the imperial sovereigns themselves had been at least nominally Christian for nearly a century, and the same could now be said of the vast mass of the population inhabiting the provinces of the Empire, from Britain to the confines of Persia. At the time of the death of Theodosius I the Christian Church was already organized in a manner which befitted a religion which was claiming the whole world as its domain. The unit of organization was the city. Here the Christian community was governed and its affairs administered by the bishop as its chief pastor and spiritual head, responsible, in the first instance at

[77] e.g. *Cod. Theod.*, XIII, v, 16 with special reference to sailors.

[78] For the history and organization of the curial bodies cf. Kübler in *Pauly-Wissowa Enc.* Art. *Decurio,* and Dill, *Roman Society,* III, ii.

[79] It even became necessary to forbid the practice of pressing a man into the local curia as a punishment for misdemeanours. See *Cod. Theod.*, XII, i, 22; 66 and 108.

[80] The oppression of the *coloni* is mentioned by Chrysostom. *Hom. in Matth.*, 61, 3. *P.G.*, 58, 591. See also Bury, *Later Roman Empire,* Vol. I, p. 56.

[81] For the condition of slaves in the fifth century see Bury, *op. cit.*, Vol. I, p. 140.

least, to his fellow bishops. In the execution of his office he was assisted by a *collegium* of presbyters (priests) and a multitude of subordinate ministers.[82] Chief among the latter were the deacons, who in some churches, doubtless owing to the limited numbers of their order, tended to overshadow in importance and influence even the presbyters themselves.[83]

Though theocratic in essence, the local church embodied in its constitution some essentially democratic principles. This characteristic is seen chiefly in the conditions governing episcopal elections, in which during the first three centuries or so both clergy and laity alike were able to express their will in making a free choice of a candidate acceptable to the local church as a whole. In course of time, however, the share of the laity in the electoral procedure tended naturally to diminish,[84] although even as late as the middle of the fourth century Martin was elected to the vacant see of Tours, chiefly in consequence of an insistent demand for him on the part of the laity. A further limitation on the lay freedom of choice arose from the insistence of neighbouring bishops that a candidate should be acceptable to them as well as to the local church, as an indispensable condition of his consecration.

As the local Christian community expanded, and places of worship within the city and outside its walls increased in number, the original ideal of unity within the community gradually gave way in practice to a form of decentralization. In some churches, mainly in the East, the local episcopate was subdivided, so that besides the ἐπίσκοπος, who remained bishop *par excellence*, other regional bishops, known as χωρεπίσκοποι, came into existence.[85] In others authority over particular "parish" churches was delegated to presbyters.

At Alexandria this development appears to have taken place rather earlier than elsewhere, and led to some difficulties,

[82] The letters of Ignatius, e.g. *Eph.* 5; *Magn.* 6, 7; *Trall.* 7 are sufficient evidence that this was the normal organization of the Christian ministry at least in Asia Minor and Syria as early as A.D. 115.

[83] For the importance of the diaconate and its usurpation of privileges reserved to the presbyterate, see Turner in *Cambridge Mediæval History*, Vol. I, pp. 154f.

[84] On the development of episcopal elections see Turner, *ibid.*, pp.152f.

[85] By Leo's time the office had largely fallen into desuetude in the West, where it had not been formally abolished. On the χωρεπίσκοπος see below, p. 109, and cf. *Inter Leon. Epp.* 52, 7.

arising from the relative independence of their bishop enjoyed by local priests.[86] Of such difficulties the revolt of Arius, parish priest of Baucalis, against the theology favoured by his bishop, Alexander, is an example. In Rome, however, where there were already numerous parish churches, there were no parish priests till the close of the fifth century. Up to that time "the bishop . . . kept under his own control all arrangements for separate services, and the presbyters, like the headquarters staff of the general, were sent hither and thither as occasion demanded." [87]

But if the bishop was the head of the local community he was also the link with neighbouring and more distant communities. To him fell the duty of despatching and also, no doubt, often of actually composing the letters in which one church informed its neighbours of events of importance affecting in a greater or less degree the welfare of the Church as a whole.[87] As time went on this sense of fellowship between neighbours came to be expressed by occasional meetings of bishops representing the local churches for mutual consultation. Originally fortuitous in composition, these gatherings or synods tended to comprise only those bishops whose see cities lay within a particular civil circumscription, so that by the beginning of the fourth century local churches were already beginning to group themselves according to the boundaries of the civil provinces demarcated by the reform of Diocletian.[88] By a natural process of development the bishop whose see was placed in the metropolis or civil administrative capital of the province came to be regarded as the *ex officio* chairman of such gatherings, and to be recognized as possessing rights, at first somewhat indefinite, in relation to the election and consecration of local bishops.[89] This development evidently took place earlier and more rapidly in the East than in the West.[90] Side by side with it was the growing recognition of the pre-eminence of certain

[86] On the growth of this system see Turner, *ibid.*, pp. 157ff.

[87] e.g. the letter despatched by the Churches of Lyons and Vienne to the Churches of Asia, ap. Eusebium, *H.E.*, 5, 1, 3.

[88] See above, p. 14.

[89] These rights were first clearly defined by the Council of Nicaea. *Canons* 4, 5 and 6, A.D. 325.

[90] In Gaul provincial organization was still lacking in definiteness as late as the beginning of the fifth century. See Chap. VII, p. 110.

sees in virtue of the civil importance of the cities to which they belonged or because of their real or supposed Apostolic origin. Such sees were those of Rome, Alexandria and Antioch, and later those of Constantinople and Jerusalem.[91] The privileges of the see of Alexandria were explicitly recognized by the Council of Nicaea, a recognition which was justified on the significant ground that similar privileges were already enjoyed by the see of Rome.[92] It is worthy of notice that the organization of the Church not only adapted itself to the civil organization of the Empire, but in more than one respect tended to assimilate the degrees of the hierarchy to equivalent ranks in the civil administration. Thus, if the metropolitan bishop was the ecclesiastical counterpart of the civil provincial governor, the exarch or patriarch[93] corresponded to the imperial prefect.

Before concluding this brief summary one further development needs to be noticed. It seems that the genius of Constantine I was in the main responsible for a notable extension of the principle of synodical administration already mentioned. To him was due in the first instance the experiment of summoning a general council, the necessity of which arose from the fact that the questions at issue, namely the problems raised by the spread of Donatism within the Western Church, affected provinces other than the one which gave birth to the schism, and were becoming a menace to the unity of the Church as a whole.[94] The Council of Nicaea itself was similarly an adaptation of the same method to meet the situation arising from the doctrinal controversy within the Church of Alexandria, which was threatening to sunder the unity of Christians in the eastern provinces. In view of the importance not only of councils of this type in the relations

[91] It is evident that as in the case of the see of Jerusalem actual or supposed Apostolic origin was not originally a decisive factor in the question as to "which of them should be the greatest." Later, however, it was used to justify a position already attained by other means, and at least in the case of the see of Constantinople, what history had denied was supplied by imagination or legend. See below, Chap. XIII, and cf. *Cons. Const., M.G.H.*, Auct. antiqu., Vol. IX, p. 239.

[92] Cf. the well known *Canon* 6 of this Council.

[93] The title of "patriarch" itself was first used (Mansi, *op. cit.*, Vol. VI, 953) at the Council of Chalcedon. Cf. Bright, *Canons*,[2] pp. 90f. It was probably borrowed from contemporary Jewish usage.

[94] i.e. the Council of Arles, A.D. 316.

of Leo with the eastern churches, but also of their decisions, as constituting the nucleus of a *Corpus Juris canonici* binding on the whole Church, we are bound to account this development something of a milestone in the history of the Church and of the Papacy in particular.

5. THE CITY OF ROME IN THE FIFTH CENTURY

Most of our information for the condition of the capital in this period is derived from a regionary survey attributed to Constantine I, preserved in a slightly modified form in the *Notitia* appended to the Philocalian Kalendar A.D. 336–354 and in the *Curiosum*.[95] Neither redaction mentions any Christian place of worship. For the sake of brevity only a bare summary of its contents can be included here.[96] Each of the fourteen regions, into which the city was divided for administrative purposes by Augustus, are described in turn and together they contained "eleven forums, ten (secular) basilicas, twenty-eight public libraries . . . two hundred and ninety . . . public warehouses . . . and besides forty-six thousand, one hundred and two tenement houses *(insulae)* and one thousand, seven hundred and ninety palaces *(domus)*."[97]

The population of the city at this time has been variously estimated at something between one and two million.[98] Its walls, built by Aurelian and restored in A.D. 403 by Honorius, were about eleven and three-quarter miles in circumference; it had fifteen gates. Nine bridges crossed the river Tiber. Its chief glory was to be found in its splendid monuments and its graceful temples. Of these some account must now be given.

It is possible that the year of Leo's birth actually coincided with the collapse of the last serious attempt to uphold the lost cause of paganism in the West. This was the battle of Aquileia, September 5th, A.D. 394,[99] in which an inferior

[95] On these documents see Richter, *Topographie,* pp. 3ff., 186ff.
[96] See further in Grisar, *History,* Vol. I, Chap. V, pp. 142ff.
[97] Grisar, *op. cit.,* Vol. I, p. 184.
[98] Homes Dudden, *St. Ambrose,* Vol. I, p. 25, accepts the latter figure for the fourth century.
[99] For details of the battle see Theodoret, *H.E.,* 5, 23, 24; Claudian, *De quarto consulatu,* 70–117; Zosimus, *op. cit.,* 4, 58.

force under the command of the Emperor Theodosius I defeated the army of the usurper Eugenius, who had given himself out to be the protector of the old religion, and had deliberately set on foot a programme of revival in the hope of rallying Rome and Italy to his standard.[100] From this time forth the ultimate triumph of Christianity was assured. Yet for a time paganism succeeded in retaining a hold, particularly among the old noble families.[101] The suppressive legislation initiated by the earlier Christian emperors had remained for the most part a dead letter and it was not till the reign of Gratian that a really decisive blow had been struck.[102]

Chief among the pagan forms of worship which had continued up to this time to enjoy an extensive popularity was that of Mithras.[103] This had two principal centres, one in the temple of Cybele, in close proximity to the basilica of St. Peter, and the other close to the present Church of San Silvestro in Capite. Similarly the Temple of Vesta[104] in the Roman Forum at the foot of the Palatine remained in use up to the year of Theodosius' victory.

Three years before his victory at Aquileia Theodosius had issued an edict prohibiting pagan worship,[105] and now that the last serious attempt of paganism to resist the progress of Christianity had been defeated the edict took effect as a matter of course. Roman temples were of two kinds; those normally used for worship[106] and those which served as government and municipal buildings.[107] The former class for the most part were simply abandoned[108] and, in spite of repeated official prohibitions,[109] served as convenient quarries.

[100] On these events see Grisar, *History,* Vol. I, pp. 1–6.
[101] Grisar, *op. cit.,* pp. 9f. mentions a number of such distinguished supporters.
[102] Zosimus, *Hist. nova,* 4, 36.
[103] On the cult of Mithras see Cumont, *Mysteries of Mithra* (E.T.), 1903.
[104] Details are given in Grisar, *op. cit.,* Vol. I, pp. 14–20.
[105] *Cod. Theod.,* XVI, x, 10, ed. Mommsen and Meyer, p. 899. Cf. XVI, x, 19 (A.D. 408), Mirbt, *Quellen,* No. 183.
[106] e.g. the Temple of Jupiter Capitolinus. Cf. Jerome, *Adv. Iovinianum,* 2, 38. *P.L.,* 23, 338; id. *Ep.* 107, 1. *P.L.,* 22, 868.
[107] e.g. the *Aedes Saturni* in the Forum below the Capitol.
[108] Only one of the greater Temples was deliberately destroyed, namely a *Mithraeum* (probably the one near San Silvestro in Capite). Cf. Jerome, *Ep.* 107, 2 and Prudentius, *Contra Symmachum,* 1, 564.
[109] *Cod. Theod.,* XVI, x, 17 renewed in *Cod. Theod.,* XVI, x, 19.

The latter merely continued to be used as before.[110]

In one direction, however, the institutions of paganism continued to flourish. Games such as the *ludi Apollinares* and festivals like the *Lupercalia*[111] outlasted the collapse of the religion, with which they had been closely associated, for at least a century. But it should be remembered that these customs were deeply rooted in the civic life of the city and as a consequence retained their hold on popular esteem long after their originally religious character had been forgotten. Nevertheless the gladiatorial combats which so long delighted the populace were early brought to an end by a peremptory edict[112] issued by Honorius, the son and successor of Theodosius.

But if the temples were deserted the churches were eagerly frequented and steadily increasing in number and in magnificence. Of those which existed before the age of Constantine we have little evidence, nor can we determine with any certainty the original site of the headquarters of the Roman see. Perhaps the best claim to this distinction is the one which can be made for the Church of St. Laurence *in Damaso,* where at least as late as Damasus' own pontificate the archives of the Roman see were still preserved.[113] By the side of the lofty spacious temples, even the largest churches, with their plain unadorned exteriors, must have seemed dull and unimpressive. Before passing on to describe the principal basilicas it is necessary to reconstruct the picture presented by a typical Christian church of this period. "Orientated" towards the west, the principal and often the only public entrance was situated at the east end. The worshipper entering the church passed through a large porch or *narthex,* which provided accommodation for catechumens and penitents, in accordance with the liturgical practice of the time. He would then find himself in the nave of the building, with aisles to the

[110] Two such Temples, namely the *Templum Sacrae urbis* and the *Rotunda Romuli,* were later converted by Pope Felix IV in A.D. 526 into the Church of SS. Cosmas and Damian. See Grisar, *op. cit.,* Vol. I, pp. 232ff.

[111] Both of these were certainly still being held in the pontificate of Leo. See below Chap. III, p. 51.

[112] Theodoret, *H.E.,* 5, 26.

[113] *Inscript. Dam.,* in De Rossi, *Inscript. Christ,* II, 1, pp. 135, 151. Cf. *Liber pontificalis,* ed. Duchesne, Vol. I, p. 213, n. 7.

north and south, separated from the nave proper by twin arcades stretching from east to west as far as the arch, beyond which opened the apse or westernmost portion of the church. On the far side of this arch, in the case of the greater basilicas, there was a transept or crossing and in the chord of the semi-circular apse would be seen the altar itself, usually furnished with a canopy resting on four columns. Round the circumference of the apse was a continuous stone bench which accommodated the members of the higher clergy, and in the centre of its arc, usually raised on a few steps, the *cathedra* of the bishop. Between the altar and the nave there was usually a square enclosure intended for the singers and inferior clergy, and on either side an *ambo* or pulpit, used for the singing of the liturgical Epistle and Gospel. This part of the Church, or else the westernmost portion enshrining the altar, was divided from the nave by a stone screen, running from north to south. When filled with worshippers and provided with its full complement of clergy, its walls glistening with the softly blending colours of various mosaics and its aisles irradiated by a multitude of lamps, the humblest church must have seemed the veritable audience chamber of a king.[114]

Of the greater churches the first to claim our attention, chiefly because it was the actual cathedral church of the city, is the *basilica Lateranensis* or *Constantiniensis*. The church itself was erected by Constantine in the time of Pope Silvester I,[115] close to the Lateran palace, itself formerly an imperial residence which the Emperor had personally bestowed on the Roman see.[116] Since that time Silvester and his successors had made the palace their headquarters, and it was doubtless there that Leo himself composed his sermons, wrote his letters and devoted himself to the manifold tasks which he felt to be incumbent upon him in virtue of his responsibility for the " care of all the churches." Of the great basilica, as it existed in Leo's time, there is little now to be seen. The *Liber pontificalis* has preserved the actual inventory of a vast treasure bestowed upon it by the Emperor's munificence,[117]

[114] For greater detail see Grisar, *op. cit.*, Vol. II, pp. 85ff.
[115] In A.D. 324.
[116] See Grisar, *op. cit.*, Vol. III, pp. 291ff.
[117] *Liber pontificalis*, ed. Duchesne, Vol. I, pp. 172ff.

which caused it to be known as the *basilica aurea*. Originally it had a double aisle to the north and south of the nave, like the old basilicas of St. Peter and of St. Paul, and even the two pier arcades retained in subsequent restorations have been encased with later work. Only the baptistery remains to-day substantially in the same state as it was when restored by Xystus III.[118]

To form a comprehensive picture of Christian Rome as it existed in the middle of the fifth century we may imagine ourselves among a group of pilgrims walking from the Lateran on the east side to the *basilica S. Petri* on the extreme west side of the city. After leaving the buildings of the Lateran, we notice first the little church of the *Quattuor Coronati*.[119] Nearly opposite to it is the *basilica Clementis*,[120] the original building of which had been erected at least as early as the pontificate of Damasus I. A little further on beyond the vast *Thermae Traiani* there stands the *basilica Apostolorum*,[121] in later times to be known as the *basilica S. Petri ad Vincula* on account of the relic which it claimed to possess. Then, as the road bends to the left of the great *Colosseum*, we pass by the triumphal arches of Constantine and Titus into the heart of the ancient city.

In Leo's time there were probably no Christian buildings in the *Forum Romanum*, with the single exception, possibly, of the Church of *S. Maria antiqua*,[122] the erection of which a doubtful tradition ascribes to Silvester I. Leaving the Forum and following the *Clivus argentarius* we pass by the north-east side of the Capitol and walking in a northerly direction along the *Via Flaminia* (the modern Corso) we turn left

[118] Grisar, *op. cit.*, Vol. II, pp. 328f.

[119] The original church replaced by the one erected by Honorius I in the seventh century has wholly disappeared. On the *Quattuor Coronati*, see Grisar, *op. cit.*, Vol. I, pp. 211f.

[120] Mentioned by Jerome, *De vir. illustr.* 15. *P.L.* 23, 633. Cf. Grisar, *op. cit.*, Vol. I, pp. 212ff.

[121] Philip, legate of Celestine I, at the Council of Ephesus A.D. 431 was in charge of this church. It was restored by Xystus III. Cf. *Liber. pont.*, Vol. I, p. 232, and received from the Emperor Theodosius II the relic mentioned in the text. See further on this point, Kirch, *Röm. Titelkirchen*, in *Stud. z. Gesch. u. Kultur d. Altertums*, Vol. IX, i, 1918, pp. 45ff.; Grisar, *op. cit.*, Vol. I, pp. 219f.

[122] On this church, the very existence of which was forgotten for several centuries, see Id. *ibid.*, Vol. I, pp. 244f. Some remains of it were brought to light at the beginning of the present century, but these were not earlier than the eighth century and belonged to the pontificate of John VII, A.D. 705.

towards the *basilica S. Marci.*[123] Further on lies the Church of *S. Laurentius in Damaso.*[124] We are now close to the river. The present road crosses the Tiber by means of the *Ponte S. Angelo* (formerly *Pons Aelius*), but in the fifth century the great *Pons Neronianus* was still in existence, and this leads us directly into the Vatican quarter. Before crossing the bridge we notice the magnificent *Mausoleum* or *Moles Hadriani*[125] and then follow the *Via Cornelia,* which brings us face to face with the easternmost buildings of the *basilica S. Petri.*[126] Erected by Constantine I, *c.* A.D. 330, on the site of the martyrdom and original burial place of the Apostle, the fourth century church measured three hundred and ninety-five feet in length and two hundred and twelve in width. It was approached by five flights of steps, at the top of which was a large open terrace, whence three lofty doors led into a spacious vestibule. This in turn opened on to the *atrium,* a large cloister in the middle of which stood the *cantharus,* with its perpetual stream of clear, fresh water. Within the church itself double aisles flanked the spacious nave with four arcades of twenty-two columns in each. On the Triumphal Arch was depicted the scene of the presentation of the Founder Emperor by St. Peter to our Lord.[127] Beyond the nave there was a large transept and further westwards the apse, on the chord of which stood the altar. The chief treasure of the church was the body of St. Peter, which reposed in the *Confessio* before the altar. The following is a description of this feature as it must have appeared in Leo's own lifetime.

[123] The original church has wholly disappeared.

[124] The earlier church built by Damasus I survived till A.D. 1486. It was then removed to make room for the new *Cancellaria Apostolica.* Cf. Lanciani, *L'Itinerario,* p. 450. It was the primitive repository of the archives of the Roman see, and owing to its proximity to the stables of the "Green Faction" was for a time known as *S. Laurentius in Prasina.* Cf. De Rossi, *Inscript. Christ.,* Vol. II, p. 134.

[125] For details and a conjectural restoration, see Grisar, *op. cit.* Vol. I, pp. 263ff. It was probably first adapted as a fortress in the time of the Emperor Honorius but with only slight alterations. Cf. Procopius, *De Bello Goth.,* 1, 22, 19. The destruction and spoliation of this great monument belongs to a later age.

[126] For a plan of the old basilica see Grisar, *op. cit.,* Vol. I, Ill. 64, facing p. 274. A conjectural restoration is on p. 304.

[127] The inscription beneath the mosaic ran, "Quod duce te mundus surrexit in astra triumphans, hanc Constantinus Victor tibi condidit aulam." Cf. *Liber pontificalis,* Vol. I, p. 193.

"The small subterranean mortuary-chamber had been overlaid by Constantine with an 'immovable' covering of bronze. Above the chamber a little shrine or 'ark' had been erected. From the floor of this 'ark' a hollow shaft descended into the chamber underneath, and through this channel small objects, such as handkerchiefs, could be let down and blessed by touching the hallowed vault. Above the 'ark' was the altar of the basilica—a silver table edged with gold and precious stones. Before the 'ark' hung a golden candelabrum adorned with fifty figures of dolphins, and at the four corners of the shrine were placed four brazen candlesticks covered with silver medallions." [128]

It is probable that in Leo's time there were twenty-five parish churches, known as *Tituli,* in existence.[129] Some of these have already been mentioned. Of the rest no more than a bare catalogue can be given. Beginning with the first of the Augustan regions, *Porta Capena,* we find the *Titulus S. Xysti* or *Crescentiae;* [130] next in *Caelimontium* the *Titulus Byzanti or Pammachii,*[131] known also as the Church of SS. John and Paul; in *Isis and Serapis* the *Titulus S. Matthaei in Merulana,*[132] and the *Titulus Equitii* or *Silvestri;* [133] in *Templum Pacis* the *Titulus Praxedis.*[134] Then in the fifth region, *Esquiliae,* the *Titulus Eusebii;* [135] in *Alta Semita* the *Titulus*

[128] Homes Dudden, *St. Ambrose,* Vol. I, p. 51. The chief source for these details is the *Liber pontificalis,* Vol. I, p. 176, No. 38. Cf. also Grisar, *History,* Vol. I, p. 299 and Lietzmann, *Petrus und Paulus,* pp. 189ff. and pp. 310ff.

[129] Hilary I, Leo's successor, provided sacred vessels for twenty-five churches. Cf. *Liber pontificalis,* Vol. I, p. 244, No. 71, and the Roman council of A.D. 499, Mansi, *op. cit.,* Vol. VIII, 23 where twenty-five *Tituli* are mentioned. See also Caspar, *Geschichte des Papsttums,* Vol. I, pp. 53–56.

[130] The *Titulus Crescentiae* is mentioned in the council of A.D. 499 and is probably the same as the *Titulus S. Xysti.* Cf. Duchesne, *Notes sur la topographie de Rome au moyen age, II: Les titres presbytéraux et les diaconies, Mélanges d'archaeologie et d'histoire,* Vol. VII (1887), pp. 217–43 esp. p. 228.

[131] Mentioned in an inscription belonging to the pontificate of Innocent I. Cf. *Liber pont.,* Vol. I, p. 236.

[132] Duchesne, *Notes, op. cit.,* p. 228. The *Titulus* had perhaps been transferred to *SS. Marcellini et Petri* by A.D. 595, *P.L.* 77, 1338. But Duchesne, *op. cit.,* p. 229 identifies it with the *Titulus Nicomedis* mentioned in the council of A.D. 499.

[133] *Liber pont.,* Vol. I, p. 187, § xxxiii. Only ruins of the original structure remain near the later *SS. Silvestro e Martino ai Monti.*

[134] Mentioned in an epitaph of A.D. 491. Cf. De Rossi, *Bullett. archaeol. crist.* (1882), p. 65.

[135] *Martyrolog. Hieron.* for August 14th, ed. De Rossi-Duchesne, p. [106].

Vestinae, later *S. Vitalis,*[136] the *Titulus Gaii* or *Susannae,*[137] the *Titulus Cyriaci,*[138] and the *Titulus Pudentis* or *Pudentianae;*[139] in *Via Lata* the *Titulus Marcelli.*[140] Next in *Circus Flaminius* the *Titulus Lucinae* or *S. Laurentii in Lucina;*[141] in *Circus Maximus* the *Titulus Anastasiae.*[142] Finally, in the twelfth region, *Piscina publica,* the *Titulus Fasciolae* or *SS. Nerei et Achillei*[143] and the *Titulus Balbinae;*[144] in *Aventinus* the *Titulus Sabinae*[145] and the *Titulus Priscae;*[146] and in the last or fourteenth region *Transtiberim,* the *Titulus Iulii* or *S. Mariae,*[147] the *Titulus Caeciliae*[148] and the *Titulus Chrysogoni.*[149] These with the five already mentioned make up the total of twenty-five already mentioned.[150]

In closing this description of Christian Rome some account must be given of at least three of the greater basilicas which are not reckoned among the list of the *Tituli.* First of these is the sister basilica to that of St. Peter in the Vatican, namely St. Paul on the Ostian Way.[151] The Church of St. Paul was the second to be erected on that site and, like the Lateran

[136] Built in the pontificate of Innocent I. Cf. *Liber pont., Innocentius,* No. 57, ed. Duchesne, Vol. I, p. 220.

[137] *Martyrolog. Hieron.* for August 11th.

[138] Since disappeared. First mentioned in A.D. 499. For its site see Grisar, *History,* Vol. I, plan in frontispiece.

[139] Mentioned in an epitaph dated A.D. 384. De Rossi, *Inscr. Christ.,* Vol. I, p. 153, No. 347.

[140] Mentioned in *Liber pont., Marcellus,* No. 31, Vol. I, p. 164. Duchesne, *Notes,* p. 227 identifies it with the *Titulus Romanus* mentioned in A.D. 499.

[141] *Coll. Avell.,* 1, 5. *C.S.E.L.,* Vol. XXXV, p. 2.

[142] *Liber pont., Damasus,* No. 54, Vol. I, p. 212. Its baptistery was erected in A.D. 403. See Grisar, *Analecta Rom.,* Vol. I, diss. 14.

[143] In existence A.D. 377. See De Rossi, *Inscr. Christ.,* Vol. I, p. 124, No. 262.

[144] Only in an inscription of the sixth century. De Rossi, *Roma sott.,* Vol. III, 515.

[145] A dedicatory inscription still survives belonging to the pontificate of Celestine I. Cf. Grisar, *Analecta Rom.,* Vol. I, 88, 146, and illustr. *ibid.* pl. i, n. 2.

[146] Mentioned in a fifth century epitaph. Marchi, *Monumenti primitivi,* p. 26. Cf. Duchesne, *Notes,* p. 226.

[147] *Liber pont.,* Vol. I, p. 205 ascribes its origin to Julius I.

[148] *Martyrolog. Hieron.* for Nov. 22nd, ed. De Rossi-Duchesne, p. [146].

[149] Mentioned in sixth century inscriptions. De Rossi, *Inscr. Christ.,* Vol. I, pp. 440, 442, Nos. 975, 977.

[150] We cannot of course be sure that other *Tituli* were not in existence in Leo's time which subsequently were transferred to some of those mentioned above.

[151] For details regarding this church see Grisar, *History,* Vol. II, pp. 103ff., and Lietzmann, *Petrus und Paulus,* pp. 211ff.

and Petrine basilicas which were standing in Leo's time, had double aisles on either side of the nave, the length of which was three hundred and ninety feet and the total width one hundred and ninety-five feet. It was thus the largest of all the great churches. The Constantinian basilica which preceded it was a comparatively small structure.[152] In its place stood the new church erected to the order of Theodosius I and his co-Emperors in A.D. 384.[153] In the centre of the transept, between the apse and the nave, lay the tomb of the great Apostle which, like that of St. Peter, was covered with an "ark" and to which a similar shaft gave access.

The orientation of the new church differentiated it sharply from the other great basilicas. This was directed eastwards and not westwards, as was usual at this time, and arose from the geographical limitations of the site. The original church was orientated like the others, but when planning a new building the presence of the *Via Ostiensis* and of sharply rising ground to the east prevented further extension. It was therefore necessary to reverse the ordinary plan. This had the additional advantage of avoiding the necessity of altering the position of the Apostle's tomb. Thus the celebrant at Mass turned his back to the people and faced the apse. Elsewhere he faced the people, standing on the far side of the altar with his back to the apse.

One other great church built in the lifetime of Constantine I, namely the *basilica Sessoriana*[154] deserves mention. It was erected on the site of *Palatium Sessorianum* where his mother Helena had formerly resided.[155]

In conclusion, a brief reference must be made to the *basilica Liberiana,* restored under Xystus III. Begun by Pope Liberius on the Esquiline, it was rebuilt in the fifth century and dedicated to the blessed Virgin,[156] and to another,

[152] For plan of both churches see Lietzmann, *op. cit.,* p. 316. Lanciani, *Pagan and Christian Rome,* p. 150.

[153] Lietzmann, *op. cit.,* p. 211. Grisar, *op. cit.,* Vol. I, p. 107.

[154] *Liber pont., Silvester,* No. 41, § xxii, Vol. I, p. 179; *ibid., Xystus III,* No. 63, *op. cit.,* p. 232.

[155] Now known as *S. Croce in Gerusalemme.* Plan in Grisar, *History,* Vol. II, p. 136.

[156] *Liber pont., Liberius,* No. 52, Vol. I, p. 208; *ibid., Xystus III,* No. 63, Vol. I, p. 232. Details of this church as of other important churches, e.g. *S. Sabina,* in Grisar, *op. cit.,* Vol. II, pp. 113ff. and Vol. I, pp. 197f.

S. Sabina, built in his pontificate. It is possible that Leo, as archdeacon, may have personally supervised some of the work of construction of these buildings.

6. CONSTANTINOPLE

Although Leo himself never visited the new capital of the East,[157] in view of the importance of its see in his correspondence no record of his times would be complete without some description of it. Constantine I, its founder, evidently intended it to reproduce at least some of the features of the ancient capital of the West. It was to be a city of seven hills and of fourteen regions. But before a century had elapsed its population had exceeded its original limits, necessitating the construction of a new wall about three-quarters of a mile westwards of the fortification erected by Constantine. One feature which differentiated it sharply from Rome was the complete absence of any public sign of pagan worship. The official centre of the city was the *Tetrastoon.*[158] Around it were grouped the principal buildings: to the north the great Church of St. Sophia,[159] perhaps founded by Constantine and known to have been completed by his son Constantius, and near by, the Church of St. Irene,[160] to the east the Senate-house, to the south lay the principal entrance to the Imperial Palace. The main street, called the *Mesa,* led through the chief *Fora* direct to the Golden Gate at the south end of the wall of Theodosius II. About a third of the distance along this street another important street led due west, past the Church of the Apostles.[161] This Church, like St. Sophia, had been begun by Constantine. It was completed and dedicated by his son Constantius. Adjoining the east end was a circular mausoleum, where the Emperor himself and a number of his successors were buried. East of the *Tetrastoon* was the Church of St. Mary *Hodegeteria.*[162] Among the more notable secular buildings were the Great Palace to the south of

[157] The chief ancient source for the topography of the city is the *Notitia urbis Constantinopolitanae,* ed. Seeck, pp. 229–43. See also Bury, *Later Roman Empire,* Vol. I, pp. 68ff.
[158] *Chron. Pasch.,* sub ann. 328. *P.G.* 92, 708.
[159] Dedicated in A.D. 360. Cf. Socrates, *H.E.,* 2, 43.
[160] Socrates, *ibid.,* 1, 16; 2, 16.
[161] Described by Eusebius, *Vita Const.,* 4, 58.
[162] Erected by Pulcheria.

St. Sophia, the Palace of *Blachernae*[163] outside the Theodosian wall to the north, and the Palace of *Hebdomon* on the shore of the Propontis, not far from the Golden Gate, at which the Emperors were crowned and acclaimed. Nearby was the Church of the prophet Samuel and that of John Baptist[164] erected by Theodosius I. West of the Great Palace stood the Hippodrome, the three axis monuments of which are still *in situ.*[165] Here were held the chariot races which played so important a part in the social and even in the political life of the city. Its population in the fifth century probably totalled little less than a million.[166]

The foundation of Constantine was developed and extended under his successors so that by the beginning of the sixth century it far exceeded any other city of the Empire in size and magnificence. Of the part which it came to play in the life and development of Christianity more will be said elsewhere.

[163] Little is known of this in early times.
[164] Sozomen, *H.E.*, 7, 24.
[165] Cf. J. Murray, *Handbook to Constantinople* (1893), pp. 39ff.
[166] Bury's estimate, *op. cit.*, Vol. I, p. 88. Sozomen, *H.E.*, 2, 3 asserts that the city equalled Rome in numbers as well as in wealth.

CHAPTER II

LEO'S YOUTH AND EARLY MINISTRY

FIFTY-ONE miles south-east of the city of Pisa there lies a place of singular historical interest, known to the Etruscans as Velathri, and in later days to the Romans as Volaterrae. The town occupies a commanding position nearly two thousand feet above sea level, and enjoys an extensive view across the mountains to the distant sea. With a population scarcely exceeding eight thousand at the present time it seems of little importance, yet the massive remains of its ancient walls, about four and a half miles in circuit, still testify to its political significance in former times. When Rome itself counted for little among its more powerful neighbours, Volterra, as it is now called, was one of the more outstanding members of the Etrurian confederacy, and even as late as the civil wars of the last century B.C. had successfully resisted the troops of Sulla. Since the creation of the Principate its status slowly declined and would have no special claim on our notice here but for the fact that it appears to possess some title to be regarded as the authentic birthplace of Leo the Great.[1]

As to Leo's birth and early years, apart from the notice supplied by the *Liber Pontificalis*[2] to the effect that he was of Etruscan origin and that his father's name was Quintianus, we are admittedly dependent largely on conjecture. Even the year of his birth cannot be fixed with any certainty, though we may reasonably infer that it took place within a short time of the conclusion of the fourth century.[3] If we are to take literally his reference to the city of Rome as his

[1] Tillemont, *Mémoires,* Vol. XV, p. 414 records that in his day (he died A.D. 1698) the inhabitants of Volterra celebrated the festival of St. Leo (April 11th) with peculiar solemnity, and claimed him as a native of their city.

[2] Ed. Duchesne, Vol. I, p. 238. "Leo natione Tuscus, ex patre Quintiano."

[3] There is no evidence as to the year. The best that can be suggested cannot be more than a guess. Cf. *D.C.B.*, art. *Leo I,* Vol. III, p. 652b.

patria in later years [4] we may suppose that his family was one of those which, in consequence of the disturbed conditions prevailing at the beginning of the fifth century in consequence of the Gothic invasions, had migrated southwards in the hope of finding greater security, and finally settled in the capital itself.

If this be so, it seems likely that he is to be identified with the acolyte mentioned by Augustine as the bearer of letters addressed by Pope Zosimus and his priest Xystus (the future Xystus III) to Aurelius, bishop of Carthage, and to other bishops of the Church of Africa.[5] Of his early life under Zosimus' successors we know little, apart from an obscure statement by Vigilius of Thapsus,[6] till we reach the pontificate of Xystus III.

The outstanding event in the Church of the East during the closing years of Pope Celestine I's reign [7] was the Council of Ephesus. Probably the seriousness of the issue debated at that council was but dimly appreciated in the West, and it was for this reason that Leo, who must have realized that something more was at stake than the right of the see of Alexandria to rank next after Rome among the greater sees of Christendom, sought the advice and co-operation of one of the outstanding theologians of the time. If the Western churches were to be awakened to the dangers underlying the teaching of Nestorius, and to the importance of lending what support they could to the side of Cyril of Alexandria, someone had to be found who should sound the alarm. The person chosen by Leo [8] for this task was John Cassian, renowned in the West for his asceticism and for his strenuous opposition

[4] *Ep.* 31, 4, JK 425. "viderer patriam et sedem apostolicam velle deserere"; cf. Prosper, *Chronicon*, sub ann. 440. *M.G.H., Chron. min.*, Vol. I, p. 478, "gaudenti patriae praesentatus." "Patria" here apparently means just "home-land" and need not be construed to imply that Rome was actually his birthplace.

[5] *Ep.* 191, 1. *P.L.* 33, 867; *Ep.* 194, 1. *P.L.* 33, 874.

[6] *Contra Eutycheten*, 4, 1. *P.L.* 62, 119. "Celestino, cui iste (sc. Leo) rectae fidei testimonium reddidit." This is sometimes understood to refer to Leo's baptism. More probably the author has in mind his attitude in relation to the Nestorian controversy.

[7] A.D. 422.

[8] The fact that the selection was made by Leo either on his own initiative or because the responsibility had been delegated to him by Celestine is clear proof of his great influence in the counsels of the Roman see even before his elevation to the papacy.

to the more advanced elements in the teaching of Augustine. A native of Scythia and a personal friend of the great John Chrysostom, he had visited Rome in the time of Pope Innocent I.[9] Some years later he withdrew to quieter surroundings in southern Gaul, and there in the neighbourhood of Marseilles founded a monastery on the eastern model. A friend of Hilary of Arles, of whom we are to hear a good deal in the story of Leo's pontificate, he had come to occupy a position of considerable influence in the West. Though, as he himself testifies, he had wished to abandon literary work, the pressure brought to bear upon him by Leo overcame his reluctance, and caused him to publish on the eve of the Council his Christological treatise, *De Incarnatione*.[10] The author himself refers to Leo's influence in the matter when he says:

"You, Leo, my honoured friend, . . . ornament of the Roman Church and of the sacred ministry, have overcome my intention and decision (sc. to set aside literary pursuits) by your praiseworthy zeal and imperious sincerity." [11]

We may conjecture that Leo owed much of his knowledge of the Christological issue, and of his comprehension of the eastern theological outlook to his study of this treatise, assets which were to serve him in good stead in the shaping of his doctrinal policy in later years.

It was about this time that Leo was ordained deacon,[12] and as such was the recipient of an urgent appeal from Cyril of Alexandria calling his attention to the ambitious designs of Juvenal, bishop of Jerusalem.[13] The latter, it seems, was aiming at obtaining from the greater sees of Christendom recognition of his *de facto* independence of his metropolitan, the bishop of Caesarea, and Cyril evidently feared the con-

[9] Palladius, *Vita Chrys.*, 3. *P.G.* 47, 13f.
[10] *P.L.* 50, 9–272; cf. Gennadius, *De vir. illustr.*, 61, *P.L.* 58, 1094.
[11] *Ibid.*, *praef.* *P.L.* 50, 10f. *C.S.E.L.*, Vol. XVII, p. 235.
[12] Gennadius, *ibid.*
[13] *Ep.* 119, 4, JK 495. "Juvenalis episcopus ad obtinendum Palestinae provinciae principatum credidit se posse proficere. . . . Quod . . . Cyrillus . . . merito perhorrescens, scriptis suis mihi quid praedicti cupiditas ausa esset praedicavit." Cf. Cyril, *Ep.* 56. *P.G.* 77, 320. The fact that Cyril addressed his appeal to Leo as archdeacon suggests that it was he who throughout the pontificates of Celestine I and Xystus III was largely responsible for the direction of papal policy. See below, p. 36, on his relations with Julian of Eclanum.

sequences of the erection of a new primacy so near the borders of his own jurisdiction. The fact that some twenty years were to elapse before Juvenal attained his goal may suggest that, at least so far as it affected the attitude of the Roman see, Cyril's appeal did not fall on deaf ears.

Pope Celestine died on July 27th, A.D. 432, and was succeeded by Xystus, the Roman priest of whom we have already heard in connexion with the record of Leo's early years. Xystus III scarcely deserves to be numbered among the more distinguished holders of the papal office; in fact in his case, as in others, mediocrity may well have seemed to the minds of his electors a sufficient recommendation. As to the suspicion, which he had incurred some twenty years previously, of being friendly disposed towards the Pelagian cause,[14] it was either forgotten or ignored. Yet there may well have been some who regretted the hostile attitude of his predecessors toward Pelagian ideas, and who now felt that they might look forward under the new regime to a greater measure of toleration. Among those who shared this hope we may number Julian of Eclanum, who in the belief that the time was ripe for regaining the confidence of the Roman see, went so far as to solicit readmission to its communion. Unfortunately, it seems that he had ignored an important factor in the situation. To win the favour of the Roman bishop it was necessary to conciliate his influential archdeacon, and it was here that Julian failed. Pope Xystus was convinced or persuaded that no good could come of the proposal, and Julian had to abandon his attempt.[15]

It was perhaps in connexion with this affair that there was published a collection of authoritative papal and conciliar documents bearing on the Pelagian controversy,[16] the com-

[14] Augustine, *Ep.* 191, 1. *P.L.* 33, 867.

[15] Prosper, *Chronicon*, sub ann. 439, *P.L.* 51, 598. *M.G.H., Chron. min.*, Vol. I, p. 477. "Julianus Eclanensis, iactantissimus Pelagiani erroris adsertor, . . . multimoda arte fallendi, correctionis speciem praeferens, molitus est in communionem ecclesiae inrepere. Sed his insidiis Xystus papa, diaconi Leonis hortatu, vigilanter occurrens, nullum aditum pestiferis conatibus patere permisit." Eclanum was near Beneventum and hence within the Roman metropolitical jurisdiction.

[16] It is given as an appendix to Celestine, *Ep.* 21, JK 381, and known as the *Syllabus*.

pilation of which on internal evidence has been attributed to Leo himself.[17]

In view of the important place occupied in Leo's pontificate by his relations with the churches of the East, some notice of those relations in the time of his predecessor seems desirable. In the very year following Xystus' election a measure of accord was achieved between two of the protagonists at the recent Council of Ephesus. The famous "Formula of Reunion," signed by Cyril and endorsed by John of Antioch, who at the time of the council had been one of the most intransigent allies of Nestorius, doubtless owed much of its success as an *eirenicon* to the support lent to it by the Emperor, Theodosius II.[18] Yet it is probable that the intervention of Xystus on the side of peace may well have had considerable influence on the ultimate issue, even if, as the event proved, the peace so effected was scarcely more than superficial, and failed to outlast the lifetime of the co-signatories.

Further proof of the pacific direction of Xystus' eastern policy will appear if we consider his relations with the see of Constantinople. Doubtless the Roman see was well aware of the dangers which lay in that quarter and of the possibility that in the near future its universal primacy might be seriously challenged by the ambition of successive occupants of the episcopal throne in the eastern capital. Only thus can we explain his policy of consolidation of the papal "vicariate" in Eastern Illyricum, as a bulwark against the westward pressure of Constantinopolitan aggression. Yet as long as that see was content to enlarge its jurisdiction in an easterly direction Xystus appears to have been willing either to acquiesce or even to approve.[19] Nevertheless, in view of what will be said presently as to Leo's attitude to this question, it is scarcely likely that Xystus' policy met with the support of his archdeacon.

When Xystus III died on June 24th, A.D. 440,[20] after a pontificate of only eight years, Leo himself was absent from

[17] Tixeront, *Histoire des Dogmes,* Vol. III, p. 290. See further Additional Note, *The "Syllabus" on Grace,* p. 41.
[18] *Ep.* 6, 6, JK 392; cf. Duchesne, *Histoire,* Vol. III, p. 670.
[19] *Ep.* 9, 3, JK 395.
[20] Prosper, *Chronicon,* sub ann. 440. *M.G.H., Chron. min.,* Vol. I, p. 478.

Rome. He had been chosen to take part in a political mission, the object of which was the adjustment of a difference then prevailing between two outstanding military authorities, Aetius and Albinus.[21] How urgent such a reconciliation was at this time will be realized if it be remembered that but a few years previously Gaiseric and the Vandal invaders had made themselves masters of North Africa and were already threatening an attack on the heart of the Empire.[22] Though we are not immediately concerned with the outcome of Leo's mission, it may be remarked that the fact that Albinus subsequently received preferment seems to imply that it was actually successful. Now that the Roman see was vacant, the one thing which mattered, so far as the Church was concerned, was that Leo should come back at once to occupy it. To secure this end a delegation of persons representative of both clergy and laity was despatched from the capital which eagerly awaited his return. No one, it seems, so much as murmured the name of a rival candidate, and when Leo re-entered the imperial city forty days after the death of Xystus he was unanimously and gratefully elected.[23]

Leo was consecrated Bishop of Rome on September 29th, A.D. 440, and marked the occasion by delivering the first of those great sermons, which year by year, at least during the earlier part of his pontificate, were to celebrate the anniversary of the event.[24] We can picture him a man in the full vigour of his life, on the threshold of his great career, surrounded by a large company of prelates and clergy, and

[21] Aetius was at this time *Magister utriusque militiae,* with a sphere of authority in southern Gaul. The office held by Albinus is unknown, but four years later he became Praetorian Prefect in Italy. See *Inter Leon. Epp.* No. 8. *P.L.* 54, 622.

[22] Cf. the edict of Valentinian III providing for the defence of Rome. *Nov. Val.* 5, ed. P. Meyer, p. 82.

[23] Prosper, *Chronicon,* sub ann. 440. *M.G.H., Chron. min.,* Vol. I, p. 478. "Defuncto Xysto episcopo XL. amplius diebus Romana ecclesia sine antistite fuit, mirabili pace atque patientia praesentiam diaconi Leonis expectans, quem tunc inter Aetium et Albinum redintegrantem Galliae detinebant, quasi ideo longius esset abductus, ut et electi meritum et eligentium iudicium probaretur, igitur Leo diaconus legatione publica accitus et gaudenti patriae praesentatus XLIII Romanae ecclesiae episcopus ordinatur."

[24] It was also the occasion of an annual synod of the bishops belonging to Leo's metropolitan jurisdiction. Such synods had been previously held in the time of Xystus III, see *Ep.* 2, 1, JK 390, and doubtless also earlier.

supported by an enthusiastic and unanimous gathering of the local church, as he addresses the assembly with these words: [25]

" 'Let my mouth speak the praise of the Lord, and my soul and spirit, flesh and tongue, bless his holy Name.' Failure to acknowledge benefits conferred by God is a mark rather of ingratitude than of modesty, and what is more fitting than that the ministry of a (newly) consecrated bishop should begin with the sacrifice of praise to the Lord. . . . I therefore will give thanks to our God, and will ever so do 'for all the benefits that He hath done unto me.' Besides this, I join with you in celebrating with fitting gratitude your favourable choice, for I, as one who with the care of a shepherd longs for the salvation of your souls, recognize how much respect, love and confidence your devoted affection has shown to myself, when in spite of my lack of merits in the past you have given your verdict so generously in my favour. So I beg of you, by the mercy of God, aid with your prayers him whom you have sought to the fulfilment of your wishes, so that the grace of God may abide in me and that your confidence in myself may not waver."

Words such as these are sufficient to suggest that "there is something of the Aristotelian μεγαλοψυχία in Leo, as he ascends the throne which was called *par excellence* apostolical; he does not think of evading the task imposed on him; he has a grave confidence that it is the task for him, that he is the man for it, and that he will be divinely enabled to satisfy its requirements." [26] Not less remarkable is the joy with which he welcomes the opportunity of undertaking a great responsibility, for the fulfilment of which he evidently believes himself to possess no less than a divine vocation. On the other hand, while he freely confesses his absolute dependence on God's grace,[27] his sermons show little sign of that artificial self-depreciation,[28] which so often occurs in the utterances of lesser men. With engaging simplicity and terse directness of language he combines an appeal for the co-operation of his hearers with a clear affirmation of his God-given authority,

[25] *Serm.* 1. *P.L.* 54, 141.
[26] Bright, *Sermons of St. Leo,* p. iv.
[27] *Serm.* 1; cf. *Serm.* 3, 1. "non desperamus . . . quia non de nobis, sed de illo praesumimus, qui operatur in nobis."
[28] e.g. Gregory I, *Registrum,* 1, *Epp.* 5 and 7. JE 1071, 1074.

suggesting that, only if the former is accorded and the latter is recognized, can the fulfilment of their common purpose be attained.

Each year, as the date of his consecration returned, Leo celebrated the occasion by delivering a sermon similar to the one which we have just considered. The second of the series opened like the first on a note of triumphal rejoicing.[29]

" As in due course the day returns, on which it pleased the Lord that I should begin my episcopal office, I have just cause to rejoice to the glory of God. For, though He found in me nothing to deserve such things, He has conferred on me great gifts, only that I might love Him much and make His grace a source of wonder. Surely such an act on His part would suggest to us, yes, convince us, that none may presume on his own righteousness, nor be distrustful of His mercy, which shows itself chiefly in sanctifying the sinner and in recovering the fallen."

Others besides Leo himself were to have good cause to rejoice. At a time when the State was a prey to civil and military chaos, when the western world was suffering the birth pangs of a new Germano-Latin civilization, and when the Church was engaged in steering the barque of faith amid the treacherous shoals of questionable doctrines and sub-Christian systems of thought, there was urgent need that the occupant of the principal throne of Christendom should be one such as Leo, " who could make the see of Peter take the place of the tottering imperial power . . . capable above all things of disciplining and consolidating western Christendom, so that it might present a firm front to the heretical barbarians, and remain in unshaken consistency throughout all that stormy period which links the ancient with the modern world." [30] In recognition of Leo's success in achieving this task the gratitude of the Church has popularly awarded him the title " great," one which he shares with Gregory I alone of all the long line of Roman bishops. It will be one of our main concerns to see how far this verdict is justified in the light of history.

[29] *Serm.* 2, 1. *P.L.* 54, 142.
[30] Gore, *D.C.B.*, Art. *Leo I, pope,* Vol. III, p. 654.

Additional Note

THE "SYLLABUS" ON GRACE

The document known as the *Syllabus,*[31] referred to in the preceding chapter and described by Duchesne as "the first attempt to define the attitude of the Roman Church itself in regard to the questions at issue"[32] (sc. in the Pelagian controversy) consists of a collection of papal and conciliar definitions on the subject of Grace and Freewill, preceded by a preface, which allows us to form some idea of the point of view of the compiler himself. He lays considerable stress on the importance of the right use of Grace and on the need of co-operation with the will of God, while he acknowledges that all good proceeds from God alone. Thus he says:

"God so works in the hearts of men and in freewill itself that holy thought, good counsel and every desire of goodwill is of God, since through Him alone are we capable of anything good, without whom we can do nothing."[33]

And later:

"Therefore we have confirmed these ecclesiastical rules and documents derived from divine authority so that we may acknowledge God as the author of all good desires and works and of all intentions and achievements by which after their conversion men strive after God, and we are convinced that all human merits are anticipated by His Grace, by whose help alone we can begin either to will or to do anything that is good."[34]

[31] It was discovered by Dionysius Exiguus among the papal archives and by him included as an appendix to Pope Celestine I's *Ep.* 21, JK 381. *Praeteritorum sedis apostolicae episcoporum auctoritates de gratia Dei.*

[32] *Histoire,* Vol. III, p. 285.

[33] *Syllabus,* c. 10. "Quod ita Deus in cordibus hominum atque in ipso libero operetur arbitrio ut sancta cogitatio, pium consilium, omnisque motus bonae voluntatis ex Deo sit, quia per illum aliquid boni possumus sine quo nihil possumus."

[34] *Ibid.,* 14. "His ergo ecclesiasticis regulis et ex divina sumptis auctoritate documentis . . . confirmati sumus ut omnium bonorum affectuum atque operum et omnium studiorum omniumque virtutum quibus ab initio fidei ad Deum tenditur, Deum profiteamur auctorem, et non dubitemus ab ipsius gratia omnia hominis merita praeveniri, per quem fit ut aliquid boni et velle incipiamus et facere." Cf. Leo, *Ep.* 1, 3. JK 398.

And again:

"He verily acts in us so that we may will and do what He wills, neither does He suffer those (gifts), meant to be used, to lie idle in us, nor award them for us to neglect: hence we too are to be fellow-workers with the Grace of God." [35]

On the other hand it is significant that the author passes over the more controversial points in Augustine's doctrine, such as the irresistibility of grace, the theory of predestination, and the question as to whether salvation is intended for all or only for a few.[36]

From internal evidence it seems probable that he had in mind not only the overt Pelagianism of Julian of Eclanum, but also its more modified form, generally known as semi-Pelagianism,[37] as taught by John Cassian and others of the school of Southern Gaul. The similarity of his thought with that of Leo's anti-Pelagian letters, e.g. *Epp.* 1 and 2, suggests, though it does not compel, the conclusion that it is of a Leonine compilation.

[35] *Syllabus,* 14. "Agit quippe in nobis ut quod vult et velimus et agamus, nec otiosa in nobis esse patitur quae exercenda, non negligenda donavit, ut et nos cooperatores simus gratia Dei."

[36] See esp. *ibid.,* 15.

[37] The term itself is probably of seventeenth century origin. See Duchesne, *Histoire,* Vol. III, p. 274, n. 1. By Leo and his contemporaries they were classed as Pelagians *tout court.* Cf. Prosper, ap. Augustine, *Ep.* 225, 7. *P.L.* 33, 1006.

CHAPTER III

LEO AS BISHOP OF ROME

THE unanimity of the Roman Church in electing Leo to fill the see left vacant by the death of Xystus III was a good omen for its internal peace during a pontificate lasting twenty-one years. No doubt an important factor which contributed to the realization of such peace was the character possessed by the new Pope, the strength of which is clearly revealed by the manner in which he dealt with the problems which arose in the course of his administration, particularly in Rome itself.

The gravest of these problems was a partial consequence of the immigration into Italy of a promiscuous number of refugees from Africa, fleeing from the violence of the Vandal invaders. Since A.D. 439 the city of Carthage and the proconsular province had been in their hands, and it was no longer possible for anyone who was not Arian in faith or barbarian by birth to enjoy there any material or personal security. Doubtless many of those who emigrated were Catholic Christians, but it is certain that their numbers included a considerable proportion of adherents of the Manichaean cult.[1]

This cult had probably first reached Rome at least a century and a half previously, but for various reasons, and not least because of the disfavour with which it was regarded by the emperors, pagan and Christian alike,[2] the Church of the capital hitherto had had little cause to regard it as a serious

[1] Leo himself refers to the Manichaean immigration and its cause in *Serm.* 16, 5. *P.L.* 54, 179A. "Hos . . . pestiferos, quos aliarum regionum perturbatio nobis intulit crebriores." For details as to the cult see Additional Note, *The Origin and Development of Manichaeism.*

[2] A rescript of Diocletian issued A.D. 290, *Cod. Greg.* XIV, iv, 4–7, ed. Haenel, p. 44, ordered the leaders of the cult when detected to be burnt alive, its books to be destroyed and its adherents to be decapitated, unless they recanted. Kirch, *Fontes,* No. 328. Similar legislation, though with some mitigation of the prescribed penalties, was enacted under the Christian Emperors, e.g. Valentinian I. *Cod. Theod.* XVI, v, 3; Theodosius I, *Cod. Theod.* XVI, v, 9; Honorius, *Cod. Theod.* XVI, v, 38, 40; Valentinian III, *Cod. Theod.* XVI, v, 62. Mirbt, *Quellen,* No. 181.

rival.[3] In Africa, however, the situation was altogether otherwise. There it could boast an elaborate organization, and embraced an extensive membership.[4] So long as Africa remained in Roman hands, in spite of the officially hostile attitude of the legislature, Manichaeans appear to have enjoyed a considerable degree of toleration. But once the Vandals obtained possession they had as good reason to fear for their safety as had their Catholic neighbours. There followed an extensive emigration in search of new homes in provinces which had hitherto remained immune from Vandal attack. Sicily and Italy, both easily accessible, seemed to promise a safe refuge, and thither came Catholics and Manichaeans side by side.

Even so, it is possible that but for the fact that the occupant of the papal chair was a man of vigorous and determined action they might have been left undisturbed. As it was the Manichaeans found in Leo an implacable adversary, whom nothing less than the total suppression of their cult could satisfy.

The report which reached Leo told of the celebration of religious rite, the details of which were sufficiently scandalous in his opinion to demand a public investigation.[5] His first step was to take counsel with the civil power, and next to summon a composite court, which embraced not only representatives of the resident and neighbouring clergy but also members of the Senate, acting in its judicial capacity.[6] To this court was brought a number of Manichaean teachers and disciples of both sexes,[7] who openly acknowledged the nature

[3] On Manichaeism at Rome see Augustine, *Confessio*, 5, 10. Cf. *Liber pont.*, ed. Duchesne, Vol. I, p. 169, n. 3.

[4] On Augustine's own association with Manichaeism see *De mor. eccl. cath. et de mor. manich.* *P.L.* 32, 1310–1378; id., *c. Faustum.* *P.L.* 42, 207–518. Cf. *Dict. Théol. Cath.*, Vol. I, col. 2292–4.

[5] The main sources are *Serm.* 16, 4. *P.L.* 54, 178; *Ep.* 7, JK 405; *Nov. Val.* 18, ed. P. Meyer, p. 103. *Inter Leon. Epp.*, No. 8. *P.L.* 54, 622.

[6] *Serm.* 16, 4. "Residentibus itaque mecum episcopis ac presbyteris ac in eundem consensum Christianis viris ac nobilibus congregatis"; *Ep.* 15, 16, JK 412, "frequentissima praesentia sacerdotum, sed etiam illustrium virorum dignitas, et pars quaedam senatus ac plebis"; *Nov. Val.* 18, *Inter Leon. Epp.*, No. 8. *P.L.* 54, 622, "in iudicio beatissimi papae Leonis, coram senatu amplissimo." On the judicial functions of the Roman senate at this time cf. Bury, *Later Roman Empire*, Vol. I, p. 22.

[7] *Serm.* 16, 4. "Electos et Electas eorum iussimus praesentari; *Ep.* 7, 1, JK 405, "Plurimos impietatis Manichaeae sequaces et doctores in Urbe investigatio nostra."

of their teaching and the details of their cultus.[8] The witnesses included so distinguished a personage as the "bishop" of the sect, whose evidence, given both verbally and in writing,[9] showed that an immoral act of a particularly gross character had taken place, namely ceremonial intercourse between a youth and a girl of ten years; the accuracy of which was sufficiently guaranteed by the presence in court of the offender himself, as well as of the two women who had been responsible for the provision of the child.[10] In giving judgment the court discriminated according to the degree of culpability of the defendants. Thus only the obdurate were severely punished. Those who were ready to condemn both in word and writing the name and teaching of Manes were subjected to lighter penalties; those who refused were consigned to lifelong banishment.[11]

Leo devotes considerable space among his sermons and letters to this affair, and in addition supplies valuable information as to the character of the cult as practised in the fifth century.

According to him the Manichaeans identified their founder with a manifestation of the Holy Ghost, Who thus continued to inspire his disciples, and unfold to them knowledge of the past.[12] He alludes to their critical attitude towards the Scriptures of the Christian Church, and draws attention to their affection for apocryphal and mythological writings. Apparently it was not difficult to recognize a Manichaean in

[8] *Serm. ibid.* "qui cum de perversitate dogmatis sui, et de festivitatum suarum consuetudine multa reserassent."

[9] *Nov. Val.* 18. *P.L.* 54, 622B. "Adeo ut eorum quoque qui diceretur episcopus, et voce propria proderet, et omnia scelerum suorum secreta perscriberet."

[10] *Serm. ibid.* "Aderant enim omnes personae, per quas infandum facinus fuerat perpetratum, puella scilicet ut multum decennis, et duae mulieres, quae ipsam nutrierant, et huic sceleri praeparabant. Praesto erat etiam adolescentulus vitiator puellae, et episcopus ipsorum detestandi criminis ordinator." *Ep.* 7, 1, "ipse qui eorum dicebatur episcopus, a nobis tentus, proderet flagitiosa in suis mysticis quae teneret."

[11] *Ep.* 7, 1. "aliquanti vero, qui ita se demerserant, ut nullum his auxiliantis posset remedium, subvenire, subditi legibus, secundum Christianorum principum constituta . . . per publicos iudices perpetuo sunt exilio relegati." On the anti-Manichaean legislation see above, p. 43.

[12] *Serm.* 76, 6. *P.L.* 54, 408. "in magistro suo Mane sanctum apparuisse Spiritum crediderunt, . . . in quo ita Spiritus Dei manserit, ut non aliud fuerit Manes ipse quam Spiritus qui per ministerium corporeae vocis et linguae discipulos suos in omnem induceret veritatem et nunquam cognita praeteritorum secreta saeculorum reseraret."

the streets of Rome. One might know him by his dingy clothing and pallid features,[13] or differentiate him from a Christian by his observance of Sunday and Monday as days of fasting in honour of the sun and moon.[14] Leo further alludes frequently to the Manichaean rejection of the essential facts of Christ's incarnate life, and to its docetic view of His human nature.[15] He also speaks of its repudiation of the validity of Christian Baptism.[16] Perhaps his general opinion of the cult is best illustrated by the following:

"He (sc. the devil) built himself a stronghold in the folly of the Manichaeans . . . where he could enjoy, not just a single kind of depravity, but a blend of every error and blasphemy. The unholiness of pagans, the blindness of the Jews after the flesh, the illicit secrets of magic, whatsoever in fact that is impious or blasphemous in every heresy, all this in a concretion of every sort of filth has flowed together into that sect as into a sort of cesspool." [17]

Leo had evidently no doubt as to the nature of the enemy with which he was dealing. Nor did he rest content with merely official action. Shortly after the trial, the details of which we have just described, he preached to a Roman congregation on the subject.[18] For the benefit of his hearers he drew a graphic picture of the whole investigation, and concluded by exhorting them to reveal to their parish priests the identity of any Manichaean sectaries known to them, appealing for their general co-operation in the task of effecting

[13] *Serm.* 34, 5. *P.L.* 54, 249A. "discretionibus ciborum, sordibus vestium, vultuumque palloribus." Cf. *Serm.* 42, 4. *P.L.* 54, 278B.

[14] *Serm.* 42, 5. *P.L.* 54, 279B. "luminaribus caeli stultam abstinentiam devoventes: siquidem in honorem solis ac lunae prima ac secunda Sabbati ieiunare delegerunt." Cf. *Serm.* 22, 6. *P.L.* 54, 198C; 27, 5. *P.L.* 54, 219A.

[15] *Serm.* 24, 4. *P.L.* 54, 206B, "nec ullum habent in Christi regeneratione consortium, qui cum de Maria virgine negant corporaliter natum: ut cuius non credunt veram nativitatem, nec veram recipiunt passionem." Cf. *Serm.* 34, 4. *P.L.* 54, 247BC.

[16] *Serm.* 9, 4. *P.L.* 54, 163C, "baptismum regenerationis totius gratiae virtute dispoliat."

[17] *Serm.* 16, 4. *P.L.* 54, 178A. "arcem tamen sibi in Manichaeorum struxit (sc. diabolus) insania . . . ; ubi non unius pravitatis speciem, sed omnium simul errorum impietatumque mixturam generaliter possideret. Quod enim in paganis profanum, quod in Judaeis carnalibus caecum, quod in secretis magicae artis illicitum, quod denique in omnibus haeresibus sacrilegum atque blasphemum est, hoc in istos, quasi in sentinam quamdam, cum omnium sordium concretione confluxit."

[18] *Serm.* 9. *P.L.* 54, 160C.

the cult's total suppression.[19] To delate a Manichaean, he tells them, is not merely an act of piety but almost a means of grace.[20] Preaching again on the same topic at a later date, he prohibits Roman Christians from all social intercourse with the sectaries, while he demands full information as to their resorts and schools, their patrons and adherents.[21]

Nevertheless, even in Rome, the effective execution of Leo's plan was beset with some difficulty. This was largely due to the fact that, as he tells us, some Manichaeans were in the habit of concealing their real profession under a cloak of occasional conformity,[22] or by representing their worship of the heavenly bodies as indirectly addressed to Christ Himself.[23]

The next step in Leo's anti-Manichaean campaign was to inform the suffragans of the Roman province of the recent course of events at the capital and to solicit their co-operation.[24] The need of doing so was the more urgent in view of the known fact that many adherents of the sect had fled from Rome to escape arrest at the hands of Leo's agents.[25] He

[19] *Ibid.*, 4. "Ad hanc vos hortamur industriam, ut Manichaeos ubicumque latentes vestris presbyteris publicetis." The use of "vestris" appears to imply the assignment of priests, at this date, to particular "congregations."

[20] *Ibid.* "Magna est enim pietas prodere latebras impiorum . . . Vobis . . . ante tribunal Domini proderit, quod indicimus, quod rogamus."

[21] *Serm.* 16, 5. *P.L.* 54, 179A. "Hos . . . ab amicitia vestra penitus abdicate; vosque praecipue mulieres, a talium notitia et colloquis abstinete . . . moneo ut si cui vestrum innotuerit, ubi habitent, ubi doceant, quos frequentent, et in quorum societate requiescant, nostrae sollicitudinis fideliter indicetis."

[22] *Serm.* 42, 5. *P.L.* 54, 279B. "Cumque ad tegendam infidelitatem suam nostris audeant interesse conventibus, ita in sacramentorum communione se temperant, ut interdum, ne penitus latere non possint, ore indigno Christi corpus accipiant, sanguinem autem redemptionis nostrae haurire omnino declinent." Later in the same passage he affirms that the refusal of the chalice by the laity is to be punished by excommunication.

[23] *Serm.* 34, 4. *P.L.* 54, 248C. "doceant in sole et luna colere Christum."

[24] *Ep.* 7, JK 405, dated January 30th, A.D. 444. The title "ad episcopos per Italiam," as given in the majority of the MSS. may suggest a range wider than southern Italy. Possibly, as Batiffol, *Siège Apostolique,* pp. 436f. thinks, copies were sent to the metropolitans of Milan and Aquileia for publication to their suffragans. The details supplied by this letter do not add much to the information already supplied by Leo's *Sermons* on the subject.

[25] *Ibid.*, 2. "aliquantos de his, quos hic, ne se absolverent, arctior reatus involverat, cognovimus aufugisse."

therefore addressed a letter, early in the year following the discovery, to the bishops of his metropolitical obedience requesting their help in effecting the general extirpation of the sectaries in southern Italy. Nor was this all. A brief description of the affair given by Prosper suggests that the Pope also took steps to acquaint the greater churches of the East with the danger which threatened society; [26] and we may suppose that they too were invited to co-operate in the measures which had been taken.[27]

We possess yet a further document of major importance bearing on the present subject, to which allusion has already been made. It is an imperial edict [28] published some eighteen months after the event. Whether it was issued as a consequence of a decision on the part of the Government to reinforce existing anti-Manichaean legislation, or because Leo, finding the ecclesiastical authorities of the provinces insufficiently active in the execution of his plans, decided to invoke the support of the secular power, cannot now be known, any more than it is possible to guage its actual effect. After alluding to earlier legislation against the sect,[29] the edict goes on to mention the recent trial in Rome, and enacts that wherever these sectaries are discovered they are to be subjected to the penalties required by the law. Trials are to be held and liberty is to be given for anyone who chooses to do so to lodge an indictment, while concealment of their whereabouts or suppression of information is severely

[26] *Chronicon,* sub ann. 443. *M.G.H.,* Vol. IX, p. 479. "Hoc tempore plurimos Manichaeos intra urbem latere diligentiae [*al.* diligentia] papae Leonis innotuit, qui eos de secretis suis erutos et oculis totius ecclesiae publicatos omnes dogmatis sui turpitudines et damnare fecit et prodere incensis eorum codicibus, quorum magnae moles fuerant interceptae, quae cura viro sancto divinitus, ut apparuit, inspirata non solum Romanae urbi sed etiam universo orbi plurimum profuit, si quidem confessionibus in urbe captorum qui doctores eorum, qui episcopi, quive presbyteri in quibus provinciis vel civitatibus degerent patefactum sit, multique Orientalium partium sacerdotes industriam apostolici rectoris imitati sunt." He mentions specifically the burning of Manichaean writings as prescribed by law.

[27] Cf. Theodoret, *Ep.* 113. *P.G.* 83, 1313; *Inter Leon. Epp.,* No. 52, 2.

[28] *Inter Leon. Epp.,* No. 8. *P.L.* 54, 622B. *Nov. Val.* 18, ed. P. Meyer, p. 103.

[29] "Manichaeos . . . quos . . . toto orbe pellendos omnium retro principum statuta iudicarunt." Strictly speaking "omnium" was an exaggeration, since there had been no legislation on the subject before the time of Diocletian, while Theodosius I had been the first to renew it after a lapse of more than half a century.

proscribed. The edict reinforces earlier laws by declaring Manichaeans excluded from civil service and from residence in urban areas,[30] and by making them incapable either of inheriting or of leaving property by will; all such property is to be confiscated to the public treasury. In addition it deprives them of the right to take proceedings for damages in the courts or to contract a legal agreement. Finally, it prescribes that any officials of the imperial civil service who are sufficiently compliant or neglectful to admit members of that cult to any office shall on conviction be penalized by a fine of ten pounds.

The whole affair is worthy of attention, not only for the light which it throws on Leo's character, as indicating his thoroughness and determination in embarking on a particular course of action, but as providing the first known example of a partnership between Church and State in carrying out a policy of religious persecution. Hitherto it was the State alone which had initiated the suppression of heterodox belief and practice.[31] Now for the first time the Church, in the person of the Pope, undertook the task of seeking out and of bringing to judgment the adherents of a rival cult, and although it may be pleaded that the extension of such a cult was not merely inimical to the very existence of the Church, but by reason of the peculiar character of its tenets and observances threatened the stability of the social fabric, it is not difficult to see that the formal adoption of such a policy was fraught with considerable danger, not so much to its victims as to its agents. It was a policy which involved the use of force and the suppression of liberty of conscience. At the same time, it should be remembered that Leo did no more than enforce the law as it then existed, and that the ultimate responsibility lay not so much with him as with those who a century and a half previously had set on foot the anti-Manichaean legislation. On the other hand it might be said that the anti-social character of the sect's beliefs and practices justified the strongest possible measures against it in the interests of public morals.

[30] *Ibid.* "Dignitate militiae et urbium habitatione privandos." It should be remembered that the term "militia" at this date had lost any military significance and was used to denote purely civil service.

[31] e.g. *Cod. Theod.*, XVI, i, 2, ed. Mommsen, p. 833. Mirbt, *Quellen*, No. 134. Published by Theodosius I, February 27th, A.D. 380.

There is good reason to conjecture that the measures taken by Leo for the total suppression of Manichaeism in Rome were largely successful, since we hear little of the cult or of its adherents in connexion with the capital.[32] Manichaeism, however, was not the only enemy of the Catholic Faith with which he had to contend. Heresy in one form or another, in spite of imperial legislation, still persisted among a population so cosmopolitan as that of Rome, and even Leo could not prevent the revival of Arianism, during the regime of the all powerful Suevian, Ricimer, himself Arian by religion.[33] It is probable, however, that a timely warning [34] issued by him against the insidious propaganda of Egyptian monophysites was successful in preventing the supporters of Eutyches and Dioscorus from winning converts among the Roman Christians.

We have no direct evidence as to Leo's relations with the Jews. Since the days of Honorius they had enjoyed certain privileges which rendered them legally immune from official interference.[35] Even if they were occasionally the victims of violence in Alexandria,[36] and in other quarters of the Empire where fanaticism flourished, it seems likely that in Rome they were usually unmolested. To this general attitude the relations between Christians and Jews there during Leo's pontificate appears to offer no exception.[37]

Paganism by the beginning of the fifth century had ceased

[32] *Liber pont., Vita Gelasii* (ed. Duchesne), Vol. I, p. 255 mentions that Gelasius like Leo detected the existence of Manichaeans in Rome and had them expelled. Their books were publicly burnt in the porch of Santa Maria Maggiore.

[33] Leo's successor, Hilary I, is called "episcopus ecclesiae catholicae urbis Romae," Mansi, *Concilia,* VII, 960, from which we may infer the existence of an Arian bishop of Rome at this time. Cf. Kidd, *History,* Vol. III, p. 390 and n. 2. Ricimer erected a central church, St. Agatha, near the Palatine. See Grisar, *History,* Vol. I, p. 114.

[34] *Serm.* 96, *P.L.* 54, 466, preached in the Church of St. Anastasia, in the Greek quarter close to the Emporium on the Tiber, a quarter much frequented by merchants and others from the East.

[35] *Cod. Theod.,* XVI, viii, 20. The quarter of Rome, known as *Transtiberim,* had been largely populated by Jews since the early days of the Empire. See Grisar, *History,* Vol. I, p. 175.

[36] e.g. in the affair of Hypatia. Socrates, *H.E.,* 7, 15.

[37] Ambrose, however, was confronted with problems arising from the presence of Jews in the East; see his *Epp.* 40 and 41; Homes Dudden, *St. Ambrose,* Vol. II, pp. 371–9. No serious difficulties arose in Rome till the pontificate of Symmachus. See Cassiodorus, *Var.,* 4, 43, ed. Mommsen, ap. *M.G.H.,* Auct. antiqu., Vol. XII, p. 133.

to exercise any profound influence over the lives or minds of the inhabitants of the city. A few of the nobility still continued to give a nominal allegiance to it,[38] and the temples, though closed, were as yet intact.[39] What popular paganism there was, was limited to the perfunctory observance of certain annual festivals such as the *Lupercalia* on February 15th [40] and the *ludi Apollinares* which lasted from July 6th to 13th,[41] and to the survival of certain pagan customs. Leo notices in one of his sermons [42] that certain worshippers, before entering the *atrium* of St. Peter's basilica, were in the habit of turning at the top of the steps and bowing to the rising sun. He reminds his audience that the sun's rays are but the reflection of God's glory and that they should revere and worship Him in church, and not imitate the folly of the heathen by such a senseless practice.

The energy and zeal of Leo, shown by the measures taken by him for the safeguarding of his flock against the insidiousness of Manichaeism or the follies of paganism, may be further illustrated by mentioning examples of his concern for the maintenance of Christian public worship. In the course of his pontificate some important improvements and additions were made to the Roman churches. First of all he was responsible for some general restorations to the basilica of St. Peter. The mosaic which adorned the main entrance to the church down to the destruction of the original building in the time of Pope Gregory IX was Leo's own work,[43] the cost of which was borne by Marinianus, ex-Prefect and *Consul ordinarius*, and his wife Anastasia.[44] He also replaced the original simple

[38] e.g. Volusianus, *Comes rerum privatarum* in A.D. 408. See *Cod. Theod.*, V, xvi, 31.

[39] Cf. *Cod. Theod.*, XVI, x, 19 of A.D. 408.

[40] Grisar, *History*, Vol. II, pp. 217f. where he mentions that a vain attempt was made to reintroduce the festival in the pontificate of Gelasius.

[41] Leo, *Serm.* 84, 1. *P.L.* 54, 433. Cf. Grisar, *op. cit.*, Vol. III, p. 281.

[42] Id. *Serm.* 27, 4. *P.L.* 54, 218. It is possible that this practice reflects Manichaean influence. We may notice, however, an interesting parallel in Ezekiel viii. 17.

[43] *Liber pontificalis*, ed. Duchesne, Vol. I, p. 239, n. 6. The details of the mosaic are known from the Farfa Codex preserved at Eton College (No. 124). Cf. Grisar, *Die alte Peterskirche*, in *Röm. Quartalschrift*, Vol. IX (1895), pp. 257ff.; id. *History*, Vol. II, pp. 72f.; *Analecta rom.*, Vol. I, pp. 463ff.

[44] *Liber pontificalis*, ed. Duchesne, Vol. I, p. cxxviia, n. 4.

decoration of the interior of the apse with something more permanent and elaborate.[45] To ensure the continuous and regular performance of divine service, but perhaps also to keep them under his close personal supervision he founded a monastery in close connexion with the basilica.[46] Finally, to protect the sanctity of the treasure which rested there, namely the relics of the Apostle, he appointed a regular service of guards, known as *cubicularii.*[47]

Leo's interest, however, was not confined to the basilica of St. Peter. The Church of St. Paul without the Walls had been entirely rebuilt in the reigns of Valentinian II, Theodosius I and Arcadius.[48] The decoration of the Triumphal Arch was Leo's special work. It happily survived the disastrous fire, in which the greater part of the basilica was consumed, though in a somewhat altered form.[49] Leo also provided for the restoration of the roof of the church, damaged by lightning,[50] and caused a fresh supply of water to flow in the *cantharus,* situated within the *atrium.*[51]

At least one parish church owed its origin to his interest. This was the Church of St. Stephen on the *Via Latina.* For many centuries its site was forgotten, and was not rediscovered till 1858. Fragments of the old metrical dedicatory inscrip-

[45] *Liber pontificalis,* ed. Duchesne, *op. cit., ibid.*

[46] *Ibid.,* probably the monastery of SS. John and Paul. Cf. Batiffol, *History of Roman Breviary,* pp. 48f. Pope Xystus III had earlier founded a monastery near the catacombs of St. Sebastian on the *Via Appia* without the walls. Jerome, *Ep.* 127, 18, shows that in his time monasticism was already tending to assert its independence of episcopal authority.

[47] *Ibid.,* Vol. I, pp. 239, 241, n. 14. The title was evidently borrowed from the usage of the imperial palaces, and occurs in Margarini, *Inscript. S. Pauli,* Rome (1654), No. 281. Leo also appointed similar officers at the basilica of St. Paul. Cf. Grisar, *op. cit.,* Vol. II, p. 73.

[48] On the reconstruction of the basilica of St. Paul see Grisar, *op. cit.,* Vol. II, pp. 73ff., pp. 103ff. Lietzmann, *Petrus und Paulus,* pp. 211ff. The work was already in hand in A.D. 384. See *Coll. Avell.* (ed. Guenther), pp. 46f.; Seeck, *Regesten,* pp. 93f.

[49] On the original form of the mosaic and its inscriptions see Grisar, *op. cit., ibid.,* where details are given.

[50] *Liber pontificalis,* Vol. I, pp. 239f., n. 7. The latter part of the inscription preserved at the Monastery of St. Paul is evidently Leo's own work. It mentions a priest Felix, who was probably the father of Pope Felix III. See De Rossi, *Inscript. Christ.,* Vol. I, p. 366, No. 831, and Grisar, *op. cit.,* p. 76.

[51] De Rossi, *op. cit.,* Vol. II, pt. i, p. 80, No. 13.

tion contains the names of Demetrias, the foundress of the church, and of Leo himself.[52]

Like that of his great successor, Gregory I, the name of Leo has been associated with liturgical composition and reform. Although the attribution to him of the so-called *Sacramentarium Leonianum* has been shown to be no more than a dubious conjecture,[53] there are perhaps better grounds for holding that the interpolation of the words, "*sanctum sacrificium, immaculatam hostiam*" into the *Anaphora* of the Roman *Canon Missae* was due to instructions issued by him. More than this, however, it is impossible to say.[54]

Of Leo's relations with the secular power we have little evidence. At the time when as a deacon the future Pope was engaged on that important mission of reconciliation between the all powerful *Magister militum* Aetius and his rival, the Prefect Albinus,[55] the nerveless Valentinian III had held the imperial dignity for more than a quarter of a century. Through all that time he had remained but a shadowy and unsubstantial figure, while others better qualified to rule assumed the reins of government over such provinces of the Empire as they could acquire, whether by force or intrigue. Most of his years were spent in idle luxury amid the blandishments of an obsequious court, and it is probable that the initiative which prompted the publication of a large number of edicts during the course of his reign is to be ascribed more to his ministers than to himself. Occasional visits to the

[52] Only the plan of the church and some fragments came to light. See Grisar, *op. cit.*, Vol. II, pp. 76f. The so-called *Epistola ad Demetriadem*, *P.L.* 55, 161, is certainly a pseudo-Leonine work.

[53] The Sacramentary was first published by Bianchini in 1735, who was himself responsible for the title based on slender evidence. The Ballerini included a reprint of Bianchini's work in their edition of the works of Leo, *P.L.* 55, 21ff., while showing that it is evidently an unofficial collection of Masses, compiled in the earlier part of the sixth century. Cf. Duchesne, *Origines* (1889), pp. 129–37; Bardenhewer, *Geschichte der altkirchl. lit.*, Vol. IV, pp. 622f.; Lietzmann, *op. cit.*, pp. 30ff., who shows convincing grounds for dating it in the pontificate of Vigilius, i.e. not earlier than A.D. 538. A further liturgical composition, *Pro Reconciliatione Penitentium, P.L.* 55, 157, has been also attributed to Leo.

[54] Duchesne, *Liber pontificalis,* Vol. I, p. 241, n. 12 regards the tradition as authentic, and suggests that it was an orthodox reaction to the Manichaean abhorrence of the use of wine in the Liturgy.

[55] See Chap. II, p. 38.

ancient imperial capital broke the monotony of the time spent amid the marshes of Ravenna, and it was while the Emperor was in Rome that the two edicts of A.D. 445,[56] one relating to the Manichaean trial and the other to the irregular conduct of Hilary of Arles, were published. In view of what is known of their respective personalities, it is reasonable to suppose that those edicts were far more the work of Leo than of Valentinian, though they bore the Emperor's name.

Five years later the Emperor, his wife Licinia Eudoxia, whom he had married at Constantinople thirteen years perviously, and his mother Galla Placidia were once again on their way southwards. By a happy coincidence their arrival in Rome synchronized with the eve of the *Cathedra Petri,*[57] a festival of pagan origin, which had been adapted by the Roman Church to the commemoration of departed occupants of the Roman see.[58] Their presence in the city provided Leo with a heaven-sent opportunity for soliciting the support of the Western sovereigns against the powerful influence of their colleague Theodosius II, wholly directed by the eunuch chamberlain, Chrysaphius, in the interests of his protégé, Eutyches, and the "monophysite" council of A.D. 449.[59]

But if Leo had some reason to fear the success of Eutyches, Valentinian himself had no less solid grounds for apprehension. In the closing years of the reign of his equally undistinguished predecessor, Honorius, a new enemy had appeared on the borders of the Danubian provinces. Travelling rapidly across the plains and steppes of eastern Europe the barbarous Huns, with their stunted bodies, mounted on surefooted, cobby horses, had made their name a terror to East and West, to Goth and Roman alike, even to the extent of imposing a handsome tribute on the Empire as the price of immunity from invasion.[60] But it was evident that respite

[56] See above and Chap. VII.

[57] *Inter Leon. Epp.*, No. 55, 1. Cf. Chap. XI.

[58] On the origin and character of this festival see Lietzmann, *Petrus und Paulus,* pp. 93–103, and below p. 79, n. 57.

[59] On the correspondence which ensued between the two courts see Chap. XI.

[60] The main sources for the Huns and their invasions are Priscus, *De leg. gent.*, fragm. 1–6; *De leg. Rom.*, fragm. 2–5; fragm. 2 in *Fragm. Hist. Graec.*, Vol. V, p. 25. Marcellus, *Chronicon* in *M.G.H.*, Auct. antiqu., Vol. XI, *Chron. min.*, Vol. II, pp. 81f.; *Chronicon Paschale, P.G.* 92, 807.

from their attacks was only temporary and with the accession of Attila to the command of the Hunnish armies conditions even more humiliating than before were accepted by the trembling court of Constantinople.[61] For the next ten years the destiny of Europe seemed to lay at Attila's disposal.

Not long after Valentinian's arrival in Rome the Hun found a convenient pretext for invading the Western provinces. It seems that Honoria, the Emperor's sister, had long begrudged the power, or rather its semblance, wielded by her incompetent brother, and at a crucial moment in her career adopted the desperate expedient of inviting the aid of Attila to her defence.[62] By the beginning of the following year (A.D. 451) Attila's preparations were complete. In his westward march none dared to oppose his progress until, after ravaging Gaul, he came face to face with a strong force of Romans and Goths in the neighbourhood of Orleans. Their commander was that last bulwark of Roman military prestige, the Patrician, Aetius.[63] The invaders' defeat, however, on the field of Maurica, a turning point in European history, only served to divert the course of the invasion.[64] Attila was now resolved to attain his end by attacking the heart of the Empire.

Within twelve months the Huns were riding across the north Italian plains and presently the rich prize of Aquileia fell into their hands. The city was razed to the ground, never again to recover its prosperity, while even Milan itself only escaped total destruction by the payment of an enormous bribe. The only man who might have saved Italy, Aetius, seems to have lacked the power or possibly the inclination to intercept the invader.

The way to Rome lay open and undefended. It seemed, humanly speaking, impossible that the capital could escape. Yet Attila, unlike Alaric the Goth, and later Genseric the Vandal, never reached the city. The story of his withdrawal, and of a dramatic climax in Leo's career, will be told later on in the course of our study. We may leave the great Pope in his episcopal see for the moment, secure in the respect of

[61] By the peace of Anatolius A.D. 443.

[62] Priscus, *De leg. gent.*, fragm. 8.

[63] Jordanes, *Hist. Get.*, 42, 10. *M.G.H.*, Auct. antiqu., Vol. V, 1, p. 115.

[64] Sometimes known as the battle of Châlons. For the site of this battle see Bury, *Later Roman Empire*, Vol. I, p. 293.

Emperor, court and populace. The Church of Rome had good cause to feel that her expectations of him had not been disappointed.

Additional Note

THE ORIGIN AND DEVELOPMENT OF MANICHAEISM

Manichaeism has always provided something of an enigma to the historian and student of religion. This is due partly to the obscurities which belong to such evidence as we possess and partly to the lack of really trustworthy information. Naturally the most reliable sources from which we might learn the doctrine and history of the cult would be the writings themselves of Mani, its founder, and of his disciples. We know that the work of the master and that of his principal adherents formed a sort of sacred book, to which the highest authority was attributed. But apart from some fragments and summaries these works are now altogether lost. In place of them there are a number of Manichaean writings recently discovered in Central Asia, which are specially valuable because they come from circles which preserved the traditions of Mani. Even so, they fail to answer all our problems; they are written in little known languages, and of uncertain date, and being for the most part in a fragmentary state they require to be supplemented by evidence from indirect sources. Among the latter the more important are those of Mohammedan provenance. Two Islamic authors, An-Nadim (A.D. 980) and Sharastani (twelfth century) compiled their works direct from the authentic books of Mani and his first disciples.[65] Among Christian writers who mention the cult, Syriac authors such as Ephrem Syrus[66] (fourth century) and Theodore Bar-Khôni[67] (eighth century) are the best informed. Latin and Greek sources include the *Acta Archelai* of Hegemonius[68] (fourth century) and the anti-

[65] On Islamic sources cf. Flügel, *Mani seine Lehre und seine Schriften*, pp. 102f.; Alfaric, *Les écritures manichéens*, Vol. II; Cureton, *Le kitab almilal*, esp. Vol. I, pp. 188–92; E. Sachau, *Chronology*, in *Oriental Translation Fund*.

[66] *Serm. adv. haer.*, ed. rom., Vol. V, 437–560.

[67] Cumont, *Recherches sur le manichéisme*, fasc. 1.

[68] Ed. Beeson in the Berlin *Corpus*, *Griechische Christ. Schriftst.*

Manichaean tracts of Augustine,[69] who is of course our chief informant for the state of Manichaeism in North Africa at the end of the fourth century.

It would take too long to describe in detail the information which we owe to these various sources, and only a very brief summary can be attempted.

From Islamic authors we learn that Mani composed seven books in a special script. These were: (1) *The Book of the Mysteries,* (2) *The Book of Giants,* (3) *The Book of Precepts,* (4) *The Shâpurakân,* or book belonging to Sapor, King of Persia, (5) *The Treasure of Life,* (6) *The Farakmatija,* apparently a book of moral teaching, and (7) *The Gospel.* Besides these some seventy-six letters are mentioned, the subjects of most of which are known.

Before leaving the subject of sources some account should be given of the recent discoveries already mentioned. Certain papers were found by travellers in the region of Turfan, on the site of the vanished city of Kouchan in Mongolia, towards the close of the nineteenth century. About the same time other documents came to light at Touen-houang in Chinese Turkestan. Alfaric thus describes these discoveries: "Most of them are very incomplete and consist of scanty scraps, more or less torn and scarcely legible. They are written in little known languages which philologists have had difficulty in deciphering and they are all the harder to understand because they appear to be simply very literal translations and ill-adapted to the spirit of the language, even derived, in certain cases, from versions equally defective. Moreover, their recent editors have taken the trouble to remark that the translation which they give is in certain respects provisional and conjectural. What is more, even the clearest texts, which are best preserved, need much caution. Their origin is little known and one may be inclined to wonder whether they are in fact authentic."[70] The most important texts are as

[69] *De moribus eccl. cath. et de moribus manich., P.L.* 32, 1309–78; *De libero arbitrio, P.L.* 33, 1221–1310; *De Genesi, P.L.* 34, 174–220; *De vera religione, P.L.* 34, 121–72; *De utilitate credendi, P.L.* 42, 65–92; *De duabus animabus, P.L.* 42, 93–112; *Acta seu disputatio c. Fortunatum, P.L.* 42, 111–30; *Contra Adamantum, P.L.* 42, 129–72; *Contra epistolam Manichaei, P.L.* 42, 173–206; *Contra Faustum, P.L.* 42, 207–518; *De actis cum Felice, P.L.* 42, 519–52; *De natura boni, P.L.* 42, 551–72; *Contra Secundinum, P.L.* 42, 571–602.

[70] *Op. cit.,* Vol. I, p. 137.

follows: (1) *The Kouastouanift,*[71] a Manichaean confession of belief, (2) *Hymns,* (3) *The Tract of Touen-houang,* (4) *Historical Fragments,* including a life of Mani, the *Ardavift.*

We must now pass on to summarize what is known of this obscure and elusive subject.[72]

Mani (or Manes), the founder of the cult, is believed to have been born near Ctesiphon in Mesopotamia about the year A.D. 216. The story of his birth and the record of his early years have been elaborated with a multitude of legendary fantasies and may be passed over here. Beginning his life's work at the early age of twenty-four, he soon showed himself to be gifted with remarkable eloquence and indomitable energy. His first missionary objective was the conversion of the Persians. As was to be expected his doctrinal propaganda met with little encouragement from the ruling hierarchy of the Magi, and after a few years he was exiled from the country. To such a one as Mani, like Mahomet some four centuries later, banishment only served as a spur to further activity. With almost incredible rapidity he traversed a considerable part of the lands of the Middle and Far East, and spread his teaching far and wide. For the benefit of his immediate disciples and also for those with whom he was unable to establish personal contact, he set down his doctrinal and ethical principles in treatises, which rapidly became disseminated through the greater part not only of the Eastern world but also of the Roman Empire itself.

After some forty years of active work Mani returned to Persia, the scene of his earlier labours, only to find the same implacable hostility on the part of the upholders of the established religion of Zoroaster, which had formerly driven him from its borders. This time the Magians determined on his destruction and within two years succeeded in accomplish-

[71] Cf. *Journal of the Royal Asiatic Society,* 1911, pp. 277–314.

[72] Among recent works should be mentioned Bevan in *E.R.E.,* Art. *Manichaeism,* Vol. VIII, pp. 394ff.; *D.T.C.,* Art. *Manichéisme,* Vol. IX, col. 1841; Burkitt, *The Religion of the Manichees,* Cambridge 1925, who argues in the light of the Turfan discoveries that the Christian elements in Manichaeism are not a late addition to the pure primitive doctrine, but that on the contrary Christianity has provided some of its fundamental principles. See also S. A. Cook, in *J.T.S.,* Vol. XXVI (July 1925), pp. 382ff.

ing their design.[73] Yet if they hoped by their action to destroy his work they were destined to disappointment. The death of the master only served to promote the more rapid expansion of his teaching, and within a quarter of a century the whole of the East was honeycombed with Manichaean propaganda.

Of what nature this propaganda was the following summary of the sect's doctrines and practices will serve to show. In regard to their origin, though we cannot be certain as to the extent to which they were derived from any one of the multitude of gnostic systems which appeared from time to time in the East, yet it is clear that their essential basis was an emphatically dualistic cosmogony, implying a recognition of the co-eternity of the two ultimate principles of Good and Evil. A natural extension of this view led to the identification of good with light, of evil with darkness, with each of which was associated an elaborate hierarchy of derived and dependent spiritual beings, comparable in some measure as to their number, function and complexity with the " emanations " of the various gnostic theogonies. By means of this dualistic hypothesis the problem of evil was provided with a solution, the chief recommendation of which was its simplicity. Thus it was held that all the good there is in the physical world is to be explained as the consequence of a mythological catastrophe, the result of which was to imprison elements of goodness (or light) within the bonds of an essentially evil creation. Equally the question of soteriology resolves itself into a theory of a theandric exploration of the means by which the good elements might be released from their enforced imprisonment. Although the human race was recognized as possessed of a greater quantity of those elements than the vegetable and the animal *genera,* at least so far as the male sex is concerned, it was thought to be only an amalgam of good and evil in almost equal measure. Ultimately, it appears, the only means by which the good could be freed from the evil was the acquisition of knowledge, of which it was held that the man Jesus, the emissary of the heavenly powers known as the " Primitive Man " and " the Spirit of Life," was the chief channel of communication. That the sect's outlook was, on the whole,

[73] He was put to death at the stake or by crucifixion about the year A.D. 276.

essentially pessimistic is seen from the fact that the majority of mankind was believed to submit willingly to the bondage of evil; while at the same time it was recognized that man has the power, and therefore the duty, to live according to the higher principles of his existence, and to achieve his liberty from the realm of darkness by seeking knowledge, by which he might distinguish aright the good and evil within himself. The chief means to such knowledge was held to be the life according to the Spirit and the mortification of man's material nature.

Mortification was therefore an important part of the Manichaean code of conduct and was systematized by the imposition of three *tabus,* known respectively as "the *tabu* of the mouth," "the *tabu* of the hand" and "the *tabu* of the heart."[74] The first of these involved an exacting rule of abstinence, not only from the moral offences of the lips, but also from all animal foods and from wine, and the second, the prohibition of all acts of violence whether to man, to beast or to plant, even to the length of excluding the faithful from participation in secular legal procedure. Of the three, the last was the most far reaching in its effect. Aimed primarily at hindering the supposed propagation of evil, it was logically destructive of the perpetuation of the human race itself, since it also prohibited all normal sexual relations.[75] With curious inconsistency, however, this absolute embargo on the satisfaction of a common human instinct was relaxed in certain particulars, though not without a highly paradoxical result. Thus, while it was held that the procreation of children in wedlock was to be ranked among the lowest grade of sins, intercourse with a concubine was treated as comparatively innocuous.[76]

Apart from such relaxations it may be supposed that the standard of conduct upheld by the sect proved unattainable by the majority of its adherents. Hence, in the interests of the weaker brethren, other modifications were introduced. This

[74] A precept difficult of reconciliation with a permissive use of the last as food.

[75] Involving the attachment of considerable prestige to an acceptance of the virgin state.

[76] Logically, of course, a strict observance of this *tabu* would require absolute continence; the less rigid standard was prone to encourage the evils of birth prevention, abortion and child exposure.

became possible by means of invoking the principle of a double standard of life,[77] including a rule of strict observance applicable only to the inner circle known as the " Elect," and another, less rigid, allowed to the outer circle of " hearers," [78] the former class alone being admitted to the privilege of Manichaean Baptism. Yet even so only the higher ranks even of the " Elect " were held to be obliged to the literal rigour of the three *tabus*, and lest they should starve by reason of the " *tabu* of the mouth " it was permitted to the inferior members of the sect to supply their material needs.

The lower grades satisfied the requirements of the sect by acknowledging a formal creed recognizing the honour due to the celestial bodies,[79] by frequent attendance at Manichaean worship, by observing monogamy and certain rules of fasting.[80] Among their positive duties was that of almsgiving, which was believed to be efficacious in obtaining the remission of lesser offences against the Manichaean code.[81]

As to the eschatology of the sect, an almost immediate *apotheosis* was promised to the " Elect " after death: for " hearers," on the other hand, it was held that a certain process of purging would be necessary; while it was taken for granted that none but adherents of some sort had any real hope of salvation. Loyal membership was to some extent secured by the forbidding prospect held out before the " sinners," namely a doom of ceaseless circumgyration of the universe in the company of monstrous apparitions, until the day of their annihilation in the final cataclysm of the material world. Unbelievers were collectively and summarily consigned to the realms of outer darkness.

Reference has already been made to public liturgical worship in connexion with the sect's religious practices. This worship found a natural focus in the observance of annual festivals, of which the most important was the one known as the " Bema," commemorating the martyrdom of the founder.

[77] On the subject of Manichaean ethics and grades of membership see Chauvanne et Pelliot, *Traité Manichéen, Journal asiatique* (1911), Ser. X, xviii, p. 564.

[78] Augustine himself had been admitted to this grade in his youth. See *C. lit. Petil.* 3, 20. *P.L.* 43, 357.

[79] Cf. Leo, *Serm.* 22, 6.

[80] *Ibid.*, *Serm.* 42, 5.

[81] Leo's own view on this point was similar. Cf. *Serm.* 16, 2.

It was held in the spring and, as time went on, came to possess a character similar to that of the Christian Easter. The sect also had an organized ministry [82] and rites of a sacramental nature resembling Baptism and the Eucharist, though it should be noticed that participation in them was restricted to the "Elect." [83] In general, however, it must be admitted that our information as to the details of their worship is distinctly meagre, due no doubt to the existence of a rigid *disciplina arcani,* which probably prevented their being described in writing and thus run the risk of their being disclosed to the uninitiated.

Enough has been said already to show that in spite of fundamental differences, as for example between their respective "Weltanschauungen," there was a considerable degree of resemblance between Manichaeism and Christianity. This may be further illustrated by the consideration of the importance attached by the former to the possession and use of certain sacred writings. Nevertheless the Manichaean "Canon of Scripture" had little in common with the Christian Bible, since it excluded the whole *corpus* of the Old Testament on the ground of its supposedly diabolical origin,[84] and while retaining the New Testament substantially as we know it, subjected it to wholesale expurgation. That this was necessary is readily intelligible if we remember that there was no room in its theology for an Incarnation of the Word of God. Thus the records of the Nativity, of the Passion and Resurrection were altogether rejected, and in their place there was introduced a docetic myth, better in keeping with the Manichaean view as to the evil origin of the material universe. In addition to this the sect repudiated all the epistolary writings except those of St. Paul, and even these were subjected to a process of drastic emendation. On the other hand it paid extravagant respect to many apocryphal

[82] Photius, *Contra Manich.,* i, 14. *P.G.* 102, 41 speaks of "twelve apostles."

[83] See Alfaric, *L'évolution intellectuelle de Saint Augustine,* p. 133, n. 2, where he points out that the Manichaeans substituted the element of water for wine.

[84] Cf. the Priscillianist view of Holy Scripture, *Ep.* 15, 15, JK 412.

books rejected by the Christian Church, such as the *Gospel of the Twelve* [85] and the *Acts of Thomas*.[86]

It is plain enough from the foregoing evidence that in no way could profession of Manichaean belief be reconciled with membership of the Christian Church. For, apart from dogmatic differences such as we have mentioned, there was a wide cleavage between their respective ethical standards. Hence for many years we see the two religions disputing the religious mastery of the Roman world, and may watch with eagerness the issue of a struggle which in some places at least seemed likely to lead to a victory for the enemies of Christianity. Yet although in reality there could be no compromise between the rival systems of thought and life, from time to time we find evidence that individuals were not innocent of attempting such compromise [87] and that Manichaeism was able by insidious means to influence movements within the Church itself.[88]

However, in the face of the combined hostility of Church and State, of which Leo's anti-Manichaean process provides so signal an example, the cult shared in the general decline which overtook the pagan religions of the ancient world. Nevertheless it maintained an esoteric clandestine existence, and in the course of the centuries emerged from time to time, whether in the form of some strange heretical distortion of the Christian Faith or in the witchcraft or black magic of the Middle Ages, some elements of which still survive as the pastime of the rich or the terror of the superstitious.

[85] Probably identical with the *apocryphon* mention by Origen, *Hom. in Luc. P.G.* 13, 1803.

[86] Augustine, *Contra Faust,* 22, 79. *P.L.* 42, 452.

[87] Augustine's view of "concupiscence" suggests that he was not wholly successful in freeing himself of the shackles of his former faith, and tends to justify the censure of him on this score by the Pelagians. See Williams, *The Ideas of the Fall and of Original Sin,* pp. 365f.

[88] The influence of Manichaeism on Priscillian's ideas is mentioned below. See Chap. VII, Additional Note G.

CHAPTER IV

LEO AND THE AUTHORITY OF THE ROMAN SEE

In an earlier chapter we have already had an opportunity of gaining from two of his sermons, preached on the occasion of his consecration and on the anniversary of that event, some first hand knowledge of the exalted conception which Leo held of his office as Bishop of Rome.[1] Our attention has been drawn to the note of solemn confidence, not unmixed with heartfelt joy, which recurs there, so significant of the speaker's conviction that he had been divinely called to fill the highest place, in relation not only to the church of Rome but to the Church as a whole.

In the latter part of the second of these sermons he touches on a theme which underlies his whole conception of authority, and which consequently plays a considerable part in his general policy. It is the theme of the perpetuation in himself of the apostolic prerogative of St. Peter.

" I am confident," he says, " that this gathering enjoys the devoted interest and unfailing affection of the most blessed Apostle Peter: and that he himself, respect for whom has brought you together, responds to your devotion. For he rejoices in your love and welcomes the regard shown by the partners of his office for that which the Lord has appointed, finding in it proof of the united love of the whole Church, which embraces Peter in Peter's see, and gives her affection as generously to his unworthy successor as to the great shepherd himself." [2]

These words, " to embrace Peter in Peter's see," will be seen to express the essence of Leo's teaching in regard to the Papacy. But for the moment we must pause to consider his

[1] Chap. II, pp. 39f.

[2] *Serm.* 2, 2. *P.L.* 54, 143C. " Nec abest, ut confido, ab hoc coetu etiam beatissimi apostoli Petri pia dignatio et fida dilectio: nec vestram devotionem ille deseruit, cuius vos reverentia congregavit. De vestro itaque et ipse gaudet affectu, et in consortibus honoris sui observantiam Dominicae institutionis amplectitur, probans ordinatissimam totius ecclesiae charitatem, quae in Petri sede Petrum suscipit, et a tanti amore pastoris nec in persona tam imparis tepescit heredis."

view as to the nature of the peculiar status which he ascribes to the Apostle, and the grounds on which that view is based.

In the following passage he describes how the stability of the Church has been divinely safeguarded, when he says:

"Although He (sc. Christ) has entrusted the care of His sheep to many shepherds, yet He has not ceased to protect His flock Himself. For it is from His supreme and eternal providence that we have received also the defence of the Apostle's aid, which never fails to be exercised: moreover the stability of the foundation, on which is erected the lofty pile of the whole Church, remains unshaken under the weight of the Temple resting thereon. For the immobility of the faith commended in the chief of the Apostles is everlasting: and just as that which Peter believed in regard to Christ endures, so there endures also that which Christ instituted in Peter." (Here Leo quotes Matt. xvi. 16–19.) [3]

At first sight this paragraph appears to suggest that the Church depends for its security, not on the permanence of St. Peter's office, but rather on that of his faith, an interpretation of the well-known Matthaean text which seems to be suggested afresh in a later sermon. Here, speaking of the nature of Christian faith, he observes:

"So the might of the Christian faith, which, being founded on a rock secure against attack, defies the gates of death, confesses . . . one Lord Jesus Christ." [4]

Yet we have only to consider the passage as a whole to realize that, while the author attaches the highest importance to St. Peter's faith, yet its significance lies not only in the fact that it was a confession of right belief in the Incarnation, but also in its value in the sight of Christ Himself, since from the author's standpoint, it was the reason for the award to St. Peter of a position of peculiar authority in relation to the Church.

[3] *Serm.* 3, 2. *P.L.* 54, 145C. "quoniam etsi multis pastoribus curam suarum ovium delegavit, ipse tamen dilecti gregis custodiam non reliquit. De cuius principali aeternoque praesidio etiam apostolicae opis munimen accepimus, quod utique ab opere suo non vacat: et firmitas fundamenti, cui totius Ecclesiae superstruitur altitudo, nulla incumbentis sibi templi mole lacessit. Soliditas enim illius fidei, quae in apostolorum principe est laudata, perpetua est; et sicut permanet, quod in Christo Petrus credidit, ita permanet quod in Petro Christus instituit."

[4] *Serm.* 62, 2. *P.L.* 54, 351A. "Christianae igitur fidei fortitudo, quae portas mortis super inexpugnabilem petram aedificata non maluit, unum Dominum Jesum Christum . . . confitetur."

That this authority is regarded as derived directly from Christ is shown by the following:

"There abides therefore that which the Truth itself has ordained, and so blessed Peter, in retaining the rock-like strength which he received, does not abandon the government of the Church committed to him. For he was appointed before the other (apostles)[5] for this reason, namely that we might understand by means of the hidden meaning of his titles—when he is called the Rock, when he is proclaimed to be the Foundation, when he is established as Porter of the kingdom of heaven, and is set up as a judge of things to be bound and loosed, so that the verdict of his decisions might abide even in heaven—of what sort is his association with Christ."[6]

Before passing on to consider the implications which Leo derives from his view of the Petrine office, it will be convenient to consider at this stage other passages in his writings which, like the foregoing, illustrate the use which he makes of scriptural authority with a view to supporting his thesis, and to meeting arguments which might be brought against it. Among the more obvious objections was the one based on a later Matthaean *logion*,[7] to the effect that this passage shows that the authority granted to St. Peter at Caesarea Philippi was subsequently extended to the rest of the Apostles. Leo admits the truth of this, but shows at the same time that St. Peter retained a privileged position.

"Admittedly," he says, "there was conveyed also to the other Apostles the right of that authority, and the office established by this pronouncement was handed on to all the chiefs of the Church: but it was not in vain that the gift which was imparted to them all was entrusted to one in particular. For it was for this reason that this (power) was

[5] The allusion here appears to be to John i. 42.

[6] *Serm.* 3, 3. "Manet ergo dispositio veritatis, et beatus Petrus in accepta fortitudine petrae perseverans, suscepta ecclesiae gubernacula non reliquit. Sic enim prae ceteris est ordinatus, ut dum Petra dicitur, dum fundamentum pronuntiatur, dum regni caelorum ianitor constituitur, dum ligandorum solvendorumque arbiter, mansura etiam in caelis iudiciorum suorum definitione, praeficitur, qualis ipsi cum Christo esset societas, per ipsa appellationum eius mysteria nosceremus."

[7] Matt. xviii. 18.

specially attributed to Peter, namely because the person of Peter is set at the head of all rulers of the Church." [8]

Nor is this all. In spite of the fact that the other Apostles received the same authority, Leo urges that they remained in some degree dependent on St. Peter, as is to be seen by the fact that when on the eve of the Passion the fidelity of them all was in the balance, it was for St. Peter that Christ prayed in particular. After quoting the relevant passage [9] he adds "the danger from the temptation of fear was common to all the Apostles, and equally they needed the help of divine protection, since the devil desired to sift and crush them all: nevertheless peculiar care is taken by the Lord of Peter, and particularly prayer is made for Peter's faith, as though the stability of them all would be more secure if the spirit of him who was chief remained unconquered. So in Peter the courage of them all is strengthened, and the assistance of divine grace is so disposed that the steadfastness, which is imparted through Christ to Peter, is conveyed through Peter to the (other) Apostles." [10]

That which chiefly distinguishes St. Peter's authority from all other gifts divinely imparted to the apostles is its universality. Leo naturally relies for proof of this on the well-known Johannine saying,[11] and infers from it the universality of the authority of the Roman see. Thus in continuation of the argument of the foregoing passage he says:

"Since, then, brethren, we see so great a safeguard divinely appointed for us, with reason and justice we rejoice in the merits and honour of our leader, giving thanks to the ever-

[8] *Serm.* 4, 3. *P.L.* 54, 151. "Transivit quidem etiam in alios apostolos ius potestatis istius, et ad omnes Ecclesiae principes decreti huius constitutio commeavit; sed non frustra uni commendatur, quod omnibus intimetur. Petro enim ideo hoc singulariter creditur, quia cunctis Ecclesiae rectoribus Petri forma praeponitur."

[9] Luke xxii. 31, 32.

[10] *Serm.* 4, 3. "Commune erat omnibus apostolis de tentatione formidinis, et divinae protectionis auxilio pariter indigebant, quoniam diabolus omnes exagitare, omnes cupiebat elidere: et tamen specialis a Domino Petri cura suscipitur, et pro fide Petri proprie supplicatur, tanquam aliorum status certior sit futurus, si mens principis victa non fuerit. In Petro ergo omnium fortitudo munitur, et divinae gratiae ita ordinatur auxilium, ut firmitas, quae per Christum Petro tribuitur, per Petrum apostolis conferatur." Cf. *Serm.* 83, 3.

[11] John xxi. 15–17.

lasting King our Redeemer the Lord Jesus Christ, because He has given such authority to him whom He made chief of the whole Church . . . and to whom after His resurrection in response to a threefold profession of everlasting love He said thrice with meaning then unrevealed, 'Feed my sheep.'" [12]

We find a similar use of this saying in two passages in his epistles. In the former of these he writes:

"For since there abides the commission of the Lord's words, with which the most blessed Apostle Peter was endued by the threefold repetition of a command of hidden meaning, that he who loves Christ the same should feed His sheep; we are constrained by respect for his see, in which we preside through the abundance of divine grace, to avoid the danger of sloth so far as we can do so: lest the profession of the chief Apostle, by which he bore witness that he was a lover of the Lord, be not found in us; for one who negligently feeds the flock so often committed to him is proved to fail in love for the Chief Shepherd." [13]

Here the Petrine charge is used to justify intervention in the affairs of the churches of Sicily, and to uphold the right of the papacy to overrule local custom.[14]

Apart from these familiar texts derived from the Gospels there is one Pauline phrase [15] to which Leo frequently alludes, though without ever actually quoting it. Like the foregoing it is employed to justify the claim to intervene in the affairs of local churches. The following passage is characteristic:

"Moreover because our care extends throughout all the

[12] *Serm.* 4, 4. "Cum itaque, dilectissimi, tantum nobis videamus praesidium divinitus institutum, rationabiliter et inste in ducis nostri meritis et dignatione laetamur, gratias agentes sempiterno Regi Redemptori nostro Domino Jesu Christo, quod tantam potentiam dedit ei quem totius Ecclesiae principem fecit . . . cui post resurrectionem suam Dominus ad trinam aeterni amoris professionem, mystica insinuatione ter dixit; Pasce oves meas."

[13] *Ep.* 16, *praef.* JK 414. "Manente enim Dominicae vocis imperio, quo beatissimus apostolus Petrus trina repetitione mysticae sanctionis imbuitur, ut Christi oves, qui Christum diligit, pascat; ipsius sedis, cui per abundantiam divinae gratiae praesumus, reverentia coarctamur, ut periculum desidiae, quantum possumus, declinemus: ne professio summi Apostoli, qua se amatorem Domini esse testatus est, non inveniatur in nobis; quia negligenter pascens toties commendatam gregem, convincitur summum non amare pastorem."

[14] See Chap. V, pp. 86ff.

[15] 2 Cor. xi. 28. The earliest use of this text by the Papacy occurs in Siricius, *Ep.* 1, 7. JK 255. See Additional Note A, p. 77.

churches, since the Lord demands this of us, who entrusted to the most blessed Apostle Peter the primacy of apostolic honour in reward for his faith, establishing the universal Church on his firmness as a foundation, we share the duty of responsibility which we possess with these who are joined with us in love of the (whole) fraternity." [16]

Similarly in a later letter he writes:

"I have delegated to you, my beloved, the vicegerency of my authority, so that you may share the care for which by divine appointment we (ourselves) are chiefly responsible in regard to all the churches." [17]

The question was bound to arise as to the position of the local bishops in relation to the authority of the Roman see, for at first sight such a view as Leo's appeared to render the local episcopate redundant. The Pope answers it thus:

"For although every shepherd presides over his own flocks with a particular responsibility . . . we have a duty which is shared with them all; in fact the function of each one is a part of our work: so that when men resort to the see of the blessed Apostle Peter from all quarters of the whole world, and seek from our bounty his love of the whole Church entrusted to him by the Lord, the greater our duty to everyone, the heavier we feel the burden to be which rests on our shoulders." [18]

Yet even if the bishops are to be regarded as partakers in the responsibility entrusted collectively to St. Peter, and so

[16] *Ep.* 5, 2, JK 403. "Et quia per omnes Ecclesias cura nostra distenditur, exigente hoc a nobis Domino, qui apostolicae dignitatis beatissimo apostolo Petro primatum fidei suae remuneratione commisit, universalem Ecclesiam in fundamenti ipsius soliditate constituens, necessitatem sollicitudinis quam habemus, cum his qui nobis collegii charitate iuncti sunt sociamus."

[17] *Ep.* 14, 1 JK 411. "Ita etiam ego dilectioni tuae . . . vices mei moderaminis delegavi, ut curam quam universis Ecclesiis principaliter ex divina institutione debemus . . . adiuvares."

[18] *Serm.* 5, 2. *P.L.* 54, 153C. "Quamvis enim singuli quique pastores speciali sollicitudine gregibus suis praesint . . . nobis tamen cum omnibus cura communis est; neque cuiusquam administratio non nostri laboris est portio: ut dum ad beati apostoli Petri sedem ex toto orbe concurritur, et illa universalis ecclesiae a Domino eidem commendata dilectio etiam ex nostra dispensatione deposcitur: tanto amplius nobis instare oneris sentiamus, quanto cunctis maiora debemus." There appears to be a reminiscence here of Irenaeus, *Adv. Haer.* 3, 3, 1. "Ad hanc enim ecclesiam propter potentiorem principalitatem necesse est omnem convenire ecclesiam, hoc est eos qui sunt undique fideles."

to his successors, they are sometimes reminded that their authority is derived only through him. It is this point which Leo emphasizes so strongly in writing to Hilary.

"Now the Lord willed that this responsibility should be the concern of all the Apostles in such a way that He has assigned it primarily to the most blessed Peter, head of all the Apostles; and intends that from him as from the head His gifts should be conveyed to the whole body, so that whoever dares to secede from the foundation of Peter may know that he is excluded from . . . the divine mystery."[19]

We pass from the consideration of the extent of the Petrine authority to the question as to the manner in which Leo believes it still to be exercised. Passages in which it is assumed that the papacy inherits the prerogatives of St. Peter have already been quoted.[20] The following serves further to illustrate the same point:

"Now he (sc. St. Peter) performs the duties entrusted to him with wider scope and greater power, and executes all parts of his obligations and responsibilities in and with that person (sc. Leo himself) through whom he has been honoured. Hence if a right action is done by us or a right decision made, if anything is obtained from God in His mercy by daily prayers, it is a consequence of his good works and merits, whose power still survives and whose authority redounds in his see."[21]

It is worth noticing that here Leo all but identifies himself with the Apostle. In the same sermon he re-emphasizes this idea when he writes:

"In such wise, beloved, is to-day's festival celebrated with reasonable service, that in my humble self he is recognized, he is honoured, with whom there abides the care of all the shep-

[19] *Ep.* 10, 1, JK 408. "Sed huius muneris sacramentum ita Dominus ad omnium apostolorum officium pertinere voluit, ut in beatissimo Petro apostolorum omnium summo principaliter collocarit: et ab ipso quasi quodam capiti, dona sua velit in corpus omne manare, ut exsortem se mysterii intelligeret esse divini, qui ausus fuisset a Petri soliditate recedere."

[20] e.g. *Ep.* 5, 2.

[21] *Serm.* 3, 3. *P.L.* 54, 146. "Qui nunc plenius et potentius ea quae sibi commissa sunt peragit, et omnes partes officiorum atque curarum in ipso et cum ipso, per quem est glorificatus, exsequitur. Si quid itaque a nobis recte agitur, recteque discernitur, si quid a misericordia Dei quotidianis supplicationibus obtinetur, illius est operum atque meritorum, cuius in sede sua vivit potestas et excellit auctoritas."

herds, together with the guardianship of the flocks committed to him, and whose privilege persists even in his unworthy heir. Therefore the presence of my brethren and fellow bishops, whom I have longed for and honour, becomes the more holy and precious, if they will assign the first place in this worship, in which they are pleased to take part, to him, whom they know not only to be head of this see, but also the primate of all bishops. When therefore we utter our exhortations in your ears, holy brethren, believe that he is actually speaking, whose vicegerent we are." [22]

The same thought recurs in the last of his "anniversary" sermons, where he says:

"There is a further reason for our celebration, namely the apostolic and episcopal dignity of the most blessed Peter, who does not cease to preside over his see and receives an abiding partnership with the eternal Priest. For the stability which the Rock himself was given by that Rock which is Christ, he conveyed also to his successors, and wheresoever any steadfastness is apparent there without doubt is to be seen the strength of the shepherd." [23]

And again later:

"Who so ignorantly or grudgingly estimates the honour of blessed Peter as not to believe that all parts of the Church are ruled by his care and prospered by his help? There flourishes and survives still in the chief of the Apostles that love of God and men which neither the bars of the prison, the chains, the onslaughts of the mob, and the threats of a king could terrify,

[22] *Ibid.*, 4. "His itaque modis, dilectissimi, rationabili obsequio celebratur hodierna festivitas, ut in persona humilitatis meae ille intelligatur, ille honoretur, in quo et omnium pastorum sollicitudo cum commendatarum sibi ovium custodia perseverat, et cuius dignitas etiam in indigno herede non deficit. Unde venerabilium quoque fratrum et consacerdotum meorum desiderata mihi et honoranda praesentia hinc sacratior est atque devotior, si pietatem huius officii in quo adesse dignati sunt, ei principaliter referunt, quem non solum huius sedis praesulem, sed et omnium episcoporum noverunt esse primatem." On the view that the bishops of Rome are the successors of St. Peter, the latter being regarded as the first occupant of the see, see Additional Note A.

[23] *Serm.* 5, 4. *P.L.* 54, 154. "Subiungit autem se ad rationem solemnitatis nostrae, non solum apostolica, sed etiam episcopalis beatissimi dignitas Petri, qui sedi suae praeesse non desinit, et indeficiens obtinet cum aeterno Sacerdote consortium. Soliditas enim illa quam de Petra Christo etiam ipse Petra factus accepit, in suos quoque se transfudit haeredes, et ubicumque aliquid ostenditur firmitas, non dubie apparet fortitudo pastoris."

and an unconquerable faith, which waged unceasing warfare, nor ever waxed cold in defeat." [24]

The idea that St. Peter is still living, that his office and work continues, and that the reigning Pope is to be regarded as his personal representative or even visible embodiment does not originate with Leo. It is to be found at least as far back as the writings of Pope Siricius.[25] Here, however, it plays an essential part in the argument. Lastly he asserts without hesitation that St. Peter's position in relation to the church of Rome was divinely ordained, when he says: "Our Lord . . . was pleased to appoint blessed Peter, chief of the apostolic order, to this city, whose solemnity of to-day, when the anniversary of the triumph of his martyrdom comes round again, has shed its brilliance and beauty over the whole world." [26]

We may now briefly summarize Leo's general thesis on this subject. St. Peter, already designated as the "Rock" at the outset of the Lord's ministry, receives in reward for his confession of his Master as "the Christ, the son of the Living God" the solemn promise that in virtue of his faith he is to be the foundation of the Church that is to be. Further confirmation of his peculiar privilege in relation to that Church is found in the charge given to him by Christ before His passion and in the commission entrusted to him after the Resurrection. Divinely commissioned and divinely guided he seeks the imperial city as a field for his missionary labours where he lays down his life in upholding the same faith which he once confessed. Nevertheless in virtue of his abiding presence there, his successors, the bishops

[24] *Serm.* 5, 4. "quis gloriae beati Petri tam imperitus erit aut tam invidus aestimator, qui ullas ecclesiae partes non ipsius sollicitudine regi, non ipsius credat augeri? Viget prorsus et vivit in apostolorum principe illa Dei hominumque dilectio, quam non claustra carceris, non catenae, non populares impetus, non minae regiae exterruerunt; et insuperabilis fides, quae bellando non cessit, vincendo non tepuit."

[25] *Ep.* 1, 1, JK 255. The same thought constantly reappears in the works of Leo's successors, e.g. Felix III, *Ep.* 8, 2. JK 601.

[26] *Serm.* 83, 1. *P.L.* 54, 429. "Dominus noster . . . apostolici ordinis primum beatum Petrum huic civitati dignatus est praerogare, cuius hodierna solemnitas, recurrente triumpho martyrii, specimen et decus contulit orbi terrarum." Evidently Leo accepted the view already prevailing in his time that June 29th was the actual date of St. Peter's death. On this date see Frere, *Studies in Early Roman Liturgy,* Vol. I, pp. 109f.; *Liturgy and Worship* (S.P.C.K.), p. 214. On the question of St. Peter's residence in Rome see Additional Note B.

of Rome, still exercise his prerogatives and wield his authority.

It is a theory of authority which is to be commended at least for its directness and simplicity. Its chief weakness lies in the absence of any real historical evidence for the exercise of powers such as Leo describes, whether by St. Peter or by any of the earlier bishops of the Roman see during the first three centuries. Nor can it be denied that, where history is silent, Leo is prone to give rein to his imagination or rather to replace real history with something little short of fantasy. For it can scarcely escape notice that in describing the divinely appointed work of St. Peter he makes little allowance for the better known and better attested work of St. Paul. Earlier popes had not hesitated to emphasize the twin apostolic origin of the church of Rome. Leo's work, on the other hand, shows the development of a process of rewriting history in which the importance of St. Paul is gradually forgotten while his fellow Apostle becomes the central and unique figure on the Roman canvas.

We have now laid bare the guiding principle which underlies the whole of St. Leo's work, namely the safeguarding and upholding of the supposed privileges of the Roman see. In carrying this principle into effect we shall do him wrong if we regard him as no more than an ambitious, self-seeking glutton for power. To him the Petrine privileges were a sacred charge and as such to be jealously protected. Hence when he came into contact with divergent or even contradictory conceptions of church organization and authority he was bound out of loyalty to his own principles to treat them as enemies to be fought and destroyed. It was largely due to him that the Papacy became an institution of such stability and permanence that neither the violence of the barbarians nor the subtleties of the Byzantines could permanently undermine its influence or destroy its prestige. That prestige was from Leo's standpoint a simple consequence of the divine commission to St. Peter, and was universally acknowledged in his time among the churches of the West. The question remains, however, whether or not the commission could be interpreted, as the petitioners on behalf of the see of Arles [27] supposed, as imply-

[27] *Inter Leon. Epp.*, No. 65, 2. *P.L.* 54, 881, "per beatissimum Petrum apostolum principem sacrosancta ecclesia Romana teneret supra omnes totius mundi ecclesias principatum."

ing the conveyance to the Roman see of a prescriptive right of the whole Catholic Church to dispose the affairs.

Additional Note A

THE EVOLUTION OF THE PETRINE PRIVILEGES

It is abundantly clear from the evidence considered in the foregoing chapter that the chief ground on which Leo rests the claims which he advances for the authority of the Roman see is to be found in his belief that the bishops of that see are the successors of St. Peter, and therefore are the heirs of the peculiar privileges believed to have been assigned to him by our Lord Himself. With this view is closely connected another, namely the supposition that St. Peter was actually the first bishop of the local Roman church.

The latter idea appears first in a clear and unmistakable form in the writings of Cyprian,[28] whose argument in favour of the claims of Cornelius, as against those of Novatian, turns simply on the truth or otherwise of his contention that Cornelius and not Novatian is the legitimate successor of St. Peter in the Roman see, whom he evidently regards as its first bishop. Earlier writers, however, while clearly sharing Cyprian's conviction as to the apostolic origin of the Roman Church, distinguish carefully between its apostolic founders and their immediate successors. This is true not only of the early list supplied by Irenaeus,[29] tracing the Roman succession from Linus to the twelfth bishop in order, Irenaeus' own contemporary Eleutherus, but also of the one cited by Epiphanius.[30] This list differs from that given by Irenaeus, in naming Cletus in the place of Anencletus, and has on this ground been held to have been derived from a source other

[28] *Ep.* 74, 2. "sub Hygino episcopo, qui in urbe nonus fuit." Comparison with earlier lists shows that Hyginus ought to have been reckoned "octavus," unless of course Cyprian was relying on an authority which duplicated Cletus with Anencletus.

[29] *Adv. Haer.,* 3, 3, 3. Mirbt, *Quellen,* No. 41. The distinction drawn by this author between the Apostles and the episcopal succession is clearly seen by comparing this section with the preceding one.

[30] *Haer.,* 27, 6. It is sometimes thought that this list is to be identified with the one generally supposed to have been compiled by Hegesippus up to the time of Anicetus; yet uncertainty as to interpretation renders it doubtful whether Hegesippus was actually the author of any such compilation. Cf. Eusebius, *H.E.* 4, 22, 3. Mirbt, *Quellen,* No. 30. It is, however, identical with the one still extant in the present Latin *Canon Missae.*

than the one from which Irenaeus obtained his information.

But in addition to the fact that each of these early lists marks a distinction between St. Peter and the Roman bishops, there is a further point of interest which they share in common, namely the mention of the name of St. Paul in association with that of his fellow Apostle. This feature is reproduced again and again by Eusebius [31] in his references to the primitive Roman Church. The earliest Western writer to mention St. Peter alone as the founder of that Church is Tertullian,[32] who in emphasizing the apostolic origin of the Catholic ministry, diverges from the Irenaeo-Epiphanian tradition by assigning Clement to the head of the list.[33] This order reappears in the *Catalogus Liberianus*,[34] which also places the names of Cletus and Anencletus side by side.[35]

We may now observe the subsequent development which followed Cyprian's statements as to the relation of St. Peter to the primitive Roman Church.[36] Originally formulated in the interests of Cornelius, they provided a convenient instrument in the hands of his successor Stephen [37] and were interpreted by him to mean that the occupant of the Roman see

[31] *H.E.* 3. 2, 4, 13, 15, 21, 34; 4. 1, 4, 5, 10, 11, 19, 30; 5 *praef.* 22, 28; 6. 21, 23, 29, 39; 7. 2, 5, 27, 30, 32. In two instances, namely 3, 2 and 3, 21, the name of St. Paul precedes that of St. Peter.

[32] *De Praescript. Haer.*, 32. Doubtless Cyprian is dependent on this passage as on others in Tertullian.

[33] The belief that Clement was the immediate successor of St. Peter persisted and reappeared in the Pseudo-Clementine writings. See *Clementina*, ed. De Lagarde (1865) 6, 7.

[34] The *Catalogus Liberianus* forms a part of the so-called Philocalian Kalendar, which was completed in the year A.D. 354. It supplies a list of popes from St. Peter to Liberius, with full information as to length of pontificate and mentions outstanding incidents; it provided the chief source of the later sixth century *Liber pontificalis*. It is edited by Mommsen, *M.G.H.*, Vol. IX, *Chron. min.*, Vol. I, pp. 73ff. Also in Mommsen's *Liber pontificalis*, *M.G.H.*, Mirbt, *Quellen*, No. 125.

[35] The problems involved in the early Roman episcopal lists are discussed in C. H. Turner's Art. in *J.T.S.*, Vol. XVIII (1917), pp. 103–134: Caspar, *Die älteste Röm. Bischofsliste*: Harnack, *Chronologie*, Vol. I, p. 187.

[36] See above. It is sometimes believed that Cyprian was actually not the first to stress the connexion of St. Peter with the see of Rome, on the ground that Tertullian, *De pudicitia*, 21, appears to censure Pope Callistus I for describing himself as the heir of the Petrine privileges. Galtier, *L'Eglise et la rémission des péchés*, pp. 143–168, however, shows good reason to hold that Tertullian is actually referring to the contemporary Bishop of Carthage. Nevertheless it still remains possible that he is the true father of Cyprian's idea.

[37] Cyprian, *Ep.* 75, 17.

was the undoubted heir to the privileges accorded to the Apostle by our Lord Himself.[38] No doubt it needed some time for the full implications of this view to be appreciated even by the Roman see itself, but the seeds were already sown from which a century or so later the universalist claims of the papacy were to spring forth.

In the interval even an assembly so pronouncedly Western in character as the Council of Sardica [39] continued to express the more primitive view that the rights of the Roman see were not so much inherent, as being derived from the privileges assigned to St. Peter, as consequent on a definite award made by a body representing or claiming to represent the Church as a whole.

It is not till we come to the Roman synod of A.D. 378 that we find an explicit claim to a privilege, made on behalf of the Roman see, which is now described as the Apostolic see for the first time in virtue of its being the see of St. Peter.[40] Nevertheless Damasus himself, the reigning pontiff on whose behalf the privilege was claimed, in contrasting the status of his see with those of Alexandria and Antioch, lays special emphasis on the fact that St. Paul in addition to St. Peter was responsible for the foundation of Roman Christianity, and thus to vindicate its superiority over its rivals, which on his own admission were equally entitled to claim Petrine origin.[41]

A few years later we notice that the evolution of the Petrine doctrine has been carried a stage further. Hitherto the writers with whom we have been concerned are content to describe

[38] E.g. Matt. xvi. 16ff. Cyprian appears to have modified his earlier view when he came to write *Ep.* 74, 11.

[39] *Canon* 3 (vers. lat.). Mansi, *Concilia,* Vol. III, 7. Mirbt, *Quellen,* No. 122. "sancti Petri apostoli memoriam honoremus." Turner, *J.T.S.,* Vol. III, pp. 370ff. upholds both the authenticity of the canons and the originality of the Latin text.

[40] Mansi, *op. cit.,* Vol. III, 624. "Et hoc gloriae vestrae . . ."

[41] *Decretum Gelasianum,* 3. The work as a whole in its present form belongs to the sixth century; the compiler, however, has incorporated three chapters 1–3, which are held by Turner, *J.T.S.,* Vol. I, 1900, pp. 554–60 to belong to the Roman synod of A.D. 382. The view that St. Peter and St. Paul were actually co-founders of the Roman Church lingered on into the fifth century at least. Cf. e.g. Xystus III, *Ep.* 4, 14, JK 392: Theodoret, *Ep.* 113, *P.G.,* 83, 1312: Leo, *Serm.* 82, 7, *P.L.* 54, 427. Nevertheless the opinion that St. Paul was the equal of St. Peter was formally condemned by Pope Innocent X in 1647. Cf. Cavallera, *Thesaurus,* No. 380, p. 212.

the Roman bishops as the heirs of Petrine privileges. Now we begin to meet with the assertion that each successive Pope is a kind of "reincarnation" of the Apostle himself, who is regarded as still living and reigning in the Roman see. The first to advance this claim is Siricius,[42] who also argues that as the rest of the Apostles derived their commission from our Lord only through St. Peter, so the episcopate generally owes its authority to papal delegation.[43] Hence he holds that, at least within the limits of the Roman province, no bishop may be consecrated without the approval of the Roman bishop[44] who is, in his view, entrusted with the "care of all churches."[45] Siricius' view as to the authority of the episcopate is extended by his successor, Innocent I, to embrace its origin, at any rate so far as concerns the West.[46] These opinions are reiterated by Boniface I; yet he is the first to extend Innocent I's use of the Pauline *dictum* to justify papal intervention in the affairs of the churches of the East,[47] so that by the time we reach the first council of Ephesus, A.D. 431, the legates of his successor, Celestine I, advance all these claims without any apparent awareness of their novelty or fear of arousing protest.[48]

It is clear therefore that Leo himself did little but re-use material which already lay ready to hand. In fact we might well do him an injustice, were we to suppose that he evolved anything new in the interests of his see. Rather we find in him a far-seeing and great-minded personality, a true artist, who fashioned of inchoate matter a structure of enduring grandeur.[49]

Additional Note B

ST. PETER IN ROME

In view of the important place which the tradition of the

[42] *Ep.* 1, 1, JK 255.
[43] The idea had already been suggested by Cyprian, *Ep.* 59, 14, "unde unitas sacerdotalis exorta est."
[44] *Ep.* 5, 1, JK 258.
[45] 2 Cor. xi. 28. "ἡ μέριμνα πασῶν τῶν ἐκκλησιῶν."
[46] *Ep.* 25, 2, JK 311. Mirbt, *Quellen*, No. 148. Cf. *Ep.* 30, 2, JK 321.
[47] *Ep.* 13, 1, JK 363. *Ep.* 14, 1, JK 364. *Ep.* 15, 1, JK 365.
[48] *Conc. Eph.*, Sessio 3. Mansi, *op. cit.*, Vol. IV, 1295.
[49] Cf. Kidd, *Roman Primacy*, p. 95.

residence and death of the Apostle St. Peter in the city of Rome occupies in the thought of Leo,[50] it is highly relevant to the present study to examine critically this tradition, and evaluate the evidence on which it rests.

The whole question has lately been investigated afresh by Lietzmann,[51] particularly in the light of certain recent archaeological discoveries made on the site of the supposed resting places of the bodies of the Apostles. It will be convenient to summarize this investigation in order to form, so far as is possible, an impartial conclusion on the whole question in the light of the new evidence.

The so-called Philocalian Kalendar,[52] compiled from a variety of sources by Furius Dionysius Philocalus, personal secretary, as it would seem, to Damasus I, serves as a starting point. In addition to a list of the "obits" of popes from Lucius A.D. 254 to Julius I A.D. 352, the *Depositio episcoporum,*[53] it includes a catalogue of feasts of martyrs, the *Depositio martyrum,*[54] and a section entitled *Catalogus Liberianus,*[55] which provides a list of popes from St. Peter to Liberius, specifying the length of their pontificates and other details. The last of these contains an interesting though historically valueless entry:

"Petrus ann. XXV, mense uno, diebus VIIII. Fuit temporibus Tiberii Caesaris et Gai et Tiberi Claudi et Neronis, a consulatu Minuci [Vinici] et Longini (A.D. 30) usque Nerone et Vero [Vetere] (A.D. 55). Passus autem cum Paulo die III Kl. Iulias, consulibus suprascriptis, imperante Nerone."[56]

There are, however, two entries in the *Depositio martyrum* which have proved to be of the highest importance:

[50] *Serm.* 72, 4, 5.

[51] *Petrus und Paulus in Rom,* Berlin, 1927. Cf. also Harnack, *Chronologie der altchristl, litt.,* Vol. I, p. 244; Duchesne, *Histoire,* Vol. I, pp. 61–3; and other ref. to be found in *D.T.C.,* Vol. XIII, Col. 262.

[52] *M.G.H.,* Auct. antiqu., Vol. IX, *Chron. min.,* Vol. I, pp. 13ff, ed. Mommsen.

[53] *Ibid.,* p. 70; *Liber pont.,* ed. Duchesne, Vol. I, p. 10.

[54] *Ibid.,* p. 71; *ibid.,* p. 11.

[55] *Ibid.,* p. 73; *ibid.,* pp. 1–9. Also in Mommsen's ed. of *Liber pont.,* printed side by side with the biography of each pope.

[56] This entry gives the traditional period of St. Peter's "episcopate," namely twenty-five years. Duchesne, *op. cit.,* pp. ccxlviff. shows that the figures of the early pontificates in the *Catalogus* are quite untrustworthy. Cf. Schwartz, *Eusebius, H.E.,* Vol. III, pp. ccxxviiiff. and pp. 6f.

[29th June] III Kal. Iul. Petri in Catacumbas et Pauli Ostense Tusco et Basso cons. [A.D. 258].

[22nd February] VIII Kal. Martias natale Petri de cathedra.

Lietzmann considers the latter entry first, and shows that it is to be explained as a Christian substitute for the pagan *Caristia,* itself analogous to the "Commemoration of All Souls," to commemorate the beginning of St. Peter's episcopate.[57] At the same time he points out its bearing on the antiquity of the tradition of St. Peter's connexion with the Roman see.

The former entry embraces a number of difficulties, not the least of which arises from the present state of the text. The plainest inference which can be drawn from it, as it stands, is that in the year A.D. 354, i.e. the date of the Kalendar in its completed form,[58] St. Peter was commemorated in the Catacombs of St. Sebastian on the *Via Appia,* and St. Paul on the *Via Ostia.* Yet the *Martyrologium Hieron.,* which is dependent on a variant copy of the Philocalian Kalendar, preserves the following entry:

"Romae via Aurelia natale sanctorum Petri et Pauli apostolorum: Petri in Vaticano, Pauli vero in via Ostense, utrumque in catacumbas, passi sub Nerone, Basso et Tusco consulibus."[59]

Various emendations of the Philocalian text have been

[57] The date of the *Caristia* or *Cara cognatio* was February 22nd, and was probably known by the popular name of the *Cathedra.* For the use of καθέδρα in connexion with the cult of the dead, see E. Rohde, *Psyche,* Vol. I, 2, p. 233, n. 2 and cf. Lietzmann, *Petrus,* pp. 19ff. who argues that the commemoration was instituted about the year A.D. 300 as an annual remembrance of the ordination days *(natalia)* of previous bishops. While the custom of formally celebrating the *natale* of the reigning bishop is probably not previous to A.D. 282, its informal celebration may well have begun much earlier. It is also probable that the *Cathedra Petri* commemorated the Apostolic confession at Caesarea Philippi. Cf. Augustine, App. *Serm.* 190, 1; *P.L.* 39, 2100. Lietzmann, *op. cit.,* pp. 93f. points out that although this feast occurs in the *Depositio martyrum* it is absent from the early Roman Mass Books, except as a Frankish addition, though it is given in *Miss. Bobbio* and *Lect. Luxov.,* under January 18th. The *Martyrologium Hieron.,* however, gives both feasts as in the *Missale Romanum* of A.D. 1570, cf. ed. De Rossi-Duchesne, p. 10. It is likely that the commemoration of February 22nd was still observed in Leo's time. Cf. *Inter Leon. Epp.,* No. 55.

[58] It is probable that the same entry was already present in the earlier form of the Kalendar, A.D. 336.

[59] The *Martyrologium Hieronymianum,* ed. De Rossi-Duchesne, p. [84].

suggested: the following alternatives are proposed by Lietzmann.[60]

"Petri [in Vaticano et Petri et Pauli] in catacumbas et Pauli Ostense. Tusco et Basso cons."

"Petri in Vaticano Pauli vero in via Ostensi utriusque in catacumbas. Basso et Tusco cons."

The first question arises as to the significance of the year A.D. 258. The most usual suggestion is that both it and the date, June 29th, mark the occasion of the translation of the Apostles' relics.[61] The well-known reply of Gaius to Proclus the Montanist, however:

"*ἐγὼ δὲ τὰ τρόπαια τῶν ἀποστόλων ἔχω δεῖξαι· ἐὰν γὰρ θελήσῃς ἀπελθεῖν ἐπὶ τὸν βασικανὸν ἢ ἐπὶ τὴν ὅδον τὴν Ὀστίαν εὑρήσεις τὰ τρόπαια τῶν ταύτην ἱδρυσαμένων τὴν Ἐκκλησίαν*," [62]

which mentions nothing about the catacombs, points to a different resting place of the relics at the time (A.D. 200) when his words were written. It is therefore supposed that they were removed from their original places in the course of the persecution initiated by the Emperor Valerian, and deposited in the catacombs of St. Sebastian for the sake of ensuring greater security. In any case it is clear that no cultus of the Apostles was possible at any earlier date since the site of the tombs, to which Gaius appears to refer, lay in close proximity to pagan cemeteries.[63] Hence there can be little doubt that the date commemorates the actual translation in the time of Pope Cornelius.

The foregoing evidence receives strong support from an inscription inserted by Damasus close to the crypt of the present Church of St. Sebastian which, though only surviving in the form of an imperfect copy made in the thirteenth century, clearly points to the existence of a tradition extant in the

[60] Lietzmann, *op. cit.*, p. 114. The second is intended to reproduce the original text used by the compiler of the *Mart. Hieron.*

[61] Id. *op. cit.*, pp. 114–22 gives numerous examples of dates in the Philocalian Kalendar which are commemorations, not of martyrdom but of translation. Nevertheless the later Missals took June 29th to be a commemoration of martyrdom, a view which already appears in the *Catalogus Liberianus, Petrus.*

[62] Cit. ap. Eusebium, *H.E.*, 2, 25, 6.

[63] Lietzmann, *op. cit.*, pp. 122f.

fourth century, connecting the Apostles' memory with the church and its surroundings.

> "Hic habitasse prius sanctus cognoscere debes,
> nomina quisque Petri pariter Paulique requiris.
> Discipulos Oriens misit, quod sponte fatemur;
> sanguinis ob meritum—Christiumque per astra secuti
> aetherios petiere sinus regnaque piorum—
> Roma suos potius meruit defendere cives.
> Haec Damasus vestras referat, nova sidera, laudes." [64]

Comparison with parallel inscriptions show that the allusion here is undoubtedly to the temporary resting place of the Apostles' relics.[65]

As to the question of its exact position, it was long supposed that this was the double grave which was found under the floor of the small chapel called the Platoma, lying to the south-west of the apse of the present Church of St. Sebastian. It has now been proved that the chapel was built for Quirinus, Bishop of Siscia in Pannonia, who perished in the Diocletianic persecution.[66] The medieval tradition, moreover, pointed to a different site, as may be illustrated by the entry which is to be found in the Salzburg Itinerary: [67]

"Postea pervenies via Appia ad S. Sebastianum martyrem, cuius corpus iacet in inferiore loco, et ibi sunt sepulchra apostolorum Petri et Pauli, in quibus XL annorum requiescebant. Et in occidentali parte ecclesiae per gradus descendis, ubi S. Cyrinus papa et martyr pausat." This indicates that the supposed resting place of the Apostles lay towards the narthex of the present church, and this was evidently accepted as the authentic position at the time when the papal privilege of 1520 [68] was granted.

The sources of our information on this point remained in this state till 1914. Ten years later careful investigations were made of the excavations which had been going on during the

[64] Diehl, *Inscr. Lat. Christ. vet.*, Vol. I, No. 951.
[65] The *Liber pontificalis*, ed. Duchesne, Vol. I, p. 212, attributes to Damasus the erection of a basilica on the site where the bodies of the Apostles lay. Excavations, however, have rendered it probable that it was erected at least as early as A.D. 350. Cf. Lietzmann, *Petrus*, p. 150.
[66] Lietzmann, *op. cit.*, pp. 151ff.
[67] De Rossi, *Roma sott.*, Vol. I, p. 180.
[68] Cit. ap. Lietzmann, *op. cit.*, p. 154, n. 3.

intervening period. Among the various discoveries which were made were a number of *graffiti*.[69] These comprise a series of invocations of the Apostles, and were all found in the remains of a subterranean room beneath the floor of the present church and known as the *Triclia*.[70] The presence of these *graffiti* serves to support the evidence derived from other sources pointing to this site as the actual place where the Apostles' relics reposed, although it is obviously impossible to fix the precise spot with anything like absolute certainty.

The further question arises as to the site of the burial places previous to the translation of A.D. 258. Lietzmann points out that the evidence of the Apocryphal *Acta* indicates the Neronian *Circus* as the original site of St. Peter's burial, and the Ostian way for St. Paul's.[71] It is clear too that Gregory I himself has the tradition of these *Acta* in mind when he refers to the subject.[72] In addition to these indications we find an entry in the *Liber pontificalis*[73] which speaks of St. Peter as follows:

"sepultus est via Aurelia, in templum Apollinis, iuxta locum ubi crucifixus est, iuxta palatium Neronianum, in Vaticanum, iuxta territurium triumphalem III Kal. Iul."

Finally we have to consider the entry which is given in the same work under the pontificate of Cornelius.[74] This in itself is plainly unhistorical since it mentions a translation of the Apostles' relics as taking place under Cornelius from the catacombs to the sites of their respective martyrdoms. But it evidently reflects an early tradition that each Apostle was actually buried near the place where he died.

We may now turn to evidence of a different kind. The

[69] Lietzmann, *op. cit.*, pp. 157–169. It must be acknowledged that the evidence falls short of being positively decisive, even if its cumulative value is considerable.

[70] Apparently a room associated with primitive Christian worship. But the character of the *graffiti* themselves point to a date not later than the end of the third century. Cf. Lietzmann, *op. cit.*, p. 165.

[71] *Acta apost. apocryph.*, ed. Lipsius, esp. the *Passio Petri et Pauli*, pp. 119–177 (vers. lat.), pp. 118–176, 178–122 (vers. graec.), cf. Lietzmann, *op. cit.*, pp. 169ff.

[72] *Registrum*, 4, 30, ed. Ewald et Hartmann, pp. 265[19]ff. The strange story of a plundering of the tombs by Eastern Christians, mentioned in the *Passio*, is repeated here.

[73] In the *Epitome Feliciana*, compiled in A.D. 530, *Lib. pont.*, ed. Duchesne, p. 52. Cf. p. 118.

[74] ed. Duchesne, Vol. I, p. 150.

early basilica of St. Peter in the Vatican was begun under Constantine I and completed probably in the reign of Constans, A.D. 337–350.[75] This church was destroyed in the rebuilding which was completed in 1615. But the final reconstruction was only finished with the erection of the *baldachino* over the papal altar in 1626. To provide sufficient foundation for the pillars of this structure considerable excavation was found necessary and careful record was kept of the discoveries made in the course of this work. These showed the existence of numerous pagan graves on the site, and the measurements of the earlier church then revealed pointed to the fact that the architect was limited on the one side by the northern walls of the Neronian circus, which he used as foundations, and by the position of the Apostle's *Confessio*. The fact that this lies somewhat south of the true centre of the apse suggests that the site of the grave was already in existence before the church was erected.[76]

A similar discovery was made in the basilica of St. Paul at the time of its rebuilding after the great fire of 1823.[77] The Church then largely destroyed had been erected by Theodosius I, probably in A.D. 384,[78] to replace the original building. Probably the *Liber pontificalis* is correct in ascribing the construction of this church to Constantine,[79] for it scarcely seems possible that the memory of St. Paul would be honoured and that of St. Peter disregarded. Here too the site of the Apostle's *Confessio* was found in close proximity to heathen graves, and it is reasonable to suppose that the church was erected here because the tradition of the actual place of St. Paul's burial, as in the case of St. Peter, had survived the period of forty years, during which the relics of both Apostles had rested in the catacombs of St. Sebastian.[80]

We have already seen that Gaius in the course of his con-

[75] Lietzmann, *op. cit.*, pp. 189f.
[76] Lietzmann, *op. cit.*, p. 208 and n. 1.
[77] *Ibid.*, p. 211.
[78] *Cod. Theod.*, XIV, i, 2; iii. 18, which records the fact that the road was diverted in order to provide room for the second and larger church.
[79] *Liber pont.*, *Vita Silvestri*, 34, xxi, ed. Duchesne, Vol. I, p. 178, where mention is also made of the burial by Constantine of the relics of St. Paul.
[80] Lietzmann, *op. cit.*, pp. 222–26, shows that the festival of January 25th probably commemorates the translation of the relics to the first church.

troversy with the Montanist Proclus claimed to be able to conduct his opponents to the actual places where the Apostles lay buried.[81] How far can we substantiate this tradition, which cannot well be later than A.D. 200, that both St. Peter and St. Paul had been martyred in Rome? Or must we dismiss Gaius' claim as no more than a controversialist's fiction? The earliest evidence as to the connexion of the Apostles with the city of Rome is to be found in the celebrated letter of Clement to the Corinthians. In the course of a passage in which the author disclaims against the harmful effects of ambition and jealousy, which he regards as the main source of the trouble in the Corinthian Church, he gives examples of those who have suffered from the effect of these vices, first from the Old Testament, then from the New. Then he goes on to say:

"λάβωμεν πρὸ ὀφθαλμῶν ἡμῶν τοὺς ἁγίους ἀποστόλους. Πέτρον ὃς διὰ ζῆλον ἄδικον, οὐχ ἕνα οὐδὲ δύο, ἀλλὰ πλείονας ὑπήνεγκεν πόνους καὶ οὕτω μαρτυρήσας ἐπορεύθη εἰς τὸν ὀφειλόμενον τόπον τῆς δόξης."[82]

The argument of this passage is simply this. St. Peter and St. Paul are examples of the kind which the writer has in mind who suffered martyrdom under Nero. At the same time he associates with the Apostles those who equally faced death for the sake of their faith. The unmistakable impression left on the mind of the reader is that Clement knew that the place of martyrdom in both cases was the city of Rome.

The same impression is created by the words of Ignatius who, in writing to the Romans, says:

"οὐχ ὡς Πέτρος καὶ Παῦλος διατάσσομαι ὑμῖν ἐκεῖνοι ἀπόστολοι, ἐγὼ κατάκριτος."[83]

It is almost inconceivable that unless Ignatius had some good reason for associating St. Peter and St. Paul with the church of Rome, he would have chosen to mention them to the exclusion of St. John, whose name would most naturally occur to one writing from the city of Ephesus.[84]

[81] See above.
[82] *Ep. ad Corinth.* 5.
[83] Rom. iv. 3.
[84] Comparison of this letter with *Trall.* 3, 3, a church of non-Apostolic origin shows an interesting contrast: while the letter to the *Ephesians* 12, 1, 2 emphasises the connexion of that church with St. Paul.

Finally when we reach the time of Dionysius, Bishop of Corinth, A.D. 170, we find him unequivocally asserting that both the Apostles were associated with the origin of the church of Rome, and that both lived and suffered martyrdom there.[85] After his time successive writers down to Gaius the presbyter, whose evidence has already been considered, treat the association of the Apostles with Rome as axiomatic.[86] It seems, therefore, that those who persist in impugning the authenticity of the tradition connecting St. Peter with Rome have to reckon with a considerable body of archaeological and literary evidence which is difficult to explain, if the tradition does not in fact enshrine the truth.

[85] Cit. ap. Eusebium, *H.E.* 2, 25, 6.

[86] e.g. Irenaeus, *Adv. haer.* 3, 1, 1; 3, 3, 2. Mirbt, *Quellen,* Nos. 39, 40: Clem. Alex. cit. ap. Eusebium *H.E.* 6, 14: Tertullian, *Scorpiace,* 15; *de Praescriptione,* 36. Mirbt, *Quellen,* Nos. 51–53.

CHAPTER V

LEO AS METROPOLITAN OF THE ROMAN PROVINCE

It is clear that by the middle of the fifth century the metropolitan jurisdiction of the Roman see embraced southern Italy with the islands of Sicily, Corsica and Sardinia, an area corresponding to the circumscription subject to the *Vicarius Urbis*.[1] We possess in all seven letters addressed by Leo either collectively or individually to bishops of his province. One of these has already been considered in connexion with the prosecution of the Manichaeans at Rome.[2]

The remaining six letters now claim our attention. Some twelve months or so previously, possibly on the occasion of the autumnal synod of A.D. 443, Leo was informed of a number of abuses in connexion with promotion to holy orders. These abuses included the ordination of men of an inferior social standing, the consecration to the episcopate of certain persons who had contracted marriage with a widow, or who had married again after the death of their first wife, and finally the prevalence among clergy and laity of the prohibited practice of usury. The letter which Leo addressed "to the bishops of Campania, Picenum, Tuscany and all the provinces"[3] sets forth his decisions on these matters. On the first point he draws attention to the unfortunate consequences of the ordination of men of low social status.[4] The practice, he says, degrades the sacred ministry[5] and inflicts injustice on their employers, in cases where the men so ordained have not been previously released from service.[6] His ruling is that such ordinations are to cease, a decision which he makes applicable to all classes of society, in any way obliged to

[1] See Chap. I, p. 14.

[2] *Ep.* 7, JK 405; see Chap. III.

[3] *Ep.* 4, JK 402, dated October 10th, A.D. 443.

[4] *Ibid.*, 1. "ad fastigium sacerdotii." The phrase may refer exclusively to the episcopate.

[5] *Ibid.* "sacrum ministerium talis consortii vilitate polluitur."

[6] *Ibid.* "Dominorum, quantum ad illicitae usurpationis temeritatem pertinet, iura solvuntur." Cf. *Canon Apost.*, 82, ed. Funk. Kirch, *Fontes*, No. 705.

hereditary labour.[7] He justifies it on the twofold ground that only so will the risk of legal claims put forward by employers be avoided and that those who are enlisted in the service of God must be free from all other obligations.[8] While the letter shows Leo's concern lest the dignity of Christian priesthood should suffer damage in consequence of the advancement of men possessing indifferent qualifications, it also illustrates his eagerness to uphold canonical principles. Thus he writes, " As to the sort of person . . . who should be associated with the ministry of the holy altar, we are instructed as well by the Apostle, as by divine commandment and by canon law." [9]

Hence he is obliged to pronounce sentence on those who have been consecrated in violation of these principles.

" Therefore we command that those, whoever they may be, who have been admitted (sc. uncanonically), are excluded by the authority of the Apostolic See from ecclesiastical positions and from the title of bishop; for they cannot claim for themselves that which, by reason of impediment in their case, they were incapable of receiving." [10]

How gravely Leo viewed the whole matter may be seen from the fact that at the conclusion of his letter he states

[7] *Ibid.* " non tantum ab his (sc. servis), sed ab aliis etiam qui originali aut alicui conditioni obligati sunt." The allusion is doubtless to the class of agricultural tenants known as *coloni* or *originarii,* which by imperial legislation had been obliged to hereditary serfdom. Cf. Bury, *Later Roman Empire,* Vol. I, pp. 56f.; Chrys., *Hom. in Matth.* 61, 31. *P.G.* 58, 591.

[8] *Ibid.* " debet enim esse immunis ab aliis, qui divinae militiae fuerit aggregandus." The use of the word *militia* for service other than military should be noticed. Cf. *Missale Romanum,* Praefationes, *passim.* The word is, of course, derived from imperial usage. See Bury, *Later Roman Empire,* Vol. I, p. 31.

[9] *Ibid.,* 2. " qualis vero . . . esse debeat sacri altaris ministerio sociandus, et Apostolo nos docente et divina praeceptione didicimus, et canonum regulis." Cf. 1 Tim. iii. 2, Tit. i. 6, Lev. xxi. 13f., and *Canon. Apost.* 17, " *ὁ δυσὶ γάμοις συμπλακεὶς μετὰ τὸ βάπτισμα ἢ παλλακὴν κτησάμενος οὐ δύναται εἶναι ἐπίσκοπος* . . . ." Funk, *Didaschalia,* 1, 564. Kirch, *Fontes,* No. 695.

[10] *Ibid.* " Hos ergo, quicumque tales admissi sunt, ab ecclesiasticis officiis et a sacerdotali nomine, apostolicae sedis auctoritate iubemus arceri; nec hoc enim sibi poterunt vindicare, cuius capaces, per hoc quod illis obstiterat, non fuerunt." The interest of this decision lies in the fact that it shows the prevalence of a view at this date that in the case of holy orders invalidity may arise from canonical impediment.

expressly that he reserves all such cases to his own judgment.[11] Possibly he had good reason to fear that the Italian episcopate could not be trusted to take an impartial view on this question.

After this he turns his attention to the practice of usury.[12] Leo's attitude to the subject is in line with earlier synodical canons on the subject, and in requiring the punishment of clergy and laity alike he enforces already existing decisions.[13] His perspicacity in dealing with the matter may be seen in the fact that he takes care also to prohibit the practice of receiving interest through a third party.

Finally he closes on a special note of warning to recalcitrant bishops,[14] and by confirming the disciplinary decrees of his predecessors, especially those of Pope Innocent I,[15] shows his determination to uphold the standard maintained by the Roman see in the past. The importance of his action lies in the fact that it enables us to trace the beginning of the process by which papal decretals, side by side with the formal enactments of important councils, came to possess the force of canon law.

The next letter to be considered [16] throws some light on a custom prevailing in the churches of Sicily at this time, and illustrates Leo's eagerness to enforce the practice of the Roman Church to the exclusion of local vagaries and peculiarities. It is concerned mainly with the custom of celebrating Baptism at the festival of the Epiphany, a practice which was wide-

[11] *Ep.* 4, 2. "huius discussionis curam nobis specialiter vindicantes, . . . quamquam ignorare nunquam licuerit sacerdotem, quod canonum fuerit regulis definitum."

[12] *Ibid.*, 3 and 4. The practice of usury by the clergy was forbidden by *Conc. Nic.*, Can. 17.

[13] *Conc. Nic.*, *ibid.* "*εἴ τις εὑρεθείη μετὰ τὸν ὅρον τοῦτον τόκους λαμβάνων . . . καθαιρεθήσεται τοῦ κλήρου.*" In the form enacted by *Conc. Carthag.* (A.D. 345) and subsequently renewed by *Conc. Carthag.* (A.D. 419), Canon 5, Mansi, *Concilia,* Vol. IV, 423, the prohibition included the laity. Cf. *Conc. Arelat.*, II (A.D. 443), Canon 14, Mansi, *ibid.*, Vol. VII, 880. Kirch, *Fontes,* No. 877.

[14] *Ibid.*, 5. "a suo se noverit officio submovendum, nec communionis nostrae futurum esse consortem, qui socius esse noluit disciplinae."

[15] *Ibid.*. "omnia decretalia constituta, tam beatae recordationis Innocentii, quam omnium decessorum nostrorum, quae de ecclesiasticis ordinibus et canonum promulgata sunt disciplinis." Cf. Innocent, *Ep.* 2, 4f., JK 286, *Ep.* 17, 1f., JK 303 and Siricius, *Ep.* 1, 8 and 11, JK 255.

[16] *Ep.* 16, JK 414, dated October 21st, A.D. 447. The mention of Paschasinus as the bearer of the reply (c. 7) suggests that it was he who brought the information as to the Sicilian custom to which Leo refers.

spread, not only in Sicily but elsewhere.[17] The Roman custom, on the other hand, was to restrict its celebration normally to the festivals of Easter and Pentecost,[18] and in denouncing the divergent usage Leo goes so far as to assert that the custom, with which he was familiar, was derived from apostolic institution.[19]

He opens his letter by recalling the threefold charge of our Lord to St. Peter,[20] and suggests that negligence of duty may imply lack of love towards God. But when he reaches the subject of Sicilian baptismal practice he gives full vent to his indignation. "I am amazed," he says, "that you or your predecessors should have followed such an absurd innovation, as by confusing the hidden meaning of the two seasons to suggest that no difference exists between the day on which Christ was worshipped by the Magi and the day on which Christ rose from the dead." [21]

Had the Sicilian bishops, he adds, taken as their rule the practice of the Roman see, whence they received confirmation of their office,[22] they would never have made such a mistake. After observing that if their conduct had already been reproved it would have deserved punishment, and that in any case ignorance of rules does not excuse contravention, the Pope goes on to show that the fitting differences between the festivals of the Christian year are to be observed by all alike, for only so will the unity of the Christian flock be preserved.[23] His argument is that of all times Easter, commemorating as

[17] Stone, *Holy Baptism,* p. 142 says, "In Jerusalem and Antioch, in Cappadocia, in Africa, in Gaul, Spain and Ireland, and in Sicily, the Epiphany was kept as a time for Baptism." Cf. Smith, *D.C.A.,* Vol. I, pp. 164–6.

[18] The earliest authority for this restriction, though not absolute, is Tertullian, *De Baptismo,* 19.

[19] *Ep.* 16, 1. "ab apostolicae institutionis consuetudine discrepare." Evidently Leo has in mind Acts ii. 37–41 and possibly Rom. vi. 3, 5.

[20] *Ibid., praef.* "Manente enim Dominicae vocis imperio, quo beatissimus apostolus Petrus trina repetitione mysticae sanctionis imbuitur."

[21] *Ibid.,* 1, "miror vos vel praecessores vestros tam irrationabilem novitatem usurpare potuisse, ut confuso temporis utriusque mysterio nullam esse differentiam crederetis inter diem quo adoratus est Christus a magis, et diem quo resurrexit Christus a mortuis."

[22] *Ibid.* "unde consecrationem honoris accipitis." We take this to refer to "confirmation" of episcopal election by the Roman see as metropolitan. It may, however, imply that the Sicilian bishops had been actually consecrated at Rome.

[23] *Ibid.,* 2.

it does the Lord's death and resurrection, is the most appropriate for the celebration of Baptism.

"Because by means of a sacramental representation and type that which is done in the members corresponds to that which was done in the case of the Head Himself; for in the rite of Baptism, death enters in by the slaying of sin, and the threefold immersion imitates the three days' burial, while the rising from the water is like the rising from the tomb." [24]

What is more, Leo urges, the fact that Christ Himself delivered to His disciples both the formula of Baptism and the authority to baptize after the Resurrection shows that it was part of His intention that that sacrament should be associated with Easter. As for the extension of the sacrament to the feast of Pentecost, he points out that this may be justified on the ground that, being the festival of the Holy Ghost, it may be regarded as, in fact, a festival of Christ Himself, and on the further ground that it has been consecrated for the celebration of this sacrament by the action of St. Peter.[25] He suggests also that such an extension makes a reasonable provision for the needs of those who by some serious hindrance have been prevented from being present at the normal time.

He therefore requires that normally Baptism shall only be given at Easter and Pentecost, though he is prepared to allow for its administration at any time in cases of real emergency.[26] Before finally leaving the subject he examines briefly the consideration, perhaps the very one put forward by the Sicilians themselves in defence of their observance, namely that the Epiphany being the commemoration of Christ's own Baptism was an appropriate time for the Baptism of Christians, and dismisses it on the ground that it was only Christ's death and the effusion of blood and water on the Cross which gave to Baptism its power of regeneration.[27] He then concludes this

[24] *Ep.* 16, 3. "in quo per similitudinem formamque mysterii ea quae geruntur in membris, his quae in ipso sunt capite gesta, congruerent: dum in baptismatis regula, et mors intervenit interfectione peccati, et sepulturam triduanam imitatur trina demersio, et ab aquis elevatio resurgentis instar est de sepulchro."

[25] *Ibid.*, 4. "Hoc autem nos . . . ex apostolica auctoritate servare, . . . sequentes beatum apostolum Petrum, qui in ipso die . . . trium milium populum . . . lavacro baptismatis consecravit," quoting Acts ii. 37–41.

[26] Such as danger of death, siege, persecution or shipwreck, *ibid.*, 5.

[27] *Ibid.*, 6. "tunc regenerationis potentiam sanxit, quando de latere ipsius profluxerunt sanguis redemptionis, et aqua baptismatis."

section of his letter by insisting that, in order to provide for the necessary period of preparation by exorcism, fasting and instruction, the Paschal rule must be kept.[28]

In the last section of the letter Leo turns to the subject of synods. After referring to the relevant canon laid down by the Council of Nicaea,[29] he requires that the bishops of Sicily shall send three representatives to the annual synod held in Rome on September 29th.[30] The purpose of such synods, he adds, is to prevent scandals and false teaching, and to maintain ecclesiastical discipline.[31]

It is difficult for us, accustomed as we are to infant Baptism as the norm and to adult Baptism as the exception, to appreciate fully the importance of the question, which Leo evidently regarded as one of some gravity. Yet once it is realized that Baptism has so largely been deprived of its solemnity by losing its public character and by being administered in the presence of a mere handful of witnesses, it will be seen that Leo had in mind an aspect of the matter which we have for the most part neglected. In addition to this we should notice that the emphasis which he placed on the proper season for the administration of the sacrament is to be explained by his anxiety lest the appropriate exercises in preparation for its reception should be omitted or neglected. To him admission to membership of the Church impressed on the neophyte a character, the dignity of which in later times was largely ignored or forgotten. Moreover, in his regulation on the subject of the annual synod he shows wisdom and consideration in the application of a general rule, such as the one defined by the council of Nicaea, to the particular conditions

[28] *Ibid.* "in baptizandis electis, qui secundum apostolicam regulam et exorcismis scrutandi, et ieiuniis sanctificandi, et frequentibus sunt praedicationibus imbuendi, duo tantum tempora, id est Pascha et Pentecosten, esse servanda; hoc vestrae indicimus charitati, ut ab apostolicis institutis nullo ulterius recedatis excessu." Cf. Siricius, *Ep.* 1, 2, JK 235.

[29] *Ibid.*, 7. "saluberrime a sanctis Patribus constitutum est, binos in annis singulis episcoporum debere esse conventus." The allusion is to *Conc. Nic.*, Canon 5.

[30] The anniversary of Leo's consecration. See Chap. II, p. 38.

[31] *Ibid.* "facilius poterit provideri ut in ecclesiis Christi nulla scandala, nulli nascantur errores, cum coram beatissimo apostolo Petro id semper in commune tractandum sit, ut omnia ipsius constituta canonumque decreta apud omnes Domini sacerdotes inviolata permaneant." The phrase "ipsius constituta" refers to earlier papal decisions. Notice that they precede "canonum . . . decreta."

of his province, and by not insisting on the attendance of the whole Sicilian episcopate, but only of representatives, he displays a reasonable consideration in making allowance for the expense and time involved in travelling.

We possess a further letter addressed to the Sicilian bishops [32] which, even if mistakenly attributed to Leo I,[33] may be considered briefly at this point. It is concerned with reports presented by the clergy of Tauromenium and by the recently elected bishop of Panormus to the effect that Church property had been alienated without the consent of the churches concerned. The matter was investigated at an autumnal synod [34] at Rome and the following ruling issued. "We decree no bishop shall venture either to present or exchange or sell any of the property of his church, saving when he does any of these things so that he may obtain better, and makes such a decision, after discussion and approval by all the clergy, as shall undoubtedly be of benefit to the Church." [35]

The writer adds that those clergy who approve of conduct which inflicts damage on their church are to be deprived and excommunicated. It may be suggested that the letter, if genuinely from Leo I's own hand, reflects his practical sense in dealing with matters of administrative detail, and shows his concern for the proper management of the material goods of the Church. His principle is that the clergy are the trustees, not the owners, of Church property.

Evidently in Leo's time the indiscriminate administration of Baptism or the observance of occasions, other than Easter and Pentecost, was not confined to Sicily. The question recurs in a further letter addressed to the bishops of Southern Italy,[36] but with this difference, namely that in this case public

[32] *Ep.* 17, JK 415, of uncertain date, perhaps October 21st, A.D. 447.

[33] The fact that Pope Hilary I refers to the same subject in *Ep.* 8, 7, JK 555, but omits any allusion to this letter, has suggested the view that it ought to be assigned to Pope Leo II.

[34] *Ibid.*, "cum totius cleri tractatu atque consensu."

[35] *Ibid. Statuta eccl. antiqu.*, Canon 32 [L]. "Irrita erit donatio episcoporum vel venditio vel commutatio rei ecclesiasticae absque conniventia et subscriptione clericorum." *P.L.* 56, 885.

[36] *Ep.* 168, JK 545, dated March 6th, A.D. 459.

baptisms were being performed on festivals of martyrs; [37] the offence, as Leo regarded it, being aggravated by the omission of the proper preparatory exercises. Here we find regulations similar to those already noticed in the Sicilian letter on the subject, with a corresponding list of emergencies, held to justify Baptism being given apart from the proper seasons.[38]

The writer then goes on to consider an entirely new question. It appears that some Italian bishops, in admitting sinners to penance, had begun to require of them, as a preliminary gesture of repentance, the public recital of their sins in detail, and were defending the requirement on the ground that it served to others as a proof of the penitent's sincerity.[39] Leo has no patience with this innovation, and prohibits its continuance. For this prohibition he gives two reasons, the practice, he says, is no real proof of sincerity, for some sins are of such a nature that their publication need cause no fear, while others may be of such a character that those who are equally conscious of them may shrink from making them known, either through shame or for fear that as a consequence of their actions being made public they may find themselves liable to legal proceedings.[40] He then proceeds:

"The confession which is presented first to God and then to the bishop, who takes the part of an intercessor for the sins of penitents, is sufficient, for only if the sins of which the person who confesses is aware are not made known to the

[37] *Ibid.* "quosdam ex vobis comperi ita esse apostolicae traditionis oblitos, . . . ut praeter Paschalem festivitatem, cui sola Pentecostes solemnitas comparatur, audeant sibimet, non aliqua humanae infirmitatis necessitate cogente, sed sola indisciplinati arbitrii libertate, ius baptismatis vindicare, et in natalibus martyrum, quorum finis aliter honorandus est quam dies Dominicae passionis, regenerationis celebrare mysteria, ac sine ullis spiritualium eruditionibus praeparationum, ita rudibus et imperitis tradere sacramentum, ut circa renovandos nihil doctrinae ecclesiasticae, nihil in exorcismis impositio manuum, nihil ipsa ieiunia, quibus vetus homo destruitur, operentur." For the stages of preparation mentioned here cf. *Ep.* 16, 6, JK 414.

[38] Cf. *ibid.*, 5.

[39] *Ibid.*, 2, "De poenitentia scilicet quae a fidelibus postulatur, ne de singulorum peccatorum genere, libello scripta professio publice recitetur, cum reatus conscientiarum sufficiat solis sacerdotibus indicari confessione secreta."

[40] *Ibid.* "ne multi a poenitentiae remediis arceantur, dum aut erubescunt aut metuunt inimicis suis sua facta reserari, quibus possint legum constitutione percelli."

ears of the congregation will many be encouraged to perform penance."[41]

There can be little doubt that the practice censured and firmly prohibited by Leo was, as he implies, an innovation,[42] misguidedly introduced by certain bishops with a view to stiffening the requirements of the penitential system. His decision shows real understanding of the weaknesses of human nature and a true pastoral sollicitude for the salvation of souls. Leo had no use either for an ostentatious parade of sin on the part of certain types of sinners, nor for the imposition of heavy burdens on the sincerely repentant.[43]

Only two examples survive of letters addressed by him to individual bishops belonging to the Roman metropolitical province. The earlier of these was written to Dorus, bishop of Beneventum, in the province of Campania, and concerned a report received by the writer from a certain Paul, priest of that city. According to the latter his bishop had arbitrarily promoted a junior cleric over the heads of senior priests and thereby caused considerable discontent. In his remonstrance addressed to Dorus on the subject,[44] Leo expresses his indignation at so grave a violation of canon law,[45] and at his suffragan's neglect to repress ambitious aims on the part of his junior clergy, even when they are supported by one or two misguided senior priests.[46] He prescribes as a punishment that the young man's supporters are to be deprived of their seniority, so as to rank below their protégé, who is to be

[41] *Ep.* 16, 2. "Sufficit enim illa confessio, quae primum Deo offertur, tum etiam sacerdoti, qui pro delictis poenitentium precator accedit. Tunc enim demum plures ad poenitentiam poterunt provocari, si populi auribus non publicetur conscientia confitentis."

[42] *Ibid.*, 2, "Illam . . . contra apostolicam regulam praesumptionem."

[43] For further consideration of Leo's doctrine of Confession and Absolution see Chap. XX.

[44] *Ep.* 19, JK 417 dated March 8th, A.D. 448.

[45] Probably referring to *Conc. Nic.*, Canon 2. The Ballerini, *P.L.* 54, 709f., n. d suggest that Dorus had been a Roman priest consecrated to the see of Beneventum by Leo, and so ought to have known better.

[46] In this connexion he quotes Luke xiv. 11 thus, *ibid.*, 2. "Dixisse Dominum quod qui se humiliat, exaltabitur: qui vero se exaltat, humiliabitur: eumque dixisse: Vos autem quaeritis de pusillo crescere, et de maiore minores esse." The additional words are found in Codex D and in the Old Latin and Curetonian Syriac versions, but are lacking in the Vulgate, thus throwing some light on the text of the N.T. used at Rome in Leo's time.

reduced to his proper status, while Paul is to be restored to his rightful place, and concludes by saying that he has commissioned Bishop Julius [47] to see that his instructions are duly carried into effect.

Three years later Leo wrote a personal letter to Paschasinus, bishop of Lilybaeum in Sicily. His primary reason for doing so was that he wished to send final instructions before the departure of his legates for the projected Council at Constantinople (actually held at Chalcedon), and to enclose a copy of the letter which he had addressed two years previously to Flavian, late bishop of that see. We shall hear a good deal of Paschasinus in connexion with the events of that council, and, as it will be convenient to consider this letter in relation to those events, it may be passed over for the present.

This group of letters serves to enlighten us considerably as to Leo's main preoccupation, namely the maintenance of the peace and good order of the Church. Whether it was a question of the administration of sacraments, or the promotion of the clergy, or the reconciliation of sinners, or even so mundane a matter as the care of Church property, his decision was conditioned by this one aim. For him there was one chief way by which it might be secured, namely by the due observance of canon law. Yet when he comes to deal with problems affecting the welfare of individuals he never loses sight of the principle that general rules need particular application. If he is impatient of undisciplined or capricious conduct, he is sympathetic with sincere repentance. In brief it may be said that behind his administration of his province, which is to him but a microcosm of the universal Church, the care of which he believes to be divinely committed to his charge, there lies his majestic conception of the papal office, as the visible embodiment of apostolic or even divine authority. We shall see how that conception governed his relations with other churches outside the limits of his own province.

[47] Probably Julius of Puteoli, who in the following year represented the Roman see at the Council of Ephesus. See Chap. X, pp. 238f.

CHAPTER VI

LEO AND THE CHURCHES OF THE WEST. I

I. NORTHERN ITALY

THE division between the area of civil jurisdiction assigned to the *Vicarius Urbis,* and that belonging to the *Vicarius Italiae,* following roughly the range of the Apennine mountains, served to mark the boundary between the metropolitical " province " of the Roman see, and the orbit of influence of the see of Milan, as it existed in the latter part of the fourth century.[1] Chosen by Maximian as his seat of government in the West in A.D. 286 [2] Milan remained for over a century one of the chief centres of imperial administration, and for a time at least overshadowed even Rome in respect of civil importance. Hence, as might be expected, its see steadily increased in influence, so much so that under the guidance of a bishop of such outstanding qualities as those possessed by Ambrose, it acquired a position in relation to other Western churches, which threatened to exceed the unique pre-eminence of the Roman see itself.[3] Yet as soon as the city ceased to be an imperial residence, and in consequence began to lose much of its civil magnificence, its ecclesiastical influence tended proportionately to diminish and it was not long before rivals to its supremacy in northern Italy made their appearance.

Aquileia, the first of these, had already been recognized during the pontificate of Ambrose as a convenient ecclesiastical centre, since it was chosen by him as the rendezvous of a council assembled under his presidency in A.D. 381, the purpose of which was to deal with certain questions, arising out

[1] It is likely that in the pre-Nicene period the see of Rome exercised an undefined primacy over the whole of Italy. Cf. Letter of the Council of Arles, A.D. 316. Mansi, *Concilia,* Vol. II, 469; Mirbt, *Quellen,* No. 100.

[2] Gibbon, *Decline* (1929), Vol. I, p. 407

[3] On the see of Milan in the time of Ambrose see Homes Dudden, *St. Ambrose,* Vol. I, p. 64, and Duchesne, *Origines du culte chrétien* (1889), pp. 32, 37.

of the later stages of the Arian controversy as it had affected the churches situated in the provinces of Western Illyricum.[4] Within a few years of the opening of the fifth century its see seems to have acquired complete independence of Milan and to have become recognized as the ecclesiastical metropolis of the churches belonging to the provinces of north-eastern Italy.[5]

It happened, however, that in forsaking Milan the choice of the fugitive Emperor Honorius fell not upon Aquileia, but Ravenna, and as a result the town which had hitherto been distinguished for little else than its dockyard and its inadequate fresh water supply found itself raised to the dignity of a city of first class rank.[6] Once more ecclesiastical predominance followed in the wake of civil aggrandisement and within thirty years of the advancement of the see of Aquileia, its sphere of influence was curtailed by the detachment of two provinces to form a new circumscription subject to the authority of the see of Ravenna.[7]

When we turn to consider Leo's relations with these northern churches we find that of the three Aquileia is the best documented.[8] Of the letters which passed between Rome and Milan during his pontificate we possess only the synodical

[4] On the Council of Aquileia, see Homes Dudden, *op. cit.*, Vol. I, pp. 200ff. Zeiller, *Les origines Chrétiennes dans les provinces danubiennes,* pp. 328ff.

[5] The list of bishops who signed the synodical letter despatched in A.D. 451 to the Roman see, *Inter Leon. Epp.*, No. 97, *P.L.* 54, 945, does not include any from the following civil provinces, Venetia, Histria, Flaminia and Picenum Annonarium. It is therefore to be supposed that at this time none of these provinces was any longer subject to Milan. The date at which the change took place is not certain, but it may be conjectured that it occurred during the episcopate of Augustine of Aquileia and may have been an indirect consequence of the Pelagian controversy. He occupied the see of Aquileia from A.D. 407–434 and wrote a *Libellus fidei* in defence of Pelagianist doctrine, see *Inter August. Op.*, Vol. X, app. 110–13, *P.L.* 45, 1732–6, and Kidd, *History,* Vol. III, pp. 124f.

[6] The earliest rescript issued from Ravenna is dated A.D. 402 so it is to be presumed that Honorius' flight took place in that year. See Bury, *Later Roman Empire,* Vol. I, p. 163, n. 2, and Seeck, *Regesten der Kaiser und Päpste,* p. 304.

[7] This development must have taken place during the regency of the Empress Galla Placidia, though there is nothing to show the precise date at which it occurred. Caspar, *Geschichte,* Vol. I, p. 469 suggests that Peter, who was elected in A.D. 432, was actually the second occupant of the see to possess metropolitical authority.

[8] There are in all four letters addressed to bishops of this province.

reply [9] addressed by Eusebius of Milan and his suffragans to the Pope on the subject of the latter's famous letter to Flavian.[10] Mention is made in the course of this document of an earlier letter from Leo himself,[11] but it has not been preserved. As the synodical letter is so closely connected with the contents of Leo's letter to Flavian it will be discussed in connection with the Eutychian controversy to which it belongs. We may therefore pass on immediately to consider his correspondence with the province of Aquileia.

This group of letters is concerned with problems connected with the heresy of Pelagianism [12] or else with difficulties arising out of the barbarian invasions. It is probable that that heresy had met with favourable reception at Aquileia, thanks to the support given to its protagonists by Augustine, bishop of that see, and had continued to flourish under his successor. In fact the position appears to have been serious enough to cause Septimus, bishop of Altinum, to send a report to Leo on the subject. To judge from Leo's reply and from his letter addressed to the unnamed metropolitan on the matter, the report alleged that certain clergy suspected of Pelagian sympathies were obtaining admission into the ranks of the clergy belonging to churches within that province, in spite of the fact that they had not produced any "letters dimissory" from their "native" churches. Leo immediately sent a reply to his informant [13] and at the same time addressed a special remonstrance to the metropolitan [14] on the matter, in the course of which he observes that the "migration" of clergy without the permission of the bishop concerned is directly contrary to canon law,[15] and goes on to protest against the negligence with which clergy suspected of heresy have been accepted without previous examination. As a remedy he urges the immediate summoning of the provincial synod, at which the *bona fides*

[9] *Inter Leon. Epp.*, No. 97.
[10] *Ep.* 28, JK 423.
[11] *Ibid.*, 2, "sicut scripta vestra signaverant."
[12] This is highly significant in view of the earlier history of this see. See above.
[13] *Ep.* 2, JK 399.
[14] *Ep.* 1, JK 398, date uncertain. The name of the metropolitan is unknown.
[15] *Ibid.* "quod per auctoritatem canonum decretorumque nostrorum ne insontibus quidem conceditur." The allusion is to *Conc. Nic.*, Can. 15 and 16, and perhaps to Xystus III, *Ep.* 9, JK 395.

of the newcomers may be investigated, and a proof of orthodoxy required in a written repudiation of all Pelagian errors, and in the formal acceptance of the existing conciliar pronouncements on Pelagian doctrine.[16] He then proceeds to utter a specific warning against the subtleties of these heretics, a warning which possibly reflects his own personal experience, and particularly mentions the Pelagian view, according to which while they acknowledge the existence of grace they nevertheless insist that it is given according to the merits of the recipient.[17] His epigrammatic reply to such an opinion is contained in the following memorable phrase: "Grace not actually given *gratis* is not grace at all." [18] Therefore the utmost caution, he adds, must be observed lest the heresy should re-establish itself in northern Italy, and all who refuse to comply with these requirements are to be excluded from the Church's fellowship. In conclusion, he renews his stipulation that discipline is to be enforced against unauthorized clerical "migration." Those who refuse to return to their "native" diocese are to be deposed and excommunicated.[19] The writer's final stricture to the effect that the shortcomings of subjects are apt to be ascribed to the fault of their ecclesiastical superiors suggests that he thought it improbable that the metropolitan concerned would be prepared to carry out his instructions.

In his reply to his informant,[20] Septimus, bishop of Altinum, he treats the allegations as a formal *relatio,* demanding a *rescriptum* in the manner prescribed by his predecessors for dealing with a *causa maior*.[21] After observing that the letter

[16] These requirements are probably based on *Conc. Nic.*, Can. 8, Mirbt, *Quellen,* No. 114. "πρὸ πάντων δὲ τοῦτο ὁμολογῆσαι αὐτοὺς ἐγγράφως προσήκει, ὅτι συνθήσονται καὶ ἀκολουθήσουσι τοῖς τῆς καθολικῆς καὶ ἀποστολικῆς ἐκκλησίας δόγμασι." "Decreta synodalia" doubtless alludes to the Canons of the African Church. Cf. also Zosimus, *Ep. Tract.*, ap. Augustine, *Opera,* Vol. X, app. *P.L.* 45, 1730.

[17] *Ibid.*, 3. "excipiunt ut gratia Dei secundum merita dari accipientium sentiatur." This became a characteristic doctrine of the "Semi-pelagians" of southern Gaul.

[18] *Ibid.* "quae (sc. gratia) utique nisi gratis detur non est gratia." Gratian in *Concord. Discord.*, II, 1 quotes this phrase at the beginning of the second part of his work, but in a form which suggests that it was copied from Humbert, *Adv. Simoniac.*, I, 4, *M.G.H.*, *Lib. de lit.*, 1, p. 108.

[19] In so saying he is applying the sanctions prescribed by *Conc. Nic.*, Can. 15 and 16.

[20] *Ep.* 2, JK 399 without date but probably A.D. 442.

[21] e.g. Innocent, *Ep.* 2, 3, JK 286.

recently received has increased his confidence in the faith of his correspondent, the writer mentions the letter which he has despatched to Aquileia and summarizes its contents. He concludes by expressing the hope that he may rely on Septimus to co-operate in any disciplinary measures which may be necessary for the sake of restoring order in the Church.

From the absence of any allusion to synodical action in Leo's reply[22] to a later letter addressed to him by Januarius, the new metropolitan, it may be inferred with some probability that no action on the lines suggested by Leo had been taken. Apparently the communication received from Januarius was concerned with a single question, namely as to the treatment which should be accorded to ex-Pelagianist clergy of whose repentance there was no reasonable doubt. In his answer Leo points out that restoration to clerical status, without expectation of preferment, is the best which can be granted in such cases: but in the event of anyone having submitted to rebaptism this provision is not to apply.[23]

When we come to the next of those letters addressed to the province of Aquileia which have survived, we find that Januarius has been replaced by Nicetas The latter, it seems, found himself confronted by a number of difficult questions consequent on the social and ecclesiastical confusion which followed the invasion of northern Italy by the army of Attila the Hun. In the year A.D. 444 Attila made himself sole ruler of the Hunnish nation. Foiled in his attempt to seize the Gallic provinces by the generalship and diplomacy of the Patrician Aetius he turned aside in A.D. 452 to attack Venetia.

[22] *Ep.* 18, JK 416. The date is dubious but perhaps should be December 30th, A.D. 447. It should be noticed that the opening section of the letter reproduces *Ep.* 2, 1, and the conclusion *Ep.* 2, 2 and part of *Ep.* 1, 5.

[23] *Ibid.* "Circa quos etiam illam canonum constitutionem praecipimus custodiri, ut in magno habeant beneficio si adempta sibi omni spe promotionis, in quo inveniuntur ordine, stabilitate perpetua maneant: si tamen iterata tinctione non fuerint maculati. Non levem apud Dominum noxam incurrit qui de talibus ad sacros ordines promovendum aliquem iudicavit." The allusion is clearly to *Conc. Nic.*, Can. 8. The exception in the case of those who had been rebaptized may refer to those who had accepted fresh baptism at the hands of Arian clergy. See *Ep.* 159, 6, JK 536, and cf. Victor Vitensis, *Historia persecutionis,* 3, 45–8, *C.S.E.L.,* Vol. VII, pp. 94–6. For similar rulings cf. Siricius, *Ep.* 2, 28, JK 258; Innocent I, *Ep.* 2, 8, JK 286, who prescribes that such persons should be subjected to a prolonged penance. *Cod. Theod.* 16, vi, 1, 5, A.D. 373, ed. Mommsen, Vol. I, pp. 880, 882. Kirch, *Fontes,* No. 838.

Aquileia, the first important city in his line of march, was taken by storm and reduced to ruins, never again to regain its ancient civil dignity.[24] Of Attila's subsequent withdrawal and the collapse of his empire we shall read elsewhere :[25] here we are only concerned with his career so far as it affected the discipline of the Church.

It appears that Nicetas took advantage of the visits of a Roman deacon, Adeodatus, to send to Rome by his hand a series of questions, including problems connected with marriage, rebaptism and lapse into paganism. In his response[26] Leo treats of each of these in turn.

The first query concerns the case of those women whose husbands had been taken prisoner by the invaders, and who had married again on the presumption that the former husband was dead or was unlikely to be liberated. In the event of the latter returning home safe, which of the two was to be regarded as the rightful spouse? Leo's answer is that the undertakings of legitimate matrimony are to be renewed and the rights of the original husband respected.[27] In which case it may be asked what is the position of the second husband? No blame attaches to him for acting, presumably, in good faith : yet he has no right to retain the woman, whom he so married, since one who has similarly become possessed of property must allow its restoration to its original owner.[28] Hence should the former husband desire to repossess his wife, he is to have her, and no blame for what has taken place is to attach to either party.[29] But supposing the woman refuses to return to him? In that case she is to be excommunicated,

[24] For the events of these years see Bury, *Later Roman Empire*, Vol. I, c. ix.

[25] See below.

[26] *Ep.* 159, JK 536, dated March 21st, A.D. 458.

[27] *Ibid.*, 1. "necesse est ut legitimarum foedera nuptiarum redintegranda credamus, et remotis malis quae hostilitas intulit, unicuique hoc quod legitime habuit reformetur, omnique studio procurandum est ut recipiat unusquisque quod proprium est," with allusion to Prov. xix. 14 and Matt. xix. 6.

[28] *Ibid.*, 2. "sic enim multa quae ad eos qui in captivitatem ducti sunt pertinebant in ius alienum transire potuerunt, et tamen plenum iustitiae est ut eisdem reversis propria reformentur."

[29] *Ibid.*, 3.

for her refusal changes a blameless act into a deliberate sin.[30] On the other hand, he remarks that those who return willingly are deserving of praise.

The second group of problems relates to those who in the course of the recent invasions had lapsed into paganism or been infected with heresy. What is the position of one who has taken part in heathen sacrifice? Leo replies that such a person is "to be cleansed by the satisfaction of penance," the duration of which is to be determined by the sincerity of his repentance;[31] while in a case where the eating of sacrificial food was prompted by fear or actual hunger, pardon may be freely given.[32] Next follow cases connected with Baptism. What of one who through fear or error has been led to submit to a fresh Baptism at the hands of heretics, and now realizes the impropriety of his conduct? The Pope's answer is that he is to be restored by means of penance and the laying on of the bishop's hand:[33] while the length of the penance is to be governed by the penitent's devotion. At the same time, in cases of real urgency such as a sudden emergency or sickness, reconciliation by the ministry of the bishop may be effected without delay.[34]

The last case to be considered concerns a person who, having been baptized once only and that by heretics, now desires admission to Catholic Communion. Leo rules that the sacrament must not be profaned by repetition: on the

[30] *Ep.* 159, 4. "merito sunt notandae; ita ut etiam ecclesiastica communione priventur: quae de re excusabili contaminationem criminis elegerunt, ostendentes sibimet pro sua in continentia placuisse, quod iusta remissio poterat expiare."

[31] *Ibid.*, 5. "poenitentiae satisfactione purgentur, quae non tam temporis longitudine quam cordis compunctione pensanda est." A significantly reasonable decision!

[32] *Ibid.* "sive hoc terror extorserit, sive fames suaserit, non dubitetur abolendum, cum huius modi cibus pro metu aut indigentia, non pro religionis veneratione sit sumptus." Evidently Leo has 1 Cor. viii. in mind.

[33] *Ibid.*, 6. "ea custodienda est moderatio, qua in societatem nostram non nisi per poenitentiae remedium, et per impositionem episcopalis manus, communionis recipiant unitatem." Evidently, as the Ballerini point out, it is the case of a layman which is in view. The clergy who have been baptized afresh are apparently to be degraded as in *Ep.* 18, JK 416; cf. Innocent I, *Ep.* 24, 3, JK 303, and *Ep.* 2, 8, JK 286.

[34] *Ibid.* "in quibus si quis ita graviter urgeatur, ut dum adhuc poenitet, de salute ipsius desperetur, oportet ei per sacerdotalem sollicitudinem communionis gratia subveniri." Cf. Innocent I, *Ep.* 6, 2, JK 293.

other hand it is necessary that such a person should be confirmed by the invocation of the Holy Ghost through the laying on of the hand:[35] since in this case the outward sign of Baptism has been received but not the grace of sanctification. The latter, which cannot be received from heretics, must be sought from Catholic bishops.[36]

This concludes the various problems reviewed and answered by Leo. It only remains for him to request Nicetas to make known the contents of his letter to the bishops of the province.

We now turn to Leo's relations with the province of Ravenna. In the same year inquiries similar to the foregoing were addressed to the Roman see by its metropolitan, Neon. In this case two problems only were raised, namely the reconciliation to the Church of those who had received Baptism at the hands of heretics,[37] and the special case of persons who after returning from captive exile among the barbarians were uncertain whether they had ever received Baptism in infancy or not.[38] Leo, it seems, took the opportunity of referring these problems to the consideration of his autumnal synod at Rome, which issued rulings, he says, in accordance with the decisions already given by him in such cases. As to the recipients of Baptism at the hands of heretics, Leo reproduces in his reply a decision similar to the one which we have already noticed in the course of his letter to Nicetas of

[35] *Ibid.*, 7. "hi qui baptismum ab haereticis acceperunt, cum antea baptizati non fuissent, sola invocatione Spiritus sancti per impositionem manuum confirmandi sunt, quia *formam* tantum *baptismi* sine sanctificationis virtute sumpserunt." Evidently, to speak technically, Leo distinguishes between the regularity and the validity of sacraments administered by heretics.

[36] *Ibid.* "cuius (sc. Domini) ablutio nulla iteratione temeranda est, sed ut diximus, sola sanctificatio Spiritus sancti invocanda est: ut quod ab haereticis nemo accipit, a catholicis sacerdotibus consequatur."

[37] *Ep.* 166, JK 543, dated October 24th, A.D. 458. The Ballerini, *P.L.* 54, 1190f., show good reason to accept the reading "Neoni" against "Leoni" and other manuscript variants. On the Roman synod see *Ep.* 166, 1, "nuper in synodo novum et in auditum antea genus consultationis exortum est."

[38] The case probably refers to some who had been made captives in the course of Attila's invasion of Italy A.D. 451–2. If they were infants at the time they would by now be at least six years old. Leo expresses the doubt thus: "utrum eiusdem mysterium baptismatis ac sacramenta perceperint, infantiae inscientia non posse reminisci." "Sacramenta" may well refer to the whole initiatory rite, i.e. baptism followed immediately even in the case of infants by Confirmation and First Communion.

Aquileia, namely that Confirmation by a Catholic bishop, yet without repetition of Baptism, is indispensable.[39]

Then he turns to the consideration of the second problem. He strongly endorses the principle that where Baptism has been validly received it must under no circumstances be renewed,[40] but suggests that excessive caution lest this principle be violated may cause individuals to be deprived of baptismal grace On the other hand mere supposition of Baptism is not enough. There must be absolute certainty on the point. Where there is any uncertainty and no witnesses of the fact of Baptism can be brought forward, the Pope rules that in such a case Baptism ought to be administered, and even if it is in fact a second Baptism, the fact that it is given in good faith absolves both the candidate and the minister of the sacrament from any blame in the matter.[41] But it should only be done after a thorough and lengthy examination so that the possibility of a witness appearing after all may not be overlooked, unless the candidate is in danger of death, in which case there should be as little delay as possible.[42] Leo concludes his letter with the usual request that Neon should communicate its contents to his suffragans.[43]

This letter exhausts the evidence which we possess as to Leo's relations with the " greater churches " of the north, but

[39] *Ep.* 166, 2. " hoc tantum quod ibi defuit conferatur, ut per episcopalem manus impositionem virtutem sancti Spiritus consequatur."

[40] *Ibid.*, 1. " inexpiabile est facinus, quoties iuxta haereticorum damnata a sanctis Patribus instituta, cogitur aliquis lavacrum, quod regenerandis semel tributum est, bis subire." Leo justifies this principle with reference to Eph. iv. 5. " Sanctis Patribus " may probably allude to Siricius, *Ep.* 1, 1, JK 255 ; *Ep.* 2, 8, JK 258 ; Innocent I, *Ep.* 2, 9, JK 286. Cf. Augustine, *Ep.* 23, 2. *P.L.* 33, 95. " Rebaptizare hominem haereticum omnino peccatum est : rebaptizare autem catholicum immanissimum scelus est." *Cod. Theod.* XVI, vi, 1, 5. Kirch, *Fontes,* Nos. 838f.

[41] Cf. also *Conc. Arelat.*, Can. 8. Mansi, *Concilia,* Vol. II, 472. Denzinger, *Encheir.*, No. 53, and *Conc. Carthag.*, A.D. 397, Can. 39. *P.L.* 56, 432.

[42] *Ibid.*, 1. " quoties persona talis inciderit, sollicita primum examinatione discutite, et longo tempore, nisi forte supremus finis immineat, indagate utrum nemo sit penitus qui testimonio suo iuvare possit ignorantiam nescientis."

[43] This use of the authority of the metropolitan bishop suggests that Leo only intervened directly in the affairs of a province and established contact with ordinary diocesan bishops in cases where he distrusted the loyalty of the metropolitan himself to canonical order. Leo himself was not directly concerned to increase centralization, even if it was the logical consequence of his theory.

it is sufficient to show how, even beyond the limits of its metropolitical jurisdiction, the Roman see in his time was regarded as the obvious centre to which there should be recourse for the solution of points of uncertainty in matters of discipline, and for support in dealing with irregularities. His letters addressed to those churches reveal points of interest similar to those which we have already noticed in an earlier chapter, namely his preoccupation with the maintenance of discipline as prescribed by canon law, but they show in addition his eagerness to ensure adequate qualifications for the clergy, and his concern for the due honour and right use of the sacraments.

2. AFRICA

At the time when Leo was elected to the see of Rome the provinces of Africa had almost ceased to be a part of the Roman Empire. The events leading up to this state of affairs may be now described in rather more detail. Soon after the death of the Emperor Honorius in the year A.D. 423, the Germanic tribe of the Vandals, under the leadership of Gaiseric, which had already established itself in Spain, invaded the African provinces and after a comparatively short time found itself in a strong enough position there to conclude a treaty with the new Emperor, Valentinian III, by which the sovereignty of Gaiseric over the three Mauretanian provinces was officially recognized.[44] In the years which followed the conclusion of this treaty (A.D. 435), the invaders made incessant raids on imperial territory and before the end of A.D. 439 the city of Carthage itself fell into their hands.[45] As a consequence of this event a new treaty was drawn up three years later, which provided for the recession of Mauretania to the Empire, while it assigned the richest areas of north Africa, namely the Proconsular-province and Byzacena, to the Vandals.[46] The latter differed from the Roman provincials both in race and in religion. They com-

[44] Prosper, *Chronicon,* sub ann. 435. *M.G.H.,* Auct. antiq., Vol. IX. *Chron. min.,* Vol. I, p. 474. Cf. Bury, *Later Roman Empire,* Vol. I, p. 249.

[45] For a description of the city at this time, see Gibbon, *Decline and Fall,* Vol. III (1929), p. 434.

[46] Victor Vitensis, *Historia persecutionis,* I, 12, 13, ed. Petschenig, *C.S.E.L.,* Vol. VII, pp. 6f.

bined with a barbarian standard of ethics a bigoted and intransigent profession of the Arian creed of Ariminum, and in respect of tolerance showed a marked difference from their Gothic co-religionists by persecuting with relentless zeal the adherents of the Catholic Faith of Nicaea. Moreover, their *odium theologicum* was sharply intensified by a vigorous national spirit, which was characterized by a persistent hatred of everything associated with Latin imperial culture. Hence the churches of Africa, with their Latin rites and Nicene standard of doctrine, owing allegiance to the primacy of the Roman see, became from the first victims of their persecuting zeal, with the inevitable consequence that bishops were banished from their sees and their churches made over to the Arian clergy; in fact, after the fall of Carthage the primatial see of Africa remained in Arian hands for no less than twelve years.[47]

In A.D. 445 a delegation from the African provinces which still remained part of the Empire arrived in Rome. Its object was to obtain from Valentinian III, in view of the economic distress prevailing in these provinces, as a consequence of the Vandal invasions, some measure of relief from taxation. The mission was successful,[48] but apart from this it has a special interest for us, since it appears to have been the means by which Leo became acquainted with certain facts as to the condition of the Church in the provinces concerned. It was alleged that grave irregularities were taking place there particularly in connexion with the choice of candidates for the episcopate. Leo, who, as we have seen, was specially concerned for the maintenance of a high standard in the episcopal order and felt it his duty to enforce the prescriptions of canon law on the subject, decided that he must have first hand information on the whole matter, and with this object despatched bishop Potentius[49] to ascertain the facts on the spot. In the course

[47] When at length in A.D. 454 a Catholic bishop of Carthage was once again tolerated by the Vandals, it was in consequence of a suppliant petition addressed by Valentinian III to Gaiseric, perhaps at the suggestion of Leo himself. Cf. Victor Vitensis, *Historia persecutionis,* I, 24, ed. Petschenig, *C.S.E.L.,* Vol. VII, p. 11.

[48] Valentinian III, *Leg. novell.* 13, ed. P. Meyer, p. 95.

[49] Since Leo refers to this person as "proficenti a nobis," it is more probable that his see was in Italy and not in Africa as Batiffol, *Siège Apostolique,* p. 480 suggests. If our view is correct, Leo's action was in accord with the provisions of *Conc. Sardic.,* Can. 7 (vers. lat.).

of the following year Potentius brought back his report, which not only confirmed the truth of the allegations, but mentioned in addition a number of other problems urgently demanding solution. It was on the basis of this report that Leo composed his instructions to the African bishops.[50]

The first question to be dealt with is the case of those who have obtained uncanonical promotion to the episcopate.[51] Evidently, as the writer himself shows, this had become specially prevalent in consequence of the social and economic disorder resulting from the recent occupation of those provinces by the Vandals,[52] and as a result the existing requirements laid down by conciliar authority had been ignored. Not only had men been elected who had not passed through the successive grades of the lower ministry, but in certain cases even simple laymen had been advanced to episcopal rank.

After pointing out that the consecration of such persons to the highest degree in the hierarchy is calculated rather to increase disorder than to restore discipline, Leo urges that the good order of the Church as a whole is dependent on due observance of the correct procedure in regard to episcopal elections.[53] Beginning with the Pauline precept,[54] he shows that the consecration of a junior, whose worth has not been tested by length of service or submission to discipline is wholly without justification.[55] After this he sets forth the qualifica-

[50] *Ep.* 12, JK 410, dated August 10th probably in the year A.D. 446. The letter is probably later than A.D. 442, the year in which the Vandals occupied Mauretania, and earlier than A.D. 455 when the whole of the African provinces passed under Vandal control. On the unity of this letter see below, p. 108.

[51] *Ibid.*, 1, "de ordinationibus sacerdotum quaedam apud vos illicite usurpata." It should be remembered that "sacerdos" unqualified in the language of this period is invariably equivalent to "episcopus."

[52] *Ibid.* "mirantes tantum apud vos per occasionem temporis impacti aut ambientium praesumptionem, aut tumultum valuisse popularem, ut indignis quibusque et longe extra sacerdotale meritum constitutis pastorale fastigium et gubernatio ecclesiae dederetur."

[53] *Ibid.*, 2, "elaborandum est ut in electione eius qui supra omnes gradus constituitur non erretur."

[54] I Tim. v. 22, "χεῖρας ταχέως μηδενὶ ἐπιτίθει, μηδὲ κοινώνει ἁμαρτίαις ἀλλοτρίαις."

[55] *Ibid.* "quid est cito manus imponere, nisi ante aetatem maturitatis, ante tempus examinis, ante meritum obedientiae, ante experientiam disciplinae sacerdotalem honorem tribuere non probatis? Et quid est communicare peccatis alienis, nisi et talem effici ordinantem, qualis est ille qui non meruit ordinari."

tions of a fit candidate. First, Leo states, such a candidate must conform to the apostolic and scriptural requirements in regard to matrimony, namely that if married he should have married once only, and that his wife should herself have been a virgin at the time.[56] These precepts he derives from St. Paul[57] and from the Mosaic law,[58] and suggests that the unique union which exists between Christ and His Church is comparable to the marriage of the Jewish priests of old time to wives of virgin integrity.[59] He then points out anew that the apostolic requirement that only those should be promoted who have passed through a period of probation,[60] implies that no one is fit for advancement to holy orders who has not passed some considerable time in each of the lower grades of the ministry.[61]

After having thus defined the qualifications for episcopal office, as prescribed by conciliar and papal authority, Leo gives judgment in the present case. Undoubtedly, he writes, abuses such as these merit severe punishment, yet in view of

[56] *Ep.* 12, 3.

[57] 1 Tim. iii. 2, "δεῖ οὖν τὸν ἐπίσκοπον ἀνεπίληπτον εἶναι, μιᾶς γυναικὸς ἄνδρα."

[58] Lev. xxi. 13f. "He (sc. the high priest) shall take a wife in her virginity. A widow, or one divorced . . . these shall he not take: but a virgin of his own people shall he take to wife."

Ezek. xliv. 22. "Neither shall they (sc. the priests) take for their wives a widow, nor her that is put away: but they shall take virgins of the seed of the house of Israel."

[59] With allusion to Eph. v. 25 and 1 Cor. xi. 3.

[60] 1 Tim. iii. 10. "καὶ οὗτοι δὲ δοκιμαζέσθωσαν πρῶτον, εἶτα διακονείτωσαν ἀνέγκλητοι ὄντες."

[61] *Ibid.*, 4. "Merito beatorum Patrum venerabiles sanctiones cum de sacerdotum electione loquerentur eosdem ut idoneos sacris administrationibus censuerunt, qui multo tempore per singulos officiorum gradus provecti experimentum sui probabile praebuissent." Among the "patrum venerabiles sanctiones" Leo would presumably include the following:—

Conc. Nic., Canon 2. "ἀνθρώπους ἀπὸ ἐθνικοῦ βίου ἄρτι προσελθόντας τῇ πίστει . . ἅμα τὸ βαπτισθῆναι προσάγειν εἰς ἐπισκοπὴν ἢ πρεσβυτερεῖον· καλῶς ἔδοξεν ἔχειν τοῦ λοιποῦ μηδὲν τοιοῦτο γινέσθαι."

Conc. Sardic., Canon 13, *P.L.* 56, 780. "si forte aut dives aut scholasticus . . . fuerit postulatus episcopus non prius ordinetur, nisi ante lectoris munere et officio diaconi et ministerio presbyteri per ordinem fuerit perfunctus, et per singulos gradus, si dignus fuerit, promoveatur ad episcopatus honorem." Cf. Siricius, *Ep.* 1, 9. 10, JK 255; Innocent I, *Ep.* 37, 3, JK 314; Celestine I, *Ep.* 4, 2, JK 369. For a further example of action based on the Canons of Sardica, see Chap. VII, pp. 114f.

the circumstances he is ready to use moderation.[62] He therefore divides the offenders into two classes according to the nature of their offence. Those who have transgressed the law which prohibits, in the case of bishops, a second marriage or marriage to a widow, are to be deposed: the same sentence to apply also in the case of one who is alleged to have been married to two women at the same time, and of another who has married a second time after divorce, if they shall be found guilty at the proposed African synod. On the other hand, he allows those who as laymen have been promoted directly to the episcopate to retain their office, without prejudice however to the strict enforcements of canonical requirements in future, offences against which, he adds, will not go unpunished.[63]

After this Leo goes on to discuss certain particular questions which have been brought to his notice. First there is the case of Donatus, bishop of Salicinum, who together with his congregation had forsaken Novatianism and been reconciled to the Catholic Church. Here his ruling is that the bishop is to retain his rank, provided that he will subscribe a statement respecting his former belief and accepting that of the Church.[64] Next comes Maximus, an ex-Donatist, who had been made a bishop while still a layman and now desired reconciliation. The verdict in his case is identical with the one pronounced in the case of Donatus.[65] Finally, Leo deals with Aggarus and Tiberianus, both of whom had been elected to the episcopate although only laymen, and whose elections had given rise to riots and public disorder, seemingly instigated by themselves. Leo remits this affair to the provincial synod

[62] *Ibid.*, 5, "cogimur secundum sedis apostolicae pietatem ita nostram temperare sententiam, ut trutinato pondere delictorum, quorum utique non una mensura est, quaedam credamus utcumque toleranda, quaedam vero penitus amputanda." The passage reflects some light on Leo's capacity for tempering justice with reason and shows him to be above the excessive rigorism of some of his contemporaries.

[63] *Ibid.* "susceptum sacerdotium tenere permittimus, non praeiudicantes apostolicae sedis statutis, nec beatorum Patrum regulas resolventes . . . quod enim nunc utcumque patimur esse veniale, inultum postmodum esse non potuit."

[64] *Ibid.*, 6. The case is interesting as showing the survival of a third century schism in Africa at this date. Leo's ruling is precisely in accord with the provisions of *Conc. Nic.*, Canon 8.

[65] *Ibid.*

for judgment, with an assurance that he will be guided by its decision.[66]

In the section which follows Leo offers a solution of the delicate question as to the attitude which a local Church ought to adopt towards those consecrated virgins, who had suffered violation at the hands of barbarian invaders. He suggests that it befits humility and modesty if they hold themselves inferior to others of their vocation, whose honour has suffered no outrage, and that a voluntary penitence will serve to detract from their disgrace, even though they have been unwilling victims.[67]

The remainder of the letter gives the appearance of having been originally a separate document. Not only is there some repetition of statements already made in the earlier part of the letter, but a number of decisions already given are reproduced in almost identical language.[68] The natural inference is that two letters originally distinct have been combined.[69]

It includes special instructions, which are transmitted through bishop David (who, it may be inferred, was the bearer of the letter), by exhorting the African Church to obedience to divine and ecclesiastical law, and by calling attention to the need of strict observance of that law in future, in spite of the fact that he has in certain cases been willing to tolerate breaches of the law in the past. In particular he observes that bishops who perform uncanonical ordinations will be deprived of their right to ordain altogether.[70]

After this he turns to a new problem, namely as to the

[66] *Ep.* 12, 7. The course followed by Leo shows his fairness in regard to matters of detail and his unwillingness to give a decision, where owing to the nature the true facts could only be ascertained on the spot.

[67] *Ibid.*, 8.

[68] Cf. c. 8 and c. 13.

[69] The Ballerini, *P.L.* 54, 645 print two versions of the document as a whole, the second being an abbreviation of the first. See Maassen, *Quellen,* Vol. I, p. 258.

[70] *Ibid.*, 9. "unde si qui episcopi talem consecraverint sacerdotem qualem esse non liceat, . . . ordinationis tam ius ulterius non habebunt, nec unquam ei sacramento intererunt, quod neglecto divino iudicio immerito praestiterunt." The passage is noteworthy as showing (1) the beginnings of a distinction between "order" and "jurisdiction," and (2) in applying the term "sacramentum" to ordination. The allusion of the phrase "divinum iudicium" must presumably be to the apostolic injunctions. See above, pp. 105ff.

relation between the so-called *chorepiscopi,* or rural bishops,[71] and the normal episcopate. He alludes to a canonical prohibition against the consecration of bishops to villages and country estates and on the strength of this declares that on the decease of a *chorepiscopus* the territory assigned to him is to revert either to the city-bishop to whom it rightly belonged or to the bishop nearest at hand.[72]

Then comes the case of Lupicinus.[73] It appears that this bishop had already appealed to the Roman see on more than one occasion with a view to obtaining the reversal of an adverse verdict pronounced by the local synod. Leo prescribes that Lupicinus is not to be excluded from communion, since the appeal of the latter to the Roman see must necessarily suspend the sentence of the local synod,[74] and severely criticizes the unwarranted haste on the part of the Mauretanian episcopate in providing a successor to the defendant. His decision is that the case is to be reheard locally, after which, it may be inferred, he expects to receive a further report.

In the succeeding paragraph he refers to the problem of the treatment of female religious who had been outraged by the barbarians. His ruling resembles the one already noticed, but in addition he enjoins that such persons are to rank below the virgins but above the widows, and so long as they continue to live in chastity are not to be refused communion.[75]

In conclusion, Leo insists that all future breaches of canonical order are to be referred, in the first instance, to the provincial synod, and that information as to the decisions

[71] The office of the *chorepiscopus* mentioned here appears to have been a modification of mon-episcopacy widely adopted in the East, and also to a limited extent in the West, with a view to making provision for the pastoral care of rural areas. Cf. *Conc. Ant.,* Can. 10; *Conc. Neocaes,* Can. 14; *Conc. Laod.,* Can. 57; Kirch, *Fontes,* Nos. 494, 389,[1] 525. In the course of the fourth century the experiment appears to have been found unsatisfactory and was prohibited by *Conc. Sardic.,* Can. 6. *P.L.* 56, 777. This canon was believed by Leo to be Nicene and no doubt is the one to which he appeals here. On the canon see Zeiller, *Les origines chrétiennes dans les Prov. Danub.,* p. 244.

[72] *Ibid.,* c. 10, evidently alluding to the Sardican canon mentioned above.

[73] *Ibid.,* 12.

[74] The case presents a close parallel to that of Celidonius, on which see *Ep.* 10, 3, JK 407 and Chap. VII, pp. 114ff.

[75] *Ibid.,* 11.

reached is to be conveyed to the Roman see with a view to their confirmation or revision.

The concluding section of this letter is highly significant of the change which had taken place during the last twenty years in the relations between the churches of Africa and the see of Rome. In the time of Celestine I the Synod of Carthage did not hesitate to express its mind freely in regard to the intervention of that see in its affairs.[76] Now, however, its place has been taken by the papacy, and the primacy of Carthage has ceased to exist. Not less significant of this change is the reliance which Leo places on the authority of the Sardican canons, apparently without any fear that their validity in the situation will be questioned.[77] The logical conclusion of this development is to be found in the words ascribed to Eugenius, Catholic bishop of Carthage, uttered some forty years later in the presence of Huneric, successor of Gaiseric. It was proposed to hold a joint conference of Arian and Catholic bishops, and Eugenius, seeing that the dice were heavily loaded against him, vainly sought a postponement of the assembly. "We must wait," he said, "till the Roman Church in particular, which is the head of all the churches, has sent a representative." [78] It is evident from these words that the successor of Cyprian and Aurelius had accepted the Leonine view of the authority of the Roman see in its entirety.

Nevertheless we are bound to recognize in this affair, as elsewhere, Leo's scrupulous adherence to principle, and at the same time his readiness in dealing with offenders to make allowances for anyone whose offence may be excused by ignorance or by exceptional circumstances. It is his treatment of such questions as have been reviewed in this chapter which help to justify his great reputation among the churches of the West.

[76] *Inter Celestini Epp.* 2. *P.L.* 50, 422–7.
[77] Cf. *Ep.* 10, 10. See below, p. 119, n. 7.
[78] Victor Vitensis, *op. cit.*, 2, 43, ed. Petschenig, p. 41. Cf. Caspar, *Geschichte*, Vol. I, p. 438.

CHAPTER VII

LEO AND THE CHURCHES OF THE WEST. 2

1. SOUTHERN GAUL

THERE were two main problems confronting Leo in his relations with the churches of Southern Gaul. The former of these was concerned with the question of organization. The grouping of dioceses into provinces, and the assignment to the presiding bishop of the province of special privileges, especially in regard to the approval and consecration of bishops elected by the local churches to fill vacant sees, had been first explicitly recognized by the canons of the Council of Nicaea. Yet with certain exceptions this provincial organization had developed less rapidly in the West than in the East and, so far as Southern Gaul was concerned, the precise limits of jurisdiction of those bishops whose sees were located in cities of greater political or commercial significance had not been clearly defined by the time that Leo was elected Pope.[1]

In the second place, the monastic movement had created some difficulties. After making considerable headway in the East it had begun to gather force in Southern Gaul and to exercise its influence in the direction of imposing on the Church generally a rigorous standard of conduct. The chief centres of influence in ecclesiastical affairs at this time were the sees of Vienne (Vienna), Marseilles (Massilia), Narbonne (Narbo) and Arles (Arelate), and it was the election of Honoratus, founder of the great abbey erected on the island of Lerins,[2] to fill a vacancy in the see of the last named which lent to the eager advocates of monasticism the support of one of the most important churches in Southern Gaul. The work of Honoratus was continued and developed by his friend, disciple and successor, Hilary, who added to his zeal for reform

[1] On this development see Additional Note A, *The organization of the Church of Gaul.*
[2] See Kidd, *History*, Vol. III, p. 142.

in Christian morals an enthusiastic belief in the opinions prevailing among monastic circles in Southern Gaul as to the nature of grace and free will.[3] The new bishop made use of every opportunity which arose for providing vacant sees with candidates of his own choosing and probably gave the impression that, if he were allowed a free hand, the whole of Gaul would be governed ecclesiastically by bishops trained in the rigorist school. Obviously it was the kind of action which, as we shall see, was calculated to arouse determined opposition.

The story of Leo's relations with Hilary[4] begins with the arrival in Rome of Celidonius, bishop of the metropolitical see of Besançon (Vesontio),[5] towards the end of the year A.D. 444. The purpose of his coming was to present an appeal against his deposition by a synod summoned by Hilary of Arles.[6] It had been alleged against the petitioner that he had been uncanonically elected to his see since, as it was stated, he was the husband of a widow,[7] and had in addition, while yet a layman occupying some secular position, been responsible for inflicting the death penalty.[8] After some brief examination of the case Leo decided that there were *prima facie* grounds for reopening the question, and that the normal procedure for dealing with a *causa maior,* since the appellant was of metropolitical rank, should be followed.[9]

[3] Cf. Augustine, *Ep.* 225, 9. *P.L.* 33, 1007.

[4] The authorities for this affair are Leo, *Ep.* 10, JK 407, Valentinian III's rescript, *Certum est, P.L.* 54, 636, *Nov. Val.* 17, ed. P. Meyer, p. 101, and *Vita Hilarii, P.L.* 50, 1213. The latter probably dates from the end of the fifth century, and represents a strongly partisan point of view.

[5] Vesontio was the metropolis of the province of *Maxima Sequanorum.*

[6] The place and date of this synod cannot be determined with certainty. Probability suggests that it took place late in A.D. 444. Most authors with Caspar, *Geschichte,* Vol. I, p. 441 locate it at Besançon. Babut, *Concile de Turin,* p. 156, n. 1, however, favours of Arles. It is scarcely possible that, if it had been held at Arles, Leo could have written, *Ep.* 10, 3, "mansisset namque in illum prolata sententia, si obiectorum veritas exstitisset," since from his point of view the see of Arles had no jurisdiction over Besançon.

[7] *Ep.* 10, 3, "quod tanquam viduae maritas sacerdotium tenere non posset." Cf. above pp. 84f., 106.

[8] *Vit. Hilar.,* 16. Innocent I, *Ep.* 6, 5, JK 293 ruled that bishops might inflict torture or even pronounce a capital sentence.

[9] The justification for reopening such a question was provided by *Conc. Sardic.,* Can. 7 (vers. lat.), Mirbt, *Quellen,* No. 122. But strictly speaking according to those canons the place of the retrial ought to have been, not in Rome, but in a province nearby, that of *Maxima Sequa-*

Presently news reached Hilary of what was taking place. Without a moment's delay he too set out for Rome, braving a journey across the Alps in the depth of winter.[10] Probably his original intention had been to protest against the intervention of the Roman see in an affair which may well have seemed to him simply the concern of the Gaulish churches.[11] As it was, he found himself obliged to justify his action in regard to Celidonius before a Roman synod. To make matters worse from his point of view, he learnt that his opponent was being openly received into communion with the Roman see, in spite of the excommunication pronounced against him in Gaul. Such action was bound to appear in his eyes as a serious violation of canonical discipline.[12] When the investigation opened and he was given the opportunity of explaining his case, Hilary lost patience and broke out into loud and emphatic protests, action which naturally did little to commend his cause from the point of view of his critics. Finding little sympathy in Rome, he thereupon withdrew from the city and returned home.[13]

Meanwhile the case of Celidonius was heard, and when it was found on the evidence of witnesses that the charges

rorum. However, Leo's action was also covered by the rescript of Gratian, *Ordinariorum sententiae, P.L.* 13, 583; cf. *Cod. Avell.* 13; *C.S.E.L.*, Vol. XXXV, p. 54, which enacted that charges against metropolitans should be submitted to the Roman see. For the association of the Sardican Canons with the Council of Nicaea see Maassen, *Gesch. d. Quell. und lit. d. Kanon. Rechts,* Vol. I, pp. 52ff.

For the treatment of a *causa maior,* see Innocent I, *Ep.* 2, 3, JK 286. The synod at Rome was probably held early in the year A.D. 445, cf. Batiffol, *Siège Apost.*, p. 450.

[10] *Vit. Hilar.* 16.

[11] The fact that our authorities show no trace of any awareness on Hilary's part of the canons of Sardica may suggest that their existence was unknown in Gaul at this time. Celidonius may well have appealed to Rome on the strength of Gratian's rescript mentioned above.

[12] *Vit. Hilar.*, 17. "adstruens aliquos apud Gallias publicam merito excepisse sententiam, et in urbe sacris altaribus interesse."

[13] Leo describes Hilary's attitude as hopelessly unreasonable. *Ep.* 10, 2. "ipsius quoque beatissimi Petri reverentiam verbis arrogantioribus minuendo," and c. 3, "ubi (sc. in synodo) postquam Hilarius rationabile quod in sanctorum concilio posset respondere non habuit, ad ea se occulta cordis ipsius transtulerunt, quae nullus laicorum dicere, nullus sacerdotum possit audire." A very different picture is presented by the author of the *Vita Hilar.*, 17. According to him, Hilary showed all due deference to the Roman pontiff, but finding his representations of no avail, his protests disregarded, and himself treated as a prisoner under arrest, decided that no course other than withdrawal lay open to him.

against him were groundless he was reinstated on the verdict of the synod.[14]

Yet this was not all. About the same time a second appeal was brought to Rome. It was presented by some friends of Projectus, a bishop in Southern Gaul,[15] and alleged yet a further misdemeanour on the part of the bishop of Arles. It was stated that while Projectus was lying dangerously ill (he was, it seems, already of an advanced age) Hilary had arrived in the place and, without waiting to ascertain the facts, had promptly consecrated a new bishop to take his place.[16] The irregularity of his action was aggravated, so it appeared, not only by the fact that his candidate was wholly unknown to the Church to which he was consecrated, but by his failure to consult the wishes and feeling of the clergy and laity concerned.[17]

The same synod, which had heard the appeal of Celidonius, now listened to the friends of Projectus. His case raised a new problem. Even supposing the old bishop was incapable of further service, had the bishop of Arles any canonical right to consecrate a successor? Hilary himself was no longer in Rome, and hence there was no one there to argue his case.

[14] *Ep.* 10, 3. "Absolutus est Celidonius episcopus, quoniam se iniuste sacerdotis fuisse deiectum, manifesta testium responsione, ipso etiam praesente; ita ut quod Hilarius nobiscum residens posset opponere non haberet. Remotum est ergo iudicium, quod prolatum in hac sententia legebatur, quod tanquam viduae maritus sacerdotium tenere posset."

[15] The Ballerini suggest that the see of Projectus was in *Narbonensis prima,* and cite in support *Ep.* 10, 4. "Quid sibi Hilarius quaerit in aliena provincia, et id quod nullus decessorum ipsius ante Patroclum habuit, quid usurpat? cum et ipsum, quod Patroclo a sede apostolica temporaliter videbatur esse concessum, postmodum sit sententia meliori sublatum." See Additional Note B.

[16] Babut, *op. cit.*, p. 161, n. 1 believes that the new bishop, Importunus, was intended by Hilary not as a successor but as a coadjutor to Projectus.

[17] *Ep.* 10, 4, "Huic negotio sic finito . . . Projecti querela successit: cuius ad nos litterae lachrymabiles et dolendae, de superordinato sibi episcopo, sunt directae. Epistola quoque ingesta est civium, ipsius et numerosa singulorum subscriptione firmata, invidiosissimis contra Hilarium plena quaerimoniis: quod Projecto episcopo suo aegrotare liberum non fuisset, eiusque sacerdotium in alium praeter suam notitiam esse translatum, et tanquam in vacuam possessionem ab Hilario pervasore haeredem viventis inductum." It is remarkable that Hilary's biographer omits to mention this case.

As a result it was not surprising that the synod decided to depose the new bishop and to restore Projectus.[18]

As soon as its deliberations were concluded Leo set to work to draw up an account of the whole affair. This he incorporated in a letter addressed to the bishops of Gaul.[19] The document is prefaced by a clear, concise statement of the view held by the writer as to the origin and nature of the Petrine primacy and as to its relation to the Divine Constitution of the Church, the purpose of which is to show that anyone who behaves as Hilary has done is attacking the authority of Peter, and so, from the author's standpoint, is undermining the stability of the whole Church.[20] After explaining the seriousness of the case from the papal point of view Leo then proceeds to assure his correspondents that his sole concern is for the good order of the Church, and that he desires to achieve this not by introducing novelty but by restoring ancient discipline.[21] In support of this statement he reminds his readers that on numerous occasions in the past bishops in Gaul have consulted the Roman see for advice and have exercised the right of hearing appeals, the outcome of which has been to promote peace and good order, since it has not been the practice of that see to deprive their churches of their rightful privileges.[22] Of this happy relationship the real

[18] *Ibid.*, 5. "Nos tamen, quod vobis credimus Deo iudice placiturum, in commune cunctis fratribus consulentes, et male ordinatum submoveri, et episcopum Projectum in suo sacerdotio permanere debere decrevimus." Leo's words seem almost to suggest that the decision taken may not prove acceptable in Gaul.

[19] *Ep.* 10, JK 407. The usual text of the address runs "universis episcopis per Viennensem provinciam constitutis." It may be inferred from internal evidence that the letter was circulated beyond the limits of that province; in fact, Sirmond cites a reading of which he was aware, "episcopis per provincias Maximam Sequanorum et Viennensem," cf. *P.L.* 54, 628, note n. Its date is probably early in A.D. 445.

[20] *Ibid.*, 1. "verum hanc petrae istius sacratissimam firmitatem, Deo, ut diximus, aedificante constructam, nimis impia vult praesumptione violare quisquis eius potestatem tentat infringere . . . cum nulli se subditum legi, nullis institutionis Dominicae credit regulis contineri."

[21] *Ibid.*, 2. "nitimur consilio maturiore corrigere, et vestrarum ecclesiarum statum communicato vobiscum labore componere, non nova instituentes sed vetera renovantes."

[22] *Ibid.* "Nobiscum itaque vestra fraternitas recognoscat apostolicam sedem, pro sui reverentia a vestrae etiam provinciae sacerdotibus, innumeris relationibus esse consultam, et per diversarum, quemadmodum vetus consuetudo poscebat, appellationem causarum, aut retractata aut confirmata fuisse iudicia . . . quoniam sollicitudo nostra, non sua quaerens sed quae sunt Christi, dignitatem divinitus datam nec ecclesiis

enemy is the bishop of Arles, who by his presumptuous behaviour shows "That by claiming for himself the rights of consecration (sc. of bishops) of all churches throughout Gaul and by transferring to himself the privilege proper to metropolitan bishops, he so desires to subjugate you to his authority, that he may not put up with being a subject of the blessed Apostle Peter."[23]

Leo then describes in detail the synodical re-examination of the cases of Celidonius and Projectus, and explains the reasons which guided the Roman synod in arriving at their verdict. He admits that if the former had actually been guilty of the charges alleged against him the synod would have been bound to confirm the original sentence.[24]

It is in the account which he gives of the case of Projectus that he comes to his chief ground for complaint in Hilary's conduct, namely the fact that, at least from the Roman point of view, Hilary had exceeded his rights. For even if it might be argued that the Roman see had accorded extensive privileges to Hilary's predecessor, Patroclus, it ought to be realized that those privileges were purely of a temporary nature, and had in fact subsequently been withdrawn.[25] And besides, by himself appointing a bishop to replace Projectus, the bishop of Arles had totally disregarded the canonical procedure prescribed for the election of bishops.[26]

nec ecclesiarum sacerdotibus abrogabat." Leo evidently alludes to the correspondence of his predecessors with the Gallic churches, e.g. JK 286, 292, 293 and to *Conc. Sardic.* (vers. lat.) Canons 3, 4, 7, 10. Mirbt, *Quellen,* No. 122.

[23] *Ep.* 10, 2. "ita suae vos cupiens subdere potestati, ut se beato apostolo Petro non patiatur esse subjectum, ordinationes sibi omnium per Gallias ecclesiarum vindicans, et debitam metropolitanis sacerdotibus in suam transferens dignitatem." There was possibly some truth in the latter allegation. Hilary was not the kind of man to allow canonical principle to hinder what he regarded as a right course of action.

[24] *Ibid.,* 3. In speaking of those who have married twice or espoused widows, he says, "ne ad sacram militiam hi permittantur accedere quibus sit tale coniugium, vel qui contra apostolicam disciplinam non unius tantum uxoris viri fuisse monstrentur. Sed sicut eos quos factum suum non potest excusare, aut non admittendos aut, si fuerint, decernimus removendos, ita quibus hoc falso obiicitur, habita necesse est examinatione purgemus et suum officium perdere non sinamus." Cf. Chap VI, 2, p. 106, on *Ep.* 12, 3, JK 410.

[25] On the nature and extent of the privileges of Patroclus, see Additional Note B, *The privileges of the See of Arles.*

[26] *Ibid.,* 4. "Expectarentur certe vota civium, testimonia populorum: quaeretur honoratorum arbitrium, electio clericorum, quae in sacer-

After this Leo proceeds to draw a highly graphic and perhaps somewhat exaggerated picture of Hilary's activities, for the details of which he was probably indebted to information supplied by the supporters of Projectus.

"Hilary," he writes, "turned up unexpectedly among people to whom he was unknown, and just as suddenly went off, making many journeys, as we have heard, at a headlong speed and rushing about through remote provinces with such haste that he appears to have acquired a reputation everywhere more for ridiculous precipitancy than for episcopal dignity. At any rate the letter sent to us by the laity suggests as much when it says, 'He was off before we knew he had got here.' . . . So Hilary seems to have been more anxious to kill off a sick man than to consecrate a bishop, and to deceive the person whom he intruded by giving him an irregular consecration." [27]

Then, after mentioning that the Roman synod had deposed Hilary's candidate and had restored Projectus, Leo enacts that wherever in the future a see shall fall vacant the right to consecrate a successor shall belong to the metropolitan of the province, to which the see in question belongs.[28] This done

dotum solent ordinationibus, ab his qui noverunt patrum regulas custodiri: ut apostolicae auctoritatis norma in omnibus servaretur, qua praecipitur ut sacerdos ecclesiae prefuturus, non solum attestatione fidelium, sed etiam qui foris sunt testimonio muniatur." Leo refers to the conditions of a regular episcopal election in similar terms elsewhere. Cf. *Ep.* 14, 5, JK 411. "Patrum regulas" may refer to *Conc. Sard.*, Can. 5 (vers. lat.) *P.L.* 56, 403. "Apostolicae auctoritatis norma" appears to allude to such a letter as Celestine I, *Ep.* 4, JK 369. Cf. Hippolytus, *Apost. Trad.*, trad. Easton, p. 33. For "qui foris sunt testimonio" cf. 1 Tim. iii. 7. On the whole question of procedure at episcopal elections see *Dict. Théol. Cath.*, Vol. IV, col. 2256ff.

[27] *Ibid.*, 5. "Sed ille insperatus nescientibus supervenit, et improvisus abscessit, cursu, ut didicimus, celeri itinera multa conficiens, et per longinquas provincias tanta immaturitate discurrens, ut videatur gloriam de scurrili velocitate potius quam de sacerdotali moderatione captasse. Haec enim directarum ad nos civium verba sunt litterarum: Ante abscessit quam eum venisse nossemus. . . . Non ergo Hilarius tam studuit episcopum consecrare quam eum potius qui aegrotabat occidere, et ipsum quem superposuit male ordinando decipere."

[28] *Ibid.* "id statuentes ut si quisquam fratrum nostrorum in quacumque provincia decesserit, is sibi ordinationem vindicet sacerdotis, quem illius provinciae metropolitanum esse constiterit." Leo hereby reinforces the requirements of *Conc. Nic.*, Can. 4 and 6. Notice that the question whether or not the bishop of Arles had metropolitical rights outside the province of *Viennensis* is simply disregarded.

he turns to describe Hilary's conduct in regard to episcopal consecrations.

"The bishop," he says, "is escorted throughout the provinces, so we are told, by a *posse* of soldiers, and wherever churches have lost their bishops he makes a tumultuous entry in their company protected in his presumption by an armed guard. This is the board before which candidates for consecration are dragged, men who are all unknown to the cities over which they are to preside." [29]

After repeating his stipulations regarding regular and canonical episcopal elections,[30] he insists that the consecration of those elected is to be performed by metropolitans assisted by the senior bishops of their respective provinces.[31] These metropolitans are to be content with their own provinces and neither to interfere with those of others nor to resign their privileges to them. But should any metropolitan attempt to transfer his rights to another they shall be assigned *ipso facto* to the senior bishop of the province.[32] Leo adds that care is to be taken only to consecrate bishops at the appropriate time, namely on Saturday night or on Sunday morning, otherwise the whole act may be regarded as invalid.[33]

[29] *Ep.* 10, 6. "Militaris manus, ut didicimus, per provincias sequitur sacerdotem, et armati praesidii praesumptione suffulto ad invadendas per tumultum famulatur ecclesias, quae proprios amiserint sacerdotes. Trahuntur ordinandi ante hoc officium, his quibus praeficiendi sunt civitatibus ignorati." Possibly in the troubled state of the Gallic provinces at this time, military escort was more necessary to a travelling bishop than Leo realized.

[30] *Ibid.* "Teneatur subscriptio clericorum, honoratorum testimonium, ordinis consensus et plebis. Qui praefuturus est omnibus, ab omnibus eligatur." Perhaps Leo had Pliny's epigram in mind, "imperaturus omnibus, eligi debet ex omnibus."

[31] *Ibid.* "Ordinationem sibi, ut ante iam diximus, singuli metropolitani suarum provinciarum cum his qui caeteros sacerdotii antiquitate praeveniunt, restituto sibi per nos iure defendant."

[32] *Ibid.* "Alienum ius alter sibi non audeat vindicare. Suis limitibus, suis terminis sit unusquisque contentus, et privilegium sibi debitum in alium transferre se posse, noverit non licere." Thus Leo hoped to prevent any attempt on the part of the see of Arles to recover a primacy over other provinces by a voluntary resignation of their rights on the part of other metropolitical sees. Cf. Duchesne, *Fastes episcopaux*², Vol. I, p. 117.

[33] *Ibid.* "nec sibi constare status sui noverit firmitatem, qui non die sabbati vespere quod lucescit in prima sabbati, vel ipso Dominico die fuerit ordinatus." Cf. *Ep.* 9, 1, JK 406 and Hippolytus, *Apost. Trad.*, pt. I, 2, trad. Easton, p. 33. It is remarkable that Leo goes so far as to assert that disregard for this rule may invalidate the order conferred.

Having thus settled the two cases which had been brought to his notice Leo turns to the main problem confronting him, namely the rights of the see of Arles. He is determined to prevent any attempt on the part of that see to assert a primacy of jurisdiction over its neighbours and, to achieve this end, utters the following ruling:

"Let each province be satisfied with its own synods and let not Hilary dare to summon synodical assemblies in future, and by interference to upset the judgments of the Lord's bishops. Let him know that in addition to his being excluded from exercising the rights of others he is deprived of that authority in the province of *Viennensis* which he had used amiss. It is fitting, my brethren, to restore the ordinances of old time, since, he who claimed rights of consecration in a province to which he had no right has been proved to be of such a character in the present case that, when with rash and insulting language he demanded a verdict of condemnation, my decision, in accordance with the generosity of the Apostolic see, has preserved for him the bishopric of his own city alone. Let him not take part in any consecration: let him not consecrate others, since conscious of his deserts when he was summoned to the hearing, he thought best to betake himself to shameful flight, an outlaw from apostolic communion, participation in which he did not deserve." [34]

[34] *Ibid.*, 7. "Suis unaquaeque provincia sit contenta conciliis, nec ultra Hilarius audeat conventus indicere synodales, et sacerdotum Domini iudicia se interserendo turbare. Qui non tantum noverit se ab alieno iure depulsum sed etiam Viennensis provinciae, quam male usurpaverat, potestate privatum. Dignum est enim, fratres, antiquitatis statuta reparari, cum is qui sibi ordinationem provinciae indebitae vindicabat, talis in praesenti etiam probatus fuerit exstitisse, ut cum ipse frequentius temerariis et insolentibus verbis sententiam damnationis expeteret, suae tantum civitatis illi sacerdotium, pro sedis apostolicae pietate, praeceptio nostra servaverit. Non ergo intersit ulli ordinationi; non ordinet, qui meriti sui conscius, cum quaereretur ad causam, turpi fuga se credidit subtrahendum, exsors apostolicae communionis, cuius particeps esse non meruit." Leo does not apparently dispute the claim of the see of Arles to be the metropolis of the province of *Viennensis*. All he does is to deprive Hilary of the right to exercise metropolitical rights and to declare that he is now no more than a simple bishop. The "antiquitatis statuta" are presumably the Nicene-Sardican canons to which we have already alluded. See above, p. 110. The "sententiam damnationis" must refer to the condemnation of Celidonius demanded by Hilary. Leo does not formally excommunicate him, but simply states the fact that he had withdrawn from the communion of the Roman see of his own accord. For a parallel sentence on a metropolitan bishop cf. Pope Hilary I, *Ep.* 8, 1, JK 555. "Quamquam notitiam."

It has already been suggested that Leo derived most of his information as to Hilary's activities in Gaul from the appellants who had recently arrived in Rome. Their information seemingly was not confined to Hilary's treatment of bishops, but contained in addition a good many details as to his inconsiderate attitude towards the laity, and especially as to his rigorous use of the power of excommunication.[35] Leo therefore adds some general admonitions on the whole subject of the administration of discipline. No Christian, he says, should be lightly deprived of communion, nor should it be done at the whim of an enraged bishop. Where, however, such a punishment is justified it ought only to be applied to the guilty person.[36]

In the concluding paragraph of his letter Leo exhorts the Gallic bishops to do their utmost for the preservation of good order and to accept the decisions of the Roman see which are not so much to his advantage as to their own. Let them not believe, as the bishop of Arles may suggest, that the Roman see is aiming at securing all rights of consecration within their provinces for itself.[37] Its sole object has been to preserve their privileges from being nullified by the presumption of another. As to the future, he makes special provision in the event of some situation arising which may necessitate the assembly of a synod embracing representatives of more than one province. Should this arise, he specifies that the approval of bishop Leontius, the senior by consecration of the bishops in the provinces of Southern Gaul, must first be obtained, provided

[35] *Ep.* 10, 8. "Cognovimus enim pro commissis et levibus verbis quosdam a gratia communionis exclusos."

[36] *Ibid.* "Nulli Christianorum facile communio denegetur, nec ad indignantis fiat hoc arbitrium sacerdotis. . . . Certe si quando causa talis emerserit, ut pro commissi criminis qualitate aliquem iuste faciat communione privari, is tantum poenae subdendus est quem reatus involvit." Leo then adds with some bitterness, "Sed quid mirum eum in laicos talem existere, qui soleat de sacerdotum damnatione gaudere?" No doubt Hilary's semi-Pelagian and monastic affinities rendered him prone to a lack of sympathy with the fallen sinner. For a critique of fifth century rigorist discipline see Kirk, *Vision of God*, p. 276: and for Hilary's semi-Pelagianism, Augustine, *Ep.* 225, 9. *P.L.* 33, 1006. On excommunication and its nature, see Brightman, *Terms of Communion* in *Early Church and Ministry*, ed. Swete, pp. 363f.

[37] Ibid., 9. "Non enim nobis ordinationem vestrarum provinciarum defendimus, quod potest forsitan ad depravandos vestrae sanctitatis animos Hilarius *pro suo more* mentiri." This recurrent bitterness in Leo's writing tends rather to weaken than to strengthen his case.

that the privileges of individual metropolitans are not thereby affected.[38]

Before passing on to observe the sequel of these events, and particularly the effect produced in Gaul by Leo's judgment, we may pause for a moment to consider the merits of the case upheld by either side in this controversy.[39] Leo's attitude throughout was based on his general determination to uphold the discipline prescribed by the canons of Nicaea, and by those subsequently issued at Sardica, which were treated at Rome at this time as possessing Nicene authority, if not actually believed to be Nicene in origin. From his point of view, as we have seen, Hilary was guilty of a serious violation of those canons, and had aggravated his offence by the lack of respect which he had shown for the jurisdiction of the Roman see and its synod. The competence of the bishop of Arles to exercise metropolitical rights within the province of *Viennensis* might not have been questioned, nor his error on the side of rigour in the administration of penitential discipline seriously regarded, if he had been content to confine his activity within a sphere which, from Leo's standpoint, constituted its proper limit. But, as it was, Hilary's conduct appeared to amount to a grave menace to the peace and order of the Church and therefore deserved to be stopped.

Hilary too, like Leo, recognized no doubt the authority of

[38] *Ibid.* "Et quoniam honoranda est semper antiquitas, fratrem et coepiscopum nostrum Leontium probabilem sacerdotem, hac, si vobis placet, dignitate volumus decorari: ut praeter eius consensum alterius provinciae non indicatur a vestra sanctitate concilium, et a vobis omnibus, quemadmodum vetustas eius et probitas exigit, honoretur, metropolitanis privilegii sui dignitate servata." The bishop thus designated was probably Leontius of Fréjus (Forum Julii) who had been consecrated to that see A.D. 419, if not earlier. Cf. Boniface I, *Ep.* 3, JK 349; Celestine I, *Ep.* 21, JK 381. The point of this provision was, of course, to prevent any attempt on Hilary's part to regain his primacy by the convocation of general councils similar to those of Riez (Regii) in A.D. 439, Orange (Arausio) in A.D. 441 and Vaison (Vasio) in A.D. 442. The principle of precedence by seniority appears to have obtained as the synods of Valence (Valentia) in A.D. 375 and Nîmes (Nemausia) in A.D. 396. It should be noticed that the use of "si vobis placet" suggests that even from Leo's point of view the plan was no more than a tentative proposal.

[39] Anglican historians have been inclined as a rule to treat Hilary as an innocent victim of papal tyranny. See Gore, *Leo the Great*, pp. 106ff.; Puller, *Primitive Saints and the See of Rome*, p. 198; Kidd, *History*, Vol. III, p. 357 and *The Roman Primacy*, p. 126.

the Nicene canons, though we cannot be certain how far he was actually aware of the special provisions of the Sardican legislation. Probably he believed that his right to exercise metropolitical jurisdiction, more or less within the borders of the *Septem provinciae,* was sufficiently justified by the privileges accorded to his predecessor, Patroclus, in the time of Pope Zosimus.[40] Moreover the chaotic condition of the greater part of Gaul, as a consequence of the Germanic invasions, had undoubtedly induced a considerable measure of laxity in the standard of Christian life and discipline, which made the need of providing men for the episcopate of undoubted integrity all the more pressing. If Hilary was guilty of some lack of consideration, in attempting to supply this need by preferring candidates from the ascetic or monastic party, the most that could be said against him was that he erred from an excess of zeal.

Yet in spite of every possible plea in defence of Hilary, we are bound to admit that conduct which involved the intrusion of men of his own choosing into churches, the clergy and laity of which were thereby deprived of an effective voice in the choosing of their pastors, was likely to be destructive of good order, if it had been widely imitated elsewhere. Hence in the interests of peace and unity in the Church as a whole, it is clear that the measures taken by Leo were inevitable.

We may now pass on to consider the immediate sequel of Leo's drastic action. It is possible that further letters passed from Rome to Gaul on the subject of the limits of metropolitical jurisdiction, but if this was so, excepting one of dubious authenticity,[41] none of them has survived. For the attitude of the Gallic episcopate we are largely dependent on conjecture. Yet the arrival of an imperial rescript[42] with reference to the whole matter unavoidably suggests that the reception given to the papal decisions in Gaul was

[40] See Additional Note B. *The privileges of the see of Arles.*

[41] JK † 446, *Quali pertinacia.* For a discussion of the authenticity of this letter see Additional Note D.

[42] *Inter Leon. Epp.,* No. 11. *P.L.* 54, 636. *Certum est,* dated July 8th, A.D. 445. *Nov. Val.* 17, ed. P. Meyer, pp. 101f. The fact that Leo despatched his letter early in the year, while the rescript was sent after a delay of several months, suggests that in the interval some difficulties had arisen of which we have now no information.

not entirely unanimous, and that some support from the secular power was necessary for their enforcement.

The rescript just mentioned, which was issued in the joint names of the Emperors Theodosius II and Valentinian III, was addressed to Aetius as *Magister utriusque militiae,* having his sphere of authority in Gaul. It opens with a clear and emphatic assertion of the primacy of the Roman see in the following terms:

"Since the authoritative decision of the sacred synod itself has confirmed the primacy of the Apostolic see as appropriate to St. Peter, who is the chief of the episcopal order and the glory of the Roman city, let no one presume to undertake any illicit act contrary to the authority of that see. For the peace of the churches will undoubtedly be preserved, if the whole body acknowledges its governor." [43]

The rescript goes on to summarize the offences committed by Hilary, making special mention of his unauthorized deprivation of bishops and his usurpation of rights of consecration, without consultation of the Roman see.[44] After describing how by force of arms Hilary had intruded bishops of his choice into churches against the will of the people concerned, the Emperors allude to the investigation recently held by Leo and to the sentence pronounced by him, and assert that "the same sentence would have been valid throughout Gaul, even apart from an imperial law. For what limit can there be to the authority of so great a bishop in the churches?" [45]

So in order to prevent Hilary or any other from using military force to settle ecclesiastical questions and from resisting the commands of the Roman bishop they enact as follows:

[43] *Ibid.* "Cum igitur sedis apostolicae primatum sancti Petri meritum, qui princeps est episcopalis coronae, et Romanae dignitas civitatis, sacrae etiam synodi firmarit auctoritas, ne quid praeter auctoritatem sedis istius inlicitum praesumptio attentare nitatur." The allusion in "sacrae synodi . . . auctoritas" seems more probably to be to the Canons of Sardica, esp. Canon 3 (vers. lat.) than to *Conc. Nic.,* Can. 6 in its later interpolated form. For the idea underlying "praeter auctoritatem" cf. Socrates, *H.E.,* 2, 17; Sozomen, *H.E.,* 3, 10.

[44] *Ibid.* "Hilarus enim, qui episcopus Arelatensis vocatur, ecclesiae Romanae urbis inconsulto pontifice, iudicia sive ordinationes episcoporum sola temeritate usurpans invasit."

[45] *Ibid.* "Et erat quidem ipsa sententia per Gallias etiam sine imperiali sanctione valitura. Quid enim tanti pontificis auctoritati in ecclesiis non liceret?"

"This is not the only thing which we prohibit (sc. conduct such as that of Hilary), highly serious offence as it is, but to prevent grave confusion among the churches or the slightest damage to ecclesiastical discipline we decree by an eternal law as follows, namely that it shall not be lawful for any bishop, whether in Gaul or in other provinces, in violation of ancient custom to undertake anything without the authority of the venerable Pope of the eternal city. For them and all men the force of law shall belong to whatever the Apostolic see has ordained or shall ordain: so that whosoever shall fail to appear when summoned to judgment by the Roman bishop, shall be compelled to present himself by the governor of that province, and those privileges conferred on the Roman church by our divine parents shall in all respects remain in force." [46]

The rescript concludes by prescribing that a fine of ten pounds shall be inflicted on any judge who fails to enforce the law as stated. The author of the rescript displays such a detailed knowledge of Hilary's misdemeanours that it has been suggested that it was drawn up at the instigation of Leo himself.[47] It is no less remarkable that he lays such repeated emphasis on the prerogatives of the Roman see. As for its immediate effect, the absence of any effective imperial control over the greater part of Gaul at this time must have rendered it to a great extent a dead letter, and the same might be said of its influence elsewhere, especially in the East.[48] On the other hand it went much further than any other document

[46] *Inter Leon. Epp.* 11. "Nec hoc solum, quod est maximi criminis, submovemus, verum ne levis saltem inter ecclesias turba nascatur, vel in aliquo minui religionis disciplina videatur, hoc perenni sanctione censemus, ne quid tam episcopis Gallicanis quam aliarum provinciarum contra consuetudinem veterem liceat sine viri venerabilis papae Urbis aeternae auctoritate tentare. Sed hoc illis omnibusque pro lege sit quidquid sanxit vel sanxerit apostolicae sedis auctoritas: ita ut quisquis episcoporum ad iudicium Romani antistitis evocatus venire neglexerit, per moderatorem eiusdem provinciae adesse cogatur: per omnia servatis, quae divi parentes nostri Romanae ecclesiae contulerunt." The rescript, of course, concedes a far greater authority to the Roman see than had been given by the *Ordinariorum sententiae* of Gratian, *P.L.* 13, 583, *Cod. Avel.* 13, *C.S.E.L.*, Vol. XXXV, p. 54; Mirbt, *Quellen*,[5] No. 133, to which it evidently alludes.

[47] Caspar, *Geschichte*, Vol. I, p. 446.

[48] Nevertheless being an official document issued in the names of the two sovereigns it was included in the *Novellae* appended to the *Codex Theodosianus*, ed. P. Meyer, Vol. II, pp. 101f.

previously issued by the imperial chancery in the direction of giving explicit sanction to the claims of the Roman see, and accorded to the Roman bishops for the first time a spiritual status analogous to that of the Sovereign himself in secular matters. Whether or not the papacy stood to gain in the long run from support of this kind is questionable. And there is room for doubt as to whether it was to the advantage of an institution claiming spiritual primacy for anyone to be able to suggest that it owed its authority, at least in some measure, to the support of the secular power.[49] For the effect of a law such as the one which we have been considering was at least to render such a suggestion distinctly plausible.[50]

We may now pass on to the story of the subsequent relations between Leo and the churches of Southern Gaul. On his return to Arles, Hilary appears to have accepted the Roman verdict and to have contented himself with the administration of his diocese as a simple bishop. Yet he must have felt a certain uneasiness at the suspension of communion between himself and the Roman see, the proof of which lies in the fact that he availed himself of the visits to Rome of two Gallic bishops, Nectarius and Constantius,[51] to plead his cause and seems to have gone so far as to send Ravennius, who presently became his successor, with that object. His biographer has recorded a letter addressed to the bishop of Arles by Auxiliaris, Prefect of Gaul,[52] in which he describes the visit of

[49] It is instructive to compare this rescript with Gratian's *Ordinariorum sententiae.* Mirbt, *Quellen,* No. 133. By the latter it was provided that (1) metropolitan bishops could be summoned to Rome for trial, or else before judges appointed by the Roman bishop; (2) ordinary bishops from the prefectures of Italy or Gaul could be summoned in like manner; (3) ordinary bishops from more remote provinces should be tried by their respective metropolitans. The new rescript, however, forbad any action on the part of bishops in all provinces which had not been first approved by the Roman see and ordered all bishops everywhere to obey a summons to Rome.

[50] Batiffol, *Siège Apostolique,* p. 460, n. 1 in agreeing that the immediate effect of *Certum est* was slight, adds "j'aimerais qu'on nous dise quelle influence cet édit a eue sur le moyen âge." Perhaps the answer is to be found in the later history of the papacy itself.

[51] Both names appear as signatories of a synodical letter, *Inter Leon. Epp.,* No. 99 and in Leo's reply *Ep.* 102, JK 479.

[52] The Ballerini, *P.L.* 50, 1238, n.h., show that this Auxiliaris was prefect of Gaul, *c.* A.D. 435 and resided at Arles. They reject the view that he was prefect of the city in A.D. 445 and suggest that after becoming prefect of Gaul for the second time that year he was on a visit to the capital.

the two bishops and mentions a conversation which he had had with them. The text of the letter is as follows:

"I received the holy bishops Nectarius and Constantius, when they came from the province of your Beatitude, with fitting respect. I often conversed with them about the courage and constancy of mind, and the contempt for worldly affairs, for which among frail creatures like ourselves you have always been distinguished . . . I also conversed with the holy Pope Leo. At this point, I suppose, you are somewhat indignant; but though you are tenacious of your purpose, and always level headed and are not carried away with any bitterness of passion, even as you are not moved by any attractions of pleasure, I for my part do not remember the slightest action of your Beatitude being darkened by a cloud of pride. But people do not take it patiently if we speak just as we think. Besides, the ears of Romans are rather humoured by a little civility; if your holiness in future condescends to such behaviour you gain a good deal and lose nothing. Do me this favour and banish tiny clouds with the fair weather of a somewhat changed attitude." [53]

Four years later (A.D. 449) Hilary died.[54] The priest Ravennius was regularly elected as his successor, and at the consecration of the new bishop twelve prelates took part, including two metropolitans, Rusticus of Narbonne and Nicetas of Vienne.[55] This would seem to suggest that in spite of all that Leo had done to reduce the see of Arles to the

[53] Ap. *Vit. Hilar.* 17. "Sanctos Nectarium et Constantium sacerdotes de Beatitudinis tuae parte venientes digna admiratione suscepi. Cum his saepius sum locutus de virtute animi atque constantia, contemptuque rerum humanarum, quo inter fragilitates nostras semper beatus est. . . . Locutus sum etiam cum sancto papa Leone. Hoc loco, credo, aliquantum animo perhorrescis: sed cum propositi tui tenax sis et semper aequalis, nulloque commotionis felle rapiaris, sicut nullis extolleris illecebris gaudiorum, ego nec minimum quidem factum Beatitudinis tuae arrogantiae memini contagione fuscari. Sed impatienter ferunt homines, si sic loquamur, quomodo nobis conscii sumus. Aures praeterea Romanorum quadam teneritudine plus trahuntur: in quam si se sanctitas tua subinde demittat, plurimum tu, nihil perditurus, acquiris. Da mihi hoc, et exiguas nubes parvae mutationis serenitate compesce."

[54] His biographer, *Vit. Hilar.* 19–22, describes with great fervour the circumstances attending his death.

[55] The names of the bishops who took part may be inferred from Leo, *Ep.* 40, JK 434. Duchesne, *Fastes*[2], Vol. I, p. 120 points out that apart from Rusticus and Nicetas, the rest belonged to the southern half of the province *Viennensis*.

status of a simple bishopric, it had nevertheless retained a sort of informal primacy among the churches of Southern Gaul. In due course the electors despatched the usual letters to the "greater churches," informing them of Ravennius' election, and it is Leo's reply [56] to the letter addressed to the Roman see which next claims our attention. The Pope hails with joy the election of one who was doubtless already a *persona grata* in Rome to be Hilary's successor, and mentions particularly his satisfaction in finding that the provisions for a canonical election have been duly observed.[57] He formally confirms the election,[58] and expresses the hope that the conduct of the new bishop will be such as to justify the confidence of his electors and to deserve the continuance of papal favour,[59] as a special mark of which Ravennius received a personal note [60] from Leo. Here the Pope renews expressions of satisfaction and of hope that his confidence in his friend will not prove to be misplaced. He particularly urges the new bishop to respect canon law in the exercise of his authority [61] and concludes with the request that he may be informed frequently as to any measures which the latter may see fit to adopt.[62]

The post carrying these letters had scarcely left Rome when a communication from Southern Gaul was received, reporting

[56] *Ep.* 40, JK 434, dated August 22nd, A.D. 449. This and the two following letters are given from the *Collectio Arelatensis* in *M.G.H., Epp.* Vol. III, ed. Gundlach, p. 15.

[57] *Ibid.* "Justa et rationabilis nobis causa gaudendi est, cum a sacerdotibus Domini ea gesta cognoscimus quae et paternorum canonum regulis et apostolicis congruant institutis." For the "canonum regulis" and "apostolicis institutis" see above, p. 118, and Chap. VI, pp. 106f.

[58] *Ibid.* "Quod ergo in Arelatensium civitate, defuncto sanctae memoriae Hilario, virum etiam nobis probatum fratrem Ravennium, secundum desideria cleri, honoratorum et plebis, unanimiter consecrastis, bonum fraternitatis vestrae opus nostro iudicio roboramus." It is remarkable that Leo can describe Hilary as "sanctae memoriae." For the conditions of a regular election of a bishop cf. *Ep.* 10, 6, JK 407.

[59] *Ibid.,* "ut dispensationis sibi creditae diligens et temperans exsecutor, vestro testimonio non inferior, et nostro per omnia favore sit dignior." Leo thus suggests that the rigorism of Hilary's regime should not be imitated.

[60] *Ep.* 41, JK 435, probably of the same date as *Ep.* 40.

[61] *Ibid.* "Ecclesiasticarum legum non ignara est dilectio tua, ut intra earum regulas atque mensuras omnia potestatis tuae iura contineas." The "leges," to which Leo alludes, are probably the same as those which guided his treatment of Hilary: see above, p. 120.

[62] *Ibid.,* "saepius nos de processu actuum tuorum facias certiores."

the unwelcome activities of a certain Petronianus, who was giving himself out to be a deacon of the Roman church. Leo lost no time in sending off a second letter to Ravennius,[63] in which, while urging him to vigilance, he affirmed that Petronianus was an excommunicate person, and instructed him to notify the bishops of the province to that effect.[64]

If, as this letter suggests, the see of Arles, through Leo's favour, was beginning to recover some of its prestige, a new development in Southern Gaul showed that its bishop was still regarded by many as the legitimate metropolitan of the province of *Viennensis*. Early in the year A.D. 450 the see of Vaison (Vasio), a city some forty-five miles north of Arles, fell vacant by reason of the death of its bishop, Auspicius. He had been one of the consecrators of Ravennius, and as such had signed the letter in which the recent election had been notified at Rome.[65] The bishop of Arles, probably at the invitation of the church of Vaison, hurried to the spot, and without delay consecrated Fonteius,[66] who had been elected to fill the vacancy, thereby issuing a direct challenge to the competence of Nicetas, bishop of Vienne, in the matter. The latter, who, since the reduction of the see of Arles to the status of a simple bishopric, in accordance with the sentence pronounced by Leo against Hilary, had good reason to regard himself as metropolitan of the whole province, hastily despatched a legation to Rome, in order to present an emphatic protest against such a flagrant violation of canonical order. His intentions, however, had already been anticipated by Ravennius, and a counter legation was hurried off to uphold the legitimacy of the latter's conduct. It must have been highly exasperating for the friends of Nicetas to find that their rivals had reached the

[63] *Ep.* 42, JK 436, dated August 26th of the same year, i.e. A.D. 449. Babut, *Concile de Turin*, p. 196, n. 1, rejects the date and places the letter later in that year.

[64] *Ibid.*, "admonitis etiam totius provinciae episcopis." This must mean the bishops of the province of *Viennensis*. Yet if *Quali pertinacia* † JK 446 be authentic, Leo had already recognized the bishop of Vienne, as the rightful metropolitan of that province, to whom properly the duty of forwarding correspondence from Rome to his suffragans should have belonged. Leo's delegation of this duty to Ravennius suggests that he was inclined after all to treat the see of Arles as metropolitical.

[65] *Ep.* 40. Cf. Duchesne, *op. cit.*, Vol. I, p. 262.

[66] Fonteius seems to have remained Bishop of Vaison for the next twenty-five years. Cf. Duchesne, *op. cit.*, *ibid.* The incident is mentioned in Leo, *Ep.* 66, 1, JK 450.

capital a few days before them, and to learn that a petition had been presented to the Roman see requesting the confirmation by the papacy of the powers claimed by the see of Arles within the province in dispute.[67]

That the Arelatine petition had evidently been drawn up with a view to doing as much as possible to win Roman favour is shown by its opening paragraph. It abounds in expressions of respect for the Roman see, and of satisfaction at the friendly relations now prevailing between that see and the church of Arles. As to its object the petitioners affirm that they desire "not so much to start something new as to restore what is long standing and ancient": [68] in a word, they wish to see the privileges of the see of Arles, once reduced for a time, now permanently renewed by fresh instructions issued by the Apostolic see.[69]

The petitioners then go on to state the reasons which justify such a renewal. "It is common knowledge in all parts of Gaul, knowledge which must be shared also by the holy Roman church, that the city of Arles was the first in the whole of Gaul to enjoy the honour of having Saint Trophimus as its bishop, a man sent by the most blessed Apostle Peter, and that from that city the blessing of faith and religion was gradually imparted to other parts of Gaul." [70]

[67] *Inter Leon. Epp.*, No. 65, *P.L.* 53, 879. *M.G.H., Epp.*, Vol. III, ed. Gundlach, p. 17, *Ep.* 12 where Nos. 66 and 67 are also given from the *Collectio Arelatensis*. The names of the bishops supporting this petition may be inferred from the address of Leo's reply, *Ep.* 66, JK 450. They belong to sees situated not only in the southern part of the province of *Viennensis*, but also in that of *Narbonensis secunda* and of *Alpes Maritimae*.

[68] *Ibid.*, 1, "suggestionem nostram, quae iustitiae partibus fungitur, audiendam a corona vestra minime dubitamus: quippe cum non aliqua nova institui, sed prisca per vos optamus et antiqua reparari."

[69] *Ibid.*, "privilegia dignitatis antiquae, quae dolebat sibi pro tempore diminuta, gauderet in perpetuum recentioribus apostolicae sedis auctoritatibus reformata." The "diminution" of privileges refers, of course, to the effect of the sentence pronounced on Hilary. "Recentioribus . . . auctoritatibus" cannot allude to instructions issued since the consecration of Ravennius, seeing that apart from *Ep.* 42, nothing of the sort had appeared. The authors of the appeal were evidently anticipating action on Leo's part favourable to the see of Arles.

[70] *Ibid.*, 2. "Omnibus etenim regionibus Gallicanis notum est, sed nec sacrosanctae ecclesiae Romanae habetur incognitum, quod prima inter Gallias Arelatensis civitas missum a beatissimo Petro apostolo sanctum Trophimum habere meruit sacerdotem, et exinde aliis paulatim regionibus Galliarum bonum fidei et religionis infusum." On Trophimus see Additional Note E, *The Trophimus Saga*.

As for the see of Vienne, they advance the argument,[71] that it has no right to claim the primacy, since other cities received bishops from Rome before it,[72] and that anyhow that privilege has always belonged to the see of Arles, in virtue of which its bishops have been invited by other churches, such as those of the petitioners, to consecrate bishops for them. Moreover the primacy possessed and exercised by the see of Arles has frequently been confirmed by earlier popes[73] (as the papal archives can show), in virtue of the principle that as the Roman church holds the first place before all other churches, because it is the see of Peter, so the see of his disciple Trophimus ought to possess the privilege of consecrating bishops throughout Gaul.[74]

From spiritual considerations the petitioners pass on to material ones. They recall the civil dignities of Arles and the honours bestowed upon it by successive Emperors. They point to its distinction as the seat of the Prefect of Gaul and of other officers of the imperial administration.[75] Next they describe the nature of the ecclesiastical primacy, which they

[71] See Additional Note A, *The organization of the Church of Gaul.*

[72] *Ep.* 65, 2, "priusque alia loca ab hoc rivo fidei quem ad nos apostolicae institutionis fluenta miserunt, meruisse manifestum est sacerdotem, quam Viennensis civitas, quae sibi nunc impudenter ac notabiliter primatus exposcit indebitos." The suggestion that Gaul owed its first bishops to initiative on the part of the Roman see suggests that the petitioners were familiar with Innocent I, *Ep.* 25, 2, JK 311.

[73] e.g. by Pope Zosimus. On which see Additional Note B, *The privileges of the see of Arles.*

[74] *Ibid.*, "ut sicut per beatissimum Petrum apostolorum principem sacrosancta ecclesia Romana teneret supra omnes totius mundi ecclesias principatum, ita etiam intra Gallias Arelatensis ecclesia, quae sanctum Trophimum ab apostolis missum sacerdotem habere meruisset, ordinandi pontificium vindicaret." The use of the phrase "ab apostolis" almost suggests that the petitioners had not forgotten the part played by St. Paul in the early history of the Church of Rome.

[75] *Ibid.*, 3. "Hae (sc. civitas) in tantum a . . . Constantino peculiariter honorata est, ut . . . Constantina nomen accepit. Hanc . . . Valentinianus [I] et Honorius . . . specialibus privilegiis et, ut verbo ipsorum utamur, Matrem omnium Galliarum appellando decorarunt. In hac urbe quicumque intra Gallias ex tempore praedictorum ostentare voluit insignia dignitatis, consulatum suscepit et dedit. Hanc sublimissima praefectura, hanc reliquae potestates, velut communem omnibus patriam, semper inhabitabant. Ad hanc ex omnibus civitatibus multarum utilitatum causa concurritur." Constantine had held a general council at Arles in A.D. 316; Honorius had issued the edict *Saluberrima* in its favour in A.D. 418. It probably became the seat of the Prefecture in A.D. 414. All the same the petitioners were evidently guilty of some exaggeration.

allege the see of Arles to have exercised in the past. They point out that:

"Thus it has come about that the bishop of the church of Arles has always held the responsibility and duty of (episcopal) consecration, not in the province of *Viennensis* alone, but in three provinces, out of regard for Saint Trophimus, as indeed the instructions issued by your holy predecessors, if consulted, will prove. Moreover such was the nature of its rank and dignity that while he ruled over these provinces in virtue of his own authority, in virtue of the vicegerency entrusted to him by the Apostolic see, he governed the whole of Gaul in accordance with canon law." [76]

Finally we come to the actual subject matter of the petition:

"We beg and implore the crown of your holiness by the name of our Lord Jesus Christ . . . and by the most blessed apostle Peter, whom we hold to have been restored to us by the grace of God in your life and conduct, that whatever the church of Arles . . . either received of old time or subsequently possessed in virtue of the instructions of the Apostolic see, an instruction of a permanent character from your Beatitude may enjoin the bishop of that church to recover it all under his episcopal authority." [77]

[76] *Ibid.* "Unde factum est ut non solum provinciae Viennensis ordinationem, sed etiam trium provinciarum, contemplatione sancti Trophimi, sicut et sanctorum praedecessorum vestrorum patefacta sibi testatur auctoritas, Arelatensis ecclesiae sacerdos ad sollicitudinem semper suam curamque revocarit. Cui id etiam honoris dignitatisque collatum est, ut non tantum has provincias potestate propria gubernaret, verum etiam omnes Gallias sibi apostolicae sedis vice mandata, sub omni ecclesiastica regula contineret."

The "tres provinciae" intended were probably, in addition to *Viennensis, Narbonensis secunda* and *Alpes Maritimae*. The former had always been more or less dependent on the see of Arles and the inclusion of the latter may be inferred from the fact that Ingenuus, bishop of Eburodunum, the civil metropolis of that province, appears among the signatories of the petition. On the title of Arles to that province from the papal standpoint see Additional Note B.

[77] *Ibid.*, 4, "quaesumus et obsecramus coronam sanctimoniae vestrae per nomen Domini nostri Jesu Christi, . . . et per beatissimum apostolum Petrum, quem vita et conversatione vestra nobis divino munere redditum credimus, ut quidquid Arelatensis ecclesia . . . vel ab antiquitate suscepit, vel postea auctoritate sedis apostolicae vindicavit, id omne ad suum pontificium revocare eiusdem ecclesiae sacerdotem beatitudinis vestrae auctoritas in perpetuum mansura praecipiat." The acceptance of the papal idea of "Petrus redivivus" is noteworthy.

So with an apology for their inability to appear before Leo in person the petitioners bring their remarkable appeal to a close. Apart from their references to the mission of Trophimus, they stated simple and incontestable historical facts, and on the basis of those facts produced a strong case. It is regrettable that the counter petition on behalf of the see of Vienne has not been preserved, yet from the nature of the controversy it may be inferred with some probability that Nicetas was content to assert a claim to metropolitical authority within the province of *Viennensis* alone.[78] In making an appeal to Leo to uphold this claim he must have felt himself to be on safe ground, since after the sentence pronounced against Hilary, Arles had ceased to have any jurisdiction within that province.

Probably the appearance of these rival groups of petitioners in Rome caused Leo some embarrassment, and he may well have found himself faced with the dilemma of choosing between a revocation of his sentence depriving the see of Arles of its privileges and the abandonment of his friend Ravennius. Evidently the only satisfactory solution of the problem from his point of view lay along the way of compromise. His reply to the supporters of Ravennius [79] shows that this was the actual course which he adopted. The letter begins by subtly limiting the extent of the petitioners' request, suggesting that all that they desire is the restoration of the privileges enjoyed by Hilary,[80] and after alluding to the counter appeal presented by the advocates of the claims of Nicetas, urges that in the interests of peace and to do justice both to ancient rights and to their requests, some adjustment is necessary.[81]

[78] Later apologists for the rights of Vienne discovered an apostolic founder in the person of Crescentius (cf. 2 Tim. iv. 10, 20 and Acts xx. 4; xxi. 29) as a rival to Trophimus of Arles. Cf. Duchesne, *Fastes*², Vol. I, pp. 148ff., and see Additional Note E, *The Trophimus Saga*.

[79] *Ep.* 66, JK 450, dated May 5th, A.D. 450.

[80] That is to say metropolitical jurisdiction within the province of *Viennensis* alone. From Leo's point of view all Hilary's acts outside this province were *ultra vires*, cf. *Ep.* 10, 7. Actually the Arelatine petitioners were now demanding this and a great deal more besides, cf. *Inter Leon. Epp.*, No. 65, 3.

[81] *Ibid.*, 1, "ad conservandam intra Viennensem provinciam pacem, adhiberetur iustitiae moderatio, quae nec antiquitatis usum, nec desideria vestra negligeret."

The Pope's decision then follows:

"After examining the statements of the clergy present, representative of both sides, we find that within your province both Vienne and Arles have held a place of importance, so that as a result of various causes, now one, now the other has been pre-eminent in ecclesiastical privileges, while it was shown that formerly in pagan times they shared an equal status. Therefore we cannot allow the city of Vienne altogether to be deprived of honour, in respect of ecclesiastical jurisdiction; especially as, in regard to the possession of privilege, it already enjoys authority by our appointment, namely the power which, after having been taken away from bishop Hilary, was in our view to be assigned to the bishop of Vienne. So, to prevent his being reduced to a status inferior to that which he now enjoys, he shall preside over the four cities near him, namely Valence (Valentia), Tarantaise (Tarantasia), Geneva (Genava) and Grenoble (Gratianopolis), so that with them Vienne itself may make a fifth, and to its bishop shall belong the responsibility for all the aforesaid churches. But the remaining cities of the province shall be comprised within the jurisdiction and ordination rights of the bishop of Arles; one who, as we believe, in a spirit of modesty and self-restraint will be so zealous of charity and peace that he will not regard that which is conceded to a brother as in any way a deprivation of himself." [82]

[82] *Ibid.*, 2. "Consideratis enim allegationibus utriusque partis praesentium clericorum, ita semper intra provinciam vestram, et Viennensem et Arelatensem civitates claras fuisse reperimus, ut quarumdam causarum alterna ratione, nunc illa in ecclesiasticis privilegiis, nunc ista praecelleret, cum tamen eisdem commune ius quondam fuisse a gentibus proderetur. Unde Viennensem civitatem, quantum ad ecclesiasticam iustitiam pertinet, inhonoratam penitus esse non patimur; praesertim cum de receptione privilegii auctoritate iam nostrae dispositionis utatur; quam potestatem Hilario episcopo ablatam, Viennensi episcopo credidimus deputandam. Qui ne repente semetipso factus videatur inferior, vicinis sibi quatuor oppidis praesidebit, id est, Valentiae, et Tarantasiae, et Genavae, et Gratianopoli, ut cum eis ipsa Vienna sit quinta, ad cuius episcopum omnium praedictarum ecclesiarum sollicitudo pertineat. Reliquae vero civitates eiusdem provinciae, sub Arelatensis antistitis auctoritate et ordinatione consistant: quem pro modestiae suae temperantia, ita futurum credimus studiosum charitatis et pacis, ut nequaquam sibi credat ablatam quod fratri videat esse concessum."

"Auctoritate nostrae dispositionis" may allude simply to the implications of *Ep.* 10, 4, or to some letter now lost, or possibly to JK † 446, *Quali pertinacia,* if that letter be authentic. The four cities assigned to Vienne all lie in the northern half of the province; cf. Heussi-Mulert,

It is evident that Leo had taken a great deal of trouble to arrive at a fair solution of this thorny problem, consistent alike with canon law and the evidence of tradition, and that both parties had good reason to be grateful to him for an impartial consideration of their respective claims. On the whole, however, the see of Arles had fared better than its rival. Not only had it received the larger share of the province in dispute, but its claim to jurisdiction over the church of Vaison, the point originally at issue, had been implicitly acknowledged. Nevertheless, although he had restored its metropolitical status, Leo had passed over in silence the more far-reaching demands of the Arelatine petitioners. There were clearly two main reasons for this. In the first place the experiment of assigning a primacy to the see of Arles over the greater part of Southern Gaul, attempted by his predecessor, Zosimus, some forty years previously, had not proved a success. Secondly, it would only have been possible to grant such extensive powers to a single see if Leo had been willing to sacrifice one of his fundamental principles, namely respect for canon law, since such a grant would have violated existing privileges of other metropolitan sees. This he was not prepared to do, even to gratify the aspirations of his friend, the bishop of Arles. Nevertheless it is plain that he still held a high opinion of Ravennius' ability, since it was to him that much of the correspondence of the Roman see relative to the churches of Southern Gaul was addressed.

The representatives of the see of Arles who had presented the petition, the outcome of which we have just reviewed, brought back with them, in addition to Leo's judgment, a personal letter for their bishop,[83] with which were enclosed documents bearing on the doctrinal controversy then prevail-

Atlas, Map IIF. "Reliquae civitates" must mean the other cities of the province *Viennensis,* i.e. the southern part. Cf. Babut, *Concile de Turin,* p. 209 and Gundlach, *Neues Archiv.* (1890), Vol. XV, p. 243; Duchesne, *Fastes*², Vol. I, p. 124 considers the expression to cover all the cities represented by the petitioners; surely much more than Leo could have meant. There is no real ground for supposing that "eiusdem provinciae" refers to the three provinces from which they came. It may be pointed out that the effect of Leo's judgment was roughly to restore the compromise arranged by the Council of Turin. See Additional Notes B and C.

[83] *Ep.* 67, JK 451, dated May 5th, A.D. 450.

ing. There were copies of Leo's letter to Flavian, bishop of Constantinople,[84] and of Cyril of Alexandria's second letter to Nestorius.[85] The purpose of sending these letters was in order that they should be widely circulated, and by this means safeguard the churches of Gaul against false teaching regarding the Incarnation. Leo also mentions in his letter that he had given other secret instructions to the Arelatine representatives, the nature of which Ravennius would learn on their arrival.[86]

To facilitate the publication of these documents the bishop of Arles summoned a general council late in the following year,[87] to which he invited representatives not only from the whole of Roman Gaul, but even from the now independent Visigothic kingdom of Aquitaine.[88] The invitation was accepted by at least forty-four bishops,[89] in fact the absentees chiefly consisted of the suffragans of the see of Vienne. Only the report containing the resolution of the synod[90] has been preserved, and this will be considered later, along with the other documents bearing on the part played by Leo in the Eutychian controversy. It has, however, certain special points of interest which are relevant to the subject of this chapter. In the first place it shows how great was the prestige enjoyed by the Roman see among the churches of Gaul at this time, as may also be seen from the consideration of a further letter,[91] addressed to that see by bishops of the

[84] *Ep.* 28, JK 423, on which see Chap. IX, pp. 225ff.

[85] *Ep.* 4, *P.G.* 77, 44.

[86] It is not impossible that Leo was seeking support for his *démarche* at Ravenna against the Eutychianism of Constantinople.

[87] The delay in summoning the council may be explained by the fact that Gaul was invaded by Attila in A.D. 451. Cf. Bury, *Later Roman Empire,* Vol. I, pp. 291–4. Yet although the synodical letter mentions "spatia" and "aurarum intemperies" it omits any reference to Attila.

[88] Aquitaine had been to some extent independent of imperial rule since A.D. 419. Cf. Kidd, *History,* Vol. III, p. 342.

[89] The names but not the sees of the bishops are preserved. It is interesting to find among them Rusticus of Narbonne and Fonteius of Vaison. The signature of Ravennius should be restored at the head of the signatories.

[90] *Inter Leon. Epp.* 99, *P.L.* 54, 966. It probably belongs to the autumn of A.D. 451.

[91] *Inter Leon. Epp.* 68, *P.L.* 54, 887. The letter is undated but from the fact that it refers to the "Tome" may be assigned to the early part of A.D. 452 at the latest.

province *Alpes Maritimae*,[93] which also has reference to Leo's letter to Flavian. In both letters the writers spare no pains to testify of their devotion and gratitude for the guidance which Leo's teaching has given them, and of their admiration for the stand which he has made in defence of the true doctrine of the Incarnation.[93] Secondly we may observe from the number and nature of the signatories to the synodical report how far the see of Arles had progressed in the direction of regaining its pre-eminent position among the churches of Southern Gaul. In fact it had become the natural intermediary between the Roman see and those churches, and for this reason it was to Ravennius that Leo wrote,[94] as he did shortly before he received the report of the synod, notifying him of the date fixed for the celebration of Easter in the following year, and asking him to convey the information "to all." [95]

The bearer of the report, already mentioned, to Rome was Ingenuus, bishop of Embrun (Eburodunum), who had reasons of his own for visiting the capital.[96] Its contents must have been highly gratifying to Leo since he did not wait for the return of the legates, whom he had sent to the council of Chalcedon, before sending his reply.[97] In this letter, after

[92] The superscription mentions Ceretius, Salonius and Veranus. Possibly the first of these is the same as the bearer of Leo's letter to Eusebius of Milan. Cf. *Inter Leon. Epp.* 97, *P.L.* 54, 946. Veranus may be the same as the bishop of that name addressed by Pope Hilary, *Epp.* 4 and 11, JK 557, 562.

[93] *Inter Leon. Epp.* 99, 2. "Multi itaque in ea gaudentes pariter et exsultantes, recognoverunt fidei suae sensum, et ita se ex traditione paterna tenuisse, ut vester apostolatus exposuit, iure laetantur." Cf. *Inter Leon. Epp.* 68, 1. "Magna praeterea et ineffabili quadam nos peculiares tui gratulatione succrescimus, quod illa specialis doctrinae vestrae pagina ita per omnium ecclesiarum conventicula celebratur, ut vere consona omnium sententia declaretur, merito illic principatum sedis apostolicae constitutum, unde adhuc apostolici spiritus oracula reserentur."

[94] *Ep.* 96, JK 477. The letter is undated. See further on this letter Additional Note to Chap. XV, *The Paschal Question*.

[95] *Ibid.*, "per dilectionem quoque tuam . . . omnibus volumus declarari."

[96] Eburodunum was at this time civil metropolis of the province *Alpes Maritimae* over which Hilary had succeeded in making good his claim to jurisdiction at the synod of Riez (Regii), A.D. 439. However, the reduction of Arles to the status of a simple bishopric had reopened the question. From Pope Hilary's *Ep.* 4, JK 562, *Movemur*, we gather that Leo's decisions in favour of Ingenuus were subsequently cancelled by him in the interests of Leontius, Bishop of Arles. Cf. Duchesne, *Fastes*[2], Vol. I, p. 126, and Jaffé, *Regesta*, Vol. II, p. 736, No. 550A.

[97] *Ep.* 102, JK 479, dated January 27th, A.D. 452.

expressing his disappointment at not having heard from Gaul before the opening of the council of Chalcedon,[98] he assures the members of the synod that unanimity of belief has been established, particularly as a result of the adoption of his letter by the council as a satisfactory statement of Christian doctrine.[99] He then sets forth briefly the errors in the doctrine of Eutyches, and concludes with the request that when they have received further information from him they should pass it on to the churches of Spain.[100]

The legates of the Roman see who, as we shall see, had been unavoidably detained in Constantinople, probably arrived in Rome soon after the departure of Ingenuus, bringing with them a Latin version of the *Acta* of the recent council,[101] and Leo lost no time, we may be sure, in fulfilling his promise of more detailed information. He addressed his letter to "Rusticus, Ravennius, Venerius and the other bishops established throughout Gaul," [102] and after announcing that at Chalcedon "the Catholic faith had been confirmed and the triumph of apostolic teaching celebrated," gave a brief summary of the decisions arrived at by the council, to which he appended a Latin version of the sentence pronounced on Dioscorus, bishop of Alexandria.[103]

For the last nine years of Leo's pontificate there is no record of any further correspondence with the see of Arles. Ravennius died a few months before him [104] and was succeeded by Leontius, who was fortunate in enjoying the favour of the new pope, Hilary I, and in consequence of this suc-

[98] *Ibid.*, 1. "Optassemus quidem fraternitatis vestrae litteras eo tempore quo promiseratis accipere, ut profecturis ad Orientem fratribus nostris, quos ad sanctam synodum vice nostra pro catholicae fidei defensione direximus, etiam vestrae sententiae professio iungeretur."

[99] *Ibid.*, 2, "evidenter apparuit hanc esse vere apostolicam et catholicam fidem, quam sinceram . . . praedicamus et universo iam mundo consentiente defendimus." Cf. *ibid.*, 4, "sancta nunc synodus humilitatis nostrae scriptis auctoritate . . . Petri apostoli et merito roboratis, religiosa unanimitate consentiens."

[100] *Ibid.*, 5, "quae volumus per curam dilectionis vestrae etiam ad fratres nostros Hispaniae episcopos pervenire."

[101] *Ep.* 103, JK 480. The letter is undated but clearly belongs to A.D. 452.

[102] The fact that the name of Rusticus occurs in the first place is to be accounted for by the fact that he was the senior by consecration.

[103] This version shows some "improvement" on the Greek text of the *Acta* of Chalcedon given in Mansi, *op. cit.*, Vol. VII, 1048.

[104] A.D. 461.

ceeded in obtaining most of the privileges refused to his predecessor. Yet in spite of the triumph of the see of Arles, the jealousy felt by the see of Vienne for its former rival persisted through the years. It is worth remembering too that in the twelfth century Vienne actually provided a successor to the papal throne.[105]

To regard the measures taken by Leo to settle the difficulties which arose during his pontificate among the churches of Southern Gaul as dictated wholly by selfish considerations is to ignore certain essential facts. In the first place, if we bear in mind the civil and ecclesiastical legislation as it then existed, once the state of affairs prevailing there in consequence of Hilary's conduct was known, it may be said that Leo had not only the right but also the duty of intervention. Moreover, both in that case and in the subsequent controversy between Ravennius and Nicetas, he appears to have acted with scrupulous fairness and in the best interests of the parties concerned. Finally, it is abundantly clear that in all these matters he consistently refused to act on expediency rather than on principle. His chief concern, as we have seen, was for the maintenance of canon law as accepted by the Roman see in his time, and to this he remained rigidly faithful.

If he had been interested simply to increase the influence of his see at the expense of the local episcopate, an excellent opportunity was afforded by a letter which he received from Theodore, bishop of Fréjus (Forum Julii) in the same year to which the correspondence just reviewed belongs. It was concerned mainly with the question as to the conditions which should govern the granting of absolution in the administration of Penance. In his reply[106] Leo takes occasion to point out to his correspondent that such an inquiry should only be made with the approval of the metropolitan bishop of the province.[107] He then proceeds to review the principles under-

[105] Quido, Archbishop of Vienne, elected as Callistus II, A.D. 1119–24. His pontificate was remarkable for the number of forgeries fabricated in the interests of his former see. Cf. Caspar, *Geschichte,* Vol. I, p. 452.

[106] *Ep.* 108, JK 485, dated June 11th, A.D. 452.

[107] *Ibid.*, 1, "hic ordo esse debuerat, ut cum metropolitano tuo primitus de eo quod quaerendum esse videbatur conferres, ac si id quod ignorabat dilectio tua etiam ipse nesciret, instrui vos pariter posceretis: quia in causis quae ad generalem observantiam pertinent omnium Domini sacerdotum, nihil sine primatibus oportet inquiri." It is possible that

lying the practice of the Church in the forgiveness of sins.

First of all he points out that Penance provides a remedy for sin committed after Baptism, adding that God's pardon can only be obtained by the prayers of the bishops.[108] Then he describes the method by which forgiveness is imparted: " For the mediator of God and man, the man Christ Jesus, entrusted this authority to the leaders of the Church, so that they might assign not only the performance of Penance to those who confess their sins, but also, when these have been cleansed by salutary satisfaction, admit them by means of the gate of reconciliation to sacramental Communion." [109]

After having defined the principle he proceeds to discuss its application to special cases. First as to those who die before actually receiving reconciliation. In such a case, says the writer, reconciliation may not be given after death; [110] nor is it necessary to discuss the merits and actions of such people, since God has reserved to His own judgment that which falls outside the scope of the bishop's ministration: showing that His purpose is to evoke fear at the fate of the half-hearted and negligent.

" For," he adds, " it is highly profitable and necessary that

Theodore, whose see lay in the civil province of *Narbonensis secunda,* approached Leo direct, because at this time it was not clear which see was to be regarded as possessing metropolitical authority. It had been exercised by Proculus of Marseilles, and later by his successor Venerius, on whose death in A.D. 451 a claim had been put forward by Auxanius, bishop of Aix (Aquae Sextiae). See Babut, *Concile de Turin,* p. 294, but cf. Duchesne, *Fastes*², Vol. I, p. 280, n. 1. It should be noticed that " metropolitanus " and " primas " are still synonymous terms at this date.

[108] *Ibid.,* 2, " non solum per baptismi gratiam, sed etiam per poenitentiae medicinam spes vitae reparetur aeternae, . . . : sic divinae bonitatis praesidiis ordinatis, ut indulgentia Dei nisi supplicationibus sacerdotum nequeat obtineri." The significance of this passage has been much disputed. Galtier, *L'Église et la remission des péchés,* pp. 70ff., discusses various opinions and argues that " supplicationibus " cannot mean merely the intercessions offered for penitents during their period of penance but must refer to the prayers recited by the bishop in the course of the rite of reconciliation. Cf. Origen, *De Oratione,* 28. *P.G.* 11, 529B, " ὡς διὰ τῆς εὐχῆς αὐτῶν . . . λυομένης . . . τῆς ἁμαρτίας."

[109] *Ibid.* " Mediator enim Dei et hominum homo Christus Jesus hanc praepositis ecclesiae tradidit potestatem, ut et confitentibus actionem poenitentiae darent, et eosdem salubri satisfactione purgatos, ad communionem sacramentorum per ianuam reconciliationis admitterent."

[110] *Ibid.,* 3, " quod manens in corpore non recepit, consequi exutus carne non poterit."

the offences of sinners should be pardoned by the prayer of the bishop before the day of death."[111]

Next comes the case of those who ask for Penance and immediate reconciliation in the face of some urgent necessity or danger. Leo points out that such people should not be refused the opportunity of satisfaction nor of reconciliation, on the ground that it is impossible to limit the measure of God's mercy or to make real conversion a matter of duration, and suggests that "we ought not therefore to be hard-hearted in dispensing the gifts of God, nor to ignore the tears and groans of those who accuse themselves, believing as we do that the desire to do Penance has been formed by inspiration of God."[112]

Nevertheless he urges that no Christian ought to postpone his conversion, lest he find himself without opportunity, either for confession or for reconciliation by the bishop. At the same time the writer allows that in a case where the sinner has put off seeking forgiveness to the last possible moment, and can no longer use his voice, both the performance of Penance and the grace of Communion are not to be refused. But if by reason of a sudden attack of sickness the penitent is prevented from requesting these for himself, the witness of faithful bystanders may suffice, so that he may receive the benefit of Penance and reconciliation at the same time:[113] provided that the provisions of canon law regarding those who have been guilty of apostasy are observed.[114]

Leo concludes his letter with the request that Theodore will

[111] *Ep.* 108, 3. "Multum enim utile ac necessarium est ut peccatorum reatus ante ultimum diem sacerdotali supplicatione solvatur."

[112] *Ibid.*, 4, "in dispensandis itaque Dei donis non debemus esse difficiles, nec accusantium se lachrymas gemitusque negligere, cum ipsam poenitendi affectionem ex Dei credamus inspiratione conceptam." Cf. *Syllabus on Grace*, above p. 41.

[113] The implication is that if the penitent recovers he will perform the allotted penance subsequently. See *Ep.* 167, 7 and 9. But we are already in sight of a method of administering reconciliation which allows the penance to follow absolution.

[114] Apostasy is treated as exceptional by Siricius, *Ep.* 1, 3, JK 255, who condemns the offender to lifelong penance. Cf. *Conc. Nic.*, Can. 11 and 12. There was evidently a movement in Gaul at this time which was favouring less rigid terms for heretics and apostates. Cf. *Conc. Arausic.*, Can. 3. Mansi, *op. cit.*, Vol. VI, 436 and *Conc. Arelat.* I, A.D. 314, Can. 22. Mansi, *op. cit.*, Vol. II, 471. *Conc. Arelat.* II, A.D. 452, Can. 10. Mansi, *op. cit.*, Vol. VII, 880.

inform his metropolitan of its contents, so that the latter may enlighten other bishops who may be in doubt regarding these questions.[115]

Some six years or so later Hermes, archdeacon of Narbonne,[116] arrived bearing three documents. These were a *relatio* from his bishop, Rusticus, reporting the resolutions passed by a synod recently held there under the latter's presidency,[117] a copy of the synodical minutes,[118] and a personal letter from Rusticus himself, in which he bewailed the difficulties of his position and expressed his desire to lay aside the responsibilities of his office. The minutes of the synod showed that the question as to what treatment should be accorded to persons convicted of adultery had aroused considerable controversy and that a minority, represented by two priests named Sabinian and Leo, had so strongly disapproved of decisions, which seemed to them to partake of laxity, that they had withdrawn from the deliberations of the synod which had approved of them. In his reply, which naturally falls into three main sections, Leo first of all offers advice as to the treatment of the rigorist minority. While leaving them to Rusticus' discretion, the writer suggests that he should use the gentle art of persuasion and respect their zeal in the cause of chastity.[119] After this he deals with Rusticus' personal grievances.

"I am amazed, however," he writes, "that your beloved self is so much upset by the difficulty of scandals, from what-

[115] It is regrettable that Leo names neither the metropolitan in question nor his see.

[116] Hermes succeeded Rusticus *c.* A.D. 461, after having been for a short time bishop of Béziers (Biterrae, Beterae). His election to Narbonne was quashed by Pope Hilary I, cf. *Ep.* 8, JK 555, who thereupon deprived that see of metropolitical status and subordinated its province to Leontius of Arles. Cf. Duchesne, *Fastes*², Vol. I, pp. 129, 304.

[117] Rusticus appears to have acted independently of the see of Arles.

[118] *Ep.* 167, *introd.*, "gestis quae in episcoporum honoratorumque examine confecta sunt recensitis." The mention of "honorati" suggests that membership of the synod included laymen, who held some State office.

[119] *Ibid.* "Circa quos quam formam quamve mensuram debes tenere iustitiae, tua relinquo moderamini: suadens tamen charitatis hortatu, ut sanandis aegris spiritalem adhibere debeas medicinam: . . . mitius agas cum eis qui pudicitiae zelo videntur modum excessisse vindictae." There is a lacuna in the text at the end of this section suggesting that Leo may have said more on this subject than now appears.

ever cause they may have arisen, that you say that you desire specially release from the travails of episcopal office and prefer to spend your life in quiet and ease, rather than persevere in the duties which have been entrusted to you." [120]

After all, he proceeds, persecution, such as the Apostle forewarned us to expect, can arise no less from differences of custom, insubordination of inferiors and malicious slander than from actual bodily suffering and torture. Leisure and toil alike are full of temptation. And what of the Church? If love of rest causes the watchman to abandon his post, who is to resist thieves and robbers? In the passage which follows Leo writes as a true pastor of souls.

"You should persevere in the duty entrusted to you and the work which you have undertaken. You should consistently maintain justice and show clemency with kindness. Let sins, not sinners, be an object of hatred. Restrain the proud, encourage the feeble and if rather severe punishment has to be awarded to sins, let it be inflicted in the spirit not of anger but of tenderness." [121]

Above all, he concludes, let not Rusticus forget that He who forewarns Christians of the possibility of suffering also promises His aid.

Leo now passes on to answer the questions which Rusticus had submitted to him by the hand of his archdeacon. It would have been better, he says, if it had been possible to discuss them with Rusticus in person. For although there are certain points which do not admit of argument, there are many which allow of modification out of consideration for age or the necessity of circumstances, so long as the principle is kept in mind that, where there is any doubt, consistency with the precepts of the Gospel and with canon law must always be observed.[122]

[120] *Ep.* 167, *introd.* "Miror autem dilectionem tuam in tantum scandalorum quacumque occasione nascentium adversitate turbari, ut vacationem ab episcopatus laboribus praeoptare te dicas, et malle in silentio atque otio vitam degere, quam in his quae tibi commissa sunt permanere."

[121] *Ibid.* "Permanendum ergo est in opere credito et in labore suscepto. Constanter tenenda est iustitia et benigne praestanda clementia. Odio habeantur peccata, non homines. Corripiantur tumidi, tolerentur infirmi: et quod in peccatis severius castigari necesse est, non saevientis plectatur animo, sed medentis." The maxims here given are of permanent value in guiding the administration of Penance.

[122] *Ibid., Resp.* 1. "Nulla ratio sinit ut inter episcopos habeantur qui

At this point he takes Rusticus' questions in turn and supplies the answer.

(1) Concerning a priest or deacon who falsely calls himself a bishop: and concerning those clergy whom such persons have ordained.

No one is to be accounted a bishop who has not been duly elected by the clergy, on the proposition of the laity, and consecrated by the bishops of the province with the approval of the metropolitan. As to those who have been ordained by false bishops, provided the ordination was performed with the approval of the "diocesans" concerned, it shall be acknowledged as valid, so long as they remain in the churches (dioceses) to which they belong.

(2) Concerning a priest or deacon who, when his offence is made known, seeks public Penance; as to whether it should be accorded to him by laying on of the hand.

Ecclesiastical custom forbids priests or deacons to receive Penance by laying on of the hand.[123] So in the case of clerical offenders withdrawal into lay communion is to be required, by means of which satisfaction, if adequate, may be profitable.[124]

nec a clericis sunt electi, nec a plebibus sunt expetiti, nec a provincialibus episcopis cum metropolitani iudicio consecrati." Leo's definition of the conditions governing a regular episcopal election reproduces what he has said frequently elsewhere. Cf. *Ep.* 10, 6, JK 407 and *Ep.* 14, 5, JK 411. Cf. Celestine I, *Ep.* 4, 3, 6, JK 369. For the stipulation that the election must be confirmed by the metropolitan, cf. *Conc. Nic.*, Can. 4. It should be noticed that Leo regards ordinations performed by bishops irregularly elected and consecrated as actually invalid if they are performed apart from the permission of the "diocesan" and without any "title," showing that in his view "jurisdiction" is closely bound up with "place." It is possible that the inquiry had reference to ordinations performed by schismatic Arian bishops, introduced by the Goths, or else by *chorepiscopi*. Cf. *Ep.* 12, 10, JK 410, and above Chap. VI, p. 111.

[123] *Ibid., Resp.* 2. "Alienum est a consuetudine ecclesiastica ut qui in presbyterali honore aut in diaconii gradu fuerint consecrati, ii pro crimine aliquo suo per manus impositionem remedium accipiant poenitendi." In support of this Leo cites 1 *Reg.*, ii, 25 with the following text, "Sacerdos si peccaverit, quis orabit pro illo?" LXX, ed. Swete, *ad loc.* reads "ἐὰν τῷ κυρίῳ ἁμάρτῃ, τίς προσεύξεται ὑπὲρ αὐτοῦ." For the prohibition of penance in the case of the clergy cf. Siricius, *Ep.* 1, 14, JK 255. It may be noted that the ceremony of admission to penance is described as "the laying on *the* hand," i.e. presumably of the right hand only.

[124] *Ibid.*, "huiusmodi lapsis, . . . privata est expetenda secessio, ubi illis satisfactio, si fuerit digna, sit etiam fructuosa." This appears to contemplate suspension from the ministry, or perhaps degradation, cf. Innocent I, *Ep.* 6, 1, JK 293.

(3) Concerning those who minister at altars and have wives, whether they may lawfully have intercourse with them?

The same law of continence, which applies to bishops and priests, also binds the ministers of the altar,[125] who when they were laymen or readers might legitimately marry and procreate children. Yet once they have ordained to the said orders what was once permissible becomes illicit. So their duty is to change a carnal marriage into a spiritual one, and though they ought not to divorce their wives, they should keep them as though they had them not. Thus, while married love remains, married intercourse ceases.

(4) Concerning a priest or deacon who has married his virgin daughter to a man who already has a wife, and has had children by her.

The first question to be determined is whether the woman who appears to be the man's wife is so in fact. For though by divine and Roman civil law alike marriage between two free born persons of equal status is valid,[126] yet there is a difference between a wife and a concubine, and between a slave and a free woman. So, while according to the primitive ordinance of marriage, even apart from actual intercourse, it embraces in itself the mystery of Christ and His Church, yet beyond doubt a woman is not married in a case in which it

[125] *Ep.* 167, *Resp.* 3. "Lex continentiae eadem est ministris altaris quae episcopis atque presbyteris." The earliest Western reference to an obligation to continence on the part of the clergy is in *Conc. Illib.*, Canon 33. Mansi, *Concilia,* Vol. II, 11. "Placuit in totum prohibere episcopis, presbyteris et diaconibus vel omnibus clericis positis in ministerio abstinere se a coniugibus suis et non generare filios." The phrase "ministris altaris" refers primarily to deacons but probably includes subdeacons. Cf. *Ep.* 14, 4, JK 411. Earlier papal decisions on the point are Siricius, *Ep.* 1, 7, JK 255; *Ep.* 5, 8, JK 258; Innocent I, *Ep.* 2, 9, JK 286; *Ep.* 6, 1, JK 293. Cf. *Conc. Carthag.* (A.D. 390), Canon 1. Mansi, *Concilia,* Vol. III, 692; *Conc. Carthag.* (A.D. 401), Canon 3, *ibid.*, 710; *Conc. Taurin,* Canon 8, *ibid.*, 862; *Conc. Tolet.* (A.D. 400), Canon 1, *ibid.*, 998; Ambrose, *De officiis,* 1, 50, *P.L.* 16, 102; Jerome, *Adv. Jovin.* 1, 34, *P.L.* 23, 268; Augustine, *De Coniug. adult.* 2, 21, *P.L.* 40, 486.

[126] *Ibid.*, *Resp.* 4. "Nuptiarum autem foedera inter ingenuos sunt legitima et inter aequales; multo prius hoc ipsum Domino constituente (Gen. ii. 24) quam initium Romani iuris exsisteret. Itaque aliud est uxor, aliud concubina." By the fifth century the old Roman forms of marriage had fallen into disuse, Bury *Later Roman Empire,* Vol. II, p. 403. A recent law enacted by Majorian in A.D. 458 had enforced prohibitions against unequal marriages. *Nov. Maior.* 6, 9, ed. P. Meyer, p. 165.

is shown that there has been no nuptial mystery.[127] Therefore, if a cleric has given his daughter in marriage to a man who has a concubine, it is not to be understood as though he had given her to a married man, unless the woman has actually been made a free woman, legally dowried and made honourable by a public marriage ceremony.

(5) Concerning girls who marry men who have concubines.

No blame attaches to those who, with parental approval, are married to men, if the women which the men "kept" were not legally married to them.

(6) Concerning those who forsake women by whom they have had children and take wives.

On the principle that a married woman is different from a concubine, to reject a slave and to take a wife of undoubted free birth is not bigamy but an honourable action.[128]

(7) Concerning those who accept Penance in time of sickness and then, when they have recovered, decline to perform it.

Such a refusal is blameworthy, but not to be treated as altogether hopeless. Such persons should frequently be urged to perform that which they requested in time of necessity.[129] For one ought not to despair of anyone in this life, since often that which is postponed by youthful irresponsibility is performed later when a more mature judgment is acquired.

(8) Concerning those who in mortal sickness accept Penance, and die before receiving communion.

Such people are to be left to God's judgment,[130] Who might have delayed their death till after Communion. But one

[127] *Ibid.* "Unde cum societas nuptiarum ita ab initio constitutasit, ut praeter sexuum coniunctionem haberet in se Christi et Ecclesiae sacramentum (Eph. v. 32), dubium non est eam mulierem non pertinere ad matrimonium, in qua docetur nuptiale non fuisse mysterium." The last phrase appears to refer not only to the consummation of the marriage, but to the whole marriage ceremony, apart from which there is, in Leo's view, no marriage at all. Ambrose alludes to Christian marriage ceremonies in *Ep.* 19, 7, *P.L.* 16, 1026.

[128] This opinion probably reflects the influence of Majorian's legislation. See above, p. 146.

[129] *Ibid., Resp.* 7. "Culpanda est talium negligentia, sed non penitus deserenda: ut crebris cohortationibus incitati, quod necessarie expetierunt, fideliter exsequantur."

[130] *Ibid., Resp.* 8. "Horum causa Dei iudicio reservanda est." Cf. *Ep.* 108, 3, JK 485.

cannot be in communion with people after their death with whom one was not in communion while they were alive.

(9) Concerning those who under pressure of great pain ask that Penance may be given to them and, when the priest comes to give what they ask, if the pain diminishes a little, evade it and refuse to accept what is offered.

Disinclination of this sort is to be ascribed not to contempt of the remedy but to fear of sinning more seriously.[131] So the postponed Penance, if it be asked for again more earnestly, is not to be refused, so that by some means or other the soul may receive the medicine of pardon.[132]

(10) Concerning those who have undertaken Penance and then start a lawsuit.

It is one thing to demand one's rights and another thing to despise even that which is one's own through love of perfection. But a person who seeks pardon for wrongdoing ought to abstain even from what is right, while if a penitent has a suit which perhaps he is bound to undertake, it would be preferable for him to have recourse to an ecclesiastical court rather than to a civil one.[133]

(11) Concerning those who carry on business while in the course of performing Penance or after having completed it.

The nature of the gain affects the case; whether the profit is honest or base. Yet it is better for one undergoing Penance to suffer loss rather than be involved in the risks of business, since in the course of trade between buyer and seller it is difficult to avoid sin.

(12) Concerning those who after performing Penance return to government service.

Canon law forbids a person to return to government service after the performance of Penance. So a man is not free from

[131] *Ep.* 167, *Resp.* 9. "Dissimulatio haec potest non de contemptu esse remedii, sed de metu gravius delinquendi." Penance could only be performed once in a lifetime according to the view prevailing in the fifth century. Cf. Augustine, *Ep.* 153, 7, *P.L.* 33, 656. But according to Siricius, *Ep.* 1, 5, JK 255, those who sin afresh after penance should be admitted to communion *in articulo mortis.*

[132] *Ibid.* This and the two foregoing answers show that Leo regards the penitential exercises in normal cases as a necessary part of the administration of penance.

[133] *Ibid., Resp.* 10. Exclusion from engaging in lawsuits and in trade (11) as part of the penitential discipline is only mentioned here.

sin who is ready to involve himself in such a vocation.[134]

(13) Concerning those who after performing Penance take wives or associate with concubines.

One who while still young has performed Penance, in fear of death or faced by danger of being made prisoner and then afterwards, in dread of the sin of youthful incontinence, has chosen to marry a wife, so as not to be guilty of fornication, appears to have done something pardonable so long as he has carnal knowledge of no one at all but his wife. In such a case the writer states that he does not so much define a rule as judge what is preferable. For, strictly speaking, nothing is so fitting for one who has performed Penance as perseverance in chastity.

(14) Concerning monks who have undertaken either government service or marriage.

A monastic vow freely taken cannot be abandoned without sin. So if anyone, after abandoning his vow of celibacy, turns aside to government service or marriage he must be cleansed by the satisfaction of public Penance. For though marriage is innocent and the other honourable, yet it is an offence to forsake the choice of better things.[135]

(15) Concerning girls who for a time wore the "religious" habit, yet were not actually professed, if they should have subsequently married.

Girls who without parental compulsion have willingly taken the vow and habit of virginity, if they marry afterwards, transgress, even if their "profession" has not taken place, which would follow if they were faithful to their vow.[136]

(16) Concerning those who were abandoned as infants by Christian parents, regarding whose Baptism there is no evidence whether they ought to be baptized.

[134] *Ibid.*, *Resp.* 12. Exclusion from civil service (12) and from sexual intercourse of any kind (13) is mentioned by Siricius, *Ep.* 1, 5, JK 255; *Ep.* 5, 3, JK 258; Innocent I, *Ep.* 2, 2 (4), JK 286. The use of "militia" for government service, not necessarily of a military nature, is general in this period. Cf. Bury, *Later Roman Empire,* Vol. I, p. 31.

[135] *Ibid.*, 14. "Propositum monachi proprio arbitrio aut voluntate susceptum deseri non potest absque peccato." Cf. Siricius, *Ep.* 1, 6, JK 255; Innocent I, *Ep.* 2, 11, JK 286.

[136] *Ibid.*, 15, "cuius (sc. consecrationis) utique non fraudarentur munere, si in proposito permanerent." Cf. Siricius, *Ep.* 1, 6, JK 255; Innocent I, *Ep.* 2, 14, 15, JK 286.

If there is no evidence among relations or servants, clergy or neighbours to show whether they have been baptized, they should be admitted to the sacrament. For to effect the salvation of those of whose Baptism there is no proof is not to repeat it.[137]

(17) Concerning those who were taken prisoner as infants by the enemy, and think that they were not baptized, but know that they were sometimes brought to church by their parents whether, when they enter imperial territory, they can or ought to be baptized.

Those who can remember coming to church with their parents can remember whether they received that which was given to their parents.[138] But if they have forgotten this they ought to be given that which is not known to have been given. To do so is to act not with rash presumption, but with merciful consideration.

(18) Concerning those who have come from Africa or Mauretania and do not know in what sect they were baptized.

They are not ignorant of the fact of their baptism, but rather of what faith the persons were who baptized them. So in whatever way they received the " form " of Baptism they are not to be baptized (again), but are to be associated with Catholics by the " laying on of the hand " with invocation of the power of the Holy Ghost, which they could not receive from heretics.[139]

(19) Concerning those who were actually baptized as infants and then been taken prisoner by the barbarians and so lived with them as barbarians; when they come as youths to imperial territory, if they ask for communion, what is to be done?

If they have simply taken part in a barbarian feast and in meat sacrificed to idols, they can be cleansed by fasts and the " laying on of the hand " : so that they may be partakers

[137] *Ep.* 167, *Resp.* 16. Cf. *Ep.* 166, 1, JK 536.

[138] *Ibid.*, 17, " possunt recordari an quod eorum parentibus dabatur acceperint." The reference is apparently to their communion as young children. For the ruling given here cf. *Ep.* 166, 1, JK 536.

[139] *Ibid.*, 18, " per manus impositionem, invocata virtute Spiritus sancti, quam ab haereticis accipere non potuerunt, catholicis copulandi sunt." Cf. *Ep.* 166, 2, JK 536 ; Siricius, *Ep.* 1, 1, JK 255 ; *Ep.* 5, 8, JK 258 ; Innocent I, *Ep.* 17, 3, JK 303. For the significance of the " manus impositio " see above Additional Note F.

of the sacraments of Christ. If, however, they have worshipped idols or been stained with murder and fornication they ought only to be admitted to Communion by means of public Penance.[140]

With this answer Leo's painstaking response to the inquiries submitted by the bishop of Narbonne comes to an end. As we look back over the rulings given by him we notice certain outstanding characteristics of his work. No one could accuse him of laxity, yet in spite of his faithfulness to canonical principle he never betrays feelings of vindictiveness or impatience.[141] His simplicity of style, and his almost studied avoidance of rhetorical exaggeration seem to suggest that he was conscious, as he wrote, that he was legislating not for a province in Southern Gaul only but for the universal Church. Characteristics such as these go far to account for the influence which he exercised, not only in the West, but, as we shall see, among churches less directly under his control. More than one of his decisions have exercised a lasting influence not only on the administration of the sacrament of Penance in the course of the centuries, but on the whole of Western canon law.

2. NORTHERN GAUL AND BRITAIN

By the middle of the fifth century the absence of any effective control by the central imperial government of the provinces of Northern Gaul and Britain meant that for a time at least there was no direct means of communication between the Roman see and the churches of those parts. Hence it is not surprising that there is no trace of correspondence between Leo and the northern sees whatever. As for Britain, there is only an isolated reference which affirms that in writing to the Gaulish and Spanish bishops, informing them of the date prescribed for the celebration of Easter in the year A.D. 455,[142] he also despatched a copy of the letter to the bishops of that country.[143] All that can be added to this

[140] *Ibid.*, 19. The distinction here is evidently based on 1 Cor. viii. 8 and Acts xv. 20.

[141] Notice esp. *Respp.* 7, 9 and 13.

[142] *Ep.* 138, JK 512, dated July 28th, A.D. 454.

[143] JK *513. Cf. *Mon. Hist. Brit.* Vol. I, p. 830. The copy has not been preserved.

scanty information is mention of the possibility that Leo had some share in instigating Germanus of Auxerre to undertake in company with Severus of Trêves a second expedition, in order to correct the influence of Pelagianism among the British Churches.[144] Otherwise there is silence.

3. SPAIN

The political and ecclesiastical confusion engendered by successive waves of barbarian invasion which had afflicted the provinces of Spain since the early years of the fifth century[145] had made it possible for the heresy attached to the name of the Spanish mystic Priscillian[146] to enjoy a fresh lease of life. As a consequence of the resultant confusion it was both difficult for the authorities of the Church to check sectarian propaganda and all but impossible to assemble synods for the restoration of discipline. But by the beginning of Leo's pontificate normal life was beginning to be possible once more under the rule of the barbarian princes, and the opportunity was to hand for a man of character and determination to undertake the restoration of order within the Church.

Such a person was to be found in Turibius, the new metropolitan bishop of Astorga (Asturica), whose see lay in the northern half in that part of the Iberian peninsula known to-day as Portugal. The fact that he appears to have travelled to some extent makes it probable that he had become acquainted with the organized unity of the Church outside Spain, and that this experience had aroused in him a desire to effect the restoration of a closer unity in the churches of his homeland. Soon after his election to the episcopate he decided to summon representatives of the Priscillianist sect and hear what they had to tell in regard to their teaching and practice.[147] This done, he informed his suffragans of all that

[144] Cf. Dom Gougaud, *Les chrétientés celtiques*, p. 34; *Dict. Théol. Cath.*, Vol. IX, col. 240. There is also a vague tradition that Patrick, the apostle of Ireland, visited Rome during Leo's pontificate. Cf. Bury, *St. Patrick*, pp. 150ff., 367ff.

[145] The earliest invasions, those of the *Suevi*, began in A.D. 409. Cf. Bury, *Later Roman Empire*, Vol. I, p. 192.

[146] See Additional Note G, *Priscillianism*.

[147] Idatius, *Chronicon*, sub ann. 445. *M.G.H.*, Auct. antiqu., Vol. XI, *Chron. min.*, Vol. II, p. 24. On the life of the author see Duchesne, *Histoire*, Vol. III, p. 588.

he had learnt. In his letter on the subject,[148] after contrasting the prevalence of heretical teaching and practice in Spain with the ordered unity existing in other parts of the Church, he set forth the fruits of his investigation. In the main he appears to have devoted considerable space to the Priscillianist use of apocryphal literature, and to have drawn special attention to the evident contradictions between that literature and the canonical books. At the same time he deplored the fact that he had experienced so much difficulty in arriving at the truth, owing to the habit of prevarication for which Priscillianists were notorious, and indicated his belief that he had not succeeded in unearthing their more secret books.[149]

At the time of Turibius' investigation Leo had probably been in occupation of the Roman see some five years or so,[150] and in the following year, perhaps as a result of receiving the Pope's letter describing the recent process against the Manichaeans in Rome, the metropolitan of Astorga summoned a synod. It is likely that the necessity for taking some definite action against the Priscillianists seemed now all the more real, if only to prevent the spread of teaching which in many respects appeared to resemble that of the disciples of Manes.[151] The synod however was largely barren of any positive decision, and contented itself with referring the whole matter to Antony of Merida, metropolitan of the province of *Lusitania*.[152] Perhaps some of Turibius' own suffragans were too much compromised with Priscillianism

[148] A letter purporting to be his addressed to Idatius, Bishop of Aquae Flaviae, and Ceponius, is given as an appendix to Leo, *Ep.* 15, JK 412. Tixeront, *Histoire des Dogmes,* Vol. II, p. 231, n. 3 regards it as a forgery.

[149] The contents of Turibius' letter may be inferred from Leo's reply.

[150] The chronology of these events is somewhat uncertain. Hefele-Leclerq, *Conciles,* Vol. II, p. 481 dates this synod A.D. 446, while Künstle, *Antipriscilliana,* p. 30 prefers A.D. 445. The latter date appears to conform better with the events of Leo's pontificate.

[151] The resemblance may have been stressed by Turibius.

[152] Idatius, *Chronicon,* sub ann. A.D. 448. *M.G.H.,* Auct. antiqu., Vol. XI. *Chron. min.,* Vol. II, p. 25 mentions that Antony banished a certain Pascentius on the charge of Manichaeism, which may suggest that he was unfavourably disposed towards Priscillianism. There was a further reason for making an appeal to the province of *Lusitania,* in that it formed part of the dominion of Rechiar, a recent convert to Catholicism.

themselves to make it possible to take any definite action on their own account.

Such hesitancy was scarcely calculated to satisfy Turibius, who thereupon came to the conclusion that the only way to galvanize the Spanish episcopate into action was to appeal for outside support. It was with this intent therefore that he addressed a letter to the Roman see, in the course of which he affirmed that the heresy of Priscillian was on the increase and, in view of the fact that it could number certain Spanish bishops among its adherents, was threatening the order and stability of the Spanish churches.[153] He enclosed with his letter a *commonitorium* summarizing the main tenets of the sect.[154]

In replying to this communication [155] Leo begins by commenting on his correspondent's references to the doctrine and character of Priscillianism in such a way as to suggest that he

[153] Leo, *Ep.* 15, *praef.* quotes Turibius in saying, "Priscillianistarum foetidissimam apud vos recaluisse sentinam . . . lethali morbo etiam quorumdam sacerdotum corda corrupta sunt." Perhaps in the province of *Gallicia,* its original stronghold, the heresy had never lost a foothold.

[154] *Ibid.,* 16, "decursis itaque omnibus quae libelli series comprehendit, et a quibus commonitorii forma non discrepat." The "libellus" here mentioned appears merely to denote Turibius' appeal. Some have sought to identify it with the "libellus in modum symboli," which Gennadius, *De vir. illustr.* 77 (76), ed. *Texte u. Unters,* Vol. XIV, p. 87, ascribes to a certain Spanish bishop Pastor, stating that it was written at the request of Turibius, cf. Babut, *Priscillien,* p.17, nn. 3 and 4.

[155] *Ep.* 15, JK 412 probably of the year A.D. 445. The authenticity of this letter has been seriously disputed, chiefly by Künstle, *Antipriscilliana,* pp. 117ff., on the following grounds. It is urged that the resemblance between c. 15 and 16 of this letter and the seventeenth anathema of the "second" Council of Braga held in A.D. 563 is to be explained best as due to a dependence of the former on the latter. Further, attention is drawn to the alleged superficiality of its comments on Priscillianist doctrines and practices and to the inconsistency between the approval expressed by its author of the execution of Priscillian and the aversion expressed by Leo himself, *Ep.* 118, 2, JK 494 for the infliction of the death penalty on heretics. Emphasis is also laid on the improbability that Leo would have spoken of the "double procession of the Holy Ghost" (*Ep.* 15, 1), and on the fact that no mention is made of the letter by certain sixth century Spanish authorities, e.g. Lucretius at the Council of Braga. Mansi, *Concilia,* Vol. IX, 773; Montanus, *Ep.* 1, 8, *P.L.* 65, 54. It may be further suggested that the occasional unwieldiness of expression employed by the author appears inconsistent with the terseness usually so characteristic of Leo's style. On the whole, it may be said that, while the case against its authenticity may be regarded as falling short of proof, we are bound to reckon the letter as among "Dubia," cf. Tixeront, *Histoire des Dogmes,* Vol. II, p. 231, n. 3. Bardenhewer, however, *Gesch. d. altkirch. lit.,* Vol. III, pp. 415f.; Vol. IV, p. 621 supports its genuineness.

did not seriously differentiate it from Manichaeism.[156] He discusses its use of apocryphal books, to its magical rites and immoral customs, and lays particular stress on its doctrine of astrological fatalism.[157] With allusion to the violent death of its founder the Pope suggests that the severity of the State in his case may well have been to the advantage of the Church since it probably compelled some Priscillianists, if only through fear, to seek reconciliation. He concludes this introductory section by deploring the cessation of normal synodical action, as a consequence of the public calamities resulting from barbarian invasions.[158]

The preface ended, Leo proceeds to review in turn the sixteen chapters of the *commonitorium,* which he has received from Turibius. It is specially interesting to note that he dismisses the Priscillianist doctrine of God as a revival of Sabellianism,[159] rejects their view of the nature of sin,[160] and pours scorn on their teaching as to the influence of the heavenly bodies on the lives of individuals. He urges that all apocryphal books should be burnt and that sectaries when detected should be required explicitly to repudiate the *Tractatus* of Dictinius.[161]

As to future action, he suggests that the minutes of the investigation recently conducted at Rome in regard to Manichaeism may serve as a guide, and after answering a special inquiry, put forward by his correspondent, as to the condition of Christ's body after death, concludes a long letter by urging the immediate assembly of a general council of all the Spanish

[156] It is clear from Maximus, *Ep. ad Siricium,* 7. *Coll. Avell.* 40, 4. *C.S.E.L.,* Vol. XXXV, i, p. 91 that Priscillian himself was regarded as infected with Manichaeism and that on this charge he was put to death. Perhaps the two sects were identified according to current Roman opinion.

[157] *Ibid., praef.,* "quod si credi liceat et doceri, nec virtutibus praemium nec vitiis poena debebitur." The comment is apposite enough to suggest Leonine authorship.

[158] *Ibid., praef.,* "inter sacerdotes Dei difficiles commeatus."

[159] It is in this section c. 1 that the author describes the Holy Ghost as "qui de utroque processit." In the following section he discards the idea of a "mutable" God, "quam enim mutatur quod minuitur, tam mutatur etiam quod augetur."

[160] *Ibid.,* 10, "quia per primi hominis praevaricationem tota humani generis propago vitiata sit, neminem posse a conditione veteris hominis liberari nisi per sacramentum baptismatis Christi."

[161] With reference to this book, which is probably the *Libra,* cf. Augustine, *Ad Consentium, P.L.* 40, 522, *C.S.E.L.,* Vol. XLI, p. 477.

provinces, at which bishops detected as adherents of Priscillianism, who decline to repudiate its teaching, are to be deposed. He mentions that he has enclosed letters addressed to the bishops of all four provinces, which he desires Turibius to forward to their appropriate destinations. Should, however, a general council prove to be impossible he urges that at least a local synod of the province of *Gallicia* should be called together, and that to this end his correspondent should invite the co-operation of bishops Idatius and Ceponius.[162]

As to the outcome of Leo's letter, we are faced with considerable uncertainty. But probability and such evidence as we possess combine to suggest that, in view of the disturbed political conditions, it proved utterly impossible to assemble a general council on the lines desired by him, and that all that could be done was to circulate the letter among the Spanish episcopate with a request for signatures of approval.[163]

It is disappointing to find that we have so little information as to Leo's relations with the churches of Spain, but perhaps the lack of it is to be explained by the supposition that owing to the political situation of the time such relations were almost impossible. Nevertheless, the one letter which we possess, if genuine, is sufficient to suggest that those churches, like others in the West, looked to the see of Rome for guidance and support and found in Leo a prudent counsellor and a rock of strength. It is even possible that the ultimate triumph of orthodoxy over Priscillianism was hastened by the realization that only the abandonment of the latter could permanently secure the unity of Spanish Christianity with the rest of Western Christendom in communion with the Apostolic see.

[162] *Ep.* 15, 17. "si autem aliquid . . . obstiterit, quominus possit celebrari generale concilium, Galliciae saltem in unum conveniant sacerdotes, quibus congregandis fratres nostri Idatius et Ceponius imminebunt."

[163] Cf. Idatius, *Chronicon,* sub ann. *M.G.H.,* Auct. antiqu., Vol. XI, *Chron. min.,* II, p. 24, "huius (sc. Leo) scripta per episcopi Thoribi diaconem Pervincum contra Priscillianistas ad Hispanienses episcopos deferuntur, inter quae ad episcopum Thoribium de observatione catholicae fidei et de haeresum blasphemiis disputatio plena dirigatur, quae ab aliquibus Gallaecis subdolo probatur arbitrio." On the question of whether or not a council was held Kidd, *History,* Vol. III, p. 374, Batiffol, *Siège Apostolique,* p. 475 supply a negative, and Hefele-Leclercq, *Conciles,* Vol. II, p. 482, Lietzmann, *RE.* Pauly-Wissowa, Vol. XII, pt. 2, col. 1963 a positive answer. It seems possible to exaggerate the value of the evidence of the Council of Braga, Mansi, *Concilia,* Vol. IX, 773.

Additional Note A

THE ORGANIZATION OF THE CHURCH OF GAUL

There can be little doubt that of the various claimants among the cities of Gaul to be the first to possess an organized Christian Church, the city of Lyons (Lugdunum) is to be regarded as the best authenticated. At the end of the second century there is little trace of any other episcopal see in that country[164] and the fact that it was chosen as the place of assembly for an important synod held about sixty years later[165] shows that at that time it must have still remained a place of considerable ecclesiastical significance. As to the source from which its Christianity had been derived, the probability is that it travelled from the East by way of the routes of commerce and, after reaching the port of Marseilles, moved slowly up the valley of the Rhône. So, although it is clear that from an early date there was contact between Gallic Christians and the see of Rome,[166] a contact which was maintained during the succeeding centuries,[167] there is nothing to show that Gaul was more indebted to that see than to any other for its knowledge of the Christian religion.[168]

An important event in its history was the assembly at Arles of a council of representatives from the western churches by the Emperor Constantine I in the year A.D. 316, with the object of settling certain controversies affecting the Church in Africa.[169] Yet apart from the prestige naturally acquired by the church and see of that city as a consequence of such an event, there is no sign as yet that any development was taking place which would assign an undoubted primacy of one see over the rest, still less of any definite demarcation of ecclesiastical provinces subject to the jurisdiction of particular metropolitan bishops. On the contrary, whenever general

[164] Duchesne, *Fastes*², Vol. I, p. 40, but cf. Harnack, *Die Mission und Ausbreitung des Christentums* (1902), pp. 319–22.

[165] Cyprian, *Ep.* 68, 1–3, probably written A.D. 254. The synod was concerned with the alleged Novatianism of Marcian, Bishop of Arles.

[166] Letter of the martyrs of Lyons and Vienne, ap. Eusebius, *H.E.*, 5, 1.

[167] Innocent I, *Epp.* 2 and 6, JK 286, 293.

[168] In spite of Innocent I, *Ep.* 25 (2), JK 311.

[169] On this Council of Arles see Duchesne, *Histoire,* Vol. II, pp. 113f. Its encyclical letter appears in Mansi, *Concilia,* Vol. II, pp. 471ff.; Mirbt, *Quellen*⁵, Nos. 100–4.

synods were summoned, as at Valence (Valentia) in A.D. 375 and at Nîmes (Nemausia) in A.D. 396,[170] the presidency was accorded, not to any particular see, but to the bishop who happened to be senior in respect of consecration, and even at the dawn of the fifth century the respective rights of the more important churches still remained undetermined.

Among the events which tended to accelerate the determination of these questions was the sack of the city of Trêves (Treveri) by the Franks in A.D. 412.[171] Since the time of the reorganization of the Empire by the Emperor Diocletian, Trêves had been one of the chief seats of imperial government in the West, and had been the actual residence of a number of his successors.[172] At the beginning of the fifth century it was still the seat of the Prefecture of the "Gauls." When, however, the city finally succumbed to the successive attacks of the invaders, it was considered expedient to transfer the centre of administration to a less vulnerable spot. The place selected for this purpose was Arles, which in consequence tended to overshadow all others by reason of its political importance.[173] Its strategic value had already been recognized in A.D. 411 by the usurper Constantine, and had been retained as his centre of administration by the Emperor Constantius III, but as yet its ecclesiastical status fell far short of its political eminence.

It happened, however, that the Emperor Constantius, in his determination to stamp out any elements of disloyalty, had deposed Heros, the existing bishop of Arles, and had raised to the see, thus rendered vacant, Patroclus, a creature of his own.[174] This person, who undoubtedly owed his preferment

[170] Caspar, *Geschichte,* Vol. I, p. 288.

[171] On the fall of Trêves see Bury, *Later Roman Empire,* Vol. I, p. 207.

[172] It was the residence of Constantius Chlorus in A.D. 305, cf. Kidd, *History,* Vol. II, p. 64.

[173] The year in which this transference took place is disputed. Bury, *op. cit., ibid.,* holds that it took place immediately after the fall of Trêves A.D. 412, although the *Notitia Dignitatum,* ed. Seeck, Berlin, 1876, which describes the political organization of Gaul up to A.D. 414 still locates the Prefecture in the latter city. In any case it had taken place before the publication in A.D. 418 of the edict *Saluberrima* by Honorius. *M.G.H. Epp.,* Vol. III, p. 17, *Ep.* 13.

[174] The deposition of Heros by Constantius was apparently quite uncanonical. Cf. Prosper, *Chron.,* sub ann. 412. *M.G.H.,* Vol. IX. *Chron. min.,* Vol. I, p. 466. "Eodem tempore Heros vir sanctus et beati Martini discipulus cum Arelatensi oppido episcopus praesideret, a populo

to the standing which he enjoyed in the favour of Constantius, used his position to the advantage of his see, and probably also to the increase of his private fortune.[175] A few years later the see of Rome fell vacant by reason of the death of Innocent I,[176] and it is likely that the influence of the bishop of Arles, who happened to be in Rome, played a considerable part in determining the choice of his successor. Within four days of his consecration the new Pope Zosimus entrusted Patroclus with a letter, addressed to the bishops of Gaul and the *Septem Provinciae,* i.e. the southern provinces, by means of which an extensive sphere of jurisdiction was created for the see of Arles.[177] It cancelled all rights, whatever they were, hitherto enjoyed by the sees of Vienne (Vienna), Narbonne (Narbo) and Marseilles (Massilia) and gave to the see of Patroclus the sole right of consecrating bishops within the three civil provinces of *Viennensis, Narbonensis prima* and *secunda,* and of revising the verdicts of synods within those provinces.[178] It is scarcely surprising that the papal decision was seriously contested by the occupants of two of the sees affected, namely of Vienne and Marseilles, and that a protest on the subject was addressed to the see of Milan as the ecclesiastical centre of northern Italy.[179] The details of this protest and of its subsequent effect are discussed fully in the ensuing notes.

Additional Note B

THE PRIVILEGES OF THE SEE OF ARLES [180]

By means of his famous letter, *Placuit apostolicae,*[181]

eiusdem civitatis insons et nulli insimulationi obnoxius pulsus est, inque eius locum Patroclus ordinatus amicus et familiaris Constantii magistri militum, cuius per ipsum gratia quarebatur, eaque res inter episcopos regionis illius magnarum discordiarum materia fuit."

[175] *Chron. Gall.* 74. *M.G.H.*, Vol. IX. *Chron. min.*, Vol. I, p. 654. "Patroclus Arelatensis episcopus infami mercatu sacerdotia venditare ausus."

[176] March 12th, A.D. 417.

[177] *Ep.* 1, JK 328, dated March 22nd, A.D. 417.

[178] See Additional Note B, *The privileges of the see of Arles.*

[179] See Additional Note C, *The Council of Turin.*

[180] The main sources are the letters of Zosimus, *P.L.* 20, 642f., of which there is a critical edition in *M.G.H. Epp.*, Vol. III, ed. Gundlach. The text given there is cited below.

[181] *Ep.* 1, JK 328. *M.G.H., ibid.*, p. 5.

Zosimus conferred the following privileges on Patroclus, bishop of Arles, A.D. 411–26.

(1) Patroclus is to possess the sole right of issuing *litterae formatae* to members of the clergy desiring to proceed to Rome or elsewhere.[182]

(2) He is to enjoy the sole right of consecrating bishops to churches within the civil provinces, *Viennensis, Narbonensis prima* and *secunda*.[183]

(3) His authority as diocesan bishop is to embrace the parishes of Cytharista and Gargaria, and to include other areas which had formerly belonged to the civil jurisdiction of his see city.[184]

(4) He is to possess jurisdiction in regard to all ecclesiastical causes which may arise within the above mentioned provinces, except where their gravity appears to demand reference to the Roman see.[185]

It is sometimes suggested that the effect of these privileges was to make him "Papal Vicar over the whole of Gaul, with powers like those of the bishop of Thessalonica in eastern Illyricum."[186] This statement appears to be open to question on the following grounds. In the first place it is clear that according to the award of Zosimus, the jurisdiction of the see of Arles was limited to three provinces of southern Gaul, while the authority of the see of Thessalonica embraced the whole of the Prefecture of eastern Illyricum.[187] Nor was the status of the two sees precisely equivalent, for however extensive the powers granted to

[182] *Ep.* 1, 1. "Si quis ex qualibet Galliarum parte . . . ad nos Roma venire contendit . . . non aliter proficiscatur, nisi metropolytani Arelatensis episcopi *formatas* acceperit." The *litterae formatae* were a kind of ecclesiastical passport, somewhat equivalent to the modern *Celebret*. See Fabricius, *Arch. f. Urk. Forsch.*, Vol. IX (1924), pp. 39ff.

[183] *Ibid.*, 2, "praecipuam, sicuti semper habuit, metropolytanus episcopus Arelatensium civitatis in ordinandis sacerdotibus teneat auctoritatem, Viennensem, Narbonensem primam et Narbonensem secundam provincias ad pontificium suum revocet."

[184] *Ibid.*, 3, "quae sibi (sc. eccl. Arel.) Cytharista et Gargariam parocias in territorio suo sitas incorporari iure desiderat. . . . quascumque parrocias in quibuslibet territoriis etiam extra provincias suas antiquitas habet, intemerata auctoritate possideat."

[185] *Ibid.*, "ad cuius notitiam, si quid illic negotiorum emerserit, referri censuimus nisi magnitudo causae etiam nostrum requirat examen."

[186] Kidd, *History*, Vol. III, p. 104.

[187] See Chap. VIII and Additional Note.

Arles might be, it still remained no more than a metropolitan bishopric: Thessalonica, on the other hand, held a position superior to that of the metropolitans and for that reason analogous to the status of one of the "greater churches," such as Antioch. But in any case it is almost inconceivable that even so short-sighted an administrator as Zosimus would have created an extensive sphere of jurisdiction in the West, such as might easily have become as resentful of papal control as the Church of Africa.[188] For while it might be said that there was good reason from the point of view of the Roman see to establish a Vicariate in Illyricum as a safeguard against the development and extension of the jurisdiction claimed by the see of Constantinople, it could not be argued that there was any similar reason for creating a like institution in Gaul. If any comparison can be drawn, therefore, between the primacy awarded to the see of Arles by Zosimus and the Illyrian vicariate the former ought to be described rather as a travesty than as a copy of the latter.[189]

Nevertheless there is this much to be said in favour of the plan devised by Zosimus, especially if we take into account the disturbed political and social condition of Gaul at this time. In the first place the provision regarding the issue of *litterae formatae* was undoubtedly a safeguard against the intrusion of clerics of doubtful origin and uncertain qualifications, in search of more secure and perhaps more lucrative employment, into the dioceses of southern Italy. Besides, in speaking of his award to Patroclus as an arbitrary act, one is bound to recognize that in the earlier decades of the fifth century the organization of the churches of southern Gaul was still in a fluid state, and it is always possible that even Zosimus himself did not intend the arrangement to be a permanent one.[190] At the same time, as we shall see, it was not Zosimus, but the

[188] Cf. Kidd, *History,* Vol. III, pp. 103–14; pp. 162–5; and Caspar, *Geschichte,* Vol. I, pp. 349–73.

[189] Cf. Caspar, *Geschichte,* Vol. I, p. 608, "Das Zosimus Privileg für Arles aber ist in jeder Hinsicht nicht ein Seitenstück, sondern ein Zerrbild der illyrischen Vikariatspolitik."

[190] Cf. his own words, *Ep.* 1, 1, JK 428, "hoc autem privilegium, formatarum sancto Patroclo . . . meritorum eius specialiter contemplatione concessimus."

synod of the province of Milan which actually modified the original scheme, at least so far as the jurisdiction of the see of Arles was concerned.

No doubt it may be conjectured that the originator of this scheme scarcely imagined that it would be carried into effect without encountering some opposition, yet it is unlikely that he anticipated what a dangerous form that opposition would take. How this came about must now be explained.

Armed with the papal award in his favour, Patroclus returned to Arles and doubtless lost no time in making its provisions known. Immediately the three metropolitans, Simplicius of Vienne, Proculus of Marseilles and Hilary of Narbonne, finding themselves deprived by a stroke of the pen of whatever metropolitical rights they had hitherto exercised or claimed, determined to make a stand against such evident usurpation. Hilary took the reasonable, though actually unprofitable, step of addressing a direct protest to the Roman see, and vigorously asserted the claim of his see to metropolitan status, on the basis of the provisions included in the canons of Nicaea. The only effect of his protest was to evoke an emphatic reproof [191] from Zosimus, who did not hesitate to suggest that such powers as Hilary had exercised had been obtained by dishonest means. As a result the latter must have abandoned any further attempt to assert his rights as hopeless, since we hear no more of him for some years. His fellow metropolitans, however, adopted a different course of action, and addressed their protest, not to Zosimus but to the see of Milan. Among the considerations which must have suggested this step was not only the proximity of that see and numerous precedents for such an appeal,[192] but the fact that Proculus had received a summons to appear before the synod of the Roman see on the charge of contempt for the recent decision.[193]

To judge from the events which followed it seems that their appeal met with a favourable reception; doubtless bishop Venerius of Milan scarcely viewed with favour the creation of a strong centre of ecclesiastical influence so close to the borders

[191] *Ep.* 6, JK 332, dated September 26th, A.D. 417.

[192] There were appeals to Milan by Spanish bishops in A.D. 381, 395 and 400; and by Gallic bishops in A.D. 390 and 405. Cf. Duchesne, *Fastes*², Vol. I, pp. 92f.

[193] Zosimus, *Ep.* 5, JK 334, dated September 29th, A.D. 417.

of his province, and was ready to support any attempt which was intended to prevent its realization. So for the convenience of the parties concerned the Milanese synod was summoned to meet, not in Milan itself, but in Turin (Augusta Taurinorum), where its proceedings opened on September 22nd, A.D. 417.[194] In addition to the members of the synod and the appellants, a representative of the see of Arles appears to have been present, in order to protect the interests of that see in regard to certain other questions which had arisen. As to the order of procedure, the appeal of the sees of Vienne and Marseilles was taken first, and after hearing the evidence the synod resolved to uphold their claims to metropolitan status within the provinces of *Viennensis* and *Narbonensis secunda* respectively.[195] This was clearly tantamount to a direct negative to the provisions made by Zosimus.

Meanwhile, it appears, information was conveyed to Rome as to the proceedings at Turin, and within seven days a further note was sent off by Zosimus to Patroclus,[196] in which the writer confirmed all the powers assigned to the see of Arles in his earlier letter, and violently attacked Simplicius and his colleague. While this was taking place, the synod seems to have reconsidered its former attitude to the see of Arles and eventually decided to effect a compromise, in virtue of which the province of *Viennensis* was divided between that see and the see of Vienne.

Possibly Zosimus came to the conclusion that his best policy was to acquiesce in this decision.[197] Nevertheless he still maintained an attitude of uncompromising hostility to Proculus, whom he probably regarded, not without justification, as the instigator of the whole affair.[198]

[194] On the date assigned here to this synod see Additional Note C, *The date of the Council of Turin,* and Babut, *Concile de Turin,* Paris (1904), where the whole question is treated at length.

[195] *Conc. Taurin.,* Canons 1 and 2. However the synod only guaranteed metropolitan rights to Proculus during his lifetime. As he was already sixty-six years of age, it was to be expected that a reconsideration of the whole matter would soon become possible. Actually he survived for a further eleven years. Cf. Duchesne, *Fastes²,* Vol. I, p. 274.

[196] *Ep.* 5, JK 334.

[197] The letter *Revelatum nobis est,* JK † 335 is, however, of doubtful authenticity. Cf. Babut, *op. cit.,* pp. 243ff., and Duchesne, *Fastes²,* Vol. I, p. 162.

[198] Cf. *Ep.* 7, JK 333, which should be dated after the synod, perhaps in November, A.D. 417. Cf. Babut, *op. cit.,* pp. 18f.

On the death of Zosimus in the latter part of A.D. 418, his successor, Boniface I, waited for four years or so before taking any action.[199] In a letter written soon after his election and addressed to the bishops of southern Gaul [200] he names Patroclus first in the address: on the other hand, in writing subsequently to Hilary of Narbonne,[201] he makes it clear that he no longer regards the jurisdiction of the see of Arles as embracing the province of *Narbonensis prima,* and encourages Hilary to assert his metropolitan rights, in accordance with the Nicene canons.[202]

When the question of the privileges of the see of Arles next arose, Patroclus was dead and Boniface I had been replaced by Celestine I. Perhaps Honoratus, the new bishop of Arles, regarded the provisions of Zosimus as still in force. In any case Celestine made it clear that in his view the status of Arles was not higher than that of other metropolitan sees.[203]

It is clear from what has been said that it is inaccurate and misleading to speak of a papal vicariate in Gaul created by Zosimus. For the origin of this institution, as it later came to exist, we have to look, not in the correspondence of Zosimus or of Leo, but in that of Hilary I and his immediate successors.

Additional Note C

THE DATE OF THE COUNCIL OF TURIN [204]

Until comparatively recently it has been generally supposed that the Council of Turin, to which we have already referred in connexion with the controversies affecting the churches of southern Gaul, is to be assigned to the early years of the fifth

[199] The delay is probably to be explained by the confused internal conditions prevailing in the Church of Rome at this time.

[200] *Ep.* 3, JK 349.

[201] *Ep.* 12, JK 362.

[202] Nevertheless the imperial government still treated the privileges of Patroclus as unabated, cf. *Cod. Theod.,* Const. Sirm. 6, ed. Mommsen-Meyer, p. 911.

[203] *Ep.* 4, JK 369, dated July 6th, A.D. 428.

[204] The canons of the council are given in Mansi, *Concilia,* Vol. III, 859, cf. *Neues Archiv.,* Vol. XVII (1891), p. 187. Mommsen, in his edition of *Chron. min.,* Vol. I, *M.G.H.,* Auct. antiqu., Vol. IX, p. 577, n. 1, argues that the place of the council was actually, not Turin, but Tours. But Babut, *Concile de Turin,* pp. 2–7 has shown from internal evidence that the case for Turin is irrefutable. Cf. also Duchesne, *Comptes rendus de l'Academie des inscriptions,* Ser. IV, Vol. XIX (1891), p. 369, and *Revue historique,* Vol. LXXXVII (1905), p. 279.

century.[205] Recently, however, some historians have shown a decided preference for a later date.[206]

The evidence for a council held at Turin appears in a synodal letter, which bears the following heading:

"Sancta synodus quae convenit in urbe Taurinatium die X Kalendas octobris [Honorio Augusto XI et Constantio II consulibus] fratribus dilectissimis per Gallias et quinque provincias constitutis." [207]

In addition there are two allusions in the letters of Zosimus to a council held there, at which charges were brought forward by Lazarus, later (*c.* A.D. 408) bishop of Aix, against Britius, successor of Martin in the see of Tours.[208]

Now, as no year is given in the heading of the synodal letter, it is reasonable to infer that it belongs to the same council as the one mentioned by Zosimus, and therefore to assign to it a date between A.D. 397, the earliest for the death of Martin, and A.D. 408, the consecration of Lazarus.[209] Moreover, internal evidence, such as the mention of the Felician controversy [210] and of the "letters of Ambrose and of the bishop of the Roman Church lately brought," [211] tends to confirm this date.

Yet there are other facts to be considered. In the first place the two first canons deal solely with questions of jurisdiction in the provinces of *Narbonensis secunda* and *Viennensis*. Secondly, it is with the same or with like questions that a number of Zosimus' letters are concerned.[212] Apart from these sources we have no evidence whatever of such disputes in southern Gaul. Hence it is natural to suppose that both refer to the same group of events. Is there any occurrence which offers a fitting explanation of their origin? The answer to this question appears to be comparatively simple. No

[205] Among those who support an early date are Duchesne, *Fastes*², Vol. I, p. 91, and Hefele-Leclercq, *Conciles,* Vol. II, p. 85.

[206] e.g. Babut, *Concile de Turin,* where the case in favour of A.D. 417 for this council is argued at length, and Bury, *Later Roman Empire,* Vol. I, p. 363, n. 4.

[207] Mansi, *op. cit.,* Vol. III, 859. Babut, *op. cit.,* p. 223. The date in brackets is his conjecture.

[208] *Ep.* 3, 3, JK 330; *Ep.* 4, 2, JK 331, both dated A.D. 417.

[209] Neither of these dates has been fixed with absolute certainty. See Babut, *op. cit.,* p. 24.

[210] *Conc. Taurin.,* Can. 6. Cf. Duchesne, *Histoire,* Vol. II, pp. 529ff.

[211] *Ibid.*

[212] *Ep.* 1, JK 328; *Ep.* 3, JK 330; *Ep.* 4, JK 331, etc.

serious difficulties arose regarding questions of jurisdiction till after the intrusion of Patroclus into the see of Arles by Constantius III in A.D. 411,[213] and the transference of the headquarters of the Gallic Prefecture to that city, following the sack of Trêves by the Franks in A.D. 412.[214] In the early years of the fifth century the city of Vienne was still the seat of the Vicarius, governing the civil diocese of the *Septem Provinciae,* and Arles was of little secular importance. It was and remained a simple *colonia.*[215] If its ecclesiastical prestige had developed since the days of Constantine I it had as yet no reason to regard itself as more than a suffragan see owing allegiance to the metropolis of Vienne.[216]

On the other hand, once the seat of the Prefecture had been transferred from Trêves to Arles,[217] it is scarcely too much to say that the relative importance of Arles and Vienne was completely reversed. Instead of Vienne, Arles now became the secular capital of the *Septem Provinciae,* and it was not long before an imperial edict formally confirmed its position as such.[218]

As to the references which occur in the sources mentioned to questions arising in regard to Britius of Tours [219] and Felix of Trêves, [220] and appear to preclude the adoption of the later date, it is not impossible that owing to confusion between the two names "Turinorum" and "Taurinorum" some matter which belongs to an earlier synod, possibly held at Tours, has here been accidentally incorporated.[221]

[213] Prosper, *Chronicon,* sub ann. 412. *M.G.H.,* Auct. antiqu., Vol. IX, p. 466.

[214] Bury, *Later Roman Empire,* Vol. I, p. 207 gives A.D. 412 for the final destruction of Trêves. Duchesne, *Fastes*², Vol. I, p. 105, n. 1 holds, without justification, that this transference took place as early as A.D. 407. Cf. Mommsen, in *M.G.H.,* Auct. antiqu., Vol. IX, p. 553 (A.D. 413).

[215] It had been created a *colonia* by Julius Caesar. Ausonius, *Opusc.* 11, 10. Teubner, p. 148, suggests that by the end of the fourth century Arles was second in importance to Trêves itself and designates it as "Gallula Roma." Yet we are bound to make some allowance for the fact that Arles was the poet's native city.

[216] Probably Leo is correct when he asserts that before the episcopate of Patroclus Arles had never enjoyed any metropolitical rights whatever.

[217] See above n. 214.

[218] Cf. the edict *Saluberrima,* April 17th, A.D. 418 in *M.G.H. Epp.,* Vol. III, p. 13. *Ep.* 8.

[219] Zosimus, *Ep.* 3, 3, JK 330 and *Ep.* 4, 2, JK 331.

[220] *Conc. Taurin.,* Can. 6.

[221] Babut, *Concile de Turin,* p. 25, says, however, "Il y a donc deux conciles de Turin."

Additional Note D

THE LETTER "QUALI PERTINACIA"[222]

Babut in his *Concile de Turin*[223] has devoted considerable space to proving the authenticity of this letter in face of a contrary opinion which has prevailed among historians since the seventeenth century. Hitherto its spurious character has been generally accepted on the following grounds:

(1) The title,[224] which in its present form appears to treat *Viennensis* as distinct from the provinces of Gaul.

(2) The use of the word *archiepiscopus*,[225] for which there is no other authority in the Latinity of this period.

(3) The expression *per vicarios suos*,[226] which has been usually understood here to refer to bishops of the Roman see; a usage which is not otherwise found earlier than the pontificate of Felix III.[227]

(4) The consular date, "Valentiano Augusto III et Anieno consulibus," which as it stands is an impossible one.[228]

(5) The fact that the letter occurs in a collection, the pseudonymous nature of which as a whole is generally acknowledged.[229]

Though M. Babut himself is constrained to admit that the hand of an editor has tampered with the title, and with the text of the letter as well, he rightly points out that the conception of the Bishop of Rome as Vicar of St. Peter is found at least as early as the writings of Leo,[230] and draws attention to the fact that the letter in question actually does little to strengthen the forger's own case. Had the latter really

[222] JK † 446, dated January 6th, A.D. 450.
[223] App. III (ii), pp. 265ff.
[224] "fratribus per Gallias et Viennensem provinciam episcopis constitutis."
[225] "sitque redintegratum Viennensi Archiepiscopo privilegium et ius antiquum."
[226] "moderationem, quam in potestate per vicarios suos semper exhibet."
[227] *Ep.* 2, 3, JK 592.
[228] Babut, *op. cit.*, pp. 271f., suggests "Nonio" instead of "Anieno," which would give A.D. 445 as the year.
[229] *Epistolae Viennenses*, ed. Gundlach. *M.G.H. Epp.*, Vol. III, pp. 84ff. The collection is believed to have been made early in the twelfth century under the auspices of Guido, Archbishop of Vienne, who later became Pope Callistus II, A.D. 1119–24, for the express purpose of upholding the claims of the see of Vienne.
[230] e.g. *Serm.* 3, 3 and 4, "cuius vice fungimur."

intended to produce a fabricated document, he would have served his purpose far better if he had drawn extensively upon the admittedly genuine letter, *Divinae cultum,*[231] of which he must presumably have been aware.

No doubt there were other letters addressed by Leo to the Gallic bishops which are not now to be found among the collection of his universally recognized writings,[232] but we are bound to feel that Babut had not wholly succeeded in justifying his contention. Apart from other difficulties already mentioned the one unsurmountable obstacle lies in the fact that the Latinity of this piece tolerates such expressions as "iustum esse videmus" or "sitque redintegratum," when Leo himself would surely have written "iustum esse videtur" and "redintegretur" respectively in these passages. Nor does "terminos antiquos canonica prolatione fundatos" seem a possible phrase in a really authentic letter of his.

To what canonical pronouncement does the author refer? And if any such had existed why was it not cited in the subsequent dispute between Ravennius and Nicetas?[233] It seems, therefore, that in spite of Babut's ingenuity the case for the genuineness of *Quali pertinacia* cannot be regarded as proved beyond doubt.

Additional Note E

THE TROPHIMUS SAGA

The name of Trophimus plays an interesting if elusive part in the history of the church of Arles. He is first mentioned in connexion with that church in the course of Zosimus' first letter relating to the authority of that see, after which his name recurs in two later letters by the same author,[234] with reference

[231] Leo, *Ep.* 10, JK 407.

[232] As appears to be implied by *Ep.* 66, 2, JK 450, "de receptione privilegii auctoritate iam nostrae dispositionis utatur."

[233] See further the Ballerini, *P.L.* 54, 1235f.

[234] *Ep.* 1, JK 328, "ad quam (sc. Arelatensium urbem) primum ex hac sede Trophimus summus antistes, ex cuius fonte totae Galliae fidei rivulos acceperunt, directus est."

Ep. 5, JK 334, "contra statuta patrum et s. Trophimi reverentiam, qui primus metropolitanus Arelatensis civitatis ex hac sede directus est . . . metropolitanis Arelatensis civitatis episcopus iam inde a Trophimo

to the same subject. In all three passages the general argument is the same. The role of Trophimus is represented as that of a missionary bishop despatched by the Roman see, presumably from Rome itself, with a view to the conversion of Gaul to Christianity and the establishment of the Church in those provinces. It is, of course, an essential point in Zosimus' argument that Trophimus chose the city of Arles as the centre of his missionary activity, and further that he came with all the prestige and authority of an emissary of the see of Rome. A variant tradition is mentioned by Gregory of Tours,[235] who mentions a Trophimus among a group of seven bishops despatched to Gaul by the Roman see in the reign of the Emperor Decius.[236] This, however, is not inconsistent with the statements of Zosimus, since the latter gives no indication of the period to which he refers.

We next come across the name in the petition of a group of Gallic bishops in support of the claims of Ravennius, bishop of Arles, to metropolitical authority,[237] thirty years or so after the above mentioned correspondence of Zosimus. By this time the tradition just described has undergone some development. Trophimus is no longer just an emissary of the Roman see, but a personal disciple of the Apostle St. Peter himself.[238] It is perhaps unfortunate that the authors do not cite any authorities in support of their statements. Yet even here we can trace the survival of a variant belief, since they assert in one place that Trophimus was the legate of the Apostles,[239] and not exclusively of St. Peter.

ordinationis seriem temporibus roboratam inviolabile in utraque Narbonensi et Viennensi auctoritate possideat."

Ep. 6, 1, JK 332. "Nam sanctae memoriae Trophimus sacerdos, quondam ad Arelatensem urbem ab apostolica sede transmissus."

Ep. 6, 2, "per s. Trophimi reverentiam."

[235] *Historia Franc.* 1, 28. *P.L.* 71, 175.

[236] i.e. about A.D. 260. It should be remembered that the Bishop of Arles at the time when Cyprian wrote his *Ep.* 68 was not Trophimus but Marcian.

[237] *Inter Leon. Epp.*, No. 65. *P.L.* 54, 879.

[238] *Ibid.*, 2, "prima inter Gallias Arelatensis civitas missum a beatissimo *Petro* apostolo sanctum Trophimum habere meruit sacerdotem . . . in sancto Trophimo primitias nostrae religionis prima (sc. Arel. civitas) suscepit. . . ."

[239] *Ibid.* "S. Trophimum ab apostolis missum sacerdotem habere meruisset." We may guess that "apostolis" alluded to SS. Peter and Paul.

It is strange perhaps to find this same variant persisting as late as the ninth century. Yet it appears once again in the so-called Martyrology of Florus as an entry for December 29th, where we read, "Trophimi episcopi, discipuli apostolorum." [240] Apart from these references there are two later documents in which the name occurs; the first of which is a tenth century catalogue of the bishops of Arles, attached to a sacramentary of the church of Arles [241] and the second, a lectionary of the eleventh century containing a series of lives of the earlier occupants of that see, and likewise incorporating an episcopal list.[242] It is noteworthy, however, that in both cases the name of Trophimus proves to be an addition made by a later hand.[243] Yet there can be no doubt that by that date the tradition was firmly established, as is shown by the fact that the principal church at Arles, dedicated to his honour, was erected in that century.[244]

There can be no doubt that the Trophimus of later tradition was generally believed to be identical with the disciple of St. Paul mentioned in a number of passages in the New Testament.[245] The question arises as to whether, if the identification be justified, we can attach any value whatever to the later story. Obviously we cannot *a priori* exclude the possibility that a disciple of St. Paul should have travelled westwards, and even perhaps settled at Arles. But this is the most we can say. To assert that he was formally commissioned by St. Peter to undertake the conversion of Gaul, as is implied by the petition in favour of the church of Arles, is not easy to reconcile with the position occupied by the churches of Lyons and Vienne in the second century, and the comparative obscurity of the church of Arles until the beginning of the fifth century. On the other hand, the known connexion between the churches of southern Gaul and Asia Minor [246] strengthens the possibility that the Trophimus saga has enshrined in a mass of legend a tiny fragment of historical fact.

[240] *Martyrologes historiques,* ed. Quentin, p. 451.
[241] This work is dated *c.* A.D. 900. Cf. Duchesne, *Fastes*², Vol. I, p. 250.
[242] Duchesne, *op. cit.,* Vol. I, p. 251.
[243] Id. *ibid.,* p. 251, n. 2.
[244] Tyrrell-Green, *French Church Architecture,* pp. 24f., et *al.*
[245] Acts xx. 4, xxi. 9; 2 Tim. iv. 20.
[246] For this connection see e.g. Kidd, *History,* Vol. I, p. 60.

Additional Note F

THE IMPOSITION OF THE HAND

The ceremony of the Imposition of the Hand was a characteristic feature according to the practice of the Western churches, not only of Confirmation,[247] but of the administration of Penance [248] as well. In view of this fact it has been disputed whether the use of the phrase by Leo is intended to denote the former or the latter.

The following are the relevant passages in which the phrase occurs:

(1) With reference to those who have been rebaptized by heretics.

(i) "Only by the remedy of Penance, and by the Imposition of the bishop's Hand may they receive reconciliation in communion." [249]

(ii) "Let that only be conferred which was lacking there (sc. in the rite administered by heretics) that the grace of the Holy Ghost may be obtained by the Imposition of the bishop's Hand." [250]

(2) With reference to those who have been baptized once only and that by heretics.

(i) "They are to be confirmed by the Imposition of Hands with the invocation of the Holy Ghost only, because they have received merely the 'form' of Baptism without the grace of sanctification." [251]

(ii) "They are not to be baptized, but are to be united to

[247] Tertullian, *De Bapt.* 8; Augustine, *Serm.* 324, *P.L.* 38, 1447; *Conc. Illiber.*, Can. 38.

[248] Cyprian, *Ep.* 71, 2; *Conc. Carthag.* (A.D. 348), Can. 1, "ut per manus impositionem in poenitentiam ecclesiae reconcilietur"; Innocent I, *Ep.* 24, JK 310, "eorum (sc. haereticorum) laicos sub imagine poenitentiae et sancti Spiritus invocatione per manus impositionem suscipimus." Vigilius, *Ep.* 2, 3, JK 907 clearly distinguishes the two; "non per illam impositionem manus quae per invocationem sancti Spiritus operatur, sed per illam qua poenitentiae fructus acquiritur, et sanctae communionis restitutio perficitur." Here he refers to those who have been rebaptized by heretics.

[249] *Ep.* 159, 6, "non nisi per poenitentiae remedium, et per impositionem episcopalis manus communionis recipiant unitatem."

[250] *Ep.* 166, 2, "hoc tantum quod ibi defuit conferatur, ut per episcopalem manus impositionem virtutem sancti Spiritus consequatur."

[251] *Ep.* 159, 7, "sola invocatione Spiritus sancti per impositionem manuum confirmandi sunt, quia formam tantum baptismi sine sanctificationis virtute sumpserint."

Catholics by the Imposition of the Hand with the invocation of the grace of the Holy Ghost, which they could not receive from heretics." [252]

(3) With reference to the clergy.

"It is unknown to the custom of the Church . . . that they should receive the remedy of Penance through the Imposition of the Hand." [253]

It is perfectly clear that in the last passage (3) the writer refers to Penance. In considering the rest it is important to remember that Leo would not normally think of Baptism as liturgically distinct from Confirmation. Hence in most cases he naturally would regard those who had been baptized by Catholics as having received Confirmation at the same time. (1) (i) must therefore refer to Penance. (1) (ii), probably refers to the special case of those who, although baptized by Catholics, had not at the same time received the sacrament of Confirmation. On the other hand, since he insists that though heretical Baptism is sufficient as a "form," the "Confirmation" which may have followed it is inoperative, and therefore the subject of such a rite must receive the Imposition of the Hand. It is evident that the phrase in (2) (i and ii) must refer to Confirmation.

Additional Note G

PRISCILLIANISM

It is by no means easy to arrive at the truth in regard to the teaching and practice of Priscillianism, mainly because much of the information which we now possess only reaches us from orthodox sources, and as such may often be unduly

[252] *Ep.* 167, 18, "baptizandi non sunt: sed per manus impositionem, invocata virtute Spiritus sancti, quam ab haereticis accipere non potuerunt."

[253] *Ibid.*, 2. "Alienum est a consuetudine ecclesiastica ut . . . ii pro crimine aliquo suo per manus impositionem remedium accipiant poenitendi." It may be observed that with one exception (*Ep.* 159, 7) the singular "manus" is used. The use of the plural in that case may be explained as a reference to the action of more than one bishop. It is not irrelevant to mention that Confirmation with the *right hand only* appears to have been the usual practice, and is explicitly ordered in the modern *Pontificale Romanum.* The same practice seems to be enjoined by the rubric contained in the *Order of Confirmation* given in the *Book of Common Prayer.*

prejudiced and therefore not wholly trustworthy, while on the other hand we cannot always be sure that those writers, who give a more favourable view, may not have deliberately suppressed or concealed some of its more objectionable features. And the possibility must be faced that owing to a certain confusion existing in the minds of contemporaries, between the tenets and observances of this sect and of Manichaeism, our authorities have occasionally ascribed to the former what was strictly only appropriate to the latter.[254]

The following passage derived from Philastrius of Brescia, a contemporary writer, may be regarded as typical of the opinion on the subject prevailing in orthodox circles.

"There are other heretics," he says, "among the Gauls and Spaniards who resemble ascetics: they follow at one and the same time the most pernicious sects of the Gnostics and Manichaeans, and do not hesitate to preach the same doctrines as they, separating married couples by their advice, and observing in regard to food a form of abstinence, though this practice had been left by Christ, as an act of His grace, to the choice of individuals, not as a precept of the Law, but to enable them to progress in the way of heaven . . . they do this in order that, by despising certain food, men may come to regard it as evil, and thus to believe that it has not been given by God to man for his nourishment, but is the creation of the Devil: those who think thus are obliged to show that creation is not the work of God but of the Devil, and by this falsehood have seduced many souls."[255]

Although Philastrius emphasizes the rigorist tendencies of the sect he does not suggest that it was part either of the founder's or of his disciples' intention to form a separate organization from the Church. On the contrary all our

[254] Among the principal sources are Sulpicius Severus, *Chronicon*, 2, 46–51; id. *Dialogi*, 3, 11–13; Orosius, *Commonitorium*, *C.S.E.L.*, Vol. XVIII, pp. 151ff.; *Conc. Caesaraug*, Mansi, *Concilia*, Vol. III, 633; *Conc. Bracar.* (A.D. 563), Mansi, *op. cit.*, Vol. IX, 773. See also works attributed to Priscillian in *C.S.E.L.*, Vol. XVIII, and Art. *Priscillian*, in *D.C.B.* and *D.T.C.* Tixeront, *Histoire*, Vol. II, pp. 229–41; Duchesne, *Histoire*, Vol. II, pp. 529–50; Kidd, *History*, Vol. II, pp. 229–310; Leclercq, *L'Espagne chrétienne*, c. 3; Homes-Dudden, *Ambrose*, pp. 224–40; Babut, *Priscillien*. The relation between Priscillian's own doctrine and that of his later adherents is discussed by Burn in *C.Q.R.*, Vol. LXXIV (April, 1912), No. 147.

[255] *De Haeresibus*, 84. *P.L.* 12, 1196.

evidence goes to show that their deliberate policy was not to compete with, but to permeate "official" Christianity,[256] and by that means to change its character from within in accordance with their ideas. But a rigorism which went so far as to stress the necessity for vegetarianism, continence and frequent fasting was bound to excite criticism, more especially when it was combined with the practice of periodical segregation, and an unwholesome devotion to the use of books rejected by ecclesiastical authority.[257] It is possible, however, that what chiefly gave rise to suspicion and indignation among their more normal contemporaries was their habit of taking part in eucharistic worship, while refraining from actual communion.[258] When we add to these peculiarities the element of mystery which seemed to shroud their behaviour, the intimate knowledge of which was jealously guarded by a rigid *disciplina arcani,* it is scarcely surprising that the Church felt that in dealing with Priscillianism she had to reckon with an enemy which was all the more dangerous because it was elusive.

[256] Priscillian himself was elected to the see of Avila. Cf. Sulpicius, *Chron.*, II, 47. *C.S.E.L.*, Vol. I, p. 100.

[257] Priscillian, *Tractatus* 3, *De fide (et) de apocryphis,* ed. *C.S.E.L.*, Vol. XVIII, pp. 44ff.

[258] *Conc. Caesaraug.*, Can. 3. Mansi, *Concilia,* Vol. III, 633f. It is improbable that they received the sacrament, but did not consume it, with the idea of using it privately at home. Had such a practice been usual, it would scarcely have escaped mention. Private reservation had altogether ceased by the end of the fourth century. Cf. Freestone, *The Sacrament Reserved,* pp. 35–50.

CHAPTER VIII

THE VICARIATE OF EASTERN ILLYRICUM

It is clear from the evidence which we have considered hitherto that so far as the churches of the West were concerned the prestige and authority of the Roman see during Leo's pontificate had nothing to fear. It issued injunctions and gave rulings on disputed points, and few questioned its right to do so. Yet as one travelled eastwards from Italy, a certain difference became perceptible. It was not that any church dreamed of denying to the successor of St. Peter a primacy of honour, the first place, in fact, among Catholic bishops. On the contrary, such a primacy was recognized in the Eastern provinces of the Empire no less than in the West, and, what is more, it was regarded as natural to have recourse to him, as well as to other bishops of the " greater churches " of the West, whenever support in the face of tyranny, secular or ecclesiastical, seemed to be needed. At the same time there was a difference in the outlook of the Eastern churches as compared with those of the West, which arose not only from divergencies in thought and language, but also from the recent creation of a new imperial capital, Constantinople or New Rome, on the shores of the Bosporus. Here resided the Eastern Emperor and the Eastern imperial court, and for this reason, if for no other, it was inevitable that its bishop, so closely in contact with the imperial government, would come to acquire a position which might seriously challenge the dignity of the Apostolic see of the West. For however much that see might be respected, convenience and accessibility would unite to commend the Eastern capital as a natural resort for the satisfaction of personal claims or the settlement of points in dispute.

To one, such as Leo, who, as we have seen, claimed before all else to be the guardian and interpreter of canon law, such a development would suggest a serious menace to the unity and peace of the Catholic Church, since it appeared that the day might come when even the decisions of the Roman see itself might be called into question. Hence, especially in his relations with the churches of the Prefecture of Eastern Illyricum, territory which lay almost midway between these two rival centres of influence,[1] we find evidence of the measures taken by him for the security of order and discipline, at least so far as those churches were concerned, and for the exclusion of intervention on the part of the see of Constantinople.

The civil and ecclesiastical capital of the Prefecture at this time was Thessalonica, the see of which naturally enjoyed a certain precedence among its neighbours, and for that reason was regarded by the Roman see as a suitable representative of its authority.

When we come to examine the measures taken by Leo to meet these dangers we find that there is little that is new in them. As far back as the time of Damasus I the Roman see realized that it was in the interests of orthodoxy and ecclesiastical discipline to maintain the closest possible relations with the see of Thessalonica.[2] It was left to his successor Siricius to make of these relations something like a permanent institution. The measures taken by him were renewed and developed by later pontiffs, such as Innocent I, Boniface I and Xystus III.[3] Hence when Leo was approached by Anastasius, bishop of Thessalonica, to obtain, as it appears, a confirmation of the powers accorded to him by papal authority in the prefecture of Eastern Illyricum, he found it necessary to do little more than renew the commission which had already been assigned to Anastasius by his predecessor. But in doing so he was extending, though probably unconsciously, and rendering more permanent the jurisdiction of his see among churches which lay far beyond the bounds of the Roman metropolitical province, an extension which demanded something more than the Nicene canons for its justification.

[1] While its limits are seldom precisely defined it is to be presumed that its area corresponded with that of the Prefecture of Eastern Illyricum, i.e. the civil "dioceses" of Dacia and Macedonia. It should be remembered that the "diocese" of Thrace, in which Constantinople itself was situated, was part of the "diocese of the East."

[2] *Epp.* 5 and 6, JK 237, 238.

[3] See Additional Note, *The development of the Illyrian Vicariate.*

In his reply to Anastasius[4] Leo begins by expressing his satisfaction at receiving letters such as that of his correspondent, since by their means, he says, he can learn where vigilance is needed, and may know what to approve as being in accord with his wishes, and what abuses to censure.[5] Referring to Anastasius' petition, he formally renews the commission previously granted by Pope Siricius to Anysius, an earlier bishop of Thessalonica, and reminds him that its purpose is for the maintenance of canonical discipline, while commending to him the example set by Anysius in the execution of his charge.[6] Since a considerable part of the responsibility committed to the bishops of Thessalonica was concerned with the consecration of bishops, the sections which follow, dealing with this subject, are of considerable importance.

After urging once again the need for due observance of canon law, Leo insists that no consideration is to be paid to favour, ambition or simony,[7] but that only those candidates for the episcopate are to be approved who have been tested by a period of service in the lower grades of the ministry,[8] and who conform to the Pauline and scriptural requirements in regard to matrimony,[9] so that even one who has been

[4] *Ep.* 6, JK 404, dated January 12th, A.D. 444.

[5] *Ibid.*, 1, "in quibus (sc. epistolis) de statu ecclesiarum certiores effecti, ad exercendae sollicitudinis vigilantiam officii nostri consideratione compellimur."

[6] *Ibid.*, 2, "petitio . . . ut tibi quoque a nobis, sicut decessoribus tuis, per Illyricum cum nostra vice propter custodiam regularum auctoritas praestaretur, praebentes assensum, nostra adhortatione compellimus ut nulla dissimulatio, negligentia nulla proveniat circa ecclesiarum regimen per Illyricum positarum, quas dilectioni tuae vice nostra committimus, beatae recordationis Siricii exemplum secuti, qui sanctae memoriae Anysio praedecessori tuo bene de apostolica sede tunc merito, et rebus post sequentibus approbato, certa tum primum ratione commisit: ut per illam provinciam positis quas ad disciplinam teneri voluit, ecclesiis subveniret." For the motive of Siricius see Additional Note below, p. 193.

[7] *Ibid.*, 3. "Divinae legis sanctio veneranda et canonum specialius decreta serventur. Per commissas tibi provincias tales Domino sacerdotes, quibus sola vitae et clericalis ordinis suffragantur merita, consecrentur. Nihil gratiae personali, nihil ambitioni, nihil redemptis permittas licere suffragiis."

[8] *Ibid.*, "per longum vitae tramitem disciplinis ecclesiasticis, qui ordinati fuerint imbuantur." For this prescription cf. *Ep.* 12, 4, JK 410 and *Conc. Nic.*, Canon 2. Siricius, *Ep.* 4, JK 259, "catholicum episcopum et vita et moribus probatum, secundum nicaenae synodi statuta vel ecclesiae romanae, clericum de clero meritum ordinari," on which see Batiffol, *Siège Apostolique*, p. 247, n. 4; Innocent, *Ep.* 37, 5, JK 314; and Celestine, *Ep.* 4, 3 (4), JK 369.

[9] Cf. Lev. xxi. 13f.; 1 Tim. iii. 2; *Ep.* 4, 2, JK 402; *Ep.* 10, 6, JK 408; *Ep.* 12, 3, JK 410.

married before Baptism and subsequently remarried is to be excluded.[10] Then come the special privileges of the see of Thessalonica in relation to the metropolitan bishops of Illyricum:

"Let no bishop be consecrated throughout those churches (sc. of Eastern Illyricum) without yourself being consulted, for by this means it will be possible for there to be carefully considered decisions as to those suitable for election, so long as your consideration of the matter, beloved, is to be anticipated. Let any bishop who shall be consecrated by one of the metropolitans contrary to our injunction without your knowledge realize that, so far as we are concerned, his status has no validity, and that those who have presumed to act in this way will have to give account for their usurpation. Notwithstanding, as the following authority is entrusted to each metropolitan, namely that within his own province he shall have the right of consecration, so it is our will that the metropolitans should be consecrated by you, only after making a carefully considered and thoughtfully weighed decision. For while it is fitting that every bishop to be consecrated should be well tried and pleasing to God, it is our wish that those who, as we shall hear, are going to preside over their fellow bishops belonging to their province, shall excel their fellows."[11]

[10] *Ep.* 6, 3, "ne se quisquam credat posse ad sacerdotium pervenire, qui uxorem antequam Christi gratiam consequeretur accepit, qua deficiente alteram post baptismum coniunxerit sibi." Perhaps it was being represented that at Baptism the whole of the individual's past life was effaced. Cf. Innocent, *Ep.* 17, 2 (4), JK 303.

[11] *Ibid.*, 4. "Nullus te inconsulto per illas ecclesias ordinetur antistes: ita enim fiet ut sint de eligendis matura iudicia, dum tuae dilectionis examinatio formidetur. Quisquis vero a metropolitanis episcopus contra nostram praeceptionem praeter tuam notitiam fuerit ordinatus, nullam sibi apud nos status sui esse noverit firmitatem, eosque usurpationis suae rationem, qui hoc praesumpserint, reddituros. Singulis autem metropolitanis sicut potestas ista committitur, ut in suis provinciis ius habeant ordinandi, ita eos metropolitanos a te voluimus ordinari, maturo tamen et decocto iudicio. Quamvis omnes antistites probatos et Deo placitos deceat consecrari, hos tamen praecellere volumus, quos praefuturos his qui ad se pertinent consacerdotibus noverimus." The powers conceded by Leo to Anastasius were therefore:

(1) The right to be consulted in regard to any episcopal consecration within the Prefecture.

(2) The right to consecrate metropolitans,

and as we shall see in c. 5,

(3) The right to settle minor points in dispute at synods.

From the subject of episcopal consecrations the writer turns to synods. He insists that any bishop who is summoned to attend shall not refuse to do so.[12] The value of these assemblies lies, he says, in the opportunity which they provide not only for the determination of disciplinary questions, but also for the preservation of unity and for the adjustment *sic.* of disputes. If, however, a matter of importance *(causa maior)* arises, which cannot be decided by Anastasius himself, a report on it is to be transmitted to himself, so that in accordance with ancient custom and due respect for the Apostolic see he may give a decision. He adds that in any case he is to be notified at once of any appeals to the see of Rome.[13]

The concluding section of the letter contains an interesting allusion to the subject of the ordination of priests and deacons. It seems that in the provinces of Eastern Illyricum, while the custom of consecrating bishops only on Sunday was being followed, some bishops were in the habit not only of ordaining priests and deacons on any day of the week, but were neglecting to take care that their candidates had already served in an inferior ministry. Leo insists that canon law on these points must be duly observed in future.[14]

[12] *Ibid.*, 5. "Ad synodum quisquis fratrum fuerit evocatus occurrat, nec sanctae congregationi se deneget."

[13] *Ibid.* "Si qua vero causa maior evenerit, quae a tua fraternitate illic praesidente non potuerit definiri, relatio tua missa nos consulat: ut . . . rescribamus: ut cognitioni nostrae pro traditione veteris instituti et debita apostolicae sedis reverentia, nostro examine vindicemus: ut enim auctoritatem tuam vice nostra te exercere volumus, ita nobis quae illic componi non potuerint, vel qui vocem appellationis emiserit, reservamus." For this treatment of a *causa maior* cf. Innocent I, Ep. 2, 3, JK 286. "Illic praesidente" may imply that Leo contemplated a single synod for the whole Prefecture. The whole passage evidently alludes to the Sardican legislation, esp. Canons 3, 4, 7, 10 (vers. lat.). Mirbt, *Quellen*, No. 122.

[14] *Ibid.*, 6, "solos episcopos tantum diebus Dominicis ordinari: presbyteros vero et diaconos, circa quos par consecratio fieri debet, passim quolibet die dignitatem officii sacerdotalis accipere: quod contra canones et traditionem Patrum usurpatio corrigenda committit . . . : ita ut per longa temporum curricula, qui sacerdos vel levita ordinandus est, per omnes clericalis officii ordines provehatur." "Diebus Dominicis" cf. *Epp.* 9, 2, JK 406; 10, 6, JK 407. "Par consecratio" must mean equal solemnity, not the same rite. Different rites already appear in the *Apostolic Tradition* of Hippolytus, ed. Easton, pp. 35–8. "Officii sacerdotalis" here evidently embraces the three "major" orders. It is not clear to what "canons" Leo refers, perhaps only to existing Roman custom. For his insistence on the qualifications of candidates cf. *Ep.* 12, 4; *Conc. Nic.*, Can. 2, and Celestine I, *Ep.* 4, 3 (4), JK 369.

While thus confirming the status accorded by his predecessors to the see of Thessalonica, Leo also took care to acquaint the Illyrian metropolitans with his action.[15] He asks them first of all to welcome the arrangements which he has made in their joint interests and to safeguard them from unwarrantable interference. Better to be protected against usurpation, he says, than to be obliged to get rid of it.[16] He goes on to explain that in virtue of the responsibility for all the churches which rests upon him as a consequence of the primacy granted to St. Peter,[17] he has made Anastasius his vicegerent and charged him to act as a sentinel to be on the watch for any illicit occurrence.[18] Obedience to him, therefore, is equivalent to obedience to the Roman see.

The section which follows is devoted to a restatement of the qualifications of candidates for the ministry in terms similar to those which we have already noticed in the letter to Anastasius.[19] Then come his rulings in regard to synods, especially as to the jurisdiction of the bishop of Thessalonica and as to his position as a channel of correspondence with the Roman see.[20] Leo's frequent insistence on the duty of

[15] *Ep.* 5, JK 403, dated January 12th, A.D. 444.

[16] *Ibid.*, 1. "Sit itaque dilectioni vestrae . . . dulcis et iucunda praeceptio, quam de sedis apostolicae auctoritate, servata charitatis gratia, manare noscatis. . . . Cautius enim usurpationibus, antequam tententur, obsistere quam quae usurpata fuerint vindicare." The allusion here is plainly to intrusions into the affairs of the Prefecture on the part of the see of Constantinople.

[17] *Ibid.*, 2. "Et quia per omnes ecclesias cura nostra distenditur, exigente hoc a nobis Domino, qui apostolicae dignitatis beatissimo apostolo Petro primatum fidei suae remuneratione commisit, universalem ecclesiam in fundamenti ipsius soliditate constituens, necessitatem, sollicitudinis quam habemus, cum his qui nobis collegii charitate iuncti sunt sociamus." On this passage see Chap IV, pp. 68f.

[18] *Ibid.* "Vicem itaque nostram . . . Anastasio, secuti eorum exemplum, quorum nobis recordatio est veneranda, commisimus et ut sit in speculis, ne quid illicitum a quoquam praesumitur, iniunximus: cui in his quae ad ecclesiasticam pertinent disciplinam, ut dilectio vestra pareat, admonemus." As to the relation between the powers assigned by Leo to the see of Thessalonica and those assigned by his predecessors, see Additional Note, *The Development of the Illyrian Vicariate.* It can well be imagined that Leo wished the eyes of his "sentinel" to be turned mainly in one direction.

[19] *Ibid.*, 3, i.e. married once only and that to a virgin, with the same provision that marriage before baptism is a real marriage. Notice that here Leo includes in his injunction priests and deacons as well as bishops. Cf. *Ep.* 6, 3 above, and Innocent I, *Ep.* 17, 1 (2), JK 303.

[20] *Ibid.*, 4. "Eius nobis relatione, si quid ad nos referendum fuerit, innotescat."

obedience to Anastasius seems to betray some fear lest the authority assigned to his "Vicar" may not be willingly recognized by some of the provinces.[21] Next he reaffirms the rights of Anastasius in regard to the consecration of bishops, and emphasizes his responsibility for informing the Roman see as to the condition of the Illyrian churches.[22] In the concluding section he repeats his instructions regarding the incidence of a *causa gravior,* namely that it is to be referred by Anastasius to the Roman see for decision,[23] and ends his letter by expressing the wish that the metropolitan shall send an acknowledgment of its receipt.

This was in A.D. 444. How far the arrangements prescribed by Leo were readily accepted throughout the Prefecture is open to some doubt. Possibly Anastasius showed himself deficient in tact in the exercise of his authority or neglectful of his duty as a "sentinel." Anyhow, scarcely two years later a petition was addressed to the Roman see by a group of Illyrian metropolitans, who were evidently dissatisfied. We may infer that it included a complaint against the treatment which they were receiving from Anastasius.

In replying to the letter of the petitioners[24] Leo repeats[25] that he has committed the care of the churches within the Illyrian Prefecture to Anastasius, and that he is to determine

[21] *Ibid.,* "ita enim vos ad illum pertinere volumus, ut ad vos provinciarum vestrarum pertinent sacerdotes." The difference in status between Anastasius and the metropolitans is evidently in Leo's view the same as that which obtains between them and their suffragans. For a further expansion of this point see *Ep.* 14, 11 below, pp. 186ff.

[22] *Ibid.,* 5. "Anastasium de ordinando antistite volumus consulatis. Cui metropolitani episcopi consecrationem statuimus reservari. . . . Ipsum vero secundum definita canonum hoc vestra dilectio nostris epistolis admonitum esse cognoscat, ut de statu ecclesiarum vestrarum certiores subinde sua relatione nos faciat." There are general allusions throughout this letter to the Sardican legislation and to the letters of earlier popes. For references see above, p. 179.

[23] *Ibid.,* 6. "Si quae vero causae graviores vel appellationes emerserint, eos sub ipsius relatione ad nos mitti debere decrevimus, ut nostra secundum ecclesiasticum morem sententia finiatur." For references see Additional Note below.

[24] The names mentioned in Leo's address are Senecio, Carosus, Theodulus, Lucas, Antiochus and Vigilantius. It is possible that Senecio is to be identified with the person of that name mentioned by Innocent I, *Ep.* 13, 3, JK 300. Quesnel, *Notae ad Ep. XIII, P.L.,* 54, 1314 quotes L. Holsten's identification of the sees of these bishops, viz., Senecio of Scodra, Lucas of Dyrrhacium, Vigilantius of Larissa.

[25] *Ep.* 13, JK 409, dated January 6th, A.D. 446.

any *causa maior* which may arise between bishops which cannot be settled within their own provinces.[26] In the most serious questions *(causa maxima)* a general synod is to be called by Anastasius, at which two or three representatives from each province shall attend.[27] Those who decline to do so without adequate reason for absence shall be liable to trial.

Leo now takes the metropolitans themselves to task on the score of a *relatio* just received from Anastasius. The papal "Vicar" appears to have reported that episcopal consecrations were being performed irregularly by the metropolitan of the province of Achaia,[28] and that clergy were being accepted by bishops from another diocese without due authorization. Referring to this report he says that no metropolitan is to consecrate any bishop in future without the approval of the clergy and laity of the church concerned.[29] As to the "migration" of clergy he insists that no cleric shall be

[26] *Ep.* 13, 1, "ut si quae maiores inter episcopos causae sunt quae in provinciis suis nequeant terminari, ad eius notitiam referantur, et eodem arbitrio sub divini timore iudicii componantur."

[27] *Ibid.*, 2, "invitati fratres in causis maximis et quae intra provincias suas finiri nequeant terminandis, si nulla gravi necessitate retinentur, fraternum studium pro ecclesiae utilitate non denegent; maxime cum moderatio nostra providerit, ut non frequens, neque pro levibus causis conveniendi necessitas indicatur: et binos ternosue episcopos de singulis, provinciis adesse sufficiat, ut leve fiat paucis, quod multis esset onerosum." "Moderatio nostra" may refer to *Ep.* 14, 10, or rather perhaps to a letter addressed to Anastasius but not preserved, such as the one referred to in c. 4 of this letter. For the provision that "two or three" bishops shall represent each province cf. *Ep.* 16, 7, JK 414. It may be noticed that what is called a *causa maior* in *Ep.* 6, 5 is here described as a *causa maxima.* On the authority of the "Vicar" in regard to a *causa maior* see p. 179.

[28] *Ibid.*, 3, "fratris nostri sollicita relatione cognovimus Achaiae provinciae metropolitanum illicitas et constitutis Patrum nostrisque auctoritatibus interdictas ordinationes saepe celebrasse, illudque suis ausibus addidisse, ut Thespiensibus invitis et repugnantibus incognitum et ante non visum episcopum consecraret." The Ballerini, *P.L.* 54, 665 suggest that the metropolitan of Achaia was Erasistratus of Corinth, who was present at the second Council of Ephesus, A.D. 449. "Constitutis Patrum" must refer to such canons as *Conc. Sard.*, Can. 5 and perhaps to the letters of earlier popes, e.g. Celestine I, *Ep.* 4, 6, JK 369. Cf. Leo, *Epp.* 10, 26, JK 407; 14, 5, JK 411. The city of Thespia was in Boeotia. It is noteworthy that the charge of consecrating bishops unknown to the local church was one of those which his opponents made against Hilary. Cf. *Ep.* 10, 6, JK 408, and Chap. VII.

[29] *Ibid.* "Nulli prorsus metropolitano hoc licere permittimus, ut suo tantum arbitrio sine cleri et plebis assensu quemquam ordinet sacerdotem; sed eum ecclesiae Dei praeficiat, quem totius civitatis consensus elegerit." The allusion of "apostolicae constitutionis" later in the section may be to 1 Tim. iii. 7.

accepted by another bishop without a written *cessio,* signed by the bishop to whom he belongs.[30] Leo concludes by expressing the hope that his rulings "may sink more deeply into their hearts," with a view to the preservation of the unity of the spirit in the bond of peace, and that the instructions which he has sent to Anastasius may be duly observed.[31]

The suggestion contained in this letter, that some feeling of unrest existed among the bishops of Macedonia and Achaia is confirmed by the tone of the next communication addressed to Anastasius.[32] Leo begins by urging that he should duly consider the nature of the commission which he has received and to this end goes on to define afresh the powers of his "Vicar." It is plain that he is much concerned lest Anastasius may be misusing his authority, and the cause of this anxiety makes itself apparent in the course of his letter.[33] Recently an appeal had been presented to the Roman see in person by Atticus, metropolitan of the province of *Epirus vetus,* against the treatment which he had received at Anastasius' hands. This had led to a formal investigation at Rome in the presence of representatives of the see of Thessalonica, and had led Leo to believe that the complaints against his "Vicar" were fully justified.

However, before referring to this matter Leo redefines the "vicarial" authority. He points out that although he has given Anastasius authority to act as his representative, yet the latter should be able to recognize when he ought to suspend judgment in the expectation of a papal verdict.[34] But in any case Anastasius ought to realize that in the administration of justice he should use self-restraint and consideration for the offender. Quoting 1 Tim. v. 1, he writes:

[30] *Ibid.,* 4, "ut nullus episcopus alterius episcopi clericum sibi audeat vindicare, sine illius ad quem pertinet cessione, quam tamen evidentia scripta contineant." Leo probably alludes to *Conc. Nic.,* Can. 15; *Conc. Sardic.,* Can. 18 and 19.

[31] The letter containing these instructions is probably one that is lost and not *Ep.* 14, q.v.

[32] *Ep.* 14, JK 411. The letter is undated but probably belongs to A.D. 446.

[33] *Ibid.,* 1. *P.L.* 54, 670.

[34] *Ibid.,* 1. "Nam cum maiora negotia et difficiliores causarum exitus liberum tibi esset sub nostra sententiae expectatione suspendere, nec ratio tibi nec necessitas fuit in id quod mensuram tuam excederet deviandi." As we shall see the affair in which Anastasius was involved concerned a bishop of metropolitan rank, and therefore should have been referred to the Roman see as a *causa maior* (or *maxima*).

"So if self-restraint is due in relation to all inferior members (sc. of the Church), according to the Apostle's injunction, how much more rightly is it to be shown to our brethren and fellow bishops? So that while admittedly there may be shortcomings in persons of ministerial rank, yet there is a place more for tenderness than for severity, more for encouragement than for anger, more for charity than for discipline in such cases. But those 'who seek their own rather than the things of Jesus Christ' (Phil. ii. 21) may more readily forsake this principle, and because it gives them pleasure to lord it over their subjects rather than to show them consideration, rank gives rise to pride, and that which is provided for the maintenance of concord only causes harm. To have to write thus causes me much mental distress. In fact I feel myself to be inculpated when I find that in your excess you have transgressed the rules committed to you. Even if you cared little about your own reputation, at least you ought to have considered my prestige; otherwise our judgment might be held to be responsible for the things of which your own caprice is guilty. Brother, you should read our letters over again, and study the documents issued by the prelates of the Apostolic see to your predecessors, and find (if you can) whether what you have done presumptuously (as we learn) was enjoined either by me or by my predecessors." [35]

Words such as these show how deeply the writer was hurt to have heard that a trusted colleague had failed him, seem-

[35] *Ep.* 14, 1. "Quae moderatio si quibus cumque inferioribus membris ex apostolica institutione debetur, quanto magis fratibus et coepiscopis nostris sine offensione reddenda est? Ut licet nonnunquam accidant, quae in sacerdotalibus sunt reprehendenda personis, plus tamen erga corrigendos agat benevolentia quam severitas, plus cohortatio quam commotio, plus charitas quam potestas. Sed ab his qui, 'quae sua sunt' quaerunt, 'non quae Jesu Christi' (Phil. ii. 21) facile ab hac lege disceditur, et dum dominari magis quam consulere subditis placet, honor inflat superbiam et quod provisum est ad concordiam, tendit ad noxam: quod, ut necesse habeamus ita dicere, non de parvo animi dolore procedit. Meipsum enim quodammodo in culpam trahi sentio, cum te a traditis tibi regulis immodice discessisse cognosco. Qui si tuae existimationis parum diligens eras, meae saltem famae parcere debuisti; ne quae tuo tantum facta sunt animo, nostro viderentur gesta iudicio. Relegat fraternitas paginas nostras, omniaque ad tuos emissa maiores apostolicae sedis praesulum scripta percurrat, et vel a me vel a praecessoribus meis inveniat ordinatum, quod a te cognovimus esse praesumptum." The last sentence is, of course, bitterly ironical.

ingly by abusing his privileges. Yet in spite of his disapproval of Anastasius' conduct, Leo's tone is rather that of disappointment than of indignation. If he counsels self-restraint, he is wise enough to exhibit the same virtue himself.

In the succeeding paragraph he explains the cause of his disappointment. It arose from the appeal which had been presented to him by bishop Atticus, to whom we have already referred. Apparently Anastasius had summoned him to attend a synod at Thessalonica, and Atticus had pleaded illness in excuse for his absence.[36] The papal "Vicar," however, regarding the plea as implying a refusal to obey his summons, as he himself admitted in the counter petition presented by his delegates, had thereupon procured the attendance of Atticus by force after invoking the civil aid of the Prefect himself.[37] It seems that in spite of his infirmity the unfortunate bishop had been dragged out of his church and compelled to travel over rough roads and in the depth of winter: in fact so exacting was the journey that some of the bishop's companions were alleged to have succumbed to its effects. Arrived at Thessalonica he was immediately compelled by Anastasius to sign on the spot a solemn promise of obedience to the see of the papal "Vicar" as to his spiritual overlord.[38]

The Pope then goes on to inquire why his "Vicar" could

[36] *Ibid.,* "De quo (sc. Attico) nihil amplius iudicaveras quam quod evocatus adesse differret, et excusationem infirmitatis obtenderet."

[37] *Ibid.* "Unde deplorationibus supradicti haec verba epistolae tuae testimonium praebuerunt, et per hoc quod non est tacitum nudatum est illud quod silentio fuerat adopertum, aditam scilicet Illyrici praefecturam et sublimissimam inter mundanos apices potestatem in exhibitionem insontis antistitis incitatam; ut missa exsecutione terribili, quae omnia sibi officia publica ad effectum praeceptionis adiungeret, a sacris ecclesiae aditis, nullo vel falso insimulatus crimine, extraheretur sacerdos, cui non ob molestiam aegritudinis, non ob saevitiam hiemis darentur induciae." Notice the use of the technical "sublimissimus" as a title one of prefectorial rank. The province of *Epirus vetus* is about one hundred and fifty miles distant from Thessalonica. On the procedure of "exhibitio" see *Cod. iur. Justin,* IX, 3, 3, ed. Krueger, Vol. II, p. 370.

[38] *Ibid.,* "quodque consensum suum etiam scripturae professione signasset, ut de illo non aliud a nobis posset intelligi, quam proprii arbitrii et spontaneae devotionis fuisse, quod venerat, quodque chartulam de oboedientiae sponsione conscripserat, in cuius tamen chartulae mentione signum prodebatur iniuriae." It is a pity that we have nothing to show what sort of a case Anastasius was able to make out in reply, but it is always possible that some of the Illyrian metropolitans were proving refractory, and that he was unfortunate in choosing Atticus in order to make an example of him to the rest.

not have waited till he received special papal instructions on the case, and suggests sarcastically that it was because he knew well enough that, if he had done so, Atticus would have been treated with reasonable consideration. If there had been any other charge against the bishop it should have been mentioned; but the absence of any such charge in Anastasius' letter proved that none could have been made.[39]

Finally he delivers an emphatic rebuke:

"We have entrusted you, beloved, with our vicegerency, so that you may be called to bear a share in our responsibility, not to possess the fullness of our authority. Therefore, while we rejoice abundantly at the things which you have faithfully performed, we are grieved by what you have done amiss. It is your duty, after experience of a number of cases, to take more care, and to be on your guard so that all occasion of scandal may be removed from the churches of the Lord which we have entrusted to you. Let the primacy of your see have the first place in those provinces and unrestrained tyranny be abandoned." [40]

The remainder of the letter consists of a series of definitions bearing on various disciplinary questions affecting the welfare of the churches of Illyricum.

(1) On the preservation of the rights of metropolitans subject to the "Vicar" of Thessalonica.

Metropolitans are to retain unimpaired their rights secured to them by canon law, as long as they avoid either negligence or presumption.[41]

[39] *Ep.* 14, 1, "cum etiam si tale aliquid mereretur, exspectandum tibi fuerit quid ad tua consulta rescriberem. Sed, ut video, bene de moribus meis existimasti, et quam civilia pro conservanda sacerdotali concordia responsurus essem, verissime praevidisti."

[40] *Ibid.* "Vices enim nostras ita tuae credidimus charitati, ut in partem sis vocatus sollicitudinis, non in plenitudinem potestatis. Unde sicut multum nos ea quae a te pie sunt curata laetificant, ita nimium ea quae perperam sunt gesta contristant. Et necesse est, post multarum experimenta causarum sollicitius prospici et diligentius praecaveri, quatemus per spiritum charitatis et pacis, omnia materia scandalorum de ecclesiis Domini quas tibi commendavimus auferatur, praeeminente quidem in illis provinciis episcopatus tui fastigio, sed amputato totius usurpationis excessu."

[41] *Ibid.*, 2. "Secundum sanctorum Patrum canones . . . metropolitanos singularum provinciarum episcopos . . . ius traditae sibi antiquitus dignitatis intemeratum habere decernimus." Evidently Leo alludes to *Conc. Nic.*, Can. 4 and 6.

(2) On persons to be excluded from promotion to the episcopate.

One to be consecrated to a vacant see must be neither a layman nor a neophyte, nor the husband of a second wife, nor of a widow.[42]

(3) On the continence of subdeacons.

While all outside the ranks of the clergy are free to beget children, carnal marriage may not be allowed to subdeacons but, like bishops, priests and deacons, they are to abstain from carnal knowledge of their wives in order to show an example of the chastity of perfect continence.[43]

(4) On inviting the clergy and people to give consent in an episcopal election.

Leo states the principle that all shall have a voice in the election of their chief pastor.[44] But if there be disagreement, the decision shall rest with the metropolitan so long as the person chosen be not imposed on a church to whom he is unknown, against its will.[45]

(5) On reference to the bishop of Thessalonica within his vicariate regarding an episcopal consecration.

Metropolitans are to consult Anastasius regarding a candidate chosen by the clergy and people of a local church, so that his approval may confirm the consecration. But unnecessary

[42] *Ibid.*, "is qui ordinandus est . . . non laicus, non neophytus, nec secundae coniugis sit maritus, aut qui unam quidem habeat vel habuerit, sed quam sibi viduam copularit." The text is evidently corrupt here. Possibly we should read "sed qui unam quidem habeat vel habuerit, nec qui sibi viduam copularit." For these conditions see *Conc. Nic.*, Can. 1 and references given above, pp. 87, 107, 118 and *Ep.* 4, 2, JK 402, etc.

[43] *Ibid.*, 4. Leo quotes 1 Cor. vii. 29 and adds, "Quod si in hoc ordine (sc. subdiaconatu) qui quartus a capite est, dignum est custodiri, quanto magis in primo aut secundo, vel tertio servandum est, ne aut levitico, aut presbyterali honore aut episcopali excellentia quisquam idoneus aestimetur, qui se a voluptate uxoria necdum frenasse detegitur." The extension of the obligation to continence to the subdiaconate is new. Siricius, *Ep.* 1, 9, JK 255 had formally exempted this order. For other references to the subject of clerical continence see p. 146, n. 125. It should be observed that it is continence, not celibacy, that is in question here.

[44] *Ibid.*, 5, "ille omnibus praeponatur quem cleri plebisque consensus concorditer postularit." For other references to episcopal elections see p. 118, n. 26.

[45] *Ibid.*, "metropolitani iudicio is alteri praeferatur, qui maioribus et studiis iuvatur et meritis: tantum ut nullus invitis et non petentibus ordinetur." The right of the metropolitan to intervene is evidently based on *Conc. Nic.*, Can. 4.

delay is to be avoided.[46] In the event of a metropolitan see falling vacant, the suffragans of the province are to meet in the metropolis, and when the wish of the local clergy and laity has been ascertained, the best of the priests or deacons of that church, whose name has been referred for approval to the see of Thessalonica, is to be consecrated. Again there should be no delay in giving effect to an election rightly performed.[47]

(6) On attendance at provincial synods.

Leo endorses the rules laid down by canon law, namely that there should be two each year to determine disputes which may arise between the different order of the Church.[48] But should a *causa de maioribus peccatis* occur, the metropolitan concerned is to inform Anastasius who, if after bringing the parties together he cannot settle the matter, is to refer the case to the Roman see.[49]

(7) On the prevention of episcopal translations.

If a bishop succeeds in obtaining his translation from a less important to a more important place, he shall be removed from the see which does not belong to him and lose his own as well.[50]

(8) On "migratory" clerics.

No one is to accept without leave of the bishop concerned a cleric from another church. If the cleric has migrated with-

[46] *Ep.* 14, 6, "quodque in provincia bene placuit, scire te faciat (sc. metropolitanus), ut ordinationem rite celebrandam tua quoque firmet auctoritas."

[47] *Ibid.*, "provinciales episcopi ad civitatem metropolim convenire debebunt, ut omnium clericorum atque omnium civium voluntate discussa, ex presbyteris eiusdem ecclesiae, vel ex diaconis optimus eligatur, de cuius nomine ad tuam notitiam provinciales referant sacerdotes . . . sicut enim justas electiones nullis dilationibus volumus fatigari. . . ."

[48] *Ibid.*, 7. "De conciliis . . . non aliud indicimus quam sancti Patres salubriter ordinarunt: ut scilicet bini conventus per annos singulos habeantur." This ruling is based directly on *Conc. Nic.*, Can. 5.

[49] *Ibid.* "Si forte . . . de maioribus (quod absit) peccatis causa nascitur, quae provinciale nequeat examini definiri; fraternitatem tuam de totius negotii qualitate metropolitanus curabit instruere, ut si coram positis partibus nec tuo fuerit res sopita iudicio, ad nostram cognitionem, quidquid illud est, transferatur." For other references to the treatment of a *causa maior* see above. The ruling given here differs slightly but only superficially from the one which appears in *Ep.* 6, 5.

[50] *Ibid.*, 8. "Si quis episcopus . . . administrationem loci celebrioris ambierit et ad maiorem se plebem quacumque ratione transtulerit a cathedra quidem pelletur aliena sed carebit et propria." This ruling is derived from *Conc. Nic.*, Can. 15 which, however, does not provide that the offender is to be deprived of his original see. Cf. *Conc. Sard.*, Can. 14 (vers. lat.).

out such leave to another church of the same province, the metropolitan shall compel him to return to the church to which he belongs, but if he has gone outside the province Anastasius himself shall determine what is to be done.[51]

(9) On summoning bishops by Anastasius.[52]

Anastasius is not to summon bishops without real cause. But if a *causa maior* arise it shall suffice that two bishops from each province, delegated by their respective metropolitans, shall attend, provided that they shall not be detained more than fifteen days after the appointed date of meeting.[53]

(10) On consulting the Roman see, should a difference of opinion arise between the Bishop of Thessalonica and the synod.

In a case where the synod disagrees with Anastasius on any matter to be determined, a full report together with the minutes of the proceedings is to be sent to the Roman see.[54]

Then follows an important statement on the subject of Church organization. Starting from St. Paul's metaphor of difference of function of the various members within the human body (1 Cor. xii. 12) he writes:

"The unity of the whole body makes it share health and beauty as a whole; moreover this unity of the whole body (i.e. of the Church) demands unanimity, and requires above all concord among bishops. For although they share the same importance their rank is not the same in each case; even

[51] *Ibid.*, 9. "Alienum clericum, invito episcopo ipsius, nemo suscipiat, nemo sollicitet. . . . Itaque si intra provinciam res agitur, transfugam clericum ad suam ecclesiam metropolitanus redire compellet. Si autem longius recessit, tui praecepti auctoritate revocabitur." Cf. *Conc. Nic.*, Canons 15 and 16, and *Conc. Sard.*, Canon 18 (vers. lat.). The latter provision is, of course, peculiar to Leo. Possibly it is aimed at a growing practice of taking up residence at Constantinople.

[52] *Ibid.*, 10. "De episcoporum a metropolita vocatione." The title is evidently corrupt and should probably read "De episcoporum ab Anastasio vocatione."

[53] *Ibid.*, "si causa aliqua maior exstiterit ob quam rationabile ac necessarium sit fraternum advocare conventum, binos de singulis provinciis episcopos, quos metropolitani crediderint esse mittendos, ad fraternitatem tuam venire sufficiat, ita ut a praestituto tempore non ultra quindecim dies qui convenerint retardentur." For this provision cf. *Ep.* 13, 2, JK 409, etc. The caution against undue delay may be derived from *Conc. Sard.*, Can. 15 (vers. lat.).

[54] *Ibid.*, 11. "Si autem in eo quod cum fratribus tractandum definiendumve credideris diversa eorum fuerit a tua voluntate sententia, ad nos omnia sub gestorum testificatione referantur." Cf. *Ep.* 6, 4, JK 404.

among the most blessed apostles, in spite of their having a similar office, there was a certain difference in regard to authority; and while all received the same call, it was given to one to be pre-eminent over the others. On this model there has arisen a difference between bishops, and by an important canon care has been taken lest all should claim everything for themselves, so that in each province there should be one whose opinion should rank first among those of his brethren: and further that certain bishops established in the more important cities should accept a more extensive responsibility, and that through them the care of the universal Church should centre in the one see of Peter, and that it should in no way be dissociated from its head. Whosoever therefore finds himself set over others let him not take it amiss that another is preferred to himself; rather let him offer the same obedience which he expects of others."[55]

If this letter actually belongs to the year A.D. 446 we must suppose, in default of any evidence as to the interval, that some three years or so elapsed before there was any further communication between Leo and his "Vicar." When Leo writes again, it is to express his satisfaction that Anastasius had

[55] *Ep.* 14, 11. "Connexio totius corporis unam sanitatem, unam pulchritudinem facit: et haec connexio totius quidem corporis unanimitatem requirit, sed praecipue exigit concordiam sacerdotum. Quibus cum dignitas sit communis, non est tamen ordo generalis: quoniam et inter beatissimos apostolis in similitudinem honoris fuit quaedam discretio potestatis; et cum omnium par esset electio, uni tamen datum est ut caeteris praeemineret. De qua forma episcoporum quoque est orta distinctio, et magna ordinatione provisum est ne omnes sibi omnia vindicarent; sed essent in singulis provinciis singuli, quorum inter fratres haberetur prima sententia; et rursus quidam in majoribus urbibus constituti sollicitudinem susciperent ampliorem, per quos ad unam Petri sedem universalis ecclesiae cura conflueret, et nihil usquam a suo capite dissideret. Qui ergo scit se quibusdam esse propositum, non moleste ferat aliquem sibi esse praelatum; sed oboedientiam quam exigit, etiam ipse dependat." It is to be noticed that Leo here almost adopts the Cyprianic idea, *De Unitate,* 4 and 5, yet with a significant alteration. Instead of "sed exordium ab unitate proficiscitur, ut ecclesia Christi una monstretur," he writes, "uni tamen datum est ut caeteris praeemineret." The phrase "in maioribus urbibus" may be compared to "qui maiores diocheseos tenes." *Conc. Arelat., Ep. ad Silv.,* on which see Caspar, *Geschichte,* Vol. I, pp. 582f. Innocent I, *Ep.* 24, 2, JK 310 and Boniface I, *Ep.* 15, 5, JK 365 held different views from the above principle. The implication of Leo's argument is that all the "greater churches," Alexandria, Antioch and Constantinople were no less than Thessalonica subject to the obedience of the Roman see. For the gradual development of this idea see Additional Note A to Chap. V, pp. 74ff., *The Evolution of the Petrine privileges.*

been prevented from attending the council held at Ephesus in A.D. 449.[56] A short time after this Anastasius must have died and his place was taken by Euxitheus. No record remains of any correspondence between the Roman see and the new bishop, apart from the mention of his name together with those of other Illyrian bishops in the course of the address at the head of an encyclical letter on the subject of the dogmatic definition of the council of Chalcedon.[57] With this letter the evidence as to Leo's relations with the Illyrian vicariate comes to an end.

The foregoing study suggests that in his dealings with the Illyrian episcopate Leo was considerably embarrassed by lack of tact or actual aggressiveness on the part of Anastasius. For in spite of all that the papacy could do to establish a "sentinel" over the East, the Illyrian churches showed an ever-increasing tendency to follow the lead given them by the see of Constantinople, and a corresponding reluctance to accept the authority of the see of Rome without question, even in matters of doctrine.[58] A typical example of the closer liaison between those churches and the bishop of the eastern capital is to be found in the attempt made by Anatolius to obtain support for the policy represented by the "twenty-eighth canon" of Chalcedon.[59] But the real test of the structure created by the papacy came some twenty years later, when Pope Felix III excommunicated Acacius, a successor of Anatolius.[60] The fact that the Illyrian episcopate went over to the side of Acacius "as one man"[61] showed that, whatever precautions were taken, they were of little avail to prevent the gradual absorption of Illyricum within the Constantinopolitan orbit. Nevertheless the ultimate failure of those precautions cannot be fairly credited to Leo. His sole objective there, as elsewhere, was the maintenance of canonical discipline, and it was only natural that he should regard its maintenance as closely bound up with implicit obedience to the injunctions of

[56] *Ep.* 47, JK 440, dated October 13th, A.D. 449.
[57] *Ep.* 150, JK 525, dated September 1st, A.D. 457.
[58] Cf. the attitude of the Illyrian bishops to certain passages in Leo's "Tome," cf. Chap. XII, p. 292, n. 19, and Mansi, *Concilia,* Vol. VII, 105C.
[59] *Ep.* 117, 5, JK 493.
[60] *Ep.* 6, 2, JK 599, dated July 28th, A.D. 484.
[61] Duchesne, *Origines* (1889), p. 40, but cf. JK 617.

the Papacy. It was not his fault that the convenient adaptability of Constantinople proved more attractive than the unbending loyalty to principle of the Roman see.

Additional Note

THE DEVELOPMENT OF THE ILLYRIAN VICARIATE

The year A.D. 379 is an important landmark in the political history of the provinces of Eastern Illyricum, for in that year the two "dioceses" of Dacia and Macedonia were formally transferred by the Emperor Gratian to the jurisdiction of his colleague Theodosius I.[62] Previously they had formed part of the prefecture of Italy, but now for the first time they became a separate prefecture under a prefect who had his centre of administration at Thessalonica.[63] It was not long before this change produced repercussions in ecclesiastical affairs. In fact it was only to be expected that now Eastern Illyricum had become subject to the control of the emperor residing at Constantinople, the whole area would soon be drawn into the ecclesiastical orbit of that see.

For the time being, however, the churches of those provinces continued to look westwards rather than eastwards, as is shown by the fact that their affairs were a subject of consideration by the synod of Aquileia, A.D. 381.[64] Yet in that same year the first council of Constantinople clearly indicated, by means of its disciplinary canons,[65] the future direction of Constantinopolitan ecclesiastical policy, and it was evident that if western influence in Illyricum was not to be gradually squeezed out some active measures would have to be taken.

Yet Damasus I, whose pontificate was contemporary with these events, was content to maintain cordial relations with Acholius, Bishop of Thessalonica,[66] and apart from this took no definite step to exclude intervention on the part of other churches in the affairs of Illyricum. It should be realized that the danger of the situation from the standpoint of the Roman

[62] Sozomen, *H.E.*, VII, 4, 1.
[63] Gibbon, *Decline and Fall*, ed. Bury, Vol. II, p. 590 (1929).
[64] Mansi, *Concilia*, Vol. III, 599–624. On this synod see Homes Dudden, *St. Ambrose*, Vol. I, pp. 200f.
[65] Cf. *Conc. Const.*, I, Can. 3. Mirbt, *Quellen*[5], No. 137.
[66] Cf. Damasus, *Epp.* 5 and 6, JK 237, 238.

see was further aggravated by the absence of any clearly defined boundaries of jurisdiction as between provinces, and by the comparatively slow development in those areas of metropolitical organization.[67]

It was left to Siricius, Damasus' successor, to make a real move in the matter. Possibly it was not till he received a report from the new bishop of Thessalonica, Anysius, that he realized how urgently attention to the absence of discipline in the Illyrian provinces was needed. This report revealed the fact that a number of cases of disputed episcopal elections had occurred in the churches of the Illyrian prefecture and, as Siricius found it necessary to write again [68] in the following year, there is some reason to think that his first reply had failed to reach its destination. In his later communication [69] he insisted that no bishop is to be consecrated before the candidate has been approved by the see of Thessalonica, and by prescribing that, as soon as a see fell vacant, Anysius was either to proceed to the city in person, or else to send written instructions to the bishops of the province, with a view to the assembly of a provincial synod and the consecration of " a catholic bishop of approved life and conduct, a cleric of good standing amongst the clergy, according to the statutes of the Nicene Council or of the Roman Church." [70]

Although Siricius made no explicit mention of the see of Constantinople in his letter, it is reasonable to suppose that the Roman see heard of its growing pretensions with considerable uneasiness. How considerable those pretensions would eventually become was foreshadowed by the fact that its bishop tended to assume, probably on the strength of the Constantinopolitan canons already mentioned, a kind of primacy or exarchate within the " diocese " of Thrace [71] soon

[67] On this development see Zeiller, *Les origines chrétiennes dans les provinces Danubiennes,* pp. 364–8. Sees with recognized metropolitical status certainly existed at the beginning of the fifth century.

[68] JK 257. For other examples of the miscarriage of papal correspondence see below.

[69] *Ep.* 4, JK 259, probably to be dated A.D. 386.

[70] *Ibid.,* " catholicum episcopum et vita et moribus probatum, secundum nicaenae synodi statuta vel ecclesiae romanae, clericum de clero meritum ordinare," on which see p. 177, n. 8. Cf. Jaffé-Kaltenbrunner, *Regesta,* Vol. I, p. 41. Notice that Siricius places the Roman Church on an equal footing with the Council of Nicaea.

[71] Socrates, *H.E.,* v. 8; cf. *Conc. Const.,* I, Canon 2. Mirbt, *op. cit.,* No. 137.

after those canons were published. Naturally the see of Heraclea, the original metropolis of the province *Europa,* was thrown completely into the shade.

The growing importance of Illyrian affairs from the standpoint of the see of Rome is clearly illustrated by the earliest surviving letter [72] of Pope Innocent I. This letter is concerned with the position of Anysius, and confirms the status assigned to the see of Thessalonica " by Damasus I, Siricius and Anastasius I," interpreting the powers already conferred on that see as including the right " to take knowledge of all things that are done in those provinces." [73]

After the death of Anysius his successor Rufus received a confirmation of the authority entrusted to his predecessor. The letter in which this was contained [74] also enumerated the following provinces as embraced within the sphere of his jurisdiction: *Achaia, Thessalia, Epirus vetus, Epirus nova, Creta, Dacia Mediterranea, Dacia Ripensis, Moesia, Dardania* and *Praevalitana.* Innocent insists that the rights of metropolitans are to be respected, since Rufus is only in the position of a *primus inter primates.*[75] Nevertheless he is responsible for all the churches of Illyricum as the vicegerent of the Roman see.[76] All communications of the local bishops with that see are to pass through him and, in addition, all but the most serious questions [77] shall be determined by him, and if he desires to do so, he may appoint episcopal assessors for the purpose. Innocent, however, does not make it clear how far he wished Rufus to intervene in episcopal elections. Possibly he intended the provision made by Siricius and himself in the case of Rufus' predecessor to fall into abeyance,

[72] *Ep.* 1, JK 285, dated A.D. 402.

[73] *Ibid.,* " omnia, quae in illis partibus gerantur, . . . cognoscenda." If Damasus ever entrusted formal powers to Acholius, no record of his action survives. Possibly Anastasius I's letters on the subject have been lost as well.

[74] *Ep.* 13, 2, JK 300, dated June 17th, A.D. 412.

[75] *Ibid.,* 3, " salvo eorum primatu." It will be observed that " primas " and " metropolitanus " are still synonymous terms at this time.

[76] *Ibid.,* " nostra vice." It is possible that Innocent derived the idea of a vicariate from the office of the *Vicarius* in contemporary civil administration. Cf. Chap. I, p. 14. This officer was the local representative in a " diocese " of the Praetorian Prefect, appointed to deal with affairs in areas remote from the centre of the Prefecture.

[77] For this special provision regarding a *causa maior* see above, pp. 179, 181f.

being shrewd enough to foresee the sort of difficulty which might arise in the event of its being abused.[78]

Some two years elapsed before the appearance of further correspondence. Meanwhile it seems that letters of complaint had been addressed to the Roman see by various Illyrian bishops, with particular reference to the conduct of the papal vicar. They alleged that Rufus and some of their fellow bishops were allowing clergy who had associated themselves with Bonosus [79] (thereby incurring the penalty of excommunication pronounced by the synod of Capua [80]), and now desired to be reconciled with the Church, to be restored to office on condition of repudiating their former allegiance; and that this treatment was being upheld on the ground that it was justified by a canon of Nicaea prescribing the treatment of ex-Novatianists.[81] Innocent was evidently in a dilemma. If he allowed the legitimacy of this action he was faced with the obvious rejoinder that the Nicene canon was irrelevant as it was capable of no more than a particular application. Yet the alternative involved the repudiation of the conduct of his own "Vicar." [82] The solution of the problem which he actually adopted does considerable credit to his statesmanship, for while he showed himself ready to allow that exceptional circumstances might justify action, technically irregular in itself, he made it clear that such action could not be tolerated in the future.[83]

Nevertheless Innocent was not prepared to permit his "Vicar" to have an entirely free hand, as we may gather from

[78] Innocent himself tells us, *Ep.* 13, 3, JK 300, that the Roman see had taken steps to make a collection of earlier letters regarding the Illyrian churches, a measure which suggests that relations with those churches were already tending to be unsatisfactory.

[79] Bonosus had been bishop of Nish (Naissus) and had been examined by Anysius, at the request of the synod of Capua, on the charge of teaching inconsistent with belief in the perpetual virginity of the Blessed Virgin Mary, and condemned. Cf. Ambrose, *De causa Bonosi,* 3. *P.L.* 16, 1172.

[80] A.D. 391. On this synod see Homes Dudden, *St. Ambrose,* Vol. II, pp. 398ff.

[81] *Conc. Nic.,* Can. 8.

[82] Cf. the situation which arose in connexion with the appeal of Atticus to Leo. See above, pp. 185f.

[83] *Ibid.,* 3. "Priora ergo dimittenda dico Dei iudicio, et de reliquo maxima sollicitudine praecavendum." A form of casuistry employed with some frequency in the later history of the papacy. Cf. Gratian, *Concordantia,* c. 41, qu. 1. A modern example may be found in Maynard Smith, *Frank, bishop of Zanzibar,* pp. 161f.

a later incident in the history of the Illyrian churches. It appears that two Illyrian bishops had been condemned by a general synod presided over by Rufus, and had thereupon appealed to the judgment of the Roman see. In spite of objections raised on behalf of their judges, Innocent decided to give the case a fresh hearing, although in the end he came to the conclusion that the original verdict had been justified. The information which we now possess on this affair is unhappily incomplete, but it is plain from the letter, in which Innocent publishes his decision,[84] that Rufus and his colleagues displayed considerable resentment at the inclination shown by the Roman see to revise a sentence which they had already pronounced.

There is nothing to indicate that Zosimus, Innocent's successor, had any direct dealings with these provinces. Perhaps it was well, so far as the prestige of the Roman see was concerned, in view of the unfortunate issue of his policy in regard to the churches of Gaul and Africa. In the meantime, however, as we shall see, the bishop of Constantinople appears to have made good use of the time at his disposal.

Boniface I, who succeeded Zosimus at the end of the year A.D. 418, soon found himself compelled to deal with a somewhat delicate situation. It arose from the fact that Perigenes, after having been consecrated to the see of Patras, presumably with the knowledge and approval of Rufus, had been refused installation by the local church, and as a result had been invited to occupy the vacant metropolitical see of Corinth. It appears, however, that Rufus had raised objections and that in consequence the Corinthian clergy had addressed an appeal to Boniface, requesting him to confirm Perigenes as bishop of their church.

The Pope approved the request of the Corinthians in spite of possible objections which might be raised on the score of the Nicene canon prohibiting translations from one see to another, and wrote to Rufus[85] expressing his impatience at not having received a report from him on the matter.[86] When

[84] *Ep.* 18, JK 304 of uncertain date but perhaps A.D. 414.

[85] *Ep.* 4, JK 350, in the middle or early part of A.D. 419.

[86] *Ep.* 5, 4, JK 351. This section is printed as the concluding section of JK 351 but probably should belong to JK 350, the last section of which should be transferred to JK 351. Cf. *P.L.* 20, 758.

at length the report arrived, Boniface wrote afresh to Rufus [87] confirming the appointment of Perigenes to the see of Corinth, and instructing him to take strong measures against those who persisted in opposition. In the same letter he reaffirmed the authority of Rufus over the Illyrian churches as the vicegerent of the Apostolic see.[88]

Yet, in spite of the decision thus given by Boniface, the matter was by no means at an end. The "opposition," nothing daunted, proceeded at once to present their case before a fresh court, in which they felt confident, and no doubt with considerable reason, of obtaining a favourable hearing.[89] Atticus, to whose see the case was now referred, had already been bishop of Constantinople for twelve years or more, and could certainly count on the support of the young Emperor Theodosius II. It cannot therefore be merely a coincidence that the year A.D. 421 saw the publication by the eastern government of a significant rescript which provided that disputed questions arising among the churches of Illyricum should not be submitted to a synodical verdict "without the knowledge of the bishop of the city of Constantinople, which enjoys the same privileges as ancient Rome." [90] This meant in effect that the see of Constantinople would in future have to be considered in connexion with Illyrian affairs, and it was not difficult to foresee the complication which might arise from such a provision.

As soon as the details of this rescript were made known to the Roman see, Boniface addressed an urgent request to the Emperor Honorius at Ravenna to procure the repeal of the offending law.[91] The Emperor thereupon addressed a private

[87] *Ep.* 5, JK 351, dated Sept. 19th, A.D. 419.
[88] *Ibid.*, 2.
[89] Cf. *Epp.* 13, 14 and 15, JK 363–5.
[90] *Cod. Theod.* XVI, ii, 45 addressed to Philip, Prefect of Illyricum, dated July 14th, A.D. 421. "Ut si quid dubietatis emerserit, id oporteat non absque scientia viri reverentissimi sacrosanctae legis antistitis urbis Constantinopolitanae, quae Romae veteris praerogativa laetatur, conventiri sacerdotali sanctoque iudicio reservari." Although the rescript is primarily concerned with the settlement of disputed points of doctrine, yet it is evident that it implies a considerable extension of the privileges assigned to the see of Constantinople by *Conc. Const.*, I, Can. 3. "Conventui sacerdotali" evidently refers to the σύνοδος ἐνδημοῦσα of that see; on which see below, p. 215, n. 44.
[91] *Ep.* 7, JK 353, dated July 1st, A.D. 420.

communication [92] to his imperial nephew and colleague to that effect, and received a satisfactory reply.[93] In spite of this, however, the bishops of Constantinople continued to exercise their newly-gained authority[94] in a way which may throw doubt on the sincerity of the Constantinopolitan government.

The Corinthian "opposition," presumably encouraged by the support which they had received from Atticus, proceeded to assemble a fresh synod, at which the verdict pronounced by the Roman see was rejected and Perigenes declared deposed.[95] When news reached Boniface of this *démarche* he was, of course, highly indignant and, besides addressing a sharp reproof to the recalcitrant Corinthians, issued further instructions to Rufus, his "Vicar." In the former letter [96] he makes a vigorous though indirect attack on the presumption of the see of Constantinople, and calls attention not only to the primacy of the Roman see, but also to the order of precedence assigned by canon law to the "greater churches." [97] In addition to this he lays special stress on the irreversibility

[92] *Inter Bonif. Epp.*, No. 10. *P.L.* 20, 769f.

[93] *Ibid.*, No. 11. The genuineness of these letters is upheld by Duchesne, *L'Illyricum ecclésiastique*, p. 531.

[94] It is possible that Theodosius never kept his word. The death of Honorius in A.D. 423 may have appeared to render the promised repeal superfluous. In any case the offending rescript was included in the collection of laws drawn up at the instance of Theodosius II, and known therefore as the *Codex Theodosianus*, A.D. 438. See p. 197, n. 90.

[95] This may be inferred from the letters of Boniface, esp. *Ep.* 15, JK 365. In any case the opponents of Perigenes, as we have seen, had canon law on their side.

[96] Mentioned in *Ep.* 13, JK 363. Whether this letter is to be identified with *Ep.* 15, JK 365 is uncertain. The subject matter of the latter supports the identification, but it is possible that besides the letter addressed to the whole Illyrian episcopate there was another document specially drawn up for the benefit of the Corinthian synod which is now lost.

[97] *Ep.* 15, 5, "si placet recensere canonum sanctiones, reperietis quae sit post ecclesiam romanam secunda sedes, quaeve sit tertia." It is likely that Boniface was making use of the Damasine theory of the three Petrine sees embodied in the manifesto of A.D. 378, *Decretum Gelasianum*, c. 3. Those who consider that Boniface refers to the later interpolated Latin version of *Conc. Nic.*, Can. 6 ignore the reference which he makes to that canon in *Ep.* 14, 1, JK 364, where it is clearly implied that he only knew the canon in its original form. On the Chieti MS. in which the interpolation occurs see Maassen, *Quellen*, Vol. I, pp. 526f. The point of the Pope's observation is, of course, to exclude the claims of Constantinople.

of verdicts pronounced by the Roman see.[98] Finally he repeats that Perigenes is confirmed by him in the possession of the see of Corinth, and points out that refusal to accept this decision will incur the penalty of excommunication by the Roman see: any further allegations against their bishop may be referred by the Corinthians to Rufus, "to whom all matters are entrusted as my vicegerent."[99]

In the other letter addressed to Rufus[100] he assured his "Vicar" that "the blessed apostle Peter has entrusted all the affairs of the church of Thessalonica to him as his representative so that he may know that he had responsibility for many, a responsibility which recent assignments have no right to diminish, because they have no authority. For we must not give way to the efforts of those people who are inspired by a desire for change and a longing for honour which is not their due."[101]

The writer goes on to express his indignation that an Illyrian synod should have presumed to review a sentence pronounced by the Roman see and, as if to show his utter contempt for the recent Theodosian rescript, entrusts the decision of a case involving a charge against an Illyrian bishop to the bishop of Thessalonica.[102]

In addition to these two communications Boniface addressed a further letter to the bishops of Thessaly.[103] This province must have contained a number of bishops who were in favour of closer relations with the see of Constantinople, and was therefore in need of a sharp reminder of its duty of

[98] *Ibid.*, 5, "nemo unquam apostolico culmini, de cuius iudicio non licet retractari, manus obvias audaciter intulit." Cf. Zosimus, *Ep.* 12, 1, JK 342. "Nobis tantum esset auctoritatis, ut nullus de nostra possit retractare sententia." The importance of this claim is, of course, difficult to exaggerate.

[99] *Ibid.*, 8, "quoniam servandus accusatori locus est. . . . Rufus cui ad vicem nostram cuncta committimus."

[100] *Ep.* 13, JK 363, dated March 11th, A.D. 422.

[101] *Ibid.*, 1, "vice sua beatus apostolus Petrus ecclesiae Thessalonicensi cuncta commisit, ut intelligat se sollicitudinem manere multorum, quam minorem facere nova, quae vires habere non possunt, testamenta non debent. Non est enim eorum cedendum studiis, quos novitas rerum et in debitae desiderium dignitatis accendit. "Nova testamenta" evidently alludes to the rescript of A.D. 421, see above, p. 197, n. 90. At the same time it is likely that Boniface has *Conc. Const.*, I, Can. 3 in mind.

[102] *Ibid.*, 2 and 3.

[103] *Ep.* 14, JK 364 also of March 11th, A.D. 422.

obedience to the "Vicar" of the Roman see. Accordingly the Pope calls their attention to the office of St. Peter in relation to the universal Church, as the source of evangelization and thus the source of ecclesiastical discipline.[104] He points out that the authority of the Roman see does not so much depend on the canons of Nicaea as on the Dominical promise to St. Peter.[105] After referring to the synod assembled by the opposition party at Corinth as deserving of censure,[106] he declares that if any objection is to be raised against the conduct of Rufus, whose privileges in regard to the churches of Illyricum are not new, but assigned to his see long ago by earlier popes, such objection should be addressed to the Roman see, instead of adopting newfangled methods contrary to canon law.[107]

By the time the next occasion arose demanding intervention by the papacy in Illyrian affairs the place of Boniface had been occupied by Celestine I. Some five years after the Corinthian controversy, to which we have just referred, Celestine received an appeal on behalf of Felix, bishop of Apollonia, regarding a verdict pronounced against him by the provincial synod of *Epirus nova*. He declared Felix guiltless and, in a letter which he addressed to the metropolitans of Illyricum,[108] took the opportunity of defining afresh, and with greater precision than that which his predecessors had used, the authority of the Thessalonian vicariate. He pointed out that all questions of appeal are to be brought before Rufus, that no bishop is to be consecrated without his approval, nor is any metropolitan to undertake the charge of the province

[104] *Ep.* 14, 1. "Institutio universalis nascentis ecclesiae de beati Petri sumpsit honore principium." Cf. Innocent, *Ep.* 25, 2, JK 311.

[105] *Ibid.* "Nicaenae synodi non aliud praecepta testantur: adeo ut non aliquid super eum ausa sit constituere, cum videret nihil supra meritum suum posse conferri: omnia denique huic noverat Domini sermone concessa." Boniface could scarcely have written these words if he had had before him the text of *Conc. Nic.*, Can. 6 in its "interpolated" form. For the use made of the "interpolated" text at a later date see below.

[106] *Ibid.*, 2. "Accipite ergo admonitionem et correptionem nostram," citing 1 Cor. iv. 21.

[107] *Ibid.*, 4, "ideo tenet sedes apostolica principatum, ut querelas omnium licentes acceptet. . . . Cesset novella praesumptio."

[108] *Ep.* 3, JK 366, dated A.D. 424. It should be observed that the name of Perigenes, metropolitan of Corinth, occurs at the head of the list.

entrusted to him with the Pope's knowledge.[109] Further, all communications with the see of Rome are to pass through his hands.[110]

The creators of the Illyrian vicariate, with the possible exception of Innocent I, seem always to have shirked dealing with the most serious obstacle to its success, namely the difficulty of relating the canonical authority of the metropolitans to the special privileges assigned by the papacy to the see of Thessalonica.

It remained for Xystus III and his successor, Leo I, to find in some way a means of adjustment. Since the election of the former in A.D. 432, a new modification of the respective spheres of influence of the eastern and western Emperors had taken place, with the result that the orbit of Constantinople was still further enlarged in a westerly direction.[111] Moreover some important changes had taken place in the episcopate. The see of Constantinople, left vacant by the death of Maximian, had been filled by the election of Proclus, while Rufus of Thessalonica had now been succeeded by Anastasius. Changes of this sort were bound to affect the situation in Eastern Illyricum, especially in view of the fact that the new bishop of Constantinople possessed a personality of the kind which was not likely to miss opportunities for extending the influence of his see.[112] Possibly some of the Illyrian metropolitans thought the time had now come to make it clear to the bishop of Thessalonica that they were no

[109] *Ibid.* "Sine eius consilio nullus ordinetur: nullus usurpet, eodem inconscio commissam illi provinciam."

[110] *Ibid.*, "per eum etiam ad nos, si quid est, referatur."

[111] The actual year is which this modification took place is doubtful. It may have taken place in consequence of the betrothal of Valentinian III to Licinia Eudoxia, daughter of Theodosius II, which occurred in A.D. 424; on the other hand it may not have happened till A.D. 437, the date of the actual marriage. The authorities are Cassiodorus, *Varia*, XI, 1, 9; Jordanes, *Rom.* 329, *M.G.H.*, Vol. V, 1, p. 42. Cf. Zeiller, *op. cit.*, p. 6, n. 1 and Bury, *Later Roman Empire*, Vol. I, p. 225, n. 5. The exact extent of the territory transferred to the authority of the eastern government is uncertain, but it appears to have embraced a considerable part of the "diocese" of Western Illyricum.

[112] Such opportunity seems to have been provided by a synod held at Constantinople probably in the year A.D. 436. See Theodoret, *Ep. ad Flavian*, 86. *P.G.* 83, 1277–81. Cf. Xystus III, *Ep.* 10, 3, JK 396. Subsequently a doctrinal statement evolved there was circulated by Proclus among certain bishops holding sees in Western Illyricum with a view to obtaining their approval. Cf. Dionysius Exiguus, ed. *Spicilegium Casin.*, Vol. I, 38, p. 144 and Zeiller, *op. cit.*, p. 371, n. 2.

longer prepared to submit to dictation from that quarter, and it is as one who shared this view that Perigenes, metropolitan of Corinth, once again came to the forefront. It appears that Xystus had received a report from his new "Vicar," Anastasius, to the effect that Perigenes was causing trouble. The immediate outcome of this report was the despatch of two letters from Rome, one addressed to Perigenes himself,[113] warning him that the same "obedience is due from him to Anastasius as from the other metropolitans of Illyricum." The other letter was sent to a synod to be assembled at Thessalonica under the presidency of Anastasius.[114] Here the Pope insisted that the privileges accorded by him to the see of Thessalonica were not different from those already assigned to it by his predecessors in the see of Rome.[115] At the same time he assures the metropolitan bishops that their rights within their own provinces remain intact:

"The metropolitans," he writes, "shall have the privilege of consecration within their respective provinces; but no one shall venture to consecrate (sc. a bishop) without the knowledge and approval of him, whom we intend to be consulted regarding all consecrations. Let all the more serious questions be referred to the bishop of Thessalonica. To him the supreme responsibility belongs of testing and examining thoroughly all who are called to the episcopate. He has the right to select from your ranks the best and most zealous and to co-opt them as judges in a task of this kind."[116]

In so defining the powers of Anastasius, Xystus was only endorsing the privileges already assigned to the see of Thessalonica by earlier popes, yet the constant need of reiterating

[113] *Ep.* 7, JK 393, dated A.D. 435.

[114] *Ep.* 8, JK 394, dated July 8th in that year.

[115] *Ibid.* "Nos . . . Anastasio tantum tribuimus, quantum decessoribus ipsius a nostris decessoribus attributum."

[116] *Ibid.* "Habeant honorem suum metropolitani singularum (provinciarum), salvo huius privilegio quem honorare debeant amplius honorati. In provincia sua ius habeant ordinandi; sed hoc, inscio vel invito quem de omnibus volumus ordinationibus consuli, nullus audeat ordinare. Ad Thessalonicensem maiores causae referantur antistitem. Ipsum maior cura respectet, eos qui ad episcopatum vocantur discutiendi sollicitius et probandi. Ipse optimos solertissimosque de vestro numero eligat, quos negotiis secum asciscat arbitros; aut sine se tribuat qui in disceptationem missa componat."

those privileges seems to suggest that considerable practical difficulties were being experienced.

The two remaining letters belonging to this pontificate which refer to Illyrian affairs were despatched late in the year A.D. 437. It was in that year, as we have seen, that Proclus of Constantinople made some notable progress in the westward extension of the authority of his see.[117] One of these letters was addressed to Proclus himself,[118] and is doubtless to be regarded as the consequence of a report having reached the Roman see that bishops or clergy who were dissatisfied with the regime of Anastasius and his supporters were being welcomed at Constantinople. Xystus, who tactfully praised the zeal of Proclus in defence of canon law, urges that no clergy should be accepted who cannot produce *litterae formatae* signed by the bishop of Thessalonica.[119]

The other letter just mentioned was addressed to the Thessalonian synod.[120] The writer, alluding apparently to the doctrinal statement produced at Constantinople earlier in the same year,[121] warns the bishops of Illyricum that no statements of this sort should be accepted except one which has been formally approved by the Roman see. He adds that controversies in which bishops are involved must be referred to the see of Thessalonica, and if the bishop there cannot settle the matter it is to be taken to the Roman see for final decision.[122]

For a few years after this there is silence. When correspondence between Thessalonica and Rome is resumed the place of Xystus has been taken by Leo I, whose relations with Eastern Illyricum form the subject of the preceding chapter.

It is sometimes suggested that it is incorrect to speak of the Illyrian vicariate as though it were either in fact or in intention

[117] See above, p. 201, n. 112.

[118] *Ep.* 9, JK 395, dated December 18th, A.D. 437.

[119] *Ibid.*, 2, "si sine eius (sc. Anastasii) epistolis atque formata venire tentaverit, tamquam disciplinae ecclesiasticae despector et contemptor canonum, quos nos temerari ex aliqua parte non patimur, habeatur."

[120] *Ep.* 10, JK 396 also of December 18th, A.D. 437.

[121] See above, p. 203, n. 112.

[122] *Ibid.*, 2, "sua (sc. Anastasii) sollicitudine, si quae inter fratres nascantur, . . . actiones distinguat atque definiat, et ad eum quidquid a singulis sacerdotibus agitur, referatur . . . , (3) . . . aut ad nos, si illic finiri non potuerit, eodem tamen suis litteris causam omnem quae vertitur prosequente, veniat examen."

a permanent institution, but rather that the privileges enjoyed by the see of Thessalonica were of the nature of personal and individual concessions made by successive occupants of the Roman see to successive bishops of Thessalonica. It is of course perfectly true that the papal correspondence on the subject show frequent repetitions and renewals of privileges. Yet the fact that it was necessary for Celestine I, for example, to endorse the power already granted to Rufus, his "Vicar," by Boniface I[123] need not necessarily imply that those powers were regarded as having lapsed with his predecessor's decease. A better explanation will probably be found in the recurring menace to canonical order, from the standpoint of the Roman see, arising from the rapidly growing influence of the see of Constantinople. The ultimate failure of the experiment was due to two main causes; first to the inevitable progress of Constantinople, which in ecclesiastical affairs led to the publication of the twenty-eighth canon of Chalcedon, and in secular matters to the reconquest, at least in part, of the western provinces by Justinian I, and secondly to the fundamental difficulty of reconciling the authority of the see of Thessalonica which rested simply on the fiat of the Roman see, with the privileges of the metropolitan bishops confirmed by the canons of Nicaea. The bishops of Constantinople were logical enough to see that if the Nicene canons could be improved upon by the see of Rome, there was no reason why the task of improvement should not be undertaken in their own interests as well. It was therefore only a question of time for the whole experiment of the Vicariate to break down. Yet it was an experiment from which the papacy learned much, which was to prove of considerable value in the future.

[123] See above, p. 197.

CHAPTER IX

LEO AND THE CHURCHES OF THE EAST. I

I. THE BEGINNING OF THE EUTYCHIAN CONTROVERSY

THE dawn of the fifth century seemed to hold little promise for the security of the Empire in the East. Theodosius I had indeed succeeded in carrying through a considerable measure of reorganization and unification, so long overdue after the political and ecclesiastical confusion of the preceding reigns. Unhappily he was removed from the scene of action too soon for the work which he had begun to be completed, and it was left to the listless hands of his son and successor Arcadius who lacked either the inclination or the ability for the task, to carry on his father's policy. As was to be expected, both Arcadius and his successor, Theodosius II, allowed the effective control of the Government to pass into the hands of women or court chamberlains, so that for a time at least a large proportion of the eastern world was subject to the will either of a eunuch or of a dominant feminine personality.

Of the political state of the eastern half of the Empire in this period we have already said sufficient elsewhere.[1] It will, however, enable us better to grasp the nature of the difficulties with which Leo had to contend, if we summarize briefly the ecclesiastical developments which had taken place there during the earlier decades of the century.

In the first place the see of Constantinople, thanks not only to its association with the seat of Empire but to the personality of such bishops as John Chrysostom and Atticus, had steadily acquired a position of predominant importance among the eastern churches. Its Achilles' heel was to be found in the silence of the Nicene canons regarding its claims to jurisdiction, the obvious reason for which was that the famous sixth canon had been framed to safeguard the interests of the sees of Alexandria and Antioch. In any case it was prior to the rise of the Constantinopolitan see to a position of influence in

[1] See Chap. I, pp. 1–13.

the Church. Hence it was easy for a doctrinal controversy such as the one which arose in connexion with the attempt made by Nestorius, bishop of Constantinople, to popularize the Christological theories of Diodore of Tarsus and Theodore of Mopsuestia, to be turned into a struggle for predominance between the sees of Constantinople and Alexandria. It should be remembered that these theories were sharply distinguished from the doctrine associated with the latter see, in that they laid emphasis on the reality of Christ's Humanity, while Alexandrine Christology tended to stress the completeness of His Godhead. Diodore, Theodore and Nestorius himself, who owed their theological training to the school of Antioch, saw no danger to belief in one Christ, in speaking of a kind of "contingent" or "moral" union between the two natures of Godhead and Manhood, and it was to assess the merits of these rival opinions that a general council was assembled at Ephesus under the presidency of Cyril of Alexandria in A.D. 431. The precise course of events at that council[2] does not immediately concern us here. We may therefore pass on to consider its immediate consequences.

With the flight of Cyril and his supporters from the city, the first council of Ephesus, now generally reckoned as the third of the oecumenical series, came to an abrupt conclusion.[3] Even so Cyril had succeeded in attaining his two principal objectives, namely the humiliation of the see of Constantinople by the deposition and banishment of its bishop, Nestorius, and the establishment of Alexandrine Christology, which upheld a "hypostatic" or personal union between the Godhead and Manhood in Christ, as opposed to the Antiochene hypothesis of a "moral" or "conjunctive" union, as the true standard of orthodoxy.

Throughout the controversy which had led to the summoning of the council, Cyril had been assured of the support of Pope Celestine I,[4] and with the promotion of Maximian to fill the vacant see of Constantinople, whose candidature was successful mainly because he was known to favour Cyrilline

[2] For a brief account of these events see Kidd, *Roman Primacy,* pp. 106ff.

[3] *Conc. Eph.,* Actio VI, 25. Mansi, *Concilia,* Vol. IV, 1465; *Collectio ad Eph.* 14, id. *ibid.,* Vol. V, 255.

[4] *Epp.* 8–20, 22–5, JK 372–80, 385–8.

Christology, he might feel content that the greater part of the Christian world had endorsed his doctrine. Only John, bishop of Antioch, together with a group of metropolitans and others subject to Antiochene jurisdiction, seemed likely to remain obdurate. Yet two years after the conclusion of the council a means was found of reconciling the apparently irreconcilable point of view of Antioch and Alexandria, and with the acceptance by Cyril and John alike of the *Formula of Reunion*, A.D. 433, a kind of façade of doctrinal unity between the two rival theological schools of the East was created. Nevertheless the question of ecclesiastical priority was bound to arise again before long, and with the election of Proclus to the see of Constantinople to fill the vacancy caused by the death of Maximian, new efforts were made to obtain for his see an ecclesiastical status not unworthy of its relation to the imperial and administrative capital of the East.[5]

Changes in the occupancy of the sees of the "greater churches" followed one another in rapid succession. Six years after the elevation of Proclus, John of Antioch was succeeded by Domnus;[6] three years more and Dioscorus was elected to the see vacated by the death of Cyril.[7] Proof of the continuance of cordial relations between that see and the papacy is to be found in the letter[8] by which Leo acknowledged the formal notification of Dioscorus' election. After expressing his satisfaction at the evidence of unity which such communications provide[9] the Pope dwells on the relation between the sees of Rome and Alexandria, and suggests that it ought to correspond[10] to the relation between St. Peter and St. Mark, saying:

[5] Proclus was elected April A.D. 434. Cf. *Les Regestes des Actes du Patriarchat de Constantinople,* Vol. I, No. 76, ed. Grumel (1932).

[6] The year of Domnus' election is uncertain. Kidd, *History,* Vol. III, p. 278 gives A.D. 440. Duchesne, *Histoire,* Vol. III, p. 390, A.D. 441 or 442; Batiffol, *Siège Apostolique,* p. 496, A.D. 441.

[7] Cyril's death is given by Kidd, *ibid.,* p. 280, as June 9th, A.D. 444.

[8] *Ep.* 9, JK 406, dated July 21st. The consular year is lacking. If the date is correct, A.D. 444 might be possible. Jaffé-Kaltenbrunner, *Regesta,* p. 60, gives A.D. 445.

[9] In *Ep.* 129, 1, JK 505, Leo shows that this custom so far as Alexandria and Rome were concerned is a long standing one.

[10] *Ibid., praef.* "Paterna . . . et fraterna collatio." Caspar, *Geschichte,* Vol. I, p. 457, n. 5, points out that the writer deliberately uses a word meant politely to conceal the Roman claim to have the right to confirm an election to the see of Alexandria.

"Since the most blessed Peter has received the apostolic primacy from the Lord, and the Roman church is loyal to his ordinances, it is wrong to suppose that his holy disciple, Mark, who was the first to rule the church of Alexandria, has laid down the canons of his traditions by rules of a different kind: since beyond all doubt disciple and teacher shared the same spirit proceeding from the same source of grace, and he who was consecrated cannot have handed down any tradition different from that which he received from his consecrator. So we cannot allow that we who acknowledge ourselves to belong to the same body and to share the same faith, should differ in any respect; and that the customs of the disciple should appear to diverge from those of the teacher." [11]

The writer then passes on to consider certain customs of the church of Alexandria, of which he has heard, and which he has noted as different from those of the church of Rome. The first of these concerns the appropriate day of the week for ordinations. Leo urges that ordinations should be performed only on Saturday night or on Sunday morning, and in justification of his contention refers to our Lord's own practice.[12] He adds that both the bishop and the ordinands must be fasting at the time.[13] Next he offers a suggestion as to what is to be done if, on the occasion of a great festival, the church proves to be inadequate for the size of the congregation. At such times, he says, the liturgy is to be repeated as

[11] *Ep.* 9, *praef.* "Cum enim beatissimus Petrus apostolicum a Domino acceperit principatum, et Romana ecclesia in eius permaneat institutis, nefas est credere quod sanctus discipulus eius Marcus qui Alexandrinam primus ecclesiam gubernavit, aliis regulis traditionum suarum decreta formaverit; cum sine dubio de eodem fonte gratiae unus spiritus et discipuli fuerit et magistri, nec aliud ordinatus tradere potuerit, quam quod ab ordinatore suscepit. Non ergo patimur, ut cum unius nos esse corporis et fidei fateamur, in aliquo discrepemus; et alia doctoris, alia discipuli instituta videantur." The earliest allusion to the traditional association of St. Mark with the see of Alexandria is in Eusebius, *H.E.*, 2, 16. For the connexion of St. Mark with St. Peter, see Papias, *ap. eund.*, *ibid.*, 3, 39.

[12] *Ibid.*, 1, "non passim diebus omnibus sacerdotalis vel levitica ordinatio celebretur; sed post diem sabbati, eius noctis quae in prima sabbati lucescit, exordia deligantur." A reference to John xx. 21f. follows. Cf. *Epp.* 6, 6, JK 404; 10, 6, JK 407.

[13] *Ibid.*, "in quibus his qui consecrandi sunt ieiunis, et a ieiunantibus sacra benedictio conferatur."

often as is necessary in order to provide for the needs of the people.[14]

The letter throws some light on Leo's view as to the relation between the Roman see and the "greater churches" of the East. It shows that from his standpoint those churches are to be regarded, not as the equals but as the subordinates of his own, and that where there is divergence of custom they should be expected to come into line with Roman practice. It would be interesting to know the reaction of Dioscorus on the receipt of Leo's communication, but unhappily we have no information. Yet it seems scarcely likely that he was content to be regarded as no more than Leo's "disciple."

The character of the new bishop of Alexandria has been so much maligned by the supporters of a "dyophysite" Christology that we ought in justice to take into account certain considerations which tell in his favour. As the nephew, and therefore probably the designated successor, of Cyril, he was of course a wholehearted supporter of the Cyrilline Christology, but being apparently far inferior as a theologian he lacked the balance of judgment which might have prevented him lending his support to a confused and unintelligent development of that doctrine. Probably from the first he was far more concerned with the prestige and authority of his own see, and regarded the doctrinal controversy in which he was later so deeply involved as largely secondary to the challenge presented by the growing importance of the see of Constantinople, to the recognized priority of the see of Alexandria among the "greater churches" of the East. He is therefore to be regarded far less as a heresiarch than as one who was unwilling to allow the provisions of canon law[15] to be lightly set aside without vigorous protest. In zeal and tenacity of purpose he deserves comparison with Athanasius

[14] *Ibid.*, 2, "cum solemnior quaeque festivitas conventum populi numerosioris indixerit, et ea fidelium multitudo convenerit, quam recipere basilica simul una non possit, sacrificii oblatio indubitanter iteretur." It is clear from what follows that this practice was already normal in Rome. The fact that such repetition was found necessary suggests that both there and at Alexandria there was a considerable Christian population.

[15] e.g. *Conc. Nic.*, Can. 6, which was currently interpreted in the West to mean that the second place in order of precedence next after the see of Rome belonged to the see of Alexandria.

himself and, if in the end he accepted a standard of doctrine which proved to be heretical, he must at least be allowed the credit of having done his utmost for what he believed to be the cause of order and discipline.

In actual fact the evil genius of the Eastern churches was far less Dioscorus than the newly-elevated court chamberlain Chrysaphius, the type of man who, under an indolent and effeminate sovereign such as Theodosius II, was capable of working untold havoc to the well-being of Church and State alike. Soon after his promotion to this all-important position in the Eastern court[16] he succeeded in persuading the Emperor to exclude his own sister Pulcheria from the palace, and a few months later to banish his wife Eudocia on the alleged ground of infidelity.[17] It happened that Pulcheria had given proof of her preference for the ecclesiastical party in the capital which favoured a "dyophysite" or Antiochene type of Christology, and it is possible that Chrysaphius in procuring her exclusion from the imperial counsels was carrying out the suggestion of his godfather and confessor, Eutyches. The latter had for many years been archimandrite of a monastery in the suburbs of Constantinople, and through the advancement of his godson was able to exert a considerable influence on the ecclesiastical policy of the Eastern government. The fact that he was a determined though unintelligent supporter of Cyrilline or Alexandrine Christology showed clearly the direction in which that influence would be exercised, and that Dioscorus would find in the archimandrite a willing ally in opposing any possible revival of "Nestorianism," whose standing in relation to the only effective force in the Eastern government would ensure that all the resources of statecraft would be more or less at his command.

In the face of so formidable an alliance the new bishop of Antioch displayed little promise of being able to put up an adequate resistance. Lacking strength of character and devoid of any real theological ability, Domnus found himself completely at the mercy of the tremendous forces presently to be let loose. Actually from the beginning of his pontificate

[16] This took place A.D. 441. Cf. Caspar, *Geschichte*, Vol. I, p. 464.
[17] On these changes see Bury, *Later Roman Empire*, Vol. I, p. 229, who says that Eudocia was already in Jerusalem, A.D. 444.

he had showed himself a supporter of the anti-Cyrilline party in Syria and elsewhere, which had never accepted the deposition of Nestorius and regarded the formula of Reunion as a betrayal of the cause of truth, and the direction of his sympathies appeared clearly enough in the attitude which he adopted when certain protagonists of the Cyrilline Christology brought forward a charge of Nestorianism against Ibas, bishop of Edessa.[18] This was in the year A.D. 445. In the following year he consecrated Irenaeus, a notorious "Nestorian," to the important see of Tyre.[19] Irenaeus, who held the rank of imperial Count after the Council of Ephesus, had been sentenced to banishment,[20] from which he had been recalled soon after the Reunion of A.D. 433. Had Pulcheria retained her influence with her brother all might have been well, but, as we have seen, her place in imperial counsels was now taken by Chrysaphius, whose theological advisers were scarcely likely to regard the preferment of an outstanding "Nestorian" with indifference.

Finding Domnus unwilling to listen to their accusations the enemies of Ibas turned to Dioscorus. This time the name of Theodoret, bishop of Cyrrhus, was specifically mentioned.[21] The bishop of Alexandria thereupon addressed emphatic protests, alike to Theodoret himself [22] and to Domnus.[23] The former replied with a carefully worded letter of self-justification.[24] At the same time Domnus directed a special appeal to Flavian,[25] the recently elected bishop of Constantinople.

Proclus who had occupied that see for the past twelve years

[18] Ibas had been consecrated to that see in A.D. 435. For the charge brought against him see Mansi, *Concilia,* Vol. VII, 196ff.; Kidd, *History,* Vol. III, p. 289.

[19] Theodoret, *Ep.* 110, *P.G.* 83, 1305B.

[20] *Synodicon adv. tragoediam Irenaei,* 188. Mansi, *Concilia,* Vol. V, 964.

[21] Theodoret, *Ep.* 83, *P.G.* 83, 1268B. If Domnus' election is rightly placed in A.D. 440 the phrase (1268CD) "*ἕβδομόν ἐστιν ἔτος . . . τοῦ κυρίου Δόμνου*" would be consistent with the year A.D. 447 for these events.

[22] Id., *Ep.* 86, *P.G.* 83, 1280A. This letter is usually attributed to Theodoret himself, but the fact that the author takes such pains to assert the apostolic claims of the see of Antioch renders the authorship of Domnus more probable. Cf. Flemming, *Die Syrische Akten der Raübersynode,* in *Abh. d. Gött. Ges. d. Wiss.,* Vol. XV, pp. 118ff.

[23] Theodoret, *Ep.* 83, 1287B.

[24] *Ibid.*

[25] Id., *Ep.* 86, *P.G.* 83, 1277.

had used the time at his disposal for the recovery of the prestige which it had lost as a result of the deposition of Nestorius.[26] His successor, however, was scarcely adequate to the task of continuing his work, and from the beginning of his pontificate found himself in a highly unenviable position.[27] Like Domnus, Flavian lacked determination and shared neither " the diplomatic urbanity of his predecessor nor the eloquent gifts of Nestorius." [28] His unfortunate relations with the court meant that sooner or later he would have to reckon with the influence of Eutyches, who seems to have been quick to appreciate the strength of his own position and, to quote the words of a contemporary, " took heart, and because he was not a bishop, set himself by means of the authority of [his] Majesty [to behave] otherwise—as bishop of bishops. For he was taking charge of the affairs of the Church, making use of Flavian, who, by reason of the greatness of his humility knew not the things which were being prepared, as of a minister in [the execution of] the things which were being commanded at Constantinople." [29]

To return to Domnus. The intervention of the see of Alexandria in the affairs of the see of Antioch appears to have galvanized him into action, which took the form, first, of a protest addressed to the court of Constantinople against an alleged revival of Apollinarianism, making particular mention of calumnious accusations directed by the archimandrite Eutyches against himself, and of teaching which appeared to him to ascribe a single nature to Christ and to predicate possibility of the Godhead [30] and, secondly, of a request addressed to Theodoret to draw up a polemical treatise against " monophysite " Christology. This request bore fruit in the publication by the latter of his series of dialogues, usually known as the *Eranistes,* the object of which was to show the unscriptural

[26] e.g. his intervention in the affairs of Asia and Eastern Illyricum. See Xystus III, *Epp.* 9 and 10, JK 395, 396.

[27] He offended Chrysaphius by not sending the customary gifts at the time of his election. Theophanes, *Chronographia,* 5940. *P.G.* 108, 256f.

[28] Caspar, *Geschichte,* Vol. I, p. 466.

[29] Nestorius, *Bazaar,* ed. Driver and Hodgson, p. 336.

[30] Mentioned by Facundus, *Pro. defens. trium cap.* 8, 5. *P.L.* 67, 723f.

and unorthodox character of Alexandrine doctrine.[31] As to the protest sent by Domnus to the Eastern court, had he realized the extent of the revolution which had taken place there he could scarcely have supposed that it would prove effective. In fact in the light of subsequent events it seems probable that it only served to stimulate anti-Nestorian activity, proof of which was seen in the issue of imperial letters addressed to himself and to Theodoret,[32] in virtue of which the bishop of Cyrrhus was forbidden to leave his diocese, while Domnus was categorically required to depose Irenaeus, the "Nestorian" bishop of Tyre, and to consecrate Photius in his stead.[33] By this means two prominent members of the Antiochene school were effectively put out of action. But it still remained to deal with Ibas of Edessa. In spite of vigorous protests against his unorthodoxy, Domnus, as we have seen, had shown himself reluctant to listen to any charge against him, and had succeeded in deferring the hearing of the case till after Easter, A.D. 447.[34] Impatient of further delay the Eastern government summarily took the matter out of his hands and, on October 26th of that year, appointed an imperial commission to investigate the charges.[35] Shortly afterwards a rescript was issued ordering the destruction of all Nestorian writings and publishing the fact of the deposition of Irenaeus.[36] Two hearings of the charges against Ibas took place, the first at Tyre and the second at Berytus, neither of which led to any decisive result.[37]

It may be gathered from what has been said that by now

[31] *P.G.* 83, 27–318.

[32] Theodoret, *Ep.* 82. *P.G.* 83, 1264B *et al.*

[33] The actual consecration of Photius took place on September 9th, A.D. 447.

[34] *Conc. Chalc.*, Actio X. Mansi, *Concilia,* Vol. VII, 213C.

[35] Seeck, *Regesten der Kaiser und Päpstte.*, p. 379, whose chronology is adopted here. See Additional Note, *The chronology of the years A.D. 446–49.*

[36] The rescript is dated February 16th, A.D. 448. Mansi, *op. cit.*, Vol. V, 420. Cf. *Cod. Justin.* 1, 1, 3, 3. Kirch, *Fontes,* No. 1016. Its contents suggest that the deposition of Irenaeus had evoked considerable opposition in Syria.

[37] These hearings took place on February 25th and September 1st. See Mansi, *op. cit.*, Vol. VII, 197, 212. A further hearing appears to have taken place early in A.D. 449 which led to Ibas' banishment later in that year. Cf. Grumel, *Regestes,* Nos. 96 and 97; Seeck, *Regesten,* pp. 379, 381, 383.

a state of extreme tension between the Alexandrine and the Antiochene parties had come about. Already both sides were busily engaged, collecting allies in the expectation of an imminent outbreak of hostilities. Significant proof of this is to be found in the letter addressed by Domnus to Flavian complaining of the growing aggressiveness of the see of Alexandria, of its contempt for the Petrine see of Antioch and of its disregard for canon law,[38] and in the representations made by Eutyches to the see of Rome, alleging that "Nestorianism" was on the increase and invoking Leo's support with a view to its immediate suppression.[39] We have nothing to show what was the outcome of the appeal addressed to Flavian. The probability is that he would have preferred to avoid being involved in the controversy altogether and, at any rate, at this stage declined to be drawn in. On the other hand Leo welcomed the representations of Eutyches.[40] At the same time he was apparently not satisfied that the evidence which he had received provided a sufficient basis for immediate intervention, and in his reply, thanking the archimandrite for his zeal in the cause of orthodoxy, as he supposed, requested more detailed information. Leo was not the sort of man who could be easily imposed upon, nor was he willing to take action on unsubstantiated statements.

2. THE SYNOD OF CONSTANTINOPLE

While Leo was awaiting further details of the "Nestorian" movement, the sees of Alexandria and Antioch had already begun a guerilla warfare of correspondence.[41] Suddenly Eutyches found himself the object of a violent attack from an

[38] Theodoret, *Ep.*86. *P.G.*83, 1277 on which see above, p.211, n.22. Notice (*ibid.*, 1280C) "*ταῦτα σαφῶς εἰδώς* (sc. *ὁ Διόσκορος*) *ὡς τοῦ μεγάλου Πέτρου τὸν θρόνον ἡ τῶν* 'Αντιοχέων *μεγαλόπολις ἔχει, ὃς καὶ τοῦ μακάριου Μάρκου διδάσκαλος ἦν, καὶ τοῦ χοροῦ τῶν ἀποστόλων πρῶτος καὶ κορυφαῖος.*" The argument bears a striking resemblance to that used by Leo in *Ep.* 9, *praef.*, JK 406. Domnus appears to allude in this letter to *Conc. Const.* I, Can. 2, suggesting that these canons were known and accepted by the see of Antioch at this time, cf. *ibid.*, 1280D.

[39] See below, JK 418.

[40] *Ep.* 20, JK 418, dated June 1st, A.D. 448. Leo's caution should be compared with the precipitancy of Celestine I in *Ep.* 11, JK 372.

[41] Fragments survive in the report of the second session of the Council of Ephesus A.D. 449. See Flemming, *op. cit.*, pp. 133ff. Martin, *Actes du brigandage.*

unexpected quarter. His assailant was Eusebius, bishop of Dorylaeum, Phrygian by race and lawyer by profession. Possessed of most of the qualities of which religious fanatics and persecutors are made, he had already given proof of his capacity for controversy, while yet a layman, by leading the attack on Nestorius himself.[42] How he came to be concerned in the present controversy may be briefly explained. For some time, it seems, he had enjoyed the personal friendship of the great archimandrite and, finding the latter's opinions on the Incarnation doubtfully orthodox, did his utmost to bring his friend to a better mind.[43] When at last his efforts in this direction proved unavailing he felt himself obliged to inform the ecclesiastical authorities. However well intentioned he may have been, it is difficult to avoid the impression that he was the sort of person who takes pleasure in stirring up trouble.

The opportunity for laying this information was provided by the autumn meeting of the "home synod"[44] of Constantinople on November 8th, A.D. 448. Doubtless to such a person as Flavian a *démarche* of this sort was as unwelcome as it was unexpected, yet nothing which he could do was sufficient to prevent a formal charge against Eutyches being preferred. In any case his position was anything but enviable, since the defendant in the case was the favourite of the imperial court, and as such could afford to treat with contempt the summons presented thrice on behalf of the synod. When at last Eutyches appeared it was not till the seventh session. He arrived with a formidable military escort, at the head of which was the patrician Florentius as the official representative of the Emperor. Florentius brought with him an imperial commission charging him to supervise the proceedings.

It now remained to be seen what Eutyches would do. In the course of the second session[45] Flavian, after suggesting

[42] Mansi, *op. cit.*, Vol. VI, 673C. Cyril, *Ep.* 2, *Acta Ephesi*, ed. Schwartz, I, I, p. 23 (Acta Graeca, No. 2).

[43] Nestorius, *Bazaar*, pp. 337ff., purports to reproduce their conversation.

[44] "σύνοδος ἐνδημοῦσα." For the *Acta* of this synod see Mansi, *op. cit.*, Vol. VI, cols. 649ff. See also Mansi, *op. cit.*, Vol. VI, 657, 697 *et al.* Its nature and origin are described by Anatolius in *Conc. Chalc.*, Actio IV; Mansi, *op. cit.*, Vol. VII, 92C. Kirch, *Fontes*, No. 944.

[45] Mansi, *Concilia*, Vol. VI, pp. 657ff.

that the basis of orthodox Christology should be discussed, had obtained the synod's approval of two Cyrilline writings, the second letter to Nestorius[46] and the letter to John of Antioch,[47] and then had put forward a doctrinal statement of his own, closely resembling the *Formula of Reunion*,[48] to which the synod had agreed. On being confronted with these documents Eutyches professed his readiness to accept only the decisions of the councils of Nicaea and Ephesus (A.D. 431). Dissatisfied with his answer, Flavian not only refused to allow such a profession to be entered in the minutes but went on to insist that he should acknowledge the consubstantiality of Christ's manhood with our own. The old man was on the point of agreeing to this, though with some reluctance,[49] when Florentius interposed with an inquiry as to whether he acknowledged two natures in Christ after the Incarnation or only one. His reply to this was that he could only allow the existence of two natures before the Incarnation; after it, he declined to acknowledge more than one. The synod thereupon came to the conclusion that his belief was inconsistent with any recognition of the reality and permanence of Christ's manhood, and encouraged by the moral support of Florentius proceeded to deprive him of his rank as priest and archimandrite and pronounce his excommunication.

No doubt the synod felt that it had good ground for such a sentence, yet at the same time a little care might have prevented a grave tactical error. In the first place no record was made in the minutes of its proceedings, that Eutyches had professed his willingness to accept the definition of "two natures," "should my fathers of Rome and Alexandria require me to do so," and secondly they ignored the fact that he had given notice of his intention to lodge an appeal with the

[46] *Ep.* 4. *P.G.* 77, 44.
[47] *Ep.* 39. *P.G.* 77, 173.
[48] Mansi, *op. cit.*, Vol. VI, 680–5. It is noticeable that in the course of this statement Flavian used the phrase "ἐκ δύο φύσεων" with reference to the Incarnation, cf. p. 222, n. 73.
[49] It should be observed that in his letter to Leo, *Inter Leon. Epp.* 21, 1, *P.L.* 54, 716 he says "non audens de natura tractare Dei Verbi, qui in carnem venit . . . immutabiliter quomodo voluit et scit, in veritate, non in phantasmate homo factus."

synods of Rome, Alexandria, Jerusalem and Thessalonica.[50] Moreover, Flavian had exceeded his authority in demanding subscription to a formula for which as yet no oecumenical basis could be claimed.[51] If an explanation of these mistakes be sought, it may be found in the fact that, in his anxiety to bring the whole distasteful business to a close, Flavian was guilty of undue haste. Yet if he seriously imagined that by a suppression of facts the affair could be tactfully settled, he was to find himself much mistaken. For in any case it was most unlikely that the court, and Chrysaphius in particular, would treat with indifference such an obvious affront to its majesty as the deposition of its protégé Eutyches. In fact Nestorius, in his biography, actually asserts that from now on the Emperor "prepared all things for the deposition of Flavian and the restoration of Eutyches."[52] Moreover Eutyches himself lost no time in addressing appeals to the "greater churches," which were supported by missives from Theodosius himself.[53]

Gratifying as the reception of such an appeal must have been to Leo, it must have been far more so to Dioscorus, who doubtless saw in it an indication that "the stars in their courses" were already favourable to the rehabilitation of the prestige of his see. Hence the reception of Flavian's letter,[54] informing him of the verdict of the Constantinopolitan synod, probably caused him more amusement than annoyance.

[50] Mentioned in the proceedings of the Council of Ephesus A.D. 449. Mansi, Vol. VI, 817f. The action of Eutyches is highly significant. It shows that at that time the see of Rome alone was not held to be the ultimate authority in matters of doctrine. The fact that he failed to appeal to the see of Antioch needs no explanation.

[51] On the contrary there was some ground, from Eutyches' point of view, for regarding "monophysitism" as the true orthodoxy. Writings reputed to be of orthodox origin, though actually inspired by Apollinaris, such as the letter of Felix I, JK 140, and of Julius I, JK † 190, spoke of "one nature" only. See Lietzmann, *Apollinaris,* pp. 92, 116, 163, 256, 318, where these pseudo-orthodox writings are quoted and discussed. "Dyophysite" statements appear in Athanasius, *Or. c. Arian.* 3, 53, *P.G.* 26, 436A, and in Greg. Naz., *Ep.* 101, *P.G.* 37, 180A.

[52] *Bazaar,* pp. 340ff. where fuller details of the Emperor's treatment of Flavian are given.

[53] *Ibid.,* p. 340, cf. Leo, *Ep.* 24, JK 421. This at least is true of the appeals addressed to the sees of Rome and Alexandria.

[54] Cf. Mansi, *op. cit.,* Vol. VI, 693B, and 836, where Flavian's letter to Domnus is mentioned. It may be inferred that the same information was sent to all the "greater churches" of the East. It was unfortunate for him that he did not think it necessary at this stage to inform the see of Rome.

It is likely that the earliest information to reach Leo on the subject of the synod was conveyed by means of the imperial letter to which we have just referred. It arrived while he was still awaiting a more detailed report from Eutyches regarding the "Nestorians," of whose activities the latter had complained, and led him to expect the arrival of a further report from Flavian. As time went on and no report made its appearance, he must have decided that the best course to adopt was to reply to the Emperor in a non-committal form, and to write to Flavian on his own initiative, requesting him for detailed information. He was on the point of composing these letters when he received Eutyches' appeal,[55] to which we have already alluded. The archimandrite's letter began by explaining how, in consequence of information laid against him by Eusebius before Flavian, he had been summoned to give an account of his beliefs before the synod of Constantinople. There he had presented a profession of faith, but when required by Flavian to acknowledge two natures in Christ after the Incarnation, he had declined to do so.[56] As a result, he said, he had been condemned by a verdict of the synod, which treated him with such violence that he was only saved from personal injury by means of a military escort. Since then other Constantinopolitan abbots had required members of their convents to subscribe to his condemnation, and had prevented his written statements of belief from being read. As a proof of his orthodoxy he asserted that he condemned all heresies which ascribe to the Incarnate Lord an unreal manhood and begged that Leo would pronounce upon him the verdict which seemed most fitting.[57]

To this letter Eutyches appended three documents, first his profession of faith, presumably a copy of the one presented to the synod, in which he stated his loyalty to the teaching of

[55] *Inter Leon. Epp.*, No. 21. *P.L.* 54, 713 undated. The Greek text is lost.

[56] *Ibid.*, 1, "expetebar duas naturas fateri et anathematizare eos qui hoc negarent. Ego autem metuens definitionem a synodo (sc. Ephesino) . . . rogabam ut innotescerent ista sanctitati vestrae, et quod vobis videretur iudicaretis, profitens omnibus modis me secuturum quae probassetis."

[57] *Ibid.*, 3, "anathematizans . . . eos qui dicunt carnem Domini . . . e coelo descendisse . . . obsecro . . . quae visa vobis fuerit super fidem proferre sententiam."

Nicaea, Ephesus, Cyril and the other great fathers of the Eastern churches, then a copy of the *libellus* in which Eusebius had set forth the charges against him,[58] and finally an extract from a letter ascribed to Pope Julius I.[59] Whether intentionally or no, the writer omitted to mention several relevant facts and in consequence succeeded in giving Leo a satisfactory impression of his orthodoxy.[60] This much at least is clear if we are to judge by the Pope's references to Eutyches in the letter which he now addressed to the Emperor,[61] in which, while deploring his lack of detailed information, he called attention to the absence of any specific evidence of heresy in the *libellus* of Eusebius,[62] and mentioned that he had expressed to Flavian his concern that as yet he had not received the minutes of the Constantinopolitan synod.[63]

Besides addressing an appeal to the see of Rome Eutyches similarly approached Peter, bishop of Ravenna, doubtless in the expectation that such a step might be the means of winning the alliance of the Western imperial court. Yet if it had once been possible to procure support of this kind by approaching a bishop of a Western imperial capital, it was now largely impossible or, if possible, of little value. Peter had little to say in reply[64] other than to warn his appellant of the dangers of speculation in the hidden mystery of the

[58] The *libellus* has not been preserved.

[59] JK † 190. In reality the letter was an Apollinarian forgery on which see above, p. 217, n. 51, and cf. Lietzmann, *Apollinaris,* p. 256.

[60] See below, JK 420.

[61] *Ep.* 24, JK 421, dated February 18th, A.D. 449. Leo speaks of Theodosius as possessing, *ibid.,* 1, "non solum regium, sed etiam sacerdotalem . . . animum," an expression capable of misuse, which may suggest that even Leo was sometimes off his guard against Caesaropapism: for a similar phrase cf. *Ep.* 23, 1 and 2, JK 422, and Celestine I, *Ep.* 19, JK 380. See also Kissling, *Das Verhältnis zw. sacerd. und. imp.,* p. 26.

[62] *Ibid.,* 2, "Eusebii . . . libellus . . . de obiectionum evidentia nihil habebat, et cum presbytero haereseos crimen intenderet, quem tamen in eo sensum argueret non evidenter expressit."

[63] *Ibid.* "Ad praedictum (sc. Flavianum) autem episcopum litteras dedi, quibus mihi displicere cognosceret quod ea quae in tanta causa gesta fuerant etiam nunc silento detineret."

[64] *Inter Leon. Epp.,* No. 25, *P.L.* 54, 739 to be dated about February A.D. 449. The original text of the second half of the letter is missing. The second chapter as it stands is probably a retranslation from the Greek version which has been preserved intact. Cf. Bardenhewer, *Gesch. d. altk. lit.,* Vol. IV, p. 607.

Incarnation, expressing his evident disgust at the ceaseless Eastern controversies on the subject, and to point out that without information from Flavian he could not adopt a decisive attitude.

Then he adds:

"We advise you, reverend brother, to attend obediently to the things now being written by the most blessed Pope of the city of Rome, since blessed Peter, who lives and presides in his own see, offers the true faith to those who seek it. For we in our zeal for peace and faith cannot decide questions of faith, apart from the approval of the Bishop of Rome." [65]

The reply is highly significant of the feeling prevailing at that time in the West regarding the doctrinal prerogative of the Roman see, and shows the extent to which the ideas of the fifth century papacy had succeeded in winning recognition even from the "greater churches" of those provinces.

Meanwhile in writing to Flavian [66] Leo scarcely concealed his annoyance that no report from Constantinople of the transactions of the recent synod had as yet reached the Roman see.[67] He indicated his desire that verdicts pronounced by bishops should be carefully weighed,[68] and, with reference to the imperial letter, mentioned with approval the promise of Eutyches to amend, if he should be found in error

[65] *Ep.* 25, 2. "'Επὶ πᾶσι δὲ προτρεπόμεθά σε, ἀδελφὲ τιμιώτατε, ὥστε τοῖς παρὰ τοῦ μακαριωτάτου πάπα τῆς πόλεως Ῥώμης γραφομένοις πειθαρχούντως προσέχειν· ἐπειδὴ ὁ μακάριος Πέτρος, ὃς ἐν τῇ ἰδίᾳ καθέδρᾳ καὶ ζῇ καὶ προκάθηται, δίδωσι τοῖς ζητοῦσι τῆς πίστεως τὴν ἀλήθειαν· ἡμεῖς γὰρ σπουδῇ τῆς εἰρήνης καὶ τῆς πίστεως ἐκτὸς συναινέσεως τοῦ Ῥώμης ἐπισκόπου πίστεως αἰτίας διαγνῶναι οὐ δυνάμεθα." "τοῖς γραφομένοις" must refer to the reply which Peter expects will be sent to Eutyches by Leo. It cannot refer to the Tome, *Ep.* 28, JK 423, which was not written till June, A.D. 449.

[66] *Ep.* 23, JK 420 of the same date as the above.

[67] *Ibid.*, 1, "miramur fraternitatem tuam quidquid illud scandali fuit nobis silere potuisse, et non potius procurasse ut primitus nos insinuatio tuae relationis instrueret." It was an error of tact on the part of Flavian not to have sent some information regarding the verdict of the synod at an earlier date, but, as we have seen, he probably considered the affair as of no interest to the churches of the West. The expression "miramur" occurs frequently in papal correspondence; cf. Innocent I, *Ep.* 37, JK 314 *et al.* For the practice of sending a *relatio* to the Roman see cf. *Ep.* 10, 2, JK 407.

[68] *Ibid.*, "sacerdotum Domini matura volumus esse iudicia." Zosimus addressed a similar reproof to the African Churches, *Ep.* 12, JK 342.

by the verdict of the Roman see.[69] He concluded by saying that the primary concern of that see must be to maintain the doctrinal standards of the fathers.[70]

In the same letter Leo had urged the need of doing everything possible to preserve charity and truth. To one such as Flavian a monition of this kind was wholly redundant, for the last thing that he desired was a general disturbance of ecclesiastical peace. What is more, by the time that Leo wrote, his request for information had already been satisfied, for, whether in obedience to the Emperor or of his own accord, Flavian had addressed to the Roman see a formal notification [71] of the synodical verdict and enclosed a copy of the official minutes of the proceedings.[72] There he sets forth the nature of Eutyches' error in the following terms:

" He is attempting to overthrow the exposition concerning the faith put forth by the three hundred and eighteen fathers, and the letter of Cyril of blessed memory which he sent to Nestorius, together with the one addressed to the Easterns, to which all consented, and is reviving the old false doctrine of Valentinus and Apollinarius . . . by asserting that our Lord Jesus Christ cannot be of two natures after the Incarnation, acknowledged by us in one substance and in one person, and that the flesh of the Lord, which is taken from us and united substantially with God the Word, is not actually consubstantial with our own: also he alleged that while the Virgin who bore him is consubstantial with us, the flesh taken by the Lord of her is not so, in fact that the body of the Lord is not the body of a man, but that the body derived from the Virgin

[69] *Ibid.*, 2, " memoratus (sc. Eutyches) presbyter libello proprio sit professus paratum se esse ad corrigendum, si quid in se inventum fuerit quod reprehensione sit dignum."

[70] *Ibid.*, " in corde nostro ea observantia . . . permaneat, ne constitutiones venerabilium Patrum divinitus roboratae et ad soliditatem fidei pertinentes, prava cuiusquam interpretatione violentur." Doubtless Leo has the definition of Nicaea foremost in his mind, but perhaps also the more recent declaration at Ephesus A.D. 431.

[71] *Inter Leon. Epp.*, No. 22. *P.L.* 54, 724–8. Of the two Latin versions the second is the older and less accurate. It was this version which Leo must have used in composing *Ep.* 28, JK 423. Flavian probably waited so long as he dare in the hope of hushing up the whole affair. On the chronological order of *Epp.* 22 and 26 see Batiffol, *Siège Apostolique,* p. 505 and Caspar, *Geschichte,* Vol. I, pp. 613f.

[72] *Ibid.*, 4. " *τὴν ἐπ' αὐτῷ* (sc. Εὐτυχεῖ) *γεγενημένην πρᾶξιν ἀπεστείλαμεν.*"

is human only in form, thus contradicting all the expositions of the holy fathers."[73]

The letter concluded with the request that Leo would make known the findings of the synod to the bishops of the western churches,[74] showing evidently that the writer treated the whole incident as finally closed.

It was probably early in March that Flavian received Leo's request for a report, by which time, as we have seen, his own letter had already left Constantinople. He found enclosed with the request a letter specially addressed to the members of the monastic section,[75] who were supporting him against Eutyches. The latter appear already to have informed Leo that dangerous doctrinal ideas were being fostered by which they probably alluded to the extreme Cyrilline sympathies of Eutyches and his friends.[76] In his reply the Pope suggested that the confession of St. Peter was a sufficient safeguard against error,[77] and requested further information if developments were to take place.

[73] *Ep.* 22, 3. "τὴν δὲ τῶν τριακοσίων δέκα καὶ ὀκτὼ ἁγίων πατέρων περὶ τῆς πίστεως γενομένην ἔκθεσιν, καὶ τοῦ τῆς θείας μνήμης Κυρίλλου πρός τε Νεστόριον γραφεῖσαν ἐπιστολὴν καὶ τὴν πρὸς τοὺς τῆς ἀνατολῆς τοῦ αὐτοῦ ὁμοίως, αἷς πάντες συνέθεντο, πειρώμενος ἀνατρέπειν, τὴν πάλαι τοῦ δυσσεβοῦς Οὐαλεντίνου καὶ 'Απολλιναρίου κακοδοξίαν ἀνανεούμενος . . . λέγων τὸν Κύριον ἡμῶν 'Ιησοῦν Χριστὸν μὴ δεῖν ἐκ δύο φύσεων μετὰ τὴν ἐνανθρώπησιν, ἐν μίᾳ ὑποστάσει, καὶ ἐν ἑνὶ προσώπῳ παρ' ἡμῶν γνωριζόμενον, μήτε μὴν τὴν σάρκα τοῦ Κυρίου ὁμοούσιον ἡμῖν ὑπάρχειν, οἷα δὴ ἐξ ἡμῶν προσληφθεῖσαν καὶ ἑνωθεῖσαν τῷ Θεῷ Λόγῳ καθ' ὑπόστασιν· ἀλλ' ἔφασκε, τὴν μὲν τεκοῦσαν αὐτὸν Παρθένον κατὰ σάρκα ὁμοούσιον ἡμῖν εἶναι, αὐτὸν δὲ τὸν Κύριον μὴ εἰληφέναι ἐξ αὐτῆς σάρκα ἡμῖν ὁμοούσιον · ἀλλὰ τὸ τοῦ Κυρίου σῶμα μὴ εἶναι μὲν σῶμα ἀνθρώπου, ἀνθρώπινον δέ σῶμα τὸ ἐκ τῆς Παρθένου, πάσαις ταῖς ἐκθέσεσι τῶν ἁγίων Πατέρων ἐναντιούμενος." The ἔκθεσις mentioned is that of Nicaea, and Cyril's letters the same as above, i.e. *Epp.* 4 and 39. The phrase "μὴ δεῖν ἐκ δύο φύσεων" is obscure and may be due to a corrupt text. Flavian appears to suggest that "of two natures" is orthodox, though it was not so regarded at Chalcedon. Cf. *Conc. Chalc.*, Definitio. Mansi, *op. cit.*, Vol. VII, 108.

[74] *Ibid.*, 4. "ὥστε καὶ τὴν σὴν ὁσιότητα γνοῦσαν τὰ κατ' αὐτὸν (sc. Εὐτυχὴν), πᾶσι τοῖς ὑπὸ τὴν σὴν θεοσέβειαν τέλουσι θεοφιλεστάτοις ἐπισκόποις δήλην ποιῆσαι τὴν αὐτοῦ δυσσέβειαν." It will be observed that Flavian does not ask for formal approval of the synod's verdict.

[75] *Ep.* 72, JK 455, without a date. This letter is evidently prior to the letter sent by Flavian, *Ep.* 22. See Caspar, *Geschichte,* Vol. I, p. 471, n. 3. Jaffé gives its date as A.D. 450 but mistakenly.

[76] Just as Eutyches in his turn had reported the activities of the "Nestorians," by which he probably meant the authors of this information.

[77] *Ibid.*, "haec fides vincit mundum, quando quis credit quia Christus Jesus est Filius Dei." The allusion is most probably to Matthew xvi. 16. St. Peter's confession was to serve as one of the main arguments against Eutychianism in *Ep.* 28, 5, JK 423. Cf. also 1 John v. 4.

Unhappily for Flavian the support of the anti-Eutychian monks was of little avail as an ally against the overwhelming forces of his opponents, and however much he might hope that the synod's verdict had settled the matter, there were other and more powerful influences in Constantinople which were determined that it should not be so. In fact he began to find himself the victim of a kind of petty persecution,[78] intended apparently either to break down his resistance or at least to effect some sort of compromise. Yet in view of the synodical verdict compromise was by now impossible. Only two courses of action remained open, either to uphold the synod and so to face the hostility of the Emperor Theodosius (or rather of his chamberlain Chrysaphius), or to resign his office. When, however, his proffered resignation had been indignantly refused [79] he must have realized, if not before, the extreme precariousness of his position, and that he and Eutyches had all but exchanged their respective rôles of defendant and judge. Nevertheless, for the time being his enemies directed the spear-head of their attack, not against himself but against his synod. An attempt was made to prove that the synodical *Acta* had been falsified [80] and, when this failed, to render the verdict ineffective by the expedient of procuring a contrary verdict from a general council. It was to this end therefore that the supporters of Eutyches now directed their efforts. In this undertaking they found a willing partner in Dioscorus, who must have seen in the present crisis an unparalleled opportunity of humiliating the see of Constantinople, and at the same time of restoring the prestige of Alexandrine Christology generally and of his own see in particular.

So by the time that Leo's original letter [81] reached Constantinople Flavian needed no prompting to send an immediate reply [82] in which he explained in detail the error of Eutyches.

[78] Nestorius, *Bazaar,* ed. Driver and Hodgson, pp. 340–2. Cf. Mansi, *op. cit.,* Vol. VI, 597.

[79] *Bazaar,* p. 343.

[80] *Ibid.*

[81] *Ep.* 23, JK 420, dated February 18th, A.D. 449.

[82] *Inter Leon. Epp.,* No. 26, P.L. 54, 744. It must have been written before the actual publication on March 30th, A.D. 449 of the edict summoning the council.

"He alleges," the bishop writes, "that though before the Incarnation of our Saviour Jesus Christ there are two natures, of the Godhead and of the manhood, yet after the union there has been but one." [83]

After recalling Eutyches' confused statement regarding Christ's manhood, Flavian affirmed that he had been justly condemned by the synod and warned Leo that in view of his persistent obstinacy all hope of his repentance was in vain. The archimandrite's assertion that he had appealed to the see of Rome in the course of the synodical proceedings was refuted by a blank denial.[84] Finally, in almost suppliant tones, Flavian implored Leo to uphold the synod's verdict by means of a confirmation in writing, "for only so," he suggests, "can the heresy be suppressed and the projected council avoided." [85]

It is probable that there were others besides Flavian who viewed the summoning of a fresh general council with distaste, if not with apprehension, and would have welcomed any alternative to such a project as a means of settling the dispute. Under the circumstances, however, the only course of action which remained open was an appeal to the Roman see.

It was now evident that the imperial government was determined on the plan of summoning a council. It came therefore as no surprise to anyone when the edict ordering the bishops to assemble on August 1st following at Ephesus was published on March 30th, A.D. 449,[86] the terms of which showed clearly enough that the friends of Eutyches had had a considerable share in its composition. Not only was Theodoret, bishop of Cyrrhus and leading theologian of the "dyophysite" party, expressly excluded from attendance, but

[83] *Inter Leon Epp.*, No. 26, 745A. "φάσκων πρὸ μὲν τῆς ἐνανθρωπήσεως τοῦ σωτῆρος ἡμῶν I. X. δύο φύσεις εἶναι, Θεότητος καὶ ἀνθρωπότητος, μετὰ δὲ τὴν ἕνωσιν, μίαν φύσιν γεγονέναι."

[84] *Ibid.*, 747A. "ὡς ὁ αὐτὸς Εὐτυχὴς λιβέλλους ἐξαπέστειλεν ὑμῖν πεπληρωμένους πάσης ἀπάτης καὶ πανουργίας, ἐν τῷ καιρῷ τῆς κρίσεως λιβέλλους ἐπιδεδωκέναι ἐκκλήτους ἡμῖν καὶ τῇ ἐνδημούσῃ ἁγίᾳ συνόδῳ καὶ ἐπικαλέσασθαι τὴν ὑμετέραν ὁσιότητα· ὅπερ οὐδαμῶς παρ' αὐτοῦ γέγονεν." Perhaps the appeal was made in the hearing of Florentius, not of Flavian.

[85] *Ibid.*, 748C. "διὰ τῶν ὑμετέρων ἱερῶν γραμμάτων κωλυθήσεται δὲ καὶ ἡ θρυλλομένη γένεσθαι σύνοδος."

[86] Mansi, *op. cit.*, Vol. VI, 588 where the imperial summons addressed to Dioscorus is given. For the invitation to Leo see *Ep.* 31, 4, JK 425B. It may be inferred that similar summonses were sent to other bishops of the "greater churches."

permission was actually given for the Syrian archimandrite, Barsumas, already notorious for his advanced monophysitism, to take part in the proceedings. Most significant of all, the presidency of the council was explicitly assigned to Dioscorus. Meanwhile the question of the genuineness of the Constantinopolitan *Acta* was revived, and a commission appointed to investigate the matter. Two sessions of the commission were held, and at the later one [87] on April 27th Flavian himself was required to produce a statement of his belief. In this statement, while assenting to the dogmatic formulae of Nicaea, Constantinople I (A.D. 381) and Ephesus (A.D. 431), he affirmed his belief in two natures after the Incarnation, in one substance and in one person, though he admitted the truth of the Cyrilline phrase " One nature of God the Word incarnate and made man." His enemies must have been more than satisfied, for here was enough to secure a verdict of deposition at the forthcoming council.

Before passing on to describe the events of that council we must pause for a moment to notice what was taking place at Rome. Flavian's second letter [88] was probably not received there till the latter part of May, A.D. 449. Meanwhile his first letter [89] had to be acknowledged. In doing so [90] Leo stated that after carefully studying its contents and the *Acta* of the Constantinopolitan synod he had arrived at the conclusion that Eutyches' opinions were open to serious objection, and promised to send a detailed treatment of the whole subject.[91]

This promise he fulfilled on June 13th, and the result was the famous letter to Flavian now generally known as the " Tome." [92] Leo begins by reiterating his surprise that Flavian

[87] Mansi, *op. cit.*, Vol. VI, 540. Liberatus, *Breviarium,* 11. *P.L.* 68, 1001. Cf. Nestorius, *Bazaar,* p. 343.

[88] *Inter Leon. Epp.*, No. 26.

[89] *Inter Leon. Epp.*, No. 22.

[90] *Ep.* 27, JK 422, dated May 21st, A.D. 449.

[91] *Ibid.*, "quae (sc. epistolae) nos de causa facerent certiores, quam apud vos pravo dolemus errore commotam. . . . Verum de hac re plenius . . . rescribimus: ut fraternitatem tuam quid de tota causa constitui debeat instruamus."

[92] *Ep.* 28, JK 423. The doctrinal significance of this letter will be further discussed in Chap. XX, on Leo as a Theologian. See also Additional Note, *The reception of the Tome and its bearing on the dogma of Papal Infallibility.*

had so long postponed the duty of sending him a report on the Constantinopolitan synod, and shows that careful perusal of that report has now convinced him that Eutyches had been guilty of both rashness and perverse ignorance.[93] Had the latter only taken the trouble to appreciate the plain teaching of the Old and New Testaments, as well as the elementary truths of the creed he might easily have avoided both pitfalls.[94] Leo then goes on to show that Eutyches' refusal to acknowledge that our Lord had the body of a man is equally inconsistent with the teaching of Holy Scripture,[95] and that nothing less than the possession of two integral natures, human as well as divine, can satisfy the requirements of the divine plan for the salvation of the human race.[96] After discussing the relation between these two natures, and proving their distinctness by means of scriptural illustrations, he urges that the truth regarding the Incarnation was proclaimed at Caesarea Philippi:

"Then," he writes, "blessed Peter with divine inspiration, destined to benefit all nations with his confession, exclaimed, 'Thou art the Christ, the Son of the Living God.' Deservedly he was pronounced blessed by the Lord, and from the chief Corner Stone derived the stability both of his courage and his name, in that by revelation from the Father he confessed the same Person to be Son of God and Christ, seeing that to

[93] *Ep.* 28, 1. "Lectis dilectionis tuae litteris, quas miramur fuisse tam seras, et gestorum episcopalium ordine recensito, tandem quid apud vos scandali contra integritatem fidei exortum fuisset agnovimus . . . Quibus Eutyches . . . multum imprudens et nimis imperitus ostenditur."

[94] *Ibid.*, "in hanc insipientiam cadunt qui cum ad cognoscendam veritatem aliquo impediuntur obscuro, non ad propheticas voces, non ad apostolorum litteras, nec ad evangelicas auctoritates, sed ad semetipsos recurrunt; . . . Et quod per totum mundum omnium regenerandorum voce depromitur, istius adhuc senis corde non capitur."

[95] *Ibid.*, 2. "Nec frustratorie loquens, ita Verbum diceret carnem factum, ut editus utero virginis Christus haberet formam hominis, et non haberet materni corporis veritatem. An forte ideo putavit Dominum nostrum Jesum Christum non nostrae esse naturae, quia missus ad beatam Mariam semper virginem angelus ait: Spiritus sanctus superveniet in te, et virtus Altissimi obumbrabit tibi; ideoque et quod nascetur ex te sanctum, vocabitur Filius Dei (Luke i. 35)? ut quia conceptus virginis divini fuit operis, non de natura concipientis fuerit caro concepti."

[96] *Ibid.*, 3, "ad resolvendum conditionis nostrae debitum, natura inviolabilis naturae est unita passibili: ut quod nostris remediis congruebat, unus atque idem mediator Dei et hominum, homo Jesus Christus, et mori posset ex uno et mori non posset ex altero."

receive one of these truths without the other would not have availed for salvation; and there was an equal risk of believing the Lord Jesus Christ either to be God only, and not man as well, or man only and not God." [97]

At the conclusion of this long letter Leo turns to the minutes of the synod and expresses his amazement that Flavian had been willing to acquiesce in Eutyches' view that there had been two natures before the Incarnation; [98] at the same time he shows that he has not yet abandoned hope of the archimandrite's repentance, though he insists that proof of this must be given by subscription to a written repudiation of his mistaken opinions.[99] Finally he states that he has sent three representatives, Julius, bishop of Puteoli, Renatus a Roman priest, and Hilary a Roman deacon, to act in the matter on behalf of the Roman see.[100]

We shall consider the doctrinal significance of this letter in a later chapter. For the moment it will be sufficient to draw attention to its importance in the ecclesiastical politics of the time. The "Tome" made an explicit claim on behalf of the Roman see, in its appeal to the testimony of St. Peter, that that see is to be regarded as the final authority in matters of doctrine. In addition to this, the fact that it was phrased in simple, concise and direct language rendered it readily intelli-

[97] *Ibid.*, 5. "Ubi beatus Petrus divinitus inspiratus, et confessione sua omnibus gentibus profuturus, Tu es, inquit, Christus Filius Dei vivi (Matthew xvi. 16). Nec immerito beatus est pronuntiatus a Domino, et a principali petra soliditatem et virtutis traxit et nominis, qui per revelationem Patris eumdem et Dei Filium est confessus et Christum: quia unum horum sine alio receptum non proderat ad salutem; et aequalis erat periculi Dominum Jesum Christum aut Deum tantummodo sine homine, aut sine Deo solum hominem credidisse."

[98] Cf. Mansi, *op. cit.*, Vol. VI, 744B, and see above, p. 222, n. 73. Leo evidently suspected that the whole affair had been mismanaged from the start and showed little grasp of Flavian's real difficulty, namely, the support of the eastern government which was Eutyches' safeguard. Later on he admitted, *Ep.* 34, 1, JK 428 that he could not understand what was objectionable in Eutyches' teaching.

[99] As in the case of others suspected of heresy. Cf. *Ep.* 1, 2, JK 398. The ruling may reflect *Conc. Nic.*, Can. 8.

[100] There is no reason to think that at the time when this letter was written Leo intended his representatives to be official legates to the projected council. Rather they were intended to be papal assessors at a re-examination of Eutyches, which the Pope doubtless expected would take place at Constantinople. It is likely that he assumed that the procedure prescribed by *Conc. Sard.*, Can. 7 (vers. lat.), Mirbt, *Quellen*, No. 122, would be followed.

gible to minds unversed in theological subtlety, and this explains the eagerness with which it was subsequently accepted as a basis of unity. But it was not the only letter which Leo entrusted to his representatives.

When they left Rome on June 13th, A.D. 449, they took with them at least five other documents directed to persons of note in Constantinople. One of them, addressed to the Emperor's sister Pulcheria,[101] is of special interest since it represents the earliest attempt on Leo's part to win support for "dyophysite" teaching by courting the favour of a member of the imperial family, and in particular of one who had good reason to resent the dominance of the theological "school" protected by Chrysaphius. Pulcheria appears already to have given proof of her willingness to support Flavian, so far as it lay in her power to do so, and for that reason seemed likely to be of some help in the delicate undertaking of winning Eutyches to repentance and settling the whole question.[102] Nor was she the only possible ally. There was also the archimandrite Faustus, of whom we have already heard as the leader of those Constantinopolitan monks who were opposed to Eutyches. A personal letter was therefore addressed by Leo to him,[103] drawing the attention of himself and his sup-

[101] *Ep.* 30, JK 425A dated June 13th, A.D. 449. There is a considerable difference of opinion as to the relation of this letter to *Ep.* 31, JK 425B, which in most codd. lacks a date and is omitted in the Greek *Acta* of Chalcedon. The Ballerini, *P.L.* 54, 786 and Hefele-Leclercq, *Conciles,* Vol. II, pp. 581f. agree in suggesting that *Ep.* 31 was never actually sent off. Langen, *Geschichte der röm. Kirche,* Vol. II, p. 26, n. 1 and Wille, *Julian v. Kios,* p. 20 hold it to be a forgery. The fact, however, that Leo mentions the repetition of a letter in *Ep.* 45, 1, JK 439, also addressed to Pulcheria, renders it probable that *Ep.* 31 is actually a second edition of *Ep.* 30, written because the original letter failed to reach its destination. It would appear that previous to the writing of this letter, Leo had not thought it worth while to address himself to the secular rulers of the East. The supporters of Eutyches, on the other hand, had taken good care to keep in touch with them from the beginning. Hence their initial advantages. For the effect of Leo's influence on the eastern court see below, Chap. XI, pp. 264, 275.

[102] It seems evident from *ibid.,* 2, "ei, qui in errore est, melius consuletur, si *ubi* desipuit, *ibi* resipiscat: et *ubi* damnationem meruit, *illic* indulgentiam consequatur," that Leo still expects that the procedure prescribed by *Conc. Sardic.,* Can. 3 and 5 (vers. lat.) is to be put into action. The letter shows clearly that he relied on Eutyches' promise to recant if the Roman see should find him to be in error. Cf. *Ep.* 21, 1, *ad fin.*

[103] *Ep.* 32, JK 426 of the same date.

porters to the letter forwarded to Flavian, and expressing the hope that Eutyches might be moved to change his mind; otherwise he must be excluded from the Church.

It is clear that Leo still supposed that a fresh synod, with his own representatives as assessors, was in prospect and that there was not as yet any question of calling together a general council. With this prospect in mind he included a special letter intended to be heard by the members of the synod.[104] Here he reiterates the theme, which has already appeared in the letter to Flavian, as to the sufficiency of St. Peter's confession for the definition of the truth regarding the Incarnation.[105] He then refers to the papal assessors whom he has despatched from Rome to take part in the rehearing of Eutyches' case,[106] and reaffirms his hope that the latter will be brought to repudiate his error.

The next letter belonging to this post introduces to us for the first time an important figure in the relations of Leo with the see of Constantinople. He is Julian, bishop of Cios in *Bithynia Pontica*,[107] who was evidently in close touch with the affairs of the Constantinopolitan church. Throughout the critical period of the councils of Ephesus and Chalcedon he remained in the closest possible touch with Leo, and was occasionally, as we shall see, the means of preventing an error of judgment on the part of the Roman see. The letter which Leo now sent[108] was actually a reply to a report already

[104] *Ep.* 33, JK 427 of the same date. Although the title reads "ad Ephesinam synodam secundam" it should be noticed that there is no mention of Ephesus in the text, and it is therefore probable that it was addressed to the new synod which Leo supposed would be assembled in Constantinople.

[105] *Ibid.*, 1, "principis fides . . . hanc reverentiam divinis detulit institutis, ut ad sanctae dispositionis effectum auctoritatem apostolicae sedis adhiberet, tamquam ab ipso . . . Petro cuperet declarari, quid in eius confessione laudatum sit." It is a mistake to interpret these words as implying that the Emperor recognized the need of papal approval for the summoning a new synod. Leo's meaning is that he welcomes the Emperor's letter as indicating that Theodosius wishes a "Petrine" definition on a matter of faith. Whether Theodosius really meant anything of the kind is open to doubt.

[106] *Ibid.*, 2, "ut pleniore iudicio omnis possit error aboleri."

[107] On the question as to the see to which Julian actually belonged see Additional Note B, *Julian, bishop of Cios.*

[108] *Ep.* 34, JK 428 of the same date. It is possible that this letter was discarded in favour of *Ep.* 35 written to meet the situation revealed by Julian's second report. On various views as to the relation between these two letters see Caspar, *Geschichte,* Vol. I, p. 614.

received. In this report Julian had evidently made it clear that there was really no hope whatever that Eutyches would change his mind. Leo himself admits that before receiving Flavian's (first) letter and the *Acta* of the Constantinopolitan synod he had been unable to understand what was amiss with the beliefs of Eutyches, yet he shows that he still clings to the hope that the archimandrite will give way to superior judgement.[109]

Just as the legates from Rome were on the point of departure a further message was received from Julian, a reply to which[110] was therefore included with the rest. Now for the first time Leo writes outspokenly on the subject of Eutyches' error as these words show:

"We added this page to accompany those letters so that you may resist with unanimity and constancy these people who wish to corrupt the Gospel of Christ: since we and you share the same instruction and teaching of the Holy Ghost, which if any man does not receive, he is not a member of the body of Christ . . . yet how can it profit that most foolish old man to attack with the name of 'Nestorianism' the belief of those whose devout faith he cannot shake, while like Nestorius himself, who departed from the truth by separating the Godhead of the Word from the substance of the manhood which it assumed, he too forsakes the right path by teaching that the only begotten Son of God was so born of the womb of the blessed Virgin, that while He wore the outward form of a human body yet the reality of human flesh was not united to the Word."[111]

[109] *Ep.* 34, 1. "Diu apud nos incertum fuit, quid in ipso (sc. Eutyche) catholicis displiceret . . . sed postquam gestorum ad nos episcopalium documenta perlata sunt, omnia illa quae fallacium querelarum velamine tegebantur, quam essent detestanda, patuerunt."

[110] *Ep.* 35, JK 429 of the same date. It will be observed that the Greek version omits several passages, e.g. in c. 3. This may be explained either as due to the blunt tone of Leo's criticism of the Constantinopolitan synod or to the translator's view that certain of his arguments would sound trivial to a Greek reader.

[111] *Ibid.*, 1, "hanc paginam quae illis epistolis consonaret adiecimus, ut unanimiter atque constanter his qui evangelium Christi corrumpere cupiunt resistatis: quoniam sancti Spiritus in nobis atque in vobis una est eruditio eademque doctrina; quam quicumque non recipit non est membrum corporis Christi. . . . Quid autem prodest imprudentissimo seni, Nestorianae haereseos nomine, eorum lacerare opinionem, quorum piissimam convellere non potest fidem; cum quantum Nestorius a

In the last of the letters entrusted to his representatives Leo addresses the Emperor Theodosius himself.[112] This is evidently a formal answer to the imperial proposal to review Flavian's verdict at a fresh synod. The Pope makes it clear that he believes the condemnation of Eutyches to have been fully justified but that even now he has not abandoned hope that the old man will modify his views in accordance with his promise.[113]

The ship carrying the Roman legates had scarcely left Italy when Flavian's second letter[114] came into Leo's hands. The same post brought a further letter from Theodosius. This was probably a formal invitation to the Pope to take part in the forthcoming imperial general council. Leo sent an immediate reply to both letters. He addressed a brief acknowledgment to Flavian,[115] mentioning that although in his view it was superfluous to discuss the doctrinal question any further,[116] yet he had sent off his representatives to take part in the projected council. In writing to the Emperor,[117] after praising his zeal on behalf of the faith, he asked him to excuse him attendance at the council partly on the ground that no precedent existed to justify the presence of a Roman bishop on such an occasion, and partly because the present conditions did not permit of his absence from the city.[118] He adds that he will do his utmost to comply with the imperial instructions and therefore has sent his delegates "who will be sufficient to cut short scandals according to the nature of the case, and will

veritate discessit, Deitatem verbi ab assumpti hominis substantia separando, tantum a recto tramite ipse desciscat, qui Unigenitum Dei Filium sic de utero beatae Virginis praedicat natum, ut humani quidem corporis speciem gesserit, sed humanae carnis veritas Verbo unita non fuerit." It is probable that by "illis epistolis" he refers to the letter addressed to Flavian, i.e. *Ep.* 28, JK 423.

[112] *Ep.* 29, JK 424 also of June 13th, A.D. 449.

[113] *Ibid.*, "hoc saltem sibi ad promerendam veniam reservaverit, ut correcturum se esse promitteret quidquid nostra sententia de his, quae male senserat, improbasset."

[114] *Ep.* 26, see above, p. 223.

[115] *Ep.* 36, JK 430 dated June 20th, A.D. 449.

[116] *Ibid.*, "quamvis evidenter appareat, rem . . . nequaquam synodali indigere tractatu."

[117] *Ep.* 37, JK 431 of the same date.

[118] *Ibid.*, "cum nec aliqua ex hoc ante exempla praecesserint, et temporalis necessitas me non patiatur deserere civitatem, praesertim cum tam evidens fidei causa sit, ut rationabilius ab indicenda synodo fuisset abstinendum."

represent my presence," though he suggests that the projected council is actually unnecessary.[119] In so saying Leo appears to betray a certain feeling of uneasiness lest the proceedings of the council may lead to the adoption of a policy at variance with his own. We shall see presently that his uneasiness on that score was amply justified.

To resume the narrative of events in the East. It seems probable that none of the letters which were entrusted to the Roman delegates on June 13th ever actually reached their destination.[120] Instead of putting in at Constantinople, Julius and his colleagues were sent on to Ephesus.[121] This meant, of course, that they had little or no opportunity of appreciating the extent to which the real state of affairs differed from the impression, which the information received at Rome had led them to form. What is more, the fact that their letter-bag contained no communication for Dioscorus, the imperially appointed president of the council, was a serious omission and one which was likely, not only to cause considerable offence, but might even suggest that they were to be regarded as partisans of the bishop of Constantinople.

Additional Note A

THE CHRONOLOGY OF THE YEARS A.D. 446–449

Some mention must be made here of the uncertainty which prevails as to the order of events in the years A.D. 446—449, at least so far as the affairs of the Eastern churches are concerned.

Thus Driver and Hodgson[122] give the following chronology:

446 Proclus dies, and is succeeded by Flavian . . .

[119] *Ep.* 37. "meum studium commodavi, ut Clementiae vestrae statutis aliquatenus pareatur, ordinatis hinc fratribus meis, qui amputandis scandalis pro causae qualitate sufficiant, quique praesentiae meae impleant vicem: quia non talis quaestio orta est de qua aut possit aut debeat dubitari."

[120] It is also probable that *Epp.* 30 and 35 miscarried. Cf. *Epp.* 31, 1, and 113, 4, with reference to *Ep.* 35.

[121] *Inter Epp. Leon.*, No. 46, 1 shows that Hilary the deacon had not visited Constantinople. Cf. Caspar, *Geschichte,* Vol. I, p. 483, n. 3. The legates were evidently conducted to Ephesus direct on the outward journey to prevent their establishing contact with Flavian's supporters, and on his return Hilary no doubt avoided the capital as a dangerous area for a fugutive from ecclesiastical "justice."

[122] *Bazaar,* pp. xxvff.

447 Count Irenaeus is recalled from banishment and consecrated Bishop of Tyre.
448 February. An Imperial Rescript proscribes the works of Porphyry and Nestorius, and orders the deposition of Irenaeus.
September. Photius is consecrated Bishop of Tyre in place of Irenaeus.
November. *Synod of Constantinople.*
449 April. The Eutychians procure the condemnation of Ibas of Edessa.
August. *The Latrocinium.*
Ibas, Irenaeus . . . and Domnus are all deposed.

The chronology supplied by Kidd [123] resembles the foregoing:

446 October. Proclus dies and is succeeded by Flavian.
447 Irenaeus consecrated Bishop of Tyre.
448 February. An Imperial Rescript proscribes the works of Porphyry and Nestorius, and orders the deposition of Irenaeus.
September. Photius is consecrated Bishop of Tyre.
October. Imperial mandate ordering the examination of Ibas.
449 February. Commission sits at Berytus.
March? Second session at Tyre.
April. Further judgment of Ibas at Edessa.
June. Rescript ordering his banishment.
August. *The Latrocinium.*
Ibas, Irenaeus . . . and Domnus are all deposed.

On the other hand Seeck [124] dates these events thus:

447 September. Photius is consecrated Bishop of Tyre.
October. Imperial mandate ordering the examination of Ibas.
448 January. Ibas leaves Edessa.
February. An Imperial Rescript proscribes the works of Nestorius and orders the expulsion of Irenaeus from Tyre.
Commission sits at Tyre.
September. Commission at Berytus.
November. *Synod of Constantinople.*

[123] *History*, Vol. III, pp. 281ff.
[124] *Regesten der Kaiser und Päpste*, pp. 379ff.

449 April. Rescript regarding the charges put forward against Ibas.

June. Instructions to the Council of Ephesus regarding Ibas.

August. *The Latrocinium.*

Ibas, Irenaeus . . . and Domnus are all deposed.

It is clear that Proclus was still alive at the time when Domnus consecrated Irenaeus to the see of Tyre, for we are told by Theodoret that he first of all obtained Proclus' approval.[125] Hence Irenaeus must have been consecrated earlier than July A.D. 446. Ibas had succeeded Rabbula in the see of Edessa in the previous year. Briefly the problem so far as Irenaeus is concerned is whether his deposition is to be assigned to A.D. 447 rather than the following year. All our authorities agree that the rescript proscribing "Nestorianism" belongs to February, A.D. 448.[126] The question is whether it refers to the deposition of Irenaeus as a past or as a future event. The text as it stands might be susceptible of either interpretation. But the fact that the consecration of Photius as his successor took place in the latter part of the previous year, A.D. 447,[127] renders the former interpretation the more reasonable. Further it seems that Kidd has inverted the order of the two examinations of Ibas. The citation read in the *Acta* of the examination held at Tyre is dated February 25th:[128] that read in the *Acta* of Berytus, September 1st.[129] The only question is whether these should be assigned to A.D. 448 or A.D. 449. But in view of the sequence of events generally it is clear that the former year is correct.

[125] *Ep.* 110, *P.G.* 83, 1306c.

[126] Unfortunately the document lacks the consular year; it concludes with the bare statement. Mansi, *Concilia,* Vol. V, 420, "Ἀνεγνώσθη ἐν τῇ ἐκκλησίᾳ τῶν μοναζόντων ἐν τοῖς ἐρημικοῖς, φαρμουθί κγ' ἰνδικτιῶνος α' ἔτους Διοκλητιανοῦ ρξδ'" i.e. April 18th, A.D. 448.

[127] *Abh. d. Gött. Ges. d. Wiss.,* Vol. XV, 1 (1917), p. 123, l. 14.

[128] Mansi, *op. cit.,* Vol. VII, 197.

[129] *Ibid.,* Vol. VII, 212. But in both dates the "Postconsulate" contradicts the "Indiction." The former indicates A.D. 449, the latter A.D. 448. Yet the latter is shown to be the more accurate from the Syrian *Acta* of the *Latrocinium,* in which documents which belong to April, A.D. 449 mention the examination of Ibas at Berytus as having already taken place. Cf. *Abh. d. Gött. Ges. d. Wiss,* Vol. XV, 1 (1917), p. 15, l. 8; p. 23, l. 47; p. 25, l. 13; p. 35, l. 50; p. 39, l. 47; p. 43, ll. 13ff. The fact that Ibas left Edessa on January 1st (*Chron. Edessa,* 64, *Texte und Unters.,* Vol. IX, pp. 84ff.) accords with these dates since his departure was evidently for the purpose of attending the first examination which was held at Tyre on February 25th of the same year.

Additional Note B

JULIAN, BISHOP OF CIOS

Until recently historians have generally held the view that the see of which Julian, Leo's *nuncio* and official representative at the court and see of Constantinople, was bishop was the city of Cos, situated on an island of the same name.[130] The island lies off the south-western coast of Asia Minor, and in the fifth century formed part of the province of *Caria*. Nevertheless here and there some doubt has been felt that the usual view was open to strong objections.[131] The most obvious difficulty is that of explaining how it could be possible for a bishop, whose see was situated some four hundred miles away from Constantinople, to find opportunity of keeping in such close contact with the city and see of the eastern capital as is implied by the frequent references to his work contained in Leo's correspondence, and at the same time to maintain the administration of the church of Cos during a period of at least ten years.

On the other hand, it is noteworthy that the titles of Leo's letters to Julian,[132] invariably describe him as *episcopus Coensis*. The question has been re-examined in recent years by Wille,[133] whose conclusions are here set forth.

It is pointed out that the evidence of the lists of subscriptions to conciliar *Acta* in which the name of Julian appears renders the traditional view open to serious doubt. Thus in

[130] The island of Cos is mentioned as a place of importance in Acts xxi. 1. It lay on the principal trade route between the cities on the coast of the Aegean Sea and the coasts of Syria and Egypt. It had formerly a Jewish colony of some size, and could boast a statue erected in honour of Herod Antipas!

[131] e.g. by Tillemont, *Mémoires,* Vol. XV, p. 915 where he draws attention to the occurrence of Julian's signature, not among the legates of the Roman see, but at a point before that of John of Rhodes, the metropolis of which Cos was a suffragan see. Cf. Mansi, *op. cit.,* Vol. VI, 1084.

[132] No less than twenty of Leo's letters were addressed to Julian, namely *Epp.* 34, 35, 48, 81, 86, 92, 107, 109, 113, 117, 118, 122, 125, 127, 131, 140, 141, 144, 147, 152. His name also occurs in many others addressed to the East, of which the last to be written is *Ep.* 156. It would appear from *Ep.* 81, JK 461, "nobis te et patriae praesentares," and *Ep.* 113, 4, JK 489, "in Latinum scilicet sermonem absolutissima interpretatione translata," that he was of Italian, if not of Roman, origin.

[133] *Julian von Cios.*

the list of subscriptions to the *Acta* of the Synod of Constantinople, A.D. 448, the Greek and Latin versions show divergent readings.[134] Similarly in the list of subscriptions appended to the canons of Chalcedon it is highly significant that the signature of Julian appears, not among the bishops of the ecclesiastical province of Rhodes, to which the island of Cos actually belonged, but immediately after the bishops of Nicomedia and Nicaea, and preceding the bishop of Chalcedon.[135] On the other hand, in none of these lists is any mention made of the see of Cios. This is at least surprising, in view of the fact that Cios was an ancient Greek colony and a city of some commercial importance in the fifth century. Moreover it is known to have been the seat of a bishop at least as early as the council of Nicaea.[136] A reasonable inference from these facts is that the transcribers confused Cios with Cos, and that the mistake once made gradually influenced all the current MSS. to the exclusion of the true reading. As Cios was situated in the province of *Bithynia,* its bishop would not find it difficult to keep in close touch with the affairs of the capital, from which his see was separated only by a short sea route, and at the same time to continue the administration of his diocese.

[134] In the session of April 13th. Mansi, *op. cit.,* Vol. VI, 749, "'Ιουλιανὸς . . . ἐπίσκοπος τῆς Κῶ": vers. lat. "Julianus . . . episcopus Coensis." Later on, Mansi, *op. cit.,* Vol. VI, 760 we read "'Ιουλιανοῦ . . . ἐπισκόπου τῆς 'Αδραμυτινῶν πόλεως": vers. lat. "Julianus . . . episcopus Conensis civitatis," with var. U. "Hadrainae, Adramyttionorum, Adrianae," and beneath in brackets "Proclus . . . episcopus civitatis Adranorum." Further on still, Mansi, *op. cit.,* Vol. VI, 1082, "'Ιουλιανὸς τῶν Κώων . . . ἐπίσκοπος καὶ πρεσβευτὴς τοῦ ἀποστολικοῦ Θρόνου": vers. lat. "Julianus . . . episcopus Coensis et legatus ecclesiae Romanae."

[135] Mansi, *op. cit.,* Vol. VII, 404; cf. *op. cit.,* Vol. VI, 1084.

[136] *Conc. Nic.* Mansi, *op. cit.,* Vol. II, 696, 701.

CHAPTER X

LEO AND THE CHURCHES OF THE EAST. 2

THE SECOND COUNCIL OF EPHESUS

In obedience to the instructions of Theodosius II the bishops and others summoned to attend the projected council assembled at Ephesus in the early part of August, A.D. 449, and met in the church of St. Mary on the eighth day of the month, where the first session was held.[1] It was clear from the beginning that the ground had been carefully prepared by the supporters of Eutyches, who were already assured of the backing of the see of Alexandria in virtue of the archimandrite's admission to communion by Dioscorus.[2] We have already seen that they could count also on the help of the Eastern government. It now gave further proof of its intentions in the instructions sent to the imperial commissioners, Elpidius and Eulogius, and also to Proclus, proconsul of Asia, of which province Ephesus was the metropolis. In addition the Emperor addressed a letter to the council setting forth its programme, namely the rehabilitation of Eutyches, the deposition of Flavian and of all other bishops suspected of " Nestorianism," and finally the maintenance of the faith, by which was meant the exclusion of any " dyophysite " doctrine.[3]

Among the one hundred and thirty or so bishops present were included Dioscorus of Alexandria and the other prelates of the " greater churches," Juvenal of Jerusalem, Domnus of Antioch and Flavian of Constantinople, together with the

[1] Mansi, *Concilia,* Vol. VI, 605. The main authorities for the council are the *Acta* recited in the course of the proceedings at Chalcedon. Mansi, *Concilia,* Vol, VI, *ibid.*, 563. The *Acta* of the later sessions are also preserved in a Syriac version, ed. Flemming, *Abh. d. Gött. Ges. d. Wiss.,* Vol. XV, 1 (1917); given in a French translation in Martin, *Actes du brigandage d'Ephèse.* Cf. also id., *Le pseudosynode connu sous le nom de brigandage d'Ephèse.* Further details are supplied by Liberatus, *Breviarium,* 12. *P.L.* 68, 1003; Nestorius, *Bazaar,* ed. Driver and Hodgson, pp. 345–62. A critical edition of the *Acta* of Chalcedon has recently been published by E. Schwartz. The references to Mansi supplied there enable the reader to use the references given here.

[2] Mansi, *ibid.,* Vol. VI, 1045.

[3] Mansi, *ibid.,* Vol. VI, 587–600, including other letters, e.g. to Dioscorus.

delegates of the Roman see. One feature of the assembly, which boded little good for the orderliness of the proceedings, was the presence of three undisciplined groups of monks and personal attendants. These had arrived in the train of Dioscorus, Eutyches and the Syrian abbot Barsumas, the presence of the latter having been specially authorized, as we have seen, doubtless as an offset to the "Nestorian" sympathies of the Syrian bishops.

The members of the council took their places in order of seniority, not according to the rank of their sees, though an exception was made in favour of the Roman legate, Julius, who sat next to the president.[4] In this way the effectiveness of the Roman legation was hindered from the start by the separation of Julius from his colleagues, whose number had already been diminished by the death of the priest Renatus on the island of Delos in the course of the journey from Italy.[5] This loss was particularly regrettable, since it seems likely that he was the one member of the legation who had been carefully "briefed." Hilary of course, being only in deacon's orders, found himself relegated to a subordinate place and thus was successfully prevented from exercising any positive influence on the course of the proceedings. Possibly he was unable even to understand what was going on.

The disadvantageous position of the Roman legation was soon clearly shown by the opening proceedings. After the recitation of the Emperor's letter, which had been addressed to Dioscorus as president, Julius requested permission to read the imperial invitation received by Leo.[6] At the same time Hilary, after apologizing for the Pope's absence on the ground that neither the council of Nicaea nor of Ephesus provided any precedent for his attendance, added "the most holy

[4] Mansi, *Concilia,* Vol. VI, 608; Liberatus, *Breviarium,* 12. *P.L.* 68, 1004 appears to suggest that the Roman legates did not sit with the rest, "eo quod non fuerit data praesessio sanctae sedi." The *Acta,* however, contradict this (see Mansi, *ibid.,* 605), so that it seems possible that Liberatus has introduced a gloss from the standpoint of his time. No doubt the precedents of Nicaea and Ephesus were held to require such a procedure. See also Additional Note A, *The relation of legates of the Roman see to the early Councils.*

[5] *Breviculus hist. Eutych.* Mansi, *ibid.,* Vol. VII, 1061. Notice that Theodoret in *Ep.* 116 confuses Renatus with Hilary the deacon.

[6] Mansi, *ibid.,* Vol. VI, 613.

(Pope) feels himself nevertheless to be among you, and rests assured that in everything you will proceed according to the orthodox Catholic faith, and in accordance with the respect due to St. Peter."[7] He then urged that the letter addressed by Leo to the council should be read next.[8] It seems that Dioscorus was on the point of acceding to his request[9] when a member of the secretariat, supported by Juvenal, insisted that a further communication from the Emperor should be heard without delay.

It now became clear that the control of the proceedings was altogether out of the legates' hands. Their repeated requests that the papal letters should be read were consistently ignored, and the council proceeded to carry out the programme already prescribed by the Eastern government, The first thing was to invite the attendance of Eutyches, and when this had been done and the archimandrite stood before the assembly, his appeal against the verdict of the Constantinopolitan synod was read. At this point Flavian entered a protest and demanded that a hearing should be given to Eusebius of Dorylaeum, but all in vain. His plea was rejected on the significant ground that the Emperor had ordered him and his supporters at the recent synod to be treated as defendants, which meant that they had no right to speak as members of the council. Instead it was proposed that the minutes of the synod should be read. This proposal met with general approval, in which even Julius concurred, but only on condition that the papal letter should be taken first. Hilary equally assented, adding that the letter had been composed with a view to its being read before the minutes. It was now the turn of Eutyches to raise an objection. This he did on the ground that from the beginning the legates had been on the side of Flavian, and that the reading of the papal letter would give rise to a prejudice against himself. Dioscorus thereupon

[7] *Ibid.* "*ὅστις ἁγιώτατος ἑαυτὸν οὐκ ἀμφέβαλεν ἐν ὑμῖν διατρίβειν ἐνταῦθα· οὓς μάλιστα ἐπίσταται ὅσα πρὸς τὴν τῆς πίστεως τῆς καθολικῆς ἀκεραιότητα καὶ ὅσα ἀνήκει πρὸς τὴν εἰς τὸν ἁγιώτατον ἀπόστολον Πέτρον εὐλάβειαν, πάντα πράττειν.*"

[8] *Ep.* 33, JK 427, on which see above, p. 229.

[9] Mansi, *op. cit.*, Vol. VI, 615. A point worth noticing in favour of Dioscorus' impartiality. It is likely that his supposedly partial conduct of the proceedings has been considerably exaggerated.

ignored the legates and gave instructions to recite the synodal minutes without further delay.[10] While this was being done numerous interruptions occurred, especially when passages of a " dyophysite " character were read. When it was over Dioscorus formally proposed a resolution condemning " dyophysite " teaching and coupling with it the explicit rehabilitation of Eutyches. The resolution was put to the vote and solemnly approved by the signatures of some one hundred and fourteen members of the council at the head of which appeared the names of Juvenal and Domnus.[11]

It is surprising that Julius allowed such an open rejection of " dyophysitism " to pass without entering a protest, even if he had no other course open than to abandon the council. Possibly he thought that no protest would be of any avail, but it is difficult to excuse his passive betrayal of the doctrine supported by the Roman see.[12]

After having condemned " Nestorianism " and restored Eutyches, the council now turned its attention to Flavian. At this point Dioscorus with considerable ingenuity requested that the minutes of the sixth session of the earlier Ephesine council should be read, in which were defined the orthodox formulae of belief. This done, he drew attention to the words of the canon which condemned all those who spoke or thought otherwise, despised or contradicted them, and invited the opinion of the assembly on those who did so.[13]

In response to his invitation some voted against any addition to the creed of Nicaea; others merely expressed a wish for its confirmation.[14] Among the latter was Hilary, who took the opportunity of pointing out that the Roman see which he represented taught and respected the faith set forth at Nicaea and subsequently confirmed at Ephesus. Then he reverted once again to the papal letter, " If you would allow it to be

[10] Mansi, *op. cit.*, Vol. VI, 649.

[11] *Ibid.*, 833. The position of Domnus was, of course, only less unenviable than that of Flavian.

[12] Caspar, *Geschichte*, Vol. I, p. 486, n. 2 suggests that since from this point onwards Hilary is the sole spokesman for the Roman see, it is possible that Julius actually did so. No doubt he is right when he says of the legates, " sie, des Griechichen unkundig, . . . den Verhandlungen nicht genügend zu folgen vermöchten."

[13] Mansi, *op. cit.*, Vol. VI, 893. Cf. Vol. IV, 1361.

[14] Mansi, *op. cit.*, Vol. VI, 905.

read," he urged, "you would see that it accords with the truth."[15] This, however, was not really the point at issue. What Dioscorus was aiming at was to find a means of procuring Flavian's condemnation; the question of reading the papal letter was by now quite irrelevant. The recital of the Ephesine canon gave him his opportunity, for the minutes of the Constantinopolitan synod showed that Flavian had endeavoured to persuade Eutyches to subscribe to a doctrinal statement, which was undeniably an addition to the statements of the Nicene creed and might be plausibly represented as a transgression of the Ephesine canon. It was on this ground therefore that Dioscorus invited the council to pronounce a sentence of deposition against Flavian and Eusebius at the same time.

Although it seems probable that such a step was unacceptable to the majority of those present, the only explicit protests were expressed by Flavian and Hilary.[16] Amid scenes of the wildest disorder a considerable number of bishops pressed forward, imploring Dioscorus to stop short of so extreme a measure. But in doing so they were asking more than they knew, for to have pardoned Flavian at this stage would have been to deprive the see of Alexandria of the real fruits of its victory. Confusion was succeeded by violence, and not even Hilary was exempt from assault in order to compel his signature to the sentence of deposition. The unfortunate Flavian and his friends then found themselves treated as condemned prisoners.[17]

At a second session held on August 22nd[18] the council carried out the second part of its programme, namely the deposition of a number of Eastern bishops who were suspected of "Nestorianism," including Ibas of Edessa, Irenaeus of Tyre (who since A.D. 448 had enjoyed a brief restoration to his see), Theodoret of Cyrrhus and finally even Domnus of Antioch.

[15] *Ibid.* "*ἅπερ εἰ κελεύσητε ἀναγνωσθῆναι, γνώσεσθε συνᾴδοντα τῇ ἀληθείᾳ.*"

[16] *Ibid.*, 908. Hilary uttered the single Latin word "Contradicitur"; Flavian's expression, according to the Greek text of the *Acta*, was "*παραιτοῦμαί σε*," which the Latin version, in anticipation perhaps of his future action, renders "Appello ad te." It should perhaps mean "I ask pardon." See Liddell and Scott, *Greek-English Lexicon*[8], s.v. II, 5.

[17] The same fate also befell Eusebius and Hilary.

[18] Martin, *Brigandage d'Ephèse*, p. 174.

But Julius appears to have been absent and by this time Hilary was under guard, so that the Roman see had no responsibility for these proceedings. Hilary, in fact, though at the cost of all his baggage, shortly afterwards made good his escape from Ephesus and embarked for Rome. But in its place he took with him a document likely to cause considerable satisfaction to Leo. It was an urgent appeal to the Roman see for help from the bishop of Constantinople.[19]

Earnestly imploring Leo's aid in the cause of orthodoxy, now so seriously threatened, the writer observes:

"It has become my duty fittingly to send a *report* at the present juncture, and to address an Apostolic appeal to your holiness, so that you may set forth to the East and bring help to the devout faith of the holy fathers now in danger, that faith which they have handed down to us by enduring persecution. For see, all things are in disorder . . . no longer is the faith of the fathers proclaimed: on the contrary the faith of Eutyches is preached and taught by Dioscorus, bishop of the Alexandrine church, and of those who hold these opinions in common with him. Their own verdict and the verdict of those bishops who were compelled by violence to give their assent has actually approved this doctrine. . . ." [20]

He went on to explain that apart from Dioscorus and his supporters, who had pursued him with relentless hostility since the day of his elevation to the see of Constantinople, the

[19] This letter was unknown until it was discovered in a Latin version by Dom Amelli in MS. 30 in the capitular library of Novara and published under the title of *S. Leone Magno e l'Oriente* (1882). It has been edited by Mommsen in *Neues Archiv.*, Vol. XI (1886), pp. 362ff. Kirch, *Fontes*, 885. Extracts are printed in Mirbt, *Quellen*[5], No. 173 and in Batiffol, *Siège Apostolique,* pp. 514ff. Caspar, *Geschichte,* Vol. I, p. 488, n. 3 suggests that Hilary himself was responsible for the version, and that his influence accounts for the "Roman" phraseology.

[20] *Ibid.*, pp. 1ff. "Oportuit quidem ad praesens tempus me dignanter referre et uti apostolica appellatione ad vestram sanctitatem, ut progrediens ad Orientem auxilium ferret periclitanti piae sanctorum patrum fidei, quam sudore ultionis tradiderunt. Ecce enim confusa sunt omnia: . . . Iam non patrum nominatur fides, sed contigit ab Alexandrinae ecclesiae episcopo Dioscoro eorum, qui haec sapiunt una cum ipso, Eutychianam iam praedicari et nominari fidem. Hanc enim firmavit sententia propria et eorum qui per violentiam coacti sunt consentire episcoporum. . . ." The phrase "sudore ultionis" is obscure and is probably corrupt. Batiffol, *op. cit.*, p. 514, n. 1 suggests "sudore vultus sui" with allusion to Gen. iii. 19 (Vulg.). Flavian evidently refers to the sufferings endured by those who upheld the faith of Nicaea.

majority of bishops were in agreement with him, and that Dioscorus in particular had shown his desire to humiliate him, by refraining from sending the appropriate notification at the time of his election to the see of Alexandria. Next he drew attention to the lack of respect shown by Dioscorus towards the see of Rome by refusing to allow the Pope's letter to be read or his legates to be heard. Then he adds:

"When I began to appeal to the throne of the Apostolic see of Peter, the prince of the Apostles, and to the whole sacred synod which is obedient to your holiness, at once a crowd of soldiers surrounded me and barred the way when I wished to take refuge at the holy altar." [21]

Finally he concludes:

"Therefore I beseech your holiness not to permit these things to be treated with indifference . . . but to rise up first on behalf of the cause of our orthodox faith, now destroyed by unlawful acts; then to make the matter your concern, because of the overthrow of canon law . . . further to issue an authoritative instruction . . . so that a like faith may everywhere be preached, by the assembly of a united synod of the fathers, both eastern and western. Thus the laws of the fathers may prevail and all that has been done amiss be rendered null and void: bring healing to this ghastly wound." [22]

Shortly before Hilary's advent in Rome a letter appeared from Eusebius of Dorylaeum,[23] followed soon afterwards by

[21] *Ibid.*, 16, "me appellante thronum apostolicae sedis principis apostolorum Petri et universam beatam quae sub vestra sanctitate est synodum, statim me circumvallat multitudo militaris, et volente me ad sanctum altare confugere non concessit." It should be observed that Flavian does not merely appeal to Leo in person but also to the synod of the Roman province.

[22] *Ibid.*, 18. "Oro itaque vestram sanctitatem, ne obdormire patiamini super his . . . sed insurgere primum quidem in causa rectae fidei nostrae quae quadam libidine deperiit; deinde propter eversionem ecclesiasticarum constitutionum curam facere . . .; dare etiam formam, . . . ut tam Occidentali quam etiam Orientali in unum facta patrum synodo similis ubique praedicetur fides, ut praevaleant sanctiones patrum, in irritum vero deduci valeant atque dissolvi omnia quae male . . . gesta sunt; afferre medicinam horribili huic vulneri." "Constitutiones" probably refers to *Conc. Const.*, I, Cans. 2 and 3, of the contents of which Leo was probably quite unaware.

[23] Ed. Mommsen, *Neues Archiv.*, Vol. XI, p. 364. Like the appeal of Flavian, this letter in a Latin version has only recently been rediscovered. An extract is given in Mirbt, *Quellen,* No. 174, and in Batiffol, *Siège Apostolique*, p. 517, n. 1.

the writer in person. The letter described historical precedents for help being sent by the Roman see to victims of injustice, and then proceeded:

"Since therefore I have received hard and unjust treatment contrary to the divine canons[24] at the hands of Dioscorus and of other faithful bishops who, compelled by fear and force, obeyed his will and assented to my condemnation (as the most faithful persons who were sent by your holiness to represent your Beatitude know well, to whom I also presented a statement of my appeal in which I requested trial before your see), I implore your Beatitude . . . declare my unjust condemnation by the most faithful bishop Dioscorus to be void and of no effect."

The letter concludes by requesting Leo to write saying that his appellant is restored to his episcopal office and enjoys the communion of the Roman see.

About the same time Leo received yet another appeal from a third victim of the "monophysite" victory at Ephesus. This came from Theodoret,[25] who from the beginning of the affair had been treated as one of the chief obstacles to the Eutychian cause.

The letter opens with a eulogy of the Roman see and says:

"If Paul, the herald of the Truth, the trumpet of the Holy Ghost, had recourse to great Peter, that he might obtain from him a decision as to those Antiochenes who were in doubt as to the way of living according to the law, with far greater reason do we, insignificant and unimportant as we are, approach your Apostolic throne, that we may receive from you

[24] *Lib. Eus.* "Quoniam igitur dura et iniqua praeter divinos canones pertuli a Dioscoro et ab aliis religiosis episcopis, qui timore et necessitate compulsi voluntati eius optemperaverunt et in condemnatione mea consenserunt (sicut sciunt qui a vestra sanctitate missi sunt in loco vestrae beatitudinis religiosissimi viri, quibus et libellos optuli appellationis meae in quibus vestrae sedis cognitionem poposci) deprecor vestram beatitudinem . . . pronuntiate evacuari et inanem fieri meam iniquam condemnationem a religiosissimo episcopo Dioscoro." The "divinos canones" are probably *Conc. Const.*, I, Can. 2. Caspar, *Geschichte*, Vol. I, p. 615 considers that the text has been subjected to interpolation, and that as "sicut sciunt . . . poposci" contradicts "misi libellos per . . . Chrysippum et Constantium diaconum," the letter in its original form is scarcely an *appellatio*, still less a *relatio* in the technical Roman sense. He points out that it is conspicuously lacking in the special language, e.g. *referre ad sedem Petri* which appears in Flavian's appeal.

[25] *Ep.* 113. *P.G.* 83, 1311. *Inter Leon. Epp.*, No. 52. *P.L.* 54, 886.

healing for the wounds of the churches. For it befits you to take the initiative in everything."[26]

He then details the special prerogatives of the Roman see or rather of Rome itself, mentioning in particular its dignity as an imperial capital, and alluding to its spiritual privileges, including its faith, both in the Apostolic Age[27] and now, and its possession of the resting places of the twin Apostles,[28] of whom he writes:

"This thrice blessed and divine pair rose in the East and sent forth their rays into all quarters, but willingly found the setting of their life in the West, and from thence even now lighten the whole world. These rendered your throne most glorious."[29]

Finally he mentions as a special mark of the divine favour, the fact that God has granted to the Roman see so orthodox a bishop as Leo. After this glowing encomium he praises the Pope's zeal against the Manichaeans[30] and alludes specially to his letter to Flavian, commenting on its "dyophysite" doctrine with approval.[31] Then he refers to the unjust sentence pronounced upon Flavian at the instigation of Dioscorus and upon other bishops including himself, and in defence of his own worthiness draws attention to his zeal in converting

[26] Theodoret had been explicitly excluded from taking part in the Ephesine council. See above, p. 224.

[27] With allusion to Rom. i. 8.

[28] *Ibid.* "Εἰ Παῦλος τῆς ἀληθείας ὁ κήρυξ, ἡ τοῦ ἁγίου πνεύματος σάλπιγξ, πρὸς τὸν μέγαν ἔδραμε Πέτρον, ὥστε τοῖς ἐν Ἀντιοχείᾳ περὶ τῆς κατὰ νόμον πολιτείας ἀμφισβητοῦσι παρ' αὐτοῦ κομίσαι τὴν λύσιν, πολλῷ μᾶλλον ἡμεῖς οἱ εὐτελεῖς καὶ σμικροὶ πρὸς τὸν ἀποστολικὸν ὑμῶν τρέχομεν θρόνον, ὥστε παρ' ὑμῶν λαβεῖν τοῖς τῶν ἐκκλησιῶν ἕλκεσι θεραπείαν. Διὰ πάντα γὰρ ὑμῶν τὸ πρωτεύειν ἁρμόττει." Theodoret's interpretation of the apostolic relations with the Antiochenes scarcely does justice to Gal. ii. 11–15.

[29] *Ibid.* "ἡ δὲ τρισμακαρία τούτων καὶ θεία ξυνωρὶς ἀνέτειλε μὲν ἐν τῇ ἑῴᾳ, καὶ πάντοσε τὰς ἀκτῖνας ἐξέμπεμψεν. Ἐν δὲ τῇ δύσει προθύμως ἐδέξατο τὰς τοῦ βίου δυσμὰς, κᾀκεῖθεν τὴν οἰκουμένην. νῦν καταυγάζει Οὗτοι τὸν ὑμέτερον περιφανέστατον ἀπέφηναν θρόνον." The writer's metaphor is derived from the chariot (ξυνωρίς) of Phoebus. For an earlier reference to the East as the source of the Christian religion cf. *Ep.* of the Council of Antioch to Pope Julius I, ap. JK 186 and Sozomen, *H.E.*, 3, 8, 5. Notice Leo's modified use of the same metaphor in *Ep.* 120, 2, JK 496.

[30] For Leo's treatment of the Manichaeans see Chap. III.

[13] *Ibid.*, 2. Apparently referring to the "Tome," *Ep.* 28. It is possible that Hilary managed to put copies of this document into circulation, in spite of the hindrance to its being read at the council.

heretics and his sufferings on behalf of the true faith. He adds that he eagerly awaits a summons to Rome so that his teaching may be pronounced apostolic, and a decision given as to his duty in regard to the sentence pronounced against him, adding that he is ready to accept whatever may be decided.[32] In conclusion he explains that obedience to the imperial edict prevents his travelling to Rome in person, so that he begs Leo to receive his messengers, to succour him in his old age and to preserve intact the inheritance which the churches have received as a legacy from the fathers.

The chief importance of these three letters lies in the evidence which they afford as to the general acceptance in the East of the Roman see as the proper court of appeal in matters of doctrine. But in recognizing this we must not lose sight of the political circumstances of the time, nor of the fact that, with the loss of prestige by the other "greater churches" of the West, no other see remained to which an appeal could be addressed to any real advantage.[33]

We must now consider the reaction of the Roman see to these events. It was not perhaps till mid-September that the Roman legates, Julius of Puteoli and Hilary, eventually reached home. The autumnal synod of the Roman "province" was at hand, and when the bishops assembled they found an agenda of exceptional importance awaiting them, so much so that no less than a fortnight seems to have been needed for the completion of the necessary business. Although no *Acta* of this synod have been preserved there is some reason to think that the letter addressed by Leo to Theodosius[34] about this time was sent off soon after the opening of its proceedings. A few days later a letter arrived

[32] *Ep.* 52, 6. "Πρὸ δὲ πάντων, μαθεῖν ἀντιβολῶ παρ' ὑμῶν, εἴτε χρή με τέρψαι τὴν ἄδικον ταύτην καθαίρεσιν, εἴτε μή. Τὴν γὰρ ὑμετέραν προσμένω ψῆφον."

[33] The appeal addressed by Eutyches to the see of Ravenna had merely elicited the reply that everything must depend on the decision of the Roman see. See above.

[34] *Ep.* 43, JK 437 without date. The Ballerini, *P.L.* 54, 818f. discuss the critical problems involved here and in JK 438 and conclude that the existing Latin texts are retranslations from the Greek version and that that version is therefore the earliest authority which we possess for JK 437. Yet even so it is at present in a fragmentary condition, with numerous *lacunae*, which Caspar, *Geschichte*, Vol. I, p. 493, n. 5 holds to be due to deliberate suppression carried out by the official censorship at Constantinople in the case of phrases offensive to Greek ears.

from Theodosius himself demanding a further communication. This was also sent together with a number of other notes at the conclusion of the synodical business.

In his earlier letter the Emperor had presumably expressed his mind somewhat freely as to the activity of the "Nestorians" and evoked an appeal from the Roman see to clear his conscience of any complicity in the damage recently done against the faith. This Leo expressed by saying:

"I, with the bishops assembled at my side, advise you, most Christian and worshipful prince, . . . that all things should remain undisturbed, as they were before this decision (i.e. of the recent council) and let them await the more weighty judgment of a council in which the whole company of bishops from all the world is assembled." [35]

The synod evidently cherished the hope that the Emperor would order a new council to meet, this time in Italy,[36] and observed in conclusion that "it is needful to observe the prescriptions of the Nicene canon and of the definition laid down by the bishops of all the world." [37] The later imperial letter was probably intended to intimate formal approval of the decisions made at Ephesus, and called for a tactful reply.[38] After expressing his confidence in the Emperor's zeal for the faith Leo goes on to suggest that if only irrelevant considerations had not prevented his letters [39] from being read at the

[35] *Ibid.*, 822C. "Ταῦτα ἐγώ, ὦ χριστιανικώτατε καὶ προσκυνητὲ βασιλεῦ, μετὰ τῶν σὺν ἐμοὶ ἐπισκόπων, εἰλικρινεῖ διαθέσει ποθῶν ὑμᾶς πρὸ πάντων Θεῷ ἀρέσκειν, ᾧ παρὰ πάσης ἐκκλησίας συμφώνως ὑπὲρ τοῦ ὑμετέρου κράτους δεήσεις ἀναπέμπονται, συμβουλεύω . . . περιμείνωσι δὲ τὸ μεῖζον τῆς συνόδου κριτήριον, ἐν ᾗ ὁ πᾶς ἀριθμὸς τῶν ἐπισκόπων ἐκ πάσης τῆς οἰκουμένης συνάγεται."

[36] *Ibid.* "ὥστε κελεῦσαι ἰδικὴν σύνοδον ἐν τοῖς τῆς Ἰταλίας ἐπιτελεσθῆναι." Whether Flavian really desired that Italy should be the place of assembly of the new council may be doubted.

[37] *Ibid.* "Πάντες οἱ ἱερεῖς, τὴν ὑμετέραν ἡμερότητα μετὰ δακρύων ἱκετεύουσι κατὰ τὴν αἴτησιν τοῦ λιβέλλου Φλαυιανοῦ τοῦ ἐπισκόπου . . . ὥστε καὶ ταῦτα ἀναγκαῖον παραφυλάξαι, ὅσα ὁ ἐν Νικαίᾳ κάνων παρακελεύεται, ὅσα τε ὁ ὅρος ὁ ἀπὸ πάσης τῆς οἰκουμένης τῶν ἐπισκόπων κατὰ τὸ ἔθος τῆς καθολικῆς ἐκκλησίας . . . ." It should be noticed that the text is defective here. "ὅρος" appears to refer to the Nicene Creed, but it is possible that the previous clause contained some allusion to the Nicaeno-Sardican canons, e.g. 3, 4 and 7 (vers. lat.).

[38] *Ep.* 44, JK 438. The Latin text is also here a retranslation from the Greek version.

[39] The letters were, of course *Ep.* 33, JK 427 and the "Tome," *Ep.* 28, JK 423.

council the whole controversy might have been avoided.

The fact that the allusions which Leo makes to the proceedings at Ephesus are more detailed here than in the previous letter suggests that Hilary had meanwhile fully informed him as to all that had taken place there,[40] and the receipt of such information doubtless explains his more marked emphasis on the culpability of Dioscorus. In concluding this letter he again draws attention to the need of assembling a fresh council in Italy so that opportunity may be given for the reconciliation of those who were intimidated at Ephesus, and for the retention of others who may repent of their rashness, and upholds his request by calling attention to the Nicene canons.[41]

Besides writing to the Emperor Theodosius Leo also addressed himself to Pulcheria[42] enclosing in addition to a copy of the letter sent to her brother, a fresh edition of his letter despatched in the previous June.[43] Here he underlines the guilt

[40] Hilary appears somewhat to have exaggerated the part played by the legates, as when Leo writes *ibid.*, 1, "*ὥστε μετὰ παῤῥησίας ἐν αὐτῇ τῇ συνόδῳ διεμαρτύραντο, οὐδαμῶς τοῦτο τὸ παρ' αὐτῶν δογματισθὲν δύνασθαι πάμπαν δέξασθαι τὴν ἀποστολικὴν καθέδραν.*"

[41] *Ibid.*, 3. "*ὅπως γὰρ μετὰ τὴν ἔκκλητον τοῦτο ἀναγκαίως αἰτοῦμεν, τῶν κατὰ Νικαίαν κανόνων αἱ ψῆφοι μαρτυροῦσι, αἵ τινες ἀπὸ τῶν πανταχοῦ τοῦ κόσμου ἐπισκόπων καθιδρύθησαν, ὥσπερ ὑπετάξαμεν.*" As in *Ep.* 43, *ad fin.*, JK 437 these words refer to the canons of Sardica which deal with the subject of appeals to the Roman see, e.g. Canons 3, 4 and 7 (vers. lat.), of which Canon 4 is quoted in the Greek *Acta* of Chalcedon, Mansi, *Concilia,* Vol. VI, 545. Cf. Maassen, *Quellen,* Vol. I, p. 57, n. 2. For the earlier history of the use of these canons as Nicene, see Kidd, *History,* Vol. III, p. 166 and Caspar, *Geschichte,* Vol. I, pp. 358ff. The text from which Leo quoted was a primitive collection of canons in Latin, of Roman origin belonging to the year A.D. 425, of which the earliest surviving form is the so-called Collection of Chieti (Cod. Vat. Regin. 1997, saec. ix.). In this collection the Sardican canons follow with consecutive numbering the authentic canons of Nicaea. For citing the former as Nicene, Leo has been accused of disingenuousness (e.g. Gore, *Leo the Great,* pp. 113ff., Bright, *Age of the Fathers,* Vol. II, p. 496), but the fact that had he known them to be falsely attributed to the Council of Nicaea, he would have been consciously risking the vitiation of the whole of his policy in relation to the Churches of the East, by quoting them as Nicene, seems to suggest that the charge is devoid of any foundation. Thus Turner in *Camb. Med. Hist.,* Vol. I, Chap. VI, p. 180 says, "We need not doubt the good faith . . . of Popes Zosimus and Boniface because they made the most of the Sardican prescriptions about appeals to Rome, which their manuscripts treated as Nicene." The same might well apply to Leo's conduct in this case.

[42] *Ep.* 45, JK 439, dated October 13th, A.D. 449.

[43] i.e. *Ep.* 30, JK 425A. The copy now enclosed was probably JK 425B. Cf. *ibid.,* 1, "ipsorum scriptorum quae ad clementiam vestram non pervenerunt, exempla subiecimus."

of Dioscorus and expresses his indignation that his letter, addressed to the council regarding the Faith, was not allowed to be read.[44]

"As to Flavian," he writes, "he remains in communion with us all, and that which was done without regard for justice, and entirely against canon law, cannot on any account be treated as valid."[45]

He continues by urging once more his suggestion of a new council in Italy and in conclusion points out that Pulcheria is to regard herself as the specially commissioned representative of the Roman see.[46]

The peculiar interest of this post is that it included a personal letter to Pulcheria from the erstwhile legate, Hilary.[47] The legate-deacon apologizes for his inability to visit the empress in Constantinople, and graphically describes his experiences at Ephesus and on the way home:

"Yet trusting in the help of Christ our God, I kept myself innocent and blameless of the condemnation of that most reverent and holy man (sc. Flavian), and no beatings, no sufferings could make me consent to his (sc. Dioscorus') verdict: but losing all that I had I fled from thence and came to Rome by way of places unknown and untrodden, and survived as a fitting messenger to the most reverend Pope of all that was done in Ephesus."[48]

He concludes by referring to the repudiation by the Roman synod of the acts for which Dioscorus was responsible and to the Pope's letter to the Empress.

[44] Apparently referring not to *Ep.* 28 but to *Ep.* 33. The attribution of the current Roman baptismal creed to apostolic authorship may be noted. *Ibid.*, 2, "ipsi Symbolo ab apostolis instituto."

[45] *Ibid.* "Flavianus episcopus in nostra omnium communione persistit, atque hoc, quod factum est sine consideratione iustitiae, et contra omnem canonum disciplinam, ratum haberi ratio nulla permittit." If Leo is referring to *Conc. Const.*, I, Can. 2, it has an important bearing on the question as to whether or no these canons were known in Rome at this time. More probably it is an allusion to *Conc. Nic.*, Can. 6.

[46] *Ibid.*, 3, "sibi (sc. Pulcheriae) specialiter a beatissimo Petro apostolo legatione commissa."

[47] *Inter Leon. Epp.*, No. 46, *P.L.* 54, 838.

[48] *Ibid.*, 2. "Verum tamen confidens de auxilio Christi nostri Dei, a damnatione reverendissimi et sanctissimi viri innocentem me integrumque servavi; licet nulla flagella, nulla tormenta me possent facere eius consentire sententiae; sed omnibus derelictis exinde discessi, per incognita et invia loca Romam veniens et reverendissimo papae, omnium quae in Epheso gesta sunt idoneus nuntiator existens."

The same post included three short letters addressed respectively to Anastasius of Thessalonica, Julian and Flavian. It appears that Leo had learnt from Hilary that Anastasius had been prevented from being present at the recent council in person, and therefore wrote to congratulate him on his good fortune in having been preserved from taking part in its misdeeds.[49] He urges Anastasius to refuse his consent to the condemnation of Flavian,[50] and declares that those who attempt to overthrow the foundations of the Catholic faith have no part in the communion of the Roman see. Julian [51] is recommended " amid the stormy blast of a single whirlwind to retain the calm of peaceful faith." The letter to Flavian,[52] which is remarkable for its omission of any reference to the appeal, is restricted to a few brief words of encouragement.

The two remaining letters which claim our attention here as having been sent off at the same time were directed to the " clergy, officers and people residing in Constantinople " [53] and to the anti-Eutychian archimandrites, Faustus and the rest.[54] The former of these is noteworthy as being the earliest example of direct intervention on Leo's part into the domestic affairs of the church of Constantinople. In this letter the writer repeats what he has said elsewhere regarding the force exercised by Dioscorus to procure subscriptions to the decisions taken at Ephesus, and urges that no fear of consequences ought to shake the allegiance of the church of Constantinople to its rightful bishop. As to Flavian he writes:

" Whosoever, while Flavian is yet safe and alive, shall dare to intrude himself into his see will never be admitted to our communion, nor can be accounted among the company of bishops. For as we have anathematized Nestorius in his perversity, so with a like censure we condemn those who deny the reality of our flesh in the Lord Jesus Christ." [55]

[49] *Ep.* 47, JK 440, dated October 13th, A.D. 449.
[50] *Ibid.*, 2. " Monemus ne vel in damnationem fratris insontis, vel in receptionem nefarii dogmatis consensum tui cordis immisceas."
[51] *Ep.* 48, JK 441 of the same date. " Saeviente unius turbinis procella, serenissimae fidei est amplectenda tranquillitas."
[52] *Ep.* 49, JK 442 of the same date.
[53] *Ep.* 50, JK 443 of the same date.
[54] *Ep.* 51, JK 444 of the same date.
[55] *Ep.* 50, 1. " quisquis enim incolumi atque superstite Flaviano episcopo vestro sacerdotium eius fuerit ausus invadere, numquam in com-

Equally Faustus and his supporters were encouraged to remain loyal to their bishop and were exhorted to constancy by the suggestion that the present trouble had been divinely permitted as a test of Flavian's constancy.

Yet by the time Leo's messenger reached Constantinople, bearing secret instructions to Flavian and Julian alike,[56] Flavian was dead.[57] After the concluding session of the council of Ephesus the inevitable sentence of banishment had been issued from the imperial chancery. But its victim, already exhausted by the strain and the violence of the treatment he had received, succumbed to his injuries before the sentence could take effect. Perhaps from the point of view of the Roman see his death was actually a stroke of good fortune. For as long as he remained alive the personal aspect of the controversy was bound to attract disproportionate attention. Once he was dead one of the chief hindrances to a possible reconciliation between Leo and Theodosius was removed.[58] The obvious plan now was to treat the council of Ephesus as a regrettable episode, to ignore its decisions and to reopen the question regarding the orthodoxy or otherwise of Eutyches *de novo*. Perhaps Leo still hoped that Theodosius might be won over to accept some plan of this sort. But if he did so he was to find himself mistaken.

From the point of view of the eastern government the recent council was evidently regarded as a perfectly normal general council. It had been convoked by the Emperor, attended by representatives of the eastern and western

munione nostra habebitur, nec inter episcopos potuit numerari. Nos enim sicut Nestorium in sua perversitate anathematizavimus, ita eos qui veritatem carnis nostrae in Domino Jesu Christo denegant, pari exsecratione damnamus."

[56] *Ep.* 49, "Perlator sane brevis huius epistolae fideli sermone poterit enarrare, quidquid illud est ad quod, adiuvante Domino, studio fidei et charitatis intendimus." Evidently Leo feared the risk that written advice to Flavian might fall into the hands of his enemies.

[57] Cf. Prosper, *Chronicon, M.G.H.*, Auctores antiquissimi, Vol. IX, *Chron. min.*, Vol. I, p. 481. "Sanctus vero Flavianus inter manus eorum, a quibus in exilium ducebatur, glorioso ad Christum fine transivit." Although Leo appears to have believed that Dioscorus was directly responsible for Flavian's death, cf. *Ep.* 105, 3, JK 482, and *Ep.* 120, 3, JK 496, it is most improbable. His fate is closely parallel to that of John Chrysostom, himself also a victim of Alexandrine aggression. Cf. Caspar, *Geschichte*, Vol. I, pp. 320f.

[58] *Ep.* 50, 1, JK 443.

churches, and as such, though inferior in point of actual numbers, was qualified to rank with the councils of Nicaea and Ephesus. Perhaps it might have done so if it had not been for the serious obstacles which stood in the way. The chief among these was the unbending attitude adopted by Leo who applied the whole weight of his influence and the strength of his personality to the task of nullifying its effects. To him it was no council but a " den of robbers," and owes the name by which it has become known to history to the sobriquet which he himself attached to it. Doubtless this attitude was due to some extent to the disregard of his letters, to the unfair pressure alleged to have been exercised on the recalcitrant minority, and to the dishonour done to the Roman see in the treatment accorded to its official representatives. But this was not all. The restoration of Eutyches showed that there was a real danger that " monophysite " doctrine was on the way to being recognized as orthodox Christology, and Leo was clear sighted enough to see that this meant the establishment of a standard of Christian belief which was irreconcilable with the Gospel.

On the other hand we must remember that most of our evidence regarding the council and its proceedings is derived from orthodox and therefore, to some extent, from prejudiced sources. It is clear that Leo lays the chief blame for its misdeeds on Dioscorus, yet it is more than doubtful how far he was really responsible. After all, the real conduct of the proceedings was in the hands of the imperial commissioners, and it must be allowed that Dioscorus made more than one attempt to give the papal letters a hearing. Nor must we exaggerate the significance of the tumultuous behaviour which characterized certain stages of the council's procedure. As we shall see, similar behaviour occurred at Chalcedon, and the enemies of that council subsequently made allegations similar to those put forward by the minority at Ephesus, for example, that constraint was used to extort signatures from the reluctant. If, however, Dioscorus may not be pronounced wholly innocent, not only of a misguided preference of the views of Eutyches to the doctrine of Leo, but of some measure of ambition and usurpation, it must be allowed on the other side that his chief opponent, Flavian, had acted, as we have seen, in a somewhat arbitrary manner in seeking to impose on Eutyches a dogmatic formula which both lacked oecumenical authority and might, with some reason, be regarded as an addition, even though, from one point of view, a legitimate interpretation, to the faith of Nicaea. Thus, while he deserves our sympathy as the unfortunate victim of a clash between imperial authority and ecclesiastical independence, he can scarcely escape responsibility for the disaster which involved him in its ruin.

The stage was being set for an ecclesiastical struggle on a titanic scale, in which questions of far greater importance than the prerogatives of bishops or the precedence of sees were at stake. Amid scenes of equivocation, betrayal and tragedy, one figure stood out like a beacon light amongst the wreckage of the storm. We shall see how in the confusion of thought resulting from the cross currents of imperial and ecclesiastical politics Leo, and he alone, offered to a distracted church security, order and peace in the recognition of the doctrinal "magisterium" of the Roman see.

Additional Note

THE RELATIONS OF LEGATES OF THE ROMAN SEE WITH THE EARLY COUNCILS

It may be said with some reason that the earliest council of the type represented by those of Nicaea and Chalcedon was the one summoned by Constantine I to meet at Arles [59] on August 1st, A.D. 314. It resembled those councils in that it was convened by means of a formal summons issued by the Emperor, and included representatives from numerous provinces, even if they came only from provinces situated in the West. While there is no definite evidence that such a summons was actually sent to the Roman see, we may reasonably conjecture that one was sent, and account for the absence of the Pope by the fact that either during or soon after the holding of the council a change took place in the

[59] For details of this council see Mansi, *Concilia,* Vol. II, 463; Optatus, *De schism. Don.*, app. 4, *C.S.E.L.*, Vol. XXVI, pp. 206–8. Mirbt, *Quellen,* No. 100. Hefele-Leclercq, *Conciles,* Vol. 275–98. No formal invitation addressed to the Roman see has survived. That such an invitation was sent is conjectured by Caspar, *Geschichte,* Vol. I, p. 115.

Roman pontificate. Our existing records of the conciliar membership show that legates of the Roman see were present, but it does not appear that they were accorded special precedence or took any leading part.[60] At the same time the somewhat " papal " character of the letter sent by the council to Silvester, reporting its proceedings and requesting its transmission to other more remote sees, may suggest that it owed something to direct Roman inspiration.[61]

When eleven years later Constantine decided to adopt the plan of summoning a new council in the East, for the settlement of the doctrinal problems created by the teaching of Arius, the Roman see evidently received an invitation to take part, since it was represented at the council by two priests, Victor (Vito) and Vincentius.[62] Since no detailed minutes of the proceedings at Nicaea have been preserved we have no means of knowing what precise part the Roman legates took in them. Yet it is clear that the traditional precedence of the Roman see was recognized by the fact that the legates signed the *Acta* of the council immediately after Hosius, who signed

[60] Miltiades died on January 10th, A.D. 314 and Silvester I was consecrated on the 31st of the same month. According to Mansi, *op. cit.*, Vol. II, 469, the papal legates were Claudian and Vitus, priests, and Eugenius and Cyriacus, deacons.

[61] Mansi, *Concilia,* Vol. II, 469. " Dilectissimo papae Silvestro Marinus etc. Communi copula caritatis et unitate matris ecclesiae catholicae vinculo inhaerentes, ad Arelatensium civitatem piissimi imperatoris voluntate adducti, inde te, gloriosissime papa, commerita reverentia salutamus . . . sed quoniam recedere a partibus illis minime potuisti, in quibus et apostoli quotidie sedent et cruor ipsorum sine intermissione Dei gloriam testatur. . . ." This early instance of the idea of the abiding presence of the " Apostles " in the Roman see is highly significant in the light of its later developments. Cf. *Ep. Antiochen. ad Julium* ap. Sozomen, *H.E.,* 3, 8, in which the authors say of the Roman Church, " φέρειν μὲν γὰρ πᾶσι φιλοτιμίαν τὴν Ῥωμαίων ἐκκλησίαν . . . , ὡς ἀποστόλων φροντιστήριον, καὶ εὐσεβείας μητρόπολιν ἐξ ἀρχῆς γεγενημένην."

[62] Eusebius, *Vita Const.,* 3, 7; Socrates, *H.E.,* 1, 8; Sozomen, *H.E.,* 1, 17. The Council of Nicaea is given in Mansi, *op. cit.,* Vol. II, 635ff. The absence of the Pope from Nicaea is explained by Eusebius as due to the fact that Silvester I was already too aged to travel. Cf. Burn, *Council of Nicaea,* p. 23. He died ten years later. It should be noted that the tradition of the Roman bishop's absence from oecumenical councils, as it existed in Leo's time, was wholly fortuitous in origin. With Leo, however, it was almost a matter of principle. See e.g. *Ep.* 93, 1, JK 473. Although the signature of Hosius always appears in the first place in our existing texts, Eusebius, *Vita Const.* 3, 13, implies that different bishops presided in turn. For a belated attempt to represent Hosius as an official representative of the Roman see cf. Gelasius Cyzicen., *H.E.,* 2, 5; *P.G.* 85, 1229. If Hosius was so in fact, at least Pope Julius I, *Ep. ad Danium,* etc. 16, JK 186 shows himself unaware of it, though writing only sixteen years later.

first either as Emperor's personal representative, or else as the president of the council at the final session.[63]

At the council of Sardica, A.D. 343, Julius I was represented by two priests, Archidamus and Philoxenus, and their signatures, as at Nicaea, follow that of Hosius.[64] At Arles, A.D. 353, Vincentius reappears as a signatory of the compromise with "official" Arianism imposed by Constantius, although at Milan, A.D. 355, the legates of Liberius, Lucifer, Eusebius and Hilary, suffered banishment rather than repudiate communion with Athanasius. There is nothing to show that at any of these councils, wholly western in character, the Roman legates received special consideration.[65] The council of Constantinople held in A.D. 381 was attended only by bishops from the East; not only were no western churches invited to take part, but even the Roman see for many years after remained in ignorance of the nature of its decisions.[66]

Hitherto, with two exceptions, we find legates of the Roman see working in cordial co-operation with the members of the council, whether predominantly western or eastern in character. It is only when we come to the African councils of the first quarter of the fifth century that we meet a discordant note, due to a strong feeling of resentment against the intervention of the Roman see in the affairs of local or "national" churches. In the course of the year 418 Apiarius, an African priest, serving under the jurisdiction of Urbanus, bishop of Sicca Veneria in the province of *Byzacium*, appealed to Pope Zosimus against the verdict of his bishop, with total disregard of the authority of the provincial or national synods of the church of Africa.[67] Zosimus' response took the form of a legation of three members headed by

[63] Cf. Caspar, *op. cit.*, Vol. I, p. 121.

[64] Athanasius, *Apol. c. Arian.* 50. *P.G.* 25, 702.

[65] No legate of the Roman see was present at the Council of Ariminum, A.D. 359 (see Socrates, *H.E.*, 2, 38; Kidd, *History*, Vol. II, pp. 166ff.) for the simple reason that in that year two popes Liberius and Felix II claimed the pontificate.

[66] See Chap. XIII, p. 304, n. 7 below, where the question as to the extent to which the canons of this council were known to the Roman see at the time of the Council of Chalcedon is discussed.

[67] The African Church had prohibited transmarine appeals as early as A.D. 407. See *Cod. can. eccl. Afric.* 105 (c. 11), *P.L.* 67, 216. On the origin of the Codex, see Duchesne, *Histoire*, Vol. III, p. 122. This prohibition was renewed in May, A.D. 418. See *Cod. can. eccl. Afric.* 125 and Hefele-Leclercq, *Conciles*, Vol. II, 1, p. 195.

Faustinus, bishop of Potentia in the province of *Picenum,* who addressed themselves first of all to Aurelius, bishop of Carthage in *Caesarea Mauretania,* in September of the same year. Here they presented their demands [68] which were received by the African bishops with sympathetic consideration.[69]

Before a general council of the African Church could be called Zosimus died, and when it assembled at Carthage on May 25th in the following year, A.D. 419, the election of Boniface I as his successor had only just been determined. Two hundred and seventeen bishops were present; Aurelius presided along with Valentine, primate of Numidia, next to them was seated Faustinus, then the bishops and lastly the papal legates in priests' orders.[70] The discussion turned largely on the question as to whether Zosimus' claim that his intervention was justified by the canons of Nicaea could be upheld.[71] As soon as the Nicene *Acta* and the Roman *Commonitorium* presented by the legate Faustinus had been read, Alypius, bishop of Tagaste, raised the objection that the first of the two canons alleged by Zosimus to be Nicene were not found in the African copy of the Nicene *Acta.*[72] Faustinus' proposal that the Roman see should be consulted was overruled [73] and it was decided to send for an authentic copy of the canons in the Nicene *Acta* from Constantinople and the East, where the originals were believed to be kept.

Meanwhile the council addressed a letter to Pope Boniface,[74] which included a request that he too would write to the East for an authentic copy of the Nicene canons and a protest against the arrogant behaviour of the legate Faustinus.

[68] *Cod. can. eccl. Afric.* 134. It is clear that Zosimus was quoting as Nicene *Conc. Sardic.,* Cans. 5 and 14. Cf. Mansi, *op. cit.,* Vol. IV, 404. There is no reason to suppose that Zosimus was not doing so in good faith. On the relation of the canons of Sardica to those of Nicaea, see Duchesne, *Histoire,* Vol. II, pp. 226–7.

[69] The African bishops knew of the existence of the Council of Sardica but confused it with the secessionist synod of Philippopolis. Cf. Augustine, *Ep.* 44, 6, *P.L.* 33, 176.

[70] Mansi, *op. cit.,* Vol. IV, 402.

[71] His claim was clearly based on *Conc. Sardic.,* Cans. 3, 4 and 7 (vers. lat.); Mirbt, *Quellen,* No. 122.

[72] *Acta* 4. Mansi, *op. cit.,* Vol. IV, 404.

[73] *Ibid.,* 5.

[74] *Cod. can. eccl. Afric.* 134.

In due course the sees of Constantinople [75] and Alexandria [76] replied to the request of the African Church, showing that the canons claimed by Zosimus and Faustinus as Nicene were absent from the authentic *Acta* of Nicaea. The Africans contented themselves by sending on the relevant documents to Boniface.[77] Even so the whole question was reopened two years or so later. This time it was a certain Antony, bishop of Fussala and friend of Augustine, who appealed to the Roman see against the sentence pronounced on him by a synod presided over by Augustine himself.[78] Boniface at once quashed the sentence and Antony returned to Africa confident that he could now obtain restoration. Augustine thereupon wrote to Pope Celestine I,[79] who by now had taken the place of Boniface, and protested gently but firmly against the action of the Roman see. It seems likely that Celestine listened and refrained from any further intervention. Shortly afterwards the notorious Apiarius once more came into public notice. Being condemned anew he again appealed to the Roman see and was immediately received into communion.[80] On his return to Africa he was accompanied by the legate Faustinus.[81] His case was reviewed by a council held at Carthage in A.D. 424, at which Faustinus peremptorily insisted that the decision given by Celestine should be treated as final.[82] In spite of frequent obstructions created by the legate the African bishops, nothing daunted, carefully examined the whole matter afresh and finally reported their findings to Celestine.[83] Their letter was a dignified and restrained assertion of the independence of the Church of Africa.

In spite of the check to the growth of Roman prestige arising from the arrogance and lack of tact on the part of

[75] *Ibid.*, 136. Atticus, *Ep.* 1. *P.G.* 65, 649. Grumel, *Regestes,* Vol. I, No. 38.

[76] *Ibid.*, 135. Cyril, *Ep.* 85. *P.G.* 77, 377.

[77] *Ibid.*, 138.

[78] Augustine, *Ep.* 209, 4, 5. *P.L.* 33, 954.

[79] *Ep.* 209.

[80] *Cod. can. eccl. Afric.* 138. The action of Celestine should be compared with that of Leo in the case of Celidonius. Doubtless Celestine, like Leo, regarded the question as still *sub iudice,* in consequence of the appeal addressed to the Roman see.

[81] *Ibid.*

[82] *Ibid.*

[83] *Ibid.* For a summary of the main points of this important letter see Kidd, *History,* Vol. III, p. 171.

Faustinus, its credit was amply redeemed by the adroitness of the legates who were present at the first council of Ephesus. In the course of the fifty years which had elapsed since the council of Constantinople the importance of the Roman see in relation to eastern affairs had vastly increased, so that when at the instigation of Nestorius the Emperor Theodosius II summoned a general imperial council to meet at Ephesus on Pentecost, A.D. 431, both that see and other western churches were invited to send representatives.[84] Celestine sent off two bishops, Projectus and Arcadius, together with Philip, a Roman priest, to act as his legates to the council.[85] From his standpoint the sole duty of the legates was to explain to the council the nature of the decision which had already been given at a Roman synod held in the autumn of the previous year.[86] Hence in his written instructions [87] he enjoined them to keep closely in touch with Cyril of Alexandria and to follow his advice, while at the same time doing everything possible to safeguard the prestige of the Apostolic see. Cyril, it should be remembered, had received,[88] as had also other bishops of the "greater churches" in the East,[89] a mandate to act as papal representative in winning Nestorius to a better mind. Celestine further reminded his legates that they were to have a deciding vote in the framing of resolutions, though he forbade them to take part in debates.[90] He added the provision

[84] The summonses were despatched from Constantinople on November 19th, A.D. 430. The copy sent to Cyril is given in Schwartz, *Acta conc. Ephesi,* I, 1, 1, p. 114 (*Acta graeca,* 25). It is worthy of mention that Martin of Milan evidently regarded the doctrinal question at issue as sufficiently answered by his predecessor Ambrose in his *De Incarnatione* from which Martin quoted in replying to the letter addressed to him by the Antiochenes. Cf. Schwartz, *op. cit.,* I, 1, 3, p. 41 (*Acta graeca,* 97). A similar view was clearly held by his successor Eusebius in relation to the Eutychian controversy. See Chap. XIII, pp. 317f. below.

[85] See below *Ep.* 17, JK 378 and JK 379.

[86] Cf. *Ep.* 11, JK 372; Schwartz, *op. cit.,* I, 2, p. 5 (*Coll. Veron.* 1).

[87] *Ep.* 17, JK 378; Schwartz, *op. cit.,* I, 2, p. 25 (*Coll. Veron.* 8).

[88] *Ep.* 11, 6; Schwartz, *op. cit.,* I, 2, p. 6.

[89] *Ep.* 12, JK 373. It is evident that Celestine was envisaging procedure on the lines prescribed by the canons of Sardica. Schwartz, *op. cit.,* p. 21.

[90] *Ep.* 17, JK 378, "vos de eorum sententiis iudicare debebitis, non subire certamen." The Roman see in particular and the western Churches generally had an ineradicable aversion to doctrinal speculation and argument. Cf. Celestine, *Ep.* 11, JK 372. Schwartz, *Acta,* I, 2, p. 5 (*Coll. Veron.* 1). It is clear that Celestine had no intention of allowing the tactical blunder of A.D. 426 to be repeated.

that should they arrive after the conclusion of the council they were to send an immediate report of its outcome, and in the event of Cyril proceeding to Constantinople they should accompany him thither and present the Pope's letter to the Emperor.[91] If, however, they should find the issue still undetermined they were to adopt the standpoint suggested by Cyril. The legates took with them a letter addressed to the council,[92] in which Celestine displayed considerable caution and reminded the assembled bishops that the duty of his legates was to assist at the proceedings as agents of that which had been already decided. He affirmed that he felt no doubt that they would support his decision, since it had been framed with a view to the security of the whole Church.

Yet, as it turned out, Celestine's "decision" had but little influence on the actual course of events. Without waiting for the arrival of the legates or of John of Antioch and his suffragans, Cyril opened the proceedings of the council on June 22nd,[93] and claimed for himself the presidency, in virtue, as he alleged, of a commission received by him from the Roman see.

In the opening stages of the session Cyril sanctioned the reading of Celestine's letter to Nestorius,[94] yet showed no readiness to allow it to play a decisive part in the proceedings. The Roman legates did not reach Ephesus till the beginning of July. On arrival they at once ranged themselves on the side of Cyril and took part in a further session held on July 10th and 11th.[95] As soon as an opportunity presented itself the legates adroitly put forward the Roman standpoint in the controversy. Philip, who appears to have excelled even his fellow-legates in tact and diplomacy, urged that the question had already been determined by Celestine, and in support of his view produced the papal letter addressed to the council.[96]

[91] *Ep.* 19, JK 380. Schwartz, *Acta,* I, 2, p. 25 (*Coll. Veron.* 9).
[92] *Ep.* 18, JK 379. Schwartz, *Acta,* I, 2, p. 22 (*Coll. Veron.* 7).
[93] Schwartz, *Acta,* I, 1, 2, pp. 3ff. (*Acta graeca,* 33ff.). Cyril so describes himself in the minutes. Yet it is doubtful whether Celestine really meant what Cyril alleged him to mean. In any case Cyril was in no sense an official legate of the Roman see. He was accorded the presidency chiefly in virtue of his tenure of the premier eastern see and of his own adroitness.
[94] *Ep.* 13, JK 374.
[95] Schwartz, *Acta Ephesi,* I, 1, 3, pp. 53ff. (*Acta graeca,* 106).
[96] *Ep.* 18, JK 379.

The letter was greeted with enthusiastic acclamations. After Projectus had explained that the purpose of the letter was only to strengthen the conviction of the well-instructed, Arcadius went on to request that the resolutions passed in the previous session should be formally brought to their notice. Philip supported this proposal and pointed out that the recent acclamations expressed the conviction of the council that their relation to the Pope was one of "members" to "head." "Thus," he added, "you know that the head of the whole Faith and of all the Apostles is the blessed Apostle Peter," and he repeated that the minutes should be read so that in accordance with the papal decision and that of the council the deposition of Nestorius might be finally confirmed by the legates' assent.

At the following session [97] Philip once more acted as spokesman of the legation and stated that he was satisfied after reading for himself the minutes of the proceedings of June 22nd that all had been done in due canonical order. At the same time he stressed the need for a public recital of the minutes, so that the papal instruction that the legates should confirm the council's decisions could be formally carried out. Eventually the concluding section only of the *Acta* was read, i.e. that part which contained the condemnation of Nestorius. This gave Philip an opening for an outspoken declaration of the theory of authority and jurisdiction now prevailing at Rome.

"No one," he said, "has any doubt, in fact it is a commonplace in all ages, that the most holy and blessed Apostle Peter, Chief and Head of the Apostles, the pillar of Faith and foundation of the Catholic Church, received from our Lord Jesus Christ, the Redeemer of mankind, the keys of the Kingdom and the power to bind and to loose: it is he who to the present day and for all time lives and passes judgment in the person of his successors. His rightful successor and lieutenant, our most blessed Pope, bishop Celestine, has despatched us as a substitute for his presence in person to this council, the assembly of which the most Christian Emperors commanded, who are ever mindful of the Catholic Faith, protecting it and

[97] Schwartz, *Acta,* I, 1, 3, pp. 59ff. (*Acta graeca,* 106, c. 25ff.).

preserving the doctrine of the Apostles, which they have received from their fathers and forbears." [98]

He concluded his speech by saying:

"In accordance with the verdict of all the churches the sentence is ratified, since the bishops of the eastern and western churches are taking part in this council either in person or through their legates." [99] The statements made by Arcadius and Projectus in support of their colleague endorsed his words, while they made it clear that in the view of the legates the papal decision came first, and the conciliar resolutions second.

The deposition of Nestorius being now confirmed, the legates took part in the subsequent sessions of July 16th and 17th.[100] There steps were taken to undo the counter-moves made by John of Antioch and his associates against Cyril.

Finally, in a letter forwarded by the council to the Emperor,[101] it was stated that the western churches represented by the legates had supported the decisions against Nestorius. A further letter [102] addressed to the Emperor by Juvenal of Jerusalem and the Roman legates emphasized the nullity of the proceedings of the *conciliabulum* conducted under the presidency of John of Antioch.

After ordering the arrest of Cyril, Nestorius and Memnon of Ephesus, the Emperor summoned a conference at Constantinople between John of Antioch on the one side and Juvenal and the legates on the other.[103] Largely thanks to Philip's diplomacy, the supporters of Cyril succeeded in winning the Emperor to their side and took part in the election of Maximian to fill the see of Constantinople, now rendered vacant by the deposition of Nestorius.[104] It is likely that the

[98] Schwartz, *Acta, ibid.*, pp. 60ff. (*Acta graeca*, 106, 31). This speech of Philip was used in the composition of the constitution *Pastor Aeternus*, 1870. Cf. *Acta et decreta sacr. conc. recent. coll. Lacensis*, Vol. VII (1890), p. 483.

[99] *Ibid.*, p. 61.

[100] Schwartz, *Acta*, 1, 1, 3, pp. 15ff. (*Acta graeca*, 87ff.).

[101] *Ibid.*, p. 63 (*Acta graeca*, 107).

[102] Schwartz, *ibid.*, p. 65 (*Acta graeca*, 108).

[103] The court cared more now as always for exterior unity than for dogmatic truth.

[104] Schwartz, *ibid.*, I, 1, 7, p. 124 (*Coll. Athen.*, 84).

legates had an important share in the composition of the letter subsequently addressed by the electors to Celestine.[105]

If the proceedings of the council of Ephesus threw into sharp relief the differences between the standpoints of the eastern churches and the Roman see on questions of authority, especially in the sphere of doctrine, they certainly served to indicate the progress of the Roman see in the direction of winning the respect and obedience of other churches. In fact it remains doubtful whether, apart from the support so opportunely given to him by the Roman legates, Cyril would have succeeded in mastering the counter-influence of the see of Antioch which, at least in the earlier stages of the council, could count on the generous and willing aid of the eastern court. If at the last moment Theodosius changed sides, most of the credit for effecting this result must belong to the undaunted courage and steadfast loyalty of Philip, priest of the *titulus, Basilica Apostolorum.*[106]

It is clear from the foregoing evidence that up to the first council of Ephesus no preponderating rôle in conciliar procedure and debates had been assigned to the legates of the Roman see. And even at Ephesus it is doubtful whether much would have been heard of them, if that see had happened to favour the cause, not of Cyril, but of Nestorius. In no case is there a single instance of Roman legates being assigned the presidency, apart from that of Cyril, who was scarcely a legate in the proper sense; on the contrary it belonged normally either to lay imperial commissioners, or to some bishop personally designated by the Emperor himself.

[105] Schwartz, *Acta,* I, 2, pp. 85ff. (*Coll. Veron.*, No. 22), JK 385, 2.
[106] Schwartz, *ibid.*, I, 1, 3, p. 13 (*Acta graeca,* 85).

CHAPTER XI

LEO AND THE CHURCHES OF THE EAST. 3

THE REACTION TO THE COUNCIL OF EPHESUS

(i) *The last years of Theodosius II*

On his way home from Ephesus to Alexandria Dioscorus may well have congratulated himself on the highly satisfactory outcome of the recent council. Not only had Alexandrine Christology been clearly proclaimed as the official doctrinal standard of the imperial Church, by the rehabilitation of Eutyches and the formal adoption of the third letter of Cyril to Nestorius together with its appended anathematisms, and Theodoret, the greatest living exponent of Antiochene teaching, safely muzzled, but a shattering blow had been delivered at the prestige of two of the greater churches of the East by the deposition of Flavian and Domnus. The confirmation of the conciliar decisions by an imperial rescript gave legal sanction,[1] and the victory thus obtained seemed final.

Meanwhile Leo eagerly awaited further news from the East. His last letter to Theodosius appeared to have been altogether ineffective. Nevertheless he made yet a further attempt to persuade the Emperor to adopt his suggestions. In his letter [2] he urges that the faith taught by himself in his letters and proclaimed by all Catholic bishops is none other than the faith of Nicaea.[3] This, he says, is proved to be true by the fact that in those documents the errors of Nestorius and of those who deny the reality of our nature taken by the Lord Jesus Christ are alike condemned. The one sure

[1] The rescript, which renewed the provisions of an earlier law of A.D. 435 against "Nestorians," and applied them to those condemned at Ephesus, also required metropolitans to obtain written statements of assent from their suffragans to the conciliar decisions, on pain of immediate deposition in case of refusal, and prescribed the destruction of all "Nestorian" writings, especially those of Theodoret. Mansi, *op. cit.*, Vol. VII, 495.

[2] *Ep.* 54, JK 445, dated December 25th, A.D. 449.

[3] *Ibid.* "Satis plene ac lucide litteris meis . . . reseratum est . . . hoc constanter asserere, quod etiam venerandi Patres, quondam apud Nicaeam congregati, secundum fidem Symboli credendum et confitendum sacratissima auctoritate sanxerunt."

way of restoring peace to the Church is to put into execution the plan of holding a fresh council in Italy.[4]

But Theodosius remained deaf to all entreaties. An imperial council had been assembled, and had delivered its verdict. The case was ended. Yet there still remained a faint possibility that, even if Theodosius would not listen to Leo, he might be moved to modify his ecclesiastical policy in deference to the express wish of his imperial colleague and cousin, Valentinian.[5] By a fortunate coincidence the young Emperor arrived in Rome from Ravenna in company with the Empress and his mother, Galla Placidia.[6] His visit happened to coincide with the feast of the *Cathedra Petri*,[7] an occasion which proved eminently appropriate for Leo's purpose. So when the imperial family were present at the liturgy in the basilica of St. Peter, the Pope, attended by the leading clergy of the capital, presented a humble petition to the Sovereigns, imploring their intervention on behalf of the cause of "dyophysite" Christology, and urging the despatch of letters to their eastern cousins in support of the repeated requests of the Roman see. The western court proved suitably attentive to these suggestions, and at once issued four letters, three of which were addressed to Theodosius in person.[8]

In the letter sent by Valentinian,[9] the young Sovereign, after referring to the petition of the Roman bishop and to the danger which appeared to threaten the safety of the Catholic faith, urged Theodosius to take action for its defence:

"It is our duty to defend it," he writes, ". . . and to preserve inviolate at this present time the honour and respect due to the blessed Apostle Peter; since the most blessed bishop of the Roman city, on whom an episcopate of universal scope

[4] *Ep.* 54, JK 445. "Ut intra Italiam haberi iubeatis episcopale concilium."

[5] A similar expedient had been adopted by Pope Julius I in favour of Athanasius, cf. Id. *Apol. ad Const.*, 4, *P.G.* 25, 601, and by Pope Innocent I in favour of John Chrysostom, cf. Palladius, *Vita Chrysostomi*, 3.

[6] For the relationships of the two imperial courts cf. genealogical table in Bury, *History of the Later Roman Empire*, Vol. I, p. i.

[7] On the origin of this feast see Frere, *Studies in Early Roman Liturgy*, Vol. I, p. 97, and Additional Note, *St. Peter in Rome*, p. 79, n. 57.

[8] These letters are preserved only in a Greek version, of which the present Latin text is a retranslation which occasionally distorts or exaggerates the force of the Greek original. See below, p. 265, n. 10.

[9] *Inter Leon. Epp.*, No. 55, *P.L.* 54, 858.

has been conferred by established custom, possesses the privilege and the right to give decisions concerning the faith and the bishops." [10]

The Emperor adds the request that a fresh council may be assembled in Italy, so that after the decisions of Ephesus have been cancelled the Roman bishop can re-examine the whole question and give a final verdict.[11]

His mother, Galla Placidia, addressed her imperial nephew in a similar strain.[12] After referring to the proceedings of the recent council and the appeal of Flavian, she writes:

"Wherefore let your Grace resist such illegality and ordain that the true faith of the Catholic religion may be preserved inviolate to the end that, in accordance with the letter and decision of the Apostolic see, which we all alike honour as the first of all, Flavian may remain in all respects secure in the rank of the episcopate, and the case may be referred to the synod of the Apostolic see, in which he who was deemed worthy to receive the keys of heaven was the first to be awarded the office of the chief bishopric: since it is fitting that in all things we should show respect for this glorious city, which is the mistress of the whole earth." [13]

[10] *Ibid.* "*ἣν ἡμεῖς ἀπὸ τῶν προγόνων παραδοθεῖσαν, ὀφείλομεν μετὰ τῆς προσηκούσης καθοσιώσεως ἐκδικεῖν, καὶ τῆς ἰδιάς εὐλαβείας τὴν ἀξίαν τῷ μακαρίῳ ἀποστόλῳ Πέτρῳ ἄτρωτον καὶ ἐν τοῖς ἡμετέροις χρόνοις διαφυλάττειν, ἵνα ὁ μακαριώτατος ἐπίσκοπος τῆς Ῥωμαίων πόλεως, ᾧ τὴν ἱερωσύνην κατὰ πάντων ἡ ἀρχαιότης πάρεσχε, χώραν καὶ εὐπορίαν ἔχειν περί τε πίστεως καὶ ἱερέων κρίνειν.*" The Latin version reads "cui principatum sacerdotii super omnes antiquitas contulit, locum habeat ac facultatem de fide et sacerdotibus iudicare." Evidently the author has in mind the Nicene-Sardican canons.

[11] *Ibid.* "*ἵνα ὁ προλεχθεὶς ἱερεὺς, συναχθέντων ἐκ πάσης τῆς οἰκουμένης καὶ τῶν λοίπων ἱερέων, ἐντὸς τῆς Ἰταλίας, παντὸς προκρίματος ἀποκινηθέντος ἐξ ὑπαρχῆς τὴν στρεφομένην αἰτίαν πεφροντισμένῃ δοκιμασίᾳ διαγνοὺς, ἐξοίσῃ τὴν ἀπόφασιν.*"

[12] *Inter Leon. Epp.*, No. 56, *P.L.* 54, 860.

[13] *Ibid.* "Τούτου *χάριν ἡ σὴ ἡμερότης τοῖς τοσούτοις θορύβοις ἀντιτιθεῖσα τὴν ἀλήθειαν ἄσπιλον τὴν πίστιν τῆς καθολικῆς θρησκείας παραφυλαχθῆναι προσταξάτω. Ἵνα κατὰ τὸν τύπον, καὶ τὸν ὅρον τοῦ ἀποστολικοῦ θρόνου, ὃν καὶ ἡμεῖς ὁμοίως, ὡς προσηνούμενον, προσκυνοῦμεν, ἐν τῇ στάσει τῆς ἱερωσύνης ἀβλαβοῦς μένοντος ἐν πᾶσι Φλαυιανοῦ ἐν τῇ συνόδῳ τοῦ ἀποστολικοῦ θρόνου ἡ δίκη παραπεμφθείη, ἐν ᾧ πρῶτος ἐκεῖνος, ὁ τὰς οὐράνου κλεῖς ἀξιωθεὶς ὑποδέξασθαι, τὴν ἐπισκοπὴν τῆς ἀρχιερωσύνης ἐκόσμησε δηλαδή· ὅποτε πρέπει ἡμᾶς ταύτῃ τῇ μεγίστῃ πόλει, ἣ τις δέσποινα πασῶν ὑπάρχει τῶν γεῶν ἐν πᾶσι τὸ σέβας παραφυλάξαι.*" The passage is of interest, not only as reflecting some acquaintance with *Conc. Sardic.* Canon 4 (vers. lat.), Mirbt, *Quellen*, No. 122, but as showing that while Placidia is mindful of the honour due to St. Peter she does not forget the civil grandeur of the ancient imperial capital.

This letter was accompanied by a personal appeal from the Empress Licinia Eudoxia to her father.[14] Like her imperial relatives she appeared to betray a certain vagueness as to the real issue at stake,[15] though she was evidently well-informed regarding the appeal received from Flavian and the papal project of a fresh council to be held in Italy.

Finally Galla Placidia addressed her niece Pulcheria.[16] She implored the Empress to lend her aid in the cause of undoing the mischief wrought by the disorderly and scandalous council,"[17] and reminded her of the appropriateness of referring causes in which the reputation of bishops is involved to the judgment of the Roman see:[18]

" For," she writes, " we ought in all things to accord the primacy to the Eternal City, which in virtue of its power has acquired a worldwide Empire, and has entrusted the earth to be administered and preserved in security by our rule."[19]

The impression given by this series of imperial letters is that they owe something, if not perhaps everything, to papal inspiration, and that the originality of the writers appears chiefly in the importance which they attach to the civil dignity of the city of Rome, as justifying or accounting for the peculiar privileges of the Roman see.

While these letters were on their way a group of interesting communications reached Leo from Constantinople in the earlier part of March, A.D. 449. They had been sent by the supporters of " dyophysite " teaching and were intended to enlighten the Roman see as to the existing state of affairs in the eastern capital. Leo sent immediate replies to his correspondents and in the one addressed to the Constantinopolitan church[20] expressed his satisfaction at the loyalty which his

[14] *Inter Leon. Epp.*, No. 57, *P.L.* 54, 862.

[15] *Ibid.*, " ὅλον τὸ δόγμα τῆς θρησκείας κατὰ τὴν ἀνατολὴν τεθορυβῆσθαι."

[16] *Inter Leon. Epp.*, No. 58, *P.L.* 54, 864.

[17] *Ibid.*, " τῇ (sc. τῇ κατὰ τὴν ''Εφεσον σύνοδον) μηδεμίαν τάξιν ἱερωσύνης φυλαξάσῃ, ἢ μηδὲ συμμετρίαν . . . τῇ τεταραγμένῃ καὶ ἀθλίᾳ συνόδῳ."

[18] *Ibid.*, " ἐν ᾧ πρῶτος ὁ μακαριώτατος τῶν ἀποστόλων Πέτρος, τὰ κλεῖθρα τῶν οὐράνων ὑποδεξάμενος, τὴν ἀρχιερωσύνην ἐκόσμησε, τοῦ ἐπὶ κλησωσαμένῃ ὑπόθεσις παραπεμφθείη." Cf. *vers. lat.*, " episcopatus causa mittatur."

[19] *Ibid.* " 'Οφείλομεν γὰρ τῇ ἀθανάτῳ πόλει ἀπονέμειν ἐν πᾶσι τὰ πρωτεῖα, τῇ διὰ τῆς ἰδίας ἀρετῆς, τοῦ κόσμου κληρῶσαι μὲν ἢ τὴν δεσποτείαν, καὶ τῇ ἡμετέρᾳ βασιλείᾳ τὸν κύκλον καὶ διοικητέον καὶ φυλακτέον ἐπιτρεψάσῃ."

[20] *Ep.* 59, JK 447, without date, but probably of March 17th, A.D. 450.

correspondents professed to Flavian.[21] He went on to insist that those like the supporters of Eutyches, who deny the reality of human nature in Christ, reject also the truth of the Passion and of the Resurrection. In opposition to such teaching he writes:

"We affirm that Christ is the Son of God, very God, born of God the Father without any beginning in time, and the same, very Man, born of a true human mother in the fullness of time." [22]

The writer concluded by suggesting that the recipients should support his request addressed to the Emperor for the assembly of a fresh council.

In writing to Pulcheria [23] the Pope expressed his pleasure at receiving the Empress's letter,[24] and after declaring his abhorrence for the teaching of the Eutychians, "which in vain pretends that it maintains the faith of the Nicene council, since it is plainly at variance with that faith," [25] urges her to further his project and affirms that the security of the Empire is assured by the orthodoxy of its rulers.[26]

Finally there was a communication for Martin and Faustus,[27] the leaders of the anti-Eutychian monks. The special interest of this letter is in Leo's allusion to the miscarriage of his post of October 13th, A.D. 449, when he writes:

"Your request would have been complied with by the time your own letter was despatched if only our communications had been delivered to your beloved selves, for they were issued by the authority of the Apostolic see and by the unanimous

[21] *Ibid.*, 1, "in sanctae plebis acclamationibus . . . omnium vestrum probavimus affectum; quia vivit ac permanet apud bonos filios optimi patris iusta dilectio."

[22] *Ibid.*, 5, "dicimus Christum Dei filium, Deum verum, natum de Deo Patre sine ullo initio temporis, eundemque hominem verum, natum de matre homine certa plenitudine temporis."

[23] *Ep.* 60, JK 448, date as above.

[24] The expression *ibid.*, "quae prius poposci" refers to his previous letter of October 13th, A.D. 449.

[25] *Ibid.*, "illudque frustra praetendens quod Nicaenae synodi fidem teneat, cuius eum esse constat alienum."

[26] *Ibid.*, "res humanae aliter tutae esse non possunt, nisi quae ad divinam confessionem pertinent, et regia et sacerdotalis defendat auctoritas."

[27] *Ep.* 61, JK 449 of the same date.

decision of the holy synod, which had assembled here in great numbers." [28]

After suggesting that they should procure the publication of his doctrinal statements in Constantinople, saying with conscious pride:

"I do not forget that I preside over the church in the name of him whose confession was commended by the Lord . . . and whose faith destroys all heresies." [29] He concluded with the statement that copies of his earlier letters are appended.[30]

Soon after this the western sovereigns received the answers to the letters which they had addressed to their eastern colleagues which, in spite of their courteously restrained language, made it abundantly clear that the eastern government had no intention of allowing the question of the orthodoxy of Eutyches, or of the legitimacy of "monophysite" Christology to be reopened. In writing to Valentinian [31] Theodosius observed that so far from the cause of truth being in danger, it had been vindicated. Flavian had been found guilty of introducing novel teaching and had received suitable punishment.[32] The Emperor's letters to Placidia [33] and to Eudoxia [34] were in a similar vein, and in writing to his daughter he

[28] *Ep.* 61, 1, "quod a nobis desiderabatis, eo vobis tempore, quo epistolae vestrae mittebantur, occurrerit, si tamen dilectioni vestrae tradi scripta nostra potuere, quae non solum apostolicae sedis auctoritate, sed etiam sanctae synodi, quae ad nos frequens convenerat, unanimitate directa sunt."

It is evident that this group of letters from Constantinople were spontaneous and are not to be regarded as replies to Leo's correspondence of October 13th of the previous year. It seems likely that the whole of this post was confiscated, and hence never reached its destination. A similar fate befell the letters from the West regarding John Chrysostom, A.D. 405. Cf. Palladius, *Vita Chrysostomi,* 4.

[29] *Ibid.,* 2. "Memor enim sum me sub illius nomine ecclesiae praesidere, cuius a Domino . . . est glorificata confessio, et cuius fides omnes quidem haereses destruit."

[30] Including no doubt a copy of the "Tome," *Ep.* 28, JK 423.

[31] *Inter Leon. Epp.* No. 62, *P.L.* 54, 875. On the use of "Patriarcha" which occurs here and in No. 63, see Additional Note A, *Eastern imperial references to the Roman see,* p. 286.

[32] *Ibid. P.L.* 54, 878. "Φλαβιανὸς δὲ ὁ φωραθεὶς αἴτιος τοῦ βλαβέρου καινισμοῦ τὴν ὀφειλομένην ἑαυτῷ τίμην ἀπηνέγκατο." The fact that at the beginning of his letter Theodosius refers to Leo as τοῦ εὐλαβεστάτου πατριάρχου need not be taken, as Batiffol, *Siège Apostolique,* pp. 525f., understands, in the sense of a deliberate slight on the Roman see.

[33] *Inter Leon. Epp.* No. 63, *P.L.* 54, 878.

[34] *Ibid.,* No. 64.

affirmed that the project of assembling a fresh council, suggested by the Pope, is altogether unnecessary.[35] The case was now finally settled. It seems that a further letter was addressed to Leo,[36] which unfortunately has not been preserved.

In referring to Flavian Theodosius made no mention of his decease, but from the fact that the arrival of the imperial post in Rome was followed shortly afterwards by the receipt of a letter from Anatolius,[37] notifying the Roman see of his election to the vacant see of Constantinople, it may be inferred that it took place in the earlier part of the year A.D. 450. The new bishop of Constantinople justified his election by explaining that in consequence of a difference of opinion prevailing in the church of the eastern capital the Emperor had ordered a suitable candidate to be chosen from among those who for various reasons were staying in the city,[38] so that without any dispute the best of them should be preferred to the episcopate. After which it had pleased the Sovereign to entrust to the clergy the election of their prelate.

"Thus," Anatolius adds, with evident satisfaction, "I . . . was elected . . . and consequently it became the duty of the holy synod residing here to proceed without delay to my consecration." [39]

The receipt of this information must have been anything

[35] *Ibid.*, "*καὶ οὐδὲν ἕτερον τοῦ λοιποῦ μετὰ ταῦτα δύνατον ὁρίσαι περὶ τῶν ἅπαξ ἤδη τετυπωμένων.*"

[36] Mentioned in No. 62; cf. No. 64. The disappearance of this letter may perhaps be due to the unacceptability of its contents to the Roman see. It would have been interesting to know what view Theodosius took of the papal allusions to the procedure prescribed by the canons of Sardica.

[37] *Inter Leon. Epp.* 53, *P.L.* 54, 854. Cf. Grumel, *Regestes,* No. 111. The present text is only a fragment. It lacks a date, but in spite of the suggestion of the Ballerini *ad loc.* that it belongs to the latter part of the year A.D. 449, it is better with Caspar, *Geschichte,* Vol. I, p. 616, to assign it to the earlier part of A.D. 450. If Anatolius had been elected before March of that year Theodosius could scarcely have failed to mention the fact. It was accompanied by a letter from Anatolius' consecrators, see *Ep.* 71, JK 454.

[38] This shows the use which could be made by the Emperor of the *σύνοδος ἐνδημοῦσα.*

[39] *Ibid., P.L.* 54, 854f. "*Καὶ ἰδοὺ φθάνει ψῆφος ἐπ' ἐμὲ τὸν ἐλάχιστον . . . ὅθεν γέγονεν ἔργον τῇ ἐνδημούσῃ ἁγίᾳ συνόδῳ ἀνυπερθέτως εἰς τὴν ἐπ' ἐμοὶ χειροτονίαν ἐλθεῖν.*" It is improbable that, as was alleged, Anatolius was consecrated by Dioscorus.

but gratifying to Leo, since it must have suggested not only that it was hopeless to look forward to a revision of the Ephesine verdict by the adoption of the procedure provided for by the Sardican canons, but that the whole of the East was at the mercy of "monophysite" bishops. The urgency of establishing direct communication with those elements in the church of Constantinople which remained faithful to "dyophysitism" was now more apparent than ever before, especially in view of the evident disadvantages of continuing to use the normal channels of correspondence.[40] Leo therefore adopted the expedient of selecting four legates to whom he entrusted a small batch of letters. Of these the one addressed to the anti-Eutychian archimandrites is the most outspoken.[41] In it Leo mentioned the receipt of letters from Anatolius and from the bishops responsible for his consecration and deplored the fact that neither letter made any reference to a formal abandonment of "monophysite" error. He then mentioned the names of his legates to Constantinople,[42] and stated that they were bringing with them a letter to the Emperor and a selection of patristic authorities bearing on Christological doctrine,[43] adding that he had not abandoned hope of reconciling those who through ignorance or fear had supported erroneous views.

In writing to Pulcheria,[44] while showing more caution, he referred once again to his dissatisfaction that no assurance had been received that Anatolius has abandoned Eutychian errors, and affirmed that he would not answer the letter which he had received from him until he learnt that the bishop had formally assented either to Cyril's letter to Nestorius or to his own letter to Flavian.[45] He mentioned the fact of the

[40] See *Ep.* 71, JK 454, "ne quod inter longinquas regiones accidere solet, in nimias dilationes tenderet veritatis examen." Obviously Leo could not express the real grounds for his anxiety regarding the fate of his correspondence.

[41] *Ep.* 71, JK 454, dated July 16th, A.D. 450.

[42] Abundius and Asterius (or Etherius), bishops, with Basil and Senator, priests. On the identity of these legates see Chap. XIII, p. 317, n. 34.

[43] A similar selection is appended to *Ep.* 165. On this dossier see Saltet, *Revue d'histoire eccl.*, Vol. VI (1905), pp. 290–4: *Le recueil patristique de St. Léon.*

[44] *Ep.* 70, JK 453 of the same date.

[45] i.e. the famous "second" letter, *Ep.* 4, *P.G.* 77, 44 and the "Tome," *Ep.* 28, JK 423. *Ibid.*, "simplex enim absolutumque quod posco ut . . .

legation and alluded to the project of a fresh council as only necessary in the event of its efforts proving a failure.

A third letter was directed to the Emperor.[46] Here Leo states that he awaited with eagerness to hear that Anatolius had given assent to the patristic catena which his legates had brought with them, and says:

"Let him (sc. Anatolius) read afresh with care the faith in the Lord's Incarnation preserved by the holy Fathers . . . and when he has noticed that the letter of Cyril . . . accords with their opinion, let him reconsider the acts of the Ephesine council . . . and let him not refuse to read once more my own letter. This he will find to be in accord with the orthodoxy of the Fathers in all respects. When he has seen that what is requested and expected of him is actually to his own advantage, let him assent to the views of Catholics with his whole heart, so that he proclaims his sincere profession of one common faith in the presence of all the clergy and of the whole body of the laity, and gives his subscription without reservation, the fact of which can be notified to the Apostolic see and to all the bishops and churches of the Lord."[47]

Nor was this all. The Pope added that Anatolius must undertake to exclude from his communion anyone who dissented from the Catholic faith and added that he had sent his legates to Constantinople for the express purpose of conveying instructions for the settlement of the whole controversy. But in the event of the "opposition" remaining recalcitrant

Cyrilli . . . epistolae, quam ipse ad Nestorium miserat, acquiescat . . . *vel* epistolae meae quae ad sanctae recordationis Flavianum episcopum est directa, consentiat." The reading given above is the one accepted by the Ballerini, *P.L.* 54, 893, in which Duchesne, *Histoire,* Vol. III, p. 424, and Kidd, *History,* Vol. III, p. 310, apparently concur. Caspar, however, *Geschichte,* Vol. I, p. 501, prefers "et," as more likely to express Leo's actual intention.

[46] *Ep.* 69, JK 452 of the same date.

[47] *Ibid.,* 1. "Relegat itaque sollicite quae a sanctis Patribus incarnationis Dominicae fides fuerit custodita . . . et cum . . . Cyrilli . . . epistolam . . . praecedentium sensui perspexerit consonantem, Ephesinae etiam synodi gesta recenseat. . . . Non aspernetur etiam meam epistolam recensere, quam pietati Patrum per omnia concordare reperiet. Cumque a se hoc quod eidem profuturum sit expeti desiderarique cognoverit, catholicorum sententiis toto corde consentiat, ita ut sinceram communis fidei professionem, absolutissima subscriptione, coram omni clero et universa plebe declaret, apostolicae sedi et universis Domini sacerdotibus atque ecclesiis publicandam."

the original project of a fresh council to be held in Italy ought to be carried out.[48]

This group of letters throws valuable light on the skill of Leo as a diplomat. Unlike his great predecessor, Innocent I, who made the rehabilitation of John Chrysostom a definite condition for the resumption of friendly relations with the church of Constantinople,[49] Leo had tacitly allowed the personal question of the status of Flavian to fall into the background, and had abandoned, apparently, the delicate problem of dealing with the appeals. The single point regarding which he had remained adamant throughout the period which followed the council of Ephesus, concerned the recognition of the "Tome" as an orthodox statement of doctrine. In so acting he had really no other course. Since the question of a right definition of the relation between the divine and human in Christ had come to the forefront, Leo had presented himself to the Catholic world as the interpreter of the Catholic faith, in the confidence that he enjoyed the peculiar prerogatives of a successor of St. Peter, the first exponent of that faith, to qualify him for that office. But this meant that once an interpretation, such as was provided by the "Tome," had been offered there could be no thought of withdrawal. Leo, in fact, "had placed the papacy in the foremost line of battle in the doctrinal struggle, the very place where the ensign goes leading the general attack in the sight of the whole force."[50]

Looking back over the events of the last ten months it is easy to see that hitherto neither Leo nor Theodosius had yielded a single inch of ground. For in spite of Leo's abandonment of the personal question regarding the status of Flavian the main issue still remained; either the "Tome" or the decrees of Ephesus. What would have happened if a wholly unexpected event had not completely transformed the whole situation is easy to imagine. Nothing less than prolonged schism between the sees of Rome and Constantinople must

[48] *Ep.* 69, 2. "Sin vero aliqui a puritati nostrae fidei atque Patrum auctoritati dissentiunt, concilium universale intra Italiam . . . clementia vestra concedat." It is remarkable that Leo should persist in his expectation that a fresh council would be possible, in spite of the fact that Theodosius had never shown the slightest interest in the proposal.

[49] *Ep.* 19, 1, JK 305. Cf. Caspar, *Geschichte,* Vol. I, p. 321.

[50] Caspar, *Geschichte,* Vol. I, p. 502.

have resulted. As it was, however, the unexpected happened and took the form of a fatal accident to Theodosius, from which he died on July 28th, A.D. 450.[51]

(ii) *The Accession of Marcian and Pulcheria*

The Empress Pulcheria, as we have seen, for the past five years or so had been excluded from the court of Constantinople, and owed her restoration after the death of her brother to the simple fact that he died without issue. From the point of view of constitutional legality Valentinian III was now sole ruler of the Empire, for it must be remembered that although for practical purposes the rulers domiciled at Ravenna and Constantinople controlled independent spheres of administration, for all this no formal or legal division of the Empire had ever been made, and its theoretical unity still continued to be symbolized by the practice of including the names of all reigning imperial colleagues in the titles of edicts, even when they were of purely local application. Yet if Theodosius I was capable of controlling the whole Empire the same was certainly untrue of his degenerate descendants: and even if Valentinian had attempted to exercise his authority in the Eastern Prefectures it is highly improbable that they would have submitted to his dictation.[52]

Hence, as soon as the news of the late Emperor's death became public, a rumour began to circulate that Marcian, a military commander of some distinction and experience (he was then 58 years old), had been designated by Theodosius as his successor. Pulcheria, to whom the origin of the rumour may perhaps be attributed, showed herself eager to support his candidature, and to legitimize him as a successor to her brother by giving him her hand in marriage.[53] Possibly the whole plan was the result of a compromise between the Empress and the *Magister utriusque militiae,* Aspar, whose barbarian origin and Arian religion rendered him incapable

[51] The immediate cause of death was a fall from horseback. Cf. Theodore Lector, *H.E.* 2, 64, *P.G.* 86, 213; *Chronicon Paschale, P.G.* 82, 812.

[52] Bury, *History of the Later Roman Empire,* Vol. I, p. 235.

[53] Prosper, *Chronicon,* sub ann. 450, *M.G.H.*, Vol. IX, *Chron. min.*, Vol. I, p. 481; *Chronicon Paschale, ibid.* For Gibbon's comments on this arrangement see *Decline,* Vol. III, p. 469 (1929).

of himself assuming the imperial diadem. Marcian was officially accorded the status of Augustus on August 28th, A.D. 450,[54] and was formally crowned either by Pulcheria or by Anatolius.[55]

The beginning of the new reign was marked by strenuous efforts to remedy the mistakes of Theodosius' last years, and as a preliminary the Chamberlain Chrysaphius was deposed and executed by order of the Empress.[56] The next step was to undertake the restoration of imperial church unity. The new Sovereigns eagerly adopted Leo's suggestion as to the importance of assembling a fresh council at the earliest date possible, with a view to revising or rescinding the recent decisions arrived at by the council of Ephesus. In notifying the fact of his election to the Roman see [57] Marcian indicated the nature of his plans to secure this end.[58] The project of a fresh council was doubtless acceptable to the new Sovereigns for the further reason that it was likely to provide an opportunity for rehabilitating the see of Constantinople in relation to the other "greater churches" of the East, and of restricting the unwelcome influence of the see of Alexandria in the affairs of the imperial Church.[59]

The receipt of this letter must have brought intense relief

[54] Marcellinus, *Chronicon, M.G.H., Chron. min.*, Vol. II, p. 83. For a brief summary of the main characteristics of the new reign see Bury, *op. cit.*, Vol. I, pp. 235–9.

[55] Or else by the Senate. See Bury, *op. cit.*, Vol. I, p. 236, n. 4.

[56] John Malalas, *Chronicon*. 14, 368, ed. Bekker (1831).

[57] *Inter Leon. Epp.*, No. 73, *P.L.* 54, 900 of the year A.D. 450. There is reason to regard the Greek text of this letter as the original and so to prefer the expression, "*τὴν . . . σὴν ἁγιωσύνην ἐπισκοπεύουσαν καὶ ἄρχουσαν τῆς θείας πίστεως*" to "tuam sanctitatem principatum in episcopatu divinae fidei possidentem." The Ballerini, however, regard the letter as having been issued in a bilingual form and cite *Inter Leon. Epp.*, No. 100, *P.L.* 54, 970 as a further example. Batiffol, *Siège Apostolique*, p. 528, n. 3 evidently accepts the Latin text as original.

[58] *Ibid.*, "*ὥστε . . . διὰ τῆς συγκροτηθείσης ταύτης συνόδου, σοῦ αὐθεντοῦντος, μεγίστη εἰρήνη . . . ὑπαρχθείη.*" The meaning of *σοῦ αὐθεντοῦντος* has been much disputed. It seems to mean less than "summoned by your authority" (*vers. lat.* te auctore), though more than "summoned in your presence." See Kissling, *Verhältnis zw. sac. u. Imp.*, p. 41, n. 132. It should be noticed that the Emperor makes no allusion to Italy as a possible place of assembly, as Leo would have wished.

[59] A rumour was mentioned at *Conc. Chalc.*, Actio III, Mansi, *op. cit.*, Vol. VI, 1032, that Dioscorus had attempted to prevent the publication of Marcian's accession. Cf. Nestorius, *Bazaar*, ed. Driver and Hodgson, p. 375.

to the mind of Leo. Since the despatch of his legates bearing important correspondence on July 16th, A.D. 450,[60] little or no news had reached him from Constantinople, and as yet he had received no assurance whatever of the orthodoxy of Anatolius. It must have been, therefore, in a mood of considerable anxiety that he wrote in the middle of September to his faithful supporters there, the anti-Eutychian archimandrites, urging them to constancy in defence of orthodox or, in other words, "dyophysite" doctrine.[61]

Yet if the imperial letter might seem to foreshadow a change for the better in the East, the Pope maintained an attitude of reserve towards the new regime and in writing once more to the archimandrites two months later,[62] while showing some renewal of confidence, he betrayed his impatience that nothing was being done at Constantinople to carry his wishes into effect.

At long last, however, the news so eagerly expected arrived in Rome. It took the form of letters from both Marcian and Pulcheria of which the latter,[63] from Leo's point of view, was by far the more important.

"Anatolius," writes the Empress, "has embraced the Apostolic confession . . . and has subscribed without hesitation the letter concerning the Catholic faith, which your beatitude sent to bishop Flavian of holy memory."[64]

Nor was this all. Pulcheria suggested that Leo himself should announce the assembly of a fresh council, so that all the bishops of the East, both of Thrace and of Illyricum, in accordance with the Emperor's wish, should meet at the most convenient city from the eastern provinces of the Empire.[65]

[60] See above, p. 270, n. 41.
[61] *Ep.* 74, JK 456, dated September 13th, A.D. 450.
[62] *Ep.* 75, JK 457, dated November 9th of the same year. Notice his phrase (c. 1) "quia propitio Domino multum catholicorum est aucta libertas."
[63] *Inter Leon. Epp.* 77, *P.L.* 54, 906 late in the year A.D. 450.
[64] *Ibid.* "Ἀνατόλιος . . . τῶν σῶν γραμμάτων τὴν ἀποστολικὴν ὁμολογίαν περιπτύσσεται . . . τῇ τε γὰρ ἐπιστολῇ ὁμοίως τῆς καθολικῆς πίστεως, ἥντινα πρὸς τῆς ἁγίας μνήμης Φλαυιανὸν τὸν ἐπίσκοπον ἡ σὴ μακαριότης ἀπέστειλε." This meant that Anatolius had accepted the "Tome," as Leo had required, *Ep.* 69, JK 454, see above, p. 271. We learn from the *Vita S. Abundii*, ap. Mansi, *op. cit.*, Vol. VI, 513, *Acta SS.* Apr. I, 94 that it took place at a session of the σύνοδος ἐνδημοῦσα at which the Roman legates were present. Cf. Grumel, *Regestes*, No. 116, where the subscription is dated October 21st, A.D. 450.
[65] *Ibid.*

Then the rehabilitation of Flavian:

"Let it be known further by your holiness, that by the command of our master and most gracious Emperor . . . the body of bishop Flavian of holy memory has been brought to the illustrious city of Constantinople, and laid to rest with due honour in the basilica of the Apostles, where the bishops who held office before him have been wont to be buried."[66]

Finally the Empress mentioned that the bishops who had been banished in the previous reign had been recalled by Marcian's order with a view to their restoration at the council now foreshadowed.[67]

The Emperor's letter[68] which accompanied this one, while assuring Leo of his support in the work of appeasement undertaken by the Roman legates, indicated quite clearly that the new regime had no more intention than its predecessor of allowing any future council to take place in Italy,[69] though it made it clear that Leo's attendance in person would be most welcome.[70]

On the surface Leo had won two of the main points for which he had contended. Anatolius had accepted, willingly or otherwise, the "Tome," and justice had been done at least to the memory of Flavian.[71] But so far as the project of a fresh council was concerned he had been less successful. The plan of such a council summoned to meet in a place chosen by the Emperor meant that it would be wholly under the control of the eastern government, and therefore there still remained a certain risk that in spite of the support given by

[66] *Ep.* 77. "Ἔτι δὲ γνώτω ἡ σὴ ἁγιότης, ὡς προστάγματι τοῦ ἡμετέρου δεσπότου καὶ γαληνοτάτου βασίλεως . . . ἐν τῇ ἐνδόξῳ πόλει τῆς Κωνσταντινουπόλεως τοῦ τῆς ἁγίας μνήμης ἐπισκόπου Φλαβιανοῦ τὸ σῶμα διακεκόμισται καὶ ἐν τῇ βασιλικῇ τῶν ἀποστόλων, ἐν ᾗ εἰώθασιν οἱ προλειτουργήσαντες ἐπίσκοποι θάπτεσθαι, τῇ χρεωστουμένῃ τιμῇ ἀποτέθειται." The basilica of the Apostles was the place of burial of Constantine and of some of his successors. See Bury, *op. cit.*, Vol. I, map facing p. 67 and pp. 77f.

[67] *Ibid.*

[68] *Inter Leon. Epp.*, No. 76, *P.L.* 54, 904.

[69] *Ibid.* "ὅπως πρός τινα ὡρισμένον τόπον, ἔνθα ἂν ἡμῖν δόξῃ, πάντες οἱ ἁγιώτατοι ἐπίσκοποι παραγένωνται."

[70] *Ibid.* "εἰ ἀρέσκῃ τῇ σῇ ὁσιότητι ἐπὶ ταῦτα τὰ μέρη παραγενέσθαι καὶ τὴν σύνοδον ἐπιτελέσαι, τοῦτο ποιεῖν τῷ περὶ τὴν θρησκείαν ἔρωτι καταξιώσῃ."

[71] Although in his more recent letters this demand had been allowed to drop.

the new regime to Leo's policy a sudden change of policy might bring about a repetition of the disaster of Ephesus.

His most notable achievement, however, had been in the doctrinal sphere, since it was evident from these imperial letters that the new Sovereigns were prepared to recognize his "Tome" as a sufficient standard of doctrinal orthodoxy and this meant not only a victory for "dyophysitism" but a signal triumph for the Roman see in its relations with the "greater churches" of the East. From Leo's point of view therefore one thing remained to be done, namely to secure the general adhesion of the eastern churches to his standard of doctrine.

Nevertheless Marcian was evidently determined to carry out the project of assembling a fresh council. Thus the object which the Pope was originally most eager to secure now became the very thing which he sought most to avoid. That this was so emerges very clearly in the letters which he now wrote in reply to the eastern Sovereigns.

His letter to Marcian,[72] while thanking the Emperor for his zeal on behalf of the Catholic faith did not so much as mention the subject of the council. Instead he contented himself with saying that he had sent brief information as to future procedure to Anatolius and had entrusted fuller instructions to his legates.

In writing to Pulcheria,[73] the Pope paid a tribute to her success in securing the defeat of Eutyches and in obtaining redress for the bishops victimized at Ephesus. As for those who were willing or eager to abandon Eutychian error he insisted that they must subscribe a formal recantation of error as a necessary condition of future restoration. Finally he recurred to the subject of Eusebius of Dorylaeum who, as we have seen, had been living as a refugee in Rome since his flight thither late in A.D. 449.[74]

"Eusebius," he writes, "is staying with us and is a partaker of our communion; we commend to you his church,

[72] *Ep.* 78, JK 458, dated April 13th, A.D. 451.
[73] *Ep.* 79, JK 459, of the same date.
[74] See Chap. X, p. 244.

which we hear is being ravaged by one who has been unjustly invited to take his place." [75]

It seems that shortly before the departure of these replies the eagerly awaited submission of Anatolius [76] was received. The document also included a report of the negotiations which had taken place with the Roman legates. Apparently it had been decided that those who regretted their assent to the decisions reached at Ephesus [77] must for the time being remain content with the communion of their own churches.[78] Acknowledging this communication [79] Leo approved the decision on the express condition that those who desired reconciliation would be ready to pronounce a formal condemnation of the things of which they once approved, and in addition gave his assent to the proposal of the legates that the names of Dioscorus, Juvenal and Eustathius [80] should be omitted from the "diptycha" of the church of Constantinople [81] on the ground that their retention would dishonour the memory of Flavian and might imply that the Church was indifferent to their offences. The letter from Anatolius had been accompanied by a communication from Julian, Leo's agent in Constantinople. In his reply to this [82] Leo mentioned the return of the Roman legation and insisted that those who desired reconciliation should only receive it when they had fulfilled

[75] *Ep.* 79, 3. "Eusebium nobiscum degere, et nostrae communionis esse consortem, cuius commendamus ecclesiam, quam dicitur vastare qui illi iniuste asseritur subrogatus." It is noticeable that no mention is made of the Sardican canons on appeals. See above, Chap. X, pp. 243ff.

[76] This may be inferred from *Ep.* 80. The letter itself has not been preserved. Cf. Grumel, *Regestes,* No. 118, dated November 22nd, A.D. 450.

[77] *Ep.* 80, 2, "communionis nostrae cupidos esse cognovimus." Cf. *Ep.* 79, 2, JK 459.

[78] *Ibid.*, "suarum interim ecclesiarum essent communionis contenti." For this partial excommunication cf. *Conc. Carthag.* (A.D. 401), Can. 11, *Cod. can. eccl. Afric.* 76.

[79] *Ep.* 80, JK 460, dated April 13th, A.D. 451.

[80] Eustathius, bishop of Berytus, had taken a prominent part in the process against Ibas, see above Chap. IX, pp. 211ff. His see had received the rank of a metropolis towards the end of A.D. 449. See Grumel, *Regestes,* Nos. 113–15.

[81] The "diptycha" in the Syro-Byzantine rite were recited at the beginning of the "Missa Fidelium" between the kiss of peace and the Eucharistic Preface. They consisted, as the name suggests, of a double list containing the names of living and dead occupants of the sees of the "greater churches." Cf. Bishop in *J.T.S.*, Vol. XI (1909), pp. 67–73.

[82] *Ep.* 81, JK 461 of the same date.

what they had promised.[83] He also announced the despatch of a fresh legation after Easter (A.D. 451).

Whatever views Anatolius might have held regarding the programme of action thus set forth by the Roman see it is unlikely that he felt particularly flattered to find himself treated in the papal correspondence as a mere assessor to a Roman legation, nor that the new Sovereigns at Constantinople would be willing to do no more than execute Leo's plans for the reconciliation of those who had supported the decisions taken at Ephesus. From the standpoint of these parties the expedient of assembling a fresh council not only seemed to be a means of averting the schism, which must have been an inevitable result of too rigid action on Roman lines, but was an obvious way to extricate themselves from an embarrassing position.

Rumours that the eastern government was set upon carrying out this plan must have reached Leo about this time and caused him to write afresh to Marcian on the subject.[84] After stressing his belief that orthodoxy is of the utmost importance as a political asset,[85] he alluded to the information which he had received, possibly through the legates recently returned to Italy, that the plans for reconciling those who had lapsed at Ephesus were to be reviewed. He added that the new legation to Constantinople, which would presently be despatched, would give full information as to his views. He concluded by saying that there ought to be no question regarding the faith; all that had to be decided was the question as to which of those who desired reconciliation ought to be accepted.[86]

Two months later, in June A.D. 451, the preparations for the promised legation were complete and its members were entrusted with a number of important communications. The legation consisted of Lucentius, a bishop of an unknown see, and Basil, a priest of the Roman church, who had been one of

[83] *Ibid.*, "reddituri hanc his quam desiderant communionem cum promissa compleverint."

[84] *Ep.* 82, JK 462, dated April 23rd, A.D. 451.

[85] Leo probably alludes to an invasion threatened by the Huns, in view of Marcian's refusal to pay the tribute promised by Theodosius II. See Bury, *op. cit.*, Vol. I, pp. 273–90.

[86] *Ibid.*, 2, "non cuiusmodi sit fides tenenda tractandum est, sed quorum precibus et qualiter annuendum."

the original delegates. Taking the letters as a whole the impression which they give is that Leo had as yet no intention of forsaking his original plan of action.[87]

In writing to Marcian [88] the Pope urged the need of taking steps to reconcile those who had lapsed at Ephesus and indicated the part assigned to the legation for carrying this into effect with the co-operation of the bishop of Constantinople. As to the question of the proposed council, while admitting that he himself had formerly requested one, he suggested that:

"The present emergency does not permit the assembly of bishops from all provinces; since those provinces from which they will have to be summoned will not be able to dispense with them from their churches owing to the chaos of warfare. So with God's favour, let your Clemency give orders for the council to be postponed to a more opportune season, when a more stable condition of peace shall have been restored." [89]

At the same time Leo assured Pulcheria [90] of his eagerness to settle all outstanding problems of reconciliation and pointed out that the Eutychian doctrine was not less deplorable than that of Nestorius. Writing of the Incarnation he says:

"Thus by the union of both states of being neither was changed into the other, nor was that which was assumed destroyed in Him who assumed it; on the contrary both the

[87] Caspar, *Geschichte,* Vol. I, pp. 507f. observes "Diese Briefe zeigen mit wie bewundernswert zäher Willenskraft Leo d. Gr. den Augenblick des Triumphs, den Flavians Appellation nach Rom für die päpstliche Doktrin bedeutete, über alle Wechselfälle der Verhandlungen dieser Monate hinweg, Dauer verleihen und die konstantinopolitanischen Rekonziliationen zu einem Anwendungsfalle päpstlicher universalkirchlicher Oberhoheit stempeln wollte." Leo's intention from the beginning, to which he persistently adhered, was that the lapses at Ephesus should be treated as *causae graviores,* and dealt with in accordance with *Conc. Sard.,* Cans. 4, 5 and 7.

[88] *Ep.* 83, JK 463, dated June 9th, A.D. 451.

[89] *Ibid.,* 2. "Sed sacerdotes provinciarum omnium congregari praesentis temporis necessitas nulla ratione permittit: quoniam illae provinciae, de quibus maxime sunt evocandi, inquietatae bello ab ecclesiis suis eos non patiuntur abscedere. Unde opportuniori tempori, propitiante Domino, cum firmior fuerit restituta securitas, iubeat clementia vestra reservari." The passage clearly alludes to the dangers of invasion by the Huns.

[90] *Ep.* 84, JK 464 of the same date.

immutability of the Word and the reality of the flesh and soul remain inseparably in the unity of Person." [91]

The Pope went on to urge that Eutyches ought to be removed from his monastery, which was much too close to the capital, "lest he may give encouragement too frequently to those whom he has won over to his error," and that the Empress should order him to be replaced by a Catholic archimandrite.

In his letter to Anatolius [92] he made special mention of the procedure to be adopted in the case of those who were chiefly responsible for the mischief at Ephesus, in the event of their being willing to repent and seek reconciliation. All such cases were reserved to the judgment of the Roman see, and meanwhile their names were not to be recited in the "diptycha." [93]

A short personal note for Julian [94] was enclosed, in which Leo mentioned his concern at the course which events were taking and added that "some things were thrown into such disorder by that rabble at Ephesus that one is bound to act with great restraint lest the evil discussions which have resulted from it may continue." [95]

Meanwhile the eastern Sovereigns had decided that the project of the council must be no longer postponed and accordingly issued an edict on May 17th, A.D. 451, summoning the bishops to meet at Nicaea in the following August.[96]

[91] *Ibid.*, 2, "cum unitione utriusque essentiae, nec altera sit in alteram versa, nec assumpta in assumente finita; sed et verbi incommutabilitas, et carnis atque animae veritas maneant inseparabiliter in unitate personae."

[92] *Ep.* 85, JK 465 of the same date.

[93] *Ibid.*, 2. "De his autem qui in hac causa gravius peccavere, et ob hoc superiorem sibi locum in eadem infelici synodo vindicarunt . . . si forte resipiscunt . . . horum si satisfactio talis accedit quae non refutanda videatur, maturioribus apostolicae sedis consiliis reservetur." Leo evidently alludes to Dioscorus, Juvenal and possibly to Eustathius as in *Ep.* 80, 3, JK 460.

[94] *Ep.* 86, JK 466 of the same date.

[95] *Ibid.*, "quaedam tamen sunt quae ita Ephesinus ille turbo confudit, ut magno moderamine sit agendum, ne mala dissensionum quae inde sunt orta permaneant."

[96] Mansi, *Concilia*, Vol. VI, 552. Cf. Seeck, *Regesten*, p. 389. It should be noticed that the *Liber pontificalis*, ed. Duchesne, p. 239, n. 1, shows how writers in succeeding centuries rewrote the history of Leo's connexion with the summoning of the council. Contrast with this the statement of the first edition of the *L.P.*, *op. cit.*, p. 90. Nestorius, *Bazaar*, ed. Driver and Hodgson, p. 345 affirms that he too regarded a

In the solemn document in which the imperial will was made known the Emperor stated that, unless prevented by a state of political emergency, he intended being present at the sessions of the council in person. It is perhaps open to question how far the receipt of this news was really welcome to the Roman see. An Italian council, such as Leo had originally requested, was one thing; the present council, summoned to meet in an eastern city, and under the immediate supervision of the eastern government, in which there could be no reasonable doubt that the eastern episcopate would possess an overwhelming majority, was quite another.

Some indication of its attitude to the new situation is provided by a group of Leo's letters which belong to the middle of this fateful year, A.D. 451. One of them is addressed to his old friend Paschasinus [97] Bishop of Lilybaeum, which served as a covering letter to a copy of the "Tome" forwarded for his information, together with a catena of patristic texts bearing on the doctrine of the Incarnation.[98] He mentioned that the "Tome" has been accepted by the whole church of Constantinople, together with all the monasteries, by many bishops, and also, as he had learnt from Anatolius,[99] by Maximus of Antioch and by the bishops of his patriarchate. He concluded by referring to the Paschal question.[100]

About the same time the Pope despatched two letters to the Emperor, in the first [101] of which he acknowledged the

council as unnecessary, though possibly the passage may refer to the Council of Ephesus, A.D. 449. Cf. Batiffol, *Siège Apostolique,* p. 535, n. 2. The whole passage shows the high value which Nestorius attached to Leo's doctrine.

[97] *Ep.* 88, JK 468 ascribed to June 24th, A.D. 451. The date of this letter is uncertain. Not only does it omit to mention the choice of Paschasinus as the leader of the Roman legation, but it appears to presuppose a state of affairs previous to the receipt of a summons to attend the council. The Ballerini, P.L. 54, 930, note q, evade the difficulty by postulating the existence of an earlier letter mentioning the fact of his appointment which has not been preserved.

[98] Cf. the catena appended to *Ep.* 165, JK 542. It is probably the one quoted in the Greek *Acta* of Chalcedon, Mansi, *op. cit.,* Vol. VI, 961ff.

[99] Cf. Grumel, *Regestes,* No. 120. Maximus had succeeded Domnus on the deprivation of the latter by the Council of Ephesus, A.D. 449, but, as the event will show, proved quite unworthy of his office.

[100] See below, Chap. XV, pp. 352ff.

[101] *Ep.* 89, JK 469, dated June 24th, A.D. 451. It is possible, as Jaffé, *Regesta,* Vol. II, p. 735, No. 468A suggests, that a further letter was addressed to Lucentius and Basil, who by now were at Constantinople, informing them that Paschasinus and Boniface had been added to their number.

invitation which he had received to attend the forthcoming council, and gave his assent to the imperial plan, while adding that he would have preferred its postponement to a more convenient season," so that the council might in a true sense be a universal one." He mentioned that he appointed Paschasinus, "who may represent my own presence," and Boniface to be his legates, with whom he associates Julian, and adds that the object of the council would be simply to arrange the terms of reconciliation for those who had lapsed. He concluded with the proposal that Paschasinus should preside at the council as his personal representative.[102] In the second letter,[103] which with three others were entrusted to the legates, the Pope stated that he would no longer oppose the imperial will regarding the new council. At the same time he stipulated that no discussion on the subject of the faith ought to be allowed; all that was necessary was to insist on the maintenance of the Nicene canons.[104]

Writing to Anatolius[105] he pointed out that although the interval before the day appointed for the assembly of the council was too short to permit of all the bishops being present who ought to be there, yet he had assented to the imperial plan and had despatched his legates. He anticipated that there would be no discussion on matters of faith, since as he had learnt that all the bishops of the eastern churches had subscribed a statement of the Catholic faith and had formally condemned Eutyches and Nestorius.[106]

In addition to these letters Leo wrote to Julian[107] expressing

[102] *Ibid.*, "praedictum fratrem (sc. Paschasinum) . . . vice mea synodo convenit praesidere."

[103] *Ep.* 90, JK 470, dated June 26th, A.D. 451.

[104] *Ibid.*, 2, "illudque potius iubeatis ut antiquae Nicaenae synodi constituta, remota haereticorum interpretatione, permaneant."

[105] *Ep.* 91, JK 471, dated June 26th, A.D. 451. A short letter *Ep.* 87, JK 467 preceded this, but it concerned merely the case of two Constantinopolitan priests who had come to Rome. Their purpose in so coming is alleged to have been to repudiate both Nestorianism and Eutychianism. Possibly the truth was that they had had some misunderstanding with Anatolius. Leo wrote to Anatolius saying that the priests had been admitted to Roman communion, on the strength of their having accepted the doctrine which we teach "by inspiration of the Holy Ghost," i.e. the "Tome."

[106] *Ibid.*, "quod in suscipienda catholica fide et damnatione Eutychis atque Nestorii omnes orientales subscripserint sacerdotes."

[107] *Ep.* 92, JK 472 of the same date. "Dum curam tuam illis con-

his confidence that with Julian's aid the Roman legates would be safeguarded from taking any false step.

But of all the letters included in this post the most weighty was the one directed to the council.[108] In this letter Leo began by attributing the invitation which he had received from the eastern Sovereigns as a signal act of consideration shown for "the privileges and office of blessed Peter."[109] At the same time he excused his absence saying:

"Neither the present emergency nor any precedent could permit my presence (with you). So let your brotherhood reflect that I am presiding at your synod in the person of my brethren . . . who have been sent by the Apostolic see . . . (through whom) I cease not to preach the Catholic faith."[110]

The Pope went on to prohibit any discussion on the subject of doctrine, which he regarded as already determined by the "Tome," in which "there has been proclaimed what is the orthodox and true confession concerning the mystery of the Incarnation."[111] Hence he wrote that the first and primary duty of the forthcoming council was to arrange for the restoration of those who have been unjustly condemned, and for the reconciliation of the lapsed.[112] Finally he pointed out that, with a view to allaying any uneasiness on the part of the upholders of Alexandrine Christology that the anticipated condemnation of Eutyches implied a slur on the memory of Cyril,

silium sociaveris in nulla parte fallantur." Leo evidently remembered clearly the difficulties which had beset his legates at Ephesus. Julian doubtless was bilingual and well acquainted with the recent course of events. Paschasinus, on the other hand, appears to have been ignorant of Greek. For the special instructions given to the legates see Mansi, *Concilia,* Vol. VI, 580; VII, 444. They included a stipulation that Dioscorus was to be excluded from a seat in the council and a requirement that the canons of Nicaea were to be upheld.

[108] *Ep.* 93, JK 473. The letter was read at the suggestion of the legate Boniface at the session of the council held on October 31st.

[109] *Ibid.,* 1, "beatissimi Petri apostoli iure atque honore servato."

[110] *Ibid.,* "quod (sc. praesentiam meam) quidem nec necessitas temporis, nec ulla poterat consuetudo permittere. Tamen in his fratribus . . . qui ab apostolica sede directi sunt, me synodo vestra fraternitas aestimet praesidere . . . et iamdudum in fidei catholicae praedicatione non desum." I.e. through the "Tome."

[111] *Ibid.,* 2, "per litteras quas ad beatae memoriae Flavianum episcopum misimus fuerit declaratum quae sit de sacramento incarnationis Domini nostri Jesu Christi pia et sincera confessio."

[112] *Ibid.,* 3, "cum si, ut cupimus, errorem omnes relinquunt nemini quidem perire suus honor debeat." It appears that Leo still hoped that the former leaders at Ephesus would give way.

the canons of the first council of Ephesus on the subject of doctrine should be explicitly confirmed.[113]

It is plain that from the Roman point of view the projected council had no concern with questions of doctrine. Instead it had only to enforce that view of the Incarnation which had been already put forth by Leo in the "Tome," and on this basis to restore those who had been unjustly deposed at Ephesus. This way of regarding the duties of the council received renewed emphasis in the last letter addressed by Leo to Marcian before its actual opening.[114] Here he wrote as before expressing his regret that the nearness of the date fixed for its assembly gave little opportunity for the gathering together of a sufficiently representative body of bishops [115] and insisted that the only possible solution of the present discord was that "all should assent to the faith proclaimed by the teaching of the gospels and of the Apostles, which we have received by tradition from the Fathers and still hold fast." [116] He hopes that "none may be found a stranger to the mystery of our common faith, and that when the blasphemy of heresy has been condemned the Catholic Church may suffer no damage from the loss of anyone." [117]

By the same post Leo despatched a personal letter to Pulcheria.[118] Here he wrote that he had entrusted his legates with a letter to the council [119] so that its members might know what line to follow in this case.[120] It is superfluous, he says,

[113] *Ibid.* "Prioris autem Ephesinae synodi, cui sanctae memoriae Cyrillus episcopus tunc praesedit, contra Nestorium specialiter statuta permaneant."

[114] *Ep.* 94, JK 474, dated July 20th, A.D. 451.

[115] Cf. p. 280, n. 89.

[116] *Ibid.*, "in eam fidem quam evangelicis et apostolicis praedicationibus declaratam per sanctos patres nostros accepimus et tenemus." The implications of his phrase "nulla penitus disputatione cuiusquam retractationis admissa" should be noticed. Yet Leo was by no means the first occupant of the Roman see to urge that definitions by a Roman bishop are above discussion. It was a claim which had already been made by Zosimus, *Epp.* 9, 2 (4) and 12, 1, JK 339, 342 and by Boniface I, *Ep.* 15, 4, JK 365.

[117] *Ibid.*, "sed damnata impietate haereseos nullum de perditione cuiusquam catholica Ecclesia sentiat detrimentum." Evidently the writer still entertains the hope that even the leaders of the opposition will submit.

[118] *Ep.* 95, JK 475 of the same date.

[119] i.e. *Ep.* 93, JK 473.

[120] *Ibid.*, 1, "quibus fraternitas advocata cognosceret quam formam servare in hac diiudicatione deberet."

to repeat the tale of the misdeeds committed at Ephesus which was "no court of justice but a den of robbers."[121] Again he repeated his hope that none might be beyond the possibility of restoration, "if they purge their offences with fitting satisfaction," and desired that every consideration may be shown to the penitent.

Preparations for holding an imperial council on a scale grander and more impressive than had ever been contemplated previously were now nearly complete. But there was still no sign that Dioscorus and his supporters had any intention of yielding either to impressiveness or imperial persuasion. On the contrary he gave the clearest possible indication of his attitude shortly after his departure from Alexandria. On his reaching the Asiatic coast, accompanied by a train of Egyptian suffragans, he took the bold and desperate step of launching a sentence of excommunication against Leo as the foremost member of the "dyophysite" party.[122] It did little to commend his cause and perhaps only served to betray his weakness. Yet it was an ill omen for the future and foreshadowed the coming disruption of imperial church unity.

Additional Note

EASTERN IMPERIAL REFERENCES TO THE ROMAN SEE

An interesting light on the attitude prevailing generally in the East towards the Roman see is supported by the occasional references to it which are to be found in secular documents and legislation of eastern origin. Perhaps the most important reference of this kind which occurs in legislation is to be found in the edict of Theodosius, dated February 27th, A.D. 380. Here it is prescribed:

"It is our will that all people, which the government of our

[121] *Ep.* 95, 2, "quidquid in illo Ephesino non iudicio sed latrocinio potuit perpetrari." The nickname was adopted later by the Byzantine chronicler, Theophanes, *Chronog.*, 5941, *P.G.* 108, 261, "σύνοδος λῃστρική." The attachment of this sobriquet to the recent council destroyed for ever the possibility of its recognition among the councils of oecumenical rank.

[122] Mansi, *op. cit.*, VI, 1009. The excommunication bore only ten signatures besides his own. See also *Inter Leon. Epp.*, No. 98, 2. *P.L.* 54, 954B.

mercifulness rules, shall abide in that religion, which the religion handed down from him even to this day proclaims to have been delivered by the Apostle Peter to the Romans, and which the pontiff Damasus and Peter, Bishop of Alexandria, a man of apostolic sanctity, evidently follow . . ."[123]

In addition to this there are three references in the replies sent by Theodosius II to the Western sovereigns. In the letter addressed to Valentinian III he mentions "the petition presented by the most reverend patriarch, Leo."[124] Writing to Galla Placidia he uses the same phrase.[125] In his reply to Licinia Eudoxia he calls him, "The most reverend archbishop."[126] Further, in the letter of Marcian,[127] written December 18th, A.D. 451, addressed to Leo, the Emperor is content to call him "holy and right reverend father."

These expressions provide a striking contrast to those used in western imperial correspondence and legislation,[128] and suggest that the East still remained a long way behind the West in accepting the Roman see's own doctrine of its relation to the Church as a whole.

[123] *Cod. Theod.* XVI, i, 2; Mirbt, *Quellen,* No. 134; on which see Kidd, *History,* Vol. II, p. 280; Turmel, *Papauté,* pp. 374ff.

[124] *Inter Leon. Epp.,* No. 62, "petitionem oblatam a Leone reverendissimo patriarcha." The use of this phrase is believed by Caspar, *Geschichte,* Vol. I, p. 499, n. 5 to be deliberate and to be intended to assign to the papacy a status, equal to but not greater than that of the "greater Churches" of the East.

[125] *Inter Leon. Epp.,* No. 63, "reverendissimus patriarcha Leo."

[126] *Inter Leon. Epp.,* No. 64, "reverendissimo archiepiscopo Leoni."

[127] *Inter Leon. Epp.,* No. 100.

[128] e.g. *Inter Leon. Epp.,* No. 55, "beatissimus Romanae civitatis episcopus, cui principatum sacerdotii super omnes antiquitas contulit."

CHAPTER XII

LEO AND THE CHURCHES OF THE EAST.

THE COUNCIL OF CHALCEDON

THE Emperor Marcian no less than Leo himself was probably desirous of bringing about the reconciliation of Dioscorus and his supporters, though doubtless with a different motive. At a time when the Huns were forcing their way through the weakened defences of the Empire, much might depend from the economic standpoint on the condition of affairs in Egypt. Hence on the eve of the assembly of the council he invited the bishops of the " greater churches " in the East to an informal conference, but as was to be expected it led to no tangible result.[1]

Apart from this setback everything went smoothly at first according to the government's plan. The latter had evidently profited by the experience of Ephesus, and by means of careful preparation had taken the utmost pains to prevent the control of the council's procedure from passing wholly into the hands of one or other of the contending ecclesiastical parties; so that it soon became evident that the ultimate issue had been carefully prescribed.

The imperial summons had named Nicaea as the place of meeting. Yet it was at Chalcedon that the bishops actually assembled. This was due to the issue of further imperial letters a short time before the appointed date, transferring the assembly thither on the reasonable ground that the uncertainty of the political situation rendered it necessary for the Emperor to be within easy reach of the capital.[2]

[1] The sole authority for this conference is Theopistus, *Historia Dioscori,* ed. Nau, *Journal asiatique,* Ser. X, 1 (1903). If it actually took place, its failure must have been a foregone conclusion. From Dioscorus' point of view the doctrinal question had been determined by an imperial council, and nothing that the Pope or anyone else might say could make any difference.

[2] Mansi, *Concilia,* Vol. VI, 557, 560. The eastern government probably avoided the choice of Constantinople in order to prevent the supporters of Eutyches from exercising undue influence on the proceedings of the council. From the point of view of accessibility Chalcedon possessed an almost equal advantage.

When the bishops met for the first time in the church of St. Euphemia [3] on October 8th, A.D. 451 they found themselves confronted with an imposing array of no less than eighteen officers of state, who constituted the official imperial commission. These occupied places facing down the church, while the bishops were ranged on either side facing "north" and "south." [4] On the left of the commission were the five representatives of the Roman see,[5] and beside them the bishops of Constantinople, Antioch, Caesarea in Cappadocia and Ephesus with others from Pontus, Asia and Thrace. On the right, Dioscorus, Juvenal, the bishop of Heraclea representing Anastasius of Thessalonica, and bishops from Egypt, Illyricum and Palestine. The total number of bishops taking part was certainly more than five hundred, a higher total therefore than that of any previous council and not much short of the aggregate present at the Vatican council of 1870.[6]

At the first session [7] the opening speech was made by Paschasinus, the principal member of the Roman legation. He began by demanding the immediate exclusion of Dioscorus from membership of the council, alleging that he had received instructions from Leo to that effect,[8] and threatening that if this were not done the whole Roman legation would withdraw forthwith from the proceedings. Bearing in mind the frequency with which Leo himself had expressed the hope that the leaders of the "monophysite" opposition might be won over,[9] it is highly probable that in so doing Paschasinus was

[3] The Church of St. Euphemia is described in Evagrius, *H.E.*, 2, 3. Cf. Leclercq, *Dict. Arch. Chrét.*, Art. *Chalcédoine,* pp. 91, 95.

[4] Further details of the personnel are given in Duchesne, *Histoire,* Vol. III, p. 430; Kidd, *History,* Vol. III, p. 315.

[5] Including Julian of Cios. Paschasinus was, of course, the chief spokesman.

[6] The council's own letter, *Inter Leon. Epp.,* No. 98, 1 (Greek text), *P.L.* 54, 952C gives "five hundred and twenty"; Leo himself mentions "about six hundred," *Ep.* 102, 2, JK 479. The *Liber Pontificalis,* ed. Duchesne, Vol. I, p. 239, n. 2 gives the astounding total of twelve hundred. Butler, *Vatican Council,* Vol. I, p. 165 mentions "679 in all" as present at the council of 1870.

[7] The *Acta* of the Council of Chalcedon are to be found in Mansi, *Concilia,* Vol. VI, 563–1102, Vol. VII, 1–453, and in Schwartz, *Acta Conc. Oecumen.,* Tom. II, Berlin 1932.

[8] We only know the details of these "instructions" through the occasional references made to them by the legates, e.g. Mansi, *Concilia,* Vol. VI, 579, "(papae) praecepta (προστάξεις) habemus prae manibus."

[9] e.g. *Ep.* 71, JK 454.

acting purely on his own initiative, but in any case it was a regrettable incident, which showed only too clearly that the spirit of prejudice, which had marred the justice of the proceedings at Ephesus, was still active and was already threatening to impair the success of the present council as a means of restoring peace in the Church.

At this point the imperial commissioners intervened, and after pointing out that Dioscorus could be excluded only by a formal resolution of the whole council to that effect, urged that his opponents should state the reasons for their demand. Whereupon Lucentius stated that without any authorization from the Apostolic see Dioscorus had usurped the place of a judge at Ephesus and had had the presumption to conduct a synod without the Pope's permission.[10] Apart from the fact that from the standpoint of imperial church administration the legality of the proceedings at Ephesus was not open to question, the commissioners dismissed the Roman plea on the ground that the same party could not play the part of judge and plaintiff, as the Roman legates wished to do, at the same time. The plea was therefore ruled out of order.

But a fresh plaintiff was not slow in coming forward. With characteristic enthusiasm the notorious litigant, Eusebius of Dorylaeum,[11] stood up and insisted that his appeal against the condemnation of himself, pronounced at the instigation of Dioscorus, should be read. After some discussion this led to the recital of the *Acta* of the synod of Constantinople, A.D. 448, which was accompanied by a good deal of disorder and by expressions of mutual recrimination. Unperturbed by interruptions the reader continued until he reached the point when the minutes referred to the exclusion of Theodoret from the council by command of Theodosius. On this the Roman legates demanded that he should forthwith be admitted to the assembly, and this time in spite of vigorous protests succeeded with the support of the commissioners in getting their way. The commissioners pointed out that his restoration to episcopal

[10] Mansi, *Concilia,* Vol. VI, 581, *Conc. Chalc.,* Actio 1, "*σύνοδον ἐτόλμησε ποιῆσαι ἐπιτροπῆς δίχα τοῦ ἀποστολικοῦ Θρόνὸυ.*" The legates evidently took the view that the absence of any former commission, such as Celestine I, *Ep.* 11, 4, JK 372, had issued to Cyril, had rendered void the whole of the proceedings of the recent council. Cf. *Acta Ephesi,* 1, 2, p. 5, *Coll. Ver.* 1 (ed. Schwartz).

[11] See Duchesne, *Histoire,* Vol. III, p. 431, n. 1, for a significant comment.

status had been approved by Marcian and that in any case he had a right to be admitted as a plaintiff. So, greeted by cheers from his supporters and abuse from his opponents, the bishop of Cyrrhus took his place beside Eusebius. The recital of the *Acta* of the recent council of Ephesus followed. When mention was made of Dioscorus' evasion of the legates' demand that Leo's letters should be read, of the restoration of Eutyches, and of the sentence of deposition against Flavian and Eusebius, it was noticed that a number of those present betrayed some uneasiness, which found expression in some earnest protestations that their agreement to these sentences had been extorted only under pressure.

After this interruption the recital of the *Acta* proceeded, until the reader came to the mention of Cyril's confession of faith. The minutes recorded Eutyches' affirmation that his belief accorded with the teaching of Cyril, but as this was one of the points in debate, the commissioners invited the assembly to express its opinion. At this Paschasinus rose in defence of Flavian, and received the support of a considerable majority of the bishops. Everyone now realized that the proceedings had taken a definite turn in favour of the "dyophysites" and, rather than risk being found on the losing side, as the session was drawing to a close in the gathering twilight, Juvenal and the Palestinians, the majority of the Illyrians and even four Egyptian representatives crossed the floor of the church and seated themselves on the same side as the Roman legates. By the light of candles it was resolved that steps should be taken to declare Dioscorus, with a number of his chief supporters, deposed from his office, and as the bishops were on the point of dispersing the commissioners suggested that individual bishops should draw up statements of belief in accordance with the doctrinal decrees of Nicaea and Constantinople [12] and the statements of the fathers, including Cyril and Leo.

When the second session of the council opened on October 10th [13] the question of doctrine was revived, and in their intro-

[12] A.D. 381. This is the Nicaeno-Constantinopolitan Creed.

[13] In the text of the *Acta* printed by Mansi, *Concilia*, Vol. VI, 937, the order of Sessions 2 and 3 is inverted. The order given above is mentioned by Facundus, *Defensio*, 5, 3, *P.L.* 67, 638ff. as the one given in certain early MSS. The inversion probably arose on account of the

ductory speech the commissioners went so far as to say that doctrinal definition was the primary purpose for which the council had been summoned. As Leo had insisted from the first that this was the very thing which must not be discussed,[14] the Roman legates would undoubtedly have raised a protest at such a statement, if the rest of the assembly had not saved them the trouble. But the commissioners evidently had had their instructions and were determined to find a way of carrying them out. Again and again they tried to form a committee of leading bishops to consider the question; each time the assembly indignantly repudiated the proposal. "The Canon states," they shouted, "that what is already defined shall suffice: it permits no fresh definition." [15]

This led Florentius, bishop of Sardis, who at the previous council had acted as interpreter to the Roman legation, to propose that the question should be postponed on the ground that the bishops had already undertaken to uphold the dogmatic statements of Nicaea and Ephesus (A.D. 431), and to assent to the doctrinal letters of Cyril, Celestine I and Leo. The assembly then requested the recital of these documents, whereat the creeds of Nicaea and Constantinople,[16] the letters of Cyril to Nestorius [17] and to John of Antioch,[18] and finally the "Tome" of Leo were read in turn. Apart from a few dissentients [19] the majority of those present loudly approved these statements of doctrine.

fact that Session III was held in the absence of the imperial commissioners and hence was not recorded in the official minutes of the proceedings. When it was inserted in the *Acta* it was introduced by some copyist after Session I in error.

[14] Mansi, *op. cit.*, Vol. VI, 952. See above, p. 284.

[15] Mansi, *op. cit.*, Vol. VI, 953. The allusion is to *Conc. Ephes.* Mansi, *op. cit.*, Vol. IV, 1362, with the infringement of which Flavian had been charged in A.D. 449, see above, Chap. X, p. 241.

[16] This creed is here ascribed to the council of A.D. 381 for the first time. Mansi, *op. cit.*, Vol. VI, 957.

[17] *Ep.* 4, *P.G.* 77, 44.

[18] *Ep.* 39. *P.G.* 77, 173. The commissioners appear to have thought this letter had been accepted at Ephesus (A.D. 449) but probably confused it with Cyril's "third" letter to Nestorius, *Ep.* 17, *P.G.* 77, 105. Cf. Duchesne, *Histoire,* Vol. III, p. 435.

[19] Mansi, *op. cit.*, Vol. VI, 959. A few asked for explanations of certain passages in the "Tome," *ibid.* 971f. Others like Atticus, bishop of Nicopolis in Illyricum, inquired why no mention was made of Cyril's "third" letter together with the XII *capitula.* Their interjections were prudently ignored, *ibid.* 973, but cf. *ibid.*, Vol. VII, 110.

"That is the faith of the Fathers," they said, "the faith of the Apostles. We all believe thus, the orthodox believe so! Anathema to him who believes otherwise! Peter has thus spoken through Leo! The Apostles taught so! Piously and truly has Leo taught thus! Cyril taught thus! Eternal memory to Cyril! Leo and Cyril taught the same thing! Anathema to him who teaches otherwise! Why was that letter not read at Ephesus? It is the letter which Dioscorus concealed!"[20]

We now pass on to the third session held on October 13th, at which the fate of Dioscorus and his supporters was sealed. As the business in hand was largely an ecclesiastical matter the commissioners left the conduct of the proceedings in the hands of the bishops.

Aetius, archdeacon of Constantinople, who acted as the head of the conciliar secretariate, opened the proceedings by bringing forward a further charge against Dioscorus, for which Eusebius was personally responsible.[21] At this Paschasinus uttered an emphatic protest that such a charge was out of order, on the ground that it had not previously been submitted to the Roman legation, to whom, according to Paschasinus, Leo had entrusted the conduct of the assembly.[22] Whether or not the council were prepared to accept his view, Eusebius' charge was passed over, and without further delay Dioscorus, who had been absent from the previous session, was thrice summoned to appear. Each summons was met with a blank refusal on the ground that the proceedings, conducted in the absence of the commissioners, were invalid.[23]

[20] Mansi, *op. cit.*, Vol. VI, 972, "*αὕτη ἡ πίστις τῶν ἀποστόλων· πάντες οὕτω πιστεύομεν· οἱ ὀρθόδοξοι οὕτω πιστεύουσιν. ἀνάθεμα τῷ μὴ οὕτω πιστεύοντι. Πέτρος διὰ Λέοντος οὕτω ἐξεφώνησεν· οἱ ἀπόστολοι οὕτως ἐδίδαξαν· εὐσεβῶς καὶ ἀληθινῶς Λέων ἐδίδαξε· Κύριλλος οὕτως ἐδίδαξε· Κυρίλλου αἰωνία ἡ μνήμη. Λέων καὶ Κύριλλος ὁμοίως ἐδίδαξαν. ἀνάθεμα τῷ μὴ οὕτω πιστεύοντι. αὕτη ἡ ἀληθινὴ πίστις. οἱ ὀρθόδοξοι οὕτω φρονοῦμεν. αὕτη ἡ πίστις τῶν πατέρων. ταῦτα ἐν Ἐφέσῳ διὰ τί οὐκ ἀνεγνώθη; ταῦτα Διόσκορος ἔκρυφεν.*"

[21] Mansi, *op. cit.*, Vol. VI, 984. "*παρὰ τοῦ θεοφιλεστάτου Εὐσεβίου ἐπισκόπου τῆς Δορυλαΐτῶν κατὰ τοῦ θεοφιλεστάτου ἐπισκόπου τῆς Ἀλεξανδρείας Διοσκόρου φανερὰ παρηκολούθησε πρᾶξις ὑπομνημάτων.*"

[22] Mansi, *op. cit.*, Vol. VI, 985. "*τὰ τῆς ἁγίας συνόδου ἐπέτρεψε.*" The Latin version is more explicit, "huic sancto concilio pro se praesidere praecepit," which certainly agrees with Leo, Ep. 93, 1, JK 473, "me synodo vestra fraternitas aestimet praesidere."

[23] Gibbon, *Decline,* Vol. V, p. 133 (1929), has no real ground for alleging that the real reason for Dioscorus' absence was the fact that he was a prisoner.

The council therefore decided to proceed against him in his absence. His condemnation was of course a foregone conclusion, and after some discussion the formal proposal of his deposition was brought forward by Paschasinus in the name of the Roman legation. In doing so he alleged the following grounds; that Dioscorus had contravened Canon Law; [24] that in spite of the sentence pronounced by Flavian against Eutyches he had admitted the latter to communion before the previous council; [25] that he had refused to permit Leo's letters to be read and thereby had inflicted serious injury on the Church; [26] that in addition to a number of other grave offences he had had the presumption to excommunicate Leo himself; [27] and finally that he had contumaciously refused to obey the summons of the present council.

"Leo, therefore," so ran the proposed sentence, ". . . through us and the present holy council, together with St. Peter, . . . who is the Rock of the Church, and the foundation of orthodoxy, deprives him of his episcopal dignity." [28]

Each bishop was then invited to sign his approval of these words. The first to do so was Anatolius himself followed by Maximus of Antioch. But it is significant of the lack of unanimity that not more than one hundred and eighty-five followed suit.[29]

This done, the verdict was formally notified to the Emperor

[24] By this Paschasinus probably meant the limitations of Alexandrine jurisdiction prescribed by *Conc. Nic,* Canon 6: though others may have understood him to mean *Conc. Const.* I, Canon 2, with which the Roman legates were to become well acquainted after their arrival at Chalcedon.

[25] See above, Chap. X, p. 237.

[26] See above, p. 239. It is probable that Dioscorus was guilty, not so much of actual refusal, as of giving way to pressure, brought to bear on him by the supporters of Eutyches.

[27] Among these other offences was that of having usurped the presidency of the council. But strictly speaking in virtue of the imperial commission Dioscorus had had a perfect right to preside.

[28] Mansi, *op. cit.,* Vol. VI, 1048. "*Λέων, δι' ἡμῶν καὶ τῆς παρούσης ἁγιωτάτης συνόδου μετὰ τοῦ . . . Πέτρου . . . ὅς ἐστι πέτρα καὶ κρηπὶς τῆς καθολικῆς ἐκκλησίας καὶ τῆς ὀρθοδόξου πίστεως ὁ θεμέλιος, ἐγύμνωσεν αὐτὸν τοῦ ἐπισκόπου . . . ἀξίας.*"

[29] Caspar, *Geschichte,* Vol. I, p. 515 comments thus on the verdict, "Es stützte das Urteil auf Verstösse Dioscors wider die Kirchenverfassung, nicht auf Abweichungen von der rechten Lehre." Cf. Gibbon, *Decline,* Vol. V, p. 133 (1929), "The purity of his faith was declared in the presence and with the tacit approbation of the fathers."

and to Dioscorus himself and communicated to the clergy and laity of Alexandria, Constantinople and Chalcedon. Without delay an edict was published banishing the offender to Gangra in Paphlagonia.[30]

When the fourth session opened on October 17th the imperial commissioners resumed their places. Following up its action in the previous session the assembly displayed some eagerness to discuss the treatment of Juvenal and of some other supporters of Dioscorus,[31] but its demands were passed over by the commissioners, who urged once more that the question of doctrine must be settled first. Anatolius then proposed that the council should agree simply to confirm the doctrinal decrees of Nicaea and Ephesus together with the dogmatic letters of Cyril and Leo. This proposal was on the point of being generally accepted when a group of Egyptian bishops brought forward a new statement of belief which significantly omitted any condemnation of the teaching of Eutyches, and passed over the "Tome" of Leo in silence.[32] Other expressions of opinion followed which served to show the absence of any real unanimity among the members of the council, but their general effect was further to postpone decision. It is even possible that the licence permitted to free discussion by the commissioners was deliberate, and had as its object the demonstration of the need of an altogether new doctrinal formula, the production of which was clearly part of the government's predetermined policy. In fact such a policy seemed now to provide the only hope of maintaining the external unity of the imperial Church.

Among the business dealt with at this session there was one matter which serves to illustrate the predominantly "eastern" character of the assembly. It concerned the status of the see of Berytus, which shortly after the late council of Ephesus had been raised by order of Theodosius II to the rank of a metropolis.[33] This order had been issued in consequence

[30] As at Ephesus in A.D. 431 and later in A.D. 449 a scapegoat was found, whose banishment served to purge the offences of others whose guilt was probably not less than that of the actual victim.

[31] Including Thalassius of Caesarea, Eusebius of Ancyra, Basil of Seleucia and Eustathius of Berytus, all of whom had favoured the deposition of Flavian.

[32] Mansi, *op. cit.*, Vol. VII, 49.

[33] Cf. Mansi, *op. cit.*, Vol. VII, 88, and Chap. XI, p. 278, n. 80.

of a resolution in favour of the change having been passed by Anatolius and his home-synod.[34] Nevertheless Photius, bishop of Tyre, whose suffragan Eustathius of Berytus had formerly been, had only accepted the change perforce, and now seized the opportunity presented by the new council for seeking the restoration of the original extent of his jurisdiction. In this he was successful, largely no doubt because the present government was unwilling to press the matter from a strictly legal standpoint, and as a result Eustathius reverted to the status of an ordinary diocesan bishop.[35]

At the beginning of the fifth session held on October 22nd a formula of belief was presented. It had been drawn up by a special committee appointed for the purpose in the course of the previous session under the presidency of Anatolius.[36] Although the text of this formula has not been preserved as a whole, it is clear that it included a definition of the Incarnate Lord as " *of* two natures," which was sufficient in itself to give rise to objections on the part of " dyophysite " members.[37] Some of them urged that such teaching was identical with the doctrine of Dioscorus. On this Anatolius rejoined with some truth that the ground for Dioscorus' condemnation was not doctrinal but disciplinary.[38] Immediately the Roman legates rose and uttered an emphatic protest against the proposed formula and threatened that, if it were adopted, they would demand permission to return to Rome, and would procure the transference of the council to Italy. This threat appears seriously to have alarmed the commissioners, who hastily put forward the suggestion that a new committee should be nominated, with the object of composing a fresh formula,

[34] The whole affair reflects the important part which the *σύνοδος ἐνδημοῦσα* was beginning to play in the ecclesiastical politics of the East. On this occasion its origin and character were discussed at some length. Cf. Batiffol, *Siège Apostolique,* p. 548.

[35] Probably the rôle of Eustathius at the recent council had some influence on the present decision.

[36] It is clear from the *Acta,* Mansi, *op. cit.,* Vol. VII, pp. 97f., that at this session Anatolius shared with two of the commissioners the presidency of the whole council.

[37] " *ἐκ δύο φύσεων*." It will be remembered that this very phrase was actually used by Flavian in his report of the proceedings of the Constantinopolitan synod, A.D. 448. Its introduction here was probably meant as a concession to the Alexandrine point of view.

[38] See above, p. 294. Mansi, Vol. VII, 104. " *διὰ τὴν πίστιν οὐ καθηρέθη Διόσκορος*."

and that it should include representatives of the Roman legation. It was now the turn of the "monophysite" party to raise objections. They professed themselves wholly satisfied with the original formula, and some went so far as to assert that it was in accordance with the "Tome." However the commissioners saw that if it were accepted it would mean the loss of the support of the Roman see. In their dilemma they referred the question to the Emperor for his decision. They received the laconic answer, "Either a new committee or an Italian council." [39] To this some of the adherents of the original statement of belief rejoined, "Those who reject the formula are Nestorians; let them clear off to Rome," but by an adroit move the commissioners won them over. "Are you for Leo or Dioscorus?" they asked. "For Leo," came the reply.[40] It was therefore agreed to appoint a new committee.[41] Later, in the course of the same day, a new formula was presented and provisionally approved. In this way the famous "Definition of Chalcedon" [42] made its appearance and came to rank among the oecumenical documents of the Christian faith.

The "Definition" opens with a brief explanation of its purpose, and goes on to insist on conformity with the doctrinal decrees of Ephesus (A.D. 431).[43] Next it refers to the pre-eminence of the creed set forth at Nicaea and explicitly confirms the formula issued by the one hundred and fifty fathers in Constantinople.[44] The text of these two creeds follows, the former in an expanded form.[45] Next it endorses

[39] *Ibid.*, 105.
[40] *Ibid.*
[41] The new committee, besides Anatolius and the Roman legates, included three representatives each from the "Diocese" of the Orient, i.e. the jurisdiction of the see of Antioch, and from the provinces of Asia, Pontus, Thrace and the Prefecture of eastern Illyricum. The fact that Thalassius of Caesarea, Eusebius of Ancyra and Atticus of Nicopolis were nominated, gave some guarantee that the "monophysite" point of view would be represented, since each of these had supported Dioscorus in the previous council.
[42] Mansi, *op. cit.*, Vol. VII, 108ff.
[43] Mansi, *op. cit.*, Vol. IV, 1362.
[44] Mansi, *op. cit.*, Vol. VII, 112. Denzinger, *Enchiridion*, No. 86. This creed had been mentioned at the first session and recited at the second. Schwartz, *Zeits. f. neutest. Wiss.*, Vol. XXV (1926) upholds its ascription to the Council of Constantinople, A.D. 381.
[45] Mansi, *op. cit.*, *ibid.*, 109.

Cyril's letters, the second to Nestorius,[46] and the letter addressed to John of Antioch,[47] and in addition confirms the authority of the " Tome " of Leo on the explicit ground that it agrees with the confession of the great Peter.[48] In defining the doctrine of the Incarnation it incorporates to a remarkable extent Leo's own teaching, as may be seen from the following characteristic passage:

" With one mind we all teach that our Lord Jesus Christ is . . . one and the same Christ, Son, Lord, Only-begotten; acknowledged in two natures, inconfusedly, unchangeably, indivisibly, inseparably; since the peculiarity of the Natures is in no way taken away on account of the union, on the contrary the properties of each Nature are preserved and concur in One Person and in One Hypostasis." [49]

Judged from the Roman standpoint the general adoption of the "Definition" undoubtedly represented a triumph in that the council had endorsed a formula which was demonstrably dependent on Leonine Christology. It meant in fact that in spite of its limitations that Christology henceforward would be the starting point of any further treatment of the problems involved in the doctrine of the Incarnation. Yet while this is recognized there is an important qualification which must be kept in mind. The authority which belongs to the " Tome " belongs to it in virtue of the council's approbation and not in virtue simply of its Roman or papal origin.

To resume the story of the council. With the acceptance of the " Definition " its task as regards the determination of

[46] *Ep.* 4. *P.G.* 77, 44–9.

[47] *Ep.* 39. *P.G.* 77, 173–81.

[48] Mansi, *op. cit.*, Vol. VII, 113. " *ἅτε δὴ τῇ τοῦ μεγάλου Πέτρου ὁμολογίᾳ συμβαίνουσαν.*"

[49] Mansi, *op. cit.*, Vol. VII, 115. " *ἑπόμενοι τοίνυν τοῖς ἁγίοις πατράσι, ἕνα καὶ τὸν αὐτὸν ὁμολογεῖν υἱὸν τὸν κύριον ἡμῶν* I. X. *συμφώνως ἅπαντες ἐκδιδάσκομεν . . . ἕνα καὶ τὸν αὐτὸν χριστὸν, υἱὸν, κύριον, μονογενῆ ἐκ δύο φύσεων ἀσυγχύτως, ἀτρέπτως, ἀδιαιρέτως, ἀχωρίστως γνωριζόμενον. οὐδαμοῦ τῆς τῶν φύσεων διαφορᾶς ἀνῃρημένης διὰ τὴν ἕνωσιν, σωζομένης δὲ μᾶλλον τῆς ἰδιότητος ἑκατέρας φύσεως καὶ εἰς ἕν πρόσωπον καὶ μίαν ὑπόστασιν συντρεχούσης.*" For " *ἐκ δύο φύσεων* " the Latin version reads " in duabus naturis," and it is generally acknowledged that the latter represents the correct reading. Otherwise the Roman legates must have raised the same objection which they had made to the earlier draft of the " Definition." Caspar, *Geschichte,* Vol. I, p. 518, n. 1, suggests that the " monophysitic " phrase was introduced by the second Council of Constantinople, A.D. 553. Cf. Hefele-Leclercq, *Conciles,* Vol. II, p. 723, n. 1.

doctrine was now finished. It only remained for the Sovereigns to give their formal approval.[50] No pains were spared to endue this act with fitting solemnity, and at the sixth session, which opened on October 25th, the Emperor and Empress entered the assembly in full state.[51] In the presence of the assembled bishops Marcian delivered an allocution in Latin, which was immediately afterwards interpreted in Greek. His words were received with great enthusiasm and after the "Definition" had been recited afresh over six hundred members of the council appended their signatures. The imperial confirmation of the "Definition" was immediately published by means of a proclamation.[52]

Passing over the subject matter of the seventh session, held on October 26th, to which we shall revert in the succeeding chapter, we come to the eighth, held later on the same day. At this session the council formally decided to reinstate Theodoret. It will be recalled that he had been deposed at the previous council and subsequently banished by order of Theodosius II. This sentence had been cancelled by Marcian soon after his accession, but it still remained to give canonical force to his restoration. This was now done.[53] In the two following sessions the sentences pronounced on Ibas[54] and Domnus[55] came in for review; Ibas was reinstated and Domnus, though not reinstated, was granted a pension. With the business conducted at the later sessions, with the exception of the last, we are not here concerned.

By accepting the "Definition" the council had made a valiant attempt to reconcile the reality of Christ's Manhood with the verity of His Godhead. If it failed, as it did, to safeguard permanently the unity of the Church on the doctrinal issue, its failure was due not so much to any inherent defects as to forces which even the imperial Church was powerless to

[50] In doing so the council had adopted the very policy which Leo had repeatedly insisted must on no account be followed.

[51] Mansi, *op. cit.*, Vol. VII, 127.

[52] *Ibid.*, 173. "Siquis igitur." Later embodied in an edict dated February 7th, A.D. 452. Seeck, *Regesten*, p. 395. Mansi, *op. cit.*, Vol. VII, 476.

[53] Mansi, *op. cit.*, Vol. VII, 189.

[54] *Ibid.*, 195.

[55] *Ibid.*, 269. Domnus had, of course, been replaced in the see of Antioch by Maximus, who was clearly a personal friend of Anatolius.

keep in check. The political and economic confusion of the Empire, spread over at least half a century, was giving birth to a new spirit of nationalism which meant that sooner or later the outlying provinces, never more than superficially latinized, would throw off the yoke of the central government at Constantinople. It comes therefore as no surprise to find the earliest symptoms of revolt making themselves felt in the sphere of religion, and manifested even in the course of a council summoned by the Emperor and conducted under his authority.

Additional Note

THE RECEPTION OF THE "TOME" AND ITS BEARING ON THE DOGMA OF PAPAL INFALLIBILITY

In the course of the preceding chapter we have had opportunity of observing the reception accorded to the "Tome" by the members of the council of Chalcedon and have had before us the consideration which chiefly commended it in their eyes, namely the fact that the teaching which it contained was in close conformation with that of the Catholic creeds and of the dogmatic letters of Cyril of Alexandria.[56] In the following chapter we shall see that similar reasons were advanced by the synods of Milan [57] and Arles [58] to justify their acceptance of it and that the specific reason mentioned in the former's synodal letter was the fact that it was in accordance with the teaching of Ambrose.[59] Plainly it would not be true to say that any of these conciliar bodies accepted the "Tome" solely on the ground that it was a doctrinal statement officially promulgated by the Roman see.

Yet the Constitution, *Pastor aeternus,* adopted by the Vatican Council of 1870, states that:

"The Roman pontiff, when he speaks from his see, that is when in the execution of his office of shepherd and teacher of all Christians he defines in virtue of his supreme Apostolic authority a doctrine concerning faith or morals to be held by the universal Church, through the divine aid promised to him

[56] See above, pp. 292f.
[57] See below, Chap. XIII, pp. 317f.
[58] See below, p. 315.
[59] See below, p. 318.

in the person of blessed Peter, is endowed with that infallibility with which our divine Redeemer willed that His Church should be enlightened in the definition of doctrine concerning faith or morals; and therefore definitions of the Roman pontiff of that sort are irreformable of themselves, and not in virtue of the consent of the Church." [60]

At first sight therefore it would seem that the theory of papal authority accepted by the Vatican Council is opposed to the view which was held in various quarters at the time of the council of Chalcedon. Yet it may reasonably be asked whether the "Tome" was in fact a definition of "doctrine concerning faith" in the sense prescribed by the Constitution. On this question there is some variance of opinion. Dublanchy, for example, in his article "Infallibilité du Pape," [61] includes it in a series of papal pronouncements, which he says, "d'après les principes que nous venons de rappeler, sont habituellement, ou assez habituellement, considérés comme contenant une définition infallible." Admittedly there is an element of ambiguity contained in the words "assez habituellement," yet it is clear that the author had in mind the fact that some authorities were satisfied that the "Tome" conformed to the conditions laid down in the Constitution. Dom Cuthbert Butler, however, in his book *The Vatican Council* [62] quotes a speech by the great historian Hefele, in which he made the downright assertion that "if ever there was an *ex cathedra* dogmatic document it was Leo's letter to Flavian." This view appears to be shared by Tixeront [63] when he writes, "Cette lettre . . . a toujours été regardée comme un document dogmatique du premier ordre . . . Saint Leo ne veut ni discuter, ni démontrer: il prononce et il juge."

On the other hand Bellarmine offered the following comment "Leo epistolam suam miserat ad concilium, non ut continentem ultimam et definitivam sententiam, sed ut instructionem, qua adiuti episcopi melius iudicarent." [64] And with

[60] *Conc. Vatican,* Sessio 4. *Const. dogm.* I, de ecclesia, 4. Denzinger-Bannwart, *Enchiridion,* No. 1832.
[61] *Dictionnaire de Théol. Cath.,* Vol. VII, col. 1665f., 1703.
[62] Vol. II, pp. 46f.
[63] *Histoire des Dogmes,* Vol. III, p. 86.
[64] Cit. ap. *D.T.C.,* Vol. IX, col. 252.

this statement Batiffol is evidently in agreement when he says, " La lettre à Flavian est devenue une constitution dogmatique revêtue de toute la majesté du magistère papal. Il suffit cependant de la lire objectivement pour se rendre compte que dans sa teneur elle n'a pas les caracteristiques d'une définition *ex cathedra*." [65]

Perhaps the right person to tell us the precise purpose of the " Tome " is Leo himself.[66] Admittedly the letter was first written in order to guide those who were responsible for the examination of Eutyches at Constantinople or elsewhere. But in the later stages of the controversy Leo did not hesitate to refer to his " Tome " as a final standard of orthodoxy and for this reason insisted, first that no further council was necessary and later, when he saw that the council was inevitable, that no discussion of doctrine should be permitted. It is difficult to avoid the conclusion that Leo himself regarded his " Tome " as a final, and therefore, in the sense of the Constitution, an infallible decision.

[65] *D.T.C.*, Vol. IX, col. 251. Cf. Id. *Siège Apostolique*, p. 509.
[66] e.g. in *Ep.* 93, 2, JK 473, see p. 284, n. 111.

CHAPTER XIII

LEO AND THE CHURCHES OF THE EAST. 5

THE ROMAN SEE AND QUESTIONS OF JURISDICTION

WITH the question of doctrine finally settled so far as the council of Chalcedon was concerned the assembly turned its attention to certain problems of jurisdiction, the most delicate of which affected the relation of the see of Jerusalem to the see of Antioch. It was now proposed to assign to the former primatial jurisdiction over the three provinces of Palestine,[1] thereby withdrawing them from the authority of the see of Antioch. After considerable discussion this proposal was approved,[2] and thus at long last the ambitious designs of Juvenal were achieved. What, however, awakens some surprise is that the Roman legates were willing to be a party to this arrangement, thereby assenting to an act which in some degree involved a repudiation of the sixth canon of Nicaea.[3] It is scarcely conceivable that if Leo had been consulted he would have approved of their action, but it is possible that they were taken unawares and thus led unconsciously to support a policy which was opposed to the declared attitude of Leo himself.[4]

Yet this was not all. From the point of view of the Roman see a more serious question, this time affecting the rights of the see of Constantinople, arose in the course of the last session of the council.[5] As we have seen, during the last fifty years

[1] For the precise extent of this area see Heussi-Mulert, *Atlas,* Map Ic, though it was not till after A.D. 553 that the jurisdiction of the see of Jerusalem included the province of Arabia.

[2] *Conc. Chalc.,* Actio 7. Mansi, *op. cit.,* Vol. VII, 180.

[3] *Conc. Nic.,* Can. 6 stated in regard to the see of Antioch "ὁμοίως δὲ καὶ κατὰ 'Αντιόχειαν καὶ ἐν ταῖς ἄλλαις ἐπαρχίαις τὰ πρεσβεῖα σώζεσθαι ταῖς ἐκκλησίαις." The privileges of the see of Jerusalem are in Can. 7. "ὥστε τὸν ἐν Αἰλίᾳ ἐπίσκοπον τιμᾶσθαι, ἐχέτω τὴν ἀκολουθίαν τῆς τιμῆς."

[4] See *Ep.* 119, 4, JK 495, in which he alludes to his earlier attitude to the same question, as it arose in the time of Cyril of Alexandria.

[5] Held on October 31st. Mansi, *op. cit.,* Vol. VII, 423.

that see had been steadily acquiring greater importance, and it was now only a question of giving formal recognition to a position which had long existed *de facto*.[6] Yet from the uncertainty and inconsistency of the attitude adopted by the Roman legation it is evident that Leo had not expected that any such question would arise, and consequently had left his legates entirely without instructions.

The subject was first tactfully introduced by Eusebius of Dorylaeum. He affirmed that in the course of his recent sojourn at Rome he had recited in the presence of Leo himself and of certain clergy belonging to the church of Constantinople the canons passed by the Constantinopolitan council of A.D. 381.[7] There is no reason to think that Eusebius was not speaking the truth, yet it was certainly a misrepresentation to suggest, as Eusebius did, that Leo had formally confirmed them. The legates, however, found themselves in a position of some embarrassment. They were neither in a position to deny the truth of Eusebius' statements, nor would it have been tactful to admit, as was probably the case, that they knew nothing of the canons in question.

So they contented themselves with reciting a seemingly relevant passage from their instructions:

[6] For examples of the exercise of this *de facto* jurisdiction see esp. Chap. VIII, p. 201, n. 112.

[7] It is suggested by Caspar, *Geschichte,* Vol. I, p. 521, that up to this time these canons were little known in the West. The probability of this view, which explains the inconsistent attitude of the legates, is supported by the fact that the edict by which Theodosius I published the decisions of the council of A.D. 381 (*Cod. Theod.* XVI, i, 3) applied only to the "greater churches" of the East. Later in A.D. 404 Pope Innocent I, *Ep.* 5, JK 288, explicitly stated that at Rome no canon other than those of Nicaea (-Sardica) was recognized. Yet there is no doubt that the Constantinopolitan canons were recognized generally in the East, as is shown by the protest against the treatment accorded to Flavian at the council of A.D. 449, mentioned in the minutes (Mansi, *op. cit.,* Vol. VI, 608), which recorded that he had been treated as an offender. "Why did not Flavian sit in his proper place? Why did they degrade the bishop of Constantinople to the fifth place?" said some of the bishops, and Paschasinus himself supported the interjection, saying, "Look, according to the will of God we honour Anatolius as the first (after the see of Rome). They set holy Flavian in the fifth place." On which Diogenes, bishop of Cyzicus, made the significant comment, "You know the canons then," by which he referred to the third canon of the Council of Constantinople. The fact that Paschasinus remained silent, suggests that he was as yet entirely disinterested in the question, and perhaps failed to understand the point of the witticism. For Leo's subsequent references to this canon see below, Chap. XIV, p. 327.

"The canon of the holy fathers (sc. of Nicaea)," they said, "must not be infringed by any headstrong action; in any case respect for myself must be shown on the part of yourselves. Should anyone relying on the importance of his city seek to cause confusion, he must be rebuked as a matter of justice." [8]

In doing so the legates at least deserve credit for some ingenuity, since it is by no means certain that Leo primarily intended these words to apply to Anatolius and the claims of the see of Constantinople. As we have seen, his chief anxiety, which he expresses again and again in his pre-conciliar correspondence, was concerned not with Anatolius but with Dioscorus and with the cause of orthodoxy. Nevertheless, in spite of their urgent objections it was clear that the rights of the see of Constantinople were now set down for immediate consideration by the council.

The sequel to this proposal put forward by Eusebius is of considerable interest. In an extraordinary session of the council held later in the course of the same day a collection of twenty-eight canons were presented for the approval of the assembly. It seems that on this occasion the Roman legation, having heard what was impending, deliberately absented themselves in spite of earnest entreaties to take part in the debate. The commissioners also refrained from attendance, but this is to be explained as due to their wish to avoid giving the appearance of exercising undue influence on the course of the discussion, so that in the final debate they might be able to play the part of impartial chairmen.

Of the whole series of canons which were agreed to in the course of this session by nearly two hundred bishops only three need concern us here. They are the ninth, the seventeenth and the twenty-eighth. The two former were mainly concerned with the subject of the appellate jurisdiction of the see of Constantinople, and state thus:

(Canon 9) ". . . But if a cleric has a matter against his own bishop or against another, let judgment be given by the synod of the province. Yet if a bishop or cleric be at variance with the metropolitan of the province, let appeal be made

[8] Mansi, *op. cit.*, Vol. VII, 444.

either to the exarch of the diocese, or to the see of imperial Constantinople, and let judgment be given upon it." [9]

Next (Canon 17). "The country or rural parishes in the case of each church are to remain undisturbed in the hands of the bishops who govern them and particularly if they (sc. the bishops) have administered them with unchallenged possession for a period of thirty years. But if within the thirty years there has arisen or may arise any matter of dispute concerning them, it is lawful for those who allege that they have been wronged to raise the matter concerning them at the synod of the province. And if any (sc. bishop) be wronged by his own metropolitan, let judgment be given by the exarch of the diocese, or by the see of Constantinople, as is aforesaid. And if any city have been reconstituted by imperial authority or shall be so reconstituted in the future, let the organization of ecclesiastical parishes (i.e. dioceses) correspond to the secular and civil boundaries." [10]

From the Roman standpoint both these canons were comparatively innocuous and provided merely a practical solution of current difficulties in the mutual relations of churches in

[9] Mansi, Vol. VII, 357. Mirbt, *Quellen*, No. 179. Can. 9 . . . "Εἰ δὲ καὶ κληρικὸς ἔχοι πρᾶγμα πρὸς τὸν ἴδιον ἐπίσκοπον ἢ πρὸς ἕτερον, παρὰ τῇ συνόδῳ τῆς ἐπαρχίας δικάζεσθω. εἰ δὲ πρὸς τὸν τῆς αὐτῆς ἐπαρχίας μητροπολίτην ἐπίσκοπος ἢ κληρικὸς ἀμφισβητοίη, καταλαμβανέτω ἢ τὸν ἔξαρχον τῆς διοικήσεως ἢ τὸν τῆς βασιλευούσης Κωνσταντινουπόλεως θρόνον, καὶ ἐπ' αὐτῷ δικαζέσθω."

[10] Can. 17. "τὰς καθ' ἑκάστην ἐκκλησίαν ἀγροικικὰς παροικίας ἢ ἐγχωρίους μένειν ἀπαρασαλεύτους παρὰ τοῖς κατέχουσιν αὐτὰς ἐπισκόποις, καὶ μάλιστα εἰ τριακονταετῆ χρόνον ταύτας ἀβιάστως διακατέχοντες ᾠκονόμησαν. εἰ δὲ ἐντὸς τῶν τριάκοντα ἐτῶν γεγένηταί τις ἢ γένηται περὶ αὐτῶν ἀμφισβήτησις, ἐξεῖναι τοῖς λέγουσιν ἠδικῆσθαι, περὶ τούτων κινεῖν παρὰ τῇ συνόδῳ τῆς ἐπαρχίας. εἰ δέ τις παρὰ τοῦ ἰδίου ἀδικοῖτο μητροπολίτου, παρὰ τῷ ἐπάρχῳ τῆς διοικήσεως ἢ τῷ Κωνσταντινουπόλεως θρόνῳ δικάζεσθω, καθὰ προείρηται. εἰ δέ τις ἐκ βασιλικῆς ἐξουσίας ἐκαινίσθη πόλις ἢ αὖθις καινισθείη, τοῖς πολιτικοῖς καὶ δημοσίοις τύποις καὶ τῶν ἐκκλησιαστικῶν παροικιῶν ἡ τάξις ἀκολουθείτω."

The frank acceptance of the principle that ecclesiastical organization should conform to civil boundaries is a noteworthy feature of this canon. It was a principle which the Roman see had more than once repudiated, e.g. Innocent I, *Ep.* 24, 1, JK 310. Nevertheless the view that the spiritual importance of any see is proportionate to its civil dignity is put forward by Leo in *Ep.* 14, 11, JK 411, and is implied in the correspondence of the Western sovereigns, *Inter Leon. Epp.*, No. 8, *P.L.* 54, 622; *ibid.*, No. 56, *P.L.* 54, 861. (Notice that in *Ep.* 58, with reference to the Roman see itself, there is a twofold view as to the origin of its primacy.) Acceptance of the principle was evidently specially distasteful to Rome. For if the claims of the see of Constantinople were admitted, the day might come when the see of Ravenna might also demand peculiar and embarrassing privileges.

the eastern provinces. It was quite otherwise with the twenty-eighth canon, which seemed to aim a direct blow at the uniqueness of the privileges claimed and already largely enjoyed by the Roman see. This canon states:

(Canon 28), "Since we follow in all respects the principles of the holy fathers and recognize the canon of the one hundred and fifty fathers just recited, we too define and prescribe by vote the same things in regard to the privileges of the holy church of Constantinople, or New Rome. For it was with good reason that the fathers assigned privileges to the see of Elder Rome, because of that city being the imperial capital, and moved by the same respect the one hundred and fifty most devout bishops awarded the same privileges to the most holy see of New Rome, judging it fitting that the city which is honoured by the government and the Senate and enjoys equal privileges with the Elder imperial Rome, should like it have an important place in ecclesiastical affairs, being in the second place after it; so that in the 'dioceses' of Pontus, Asia and Thrace the metropolitans only should be ordained by the aforesaid most holy see of the most holy church at Constantinople, and in addition ordinary bishops of the aforesaid 'dioceses' in areas populated by barbarians, while as a matter of course every metropolitan in the said 'dioceses' with the bishops of the province is to ordain the bishops of the province, even as it is prescribed in the holy canons. But that, as is aforesaid, the metropolitans of the aforementioned 'dioceses' are to be ordained by the archbishop of Constantinople, after a favourable vote has been accorded to a particular candidate according to custom." [11]

[11] Mansi, *op. cit.*, Vol. VII, 369f. "Πανταχοῦ τοῖς τῶν ἁγίων πατέρων ὅροις ἑπόμενοι καὶ τὸν ἀρτίως ἀναγνωσθέντα κανόνα τῶν ἑκατὸν πεντήκοντα θεοφιλεστάτων ἐπισκόπων γνωρίζοντες, τὰ αὐτὰ καὶ ἡμεῖς ὁρίζομεν καὶ ψηφιζόμεθα περὶ τῶν πρεσβείων τῆς ἁγιωτάτης ἐκκλησιάς Κωνσταντινουπόλεως νέας Ῥώμης. καὶ γὰρ τῷ θρόνῳ τῆς πρεσβυτέρας Ῥώμης, διὰ τὸ βασιλεύειν τὴν πόλιν ἐκείνην, οἱ πατέρες εἰκότως ἀποδεδώκασι τὰ πρεσβεῖα, καὶ τῷ αὐτῷ σκοπῷ κινούμενοι οἱ ἑκατὸν πεντήκοντα θεοφιλέστατοι ἐπίσκοποι τὰ ἴσα πρεσβεῖα ἀπένειμαν τῷ τῆς νέας Ῥώμης ἁγιωτάτῳ θρόνῳ εὐλόγως κρίναντες, τὴν βασιλείᾳ καὶ συγκλήτῳ τιμηθεῖσαν πόλιν καὶ τῶν ἴσων ἀπολαύουσαν πρεσβείων τῇ πρεσβυτέρᾳ βασίλιδι Ῥώμῃ καὶ ἐν τοῖς ἐκκλησιαστικοῖς ὡς ἐκείνην μεγαλύνεσθαι πράγμασι, δευτέραν μετ' ἐκείνην ὑπάρχουσαν· καὶ ὥστε τοὺς τῆς Ποντικῆς καὶ τῆς Ἀσιανῆς καὶ τῆς Θρᾳκικῆς διοικήσεως μητροπολίτας μόνους, ἔτι δὲ καὶ τοὺς ἐν τοῖς βαρβαρικοῖς ἐπισκόπους τῶν προειρημένων διοικήσεων χειροτονεῖσθαι ἀπὸ τοῦ προειρημένου ἁγιωτάτου

At the last session, held on November 1st, the commissioners again presided and the Roman legates were in their places. In the course of the introductory proceedings Lucentius took the opportunity of making a solemn pronouncement.

"The Apostolic see charged us that everything must be done in our presence; if therefore anything took place yesterday in our absence, contrary to the canons, we now request your Highness (i.e. the presiding commissioner) to cause it to be annulled."[12]

The canons were then recited at the request of the legates and when the twenty-eighth canon was finished Lucentius again interposed by questioning the independence of the signatories and the sincerity of the council. On receiving the answer "None of us has acted under compulsion," he repeated his protest that the twenty-eighth canon was contrary to existing Canon Law.[13] "Besides this," he added, "the council ignores the decrees of the three hundred and eighteen fathers, and only mentions those of the one hundred and fifty fathers, which are not included in conciliar canon law and were published even on your evidence not more than eighty years ago. If then Constantinople has enjoyed privileges of this sort for all this time what is it demanding now?"[14]

θρόνου τῆς κατὰ Κωνσταντινούπολιν ἁγιωτάτης ἐκκλησίας, δηλαδὴ ἑκάστου μητροπολίτου τῶν προειρημένων διοικήσεων μετὰ τῶς τῆς ἐπαρχίας ἐπισκόπων χειροτονοῦντος τοὺς τῆς ἐπαρχίας ἐπισκόπους, καθὼς τοῖς θείοις κάνοσι διηγορεύεται. χειροτονεῖσθαι δὲ, καθὼς εἴρηται, τοὺς μητροπολίτας τῶν προειρημένων διοικήσεων παρὰ τοῦ Κωνσταντινουπόλεως ἀρχιεπισκόπου, ψηφισμάτων συμφώνων κατὰ τὸ ἔθος γενομένων, καὶ ἐπ' αὐτὸν ἀναφερομένων."

[12] Mansi, *op. cit.*, Vol. VII, 453. The Greek *Acta* read:—"*ὁ ἀποστολικὸς θρόνος ἡμῶν παρόντων προσέταξε πάντα πράττεσθαι. καὶ διὰ τοῦτο εἴ τι δήποτε πρὸ τοῦ δικαστηρίου παρὰ κανόνας τῇ χθὲς ἡμέρᾳ ἐπράχθη ἀπόντων ἡμῶν, τὴν ὑμετέραν ὑπεροχὴν αἰτοῦμεν, ὥστε κελεῦσαι περιαιρεθῆναι.*" In the Latin version, however, the protest appears to have been intentionally suppressed: "Sedes apostolica nobis praesentibus humiliari non debet, et ideo quaecumque in praeiudicium canonum vel regularum hesterna die gesta sunt nobis absentibus, sublimitatem vestram petimus, ut circumduci iubeatis."

[13] Mansi, *op. cit.*, Vol. VII, 442. "*πρωὴν ἡ ὑμετέρα ἐνδοξότης ἐδοκίμασεν ὅσα ἐπί παρουσίᾳ τῶν ἐπισκόπων ἐπράχθη, ἵνα μή τις κατὰ ἀνάγκην ὁρίσας ὑπόγραψαι τοῖς μνημονευθεῖσι κανόσι βιασθῇ.*" The Latin version shows some significant changes. "Primo gloria vestra perpendat, quia circumventione cum sanctis episcopis gestum sit, ut non conscriptis canonibus, quorum mentionem fecerunt, subscribere sint coacti."

[14] Id. *ibid.* "*τοῖς μετὰ ταῦτα ἑκατὸν πεντήκοντα τὰ νῦν μνημονευθέντα μὴ ἐμφερόμενα δὲ ἐν τοῖς συνοδικοῖς κανόσι ταῦτα φάσκουσι ὡρίσθαι. εἰ τοίνυν ἐν τοῖς χρόνοις τούτοις τῷ βενεφικίῳ ἐχρήσαντο, τί νῦν ζητοῦσιν ᾧ μὴ κατὰ κανόνας ἐχρήσαντο*"; Latin, "... centum quiquaginta, qui in

It is fairly clear that the appeal of the supporters of the twenty-eighth canon to the third canon of Constantinople put the Roman legates at a disadvantage, since they were unaware of the existence of any such canon. At the same time they refrained from affirming that the Roman church at this time recognized no canons other than those of Nicaea.[15] But in any case they had laid themselves open to the charge of deliberate obstructiveness. Although invited they had refused to be present at the session at which the canons were given preliminary approval, and then objected to them on the ground that they had been passed in their absence.

Finding that matters had now reached a deadlock, the commissioners invited both sides in the debate to bring forward documentary evidence in support of their respective points of view. Thereupon, on behalf of the legates, Paschasinus recited the sixth canon of Nicaea in the following form :

" The Roman church has always held the primacy. Let Egypt moreover hold (authority) [over Libya and Pentapolis] : so that the Bishop of Alexandria may possess authority over all [these] (provinces) : since this custom belongs also to the Roman bishop. In like manner too the bishop who is established at Antioch. And [so] let the privileges of the churches be preserved in the other provinces also." [16]

synodicis canonibus non habentur, mentionem tantum fuisse noscuntur, quae dicunt ante octaginta prope annos constituta fuisse. Si ergo his temporibus hoc beneficio usi sunt, quid nunc requirunt? si nunquam usi sunt, quare requirunt?" Both this and the above quotation again show interesting contrasts between the Greek and Latin texts. Notice especially the omission of " non conscriptis canonibus " in the Greek text, unless its counterpart is possibly " μη ἐμφερόμενα δὲ ἐν τοῖς συνοδικοῖς κάνοσι." The Roman legate is, of course, alluding to the Constantinopolitan defence of Canon 28 based on *Conc. Const.*, Canon 3, which they regarded as no part of oecumenical Canon Law and as inconsistent with *Conc. Nic.*, Canon 6, on which see below, n. 16. It is evident that he had in mind the latter canon in its interpolated form.

[15] Turner in *Camb. Med. Hist.*, Vol. I, c. vi, p. 180 points out that the earliest eastern code of canon law was compiled about A.D. 400 and that " the canons of Constantinople were the first appendix to the code." It seems probable that this appendix had already been added by the year A.D. 451.

[16] Mansi, *op. cit.*, Vol. VII, 443. " Ecclesia Romana semper habuit primatum. Teneat autem et Aegyptus [Libyae et Pentapolis] ita ut episcopus Alexandriae (harum) omnium habeat potestatem : quoniam et Romano episcopo haec est consuetudo. Similiter autem et qui in Antio-

When he had finished the supporters of the new canon raised no objection to the form in which the Nicene canon had been quoted, but proceeded without delay to recite the first three canons of Constantinople. In the discussion which followed the only Eastern bishop to adopt an attitude which was in any way unfavourable was Thalassius, exarch of the "diocese" of Pontus, who urged that a conference with Anatolius should be arranged in order to settle details. It was a suggestion which could be safely ignored.

The commissioners then proceeded to sum up the debate in the following words:

"The primacy before all others and the chief dignity shall belong to the archbishop of old Rome, yet the archbishop of New Rome shall enjoy the same privileges of honour and possess the right to ordain metropolitans in the 'dioceses' of Asia, Pontus and Thrace." [17]

Their proposal was greeted with general approval and passed by acclamation. Only the papal legates persisted in their opposition, and demanded its rejection. "If this may not be," they added, "let our protest be recorded in the minutes, and we shall know what we have to report to the Apostolic Pope of the universal Church, that he may condemn what has been done to the damage of his own see and to the confusion of Canon Law." [18]

It was regrettable that the council which had opened with harmonious acceptance of the authority of the Roman see in matters of doctrine closed on a note of discord regarding questions of rank and precedence. Perhaps if the legation had included one possessed of diplomatic ability similar to that of Philip, legate to the council of Ephesus A.D. 431, the whole business of the council might have been guided to a conclusion less unfavourable to papal prestige. As it was the tactlessness of the legates on this occasion was responsible for

chia constitutus est. (Itaque) et in caeteris provinciis privilegia salva sint ecclesiarum." On the origin of this text see above, Chap. VIII, p. 198, and Maassen, *Quellen Can. Rechts,* Vol. I, p. 19.

[17] *Ibid.*, 452.

[18] *Ibid.*, 453. The Greek text adds "*ἵνα μὴ φιλονεικίᾳ τις ἐξ ἡμῶν ἐγκεῖται τούτοις τοῖς ὑπομνήμασι*," the sense of which is obscure. Apparently they wished to prevent the possibility of anyone suggesting that the canon had been adopted without protest.

the loss of a considerable measure of the gains won by them for the Roman see in the course of the earlier debates.

The letter which the council composed as an official report to the Roman see of its proceedings is a notable document,[19] and although allowance should be made for the underlying motive, namely to obtain papal approval for the authority conferred on the see of Constantinople, it clearly shows the high esteem in which the Roman see was held at this time in the East. Its courteous deference to Leo as the present occupant of that see is expressed in the following terms:

"You have indeed safeguarded the faith, which is to be likened to a golden stream coming down to us by commandment of Him who first gave it being, you were an interpreter of the words of blessed Peter to all mankind, and poured forth on all the blessing pronounced on his faith; wherefore we regarded you as the captain of our religion with great gain to our salvation . . ."[20]

And later with allusion to the respective parts played by the legates and the eastern Sovereigns:

"Your gracious leadership of us in the things which belong to orderliness was like the head is to the members. The faithful Emperors indeed as an ornament (of our assembly) took the first place . . . for they were eager to renew their education in doctrine."[21]

The letter passed on to describe the deposition of Eutyches and Dioscorus and affirms that:

"He (sc. Dioscorus) extended his fury even against him who had been entrusted by the Saviour with the guardianship of the vine—we mean your holiness—and planned the excommunication of him who was most zealous to unite the body of the Church. And though he ought to have repented of this and begged mercy with tears, he rather rejoiced in it as in

[19] *Inter Leon. Epp.*, No. 98. *P.L.* 54, 951.

[20] *Ibid.*, 1, "ἣν (sc. τὴν πίστιν) αὐτὸς ὥσπερ χρυσῆν σειρὰν τῷ προστάγματι τοῦ θεμένου καταγομέμην εἰς ἡμᾶς διεφύλαξας, πᾶσι τῆς τοῦ μακαρίου Πέτρου φωνῆς ἑρμηνεὺς καθιστάμενος καὶ τῆς ἐκείνου πίστεως τοῖς πᾶσι μακαρισμὸν ἐφελκόμενος· ὅθεν καὶ ἡμεῖς ὡς ἀρχηγῷ σοι τοῦ καλοῦ πρὸς ὠφέλειαν χρησάμενοι. . . ."

[21] *Ibid.*, 1, "ὧν (sc. ἡμῶν) σὺ μὲν, ὡς κεφαλὴ μελῶν, ἡγεμόνευες ἐν τοῖς τὴν σύνταξιν ἐπέχουσι τὴν εὔνοιαν ἐπιδεικνύμενος. Βασιλεῖς δὲ πιστοὶ πρὸς εὐκοσμίαν ἔξηρχον . . . τὴν ἐν τοῖς δόγμασι οἰκοδομίαν ἀνανεοῦν προθυμούμενοι."

something noble, despising the letter of your holiness and resisting every true doctrine." [22]

They go on to relate how Dioscorus had been fittingly deposed and then describe the steps which led to the adoption of the "Definition":

"Since we had received authority to plant as well as to pluck up we limited our pruning to one individual, and with due care cultivated the fertility of those who were well disposed. For it was God who worked in them, with the co-operation of the triumphant Euphemia, who with her bridal chamber lent adornment to the assembly and, receiving the Definition of Faith from us, presented it to her Spouse as her own confession, by the medium of our most devout Emperor and our Empress beloved of Christ . . . This we have accomplished with your aid, present in the spirit and in full concord with your brethren, all but visible to us in the prudent conduct of your legates." [23]

So far the task of representing the work of the council in a favourable light from the Roman standpoint had been comparatively easy. It became less simple when the adoption of the twenty-eighth canon came to be described. At this point, as the following paragraph shows, a good deal of tactful diplomacy was needed.

"We mention further that for the sake of good order in our affairs and of the stability of canon law we have made certain other decisions in the confidence that your holiness, on learning of them, will accept and confirm them. We have, in fact, endorsed by a vote of the assembly a custom which is

[22] *Ep.* 98, 2, "*καὶ πρὸς τούτοις ἅπασιν, ἔτι καὶ τὰ κατ' αὐτοῦ τοῦ τῆς ἀμπέλου τὴν φυλακὴν παρὰ τοῦ σωτῆρος ἐπιτετραμμένου τὴν μανίαν ἐξέτεινε · λέγομεν δὴ τῆς σής ὁσιότητος · καὶ ἀκοινωνησίαν κατὰ τοῦ τὸ σῶμα τῆς ἐκκλησίας ἑνοῦν σπουδάζοντος ἐμελέτησε · καὶ δέον ἐπὶ τούτοις μετανοῆσαι, δέον δάκρυσιν αἰτῆσαι τὸν ἔλεον, ὡς ἐπὶ σεμνοῖς ἐπηγάλλετο · τὴν μὲν ἐπιστολὴν τῆς σῆς ὁσιότητος διαπτύων, πᾶσι δὲ σοῖς τῆς ἀληθείας δόγμασιν ἀνθιστάμενος.*"

[23] *Ibid.*, 3, "*καὶ ὡς ἐκριζοῦν καὶ καταφυτεύειν τὴν ἐξουσίαν δεξάμενοι, τὴν μὲν ἐκτομὴν μέχρις ἑνὸς ἐστενώσαμεν, τῶν δὲ καλῶν τὴν εὐκαρπίαν ἐπιμελῶς ἐρριζώσαμεν. Θεὸς γὰρ ἦν ὁ ἐνεργῶν, καὶ ἡ τὸν σύλλογον τῷ νυμφῶνι στεφανοῦσα καλλίνικος Εὐφημία · ἣ ὥσπερ οἰκείαν ὁμολογίαν, τῆς πίστεως παρ' ἡμῶν δεξαμένη τὸν ὅρον, τῷ ἑαυτῆς νυμφίῳ διὰ τοῦ εὐσεβεστάτου Βασίλεως καὶ τῆς φιλοχρίστον Βασιλίδος προσήγαγε, . . . Ταῦτά ἐστιν, ἅπερ σὺν σοὶ τῷ πνεύματι παρόντι καὶ συνευδοκεῖν ὡς ἀδελφοῖς ἐγνωκότι καὶ μονονουχὶ διὰ τῆς τῶν σῶν τοποτηρητῶν ὁραμένῳ σοφίας εἰργάσμεθα.*"

longstanding in its observance by the holy church of God at Constantinople, namely of consecrating metropolitans in the 'dioceses' of Asia, Pontus and Thrace, not adding thereby anything to the see of Constantinople, but rather providing for the good order of sees of metropolitical rank. For frequently when bishops die much disorder has arisen, and clergy and laity have been without leaders and have disturbed the peace of the Church. Of this your holiness must be well aware since, especially in regard to the affairs of (the Church of) Ephesus, appeals have been frequently made to you. Moreover we have confirmed the canon of the one hundred and fifty fathers, who were assembled at Constantinople in the time of Theodosius the Great of blessed memory, which states that the see of Constantinople shall have privileges so as to rank second after your own most holy and Apostolic see, in the assurance that, as (previously) with your accustomed interest you have often shed forth that shining Apostolic radiance of yours even upon the church of Constantinople, you will increase it many times, since you share your own privileges ungrudgingly with your brethren." [24]

Next comes the delicate question of the behaviour of the Roman legates.

"Therefore, most holy and blessed father, deign to accept our definition, the purpose of which is the removal of all confusion and the stabilizing of ecclesiastical discipline in the

[24] *Ep.* 98, 4. "Γνωρίζομεν δὲ, ὡς καὶ ἕτερα τινα τῆς τῶν πραγμάτων εὐταξίας, καὶ τῆς τῶν ἐκκλησιαστικῶν θεσμῶν εὐσταθείας ἕνεκα ὡρίσαμεν, πεπεισμένοι καὶ τὴν ὑμετέραν ἁγιωσύνην διδαχθεῖσαν ἀποδέχεσθαί τε ταῦτα, καὶ βεβαιοῦν. Τὸ γὰρ ἐκ πολλοῦ κρατῆσαν ἔθος, ὅπερ ἔσχεν ἡ Κωνσταντινουπολιτῶν ἁγία τοῦ Θεοῦ ἐκκλησία εἰς τὸ χειροτονεῖν μητροπολίτας τῶν διοικήσεων τῆς τε Ἀσιανῆς καὶ Ποντικῆς καὶ Θρακικῆς, καὶ νῦν κατὰ συνοδικὴν ἐκυρώσαμεν ψῆφον, οὐ τοσοῦτον τῷ θρόνῳ Κωνσταντινουπόλεως τι παρέχοντες, ὅσον ταῖς μητροπόλεσι τὴν εὐταξίαν πρυτανεύοντες, διὰ τὸ πολλοὺς πολλάκις, τελευτώντων τῶν ἐπισκόπων, ἀνακύπτειν θορύβους, ἀνηγεμονεύτων ὄντων τῶν ἐν αὐταῖς κληρικῶν τε καὶ λαϊκῶν, καὶ τὴν ἐκκλησιαστικὴν τάξιν συγχεόντων. Ὅπερ οὐδὲ τὴν ὑμετέραν λέληθεν ἁγιότητα μάλιστα τῶν Ἐφεσίων ἕνεκεν, πλεόνακις ὑμῶν διενοχληθέντων. Ἐβεβαιώσαμεν δὲ καὶ τὴν τῶν ρύ ἁγίων πατέρων, τῶν ἐν Κωνσταντινουπόλει συναθροισθέντων ἐπὶ τοῦ τῆς εὐσεβοῦς μνήμης τοῦ μεγάλου Θεοδοσίου, κανόνα τὸν διαγορεύοντα, μετὰ τὸν ὑμέτερον ἁγιώτατον καὶ Ἀποστολικὸν θρόνον τὰ πρεσβεῖα τὸν Κωνσταντινουπόλεως ἔχὲιν δεύτερον τὲταγμένον· πεπεισμένοι ὡς τῆς ἀποστολικῆς παρ' ὑμῖν κρατούσης ἀκτῖνος, καὶ ἐπὶ τὴν ἐν Κωνσταντινουπόλει ἐκκλησίαν συνηθῶς κηδόμενοι πόλλακις ταύτην ἡπλώσατε· διὰ τὸ ἄφθονον ὑπάρχειν ὑμῖν τὴν τῶν οἰκείων ἀγαθῶν πρὸς τοὺς γνησίους μετάδοσιν."

interests of the extension of peace as though it were your very own. Yet your holiness's representatives, the most holy bishops Paschasinus and Lucentius, with the divinely loved priest Boniface, vehemently essayed to oppose our proposals, because they were eager that the credit for this beneficial act should be given to your watchful interest, and you should earn the merit of having restored not faith only but discipline as well. We ourselves, in obedience to the will of the most devout and Christian sovereigns, who approved of the proposal, and of the illustrious senate and, so to speak, of the whole capital, regarded the confirmation of this privilege by the present council as fitting, and we confidently endorsed it as proceeding from your holiness through those (letters) with which you have ever been willing to strengthen our hands. . . . We beg you therefore to honour our decision with your approval. Thus, as we have shown our concord with the head in all that is right, so the leader himself may do what is fitting for his children. Thus the devout sovereigns will be obeyed, who have given legal confirmation to your decision, and the see of Constantinople, which has shown all eagerness in carrying out your proposals, and has accorded with your wishes, will receive its recompense. Yet so that you may be assured that we have so acted, not by favour nor by malice, but only in accordance with the divine will, we have informed you of the whole tenor of our actions, thus proving our loyalty and expecting confirmation and assent to all that we have done." [25]

[25] *Ep.* 98, 4. "Ἅπερ τοίνυν ὡρίσαμεν πρὸς ἀναίρεσιν μὲν πάσης συγχύσεως, βεβαίωσιν δὲ τῆς ἐκκλησιατικῆς εὐταξίας, ταῦτα ὡς οἰκεῖά τε καὶ φίλα καὶ πρὸς εὐκοσμίαν ἁρμόδια περιπτύξασθαι, ἁγιώτατε καὶ μακαριώτατε πάτερ. Οἱ γὰρ τὸν τόπον τῆς ὑμετέρας ἁγιότητος ἐπέχοντες ὁσιώτατοι ἐπίσκοποι Πασχασῖνος καὶ Λουκήνσιος καὶ ὁ σὺν αὐτοῖς θεοφιλέστατος πρεσβύτερος Βονιφάτιος, τοῖς οὕτω τυπωθεῖσι σφοδρῶς ἀντειπεῖν ἐπειράθησαν, πάντως ἀπὸ τῆς ὑμετέρας ἄρξασθαι καὶ τοῦτο τὸ κάλὸν προνοίας βουλόμενοι, ἵνα καθάπερ τῆς πίστεως, οὕτω καὶ τῆς εὐταξίας ὑμῖν λογισθῇ τὸ κατόρθωμα. Ἡμεῖς γὰρ θεραπεύοντες τούς τε εὐσεβεστάτους καὶ φιλοχρίστους βασιλέας ἐπὶ τουτῷ ἡδομένους, τὴν τε λαμπρὰν σύγκλητον καὶ πᾶσαν, ὡς εἰπεῖν, τὴν βασιλεύουσαν, εὔκαιρον ἐνομίσαμεν τὴν ἐπ' αὐτῇ παρὰ τῆς οἰκουμένης συνόδου βεβαίωσιν τῆς τιμῆς· καὶ ὡς ἐκ τῆς σῆς ὁσιότητος ταυτὴν ἐναρχθεῖσαν, δι' ὧν ἀεὶ θάλπειν ἐσπούδακας, θαῤῥήσαντες ἐκυρώσαμεν . . . παρακαλοῦμεν τοίνυν, τίμησον καὶ ταῖς σαῖς ψήφοις τὴν κρίσιν, καὶ ὥσπερ ἡμεῖς τῇ κεφαλῇ τὴν ἐν τοῖς καλοῖς συμφωνίαν εἰσενηνόχαμεν, οὕτω καὶ ἡ κορυφὴ τοῖς παισὶν ἀναπληρώσοι τὸ πρέπον. Οὕτω γὰρ καὶ βασιλεῖς εὐσεβεῖς θεραπευθήσονται, οἱ τὴν τῆς σῆς ὁσιότητος, ὡς νόμον, βὲβαιώ-

Before describing the kind of reception accorded in Rome to this noteworthy letter we must see what had been happening there since the departure of the Roman legates. Soon after the deliberations of the council had concluded early in November Leo received a communication from Ravennius bishop of Arles, reporting that the bishops of the provinces of Southern Gaul had unanimously approved the "Tome."[26] The writers apologized for the fact that there had been some delay owing to the obstacles in the way of summoning a general council, but however sincere their apology the fact remained that it was then already too late for the letter to be of any use from the point of view of Leo's relations with the council. At the same time he must have read words such as the following with a good deal of satisfaction.

"He who is familiar with the revelation of our redemption writes your Apostolic letter, like the symbol of faith, on the tables of his heart, and that he may more readily refute the errors of heretics, commits it to a retentive memory. Many, exulting and rejoicing at it with one accord, have found in it the substance of their faith, and are rightly glad that their constant belief, handed down to them from the past, is in fact the teaching of your Apostolic self."[27]

It had been their intention, said Ravennius, to write to the eastern Emperor in defence of the truth, but information subsequently received had suggested that this was unnecessary.[28] He concluded with enthusiastic expressions of gratitude for Leo's defence of the truth.

In the course of the same winter Leo also heard from Marcian and from Anatolius, and it was on the basis of this

σαντες κρίσιν, καὶ · ὁ Κωνσταντινουπόλεως θρόνος τὴν ἀμοιβὴν ἀποδέξεται, πάσαν ἀεὶ σπουδὴν πρὸς τὴν τῆς εὐσεβείας ὑμῖν ἐκπληρώσας ὑπόθεσιν καὶ τῷ ζήλῳ συνάψας ἑαυτὸν ὑμῖν πρὸς ὁμόνοιαν. Ἵνα δὲ γνῶτε, ὡς οὐδὲν πρὸς χάριν ἢ προς ἀπέχθειαν πεποιήκαμεν, ἀλλ' ὡς θείῳ κυβερνώμενοι νεύματι πᾶσαν ὑμῖν τῶν πεπραγμένων τὴν δύναμιν ἐγνωρίσαμεν εἰς σύστασιν ἡμετέραν καὶ τῶν παρ' ἡμῶν πεπραγμένων βεβαίωσίν τε καὶ συγκατάθεσιν."

[26] *Inter Leon. Epp.*, No. 99, *P.L.* 54, 966.

[27] *Ibid.*, 2. "Quae apostolatus vestri ita ut symbolum fidei quisquis redemptionis sacramenta non neglegit, tabulis cordis ascribit et tenaci quo ad contundendos haereticorum errores paratior sit, memoriae commendavit. Multi itaque in ea gaudentes pariter et exsultantes recognoverunt fidei suae sensum, et ita se semper ex traditione paterna tenuisse ut vester apostolatus exposuit, iure laetantur."

[28] The use of the phrase "filium vestrum" suggests that it is Valentinian III to whom he refers.

information that he composed his reply to the Gallic bishops.[29] After expressing his disappointment that their letter had not been received in time to be entrusted to the legates on their departure for Chalcedon he informed them that "the council, embracing about six hundred of our brethren and fellow bishops, has allowed no device of argument, no eloquence of speech to blast the divinely founded faith. With the help of God and by the efforts of our brethren and legates, who gave their willing co-operation at every session, it was fully and distinctly made known not only to the bishops of Christ but to the Christian princes and officials, to all ranks of clergy and people that our teaching (which as we have received it is pure and free from any taint of error and which we uphold with the accord of the whole world) is the Catholic and Apostolic Faith."[30]

He went on to point out that the council had repudiated Eutyches no less than Nestorius.

"Because he essayed to teach that the word of God was so made flesh that He did not take the actual flesh of His Mother; and that He had not a human body, but that there was but one nature of His Godhead and His flesh, so that he said that our one Lord Jesus Christ was both unreal man and passible God."[31]

Dioscorus, he said, had been condemned by the council, which had approved the "Tome," as confirmed by the authority of St. Peter, "lest the church of Alexandria should be brought into bondage to heresy."[32] The letter ended with

[29] *Ep.* 102, JK 479, dated January 27th, A.D. 452.

[30] *Ibid.*, 2, "cum ob hoc ipsum sexcentorum fere fratrum coepiscoporumque nostrorum synodus congregata, nullam artem ratiocinandi, nullum eloquium disserendi contra fundatam divinitus fidem spirare permiserit: quoniam annitentibus per auxilium gratiae Dei fratribus et vicariis nostris quorum plenissima exstitit in omni actione devotio, non solum sacerdotibus Christi, sed etiam principibus et potestatibus Christianis cunctisque cleri et plebis ordinibus, plene atque evidenter apparuit hanc esse vere apostolicam et catholicam fidem ex divinae pietatis fonte manantem, quam sinceram et ab omni faece totius erroris alienam, sicut accepimus, praedicamus et universo iam mundo consentiente defendimus."

[31] *Ibid.*, 3.

[32] *Ibid.*, 4. It cannot be said that Leo deliberately misrepresented the ground on which the condemnation of Dioscorus was actually based (see above, p. 294, n. 29), for in any case at the time when the letter was written he was dependent on rumour and had not yet received the report brought by his legates.

the request that the information which it contains shall be passed on to the churches of Spain.

Not only Gaul but northern Italy as well testified to its wholehearted acceptance of the teaching contained in the "Tome," as appears from a further letter received from Eusebius of Milan about this time.[33] The "Tome" had been conveyed to Milan by Abundantius and Senator, who had recently served as legates of the Roman see at Constantinople, and whose churches were situated in the Milanese province.[34] It was considered at a synod of the province held in the latter part of the year A.D. 451 and Eusebius' letter is a formal report of the opinions expressed by the synod on the subject. It redounds with expressions of enthusiasm for Leo's doctrine, of which the following is characteristic:

"It is not a matter of surprise that our Lord Jesus Christ has granted the favour and protection of His majesty to the Catholic Faith, which we hold, seeing that He has established you as prelate in the see of His Apostle to be a fitting protector of His religion, who are competent both to believe aright concerning the mystery of the Lord's Incarnation and also rightly to defend it." [35]

And later, again with reference to the impression made on the synod:

"It was clear that it (sc. the 'Tome') was brilliant with perfect purity of Faith, and blazed out with a kind sparkling light and truthful radiance, embracing the words of the

[33] *Inter Leon. Epp.*, No. 97, *P.L.* 54, 945. It is clear that at this time the legates had not yet returned, for Leo writes (*Ep.* 102, 5), "Oret nobiscum vestra dilectio, ut fratres nostros, quos expectatio nostra desiderat, incolumes quam primum rediisse laetemur." Caspar, *Geschichte,* Vol. I, p. 525, n. 4, suggests that their return was delayed by the time taken in providing a Latin version of the conciliar *Acta,* which must have been a labour occupying some weeks. On the other hand, Anatolius, *Inter Leon. Epp.* 101, 1, *P.L.* 54, 978, writing probably on December 18th, A.D. 451, implies that his letter was composed after their departure.

[34] *Ibid.,* 2, "frater et coepiscopus noster Abundantius (Abundius) et compresbyter meus Senator." They had been in Constantinople in the year A.D. 450 (see above, p. 270, n. 42). Cf. *Ep.* 69, 2, JK 452. Abundantius was probably bishop of Comum (Como) and Senator a priest of the church of Milan, who later became a bishop of the see.

[35] *Ibid.,* 1. "Nec mirum quod Dominus noster Jesus Christus catholicae fidei, quam tenemus, maiestatis suae gratiam custodiamque praestiterit; quando vos idoneos cultus sui assertores in apostoli sui sede praesulem collocavit, qui et recta sentire de incarnationis dominicae sacramento, et eadem potestis rectius custodire."

prophets, the utterances of the Gospels and the testimony of Apostolic preaching and was in accord with the beliefs which blessed Ambrose had expressed in his books on the mystery of the Lord's Incarnation by the inspiration of the Holy Ghost." [36]

The writer then stated that "as everything (sc. in the 'Tome') was wholly in agreement with the Faith of our fathers handed down to us of old," [37] the synod resolved, in accordance with the suggestion of Leo's own letter, to pronounce condemnation on those whose faith concerning the Incarnation was at fault, though they stood self-condemned. He concluded by suggesting that the "Tome" ought to be preserved so that future generations might know the nature of the heresy condemned and might find security in its teaching. The signatures of the bishops present follow the letter.

Early in the new year, A.D. 452, Leo received a letter from the Emperor Marcian.[38] It had been brought by a special legation, who also carried a communication from Anatolius. Marcian began by describing the decisions reached at Chalcedon as a victory of Christ over error and referred with satisfaction to the assent given by the council to the contents of the "Tome." But evidently the real purpose of the letter was to ensure that Leo would give approval of the twenty-eighth canon before he could be prejudiced against it by the report of his legates. So the Emperor urged as a reason for such approval:

"That this decision actually was made so that the resolutions of the one hundred and fifty most holy bishops in the time of the divine Theodosius the Elder concerning the honour of the venerable church of Constantinople and the recent prescription of the holy synod on the same subject should be

[36] *Ep.* 97, 2. "Claruit eam plena fidei simplicitate fulgere, prophetarum etiam assertionibus, evangelicis auctoritatibus et apostolicae doctrinae testimoniis, nitore quodam lucis ac veritatis splendore radiare, omnibusque sensibus convenire, quos beatus Ambrosius de incarnationis dominicae mysterio suis libris, Spiritu sancto excitatus inseruit." The allusion is probably to Ambrose, *De Incarnatione, P.L.* 16, 817.

[37] *Ibid.*, 3, "quia omnia maiorum fidei nobis antiquitus traditae tota puritate conveniunt."

[38] *Inter Leon. Epp.*, No. 100, *P.L.* 54, 970. The original Latin text is here preserved.

upheld intact; namely that after the Apostolic see the bishop of the city of Constantinople receives the second place; because the said most glorious city is called Rome the Younger." [39] Unhappily, he added, the Roman legates strongly opposed the settlement of anything concerning this venerable church; yet in spite of their opposition he asked for Leo's assent to the canons.[40]

Anatolius,[41] after referring to the decisions of the council, mentioned specially the deposition of Dioscorus on the ground that he "had filled the whole world with storm and tempest." [42] Writing of the "Definition" he said that it had been approved by unanimous consent. Then he comes to the twenty-eighth canon. This decision had been reached, he said, "so that the most holy see of this imperial city of Constantine may receive some additional honour." [43]

It was in fact, according to the writer, a confirmation of the canon approved by all the leaders of the Church at the council of A.D. 381, and in view of the concern which the Roman see has expressed in the past for the due honour of the see of Constantinople, no doubt Leo would be eager to give his assent to it. Nevertheless, he added with ingenious tactfulness, so far from enlarging the privileges of that see, the canon actually deprived it of the right of consecrating diocesan bishops within the prescribed "dioceses," a right which it had enjoyed for the past sixty or seventy years.[44] Alluding to the

[39] *Ibid.*, 3, "Quoniam vero et hoc statutum est ut ea quae centum quinquaginta sanctissimi episcopi sub divo Theodosio maiore de honore venerabilis ecclesiae Constantinopolitanae statuerunt et quae nunc a sancto synodo de eadem re statuta sunt firma serventur: scilicet ut post sedem apostolicam Constantinopolitanae urbis antistes secundum obtineat locum: quoniam et eadem splendidissima civitas iunior Roma nuncupatur." The allusion to a decision by the "sancta synodus" probably refers to a canon passed by the *σύνοδος ἐνδημοῦσα* in the previous year. Cf. Grumel, *Regestes,* No. 119, and *Ep.* 85, 3, JK 465, the nature of which had been communicated by Anatolius to Leo.

[40] *Ibid.*, "huic parti proprium adhibere consensum."

[41] *Inter Leon. Epp.*, No. 101, *P.L.* 54, 976.

[42] *Ibid.*, 2, "*τὸν καὶ πᾶσαν τὴν οἰκουμένην χειμῶνος καὶ ζάλης ἐμπλήσαντα.*" Once more there is no condemnation of his doctrine.

[43] *Ibid.*, 4, "*προσθήκης τινὸς εἰς τιμὴν, τὸν κατὰ τὴν βασιλεύουσαν ταύτην Κωνσταντίνου ἁγιώτατον θρόνον.*"

[44] *Ibid.*, "*ἀφαιρεῖσθαι μᾶλλον τοῦ θρόνου Κωνσταντινουπόλεως χειροτονίας πλείστων ἐπισκόπων, ὥσπερ ἀπὸ ἑξήκοντα καὶ ἑβδομήκοντα ἐνιαυτῶν ἐτύγχανεν ἐπιτελῶν.*" There appears to be a contradiction, which is doubtless only verbal. It was most unlikely that the see of Constantinople stood to lose by the passing of the canon in question. Nor did it do so in fact.

unfavourable attitude of the legates Anatolius alleged that he could only account for it by supposing that they acted as they did in ignorance of Leo's real wishes [45] and, after pointing out that it had been approved both by the sovereigns and the imperial commissioners, requested that Leo would send his confirmation in writing by the hands of the imperial legate.

It is evident that both Emperor and bishop alike were extremely anxious to obtain the general approval of the western churches to the Chalcedonian decisions. From the Emperor's point of view much depended on it for maintaining the political unity of the Empire; from the bishop's for the regularization of the *de facto* authority of his see. But from Leo's standpoint doctrinal orthodoxy and respect for Canon Law were primary considerations. Hence he refrained from replying to either of these communications till he had had the opportunity of consulting personally with his legates, and of hearing from their own lips an account of what had taken place at Chalcedon.

The significance of the twenty-eighth canon, which as a point of controversy occupies so large a space in the correspondence of the last nine years of Leo's pontificate, lies chiefly in the fact that it was a naked and unashamed expression of the principle that the rank and jurisdiction of episcopal sees ought to follow the civil importance of the cities to which they belonged. This principle, not without some reason, had always been normative in the East, yet it had frequently been repudiated either directly or by implication by the Roman see. Nevertheless, however emphatic that repudiation might be, at least so far as the eastern churches were concerned, it was a principle which, as we shall see, was destined to prevail.

[45] *Ep.* 100, 5, "ἀγνοοῦντες δὲ τὸν σκοπὸν τῆς ὑμετέρας ἁγιωσύνης." It was quite true that the legates had received no instructions on the point. But to imagine that they had acted contrary to Leo's intentions was somewhat wide of the mark.

CHAPTER XIV

LEO AND THE CHURCHES OF THE EAST. 6

THE REACTION TO THE COUNCIL OF CHALCEDON

It is clear from the evidence supplied by the letters addressed to the Roman see by the synods of Milan and Arles that there was no danger of the doctrinal decrees of Chalcedon being rejected by any of the western churches. They were content to accept the guidance of the papacy in questions affecting dogma and leave it so. With the new canons dealing with the jurisdiction of the see of Constantinople they had no immediate concern. On the other hand, as we have seen, from the standpoint of the Roman see those canons were a flagrant violation of existing canon law and a direct challenge to the Roman theory of ecclesiastical jurisdiction.[1] Leo was therefore determined to resist their adoption to the utmost, in particular the twenty-eighth canon, and in his subsequent correspondence with the eastern Sovereigns and churches adopted a stiffly negative attitude.

Yet unhappily for the eastern government's policy of safeguarding imperial unity by means of decisions arrived at by a general council, resistance to those decisions was by no means confined to the papacy, and in spite of all that had been done to conciliate the supporters of Alexandrine Christology there remained a vigorous and numerous party in opposition.

Among the chief centres of this opposition were the monasteries in Jerusalem where, since her exclusion from the eastern court, Eudocia, widow of Theodosius II, had resided,

[1] e.g. as set forth in the Manifesto of the Roman synod, A.D. 382 (*Decretum Gelasianum*, ed. Dobschütz in *Texte u. Unters.*, Vol. XXXVIII, 4 (1912), Mirbt, *Quellen*, No. 191) where the view is put forward that the precedence accorded to the sees of Rome, Alexandria and Antioch is due solely to their Petrine origin. In support of the view that these chapters of the *Decretum* actually belong to the above synod, cf. Caspar, *Geschichte*, Vol. I, pp. 598f. Batiffol, *Siège Apostolique*, pp. 146ff., however, accepts the conclusions of Dobschütz as to its date (late fifth century) and non-Roman origin.

nursing her grievance against the Theodosian house, and while continuing to enjoy imperial honours was employing her time and her ample revenues in works of charity and religion.[2] The news that the council of Chalcedon had betrayed the cause of Cyril and reinstated "Nestorianism" as the official theology of the Empire afforded her an admirable opportunity for increasing the difficulties of the regime of Marcian and Pulcheria, and we may attribute to her influence the hostile reception accorded by the monks to their bishop, Juvenal, on his return from the council. So great was this hostility that he was compelled to flee from the city. A local synod declared him deposed and Theodosius, a prominent member of the monastic party and a determined adversary of the council, was installed in his place.[3]

Before pursuing further the course of these events we must turn back to see what was happening in Rome. Early in the year A.D. 452, perhaps as late as March, the legates returned and presented to Leo not only the *Acta* of the council but also the detailed information as to what had taken place at the council, which he so eagerly awaited. In the course of May he received an urgent appeal from Julian, begging him to give his assent to the decisions of the council, in which was included the twenty-eighth canon. The appeal probably reached him when he was in the process of composing his answers to the letters received earlier in the year,[4] which he had delayed to send in order that he might be better informed before doing so. These were actually despatched on the twenty-eighth of the month.

In writing to the Emperor[5] he stated that he was overjoyed at the unanimity with which the council had vindicated the truth, yet he took no pains to conceal his indignation regarding the attempt to change existing Canon Law by means of the twenty-eighth canon for which, in his view, Anatolius was personally responsible.

"Let the city of Constantinople retain her greatness, for such is our will, and by the protection of God's right hand let

[2] For details see Bury, *Later Roman Empire,* Vol. I, pp. 230, 358.
[3] See Duchesne, *Histoire*, Vol. III, pp. 466–71.
[4] *Inter Leon. Epp.* 98, 100, 101, on which see above, pp. 311–15, 318f.
[5] *Ep.* 104, JK 481, dated May 22nd, A.D. 452.

her enjoy many years of government by your Grace. Yet the principles which regulate secular affairs and those which regulate the affairs of God are not the same: nor can any structure be stable apart from that Rock which the Lord laid as a foundation. He who covets what is not his due loses that which is his own. Let it suffice him (sc. Anatolius) that with the aid of your favour and by my gracious approval he has received the bishopric of so great a city. Let him not think too little of a city which has imperial rank, but which he cannot make into an Apostolic see; nor let him hope that its prestige can be increased by wrongs inflicted on others." [6]

He then stated clearly the principle which governed his present attitude.

"The privileges of the churches, established by the canons of the holy fathers and prescribed by the decrees of the Nicene council, cannot be disturbed by presumptuous action or modified by innovation. In carrying out my responsibility faithfully with the help of Christ I am bound to give unremitting service." [7]

He suggested to Marcian therefore that he should use his authority to restrain the unlawful ambition of Anatolius who, in view of the attitude of the legates at the council, could pretend that his wishes were acceptable to the Roman see. It was enough that he had presumed to consecrate Maximus as a successor to Domnus in the see of Antioch,[8] and though for the sake of peace, in spite of the absence of any precedent and of the intrinsic irregularity of such a consecration in defiance of Canon Law, his action in this respect could be over-

[6] *Ibid.*, 3. "Habeat, sicut optamus, Constantinopolitana civitas gloriam suam, ac protegente dextra Dei, diuturno clementiae vestrae fruatur imperio. Alia tamen ratio est rerum saecularium, alia divinarum; nec praeter illam petram quam Dominus in fundamento posuit, stabilis erit ulla constructio. Propria perdit, qui indebita concupiscit. Satis sit praedicto (sc. Anatolio) quod vestrae pietatis auxilio et mei favoris assensu, episcopatum tantae urbis obtinuit. Non dedignetur regiam civitatem, quam apostolicam non potest facere sedem; nec ullo speret modo quod per aliorum possit offensiones augeri."

[7] *Ibid.* "Privilegia enim ecclesiarum, sanctorum Patrum canonibus instituta, et venerabilis Nicaenae synodi fixa decretis, nulla possunt improbitate convelli, nulla novitate mutari. In quo opere, auxiliante Christo, fideliter exsequendo necesse est me perseverantem exhibere famulatum."

[8] Leo must presumably have been informed by his legates of this fact.

looked, yet he must realize that should he persist in doing things of this sort he would find himself deposed.[9]

A letter to Pulcheria [10] was included in this post. Compared with the reply to the Emperor it is, as one might expect, more outspoken, particularly on the subject of the objectionable canon. After suggesting that force had been used to obtain signatures of approval Leo described the nature of the offence committed by Anatolius in desiring its adoption.

" It is a mark of excessive pride and of the absence of modesty to reach out beyond one's proper limits, and by spurning ancient custom to desire to snatch the rights of another, and in the interests of the rank of one individual to violate the primacy of so many metropolitans, in a word to inflict a war of fresh disorder on peaceful provinces, the boundaries of which were determined of old time by regulation of the Nicene council and, finally, in order to dispose of the decrees of the venerable Fathers, to put forward a resolution approved by certain bishops, the validity of which is excluded by the precedent of so long a period of years. For it is alleged that connivance at this sort of thing has been going on for about sixty years, a fact which the aforesaid bishop supposes will help his cause, while he vainly hopes that the thing which no one could have allowed, even if he were bold enough to wish for it, will really be of benefit to himself." [11]

[9] It is sometimes inferred from this letter c. 2, " ordinatorum suorum errorem deserens," that Anatolius had been consecrated by Dioscorus. Yet Anatolius himself, *Inter Leon. Epp.*, No. 53, affirmed that he had been consecrated by members of the " home synod," at which it is unlikely that Dioscorus himself was present. Perhaps Leo only intended to suggest that after the council of A.D. 449 the whole eastern episcopate had succumbed to " monophysitism." At the same time in view of the fact that Anatolius had been for a time the " apocrisiarius " of the see of Alexandria at Constantinople shows that he must have been personally acceptable to Dioscorus.

[10] *Ep.* 105, JK 482 of the same date.

[11] *Ibid.*, 2. " Superbum nimis est et immoderatum ultra proprios terminos tendere et antiquitate calcata alienum ius velle praeripere, atque ut unius crescere dignitas tot metropolitanorum impugnare primatus, quietisque provinciis, et olim sanctae synodi Nicaenae moderatione dispositis bellum nova perturbationis inferre ; atque ut venerabilium Patrum decreta solvantur, quorumdam episcoporum proferre consensum, cui tot annorum series negavit effectum. Nam sexagesimus fere annus huius conniventiae esse iactatur, qua se praedictus episcopus aestimat adiuvari, frustra cupiens id sibi prodesse quod etiam si quisquam ausus est velle, nullus tamen potuit obtinere." Leo obviously refers here to *Conc. Const.*, I, Canon 3, with which he had become acquainted through his legates.

In the subsequent paragraph Leo formally cancelled the canon:

"Resolutions of bishops which are repugnant to the rules of the holy canons laid down at Nicaea, in co-operation with the loyalty of your faith, we annul and cancel with a decision of general application for the future by the authority of blessed Peter the Apostle, since in all ecclesiastical questions we respect those laws which the Holy Ghost defined, through the three hundred and eighteen, to be kept peaceably by all bishops." [12]

So, after apologizing for the length of his letter, Leo concluded by commending his messengers, and by expressing the hope that the Empress will succeed in bringing Anatolius to a better mind.

His letter to Anatolius [13] opened with expressions of satisfaction at the doctrinal achievements of the council, but quickly changed to a tone of sharp reproof. Leo pointed out that apart from what has recently occurred the circumstances of Anatolius' consecration were an unfortunate augury for the future,[14] but in spite of them all might have been well if he had not yet yielded to the temptations of ambition. Not only had he presumed to consecrate Maximus to the see of Antioch, but had actually attempted to infringe the sacred canons of Nicaea. All this was true up to a point, yet in the description of the powers acquired by the see of Constantinople, in virtue of the new canons, Leo appears to be guilty of some inaccuracy.

"It seems," he writes, "that the present is a favourable opportunity for the see of Alexandria to lose the privilege of

[12] *Ibid.*, 3. "Consensiones vero episcoporum, sanctorum canonum apud Nicaeam conditorum regulis repugnantes, unita nobiscum vestrae fidei pietate *in irritum mittimus, et per auctoritatem beati Petri apostoli, generali prorsus definitione cassamus,* in omnibus ecclesiasticis causis his legibus obsequentes quas ad pacificam observantiam omnium sacerdotum, per trecentos decem et octo antistites spiritus sanctus instituit: ita ut etiam si multo plures aliud quam illi statuere decernant, in nulla reverentia sit habendum, quidquid fuerit a praedictorum constitutione diversum." Here we find the principle which moulded Leo's policy in relation to the see of Constantinople for the next few years, namely the divine origin and therefore the finality and irreversibility of the Nicene canons. Notice also that in his view mere numbers do not count.

[13] *Ep.* 106, JK 483, of the same date.

[14] Leo alludes once more to the belief which he appears to have held that Anatolius had been consecrated by Dioscorus.

the second place, and for the church of Antioch to be deprived of its right to the third rank; with the result that, when these provinces are subjected to your authority, all metropolitan bishops are stripped of their rightful office." [15]

Leo shows himself specially indignant that a council which, as he says, was assembled for the express purpose of confirming the Catholic Faith should be diverted to serve the lusts of ambition, as though it were possible to undo what was once appointed by the canons of Nicaea. No mere boast as to the size of the council which has supported his claims can avail Anatolius anything.

"For the Nicene council has been endowed by God with so high a privilege that if ecclesiastical decisions are approved, whether by few or many, whatever is inconsistent with its decrees is altogether devoid of authority." [16]

As to the attitude of the Roman legates Leo affirms that they were well justified in making their protest against so evident a violation of Canon Law, and for the following reason:

"Those holy and venerable fathers, who in the city of Nicaea condemned the impious Arius with his error and laid down laws consisting of ecclesiastical canons to abide till the end of the world, still live on in their decrees among ourselves and throughout the whole earth." [17]

[15] *Ep.* 106, 2, "tanquam opportune se tibi hoc tempus obtulerit, quo secundi honoris privilegium sedes Alexandrina perdiderit, et Antiochena ecclesia proprietatem tertiae dignitatis amiserit: ut, his locis iuri tuo subditis, omnes metropolitani episcopi proprio honore priventur." Leo has in mind, of course, *Conc. Nic.*, Canon 6. "His locis" is here taken to refer to the "dioceses" of Pontus, Asia and Thrace in accordance with the terms of *Conc. Chalc.*, Canon 28; it may, however, refer to the jurisdictions of Alexandria and Antioch, though it is scarcely possible that Leo supposed that the consecration rights of *all* the eastern churches were being handed over to the see of Constantinople.

[16] *Ibid.*, "cum tanto divinitus privilegio Nicaena sit synodus consecrata, ut sive per pauciores, sive per plures ecclesiastica iudicia celebrentur, omni penitus auctoritate sit vacuum, quidquid ab illorum fuerit constitutione diversum." "Pauciores" alludes to the council of A.D. 381; "plures" to Chalcedon itself.

[17] *Ibid.*, 4. "Sancti illi et venerabiles Patres, qui in urbe Nicaena, sacrilego Ario cum sua impietate damnato, mansuras usque in finem mundi leges ecclesiasticorum canonum condiderunt, et apud nos et in toto orbe terrarum in suis constitutionibus vivunt." The idea that the Council of Nicaea still survives in the canons passed by it resembles Leo's insistence on the survival of St. Peter in his see. Cf. *Sermo*. 5, 4, P.L. 54, 155. It is, of course, merely a concrete way of expressing the immutability of its decisions.

After thus reasserting the Roman view as to the permanency and sufficiency of the Nicene legislation he referred to the alleged approval given by certain bishops to the authority of the Constantinopolitan see.[18] Such a canon, he said, was never formally brought to the notice of the Roman see and being invalid from the outset could not now be validated by a belated notification.[19] In conclusion he repeated that assent to the ambitious designs of Anatolius would infringe the rights of the Petrine sees of Alexandria and Antioch.[20] Let the see of Constantinople acquire a better fame by its obedience to the canons.

Last of all there was a personal letter addressed to Julian.[21] The note to which it was a reply appears to have urged Leo to delay no longer in sending his formal approval of the decisions of the council. The Pope was highly indignant at Julian's suggestion that the required assent would be a personal favour to himself and asserted that neither persuasion nor pleading would procure his endorsement of proposals which he held to be destructive of order in the Church. To grant such a request, he says, would mean that both Julian and himself would be involved in responsibility for an illicit act.[22]

In spite of Leo's evident indignation at the use which had been made of the council to obtain approval for the enlarged jurisdiction of the see of Constantinople there is a remarkable tone of restraint in these letters, not least in those addressed

[18] i.e. *Conc. Const.* I, Canon 3.

[19] This seems to support the view that the Roman see was unaware of this canon till Eusebius of Dorylaeum brought it to its notice in A.D. 449; on this question see above, Chap. XIII, p. 304, n. 7.

[20] *Ibid.*, 5, "nihil Alexandrinae sedi eius, quam per sanctum Marcum evangelistam beati Petri discipulum meruit, pereat dignitatis . . . Antiochena quoque ecclesia, in qua primum, praedicante beato apostolo Petro, Christianum nomen exortum est, in paternae constitutionis ordine perseveret et in gradu tertio collocata nunquam se fiat inferior." The thought here bears some resemblance to that of the Roman synodal letter of A.D. 382, on which see above, p. 321, n. 1. Nevertheless the theory that the three greatest sees enjoyed their privileges in virtue of their supposed Petrine origin was not without its difficulties. Cf. Innocent I, *Ep.* 24, 1, JK 310, where he attempts to repudiate the view that the privileges of Antioch are due solely to its secular importance. For the connexion of St. Mark with the see of Alexandria, cf. *Epp.* 102, 4, JK 479; 129, 1, JK 505.

[21] *Ep.* 107, JK 484, of the same date.

[22] *Ibid.*, "quae sine reatu utriusque nostrum, nec mihi concedere, nec tibi liceat obtinere."

to Anatolius and Julian.[23] Nevertheless it must have been a great disappointment to one who had the cause of the peace and unity of the Church so much at heart to find that the high hopes which he had set upon the council as a means of achieving that end were being dashed to the ground. For from the Roman standpoint the elevation of the see of Constantinople to the second place of honour in the Church, with the suggestion that because it was the imperial capital of the East it had a right to share the same privileges as the see of ancient Rome itself, was a direct challenge to the unique position which the latter claimed for itself.

Yet besides showing considerable perspicacity Leo had behaved with remarkable courage in upholding, as against the imperial theory that ecclesiastical precedence should accord with civil importance, the Roman view that nothing less than apostolic foundation could justify the attribution of major jurisdiction to any particular see. The fact that the stand which he made caused such serious concern to the eastern Sovereigns only serves to illustrate the extent of the change which had taken place during the last seventy years or so in the relations between the eastern government and the see of Rome. In the reign of Theodosius I no representatives of the Roman see had been summoned to attend the council of A.D. 381, and yet its canons acquired recognition in the East in virtue of imperial approval and were included in eastern Canon Law. The attitude of the West at that time scarcely mattered. Now, however, all was different. Council, Emperor and bishop hastened to request papal approval for the disciplinary canons passed at Chalcedon: and were considerably embarrassed when that approval was refused. Yet the effect of Leo's refusal, so far from procuring the abandonment of the offending legislation, only served still further to enlarge the already widening gulf between the two great sees of Rome and Constantinople, in respect both of policy and outlook.

That relations between these two sees were already somewhat embittered is suggested by the fact that no replies to Leo's letter were received. In fact the next information to

[23] We may contrast the almost abusive language used by Celestine I in *Ep.* 21, 1 (2), JK 381.

reach him as to what was taking place in the East came from Julian. The story which Julian had to tell was by no means encouraging. He appears to have mentioned further difficulties with the monophysite party in Palestine, a growing wave of sympathy with Eutyches and Dioscorus and, in addition, had hinted that objections were being raised against the " Tome " on the ground that it failed to accord with the doctrine of the fathers. In replying to this letter [24] Leo expressed his regret that monastic circles in Palestine were still rousing opposition to the doctrinal decrees of the council but, while sympathizing with the misfortunes of Juvenal, suggested that the bishop had only himself to blame.[25] As for Eutyches and Dioscorus he urged that measures should be taken to banish them to localities sufficiently distant to prevent communication with their supporters.[26] Turning to the question of the objections which have been raised to his teaching, he wrote that he had forwarded a copy of Athanasius' letter to Epictetus [27] which he believed to be sufficient to refute the teaching of Eutyches and Nestorius alike.

It is possible that Leo would have expressed more definite sympathy with Juvenal, if that bishop had referred his case to the Roman see. Yet instead of doing so the bishop of Jerusalem had simply appealed to Marcian with the happy result that, after the occupation of Jerusalem by a military force, he had been securely reinstated.[28]

It is clear from the foregoing that the task of securing general approval of the decisions of the council in the East was by no means easy. The resistance which was already

[24] *Ep.* 109, JK 486, dated November 25th, A.D. 452.

[25] *Ibid.*, 4. Leo here refers to the injudicious part played by Juvenal at the second council of Ephesus.

[26] Hitherto Eutyches had been residing in his own monastery in the suburbs of Constantinople.

[27] *Ibid.*, 3, " audeant hunc tantae auctoritatis virum (sc. Athanasium) Eutychis et Dioscori sectatores aut imperitiae aut pravitatis arguere, qui praedicationem nostram a doctrina atque intelligentia Patrum iactitant deviare." Leo mentions that Cyril had referred to this letter in writing against Nestorius (Cyril, *Ep.* 39), and a copy of it was probably among those received by Xystus III from Cyril; cf. Xystus, *Ep.* 5, JK 391. It is *Ad Epictetum,* 1, *P.G.* 26, 1049, on which see Bardenhewer, *Gesch. d. altk. lit.*[2], Vol. III, p. 71.

[28] Marcian issued an edict in his favour, dated July 6th, A.D. 452. *Cod. Iust.* I, 3, 23. Cf. Seeck, *Regesten,* p. 397. Mansi, *Concilia,* Vol. VII, 497.

showing itself in Palestine was being reproduced and actively fostered in Egypt, with the result that some difficulty was experienced in filling the see of Alexandria, left vacant by the deposition and banishment of Dioscorus. Proterius, the elected bishop, encountered the most determined opposition and could only maintain his tenure by invoking, like Juvenal, imperial support.[29] Even in Constantinople itself Eutyches still had his supporters[30] and there were rumours that in spite of Anatolius' eagerness to secure the acceptance of the disciplinary canons of the council he was showing signs of wavering in his loyalty to its doctrinal position. These rumours were possibly based on his treatment of Aetius, who at the time of the council had been archdeacon of the city. It seems that Aetius had owed his promotion to the intervention of Pulcheria, and had displaced a certain Andrew in that position.[31]

Now some twelve months after the conclusion of the council Anatolius ordained Aetius to the priesthood, giving him the charge of the urban cemeteries and then reinstated Andrew as archdeacon. This change, which probably took place late in A.D. 452, was reported to Leo by Julian early in the following year.

In consequence of this report Leo decided that immediate intervention in the affairs of the see of Constantinople was urgently necessary and wrote at once to the eastern Sovereigns and to Julian, the sequel of which, as we shall see, was a rapid interchange of correspondence between Constantinople and Rome.

As usual Leo informed Marcian[32] of the anxiety which he felt at hearing this news,[33] and made it clear that he regarded

[29] Evagrius, *H.E.* 2, 5; *P.G.* 86, 2511.

[30] A succession of edicts was issued in the same year prohibiting criticism of the council, i.e. February 7th. *Cod. Iust.* I, 1, 4; Mansi, *op. cit.*, Vol. VII, 476; March 13th, Mansi, *op. cit.*, Vol. VII, 477; July 28th, Mansi, *op. cit.*, Vol. VII, 501.

[31] See Grumel, *Regestes*, Vol. I, Nos. 121, 122. The post of cemetery chaplain no doubt was politically insignificant and probably involved distasteful duties.

[32] *Ep.* 111, JK 487, dated March 10th, A.D. 453.

[33] Leo makes a special grievance of the day of the week on which Aetius was ordained to the priesthood. *Ibid.*, 2, "consecrationem . . . sexta sabbati, traditionis apostolicae aut nescius aut oblitus, inferret." For the Roman rule that ordinations are to take place on Saturday night or Sunday morning cf. *Ep.* 9, 1, JK 406, and see above, Chap. IX, p. 208. For Aetius' part in the council, see p. 293.

the preferment of Andrew as an act prejudicial to the cause of the Catholic Faith. He urged the Emperor to see that Anatolius did not continue to act in this way and pointed out that Andrew should only be restored to the status of a deacon if he were prepared to give proof that he had abandoned the cause of Eutyches; in any case it was appropriate that his rank should be inferior to those who had been loyal to the orthodox faith. He added that the Emperor should regard Julian as the accredited representative of the Roman see.[34]

Equally in writing to Pulcheria [35] Leo suggested that by his promotion of Andrew, Anatolius had shown himself an abetter of heresy and recommended her to support Julian in whatever steps he might recommend for the rectification of the matter.

In thanking Julian [36] for his letter and for sending the information Leo laid emphasis on a particular objection to the suitability of Andrew for the office to which he had been advanced in that he had been one of the accusers of Flavian. He urged Julian to play the part of a watchman in regard to the affairs of the see of Constantinople,[37] by sending frequent reports of what was taking place therein, and incidentally requested that he would advise him as to the attitude which he should adopt in relation to any particular question. Thus he writes:

"At the same time as you, my friend, consult me regarding any affairs as to which you think there is room for doubt, include a suggestion in your reports as to the form which my reply should take: so that apart from the conduct of those cases which ought to be determined by examination, carried out by bishops of individual churches, you may undertake this duty as my legate, lest anywhere either the Nestorian or the Eutychian heresy may revive." [38]

[34] *Ibid.*, 3, "cuius suggestiones . . . tamquam meas audire dignemini."
[35] *Ep.* 112, JK 488, of the same date as the above.
[36] *Ep.* 113, JK 489, of the same date as the above.
[37] *Ibid.*, 2, "speculari de Constantinopolitanae urbis opportunitate non desinas." The phrase "apostolicae sedis . . . quae tibi apud se nutrito catholicam . . . actionem materno iure commendat" appears to imply that Julian himself was of Roman origin.
[38] *Ibid.* "Consulente autem dilectione tua de his in quibus putaveris ambigendum non deerit relationibus tuis meae responsionis instructio; ut sequestrata earum actione causarum, quae in quibusque ecclesiis, praesulum suorum debent cognitione firmari, hanc specialem curam vice mea functus assumas, ne haeresis vel Nestoriana vel Eutychiana in aliqua parte revirescat."

Leo passed on to refer again to the disorders created by monks in Palestine, but he mentioned that he was uncertain whether they had so acted in support of Eutyches or on account of their resentment of the opinions once favoured by Juvenal.[39] As to the case of Aetius he pointed out that neither the documents mentioned by the former archdeacon in his letter nor the "Summary of the Faith," which Julian had stated that he had sent off, had yet reached him.[40] He requested reliable information as to the state of affairs in the Alexandrine church, and desired Julian to indicate the names of responsible persons there to whom letters might be addressed.[41] In conclusion he referred to a copy of the "Tome" which he had sent in response to a request and wished to know if it had arrived safely. Julian was asked to make an accurate translation into Latin of the *Acta* of Chalcedon, which might be the means of clearing up doubt as to the trustworthiness of the existing version.[42]

This group of letters shows a number of points of special interest. In the first place we see the Roman see intervening in the administration of the church of Constantinople in precisely the same manner as it has already intervened in the affairs of the church of Beneventum.[43] Next we observe that Leo felt the situation which had arisen, in view of the pressure being brought to bear upon him to confirm the twenty-eighth canon, to be sufficiently grave to require that he should explicitly renew the credentials of Julian, bishop of Cios, as the *legatus a latere* of the Roman see in Constantinople. It was evidently his intention that he should be promptly

[39] The point is that Leo could not make up his mind whether the monks were rioting in support of the intruder Theodosius, or because they were dissatisfied with Juvenal's loyalty to the Chalcedonian "settlement." Yet in *Ep.* 109, 4 he shows that he regarded them as "monophysites." Perhaps some conflicting information had recently arrived.

[40] *Ep.* 113, 4. "Chartas etiam quae Aetius presbyter ante indicavit esse directas, et Breviarium fidei, quod te misisse significas, necdum ad me noveris pervenisse." The Ballerini, *P.L.* 54, 1433, n. (a) argue that this is a Latin compendium containing *Actio* III and VI of the council preserved in *Cod. Vat.* 1322.

[41] Leo refers to the difficulties experienced by the Chalcedonian Proterius in obtaining possession of his see in face of "monophysite" opposition.

[42] Possibly this reflects dissatisfaction in the West with the doctrinal decisions of the council. If there was any it counted for very little in view of Leo's wholehearted support. On the translation see Chap. XXI, p. 506.

[43] See above, Chap. V, p. 94.

informed of any new development, and he had good reason to wish to be independent of the precarious means of communication provided by the imperial posts. If he now remained silent on the subject of the offending canon it is perhaps because he hoped that his earlier strictures on the subject had been adequate and that the Emperor would see that nothing more would be heard of it.

Yet from the point of view of the eastern government any such withdrawal was unthinkable. The canon had been approved by an imperial general council, the decisions of which had by now received the force of imperial law. Nevertheless, the fact that it was becoming widely known that the Roman see was raising objections was only serving to strengthen the hands of the "opposition," who were already doing all that was possible to resist the acceptance of the council on doctrinal grounds, and this knowledge was proving highly embarrassing to the government. It was for this reason that the Emperor once more took the initiative in seeking to persuade the Roman see to withdraw its objections and to give its unconditional assent to the conciliar decrees as a whole. His letter [44] opened on a note of polite amazement. "We are considerably surprised," he writes, "that since the council of Chalcedon and the despatch of the letter sent by the reverend bishops to your holiness, in which all that took place at the council was reported, your grace has sent no reply whatever of the sort which could be read in the most holy churches and so be generally published; your omission to do so has given rise to considerable doubt in the hearts of certain people, who still follow the erroneous heresy of Eutyches, as to whether your blessedness has actually confirmed the decrees of the holy council or not." [45]

[44] *Inter Leon. Epp.*, No. 110, *P.L.* 54, 1017, dated February 15th, A.D. 453. This letter evidently crossed the one which Leo addressed to Marcian, *Ep.* 111, JK 487, on March 10th.

[45] *Ibid.* "Miramur supra modum quod post Chalcedonensem synodum, et litteras venerabilium episcoporum ad tuam sanctitatem missas, quibus omnia in ipsa synodo acta significabant, nullo prorsus pacto a tua clementia eiusmodi epistolae remissae sunt, quas videlicet in sanctissimis ecclesiis perlectas in omnium oportebat notitiam venire. Quod non nullorum animis qui Eutychetis etiam nunc pravam opinionem et perversitatem sectantur, ambiguitatem multam iniecit, utrum tua beatitudo quae in sancta synodo decreta sunt confirmaverit." "Litteras vener-

The Emperor tactfully praised Leo's energy in the defence of Canon Law and concluded with the suggestion that in view of the attitude of the "opposition" immediate assent to the conciliar decisions would be of the utmost value.

The Emperor's letter was phrased in highly diplomatic terms, and revealed clearly enough the extent of the dependence of the eastern government on the Roman see. It must have reached Rome early in March, A.D. 453,[46] and evoked a number of communications in reply.

The first of these was addressed to the members of council.[47] Its special interest is that it reveals a certain change of attitude on Leo's part. In his earlier letters addressed to the East since the conclusion of the council, he had referred only to the deposition of Dioscorus and Eutyches;[48] now, however, he stated his formal approval of the council's Definition of Faith.[49] Yet if he approved the Definition he was not prepared to move a fraction from his former position in relation to the claims of the see of Constantinople, based on the new synodal canons.

"However much," he writes, "presumptuous vanity may build upon votes of approval given under pressure, and may suppose that its ambitious designs are supported by the name

abilium episcoporum" refers to *Inter Leon. Epp.*, No. 98, *P.L.* 54, 952, which Leo must have received in the earlier part of A.D. 452. The pope had already written to Marcian, Pulcheria and Anatolius on May 22nd, A.D. 452, but hitherto had ignored the synodal report. See *Epp.* 104–6.

[46] Caspar, *Geschichte*, Vol. I, p. 534 and n. 2 appears to be mistaken in dating this group of letters *June* A.D. 453. Cf. Jaffé-Kaltenbrunner, *Regesta*, p. 69 and Seeck, *Regesten*, pp. 396, 398.

[47] *Ep.* 114, JK 490, dated March 21st. To address a letter to the council sixteen months after the dispersal of its members is, of course, of the nature of a polite fiction.

[48] e.g. in *Epp.* 104–6, JK 481–3. The view formerly taken by Leo was that the purpose of the council was simply to arrange for the reconciliation of those who had "lapsed" at Ephesus in A.D. 449 and to pass judgment on the unrepentant.

[49] *Ibid.*, 1, "non ambigo definitionem sanctae synodi, quae ob confirmationem fidei in Chalcedonensi civitate celebrata est, toto corde me fuisse complexum." He goes on to suggest that if there is any doubt, then it is the fault of Anatolius who must have suppressed his letters. Perhaps there was some truth in this. It was evidently against Anatolius' interests to publish the fact that the Roman see objected to the twenty-eighth canon. Yet it should be noticed that Leo here adopts the very view of the purpose of the council which formerly he had emphatically repudiated. Cf. *Ep.* 93, 1 and 2, JK 473, and above Chap. XI, p. 284.

of councils, everything which is at variance with the canons of the aforesaid fathers will be null and void in effect." [50]

He concluded by pointing out that anyone who read his letters might see that the Apostolic see showed due respect for those canons and that he was "the guardian of the Catholic Faith and of the decrees of the fathers." [51]

Writing to the Emperor himself [52] Leo again displayed considerable tact. He began by ascribing to him royal authority and priestly zeal and then suggested that "all sacrilegious error will be deprived of its power . . . if the fact that the Apostolic see has approved the definition of the holy council of Chalcedon is published throughout all the churches," [53] although, he adds, there was really no doubt on the point, seeing that the council had given its assent to the "Tome." [54] As before, Leo laid the chief blame for the present misunderstanding on Anatolius, and on his failure to publish the letter which he had received from the Roman see.[55] He mentioned that he had been informed by Julian of the disorders created in Palestine by the opponents of the council, and of the measures which had been taken to suppress them, and pointed out that Julian should be regarded as his own accredited representative.[56]

As for the twenty-eighth canon Leo is content with an indirect allusion to the subject.[57] Evidently he realized that

[50] *Ibid.*, 2. "Quantumlibet enim extortis assentationibus sese instruat vanitatis elatio, et appetitus suos conciliorum aestimet nomine roborandos, infirmum atque irritum erit quidquid a praedictorum Patrum canonibus discreparit."

[51] *Ibid.*, "me . . . catholicae fidei et paternarum constitutionum esse custodem."

[52] *Ep.* 115, JK 491, of the same date as the above.

[53] *Ibid.*, 1, "omnes vires sacrilegus error amitteret . . . si per universas ecclesias definitiones sancti synodi Chalcedonensis apostolicae sedi placuisse doceantur."

[54] *Ibid.*, 1, "de quo quidem ratio non fuit ambigendi, cum ei fidei omnium subscribentium consensus accesserit, quae a me secundum formam apostolicae doctrinae ac paternae traditionis emissa est."

[55] i.e. *Ep.* 106, JK 483. As we have seen Anatolius could scarcely be expected to be very eager to publish a letter of this sort.

[56] *Ibid.*, 2. "Fratri autem meo Juliano episcopo noverit vestra clementia hoc me proprie delegasse, ut quidquid illic ad custodiam fidei pertinere probaverit, meo nomine vestrae fiducialiter suggerat pietati."

[57] *Ibid.*, 1, "cum vobis religiossime placere cognosco, ut et fides Nicaena suam teneat firmitatem, et privilegia ecclesiarum illibata permaneant." Yet from the eastern standpoint the latter requirement was satisfied if the principle underlying *Conc. Const.* I, Canon 3 was enforced so far as the see of Constantinople was concerned.

this was a time to emphasize agreement rather than difference of opinion. The same indirectness is noticeable in a parallel letter addressed to Pulcheria.[58] Writing to Julian[59] at the same time the Pope explained what action he had taken in deference to the Emperor's wishes and acknowledged the receipt of a copy of the edict published against the rebellious Palestinian monks,[60] and of the letter from the Empress Eudocia which laid the blame for the disturbances on the conduct of the archimandrites.[61] He pointed out further that at the request of Marcian, addressed to him secretly, he had himself written to Eudocia and persuaded her son-in-law, the Emperor Valentinian III, to do the same,[62] adding "if those who oppose the council will not accept the teaching contained in the 'Tome' let them acknowledge the doctrine of Athanasius, Theophilus and Cyril, with which it is in all respects identical."[63] So far as the case of Aetius is concerned, he urged the need of patience and stated that, as he had emphasized in his letter addressed to Marcian, the former archdeacon of Constantinople was assured of the support of the Roman see.[64]

In answer to Julian's explicit request that he should write to Anatolius he explained that he had refrained from doing so, in view of what he had heard from the messenger who had recently brought the official notification of the election of Euxitheus to the see of Thessalonica,[65] namely that the bishop

[58] *Ep.* 116, JK 492, of the same date. Leo appears to imply that he had heard that Pulcheria had intervened in the affairs of Palestine on her own account.

[59] *Ep.* 117, JK 493, of the same date.

[60] Mansi, *Concilia,* Vol. VII, 501. Seeck, *Regesten,* p. 337.

[61] Possibly the Empress made little of her own responsibility in the matter.

[62] It was not the first time that Leo had invoked the support of the western Emperor, see above, Chap. XI, p. 264.

[63] *Ibid.,* 3. "Cum quibus ita fidei nostrae forma concordat, ut in nullo a nobis discrepet, qui se illis consentire profitetur." Leo probably alludes to Athanasius, *Ep. ad Epictetum,* 1. *P.G.* 26, 1049; to some work of Theophilus now lost, possibly quoted in *Ep.* 165, *Catena* 8, and to the letters of Cyril endorsed by the council (see above, Chap. XII, p. 292). Superficially, Leo seems for a moment to abdicate the claims of the Roman see to a supreme *magisterium* in the sphere of doctrine.

[64] *Ibid.,* 4. "Filio nostro Aetio presbytero in suo maerore compatimur." Cf. *Ep.* 111, JK 487.

[65] Euxitheus' election had taken place after the council, since Juvenal of Heraclea is mentioned as Anastasius' representative. Cf. Mansi, *op. cit.,* Vol. VI, 580.

of Constantinople had been summoning a synod, at which he invited the approval of bishops from Eastern Illyricum to the canons of Chalcedon.[66] In the final sentence of this letter Leo revealed the highly delicate nature of the situation.

"I have composed two letters to the council at the same time; one to which I have appended copies of my letter addressed to Bishop Anatolius and the other which lacks the addition of those copies; leaving it to your judgment to decide which of the two you will present to his Grace the Emperor and which you will keep to yourself." [67]

This appears to suggests that although Leo was uncertain of his ground yet his chief anxiety was to conciliate Constantinopolitan feeling as far as he could. What mattered to him was the peace and unity of the Church.

These letters had scarcely left Rome when a further communication arrived from Julian, informing Leo that irregularities on the part of monks were not confined to Palestine but were becoming prevalent in the province of Cappadocia, where the metropolitan of Caesarea, Thalassius, who was already suspected of being a supporter of Eutyches owing to the part which he had played at Ephesus in A.D. 449, had allowed monks to exercise the office of public preaching. In his reply [68] Leo pointed out that while it belonged to the civil power to deal with riotous behaviour, it was equally the duty of the episcopate to suppress illicit preaching, and requested Julian to guide him as to the advisability of addressing a direct admonition to Thalassius on the subject, and of enclosing relevant documents.[69] At the same time he urged

[66] *Ibid.*, 5. "Anatolium episcopum post coercitionem nostram (*Ep.* 106, JK 483) in suae praesumptionis adeo temeritate persistere, ut Illyricianos episcopos, ut sibi subscriberent, conveniret." Cf. Grumel, *Regestes*, No. 132. But from the eastern standpoint, in view of the edict of A.D. 421, *Cod. Theod.* XVI, ii, 45, Anatolius' action was reasonably justifiable.

[67] *Ibid.* "Duas a pari ad synodum epistolas feci: unam cui exemplaria epistolae meae ad Anatolium episcopum datae subdi feci, alteram, quae exemplaria subdita non haberet; tuo permittens arbitrio, ut quam dandam esse clementissimo principi duxeris, hanc tradas, altera apud te retenta."

[68] *Ep.* 118, JK 494, dated April 2nd, A.D. 453.

[69] i.e. no doubt Celestine I, *Ep.* 21, JK 381.

that whatever measures might be taken to suppress disorder, infliction of capital punishment ought to be excluded.[70]

During the next six months correspondence between Rome and Constantinople was in suspense, apart from those letters in which reference was made to the Paschal Question. At long last the eastern government had obtained the formal approbation of the Roman see to the Definition of Chalcedon, and from the political standpoint that was all that mattered. It made little difference in practice if that see persisted in its opposition to the twenty-eighth canon for, so far as the "dioceses" in question were concerned, that canon was already in force. The real significance of the events which had taken place since the conclusion of the council was to show that, if the Roman see depended on the support of the eastern Emperor to maintain its doctrinal prestige and its claims in the sphere of jurisdiction, the eastern Emperor was no less dependent on the Roman see for support in the maintenance of imperial unity.

The council of Chalcedon, as we have seen, had been a victory for the "dyophysite" view of the Incarnation in the sphere of doctrine. But from Leo's point of view it had been more. It had been a personal triumph. Further proof of this is to be found in the letter which he received early in June of A.D. 453 from Maximus, consecrated bishop of Antioch after the deposition of Domnus by the second council of Ephesus.

Probably the main topic in the letter of Maximus was the deprivation which his see had suffered, in consequence of the canon passed by the council of Chalcedon, of his jurisdiction over the Palestinian provinces which, as we have seen, had thereby been assigned to the jurisdiction of the see of Jerusalem.[71] In answering Maximus[72] Leo took the opportunity

[70] *Ep.* 118, 2, "quem (sc. Marcianum) superna inspiratione ita instruendum esse confido, ut et disciplina inquietos revocari, et a sanguine eorum iubeat abstineri." Cf. the desire expressed by the Roman synod of A.D. 378 that the clergy should be exempt from torture, *P.L.* 13, 584; Ambrose, *Ep.* 21, 2, *P.L.* 14, 1045.

[71] *Ep.* 119, 4, "in Ephesina synodo . . . Juvenalis episcopus ad obtinendum Palestinae provinciae principatum credidit se posse proficere, et insolentes ausus per commentitia scripta firmare." Unhappily history is silent as to the nature of these fictitious writings.

[72] *Ep.* 119, JK 495, dated June 11th, A.D. 453.

of referring to the information which he had received (probably through Julian) that some were incapable of distinguishing the error of Nestorius from that of Eutyches.[73] He urged that Maximus should consider the teaching of St. Peter:

"Which he proclaimed by means of his consistent preaching throughout the whole world, and which by a special exercise of his authority he laid down in the cities of Antioch and Rome; so that you may recognize that he who still reigns in the home of his martyrdom insists on those principles which he handed on as he had received them from the Truth Itself which he had confessed."[74]

Therefore, he insisted, no divergence from the truth of the Gospel either towards Nestorianism or towards Eutychianism ought to be permitted among the churches of the "Diocese" of the East, since "The Rock of the Catholic Faith, the name of which the blessed Apostle Peter received from the Lord, is not marked by any trace of either heresy."[75]

Leo expressed the wish that Maximus would keep him frequently informed of the state of the churches of the East and would confidently uphold the privileges of the see of Antioch.[76] He assured him that the copy of Cyril's letter with reference to the aggressive claims of the see of Jerusalem presented at the first council of Ephesus was accurate, as had

[73] *Ibid.*, 1, "non habentes intelligentiam qua . . . blasphemiam Nestorii ab Eutychis impietate distinguant." Leo probably alludes to those who regarded the Council of Chalcedon as a capitulation to Nestorianism.

[74] *Ibid.*, 2, "quem praecipuus apostolorum omnium beatissimus Petrus, per totum quidem mundum uniformi praedicatione, sed speciali magisterio in Antiochena et Romana urbe fundavit: ut illum in suae glorificationis domicilio praeeminentem ea intelligas reposcere instituta, quae tradidit, sicut ab ipsa quam confessus est veritate suscepit." The allusion is evidently to St. Peter's doctrine, as illustrated by Matthew xvi. 16.

[75] *Ibid.*, "catholicae fidei petra, cuius cognomen beatus apostolus Petrus sumpsit a Domino, nullum recipit ab utraque impietate vestigium."

[76] *Ibid.*, 3, "cum te deceat . . . nosque saepius de profectu ecclesiarum tuis relationibus quid agatur instruere. Dignum est enim te apostolicae sedis in hac sollicitudine esse consortem, et ad agendi fiduciam privilegia tertiae sedis agnoscere, quae in nullo cuiusquam ambitione minuentur." Leo alludes to *Conc. Nic.*, Canon 6, and perhaps also to the *Decretum Gelasianum*, 3, see above, p. 321, n. 1. It is plain that he deliberately disregards *Conc. Chalc.*, Canon 28, in virtue of which the see of Antioch was to be reckoned as the "quarta sedes." He has also in mind the recent award made by the latter council in favour of the see of Jerusalem, see above, Chap. XIII, p. 303.

been ascertained by its comparison with the copy preserved in the Roman archives.[77]

No resolutions of any council which infringe the provisions of Nicaea, he said, possessed any validity, as had been shown by the protest uttered by the legates of the Roman see at the council of Chalcedon against those canons which were not concerned with questions of faith. This, Leo pointed out, was further indicated by the letter which he addressed to Anatolius,[78] and of which he now enclosed a copy, with the intention that it should be published throughout the "Diocese" of the East. He concluded by urging that Maximus should suppress illicit preaching on the part of monks or laity, on the ground that preaching was a function reserved to the priesthood.[79]

On the same day he despatched a further letter to Theodoret, bishop of Cyrrhus,[80] which we may regard as a belated reply to the appeal [81] which he had received nearly three years previously.

After expressing his joy at the vindication of Theodoret's orthodoxy through the verdict of the council of Chalcedon [82] he pointed out that the opposition encountered by the faith defined by the Roman see had actually proved to be advantageous in that it had served to bring out the truth into a clearer light, adding that he regarded the council as a kind of renewal of the Incarnation.[83] He then passed on to call attention to the part played by the Roman see in defence of the orthodox faith.

"Now," he writes, "the brightness of the Sun of Righteousness, darkened for a time in the East by the heavy clouds (arising from the teaching) of Nestorius and Eutyches has

[77] *Ep.* 119, 4. The letter itself has unfortunately not survived. The allusion is valuable as pointing to the practice of preserving letters of doctrinal or disciplinary importance at Rome. Cf. *Ep.* 69, 1, JK 452.

[78] *Ep.* 106, JK 483.

[79] *Ibid.*, 6, "praeter eos qui sunt Domini sacerdotes, nullus sibi docendi et praedicandi ius audeat vindicare, sive ille monachus, sive sit laicus." Cf. *Ep.* 118, 2, JK 494.

[80] *Ep.* 120, JK 496, dated June 11th, A.D. 453.

[81] *Inter Leon. Epp.*, No. 52. *P.L.* 54, 848, on which see above, Chap. X, p. 244.

[82] *Ibid.*, 1, "agnovimus dilectionem tuam, superno adiutorio, nobiscum tam Nestorianae impietatis quam Eutychianae vesaniae exstitisse victricem."

[83] *Ibid.*, 2. "Secunda est post adventum Domini haec orbi festivitas."

shone forth anew with unsullied radiance from the West, where He has placed the high zenith of His course in the persons of His Apostles and teachers." [84]

Dioscorus, "that second Pharaoh," he added, had met with fitting retribution for his offences, and particularly for his novel and unheard of presumption.[85] As to the doctrinal Definition of Chalcedon it could not be a subject for doubt or reconsideration, nor could concessions be made either to Nestorians or to Eutychians. Not that there could be any doubt as to the orthodoxy of Theodoret himself; the confidence in him already expressed by the Apostolic see was enough to show that he was beyond suspicion.[86] Yet the persistence of error demanded continued vigilance and made it necessary that Theodoret should report frequently to the Roman see the course of events. Finally Leo referred to the disciplinary legislation of Chalcedon and recommended Theodoret to consult the letter which he had addressed to Maximus, and to note his admonitions of the subject of preaching by monks.[87]

The letter illustrates Leo's tireless zeal for the conversion and reconciliation of all who still remained hostile to the doctrinal standard of the council, a feature recurring again and again in the correspondence of his later years. It is especially apparent in a group of letters belonging to this time,[88] bearing on the situation in Palestine.

The first of these is addressed to the Empress Eudocia [89] at Jerusalem. Referring to the disturbances which have taken

[84] *Ibid.* "Solis iustitiae iubar, densis per Orientem Nestorii et Eutychis nebulis impeditum, pure ab Occidente resplenduit, ubi culmen summum in apostolis et doctoribus principaliter collocarit." Cf. I Cor. xii. 28.

[85] *Ibid.*, 3, "nova atque inaudita prius atque incredibili audacia inferre contra suum caput est molitus iniuriam." The allusion is probably to the attempt made by Dioscorus and others to excommunicate Leo.

[86] *Ibid.*, 5. "Deus noster, cuius invincibilis veritas ab omni haereseos macula mundum te, secundum sedis apostolicae iudicium, demonstravit."

[87] *Ibid.*, 6, "hoc specialiter statuentes ut praeter Domini sacerdotes nullus audeat praedicare, seu monachus, sive ille sit laicus."

[88] *Epp.* 123, 124 and 139, JK 499, 500 and 514. The last of these is dated September 4th, A.D. 454; the first June 15th, A.D. 453, the second being without a date. Yet in view of the allusion in *Ep.* 117, 3, JK 493, dated March 21st of that year to a letter already sent to the Empress Eudocia, it seems not impossible that the date of *Ep.* 123 is corrupt and should perhaps read JAN. instead of JUL.

[89] *Ep.* 123, JK 499, usually dated June 15th, A.D. 453.

place there in consequence of the intransigent attitude of the monophysite monks to the Chalcedonian Definition, Leo insisted that the time had come to take strong measures.[90] He pointed out that the Catholic Faith condemned Eutyches and Dioscorus alike, and that he relied on the support of the Empress herself in bringing the opponents of the council to a better mind. He requested her to send him information as to her success in achieving this result.[91] The second letter is directed to the monks themselves.[92] Referring to the strong feeling of opposition to the Christological doctrine of the "Tome," he suggested that it had probably arisen as a consequence of some mistranslation,[93] and he assured them that in none of his writings had he departed in any way from the confession of the holy fathers.[94] In the latter part of his letter he set forth at length the dyophysite view of the Incarnation, and emphasized not only the necessity of a true Incarnation to provide for a real Atonement, but on the uniqueness of our Lord's incarnate activity.[95]

Finally he expressed his deep indignation at acts of violence which had resulted in the deaths of priests and bishops, pointing out that such conduct was totally inconsistent with the peace of the religious life. He concluded with an earnest appeal to the monks to abandon their errors.[96]

For some months no news whatever came from the East. Even Julian remained silent. This continued absence of

[90] Leo also calls attention to the bearing of the sacred sites of our Lord's incarnate life on the truth that the humanity which He assumed was a real one. *Ibid.*, 1, "quos enim . . . nec ipsa sacratorum locorum testimonia commovebant, quid eis nisi abruptum periculum timeretur?" For this allusion to the sacred sites cf. *Ep.* 113, 3, JK 489.

[91] It is most unlikely that Eudocia was willing to do anything of the sort, seeing that she was probably responsible for a considerable share in creating the trouble.

[92] *Ep.* 124, JK 500, without a date.

[93] *Ibid.*, 1, "aut imperiti, ut apparet, interpretes aut maligni, quaedam vos aliter intelligere, quam a me sunt praedicata, fecerunt, non valentes in Graecum eloquium apte et proprie Latina transferre." The supposition was possibly not without foundation, and illustrates the growing cleavage between East and West.

[94] *Ibid.*, "in nullo a sanctorum Patrum confessione (sc. Nicaena) discessi."

[95] *Ibid.*, 2–7.

[96] *Ibid.*, 8, "doleo vos evangelicae et apostolicae doctrinae, ut audio, resultare, exagitando seditionibus civitates, conturbando ecclesias, nec solum iniurias sed etiam caedes presbyteris atque episcopis inferendo."

information evidently caused Leo considerable anxiety and led him to address a strongly worded reproof to his representative.[97] Perhaps the temporary cessation of correspondence was to be accounted for by the simple fact that there was no news to be sent such as would have been acceptable to the Roman see.

When at last the long-expected report from Julian arrived it was accompanied by two letters from the Emperor. Marcian informed Leo that the opposition in Palestine had been finally crushed and that Juvenal had been restored to his see. At the same time he bewailed the continuance of monophysite resistance to the council in Egypt. The contents of Julian's letter must have been similar, though there were some additional points, including mention of the fact that Proterius, the successor of Dioscorus in the see of Alexandria, had addressed a letter to the Roman see in proof of his orthodoxy.

He also appears to have alluded to a recent meeting of the "Home Synod" at Constantinople at which Leo's letter to the council had been read, though with the significant omission of the second part, in which Leo had repudiated the twenty-eighth canon,[98] and to have signified that Aetius had been declared innocent of the charge laid against him.[99]

In replying to the Emperor[100] Leo wrote of his satisfaction at the restoration of order in Palestine,[101] and of his anxiety as to the security of the Church in Egypt.[102] At the same time he thanked Julian[103] for his information regarding Juvenal's restoration, and the satisfaction promised by Proterius which, he said, he was all the more anxious to receive, so that the see of Alexandria might lose none of the privileges which

[97] *Ep.* 125, JK 501, dated June 25th, A.D. 453. *Ibid.,* "quibusdam . . . scriptis meis, id est, per . . . Rodanum . . . datis, nullum responsum tuae fraternitatis accepi." Leo refers to *Epp.* 115 and 117, JK 491, 493.

[98] The letter was *Ep.* 114, JK 490.

[99] There is nothing to show what these charges were. We may surmise that the whole affair arose from a personal difference between Anatolius and his former archdeacon.

[100] *Ep.* 126, JK 502, dated January 9th, A.D. 454.

[101] *Ibid.,* "compressis errantium motibus . . . Juvenali ad sacerdotii sui sedem tandem licuit, non iam resultante populo, sed desiderante, remeare."

[102] *Ibid.,* "adhuc apud Aegyptum caligo residet."

[103] *Ep.* 127, JK 503, dated January 10th, A.D. 454. Leo on this occasion answered Julian's letter as soon as it arrived (*ibid.,* 1). Possibly the Emperor's second letter reached him by the same post.

belonged to it in virtue of Canon Law.[104] He passed on to allude to his uncertainty as to the correct date for the observance of Easter in the year A.D. 455 and requested Julian to urge the Emperor to prevent any divergence on the point arising between the Roman and the Eastern churches.[105] Alluding to Julian's information regarding the recent synod at Constantinople, he deplored the omission of the passage in which he had reproved Anatolius' ambition,[106] and expressed his satisfaction at the favourable verdict accorded to Aetius.[107] Finally he mentioned the delicate subject of correspondence with Anatolius, and the Emperor's request that, in virtue of the promise made by the bishop to give satisfaction in regard to his belief, he would be willing to renew friendly relations.[108]

No doubt Leo would have been pleased to be reassured as to Anatolius' orthodoxy, but what he most desired, and hitherto had treated as indispensable, was a formal withdrawal of claims based on the twenty-eighth canon.

It is clear that the reserve of the Roman see in regard to Anatolius was causing the eastern government some embarrassment, as is shown by a further letter received by Leo from Marcian at the beginning of March, imploring him to show some gesture of friendship towards the see of Constantinople. In his reply [109] Leo pointed out that the sole responsibility for any breach of unity rests with Anatolius himself, who had consistently failed to answer Leo's correspondence [110] and to inform him as to the present position regarding the case of the former archdeacon, Aetius. The fact was, Leo added, that Anatolius had not yet given any sign of abandoning his

[104] *Ep.* 127, 1, "sedis suae privilegia, paternae antiquitatis exemplo, iuxta canonum illibata iura possideat." Leo evidently alludes to *Conc. Nic.*, Canon 6, and to *Conc. Chalc.*, Canon 28.

[105] *Ibid.*, 2, "ne vel apud nos vel apud Orientales nascatur ex hac parte diversitas."

[106] *Ibid.*, 3, "cum maxime omnibus innotescere debuisset (sc. Anatolius) improbum a nobis ambitum notatum fuisse."

[107] *Ibid.* "Aetium . . . gratulamur, cognitione habita, in omnibus fuisse purgatum."

[108] *Ibid.*, "interveniens pro Anatolio episcopo, ut nostri illi animi gratia praebeatur, quoniam correctionem eius promittit et in omnibus se satisfacturum esse quae ad fidei observantiam pertinent pollicetur."

[109] *Ep.* 128, JK 504, dated March 9th, A.D. 454. It will be remembered that Marcian had been pressing for some such gesture on Leo's part since the end of the previous year.

[110] i.e. *Ep.* 106, JK 483.

ambitions.[111] If the bishop would only do this, and show himself ready to conform to Canon Law, Leo would be ready at once to receive him as his colleague.[112]

The effect of this outspoken remonstrance was immediate, and in the course of May a letter arrived from Anatolius,[113] which went some way in the direction of satisfying the Pope's demands. Anatolius began by assuring Leo of the anxiety which he had felt by reason of the cessation of letters from the Roman see, which was only increased by the fact that that see continued to correspond with others.[114] But as soon as the Emperor had shown him Leo's letter,[115] he had hastened to fulfil Leo's wishes. He went on to say that Aetius, after giving satisfaction,[116] had been restored and that Andrew, who had been promoted, not for himself but in virtue of his rank, had been excommunicated, together with other adversaries of Flavian and supporters of Eutyches, although they had given satisfaction by subscription to Leo's letter.[117] He therefore hoped to receive a letter from Leo immediately as a sign that the breach had been healed. Finally he referred to the controversial subject of the twenty-eighth canon.

"The fault is not mine," he wrote, "who from my earliest days am one who has loved ease and repose in modest humility. It was the clergy of the church of Constantinople who were eager for this proposal, and were supported by the most reverend bishops of those provinces, who were in agreement with them: though even so the validation of their acts and

[111] *Ibid.*, "nihil de ambitionis poenitudine voluerit profiteri."
[112] *Ibid.*, "in omnibus quae sunt Domino placitura consortium eius amplectar."
[113] *Inter Leon. Epp.*, Nos. 132. *P.L.* 54, 1082. Grumel, *Regestes,* No. 133, who assigns the letter to April or May, A.D. 454. The Ballerini, *ad loc.* suggests that the Latin text is a version provided by Anatolius himself.
[114] *Ibid.*, 1, "maxime cum mihi, quae scripta essent a vobis aliis, ostenderentur epistolae," e.g. *Ep.* 119, JK 495 possibly.
[115] i.e. *Ep.* 128, JK 504. It seems likely that Anatolius acted as he did under pressure.
[116] *Ibid.*, 2, "omne quod episcopi nostri est modeste faciens ipse responsum." This again appears to suggest that the difference between Aetius and his bishop was of a personal nature. The passage is evidently corrupt.
[117] *Ibid.* Anatolius refers presumably to the subscription to the "Tome" given in November, A.D. 450. Cf. *Inter Leon. Epp.*, No. 77; *P.L.* 54, 906, and Grumel, *Regestes,* No. 118.

confirmation of them was altogether reserved to your blessedness's authority." [118]

It was an ingenious letter carefully composed with an eye to the susceptibilities of the Roman see. Yet it scarcely concealed the one relevant fact, namely that the twenty-eighth canon was to all intents and purposes already in force, and that the absence of Roman approval made no practical difference. It is most unlikely that the letter succeeded in deceiving one so astute as Leo, yet it evoked from him a generous answer.[119] He pointed out that he would have had the same confidence in Anatolius' zeal for the protection of the Catholic Faith and the preservation of Nicene discipline as he had had in the teaching of John (Chrysostom), in the authority of Atticus, in the zeal of Proclus and in the faith of Flavian if attempts had not been made to infringe the Nicene canons. So when, as he pointed out, he received no reply to his letter on the subject, it was Anatolius himself who was responsible for the cessation of correspondence.[120] Now, however, he rejoiced that through the intervention of the Emperor the breach had been healed. As to the case of Aetius and Andrew, while he showed his pleasure that the former had been restored to favour he suggested that now that Andrew has been removed from the office of archdeacon, together with Eufrates, who had been one of Flavian's accusers, Anatolius should ordain them priests, if they present a written repudiation of Nestorianism and Eutychianism, and that the same conditions should apply to others who had lapsed into error.[121]

Referring to the explanation offered by Anatolius regarding the twenty-eighth canon, Leo suggested that the proposal could never have been made without Anatolius' approval, but

[118] *Ep.* 132, 4, " nullam esse culpam in me, homine qui semper otium et quietem in humilitate me continens ab ineunte mea aetate dilexerim, sed Constantinopolitanae ecclesiae reverentissimus clerus est, qui hoc habuit studium et istarum partium religiosissimi sacerdotes qui in hoc fuere concordes et sibi pariter concordes; cum et sic gestorum vis omnis et confirmatio auctoritati vestrae beatitudinis fuerit reservata." It is doubtful whether Anatolius was wholly sincere in writing these words.

[119] *Ep.* 135, JK 509, dated May 29th, A.D. 454.

[120] *Ibid.*, 1. " Ad quas (sc. litteras meas) cum non rescriberes, ipse te a colloquii mei consortio separasti."

[121] This requirement reflects the relative unimportance of the priesthood compared with the diaconate at this time.

The letter is chiefly concerned with the subject of doctrine and reproduces arguments in favour of dyophysite Christology which we have already noticed elsewhere, particularly in regard to the appeal which Leo makes to the sacred sites of Palestine as evidence of the reality of our Lord's humanity.[135] In general it is a defence of the standpoint of the "Tome" to which Juvenal himself appears to have referred in an earlier letter.[136]

The reign of Marcian was drawing to a close. Pulcheria had already passed to her rest, and the aged and now lonely Emperor could regard with satisfaction the measure of success which had rewarded his efforts to maintain the ecclesiastical unity of his Empire. But the forces which were productive of schism, though suppressed, were still active and even so seemingly trivial a question as the fixing of the Paschal Feast was sufficient to reveal the growing cleavage between the churches of the East and the Apostolic see of the West. The special interest of the Paschal question as it arose during Leo's pontificate, which next claims our attention, is that it shows his capacity for dealing with the delicate problem of meeting the rival claims of œcumenical principle and local Roman custom.

[135] Cf. *Ep.* 123, 1, JK 499.
[136] *Ibid.*, 4, "scripta mea ad sanctae memoriae Flavianum data, quorum mentionem ipse fecisti."

CHAPTER XV

LEO AND THE CHURCHES OF THE EAST. 7

THE PASCHAL QUESTION

THE problem of ascertaining the correct date for the celebration of Easter in A.D. 455 was not a new one so far as the Roman see was concerned, nor in fact was it the first time that the question had arisen in the course of Leo's pontificate. It actually arose as early as the year A.D. 444, and formed the subject of letters addressed by him to Cyril of Alexandria [1] and to one of his own suffragans, Paschasinus, bishop of Lilybaeum in Sicily.[2]

As early as the council of Nicaea, as part of the Emperor Constantine I's general policy of establishing doctrinal and disciplinary uniformity throughout the Empire, an attempt had been made to secure the universal observance of Easter on the same day, but in spite of this divergencies of reckoning still remained, more particularly between the mode of calculation in use at Rome and that employed by the see of Alexandria.[3] By Leo's time some of the causes of this difference had been removed, yet the fact that the Roman see continued to insist on March 22nd and April 21st [4] as the extreme limits of incidence for the Paschal feast, as against March 22nd and April 25th fixed by the see of Alexandria,[5] was cer-

[1] The existence of this letter is to be inferred from *Inter Leon. Epp.*, No. 3, *P.L.* 54, 606. The document given in *P.L.* 54, 601, JK 400, purports to be Cyril's reply. Krusch, *Studien z. christ.-mittelalt. Chronologie*, p. 345, n. 1, shows that it is a later forgery of western origin.

[2] JK 401. Its existence is equally to be inferred from the above. Paschasinus later headed the Roman legation to Constantinople, A.D. 451, and took a leading part in the debates at Chalcedon. See above Chap. XII and XIII.

[3] Details of these modes of reckoning are given below in Additional Note, *The early history of the Paschal controversy*, pp. 358ff.

[4] Leo refers to these dates in *Ep.* 121, 2, "Siquidem ab undecimo kalendarum Aprilium, usque in undecimum kalendarum Maiarum, legitimum spatium sit praefixum, intra quod omnium varietatum necessitas concluditur: ut Pascha Dominicum nec prius possimus habere nec tardius." This tradition was held in Rome to be of Petrine origin.

[5] *D.T.C., Pâques*, Vol. XI, col. 1958. Cf. Krusch, *op. cit.*, pp. 64f.

tain to involve difficulty, if the date prescribed by Alexandria should happen to fall outside the limits recognized at Rome.

The year A.D. 444 was just such an occasion. For that year Cyril of Alexandria gave notice of April 23rd as the correct date [6] and, in spite of Leo's inquiry,[7] continued to insist that it alone could be regarded as the right day. This was a direct challenge to the Roman principle that April 21st was the latest possible date for the celebration of the festival. Yet since at this time it was generally believed in Rome and elsewhere that, in virtue of the decisions of Nicaea, the see of Alexandria was in possession of a prescriptive right in the matter, and that in consequence its ruling could not be lightly disregarded, the Roman see felt it necessary to proceed with some caution. It was for this reason that Leo wrote to ask the advice of Paschasinus,[8] who by reason of his canonical allegiance to the Roman see, and of his acquaintance with the eastern standpoint might be expected to be able, if anyone was, to find a way out of the impasse.

In his reply [9] Paschasinus pointed out that the date prescribed by the see of Alexandria, namely April 23rd, arose from the fact that the year in question, i.e. A.D. 444 was reckoned by that see to be an "embolic" one.[10] In support of his conviction that the Alexandrine date was correct he mentioned a similar divergence between the Roman and Alexandrine dates which had occurred in A.D. 417 in the pontificate of Zosimus, when in spite of the fact that the see of Alexandria had indicated April 22nd as the day to be observed, March 25th had been kept at Rome and throughout

[6] *Inter Leon. Epp.*, Fragmentum, *P.L.* 54, 601. "Simul Pascha celebremus kal. IX Maii."

[7] Cf. *Inter. Leon. Epp.*, No. 3, 1. *P.L.* 54, 606. "Quod ab Alexandrinae ecclesiae antistite beatitudini vestrae rescriptum est."

[8] *Ibid.* "Iubere dignata est corona vestra, ut quid paschalis supputationis veritas anni post hunc futuri haberet, sacrosanctis auribus vestris exiguitas mea intimaret."

[9] *Inter Leon. Epp.*, No. 3. *P.L.* 54, 606.

[10] The term "embolic" (*ibid.*, "anni embolismi") was applied to a year, which required the intercalation of an additional month, in order to adjust the difference between the lunar and the solar kalendar. The question as to the introduction of these intercalations became the cause of much divergence between different modes of reckoning. Cf. Duchesne, *La question de la Pâque au concile de Nicée* in *Revue des questions historiques* (1880), p. 17, and Additional Note to this chapter, pp. 358ff.

the Roman ecclesiastical province.[11] Yet on that occasion proof of the correctness of the Alexandrine date was provided by the failure of the baptismal spring in the Sicilian town of Meltinas on March 24th, so that baptisms had to be postponed till April 21st when, as Paschasinus alleged, it spontaneously gushed with water.[12]

The result was that in that year Leo decided to abandon the Roman date and to accept the one prescribed by the see of Alexandria, as we learn from Prosper, who justified the decision by saying:

"It (sc. the date) was not incorrect since (in that year) the Lord's Passion (i.e. Good Friday) fell on April 21st."[13]

Nine years later a difficulty of a similar nature arose. In spite of determined efforts on Leo's part to amend the Roman Paschal cycle,[14] in order to avoid the possibility of serious discrepancy in the future, the essential cause of discrepancy remained, namely the use at Rome of a basis of calculation different from that which obtained at Alexandria.[15] Thus for the year A.D. 455 the Alexandrine calculation prescribed April 24th while the Roman reckoning gave April 17th.[16]

Leo evidently grasped the difficulty sometime beforehand and, realizing that on this occasion not even the justification put forward in A.D. 444 could be used in order to apologize for a date so far outside the Roman limit (sc. April 21st) as April 24th, wrote once again to Paschasinus on the subject.[17]

[11] Embracing therefore the churches of the island of Sicily.

[12] The dates mentioned are, of course, the dates of the Paschal vigil in each case. Paschasinus, *ibid.*, 3, concludes, "evidenti ergo miraculo claruit Occidentalium partium fuisse errorem."

[13] *Chronicon,* sub ann. 444, *M.G.H.*, Vol. IX, *Chron. min.*, Vol. I, p. 479; cf. Leo, *Ep.* 121, 2, JK 497. Caspar, *Geschichte,* Vol. I, p. 460 suggests that Prosper acted as Leo's secretary in the correspondence on this subject. Cf. Beda, *De ratione temporum,* 43. *P.L.* 90, 483.

[14] *Liber Pasch.*, A.D. 447. *M.G.H.*, Vol. IX. *Chron. min.*, Vol. I, pp. 501–10. The amendment aimed at harmonizing the Roman Paschal cycle of 84 years with the Alexandrine cycle of 19. Cf. Krusch, *op. cit.*, pp. 116f.

[15] See Additional Note on the different cycles in use, pp. 362ff.

[16] *Ep.* 88, 4, JK 468, dated June 24th, A.D. 451, "quarto (sc. anno) sanctae memoriae Theophilus (octavo) kalendas Maii constituit observandum: quod regula ecclesiastica penitus invenimus alienum; in nostris autem paschalibus cyclis, quod bene nosse dignaris, decimo quinto kalend. Maii eiusdem anni Pascha celebrandum esse sit scriptum."

[17] *Ep.* 88, JK 468. In the earlier part of the letter he informs Paschasinus of the nature of the Eutychian heresy.

"Since you are well acquainted," he says, "with the method of reckoning the Paschal feast, we hold that it falls to you to make careful inquiry there (sc. in Constantinople), concerning a point which we have detected with dismay in the reckoning of Theophilus, and discuss it with people who are familiar with his calculation and method: namely as to when the day of the Lord's Resurrection ought to be kept in the fourth year from now."[18]

Paschasinus' reply has not been preserved, but probability, supported by his known advice on the previous occasion, suggests that it was favourable to the Alexandrine date.

Evidently Leo was not satisfied with the advice of his suffragan, as two years later he wrote once again on the subject; this time to Proterius of Alexandria.[19] In addition he sought the Emperor's co-operation[20] and mentioned that in view of the variation to which the date of Easter was subject, and the importance of a common uniform observance of the festival throughout the Church, the council of Nicaea had sought to remove occasion of error by authorizing the see of Alexandria to take full responsibility in the matter and to inform the Apostolic see of the correct date, so that the information could be conveyed to the more remote churches by letter from that see.[21]

He then went on to explain that, according to the Paschal cycle of Theophilus of Alexandria,[22] Easter of the seventy-

[18] *Ibid.*, 4. "Illud quoque curae tuae credimus iniungendum, ut quia ratio paschalis festi experientiam tuam non latet, de eo quod in Theophili annotatione invenimus, quodque nos permovet, diligentius inquiras illic, atque pertractes cum his qui possunt supputationis et regulae istius habere peritiam: qualiter quarti anni futuri Dominicae resurrectionis dies sit tenendus."

[19] Only the reply of Proterius has been preserved, see below p. 355.

[20] *Ep.* 121, JK 497, dated June 15th, A.D. 453.

[21] *Ibid.*, 1, "ita tamen est lunaris cursus conditione mutabile, ut plerumque sacratissimae diei ambigua occurrat electio, et ex hoc fiat plerumque quod non licet, ut non simul omnis ecclesia, quod non nisi unum esse oportet, observet. Studuerunt itaque sancti Patres occasionem huius erroris auferre, omnem hanc curam Alexandrino episcopo delegantes (quoniam apud Aegyptios huius supputationis antiquitus tradita esse videbatur peritia) per quem, quotannis dies praedictae solemnitatis sedi apostolicae iudicaretur, cuius scriptis ad longinquiores ecclesias indicium generale percurreret." As to the nature of the decisions arrived at by the Council of Nicaea in regard to the observance of Easter, see Additional Note, pp. 365ff.

[22] On the Paschal cycle of Theophilus see Additional Note, pp. 369f.

sixth year was prefixed for April 24th, for which date no precedent whatever was to be found, while according to others (i.e. the Roman cycle) April 17th was determined. After mentioning the limits prescribed by Roman custom he admitted that April 22nd and 23rd could be justified on the ground that in those cases the commemoration of the Passion would not exceed those limits, but the deferring of the observance of Easter to April 24th was an "unwonted and obvious error." He therefore requested the Emperor to cause the question to be investigated by the Egyptians or by other experts, with a view to the removal of doubt in the matter, and "so that general observance may be enjoined on that day which neither abandons the rules of the fathers nor exceeds the prescribed limits."[23] He concluded with the suggestion that Marcian should send an immediate report of the outcome of his consultation of experts.

By the same post Leo wrote to Julian[24] informing him of the request which he had addressed to the Emperor and repeating his view that the Alexandrine calculation was in some way at fault. He expressed his concern lest the adoption of the disputed date should be ascribed to his connivance or neglect,[25] and requested Julian to co-operate with the Emperor in causing the error to be corrected. Yet for some reason or other the Emperor delayed taking action and it was not till sometime in the following December that Leo heard from him to the effect that reinvestigation of the question had been entrusted to the see of Alexandria. The Pope immediately wrote and informed Julian[26] of the fact. Yet when at length

[23] *Ep.* 121, 3, "ut in eum diem generalis observantia dirigatur, qui nec paternarum constitutionum normam relinquat, nec ultra praefixos terminos evagetur."

[24] *Ep.* 122, JK 498, of the same date as the above.

[25] *Ibid.*, "ut eos qui huius supputationis perfectam videntur habere notitiam, in unum iubeat convenire et diligenter inquirere: ne forte haec definitio teneatur, et hic excessus, qui prioribus videtur repugnare temporibus, nostrae conniventiae vel negligentiae deputetur, et fiat in nostris diebus quod nunquam ante praesumptum est." In his letter to Proterius, Leo appears to have suggested that the date prescribed by the Alexandrine see must have arisen from a corruption in the text of Theophilus' Paschal table. Cf. *Inter Leon. Epp.*, No. 133, 1; *P.L.* 1085, "Sed forte, sicut tua sanctitas scribit, mendosi codicis aut librarii error est, et propterea nos oporteret diem sanctae illius festivitatis transferre, quod absit."

[26] *Ep.* 127, JK 503, dated January 9th, A.D. 454.

the promised letter from Proterius [27] arrived it contained no mention of the question whatever.[28] Once again therefore Leo wrote to Julian [29] urging the need of haste in the matter, "Since the day approaches when we ought to know what date we should insert in the letters of instruction." [30]

It was not until April 15th, A.D. 454 that the Emperor Marcian informed Leo that he had despatched a state official to Alexandria with instructions to advise Proterius of the error alleged to exist in the cycle of Theophilus, undertaking that the Pope should be notified of the result as soon as it was known. This letter was briefly acknowledged.[31]

But when in the course of the following month the promised notification arrived it bore the signature not of the Emperor but of the bishop of Alexandria.[32] It was a lengthy communication, evidently drawn up by a chronological and mathematical expert, the purpose of which was simply to explain and justify the Alexandrine mode of calculation. The author nowhere explicitly mentioned the Roman date, though he appears to refer to it when he contemptuously dismissed all non-Alexandrine Paschal cycles as "based on the spurious and feigned wisdom of pagans." [33]

[27] It had been promised by Julian and Leo mentions that he was expecting its arrival, *ibid.*, 1.

[28] Possibly Proterius had not yet heard of the question from the Emperor at the time when he composed his letter to which Leo refers in *Ep.* 129, 1, JK 505. The fact that Leo, in his reply, makes no mention of it either, may be due to tactful reserve on his part, since he was under the impression that it was already *sub iudice*.

[29] *Ep.* 131, JK 507, dated March 10th, A.D. 454.

[30] *Ibid.*, 2, "quoniam imminent dies ut nosse possimus quam diem formatis ascribere debeamus." The "(litterae) formatae" in this case are evidently official notifications sent by the Roman Church to other western sees, a custom to which Leo alludes in *Ep.* 121, 1, JK 497 and of which *Ep.* 96, JK 477 addressed to the see of Arles is evidently a typical example. That letter prescribes the date of Easter in A.D. 452. Cf. *Conc. Arel.* I, Canon 1; Petavius, *De doctrina temporum,* 1, app., p. 502; Kirch, *Fontes,* Nos. 368, 792. Cf. *Ep.* 138, JK 512.

[31] *Ep.* 134, 3, JK 508, dated April 15th, A.D. 454.

[32] *Inter Leon. Epp.,* No. 133, *P.L.* 54, 1084. The present text is a sixth century Latin version made by Dionysius Exiguus. Cf. Krusch, *op. cit.,* p. 267. Proterius himself, *ibid.,* 9, states that in order to avoid possible errors in rendering it into Latin he has sent the letter in its original Greek text. Its interest was naturally confined to chronologists, and as such the Latin translation made in Leo's time would easily be lost. Krusch, *op. cit.,* pp. 269ff. gives a critical edition of the letter.

[33] *Ibid.,* 7, "non iuxta Iudaeorum nunc indoctas atque ineptas actiones, neque secundum exterorum putativam fictamque prudentiam sed secundum gratiam Spiritus sancti instituti."

Its main burden may be summarized thus. "In deference to the Emperor's request, who, not on his own account, but simply in order to meet your wishes, desired that the question of the date of Easter in the coming year should be examined, a most careful investigation of the whole matter has been made, the basis of which has been the cycle of Theophilus. We have found it to be devoid of any trace of inaccuracy. It prescribes April 24th as the correct date in the coming year, and on that date Easter will be kept in Egypt and throughout the churches of the East." [34]

The question as to what date the Roman church happened to prescribe simply did not arise for the see of Alexandria. For Proterius the verdict of the cycle of Theophilus was final.

Nevertheless, in spite of the fact that the verdict had gone against the date upheld by the Roman see, Leo came to the conclusion in the interests of peace and of uniform observance throughout the Church that the right course for him to adopt was to give way. He therefore addressed a letter to the Emperor [35] saying that though he was not convinced by the argument advanced by the see of Alexandria in favour of the date indicated by the Paschal cycle of Theophilus, yet in the cause of unity he was ready to agree to the observance of Easter on that day in the coming year.[36] Letters of notification [37] were accordingly transmitted to the Western churches,

[34] *Ep.* 133, 6. The substance of the writer's argument is as follows. In A.D. 455 the fourteenth day of the Paschal moon falls on Sunday, April 17th, and since according to Alexandrine rules Easter may not be celebrated earlier than the fifteenth day, it is necessary to postpone the festival for eight days, otherwise Sunday would be a fast day; so that April 24th becomes the correct date. He points out that the same situation occurred in A.D. 373, 377 and 387 and again in 444 and will recur in A.D. 550. It is clear that the whole force of Proterius' case depends on the identification of April 17th with the fourteenth day of the Paschal moon. In Rome, however, according to the Paschal Table in use there, April 17th was not the fourteenth but the eighteenth day. Hence it is not surprising that the Roman see remained unconvinced by the Alexandrine contention.

[35] *Ep.* 137, JK 511, dated May 29th, A.D. 454. Bede, *De ratione temporum,* 44. *P.L.* 90, 484, suggests that Leo wrote also to this effect to Proterius himself.

[36] *Ibid.,* 1. "Litteras . . . Proterii . . . me accepisse significo, quibus apud pietatem vestram de mea consensione respondi, non quia hoc ratio manifesta docuerit, sed quia unitatis, quam maxime custodimus, cura persuaserit."

[37] e.g. *Ep.* 138, JK 512, dated July 12th, A.D. 455. Jaffé-Kaltenbrunner, *Regesta,* Vol. I, p. 71, mentions another such letter, JK 513, addressed to the churches of Britain, which has not survived.

in which Leo took the opportunity of narrating the recent course of events and explaining the reasons which had led him to adopt the Alexandrine date. Shortly afterwards he informed the Emperor [38] that in accordance with his rescript [39] the western churches had been notified that that date was to be observed.

It is probable that Leo himself, who believed that in virtue of the Nicene decisions the see of Alexandria possessed the right to determine the Paschal date,[40] was not seriously concerned by the fact that the adoption of that see's ruling involved the admission that the Roman cycle was undependable. Yet in some quarters such a concession to eastern superiority was felt to be extremely galling. Prosper himself probably acted as the mouthpiece of western feeling when he wrote:

"In the same year the Lord's Passover was celebrated on April 24th by reason of the unbending determination of the bishop of Alexandria, with whom all the Easterns held that they were bound to agree: though the most holy Pope Leo expressed his opinion that instead April 17th should be kept. There survive some letters of his addressed to his Grace the Emperor Marcian in which the justification of the truth investigated was plainly set forth, from which the Catholic Church can learn that this point of view was conceded rather in the interests of unity and peace than because it was demonstrated as true, and must never be followed henceforth, so that being the cause of deadly wrong it loses all force for ever." [41]

[38] *Ep.* 142, JK 517, dated March 13th, A.D. 455.

[39] *Ep.* 138. "Quo rescribente, octavo kalendas Maias definitus est dies." It is clear from this that the letter of Proterius, *Inter Leon. Epp.*, No. 133, was supported by an imperial rescript.

[40] See *Ep.* 121, 1, JK 497.

[41] *Chronicon,* sub ann., A.D. 455. *M.G.H.*, Vol. IX; *Chron. min.*, Vol. I, p. 484. "Eodem anno Pascha Dominicum die VIII kal. Maas celebratum est pertinaci intentione Alexandrini episcopi, cui omnes Orientales consentiendum putarunt; cum s. papa Leo XV kal. Mai potius observandum protestaretur in quo nec in ratione plenilunii nec in primi mensis limite fuisset erratum. Exstant eiusdem papae epistolae ad clementissimum principem Marcianum datae, quibus ratio veritatis sollicitate evidenterque patefacta est, et quibus ecclesia catholica instrui potest, quod haec persuasio studio unitatis et pacis tolerata sit potius quam probata, numquam deinceps imitanda, ut, quae exitialem attulit offensionem, omnem in perpetuum perdat auctoritatem." The letters addressed to Marcian to which Prosper refers are, of course, *Epp.* 121, 134, 137 and 142.

The subsequent history of the Paschal controversy[42] shows that in actual fact Prosper and his western supporters were wrong, and that Leo in adopting the Alexandrine date was right and in so doing foreshadowed the time when West and East alike would acknowledge the superiority of Alexandrine mathematical principles. A lesser man than Leo might easily have made of the whole question a cause of lasting schism.

Additional Note

THE EARLY HISTORY OF THE PASCHAL CONTROVERSY[43]

In the absence of direct evidence it is reasonable to suppose that Christians of at least the first two generations continued to observe an annual commemoration of the Passion and Resurrection on the same date as the Passover of the Jewish Church.[44] At first, therefore, there was no question of deciding when that commemoration should be kept, since its date was predetermined by the Jewish reckoning.[45] Doubtless the Christians of that time would mark their observance by specifically Christian rites, but for them there could have been no alternative to the celebration of the fourteenth day of the month Nisan.[46]

[42] See Additional Note, pp. 370ff.

[43] The chief modern authorities on the Paschal question are Krusch, *Studien zur christl.-mittelalt. Chronologie,* Leipzig (1880). Schmid, *Der Osterfestberechnung in der abendlandischen Kirche,* Freiburg in B. (1908). Schwartz, *Christliche und jüdische Ostertafeln* in *Abh. d. Gött. Ges. d. Wiss. phil. hist. Kl. N.F.,* Vol. VIII, pt. 6 (1905). Schwartz has shown that there are grounds for disputing the view put forward by Krusch in regard to the dates shown in the Paschal table included in the Philocalian Kalendar of A.D. 354 and in the list of the dates on which Easter was celebrated from A.D. 312–411, in *M.G.H.,* Auct. antiqu., Vol. IX, p. 62. Krusch, pp. 64ff., argues that the dates from A.D. 312–42 alone represented Easter days actually observed, while those of A.D. 343–54 and A.D. 355–411 stood for dates computed but not observed, with the result that in the majority of cases he believes that the see of Alexandria gave way to the Roman date. Schwartz, pp. 50ff., on the other hand, shows that the discrepancies are more often due to concessions on the part of the Roman see even in the fourth century. For a restatement of the part played by the Council of Nicaea in the solution of Paschal problems see Duchesne, *Revue des questions hist.,* Vol. XXVIII (1880), pp. 1–42. His views have been embodied in the text of this Additional Note.

[44] The rules governing the observance of the Jewish Passover in the first century A.D. were based on Exodus xii. 1–6.

[45] The Jewish Kalendar of this time was partly Babylonian in origin, at least so far as the names of the months were concerned. Hence the first month of the year was known as Nisan.

[46] The months were lunar, so that the first of the month coincided with the "new moon."

Nevertheless there was one consideration, which was bound sooner or later to be taken into account, namely the evidence of the Gospels that the Resurrection itself took place on "the first day of the week,"[47] and in those communities where the Gentile element was in the majority and the influence of Jewish tradition proportionately less strong it would naturally be felt that attention ought to be given to the day mentioned in New Testament records, rather than to the date prescribed by the Old Covenant. As a result in Gentile churches the practice of keeping, not the fourteenth day of the month Nisan, but the Sunday immediately after that day, began to make headway. It would seem that this change made itself felt in the West sometime before the middle of the second century and was introduced in the Roman church at least as early as the pontificate of Xystus I.[48] In fact so rapidly did the practice become general in the West during the course of that century that long before its conclusion the earlier custom was being already regarded as exceptional, and those churches which continued to observe it stigmatized as "Quartodeciman."[49]

Yet although diversity of observance must have arisen quite early, it did not at first attract serious notice, so that it was not till the middle of the second century that attention was drawn to its existence by the visit of Polycarp of Smyrna to Rome.[50] Even then the advocates of the rival customs were able to agree peacefully to differ, though Anicetus, who was bishop of Rome at the time[51] made it clear that he regarded the Roman custom as the better one of the two. Nevertheless the earliest actual controversy on the subject seems to have arisen, not between those who observed Sunday and the "Quartodecimans," but rather between the latter and a rival Asian usage, which chose to keep the *fifteenth*

[47] Mark xvi. 2.

[48] i.e. *c.* A.D. 115–125. See Irenaeus, cit. ap. Eusebius, *H.E.*, 5, 24.

[49] i.e. the "fourteenth-ites." Eusebius, *ibid.*, mentions Polycrates, bishop of Ephesus, as a supporter of the "Quartodeciman" usage. As Ephesus was the capital of the proconsular province of Asia, it is to be inferred that that usage was general throughout the whole peninsula at this period. It survived there in certain places as late as the Council of Nicaea.

[50] Irenaeus, ap. Eusebius, *ibid.*

[51] *c.* A.D. 155–166.

rather than the fourteenth day of the lunar month. We learn from Melito of Sardis [52] that a Paschal dispute of some sort took place at Laodicaea,[53] and to judge from a citation from a lost work of Apollinaris of Hierapolis [54] preserved in the *Chronicon Paschale*,[55] it is probable that the dispute in question was concerned with the emergence of a local rival to the "Quartodeciman" practice.[56] The whole affair is little known, and in any case the fact that after the middle of the second century we find no further allusion to the "Quintodecimans" appears to indicate that their peculiarity only enjoyed a comparatively brief existence, and that for the future the issue lay solely between the "Quartodecimans" and those who upheld the "Dominical" usage.[57]

Obviously so long as the fixation of a date for universal observance was not felt to be a matter of principle, as it came to be regarded at a later date, the existence of divergent usages would only be realized in such Christian communities as were of a cosmopolitan character and therefore included

[52] Melito of Sardis is chiefly known for his authorship of an *Apology* addressed to the Emperor Marcus Aurelius, *c.* A.D. 172. Only fragments of this work have survived. Cf. Eusebius, *H.E.*, 4, 26.

[53] Eusebius, *ibid.*, mentions his two books "Περὶ τοῦ Πάσχα," and quotes the following, "Ἐπὶ Σερουιλλίου Παύλοὺ ἀνθυπάτου τῆς Ἀσίας . . . ἐγένετο ζήτησις πολλὴ ἐν Λαοδικείᾳ περὶ τοῦ Πάσχα." Waddington, *Fastes Asiatiques*, p. 226, suggests that the proconsul mentioned is Sergius Paulus, which would date the event A.D. 165.

[54] Apollinaris of Hierapolis is similarly stated to have addressed an *Apology* to Marcus Aurelius. The citation from his work "on the Passover" is given in *Chron. Pasch.*, *P.G.* 92, 80.

[55] The *Chronicon Paschale*, probably of Constantinopolitan origin, in its present form dates from the earlier half of the seventh century. The work was so called by Ducange, because it denotes each year by the date of the Paschal cycle. Cf. Rauschen-Wittig, *Grundriss der Patrologie*, p. 143.

[56] The rival custom to observe not the fourteenth but the fifteenth day of the month Nisan was justified doubtless on the ground that the Synoptists' record pointed to the latter as the actual day of the Crucifixion. The "Quartodeciman" practice was evidently based on the evidence of the Fourth Gospel. The existence of the discrepancy is, of course, well known at the present time to students of the N.T. See e.g. Bernard, *St. John*, Vol. I, pp. cviff.

[57] The adoption of this usage probably made more rapid headway, as we have seen, in Gentile Christian communities, where the Kalendar in use was solar rather than lunar in character. It is even possible that it owed something to the prevalence of those mystery cults, in which the "Sol invictus" held a prominent place. Equally the "Quartodeciman" practice remained vigorous where Semitic influence with its lunar reckoning of time was still strong.

members who had been brought up in a custom different from the one observed by the majority. Cosmopolitanism was nowhere so noticeable as in the church of Rome,[58] and hence it was to be expected that the inconvenience of divergency would be appreciated more readily there than elsewhere. There is evidence of a certain coolness between the bishop and the local "Quartodeciman" congregations there so early as the time of Pope Soter,[59] but it was not till some fifteen years later that definite measures were taken by the Roman see to insist on conformity with the local Roman custom by all alike.

The evidence is admittedly obscure and as such was probably not clearly understood even by early ecclesiastical historians.[60] It seems that the inconvenience of rival usages was felt even more keenly by Pope Victor than by his predecessor, and that in this instance the bishop sought to enforce uniformity on the "Quartodecimans" of Rome by the infliction of the supreme penalty of excommunication. Evidently his view as to the importance of uniformity was not shared by many of his contemporaries[61] and under his successor a policy of toleration was revived.[62] Yet the incident served to show that as the Church gradually came to appreciate her universal character, the need of uniformity

[58] Cf. Irenaeus, *Adv. Haer.* 3, 3, 2. Mirbt, *Quellen,* No. 40.

[59] *c.* A.D. 166–174. Irenaeus, cit. ap. Eusebius, *H.E.,* 5, 24, explicitly states that the presidents of the Roman Church *before* Soter continued to send the Eucharist to the Christians from those parishes (? dioceses) which kept the "Quartodeciman" custom, from which it may be inferred that Soter was the first to cease to do so. Soter's action amounted to a partial excommunication. On the practice of "sending the Eucharist," see Freestone, *Sacrament Reserved,* pp. 73–7.

[60] The treatment accorded by Victor to the "Quartodecimans," and the reaction of his contemporaries in Gaul and Asia, is described by Eusebius, *H.E.,* 5, 23–25. His evidence has been usually interpreted to mean that Victor excommunicated the local churches of Asia. Cf. e.g. Duchesne, *Histoire,* Vol. I, pp. 289ff. Recently, however, an alternative explanation has been put forward by La Piana, *Harvard Theological Review,* July, 1925, pp. 209ff., 221ff., 231 and adopted by Zernov, *C.Q.R.,* Vol. CXVI, April 1933, pp. 24ff. It is argued that Eusebius misread his authorities and interpreted their evidence in the light of contemporary history, and in so doing made the mistake of reading back into the second century the conditions of the fourth.

[61] See Eusebius, *H.E., ibid.* In *H.E.* 5, 15 and 20 he mentions a temporary schism in the Roman Church for which Florinus was primarily responsible. His coadjutor, Blastus, may have been the leader of the "Quartodeciman" party. Cf. Zernov, *art. cit.,* p. 35.

[62] Zephyrinus, *c.* A.D. 199–217.

began to be felt to be a matter not so much of convenience as of principle.

The adoption of the "Dominical" usage which, as we have seen, seems at first to have taken root as a predominantly western custom, represented the earliest departure from Jewish custom. Even so the determination of the correct Sunday still remained dependent on the Jewish reckoning, and for the first two centuries no attempt was made to arrive at an independent Christian mode of calculation. During this period it does not appear to have occurred to anyone to question the propriety of this dependence, but as the Gentile influence increased and the tendency to regard the Jews as aliens and "deicides" developed, the demand for a wholly non-Jewish method of reckoning the correct date became more insistent.

At this point we may summarize briefly the factors which every Paschal chronologist had to take into account. In the first place it has to be remembered that any Paschal calculation involves the difficulty of reconciling the lunar with the solar year. Now it happens that twelve lunar months are together less than the number of days in the solar year by approximately eleven and one quarter days, and for this reason in order to prevent an ever increasing discrepancy between the lunar and the solar year it is necessary periodically to intercalate an additional lunar month; the year in which such an intercalation takes place being known as the "annus embolismus." The essential problem therefore lay in discovering, not only how often the intercalation should be made, but also how many solar years should be allowed, "so that when that number has elapsed, the Paschal dates, that is to say the fourteenth days of Nisan, should recur in the same order on the same days in the Kalendar." [63] The name given to such a period of years was a Paschal cycle, and a list of dates to be observed based on such a cycle was known as a Paschal table.

The earliest known attempt to calculate a Paschal cycle is that made by Hippolytus.[64] It was set forth by him in a

[63] Duchesne, *La question de la Pâque au concile de Nicée* in *Revue des questions historiques* (July 1880, p. 17).

[64] On this elusive figure in the history of the Roman Church, see e.g. Duchesne, *Histoire,* Vol. I, pp. 296–323.

work now lost entitled the "'Ἀπόδειξις χρόνων."[65] The Paschal table, however, which was based on it has been found inscribed on the base of a statue discovered in Rome in 1551,[66] and believed to be a representation of the author himself. From this table it is possible to reconstruct the Hippolytean cycle. It covers a period of one hundred and twelve years, beginning with the year A.D. 222, and is based on a cycle of *sixteen years.* It does not allow the celebration of Easter before the sixteenth day of the lunar month; so that if the fourteenth should fall on a Saturday, Easter is to be postponed till the Sunday next but one. This Roman principle remained in force for some time and was the source of a considerable amount of controversy.

The Hippolytean cycle of sixteen years was soon found to be unsatisfactory. It was discovered that at the end of that period there was a difference between the solar and lunar years actually of three days, so that the fourteenth day of Nisan was three days late. An anonymous Latin writer of African origin undertook the task of effecting a correction, but was hampered by his conviction that the error was due to Hippolytus' failure to allow for the supposed creation of the moon on the "fourth day." His correction therefore only amounted to the addition of three days to each of the Hippolytean dates,[67] and left the real solution of the problem still to be found.

Some years later a new Paschal cycle was evolved by Augustalis, on the basis of which he constructed a fresh Paschal table which he entitled the "Laterculus."[68] His cycle was one of *eighty-four years,* which reduced the discrepancy between the solar and lunar kalendars to one day and a quarter for the whole period. It also possessed a further advantage in that not only did the Paschal dates, the fourteenth of Nisan, recur in the same order, but also the Paschal Sundays. The author reckoned the date of Easter from the

[65] Referred to by Eusebius, *H.E.*, 6, 22.
[66] *Corpus inscriptionum graec.*, Vol. IV, No. 8613.
[67] His work, *De Paschae computu,* is given in Cyprian, *Opera, C.S.E.L.*, Vol. III, iii, pp. 248ff. Its date is generally given as A.D. 243.
[68] The "laterculus" has been reconstructed by Krusch, *op. cit.*, pp. 5f., from the data supplied by a Carthaginian writer of A.D. 455, Krusch, *op. cit.*, pp. 279ff. His Paschal table is also given; id. *ibid.*, p. 17. Schwartz, *op. cit.*, however, regards the work as a clumsy invention of the fifth century.

age of the moon on January 1st. Now since, as we have seen, the lunar year is eleven days shorter than the solar year, it meant that by the following January 1st the moon was eleven days older than its age at the beginning of the previous solar year. (We are probably indebted to Augustalis for the term "epact" to describe the age of the moon on January 1st at the beginning of each year.) Thus, if the "epact" at the beginning of the cycle be 1, by the beginning of the second year it will be 12, of the third 23, and so on. Each time the epact exceeds 30 Augustalis held that a lunar month should be intercalated, and that the new "epact" should be reckoned by subtracting 30 from the old one. Thus in the fourth year the epact would be 4. So in the course of eighty-four years it would be necessary to intercalate a lunar month thirty times ($84 \times 11 = 924$ days). But as this would still leave a discrepancy of twenty-four days ($924 - 900 = 24$), to avoid beginning the new cycle with an epact of 25, Augustalis proposed to increase the epact every fourteenth year from eleven days to twelve. This modification would occur six times in the course of the cycle and was known to later chronologists as the *saltus lunae*.

This cycle of Augustalis was adopted by the church of Rome; but after the year A.D. 312 [69] its place was taken by a new mode of calculation known as the *Supputatio romana vetus*.[70] Two features distinguished this new basis of reckoning from the old; first it provided that the *saltus lunae* should recur every twelfth instead of every fourteenth year, as allowed in the cycle of Augustalis, and secondly, it appears to have required that the celebration of Easter should not occur earlier than March 25th nor later than April 21st.[71]

Meanwhile parallel developments were taking place in the East. The earliest Eastern cycle, of which evidence survives, is the one calculated by Dionysius of Alexandria,[72] which thus belongs to the middle of the third century. Like the Hippolytean, it also consisted of *sixteen years*, but apart from the fact

[69] The Church of Africa continued to use the cycle of Augustalis into the fifth century and by means of the calculations of Agriustia provided a continuation of his Paschal table. See Krusch, *op. cit.*, pp. 23f.

[70] Krusch, *op. cit.*, pp. 32f.; pp 227–44. Schwartz, *op. cit.*, denies that a change in reckoning the *saltus* took place at this time.

[71] i.e. not before the Roman equinox.

[72] Mentioned by Eusebius, *H.E.*, 7, 20.

that it embodied the principle that Easter might not be observed before the equinox, we are ignorant of its details. Some years later a new basis of calculation was provided by Anatolius of Laodicaea in Syria. His Paschal cycle[73] comprised *nineteen years* and assigned the equinox to March 19th. In addition it was stipulated that Easter should not occur earlier than March 20th nor later than April 25th.

So far as our evidence goes there is no sign that these divergent methods of calculating the date of Easter caused any serious controversy during the third century. The *Chronicon Paschale* provides us with a reference to a controversial work by Peter of Alexandria on this subject dated at the beginning of the fourth century, but in this case the author was only concerned to uphold the accuracy of the Jewish reckoning up to the time of the destruction of the Temple.[74]

Notwithstanding the absence of actual controversy the existence of divergencies must have caused considerable inconvenience, at least so far as the Western churches were concerned, a fact which is sufficient to explain the canon passed by the council of Arles on the subject. This canon prescribed that " in regard to the observance of the Lord's Passover it is to be kept by us on the same day and at the same time throughout all the world, and as is customary you (sc. Pope Silvester) should send letters (of information) to all." [75]

The subject of divergencies in the observance of Easter is mentioned next by Eusebius of Caesarea as having been discussed at the Council of Nicaea. He alludes to the custom of some of conforming to the practice of the Jews, while others affirm that the exact time of the occasion (i.e. of the

[73] The cycle of 19 years had been discovered by Meton of Athens in B.C. 432. In this case the discrepancy between the lunar and solar years only amounted to about two hours. His Paschal calculation is mentioned by Eusebius, *ibid., P.G.* 20, 728. Cf. Duchesne, *art. cit.*, p. 20.

[74] *Chron. Pasc. P.G.* 92, 72. Clearly Peter was in agreement with his opponent as to the inaccuracy of contemporary Jewish observance.

[75] *Conc. Arel.*, Canon 1. Mirbt, *Quellen,* No. 101. " Primo loco de observatione paschae domini, ut uno die et uno tempore per omnem orbem a nobis observetur et iuxta consuetudinem literas ad omnes tu (sc. Silvester papa) dirigas." The probability is that this canon was aimed primarily at rectifying divergencies between African and Roman usage. Cf. Krusch, *op. cit.*, pp. 32, 227–44.

Passion) should be kept." [76] But it appears that the "Judaizing" minority was persuaded to accept the rival custom, and that as a result the council was able to report in its synodical letter that "All our brethren in the East, who formerly acted with the Jews, henceforth are in harmony with the Romans, with us and all of you who from of old have kept Easter with us." [77]

There is no reliable evidence that the council actually passed a canon on the subject. It certainly did not sanction explicitly, as is often supposed, the Paschal cycle of nineteen years at that time in use at Alexandria,[78] still less did it prescribe that the see of Alexandria should each year notify the date determined to the see of Rome,[79] with a view to its publication elsewhere. The most that can be attributed to it

[76] *Vita Constant.* 3, 5. *P.G.* 20, 1057. *G.C.S.*, Eusebii *Opera,* Vol. I, p. 79, ll. 10ff. "... *τῆς σωτηρίου ἑορτῆς διαφωνία, τῶν μὲν ἕπεσθαι δεῖν τῇ Ἰουδαίων συνηθείᾳ φασκόντων, τῶν δὲ προσήκειν τὴν ἀκριβῆ τοῦ καιροῦ παραφυλάττειν ὥραν μηδὲ πλανωμένους ἕπεσθαι τοῖς τῆς εὐαγγελικῆς ἀλλοτρίοις χάριτος.*" The "Judaizing" custom to which the author alludes is evidently not "Quartodecimanism," which at this date was confined as an archaic survival to certain churches in the province of Asia, but the practice which must have been still general at this time, in the "diocese" of the Orient, that is to say, within the jurisdiction of the see of Antioch, of keeping the Sunday after the day on which the Jews determined the fourteenth of Nisan. Socrates, *H.E.*, 5, 22 clearly distinguishes the two, and Athanasius refers to the latter in *Epistola ad Afros,* 2, *P.G.* 26, 688; 1032, and in *De synodis,* 5. *P.G.* 26, 687. The custom of those who urge "*προσήκειν τὴν ἀκριβῆ τοῦ καιροῦ παραφυλάττειν ὥραν*" is that followed by the Church of Alexandria. The chief objection to contemporary Jewish custom arose from the fact that since the second century in fixing the date of the Passover the Jews had ignored the incidence of the equinox, so that contrary to Mosaic legislation it might occur twice within a single year. The Alexandrine cycle, as we have seen, explicitly excluded this possibility.

[77] Socrates, *H.E.*, 1, 9; Theodoret, *H.E.*, 1, 9. Cf. encyclical letter of Constantine, *Vita Constant.* 3, 19. *G.C.S.*, Eusebii Opera, Vol. I, p. 88, ll. 24ff.

[78] This was evidently believed by Ambrose, *Ep. ad epp. Aemil. P.L.* 16^2, 1070f. His statement is repeated by Dionysius Exiguus. *Tabula Pasch., praef., P.L.* 67, 484f. It is scarcely conceivable that if the council had done so that it would have failed to mention the fact in its synodical letter addressed to the see of Alexandria. Cf. Socrates, *H.E.*, 1, 9.

[79] The evidence for the attribution of this prescription to the Council of Nicaea is supplied by the *Prologus Paschalis,* 2 (Krusch, *op. cit.*, p. 338, Kirch, *Fontes,* No. 791), a late composition which appears to be based on Leo, *Ep.* 121, 2, JK 497. If it is correct it is difficult to account for the silence of all contemporary authorities, particularly for the omission of any mention of such a prescription in the letter of Constantine. See *Vita Constant.* 3, 19.

with any certainty is the agreement already described which was primarily concerned with a divergent usage obtaining in the "diocese" of the Orient. The divergencies between the cycles in use at Rome and at Alexandria respectively remained unaffected.[80]

Nevertheless the general concord reached by members of the council in favour of the Alexandrine reckoning bore fruit in due course. The council of Antioch, sixteen years later, explicitly condemned any divergence from the decisions reached at Nicaea,[81] and although John Chrysostom found himself obliged to denounce certain supporters of an earlier Antiochene usage,[82] the latter seems to have disappeared wholly by the beginning of the fifth century.

The divergencies between the customs in vogue at Rome and Alexandria in the middle of the fourth century, of which the council of Nicaea either was ignorant or simply disregarded, may be briefly summarized as follows. First of all, at Rome a Paschal cycle of *eighty-four years* was in use,† while at Alexandria the cycle consisted of *nineteen years*. Roman chronologists, following the Kalendar of Julius Caesar, reckoned March 25th as the equinox, while the Alexandrines correctly assigned it to March 21st. At Rome it was held that Easter could not be celebrated before the sixteenth day of the lunar month. At Alexandria the fifteenth day was considered possible. Finally the limits of incidence varied; at Rome they were March 25th and April 21st; at Alexandria March 22nd and April 25th.[83]

It is possible that these divergencies might have continued to go unnoticed for a more or less prolonged period if it had not been for the fortuitous alliance of the see of Alexandria, in

[80] Various rules regarding the observance of Easter have been ascribed to the council, e.g. Petan, *De doctrina temporis,* 6, 6: 5, 1, who mentions that its prescriptions regarding the feast were that it should be held (1) on Sunday only; (2) always on a day other than the Jewish Passover; (3) after the full moon following the equinox. He derives his view from Isidore of Seville, *De officiis ecclesiasticis,* 1, 32, *P.L.* 83, 768, whose testimony was accepted by Pope Gregory XIII in his bull *Inter gravissimas* dated February 24th, A.D. 1582.

[81] *Conc. Antioch,* A.D. 341, "*In encaeniis,*" Canon 1. Mansi, *Concilia,* Vol. II, 1307.

[82] *Hom. 3 adv. Iudaeos. P.G.* 48, 861f. The usage was presumably that of following the Jewish reckoning, see p. 366, n. 76.

† Or of *sixteen* according to the Hippolytean cycle, if Schwartz's view as to Augustalis is correct. See p. 364, n. 70.

[83] Krusch, *op. cit.,* pp. 64f.

the person of Athanasius, with the see of Rome, in the person of Julius I, in resisting the menace of Arianism. This alliance was cemented at the council of Sardica, and the fact that the amendments made to the *Supputatio romana vetus* [84] date from the year of that council, i.e. A.D. 343, render it probable that some compromise was made there between the two sees on the subject of Paschal observance.[85] By that time a new Paschal table had been drawn up to take the place of the "laterculus" of Augustalis (or of the Hippolytean table). It began with the year A.D. 312 and was later enlarged so as to extend to the year A.D. 411. Yet a comparison of the dates given in the Philocalian Kalendar, embodying this table [86] and those which are shown in the Syrian chronicle,[87] which is given as an introduction to the twenty-first "festal" letter of Athanasius, and mentions the dates on which Easter was observed at Alexandria from A.D. 328–73, show divergencies in the following years: A.D. 333, 346, 349, 350, 357, 360, [387 and 417]. It seems that the Alexandrines adopted the Roman date in A.D. 333, 346 [88] and 349, while the Romans gave way in A.D. 350, 357 and 360. In the two other years, viz. A.D. 387 and 417, each church followed its own custom. How this came about may be briefly explained.

In the year A.D. 385 Theophilus succeeded to the see of Alexandria and made a determined effort to obtain oecumenical authority for the Alexandrine mode of reckoning. He

[84] The amendment fixed the equinox on March 21st so that for the future the celebration of Easter could take place between March 22nd and April 21st. Cf. Krusch, *op. cit.*, pp. 64f.

[85] It is possible that the arrangement in virtue of which the see of Alexandria was to notify the see of Rome regarding the correct date, with a view to wider publication, which, as we have seen, has been mistakenly attributed to the Council of Nicaea, was actually made at the Council of Sardica, and later, like the canons of that council, came to be reckoned as "Nicene." It was certainly believed to be Nicene in Alexandria by the time of Theophilus, *Prologus paschalis,* 2, and was accepted as such by Cyril, *Ep.* 87, 2, *P.G.* 77, 385. Cf. Caspar, *Geschichte,* Vol. I, p. 612.

[86] The Philocalian Kalendar was compiled in A.D. 354. It has been edited by Mommsen, *M.G.H.*, Vol. IX, pp. 62f.

[87] In a Latin version, *P.G.* 26, 1351f.

[88] Krusch, *op. cit.*, pp. 69f. Schwartz, *Ostertafeln,* pp. 50ff. on the other hand argues that the dates of Easter given in the Philocalian Kalendar for the years previous to its publication, i.e. in A.D. 333, 346, 349, 350 do not necessarily represent the dates on which the festival was actually celebrated. He believes that in every case except A.D. 387 and 417 the Alexandrine date was accepted at Rome.

published a detailed treatise on the Paschal question, which in the course of the prologue he formally dedicated to the Emperor Theodosius I.[89] Even if the Emperor declined to accept Theophilus' proposal that he should impose the Alexandrine usage legally on the whole Church, his efforts were largely successful in an indirect way. Yet it was not till the pontificate of Innocent I that attention was paid to his work in Rome. In A.D. 387 the Roman Church must have simply ignored the Alexandrine reckoning altogether. But by the early years of the fifth century the defects of the Roman *Supputatio* were clearly recognized, and Innocent himself evidently felt the need of taking into account the dates prescribed by the calculations of Theophilus.[90] Perhaps too it was coming to be believed that the only hope of establishing uniformity of Paschal observance lay in the general acceptance of the date prescribed by the see of Alexandria. Yet it took nearly four centuries more for the ideal to be achieved.

In the case of the year A.D. 417, in spite of the fact that Cyril had already notified the see of Rome that the proper date was April 22nd,[91] a date which fell outside the Roman limits of incidence, Zosimus insisted on the date given in the Roman table, i.e. March 25th, being kept.[92] We may infer, however, from the absence of similar differences for the next thirty-five years or so, that the Alexandrine date was normally accepted by the Roman see during this period.

When the date prescribed by the see of Alexandria exceeded the limits of incidence, i.e. March 22nd and April 21st, which occurred, as we have seen, in A.D. 444 and again in A.D. 455,

[89] It must be remembered, however, that the genuineness of this document is open to question. In any case all that Theophilus did was to continue the existing Paschal table of Anatolius to the end of the fourth century. It was subsequently extended by Cyril so as to reach the year A.D. 531.

[90] Cf. *Ep.* 14, JK 301, addressed to Aurelius, bishop of Carthage, in which he expresses his uncertainty as to whether the date prescribed by the see of Alexandria for the year A.D. 414 was correct or not, owing to the fact that it was the fifteenth day of the lunar month. Leo's belief as to the responsibilities of the see of Alexandria (*Ep.* 121) may owe something to this letter.

[91] Cyril Al., *Hom.* 5, 8. *P.G.* 77, 497. Cf. *Inter. Leon. Epp.*, No. 3, 2. *P.L.* 54, 608f.

[92] See *Inter Leon. Epp.*, No. 3, and Chap. XV, pp. 351f. The letter of Paschasinus, c. 1, mentions an official Roman Paschal Table, beginning in A.D. 382, the dates of which appear in the Paschal cycle of *Cod. Vat. Regin.* 2077, ed. Mommsen in *M.G.H.*, Vol. IX, pp. 740ff. Cf. Leo, *Ep.* 127, JK 503.

during the pontificate of Leo I, there was no longer any question as to whether the see of Alexandria had the right to prescribe the date. All that could be said in defence of the Roman standpoint in the matter was that the Alexandrine table must contain some mathematical error or copyist's blunder.[93]

So when, in spite of the principles of the Roman see, Leo felt obliged in the interests of unity to adopt the Alexandrine date prescribed by Proterius for the year A.D. 455,[94] he appears to have wished to ensure that similar divergencies between the Alexandrine and Roman dates should not recur, and with this end in view entrusted the task of revising the Roman Paschal rules to his archdeacon Hilary.[95] Finding himself unable to wrestle with the difficulties involved, Hilary invoked the aid of a distinguished mathematician, Victorius of Aquitania.[96] Victorius boldly abandoned the Roman cycle of eighty-four years and adopted as a basis the Alexandrine one of *nineteen;* by reducing the Roman cycle to twenty-eight years (i.e. a third) and multiplying this by the Alexandrine figure he arrived at a Paschal period, after the elapse of which the Paschal full moons would recur not only on the same dates of the lunar month but also on the same days in the week. It was a period of no less than five hundred and thirty-two years. In his view this period had begun in the twenty-eighth year of our Lord, which he regarded as the actual year of the Passion and Resurrection. In addition, like the Alexandrine reckoning, he admitted the *saltus lunae* only once every nineteen years. Notwithstanding he retained the Roman limits of incidence, which in his time were considered to be March 22nd and April 24th, and thus was prevented from achieving complete accord with the Alexandrine calculations. In his Paschal table, where the Alexandrine date differs from the Roman one, he entered both dates side by side.

[93] Proterius, *Ep., Inter Leon. Epp.,* No. 133, 1. *P.L.* 54, 1085.
[94] See *Ep.* 137, 1, JK 511. Cf. Chap. XV, p. 356.
[95] This measure adopted by Leo is known only from the Paschal table of Zeitz given in *M.G.H.,* Vol. IX, pp. 501–10. Cf. Krusch, *op. cit.,* pp. 116f.
[96] *Alias* Victorinus. His Paschal canon is given in *M.G.H.,* Vol. IX, pp. 669f. It never received official approval at Rome but had a considerable vogue in Gaul and also in Italy itself. For Hilary's letter, the cycle of Victorius and the Paschal Table of Dionysius Exiguus see Krusch, *Studien z. ch.-mitt. Chron.,* Berlin (1938).

As a consequence of the divergence which still remained a fresh difficulty arose in the year A.D. 501. In that year the Roman table gave March 25th, while Victorius prescribed April 22nd, with a note that March 25th was the date of the "Latins." Pope Symmachus accepted the former and with his supporters celebrated Easter at Rome on that day.[97] The Victorian alternative, however, was adopted by Lawrence, a rival claimant to the Roman see, and by command of Theoderic the Great was celebrated as the true Paschal date by a bishop acting under his orders, even in Rome itself.[98] As a consequence of this *démarche* the Symmachian party drew up a number of documents, a collection of twenty canons purporting to have been passed by a local Roman synod of A.D. 324,[99] together with two letters alleged to have been addressed by Pope Silvester I to the council of Nicaea,[100] the evident purpose of which was to invalidate the calculations of Victorius. The result of the ultimate triumph of Symmachus over his rival was the re-establishment of the earlier Roman cycle of eighty-four years.[101]

But the day of reconciliation was already near at hand. The Alexandrine Paschal table was due to expire in A.D. 531.[102] With this in view a certain bishop, Petronius, requested a Scythian monk, Dionysius Exiguus, who was then residing at Rome, to draw up a new table.[103] Taking the year A.D. 532 as his point of departure Dionysius adopted the Alexandrine cycle of nineteen years, which he evidently believed to have been sanctioned by the authority of the council of Nicaea. His table extended to the year A.D. 626 (ninety-five years) and therefore embraced five cycles of nineteen years each. It fixed March 8th and April 5th as the limits of incidence for the Paschal new moons, and those of the Paschal full moons on March 21st and April 18th, which thus allowed March 22nd

[97] On these events see Caspar, *Geschichte,* Vol. II, p. 91.
[98] Cf. Duchesne, *op. cit.* Caspar, *Geschichte,* Vol. II, p. 93.
[99] Given in Mansi, *op. cit.,* Vol. II, 266.
[100] *Ibid.,* Vol. II, 720. *P.L.* 56, 214. The discovery that these documents were forgeries was first made by Duchesne, *Études sur le Liber pontificalis,* pp. 30f.; 179f.; 201f.
[101] Cf. Krusch, in *Neues Archiv. der Gesells. f. ält. deutsche Geschichtskunde,* Vol. IX, p. 106.
[102] See above, p. 359.
[103] *P.L.* 67, 483f.

and April 25th as the limits for the incidence of the feast itself, since Dionysius admitted the Alexandrine custom of keeping Easter if necessary on the fifteenth day of the lunar month. Moreover he abandoned the practice, hitherto in force, of dating years by the era of Diocletian.[104]

By the end of the sixth century, in spite of persistent opposition, the cycle of Dionysius had completely ousted at Rome and in Italy both the old Roman cycle and the one drawn up by Victorius.[105] Yet the *Supputatio vetus* was retained for nearly a century longer in certain churches of the British Isles,[106] and the cycle of Victorius lingered on for nearly two centuries in parts of Gaul.[107]

[104] Later calculations showed that Dionysius was responsible for an error which had placed the birth of Christ four years too late.

[105] Cf. Victor of Capua, *De Pascha,* ap. Bede, *De ratione temporis,* 51. *P.L.* 90, 500f.

[106] The Dionysian cycle was adopted generally at the synod of Whitby. Bede, *H.E.,* 3, 25, 26. *P.L.* 95, 158f. In Cornwall and Wales supporters of the *Supputatio* were found as late as the end of the eighth century. Bede, *H.E.,* 5, 18. *P.L.* 95, 260.

[107] Greg. Turin., *Hist. Franc.* 5, 17. *P.L.* 71, 332; *M.G.H.,* Script. rer. Merov., Vol. I, p. 207; id. *ibid.,* 10, 23. *P.L.* 71, 564. Cf. Krusch, *Neues. Archiv.,* Vol. IX, pp. 137f.

CHAPTER XVI

LEO AND THE CHURCHES OF THE EAST. 8

THE REIGN OF LEO I

It must have been with some feeling of relief that Marcian received the news in the latter part of A.D. 454 that Dioscorus, the deposed and exiled bishop of Alexandria had died on September 4th of that year.[1] The information was at once transmitted by Julian to the see of Rome, where no doubt it must have been equally welcome. In his letter of acknowledgment [2] Leo expressed the hope that the event might do something to facilitate the reconciliation of the "monophysite opposition," especially in Egypt.

How vain was that hope was clearly shown by the contents of a further report on the affairs in the Eastern churches received by Leo from Julian early in the following year. Not only did it mention the outbreak of serious disorders in Alexandria which had caused the Emperor to despatch John, his personal representative, with a view to procuring their suppression, but the existence of some sort of scandal at Antioch, involving the reputation of Maximus. At the same time it stated that a certain Constantinopolitan, Carosus, had been admonished on some point of doctrine, yet because of his equivocal attitude had not yet been admitted to communion by Anatolius. Shortly afterwards the Emperor's letter arrived notifying the see of Rome of the findings of the imperial commission regarding the date prescribed for the celebration of Easter in the current year by the see of Alexandria, and also contained the news that two Constantinopolitan monks, Carosus and Dorotheus, convicted of erroneous beliefs, had been banished from their monasteries. Leo briefly acknow-

[1] Evagrius, *H.E.*, 2, 5, 8. *P.G.* 86, 2509f.; Liberatus, *Breviarium*, 14, 15. *P.L.* 68, 1016f.; Zacharias Mit., *Chronicon*, 4, 1. *P.G.* 85, 1150f. He died at Gangra in Paphlagonia, his place of exile.

[2] *Ep.* 140, JK 515, dated December 6th, A.D. 454.

ledged each of these letters in turn.[3 and 4] In doing so he addressed Marcian for the last time. The Emperor breathed his last sometime in January of the following year,[5] and it soon became apparent how closely the success of the policy adopted by Leo was dependent on imperial support.

Marcian had died without nominating a successor. Apart from the overwhelming influence exercised by the Patrician, Aspar,[6] the obvious candidate for the vacant throne was Anthemius, the late Emperor's son-in-law.[7] Yet Aspar's race and religion alike disqualified him from assuming the diadem. It was therefore given by him to Leo, a nominal Catholic, and one who held the post of military tribune in a legion which was closely attached to the person of the Patrician. As a native of Dacia he must have been only too familiar with the comparatively defenceless state of the Danubian frontier, and yet at the same time sufficiently Western in outlook to appreciate, no less than his predecessor, the importance of maintaining at this critical juncture in the history of the Empire the fiction of imperial unity. It is this consideration which goes far to explain the somewhat ambiguous character

[3] *Ep.* 141, JK 516, dated March 11th, A.D. 455. The "Joannem" mentioned in this letter is qualified as "spectabilem virum," which shows him to have belonged to the second order of the Senate, and suggests that he enjoyed some post in the civil administration. It is probable that the disturbances referred to at Alexandria arose from an attempt made by the "monophysites" to hold an election, with a view to providing an anti-Chalcedonian in succession to Dioscorus and in opposition to Proterius. There is nothing to show the nature of the charges which were being preferred against Maximus of Antioch. The Ballerini, *ad. loc., P.L.* 54, 1109, n. g, point out that the Carosus mentioned here is to be distinguished from the monk of the same name to whom Leo refers in *Epp.* 136, 4; 142, 2.

[4] *Ep.* 142, JK 517, dated March 13th, A.D. 455 addressed to Marcian. The fact that Leo writes *ibid.*, 1, "pro incolumitate gloriae vestrae vota offerre et supplicare non desinam: quia multum et sanctae ecclesiae et Romanae rei publicae divinitus vestra salute consulitur," suggests that at that time the Emperor was already the victim of a fatal illness. Not only the Roman see but the Catholic Church as a whole had good reason to desire the prolongation of Marcian's reign.

[5] Theodore Lect., *H.E.* 1, 12. *P.G.* 86, 169. The actual date of Marcian's death is uncertain. Cf. Bury, *Later Roman Empire,* Vol. I, p. 239, n. 1. A probable date is January 26th, A.D. 457.

[6] Aspar had probably regained some influence in Constantinople since the death of Pulcheria.

[7] Anthemius, who later succeeded to the western throne in A.D. 467, had married Euphemia, Marcian's daughter by his first wife. He had held important military commands and civil posts under the eastern government.

of his ecclesiastical policy and particularly his well-intentioned efforts to retain the favour of the see of Rome.[8]

His nomination as Augustus by Aspar was duly accepted by a compliant Senate, acknowledged by an obedient army and acclaimed by a servile people.[9] Yet in spite of this his title to the imperial diadem must have been regarded as in some degree defective if it had not been awarded him by Anatolius, in default of any surviving representative of the Theodosian dynasty.[10] But he was not long to enjoy in peace the fruits of his success.

As soon as the news of Marcian's death reached the provinces it was welcomed as a relief from oppression, particularly in Egypt, where national aspirations were stimulated by ecclesiastical fanaticism. Even in the late Emperor's lifetime the tenure of the see of Alexandria by Proterius had been largely dependent on military support, since the great majority of the Egyptian clergy and laity had firmly refused to accept the Definition of Chalcedon, and after the death of Dioscorus had for the past year or more been eagerly awaiting an opportunity to elect one of their own number as his successor. When it was known that the old Emperor was dead it happened that Dionysius, the count of Egypt, was absent from Alexandria, being engaged in a punitive expedition. A more favourable occasion for the execution of the plans of the "opposition" could scarcely be desired.[11] At once a tumultuous mob forcibly occupied the cathedral church, known as the *Caesareum,* and after ejecting the orthodox clergy proceeded to elect and enthrone Timothy, surnamed Aelurus,[12] who had for some time been regarded as one of their leaders. Although no more than two bishops could be found who were willing to perform his consecration, yet the fact that they were both under sentence of excommunication

[8] On Leo I, Emp., see Candidus, *Fragm. Hist. Graec.,* Vol. IV, p. 135.
[9] It took place on February 7th, A.D. 457.
[10] Theophanes, *Chronographia,* 5950. *P.G.* 108, 280; *M.G.H.,* Auct. antiq., Vol. XI, *Chron. min.,* Vol. II, p. 87.
[11] For this affair see Mansi, *op. cit.,* Vol. VII, 525, 531, 536; Zacharias, *H.E.,* 4, 1–3; *P.G.* 85, 1152f.; *Vita Petri Iberiae* (ed. Raabe), p. 65.
[12] Gardner in *Cambridge Med. Hist.,* Vol. I, p. 512, mentions that he was "a Teuton whose tribal name, The Herul, was appropriately twisted into Aelurus, The Cat."

and banishment probably served to commend them in the eyes of the rebels. It took place in the *Caesareum* on March 16th amid scenes of wild enthusiasm; in fact so widespread was the popular satisfaction at this event that after making a vain attempt to secure Timothy's banishment Count Dionysius came to the conclusion that it would be more prudent to let things take their course. Twelve days later, on the vigil of Easter itself, the mob broke into a smaller church, called *Quirinus,* and there murdered the Catholic bishop Proterius in the baptistery. His body was dragged through the streets of the city and publicly cremated.

Timothy was now in undisputed possession of the see of Alexandria and lost no time in promoting resistance to the imposition of the Definition of Chalcedon by every means which lay to his hand. Fourteen members of the party favourable to the Definition presented an urgent appeal to the Emperor and to the see of Constantinople, and were presently followed by representatives of Timothy seeking allies in the prosecution of his anti-Chalcedonian campaign.

The new Emperor duly notified to the Roman see the fact of his election and elevation to the Principate in a letter which was courteously acknowledged by Leo.[13] As yet, however, the Pope remained in ignorance as to the ecclesiastical policy which was favoured by the new regime and it was not till a letter arrived from Julian that he had any information as to what was proposed. In his reply [14] Leo expressed his satisfaction at Julian's faithfulness in the performance of his duty, and at the news that disorders created by the Eutychian party at Constantinople had been suppressed, while he mentioned rumours which had reached him as to disturbances in Alexandria, regarding which he was imperfectly informed.[15]

[13] The existence of this correspondence is to be inferred from *Ep.* 145, 1, JK 521. Neither the letter of the Emperor nor the Pope's reply has survived. We gather from *Ep.* 144, JK 520 that the Emperor assured Leo of his adherence to the Catholic cause, *ibid.,* "glorioso et catholico, ut probamus, Augusto." Cf. *Ep.* 148, JK 524, "sancto et catholico spiritu."

[14] *Ep.* 144, JK 520, dated June 1st, A.D. 457.

[15] *Ibid.,* "quidam ad nos rumores de Alexandrini populi ausibus deferuntur, quos ideo plenius indicare non possumus, quia necdum ex integro quae dicuntur gesta cognovimus." Evidently Leo had not yet heard of the murder of Proterius. Duchesne, *Histoire,* Vol. III, p. 480, takes the view that Leo here refers to an appeal to the Roman see pre-

It must be Julian's task, he said, to see that " the Definition of Chalcedon, taught by the Holy Ghost for the salvation of the whole world, remains inviolate." [16]

Further proof of the new Emperor's eagerness to assure himself of the support of the Roman see was to be found in a letter from Anatolius which reached the Pope a month or so later. Anatolius testified to Leo's zeal in the cause of orthodoxy [17] and retailed the news which had recently been received at the hands of the Catholic appellants from the see of Alexandria as to the fate of Proterius.[18] In replying to Anatolius [19] the Pope showed his pleasure at receiving so signal a proof of the bishop's concern for the wrong inflicted on " all the churches " and urged him to use his influence to prevent any further outrage on the church of Alexandria,[20] and specially to urge the Emperor to secure the maintenance of the decisions of Chalcedon.[21] At the same time he wrote to the Emperor [22] pressing him to intervene on behalf of the orthodox at Alexandria. The cause of orthodoxy there and elsewhere, he pointed out, would best be served if the Emperor refused to allow any reconsideration of the Definition.[23] He

sented by members of the orthodox party at Alexandria. Yet if this were so, it is scarcely conceivable that they would have failed to mention the tragic death of their bishop, which had taken place in the previous March. Moreover, *Ep.* 155, 2, JK 531 implies the receipt of an appeal at a later date.

[16] *Ibid.*, " hoc vobis . . . laborandum est, ut . . . sanctae Chalcedonensi synodo praeiudicare non possint, ut quae instruente spiritu sancto ad totius mundi salutem definita sunt, inviolata permaneant."

[17] See *Ep.* 146, 1. " Cuius (sc. imperatoris) quidem tam laudabilis fides et tam prompta devotio est, ut quae paci ecclesiasticae congruebant, sine intercessione cuiusquam, sicut ipse indicas, sponte praestiterit, omnes haereticorum insidias repellendo."

[18] See *Ep.* 145, 1. " Nam talia in Alexandrina ecclesia perpetrata, . . . Anatolii relatione cognovi." It is possible that Anatolius was less anxious regarding the fate of the " Definition " than as to the security of the twenty-eighth canon, which in the event of a revival of an Alexandrine primacy in the East was likely to become largely ineffective.

[19] *Ep.* 146, JK 522, dated July 11th, A.D. 457.

[20] *Ibid.*, 2, " ne in pervasionem Alexandrinae ecclesiae aliquid ulterius sibi possit haeretica audacia vindicare."

[21] *Ibid.*, " studeat (sc. fraternitas tua) enixius deprecari de statutis sanctae synodi Chalcedonensis sine ulla retractatione servandis ; cum ea, quae Deo aspirante decreta sunt, nulla se patiantur varietate corrumpi."

[22] *Ep.* 145, JK 521, of the same date as the above.

[23] *Ibid.*, 1, " si apud sanctam Chalcedonensem synodum de D. Christi incarnatione firmata nulla permiseritis retractatione pulsari : quia in illo concilio per Spiritum sanctum congregato, tam plenis atque perfectis definitionibus cuncta firmata sunt, ut nihil ei regulae, quae ex divina

went on to mention his satisfaction at hearing of the measures taken by the Emperor to suppress attacks on the council made by heretics,[24] and requested that he would take steps to provide for the election of a fitting and orthodox bishop to the see of Alexandria.[25]

But it was evidently a cause of annoyance to Leo that the earliest news of the catastrophe at Alexandria had not reached him through the instrumentality of Julian. He therefore wrote by the same post to his "agent"[26] to express his disappointment.

"I am surprised," he says, "that you have passed over in silence an opportunity, which was used by our brother Anatolius as a matter of course, for sending a report, although in view of the times and the issues at stake communications ought to be the more frequent."[27]

Leo added that Julian should use his influence to procure the re-establishment of the orthodox cause at Alexandria, and the election of a bishop of whom the Roman see could approve.[28]

Possibly he was beginning to fear that the new regime was not proving so trustworthy as he had hoped at first. If so the absence of any direct communication from the Emperor himself must only have served to increase his anxiety. That his fear was not without some justification was shown by the

inspiratione prolata est, aut addi possit aut minui." Evidently Leo regards the "Definition" as possessing a status equal to the decrees of the Council of Nicaea. His anxiety possibly reflects the prevalence of rumours to the effect that the new regime at Constantinople was already contemplating some reconsideration of the "Definition" with a view to reconciling the opposition and restoring unity. It is remarkable that Leo appears to have forgotten the existence of the twenty-eighth canon.

[24] *Ep.* 145, 2, "ut multorum ante relatione comperimus, molitiones haereticorum, quae contra praedictae synodi auctoritatem conabantur assurgere, nihil ex hoc permiseritis audere." Cf. *Ep.* 146, 1.

[25] *Ibid.*, "sanctae primitus Alexandrinae ecclesiae pacis reparatione consulite, et per catholicos sacerdotes talem provideri iubete pontificem, in quo et in actuum probitate et in fidei professione nihil possit reprehensibile reperiri." It is to be noticed that nowhere in these letters is any mention made of the *name* of Proterius.

[26] *Ep.* 147, JK 523, of the same date as the above. The addition of "et Aetio" to the title is probably spurious.

[27] *Ibid.*, 1, "miror tamen eam rescribendi opportunitatem, qua frater Anatolius necessarie usus est, silentio praeteriisse, cum pro ratione temporis atque causarum crebriora oporteat esse colloquia."

[28] *Ibid.*, 2, "cui cum securitate concordiae communio sedis apostolicae praebeatur."

steadily increasing confidence of the monophysite party and by the growing demand that steps should be taken to summon a fresh council, with a view to revising the measures adopted by its predecessor. In view of Leo's policy in regard to those measures it can well be imagined what indignation such a demand would arouse in Rome as soon as it became known there.

Some sort of information regarding a plan of this kind must have reached Leo in the early autumn, and as a result a gigantic post was despatched consisting of letters addressed to all the principal interested parties. The most important item in this series was an "Encyclical," of which apparently two separate copies have been preserved.[29] It was addressed in the first instance to the see of Antioch, and also to the sees of Jerusalem, Thessalonica, Corinth and Dyrrhachium.[30] In the case of the see of Antioch the addressee was the new bishop Basil, who had recently been consecrated to succeed Maximus.[31] The letter opened with an allusion to the recent tragedy at Alexandria and urged the recipients that they should resist attacks on the faith with courage and tenacity, especially in view of the known policy of the new Emperor, which Leo professed to regard as identical with that of his predecessor.[32] He was confident, he wrote, that the Emperor would not assent to the plan which the opponents of Chalcedon had proposed, namely that its Definition should be cancelled and a fresh council summoned.[33] The purpose of such a project, he suggested, could only be the subversion of the Gospel; he requested, therefore, that they should remain loyal to the Definition, for if the bishops remained constant,

[29] *Epp.* 149, 150, JK 526, 525, dated September 1st, A.D. 457.

[30] The last three sees were all situated within the Prefecture of eastern Illyricum. Corinth was the metropolitical see of the province of Achaia; Dyrrhachium of the province of *Epirus nova*.

[31] Apparently Maximus had been deposed as guilty of the charges which had been made against him. See above, pp. 373f., n. 3, and cf. *Ep.* 141, 2, JK 516. The new bishop was probably the same person who as deacon of the Church of Constantinople had brought the letters to Rome, to which Leo had replied in *Epp.* 104 and 106, JK 481 and 483.

[32] *Ep.* 150, JK 525, "non aliud de illo credendum sit quam probavimus de augustae memoriae Marciano."

[33] *Ibid.*, "ut sanctae Chalcedonensis synodi definitionibus resolutis, in alios tractatus vocaretur episcopale concilium."

the Emperor and Aspar himself would be the more determined to resist the efforts of heretics.[34]

The form of this letter, as transmitted to the see of Antioch,[35] was prefaced by a special paragraph addressed to Basil himself,[36] which opened with a gently worded reproof that the Roman see had not been informed of his election either by Basil himself or by his comprovincials,[37] though admitting that the writer had learnt of the fact from the Emperor Marcian.[38]

In addition to the " Encyclical " a letter was directed to the Emperor Leo,[39] in which the Pope, after referring to his two previous communications, reaffirmed his confidence in the Emperor's orthodoxy, and urged the need of strong official measures if heresy was to be effectively suppressed. Next he addressed Anatolius,[40] and while praising his diligence in correspondence insisted that more definite steps ought to be taken to suppress monophysitism. In particular he mentioned the allegations of heretical proclivities which had been made against Atticus, a Constantinopolitan priest, and urged that they should become the subject of private investigation.[41] Personal letters were also directed to Julian [42] and to Aetius of Constantinople.[43] In the former of these he requested Julian's co-operation in resisting the influence of heresy and in procuring the despatch of his Encyclical letter. At the same time he expressed his surprise that it should still be felt that his

[34] *Ep.* 150. " Certus enim sum quod clementissimus imperator et vir magnificus Patricius cum omni coetu illustrium potestatum, nihil in perturbationem ecclesiae patientur haereticos obtinere, si pastorales animos in nullo viderint fluctuare." *Ep.* 153, 1, indicates that there was also a letter addressed to Aspar himself which has not survived.

[35] *Ep.* 149, JK 526.

[36] *Ibid.*, 1.

[37] References to such letters occur in *Inter Leon. Epp.*, No. 53; 171, 2, JK 548; 172, JK 549; 173, JK 550. The election of a Constantinopolitan presbyter to the see of Antioch was significant of the gradual centralization of the eastern churches.

[38] *Ibid.*, " sanctae memoriae Marcianus princeps suis scriptis consecrationem tuam nobis cognitam fecit." The letter has not been preserved. It probably was sent in the latter part of the year A.D. 455.

[39] *Ep.* 148, JK 524, dated September 1st, A.D. 457.

[40] *Ep.* 151, JK 529, of the same date as the above.

[41] *Ibid.* " Atticum presbyterum, qui perhibetur Eutychianorum errorem apertis intra ecclesiam disputationibus confovere, secreta primum disquisitione discutias."

[42] *Ep.* 152, JK 527, of the same date as the above.

[43] *Ep.* 153, JK 528, of the same date as the above.

"Tome" contained doctrinal obscurity, and was in need of more plain exposition, since its doctrine was derived solely from the teaching of the New Testament.[44] Equally he requested the help of Aetius in the matter and mentioned that he had enclosed copies of the letters which he had received regarding the "Tome" from the churches of Gaul and Italy.[45]

The paradox of the situation was that the Pope and Anatolius now found themselves yoked together in a common cause, namely the defence of the council of Chalcedon. Nevertheless it is certain that their respective motives in upholding the council were in no sense the same. Both, it is true, feared the restoration of an Alexandrine primacy, yet the fear of Anatolius arose from his unwillingness to abandon the dominant position which the twenty-eighth canon had secured for his see, while Leo's apprehension was due rather to his anxiety that such a restoration might imperil the doctrinal hegemony of the Roman see, now vindicated by the Definition. In any case Leo found himself driven, in the cause of orthodoxy, to rely to an ever increasing extent on the influence of the see of Constantinople.

Earlier in the year the Emperor had informed him of the arrival at Constantinople of the orthodox refugees from Alexandria,[46] and while waiting to hear further news of the success of the measures, which he had urged against the monophysites Leo found opportunity to address to them a personal letter of encouragement.[47] After reaffirming his confidence in the Emperor's orthodoxy he expressed the hope that the time might not be far distant when in consequence

[44] *Ep.* 152, JK 527, "miror sane calumniantium vanitati aliquid adhuc in epistola mea, quae universo mundo placuit, obscurum videri, ut de ea putent apertius exponendum; cum illius praedicationis tam plana et solida sit assertio, ut nihil recipiat vel in sensu vel in sermone novitatis: quia quidquid tunc a nobis scriptum est, ex apostolica et evangelica probatur sumptum esse doctrina." The appeal to Scripture is characteristic of Leo's doctrinal writings.

[45] *Ep.* 153, 2, i.e. *Inter Leon. Epp.*, Nos. 97 and 99.

[46] The letter is mentioned in *Ep.* 154 but now lost.

[47] *Ep.* 154, JK 530, dated October 11th, A.D. 457. A similar letter *Ep.* 158, JK 533, followed on December 1st of the same year.

of their loyalty the church of Alexandria might recover its ancient dignity.[48]

By the same post Leo also despatched a reply [49] to a letter recently received from Anatolius, in which reference was made to the arrival of deputations from Egypt.[50] While urging the need of inflexible constancy in the face of the boldness of the heretics he insisted that no opportunity should be allowed to them of arguing against the Faith lest the same injury of which the Egyptian refugees complained should be inflicted on others. Leo then passed on to allude to reports which had reached him regarding the existence of some secret supporters of monophysitism among the Constantinopolitan clergy. Anatolius, he said, should examine them and punish the guilty; those who were unamenable to correction must be deposed.[51] He further recommended that Anatolius should use his influence with the Emperor to persuade him to prohibit their having any part in the Church, lest they should enjoy sacramental privileges whose crimes deprived them of the right either to dwell or to pray in the house of God.[52]

The cause of the reaction against the council of Chalcedon had evidently made some progress during the last few months at Constantinople, so much so that the eastern government appears to have come to the conclusion that peace could only be procured at the price of summoning a fresh council. Accordingly the Emperor wrote once more to Leo explaining the need of such a council and expressing the hope that he would be able to attend in person. Its purpose, so he said, was solely to vindicate the faith of Nicaea. The receipt of such a letter evidently caused the Pope considerable dismay. Not

[48] *Ep.* 154. "Alexandrina ecclesia depulsis haereticis antiquam recipiat dignitatem." Possibly Leo was alluding to his rejection of the twenty-eighth canon of Chalcedon.

[49] *Ep.* 155, JK 531, of the same date as the above. He alludes to a letter which he had received from the Emperor and to which he is now replying. Neither the letter nor the Pope's reply have survived.

[50] Including one from the supporters of Timothy. *Ibid.*, 1. "ut etiam apud Constantinopolim audeant insanire."

[51] *Ibid.*, 2. "ita ut his quibus prodesse non potuerit correctio, non parcat abscissio." There is a noticeable change here as compared with Leo's earlier attitude to those convicted or suspected of heresy.

[52] *Ibid.* "neque quidquam illis in ecclesiis Christi licere patiatur, ne in eorum potestate sint divina mysteria, quibus in domo Dei pro scelerum suorum magnitudine, nec habitandi ius residet, nec orandi."

only did it show that the very thing which he feared and had consistently rejected was now being urged upon him with all the weight of imperial authority, but that the purpose of the council was to be no other than the reconsideration of doctrine. Not a word was mentioned in the Emperor's letter of judicial proceedings against Timothy Aelurus and the Egyptian "parricides," but, as it seemed that his representatives were enjoying the hospitality of the imperial capital and the imperial church, it might be expected that he too would be invited to the capital. Nor did the fact that the Emperor enclosed copies of the appeals which he had received from the rival Alexandrine parties serve to disarm criticism.[53] From Leo's own standpoint there could be but one answer to such appeals. The Chalcedonians were in the right; their opponents in the wrong.

Thus, in the main, within a year of the accession of the new Emperor, Leo I, the situation of A.D. 449 had been reproduced. Then as now the issue was a doctrinal one; then as now the eastern government was set upon determining the question at issue by the expedient of summoning a general council; then as now there was a prospect that the see of Alexandria would be able to exercise a preponderating influence on its decisions. And in one respect the position of the see of Rome in relation to the situation was even less favourable than it had been on the former occasion. In A.D. 449 it was at least assured of the whole-hearted support of the sees of Constantinople and Antioch.[54] Now there was a very real danger that if a way could be found of securing to the former the gains which it had secured through the adoption at Chalcedon of the twenty-eighth canon it might accept some compromise at the price of abandoning the Chalcedonian Definition, while the attitude of the see of Antioch was too indeterminate for reliance to be placed on it to put up any effective resistance.

The gravity of the situation from the standpoint of the Roman see was clearly shown by the character of the reply[55] sent by Leo in answer to the Emperor's invitation.

[53] These details are to be inferred from Leo's reply, *Ep.* 156, JK 532.
[54] See Chap. IX, pp. 211ff.
[55] *Ep.* 156, JK 532, dated December 1st A.D. 457.

Referring to the Emperor's request that he would take part in the projected council, Leo on this occasion did not waste time in pointing out the grounds on which he was unable to do so. On the contrary he asserted bluntly that the whole project was altogether unnecessary, since all that had to be done for the preservation of the peace of the Church and the defence of the Faith was to remain loyal to the Definition of Chalcedon.[56] The only effect, he wrote, of conceding the request of the heretics would be to introduce fresh causes of division between the churches. In proof of this he adduced the fact that the council of Chalcedon had been found necessary to remove the causes of scandal created by the second council of Ephesus;[57] yet opportunity for reconciliation was still available by all who sought it. The only policy open to the Emperor was to uphold the Chalcedonian decrees. Then follows a characteristic appeal to the doctrinal authority of the Roman see:

"Since therefore the universal Church has been made like a rock by the fashioning of that original Rock, since the most blessed Peter, the first of the Apostles, has been told by the lips of the Lord Himself: 'Thou art Peter, and upon this Rock I will build my Church'; who but an Antichrist or devil would dare to strike its impregnable solidity? Who but one, who remaining unrepentant in his wickedness, longs to sow lying seed, by means of vessels of wrath fit implements for his guile, while under the false pretext of zeal he pretends that he is seeking the truth?"[58]

[56] *Ep.* 156, 1. "nihilque sit convenientius fidei defendendae quam his quae per omnia instruente spiritu sancto irreprehensibiliter definita sunt, inhaerere."

[57] *Ibid.* "Unde quia post illas Ephesinae synodi impietates . . . nihil ad conservationem fidei Christianae potuit ordinari, quam ut praedicti facinus sancta synodus Chalcedonensis aboleret." This was, of course, a two-edged argument and appeared to ignore the obvious retort of the "monophysites" that in their view, not Ephesus, but Chalcedon had been a cause of scandal and needed correction by means of a fresh council. Nor, in fact, does it represent Leo's original view before the Council of Chalcedon was held. At that time he was urging that subscription to his "Tome" and to other doctrinal statements in agreement with us would suffice to correct the errors of Ephesus, without the necessity of a council at all. Cf. Chap. XI, p. 277.

[58] *Ibid.*, 2. "Cum ergo universalis Ecclesia per illius principalis petrae aedificationem facta sit petra, et primus apostolorum beatissimus Petrus voce Domini dicentis audierit: *Tu es Petrus, et super hanc petram aedificabo ecclesiam meam;* quis est, nisi aut Antichristus, aut

Those who were outraging the church of Alexandria, he writes, showed the true character of the opponents of Chalcedon. They urged that nothing should be held which is at variance with the faith of the council of Nicaea, and pretended that they themselves hold that faith, while they forgot that the Nicene Creed asserted the consubstantiality not of the manhood of the Son, but of His Godhead with the Father, and that the Definition of Chalcedon proclaimed that He took the reality of our human nature from the substance of His Virgin Mother.

The duty of the Emperor therefore and of all who preach Christ was to abide in the fellowship of the Apostles and prophets. The Emperor had received his imperial authority not only for the governance of the world but for the protection of the Church. In virtue of that authority those guilty of outrages should be punished, and salutary decrees upheld by banishing the usurpers of an authority which was not theirs and restoring the see of Alexandria to the ancient Faith. Let him pardon the offences of that city if he will, but let him know that the bishops of the universal Church are imploring him to do justice on the usurpers of the Alexandrine church who are persecutors of the Catholic Faith. Such men were unworthy not only of the episcopate, but even of the Christian name.[59] The fact that those who demand a fresh council were "parricides" did not really affect the issue; such a demand could not be granted even if the petitioners were innocent.

Leo then passed on to examine the petitions from the two Alexandrine parties, copies of which he has received from the Emperor. He pointed out that the one presented by the Catholics is supported by signatures, which included mention of positions of honour. The rival document, on the other hand, omitted to mention any particular names and concealed a lack of distinction and of merit in its supporters by the use

diabolus, qui pulsare audeat inexpugnabilem firmitatem; qui in malitia sua inconvertibilis perseverans, per vasa irae et suae apta fallaciae, falso diligentiae nomen, dum veritatem se mentitur inquirere, mendacia desiderat seminare?" It is not clear whether "principalis petrae" refers to our Lord Himself or to St. Peter, probably the former. The whole passage is steeped in scriptural allusion.

[59] *Ibid.*, 3. The allusion here is of course to Timothy Aelurus and to his associates.

of an obscure general expression.[60] Evidently fear of deserved condemnation was causing them to suppress mention of their places of origin. One, he said, was a petition of Catholics, the other a pack of lies originating from heretics.

He therefore argued that there was but one course of action open to the Emperor, since the Church of Alexandria, through the persecuting zeal of heretics, was deprived of all light of the heavenly mysteries.[61]

"The offering of sacrifice was interrupted, the chrismal consecration was omitted and all sacraments were withdrawn by the hands of parricides."[62] Now the heretics have even the audacity to demand the right to a usurped dignity which they have obtained by an outrageous murder,[63] and presume to call in question the impregnable faith of Apostolic teaching before councils.[64] The Emperor, he added, could not obtain a more glorious triumph than by delivering the church of Alexandria from such an insensate tyranny.

In conclusion Leo promised that he would write later on the subject of the faith, in a fashion which would disclose the ambushes of the heretics.[65] The fact that the church of Constantinople itself was besmirched by the presence of supporters of heresy among its clergy ought to be enough to arouse him to take just vengeance and to exclude such not only from the church but to banish them from the city.[66] He com-

[60] *Ep.* 156, 4. "sub incerto confusae universitatis vocabulo, ideo certum nomen retrahitur." Leo means that the heretical petition contains no signatures of individuals nor mention of the name of Timothy Aelurus.

[61] *Ibid.*, 5. "omne illic coelestium sacramentorum lumen exstinctum," alluding to the nocturnal ceremonies of the Easter vigil.

[62] *Ibid.* "Intercepta est sacrificii oblatio, defecit chrismatis sanctificatio et parricidalibus manibus impiorum omnia se subtraxere mysteria." The allusion is, of course, to the interruption of the Easter Liturgy, including Confirmation, "chrismatis sanctificatio," and the Eucharist "sacrificii oblatio," by the murderers of Proterius, who doubtless took advantage of the fact that the time of its celebration was in the course of the night.

[63] *Ibid.* Leo mentions the cremation of the body of the murdered bishop.

[64] *Ibid.* "audent . . . apostolicae doctrinae inviolabilem fidem ad concilia provocare." The idea in his mind is that the "Tome" is being arraigned before a conciliar tribunal.

[65] *Ibid.*, 6. At the same time Leo suggests that the "Tome" is sufficient for the purpose, "licet ea quae a sede apostolica sunt praedicata sufficerent."

[66] *Ibid.* "ut tales non solum ab ordine clericatus, sed etiam ab urbis habitatione pellantur." He suggests that Anatolius has been somewhat remiss in taking action in the matter.

mended the good offices of Julian and Aetius and begged that the Emperor would give ear to their advice.[67]

This letter is of singular interest. Not only does it show that at this time the Roman see was the only substantial bulwark of the Chalcedonian decrees, but it reveals the present holder of that see as a man of imperious will who does not fear to remind the Sovereign of his duty and even to dictate to him an appropriate course of action. When elsewhere all was change, transition and uncertainty the Roman Pontiff stands out as one who is conscious of a supreme vocation to be the arbiter of the world's spiritual destiny and who is determined to allow nothing to hinder him in the fulfilment of his responsibility.

By the same post Leo wrote to Anatolius[68] in reply to a letter which he had received mentioning the appeal addressed to the see of Constantinople by the orthodox Egyptians.[69] Their present duty, he said, was not so much to bewail the past as to provide for the welfare of the Church and to exclude heretics. He mentioned that he had strongly urged the Emperor to give instructions that the Definition of Chalcedon was to remain intact and that the "usurpers" at Alexandria were to be banished.[70] It was cause for satisfaction, he added, that only four Egyptian bishops, themselves already condemned, could be found to support Timothy. Even should they accept the Catholic Faith their responsibility for the murder of Proterius made them unfit for a place in the Church.[71] Hence the crying need of the Church of Egypt was that it should be freed from persecution and its secret resorts cleansed from this evil. As to the orthodox Egyptian exiles, he stated that he had repeatedly commended their cause

[67] It is the last time that these two names occur in Leo's correspondence. But Julian was undoubtedly present at the synod of Constantinople, A.D. 457. Mansi, *op. cit.*, Vol. VII, 919.

[68] *Ep.* 157, JK 534, of the same date as the above.

[69] *Ibid.*, 1. "quae Alexandriae insanissime gesta sunt cum magno dolore cognovi."

[70] *Ibid.* "nec alio modo totam causam posse esse consumi nisi praedictae synodi constitutiones perennitatis robur accipiant, et insanissimi pervasores ab aliena sede pellantur."

[71] *Ibid.*, 2. "cum autem . . . interficiendo episcopum inauditum facinus perpetrarint, quid illis in ecclesia loci est etiamsi catholicam suscipiant veritatem?"

to the Emperor.[72] Anatolius should help them with his encouragement and see to it that no approval was given to the request for a fresh council. Any who connived at the devices of the heretics would automatically exclude himself from the communion of Catholics,[73] for among the western churches to depart from apostolic tradition in the slightest would be regarded as a highly sacrilegious act.[74] In the final paragraph Leo alluded once more to the failure of Anatolius to bring to book those of his clergy, particularly Atticus, who were prone to argue against the authority of Chalcedon.[75]

He was surprised, he said, that in spite of previous admonition,[76] Anatolius had so far failed to take any action. Atticus should be ordered to defend the Catholic Faith in the same place where he had attacked it and openly to condemn Eutychian teaching. Otherwise, if he and Andrew went uncorrected, Anatolius could not be held guiltless of prevarication.[77]

Yet in spite of everything it seemed for the moment that Leo's demands addressed to the Emperor and to Anatolius were being simply disregarded and that, whether he liked it or not, plans for the projected council were being pushed forward. This impression must have been confirmed by a letter received from the Emperor early in March of the following year, requesting the Roman see to despatch representatives to Constantinople with a view to taking part in the council's deliberations. In his reply [78] Leo insisted that to call in question the Definition of Chalcedon was tantamount to showing ingratitude to God Himself.[79] In fact he suggested that to permit dissension regarding the decisions of the council between the disciples of Eutyches and Dioscorus and the legate

[72] *Ep.* 157, 3. "litteris meis imperatori commendare non destiti." Cf. *Epp.* 145, JK 521; 156, JK 532.

[73] *Ibid.* "ipse se a communione catholicae ecclesiae separabit."

[74] *Ibid.* i.e. by their assent to the "Tome" which to Leo is "traditio apostolica."

[75] This complaint had already appeared in *Ep.* 155, 2, JK 531.

[76] i.e. *Ep.* 155, 2.

[77] The case of Andrew had already been a cause of anxiety on Leo's part. See *Epp.* 111, 112, 113, JK 487–9, and Chap. XIV, pp. 330f.

[78] *Ep.* 162, JK 539, dated March 21st, A.D. 458.

[79] Leo even compares it to the offence of Adam, *ibid.*, 1, "quid aliud quam . . . ad interdictae arboris cibum improbus appetitus mortiferae cupiditatis extendere?"

of the Roman see was to inflict injury on the council of Nicaea itself.[80] There must, therefore, he said, be no discussion whatever on the subject of the Definition. For there could be no communion with those who venture to gainsay the divine mysteries.[81] To act otherwise would be to render oneself liable to the very penalties enjoined by Marcian and sanctioned by the writer himself.[82]

Referring to the Emperor's request that representatives of the Roman see should be despatched to Constantinople Leo promised that they should be sent [83] but expressly only to make known what was the rule of the apostolic faith and not to engage in controversial discussion with its enemies.[84] He concluded by insisting that no freedom for discussion should be permitted to such people and that it was enough, after excluding "the robber and parricide," to leave him to the judgment of God.[85] Let not the Emperor allow the captivity of the Alexandrine church to be prolonged further.

This letter was accompanied by two others, the first of which was addressed to the Egyptian exiles at Constantinople.[86] Leo encouraged his friends to hold fast, in spite of the apparent success of their enemies and told them that he had complied with the Emperor's request to send a representa-

[80] *Ibid.* "quod enim nostris temporibus apud Chalcedonam de . . . incarnatione firmatum est, hoc etiam apud Nicaeam mysticus ille Patrum numerus definivit." The allusion is to the belief, already traditional in Leo's time, that the membership of the Nicene council was three hundred and eighteen, i.e. the number of Abraham's servants who delivered Lot. Cf. Gen. xiv. 14–16 and *Ep. Liberii,* ap. Socr. *H.E.* 4, 12.

[81] *Ibid.,* 2. "ut qui divinis audent contradicere sacramentis aliqua nobis communione socientur." "Divina sacramenta" is used to designate the fact of God's self revelation in the Incarnation.

[82] The allusion is to the edicts issued by Marcian against those who defamed the council. Mansi, *op. cit.,* Vol. VII, 476, 477. For Leo's confirmation of these laws cf. *Ep.* 114, JK 490.

[83] *Ibid.,* 3. "praeceptioni tamen vestrae in eo adnitar obedire, ut aliquos de fratribus meis dirigam, qui apud vos praesentiae meae instar exhibeant et quae sit apostolicae fidei regula, licet, ut dixi, vobis bene sit nota, demonstrent." In c. 1 he mentioned "*eum,* quem apostolica sedes direxerit."

[84] *Ibid.* "hos quos spondeo dirigendos, non ad confligendum cum hostibus fidei."

[85] *Ibid.,* 4. "Cuius vindictam sic Domini iudicio volumus reservari, ut improbus praedo et parricida crudelis in seipsum recidat, et nostra non teneat." The allusion is, of course, to Timothy Aelurus. Besides comparing him to Cain (Gen. iv. 10) Leo here suggests a comparison with Judas (Acts i. 25).

[86] *Ep.* 160, JK 537, of the same date as the above.

tive of the Roman see who might proclaim the true faith to those who refuse it.[87] Let them not bewail, he said, the fact of their expulsion from their sees[88] since no one could be exiled from the presence of God. He added that there must be no discussion regarding the Definition which the Emperor and the Apostolic see had approved.[89] To allow controversial disputes to take place with the heretics could only endanger the faith and the loyalty of bishops.[90]

The other letter[91] was addressed to the supporters of the council of Chalcedon among the clergy of the church of Constantinople. Here Leo expressed his joy at their faithful adherence to the teaching of the New Testament[92] and exhorted them to repudiate alike the errors of Nestorius and Eutyches. He mentioned that he had urged the Emperor not to accede to the demand of the heretics and so allow the Definition of Chalcedon to be called in question, and to be made a subject of discussion which could only serve to weaken its authority.[93] As to Atticus and Andrew he insisted that unless they presented a verbal and written repudiation of Eutychianism and openly in the presence of the laity professed their adherence to the faith of Chalcedon they should be deprived of their status.[94]

[87] *Ep.* 160, 1. " desiderat (sc. imperator) a nobis tamen dirigi, qui fidem . . . non recipientibus, tamquam sit adhuc dubia, possit asserere."

[88] The address of the letter mentions fifteen names, whom it qualified as " episcopis et clericis," the first, namely Nestorius, being probably the same as the bearer of the letter from Proterius. Cf. *Ep.* 129, 1, JK 505. He was probably one of the consecrators of Proterius. Liberatus, *Breviarium,* 14. *P.L.* 68, 1016. Yet the appeal presented to the Emperor and forwarded by him to Leo shows only fourteen signatures, yet there the order is different, while the names of Pulsanimon and a second Athanasius appear. On the other hand, three names mentioned here, i.e. Isidore, Elpidius and Apollonius, are omitted from the appeal, though possibly the second Apollonius here is the same as " Apollo " among the signatures. The names of Elpidius and of an Apollonius are mentioned among the signatures to the resolutions of the synod of Constantinople held under Gennadius, Mansi, *op. cit.,* Vol. VII, 912–16; Grumel, *Regestes,* No. 143.

[89] Notice how frequently this theme recurs in Leo's correspondence of this time.

[90] *Ibid.,* 2. Possibly Leo was apprehensive regarding the " loyalty " of Anatolius.

[91] *Ep.* 161, JK 538, of the same date as the above.

[92] It should be remembered that the teaching of the New Testament for Leo means the doctrine of the " Tome."

[93] *Ibid.,* 2. " dum disceptatio admittitur, auctoritas auferatur." Cf. *Ep.* 162, 3, JK 539.

[94] *Ibid.,* 3. Cf. *Ep.* 157, 4, JK 534.

Since the restoration of intercommunication between the see of Rome and the see of Constantinople, after the temporary breach arising from the resentment felt by the former for the twenty-eighth canon, and the receipt of Anatolius' "apology," [95] mutually friendly relations had existed between Leo and the Constantinopolitan bishop. But it is significant of the extent to which those relations were dependent on the policy of the Sovereign for the time being, and of the change in the situation which had taken place since the accession of the new Emperor, Leo I, that Anatolius appears to have resented the demands made on him by the last letter addressed to him by the Roman see, and to have written immediately expressing his annoyance.[96] His letter must have reached Leo soon after the post carrying the communications dated March 21st had left for Constantinople, and was answered [97] by the Pope a week later. Leo pointed out that in entrusting Anatolius with the duty of investigating the allegations made against the priest, Atticus, of preaching Eutychianism he was not infringing the bishop's rights.[98] As for the document which he has received from Anatolius, purporting to be a doctrinal statement composed by Atticus, it rather tended, he thought, to confirm the impression which he had derived from other sources.[99] The Pope repeated that Atticus must be required explicitly and in writing to repudiate Eutychianism and to acknowledge his acceptance of the Definition of Chalcedon, and that his statement should be published in church. Otherwise he must incur the penalty prescribed by the council.[100]

No doubt the Eutychian party at Constantinople viewed the

[95] *Inter Leon. Epp.*, No. 132. *P.L.* 54, 1082.

[96] This is to be inferred from *Ep.* 163, 1, JK 540. "intellexi tibi studium meae sollicitudinis displicere." Possibly Anatolius specially resented the letter addressed by Leo, *Ep.* 161, to the clergy of Constantinople.

[97] *Ep.* 163, JK 540, dated March 28th, A.D. 458.

[98] *Ibid.* "neque in aliquo honorem tuum laesi, cui discutienda ea quae ad me erant perlata commisi."

[99] *Ibid.* "scilicet Atticus presbyter, quem talia audere cognoveram, . . . qui scripta mittendo dubiae fidei et professionis incertae confirmavit magis quam diluit, quidquid ad nos de eo fama pertulisset."

[100] *Ibid.* "Qui si eadem pravitate perduratis, praeceptis salutaribus parere noluerit, sententiam synodi Chalcedonensis, cuius definitionibus resultat, excipiat."

prospect of a fresh council with considerable satisfaction. But they were destined to be disappointed. Instead of issuing the usual invitations to the bishops the Emperor changed his mind and circulated a *questionnaire* consisting of two articles, both very much to the point in the present situation.[101] The first article asked the question, " Ought the council of Chalcedon to be upheld? " the second, " Ought Timothy to be recognized as bishop of Alexandria? " How much responsibility for this step should be put down to the credit of Anatolius is hard to say; yet it seems highly probable that the eventual abandonment of the original plan was due in some degree to his influence. After all, if the new council were to declare the proceedings of Chalcedon null and void, as it seemed most likely to do, the Definition, in the composition of which Anatolius had played so important a part, would have been struck out of the list of oecumenical statements of belief: yet, from his point of view, even this would not be so serious as a possible cessation of the twenty-eighth canon. The alternative therefore had everything to commend it from his standpoint.

Actually its results proved highly satisfactory. Out of all the answers of which any record survives we only find one negative to the former question, namely the reply presented by the synod of the province of Pamphylia,[102] while to the latter all provinces unanimously replied in the negative. Yet in spite of receiving this significant expression of prevailing opinion, for the time being the eastern government held its hand. No steps were taken to remove Timothy from

[101] The documents of this affair were included in a single collection known as *Encyclia,* Evagrius, *H.E.* 2, 9, 10, and in a Latin version, Cassiodorus, *Divin. et saec. instit. litt.*, 11. Out of fifty-six provinces, the total number in the eastern half of the Empire less the " diocese " of Egypt, the answers of twenty-two are unknown.

[102] The synodical letter of this province, drawn up by the metropolitan Amphilochius of Side, is mentioned by Evagrius, *H.E.*, 2, 10, from the history written by Zacharias. In the Syriac text there is only a summary of it. A short passage of the original Greek has been preserved, *P.G.* 86, ii, 1841, and some Syriac extracts in the *Chronicon* of Michael Syrus (ed. Chabot, Vol. II, p. 145). However, the synod of Perga also criticized the council and considered the use of the phrase " in two natures " unsuitable in a doctrinal formula intended for the general public. It must be remembered that Amphilochius himself was suspected of Eutychianism at the time of the council and in the course of the eighth session was required expressly to anathematize that doctrine.

Alexandria, nor was it officially stated at once that after all no council would be summoned. As we have seen, Leo had received no information of what was taking place at Constantinople since the previous March. Possibly, so far as the Roman see was concerned, it might be said that under the circumstances "no news was good news." Yet, perhaps just because of the absence of information, Leo decided that no opportunity should be allowed to the eastern government to steal a march. He therefore despatched bishops Domitian and Geminian [103] to Constantinople on August 17th, A.D. 458 and entrusted them with two letters to the Emperor. In the former [104] of these Leo began with a brief introduction of his legates. He implored the Emperor not to allow old controversies to revive, nor to permit open and unchecked discussion which could only tend to mislead.[105] After drawing attention to the essential truth regarding the Incarnation proclaimed at Chalcedon and its identity with the decrees of Nicaea,[106] he insisted that no course was open but to demand submission from the heretics. As for Timothy and his associates in the murder of Proterius, though forgiveness by human means was impossible,[107] if they were sincerely repentant they might at least hope for the prayers of Catholics, but only if they ceased in addition from persecuting the Church. In conclusion, Leo begged the Emperor to follow the advice of the Roman legates, who had been sent not to discuss doctrine [108] but to solicit imperial succour for the stability of the Catholic Faith. Most of all he urged the consecration of a new bishop to the see of Alexandria, whose

[103] From *Ep.* 170, JK 547, we may infer that they were well acquainted with the state of things at Constantinople. Their sees are not known.

[104] *Ep.* 164, JK 541, dated August 17th, A.D. 458.

[105] *Ibid.*, 2. "ita fit ut quod maiore facundia defenditur, verius aestimetur." Leo had probably good reason to be contemptuous of the rhetorical art, especially as practised by inferior Greek theologians.

[106] *Ibid.*, 3. "sancta synodus Chalcedonensis, quae ab universis Romani orbis provinciis cum totius mundi est celebrata consensu, et a sacratissimi concilii Nicaeni est indivisa decretis. . ." This may suggest that Leo had heard unofficially of the result of the Emperor's *questionnaire,* yet after all the identity of the doctrine of Chalcedon with that of Nicaea was the very point which the "heretics" disputed.

[107] Leo's view that the sin of the Egyptian monophysites, who had been responsible for the death of Proterius, was unpardonable, appears to reflect the primitive view as to the irremissibility of certain grave sins, including the sin of murder.

[108] He refers to his previous letter to the Emperor, *Ep.* 162, JK 539.

loyalty to the decrees of Chalcedon was undoubted,[109] and the restoration of all those bishops and clergy whom Timothy had driven from their churches. Finally, with all the weight of his authority as primate of the universal Church he uttered the following pronouncement:

"If any man be so regardless of Christian hope and of his own salvation as to presume to attack controversially the evangelical and apostolic Definition of the holy council of Chalcedon to the overthrow of the most holy council of Nicaea, him and all heretics, who have held ungodly and abominable opinions concerning the Incarnation of our Lord Jesus Christ, we condemn with a common anathema and a like execration: thus, while to those who have made amends with the satisfaction required by law the remedy of penance is not refused; on those who remain obdurate the sentence of the council, as the mouthpiece of truth, abides." [110]

The second letter [111] is wholly of a dogmatic nature, and was sent in fulfilment of Leo's promise mentioned in an earlier communication.[112] Its purpose is to set forth the doctrinal position of Chalcedon and to emphasize that council's repudiation of the doctrines of Eutyches and of Nestorius alike, and to emphasize the need of a real humanity in our Lord as a necessary condition of a real Redemption. It is followed by a formidable catena of patristic texts in support of the Chalcedonian position.[113] The author phrased his letter in significantly conciliatory language, as may be recognized from the fact that he nowhere made use of the expression "in two

[109] For the fulfilment of Leo's request see below, p. 397.

[110] *Ep.* 164, 5. "Nam si quis ita Christianae spei ac propriae salutis oblitus est, ut ad convulsionem sacratissimi concilii Nicaeni sanctae Chalcedonensis synodi evangelicum apostolicumque decretum violare aliqua disputatione praesumat, hunc cum omnibus haereticis, qui de incarnatione Domini nostri Jesu Christi impia et detestanda senserunt, simili anathemate parique exsecratione damnamus: ut et legitima satisfactione correctis poenitentiae remedium non negetur, et in resultantes sententia synodalis, quae veritatis est plena, permaneat."

[111] *Ep.* 165, JK 542, of the same date as the above. It has been called the "Second Tome"; its standpoint closely resembles that of its predecessor. For details as to Leo's Christology, see Chap. XX, pp. 451ff.

[112] Cf. *Ep.* 156, 6, JK 532.

[113] The dossier includes a considerable proportion of Alexandrine writings, namely extracts from the works of Athanasius, Theophilus and Cyril. Cf. Saltet, *Revue d'hist. eccl.*, Vol. VI (1905), pp. 301–3. The selection may owe some inspiration to Theodoret, *Dial* 2, *P.G.* 83, 169.

natures," and in criticizing the doctrine of Eutyches contented himself with repudiating a particular interpretation of that doctrine.[114]

The Emperor appears to have welcomed the opportunity thus presented to him of extending an olive branch to Timothy. But the monophysite " diehard " would have none of it and the imperial legate returned to the capital with an obstinate refusal of the offer of peace.[115] After a year's delay the patience of the government seems to have been exhausted, and goaded into activity perhaps by Gennadius, who had recently succeeded to the see of Constantinople, vacant since July A.D. 458 by the death of Anatolius,[116] it entrusted the task of arresting Timothy and restoring the supporters of the council in Egypt to Stilas, " Vicar " of the Egyptian " Diocese." Such a duty was no doubt anything but enviable and was in fact only executed at the price of a considerable civil disturbance. Eventually, however, Timothy was secured and brought under escort to Constantinople.[117] The Emperor then duly informed the Roman see of these events and received in reply a letter,[118] in which Leo showed clearly his view as to the procedure to be adopted. He congratulated the Emperor on the success of his measures for the restoration of the Catholic cause in Egypt, and begged him to secure the appointment of a Catholic bishop to the see of Alexandria.[119] Next he warned him of

[114] *Ibid.*, 2. " ne convincatur (sc. Eutychianus) . . . Verbi incarnati, id est Verbi et carnis, unam audet pronuntiare naturam." Cyril himself had taught, *Ep.* 40, *P.L.* 77, 193, " μία φύσις τοῦ Θεοῦ Λόγου σεσαρκωμένη " ; Eutyches modified this so as to read " μία φύσις τοῦ Θεοῦ Λόγου σεσαρκωμένου," but he had not explicitly asserted identity of nature between the " Word " and the " flesh." In fact he himself would probably have repudiated such an assertion.

[115] Zacharias Mit., *H.E.* 4, 6. *P.G.* 86, i, 273, cf. Michael Syrus (ed. Chabot), 9, 1.

[116] Grumel, *Regestes,* p. 62. Gennadius was a convinced Chalcedonian. His election was probably entirely due to the strong feeling in favour of the council prevailing among the clergy of the capital.

[117] Zacharias, *H.E.*, 4, 9. Cf. Michael Syrus (ed. Chabot), pp. 126 and 130.

[118] *Ep.* 169, JK 546, dated June 17th, A.D. 460. *Epp.* 169–73 are to be found edited by Guenther from the *Collectio Avellana* in *C.S.E.L.*, Vol. XXXVA (1895), pp. 117–24, Nos. 51–55.

[119] *Ibid.*, 1. " ut de catholico civitatis illius praesule quod Deo placeat decernatis." In other words Leo asked the Emperor to " provide " a successor to the see of Alexandria by means of an imperial edict. The plan bears some resemblance to the modern *congé d'élire* issued to cathedral chapters, and shows the beginning of the breakdown of the

the danger which might result from the acceptance of any subscription to orthodoxy on the part of Timothy,[120] and rejected the suggestion that the latter was actually innocent of responsibility for the murder of Proterius. However orthodox Timothy might pretend to be, Leo said, he must never be restored.

By the same post Leo wrote to Gennadius,[121] the new bishop of Constantinople, acknowledging a letter which he had received recently,[122] and particularly the information that the exiled Timothy had been allowed to come to the capital. He pointed out the possibility that Timothy might be persuaded to acquiesce in "apostolic doctrine" in order to regain his see.[123] Such a step was, however, unthinkable, particularly in view of the imperial edict. The best way, he suggested, to prevent its occurrence was to secure the election of a Catholic bishop.[124]

In this case, however, Timothy was on the side of the Roman see and, in spite of all that was done to win him over, remained persistently obdurate.[125] The government had therefore no alternative but to execute the sentence of banishment and send him off to Gangra, where Dioscorus had spent his last years.[126] Now that the "parricide" was safely out of the way it was felt that the time had come to carry out Leo's

primitive procedure of election by the clergy and laity of the local church. No doubt Leo was prompted to make this suggestion by the fear that serious disturbances would be renewed in Alexandria if a normal election were to be held, as well as by the probability that the *vox populi* would make an error of judgment.

[120] Possibly a rumour had reached Leo that some such plan was afoot.

[121] *Ep.* 170, JK 547, of the same date as the above.

[122] Since this letter contained the news of Timothy's deportation it could not have been written earlier than the spring of A.D. 460, whereas Gennadius had been consecrated to the see of Constantinople some eighteen months previously. If Gennadius formally notified the fact of his election to the Roman see his letter is now lost.

[123] Cf. *Ep.* 169, 2.

[124] Cf. *ibid.*, 1.

[125] In view of his attitude to Leo's *Ep.* 165, this was only to be expected.

[126] See above Chap. XII, p. 295. A few years later he was deported to the far north of the Black Sea, to Cherson in the Crimea, where he remained till the flight of the Emperor Zeno from Constantinople in A.D. 475, when he was recalled by the usurper Basiliscus. Meanwhile he continued his incessant literary polemic against the Council of Chalcedon. Cf. Lebon, *La christologie de Timothée Élure,* in *Revue d'hist. eccl.,* Vol. IX (1908), p. 677.

request and provide a Catholic successor to the see of Alexandria. The person nominated by the Emperor was also called Timothy, and to distinguish him from his monophysite rival namesake he received the nickname of "Melkite," the "emperor's man," or "Solofaciol," "the man with the white turban." [127] The fact that only ten Egyptian bishops could be found to proceed with his consecration served to show how deep now were the roots of monophysitism in that country and betrayed the degree of his dependence on imperial support for the security of his tenure. In due course his election was notified to the Roman see both by Timothy II himself, by the clergy of Alexandria and by his Catholic comprovincials,[128] each of whom in turn received a letter of gratitude and appreciation from Leo. Writing to Timothy,[129] the Pope expressed his unfeigned satisfaction that at long last the see of Alexandria had regained a Catholic bishop, and exhorted him to use moderation in his relations with the erstwhile supporters of his monophysite rival.[130] He encouraged him to take all possible measures for the repression of the Nestorian and Eutychian heresies, and requested him to report as often as possible on the progress of his reconciliatory programme. Addressing the Alexandrine clergy [131] Leo congratulated them on the removal of the "wild beast," and urged them to teach only the doctrine of the Catholic bishops of their see.[132] Equally he exhorted the Egyptian bishops [133] who had shown their loyalty to the change of regime to support the new Timothy in his delicate task of undoing the damage caused by "the most bloody usurper," and to prove themselves worthy members of the episcopate

[127] Evagrius, *H.E.*, 2, 11.
[128] Their names are given in the title of *Ep.* 173, JK 550.
[129] *Ep.* 171, JK 548, dated August 18th, A.D. 460.
[130] This advice is a marked characteristic of Leo's attitude to repentant heretics. But in this case at any rate it proved superfluous. We learn from Zacharias, *H.E.*, 4, 10, that Timothy II proved highly accommodating to the monophysites, and went so far as to restore the name of Dioscorus to the diptychs of the Alexandrine Church, for which he was duly reproved by the Roman see. Cf. Simplicius, *Ep.* 11, JK 580. Thiel, Vol. I, p. 197.
[131] *Ep.* 172, JK 549, of the same date as the above.
[132] i.e. especially of Athanasius, Theophilus and Cyril, extracts from whose writings Leo had appended to his *Ep.* 165.
[133] *Ep.* 173, JK 550, of the same date as the above.

in assisting him in his duty of providing for the reconciliation of those who desired "healing for their wounds."

It is fitting that the last of the surviving letters which were issued by the Roman see in the course of Leo's pontificate should close on a note of reconciliation and with an expression of the hope that "all the sheep of Christ may know that they have one Shepherd."[134] Throughout the twenty years of his rule he had laboured incessantly for the peace and unity of the Church, and in spite of the persistence of uncertainty elsewhere it must have been a consolation to him in his last years to know that the Petrine see of Alexandria was once again restored to Catholic communion. The tragic future of more than one of the "greater churches" of the East was happily veiled from his sight.

[134] *Ep.* 173, JK 550. "Omnes Christi oves unum se sentiant habere pastorem." The allusion is probably to 1 Pet. ii. 25. It is probable that Leo has also in mind the return to the Egyptian Churches to unity with the Roman see.

CHAPTER XVII

LEO AND WORSHIP

IN the following chapter we shall summarize the evidence provided by Leo's writings as to the normal public worship of the church of Rome in the middle of the fifth century, and also give a short account of his work as a preacher.

(1) THE PUBLIC WORSHIP OF THE CHURCH OF ROME

(i) THE DIVINE OFFICE. The works of Leo contain no direct allusion to any cycle of the Divine Office in use at Rome in his time. The most that we can find is mention of the Saturday vigil in the Ember season,[1] which probably covers the celebration of some vigil office. On the other hand there can be no doubt that some form of the Divine Office was regularly celebrated by the Roman Church at this time,[2] and that Leo himself took active steps to secure its regular maintenance by founding a monastery in close proximity to the basilica of St. Peter.[3]

(ii) THE LITURGY. It is possible that in Leo's time the Mass was celebrated daily, though Leo himself mentions specifically no other day but festivals as liturgical.[4] He implies, however, that it was already the custom at Rome to celebrate the liturgy more than once on such days, in the event of the church being inadequate to accommodate all those who desired to be present.

[1] e.g. *Serm.* 16, 6, *et al.*

[2] Jerome, *Ep.* 109, 3, 9, refers to Vigils; *Ep.* 107 to Vigils, Nocturns, Morning Prayer, Terce, Sext, None and Vespers. An apocryphal letter of his attributed to Damasus the arrangement of the Psalms in the *Breviarium Romanum* on which see Baümer, *Histoire du Brévaire,* Vol. I, pp. 199ff.

[3] *Liber pontificalis,* ed. Duchesne, Vol. I, p. 234. See also n. on p. 236. Batiffol, *History of the Roman Breviary,* pp. 48f. says, "The foundation, in the fifth century, of this monastery thus attached to the basilica of St. Peter is a very important fact; this monastery is the most ancient of the basilican monasteries of Rome. . ." It "is believed to have been that of SS. John and Paul," mentioned in the life of Leo III, *Liber pont.,* Vol. I, p. 324.

[4] *Ep.* 9, 2. "solemnior quaeque festivitas."

(a) *The Mass of the Catechumens.* Leo alludes frequently in his sermons to the Liturgical Lessons, to the Epistle,[5] and to the Gospel.[6] It is clear that the sermon followed the Gospel.[7] Normally it is to be presumed that the bishop himself preached,[8] but licence to preach was evidently given at least on occasion to presbyters.[9]

(b) *The Mass of the Faithful.* Allusions to the more solemn part of the Liturgy are extremely sparse. The recital of the names of the living and the dead at the altar is mentioned, though nothing is said as to the place in the service at which this recital occurred, nor is it clear whether such a recital was normal at Rome or not at this time.[10] While Leo more than once describes the Mass as a sacrifice,[11] he nowhere supplies any material from which we might reconstruct the Canon as it existed in his time. At the words of administration which are implied to have been "The Body of Christ,"[12] each communicant answered "Amen."[13] Communion was administered under both species,[14] and to the baptized of all ages, not excluding young children.[15]

(iii) THE CHURCH'S YEAR. Apart from occasional allusions to liturgical practice contained in his letters the titles of Leo's

[5] *Serm.* 40, 2, a sermon on Lent quoting from the Epistle of Lent I in the *Missale Romanum.*

[6] Of the Epiphany, *Serm.* 33, 1; 34, 1; 35, 1; 38, 1. Of the Passion, *Serm.* 52, 1; 54, 5; 56, 1; 66, 1; 70, 1. Of Easter, *Serm.* 72, 1.

[7] See reff. above, esp. *Serm.* 72, 1.

[8] Leo refers to his preaching in such a way as to imply that it was the regular practice of the Roman bishops, *Serm.* 33, 1; 38, 1; 58, 1; 62, 1; *Ep.* 139, 1.

[9] *Ep.* 119, 6. "non tamen permittendum est ut quisquam extra sacerdotalem ordinem constitutus gradum sibi praedicatoris assumat." This might mean that no one but the bishop was permitted to preach, but in view of the emphatic refusal of licence to do so to monks and laymen expressed in *Epp.* 118, 2: 120, 6, it is possible that "sacerdotalis ordo" may include priests if not deacons as well.

[10] *Ep.* 80, 3, with reference to the recital of the names of Dioscorus, Juvenal and Eustathius still alive and of Flavian who by then was dead. The allusion is, of course, to the so-called "diptycha."

[11] *Serm.* 59, 7; 91, 3. *Ep.* 9, 2, "sacrificii oblatio."

[12] Cf. *De Sacramentis,* 4, 25.

[13] *Serm.* 91, 3. "Frustra ab illis (sc. Eutychianistis) Amen respondetur, a quibus contra id quod accipitur, disputatur." Cf. *Ep.* Cornelii, ap. Eus., *H.E.* 6, 43; Augustine, *Serm.* 272.

[14] *Serm.* 42, 5, referring to the abstention of Manichaeans from the chalice.

[15] *Ep.* 59, 2. "nec ab infantium linguis veritas corporis et sanguinis Christi inter communionis sacramenta taceatur."

sermons supply some evidence as to the seasons and festivals observed by the Roman Church in the fifth century. The Christian year opened with the feast of the Nativity of our Lord.[16] This was succeeded by the Epiphany,[17] a commemoration which at any rate at Rome has already lost its original meaning and associations, and has come to be regarded solely as the remembrance of the worship paid by the Magi to the Infant Christ.[18] The forty days of Lent [19] still retained their primitive character as the season of preparation for Baptism, though their observance as a time of prayer, fasting and almsgiving was regarded as binding on the whole body of the faithful; its concluding week is particularly associated with the Passion.[20] The festivals of Easter [21] and Pentecost [22] were of central importance, and both were regarded as the normal if not the exclusive occasions for the celebration of the ceremonies of Christian initiation.[23] Ember days, not yet associated with ordinations,[24] but primarily seasons of prayer, fasting and almsgiving were observed in December,[25] in the octave of Pentecost [26] and in September.[27] The immoveable festivals for which surviving sermons are provided are the following, SS. Peter and Paul,[28] St. Lawrence,[29] the anniversary of Leo's

[16] *Serm.* 21–30.

[17] *Serm.* 31–8.

[18] Some trace of these associations is to be found in *Ep.* 16, 6.

[19] *Serm.* 39–51. It is clear from *Serm.* 48, 1, that the duration of this season was already forty days in Rome at this time and began after *Quadragesima Sunday*. Cf. *Serm.* 40, 2. The addition of days carrying back the beginning of Lent to the previous Wednesday had already been made before the compilation of the *Sacramentarium Gelasianum;* see *The Gelasian Sacramentary,* ed. Wilson, pp. 15–17. For the general obligation of Lenten observance see *Serm.* 45, 1.

[20] *Serm.* 52–70.

[21] *Serm.* 71–2. The inclusion of *Serm.* 73–4 on the Ascension shows that this feast had already been introduced by this time.

[22] *Serm.* 75, 77.

[23] See esp. *Epp.* 16 and 168.

[24] The absence of any reference to ordinations in the Prayers of the Ember Days bears this out, though the association was already customary before the appearance of the *Sacramentarium Gelasianum,* and may date from the conclusion of the fifth century, since the *Liber pontificalis* makes frequent mention of ordinations in the month of September.

[25] The observance of Ember Days in the first week of Lent is evidently later than Leo's time and probably arose from the choice of this week as suitable for ordination. For the December days see *Serm.* 12–20.

[26] *Serm.* 78–81.

[27] *Serm.* 86–94.

[28] *Serm.* 82, 83.

[29] *Serm.* 85.

own consecration.[30] For the mention of the feast of the *Cathedri Petri* we are indebted to one of the imperial letters [31] included in the Leonine collection. Finally there are the fast days of the "Collecta" belonging to July 6th and coinciding with the pagan *ludi Apollinares*.[32]

(2) LEO AS A PREACHER

The fact that not less than ninety-six sermons [33] have survived, the attribution of which to Leo is not seriously doubted, is some indication of his activity as a preacher. It equally serves to show the depth of the impression which he made on the Church of his time. The needs of the Church then differed in few respects from the needs of the Church to-day. They were primarily popular edification and instruction. In his fifth sermon on the Incarnation Leo tells his hearers explicitly that his purpose in preaching is "that some utterance may be made by us which may serve to edify our hearers." [34]

Equally in a later sermon on the Passion he points out: "It pertains most to the permanence of the Christian faith, that according to the teaching of the Apostle, 'we all speak the selfsame thing, and be perfect in the same mind and in the same knowledge,'" [35] and says that it is with a view to securing this unity of mind that he is addressing his congregation.

Leo appeals therefore first to the understanding of his

[30] *Serm.* 1–5.
[31] *Inter Leon. Epp.*, No. 55.
[32] *Serm.* 6–11.
[33] Besides the ninety-six sermons printed by the Ballerini, *P.L.* 54, and of which the authenticity is generally accepted, no less than sixty-one others have been attributed to him. Of these forty-one have been identified as the work of various authors such as Ambrose, Augustine, Caesarius of Arles, and Maximus of Turin. The remaining twenty are given in Migne's reprint, *P.L.* 54, 477–522. Of these only the first has any relation to the genuine sermons in respect either of style or vocabulary, and is to be explained as a *cento* derived from Leo's authentic writings. Eight further sermons are given in *P.L.* 56, 1131–54, but these are certainly unauthentic. Cf. Pschmadt, *Leo als Prediger*, p. 39; Bardenhewer, *Geschichte*, Vol. IV, p. 622. *Serm.* 14 of this collection, *In Cathedra S. Petri*, of fifth century date, is also discussed by Morin, *Études, textes, découvertes*, 1913, p. 35.
[34] *Serm.* 25, 1. "ut . . . aliquid a nobis quod audientes possit aedificare promatur."
[35] *Serm.* 69, 1. "ut secundum apostolicam doctrinam 'id ipsum dicamus omnes, et simus perfecti in eodem sensu et in eadem scientia'" (1 Cor. i. 10).

hearers;[36] yet he does not fail to appeal also to their wills.[37] He is concerned not only with the duty of promoting the spiritual welfare of the devout but of exhorting the negligent and careless.[38] Neither one nor the other is to him outside the pastoral responsibility of the bishop.[39] In his capacity as pastor he is much preoccupied with the dangers to which the faithful are exposed through contact with persons of insufficient or false faith. Thus in his sermons on the Epiphany and the Passion he devotes considerable space to pointing out the defects of Judaism;[40] elsewhere he describes, often with a wealth of detail, the false elements in the heresies or sects of Priscillian and Manes,[41] and in one of the latest of his surviving sermons draws attention to the insidious nature of monophysite propaganda in Rome.[42]

Among the authorities to which he appeals there is, of course, in the first place Holy Scripture,[43] from which every sermon contains at least one quotation. Next comes the local Roman baptismal Creed, which Leo constantly describes as apostolic.[44] Occasionally, however, he speaks of the " Catholic Faith " and by this phrase he appears to mean the symbol of Nicaea.[45]

Frequently he grounds his arguments on the authority of the Apostles or of the " holy fathers," by which he means

[36] *Serm.* 32, 2. "ut rerum gestarum ordinem non solum credendo, sed etiam intelligendo veneremur." Cf. *Serm.* 52, 1. In both these passages he refers to the need of an intelligent grasp of the facts of history. Elsewhere e.g. *Serm.* 33, 1; 38, 1; 64, 1 and 67, 1 he mentions the value of understanding the true significance of the festival being celebrated that day.

[37] *Serm.* 71, 1. "Moriendum ergo est diabolo et vivendum Deo." Cf. *Serm.* 72, 1.

[38] *Serm.* 86, 1. "ut si qui sunt in hoc exercitio tardiores, in his saltem diebus communi abstinentiae se obedienter adiungant."

[39] *Serm.* 94, 1. "sacerdotalis officii est erga omnes ecclesiae filios curam habere communem, in id quod et rudibus prosit et doctis, quos simul diligimus, pariter incitamus." Cf. *Serm.* 96, 1.

[40] e.g. *Serm.* 29; 32; 33; 35; 55; 57; 58; 59; 60; 61; 68; 70.

[41] e.g. *Serm.* 9; 10; 16; 22; 24; 27; 34; 42; 43; 47; 76.

[42] *Serm.* 96.

[43] Cf. *Serm.* 26, 5. Of the New Testament Leo makes frequent use of the epistles of St. Paul and of the Gospel according to St. Matthew. He nowhere cites St. Mark. Of the Old Testament the books most commonly quoted are the Psalms and Isaiah.

[44] *Serm.* 24, 6; 34, 4; 62, 2; 72, 7; 96, 1. For his view as the origin of this Creed see *Ep.* 31, 4.

[45] *Serm.* 24, 5; 30, 3; 91, 2.

either the Apostles themselves or the "fathers of the Church," including in particular the council of Nicaea and his predecessors in the see of Rome.[46] Nevertheless he sometimes makes use of an appeal to the "common sense" of men and women, especially in connection with exhortations to almsgiving.[47]

His sermons never fail to lead up to a practical application in the development of which he shows his intimate knowledge of the circumstances and manner of life of his flock.[48]

It is evident that the sermons which we possess belong to the period of Leo's life subsequent to his election to the episcopate. Not only can we remark a tone of authority in many of them, inconceivable if the preacher were not possessed of the right to instruct his hearers as to the manner of their faith and conduct;[49] we notice also that his words frequently apply not to a single congregation but to the whole local Church.[50] In addition the numerous references to contemporary events, such as the detection of the Manichaeans, the emergence of Eutychianism and the deliverance of Rome from hostile invasion all belong to the period of his pontificate.[51] Actually it is possible on closer examination to assign to them a more exact date. Apart from a few sermons on special topics,[52] it is reasonably clear that the majority belong to the first ten or twelve years of his rule. As to the remaining period it is impossible to determine whether the sermons of the later years have for the most part perished or whether, owing to the Pope's preoccupation with his relations with the churches of the East, few were actually preached. Even so, it is doubtful whether we possess more than a fraction of those which were uttered during the earlier period, since it will be noticed that those which belong to specific feasts or seasons

[46] *Serm.* 7. "primus collectarum dies saluberrime a sanctis Patribus institutus." Cf. 16, 2; 9, 3; 10, 1; 96, 2, etc.

[47] *Serm.* 12, 1. "Nam si inter homines ea demum firma amicitia est, quam morum similitudo sociarit . . . quantum nobis optandum . . . est ut in nullo ab iis quae Deo sunt placita discrepemus." Cf. *Serm.* 20, 3; 41, 3; 45, 3; etc.

[48] e.g. *Serm.* 21; 23; 25; 26, etc.

[49] e.g. *Serm.* 86, 1.

[50] Especially with reference to the duty of almsgiving. *Serm.* 8; 9, 3; 11, 2.

[51] Manichaeism, A.D. 444/5, *Serm.* 9, 4; 16, 4; 24, 4; 34, 4; 42, 4; 76, 6–7. Eutychianism, A.D. 449, *Serm.* 28, 5; 91, 2; 96. The Vandal Invasion, A.D. 455, *Serm.* 84.

[52] e.g. *Serm.* 84; 91; 96.

range from the Ember season in December to Pentecost, and it is possible that those which belong to the period of the year from Pentecost to the end of Advent were accidentally lost.

A marked characteristic of many of the sermons is their brevity, and this feature has prompted the suggestion that we do not now possess them in their original form, and that they are in fact mere abbreviations.[53] Close examination of the sermons, however, reveals that as they stand they are complete in themselves.[54] An alternative and probably more correct explanation of their brevity is to be found in the view that in certain cases, at least, we no longer possess the actual liturgical sermon for a particular day, but rather a brief personal exhortation given at the conclusion of the rite and bearing on the practical application of the spiritual significance of the occasion to which it belongs. This is particularly clear in the case of the sermons on the feast of Pentecost [55] and seems likely to be true in other cases as well.

We may pass on to enumerate the allocation of the surviving sermons to particular festivals and seasons. There are ten on the festival of Christmas,[56] eight on the Epiphany,[57] two on Easter,[58] two on the Ascension,[59] three on Pentecost,[60] and one each on the *natale* of St. Peter,[61] of St. Lawrence,[62] and on the feast of the Transfiguration.† For the seasons of fasting we find twelve on Lent,[63] nineteen for Passion or Holy Week; [64] the autumnal [65] and winter [66] Embertides have each a group of nine and six are devoted to the annual observance of the "Collecta." [67] Finally there are five sermons on his *natale* [68]

[53] Comparison e.g. with the sermons of John Chrysostom show how relatively short most of Leo's sermons are.
[54] e.g. *Serm.* 1; 6; 7; 8; 13; 14; 15; 78; 79; 80; 81; 84; 86.
[55] *Serm.* 78–81.
[56] *Serm.* 21–30 on Christmas.
[57] *Serm.* 31–8 on the Epiphany.
[58] *Serm.* 71, 72 on Easter.
[59] *Serm.* 73, 74 on the Ascension.
[60] *Serm.* 75–7 on Pentecost.
[61] *Serm.* 83.
[62] *Serm.* 85. † *Serm.* 51.
[63] *Serm.* 39–50.
[64] *Serm.* 52–70.
[65] *Serm.* 86–94.
[66] *Serm.* 12–20. The Pentecostal Embertide sermons are 78–81.
[67] *Serm.* 6–11.
[68] *Serm.* 1–5. See Chap. V. One Sermon, No. 95, on the Beatitudes is omitted from the above classification.

or its anniversary of considerable value for the light which they throw on Leo's own conception of his office, which we have described elsewhere.

Generally speaking the sermons as a whole reveal the care exercised by the author in their composition. Thus Bardenhewer says: "The delicate construction of periods, the completeness of their antitheses, the rhythmical cadences must have delighted the ears of his Roman audiences, though the modern reader can scarcely avoid the impression of an excessive affectation. As an example of the antithetical parallelism with homoioteleuton we may refer the reader to *Serm.* 82, 2." [69]

As the main points of doctrinal interest contained in the sermons will be set forth in a later chapter we may confine our attention here to certain points of importance. Leo's references to the season of Lent [70] show that already in his time the Roman Church was accustomed to observe it as a period of forty days.[71] He urges the obligation to carry out the duties of fasting, almsgiving and penance,[72] which belong to that season, is binding not only on those who are preparing for Baptism, but on the whole Church.[73] Those who are

[69] *Geschichte,* Vol. IV, 622. *Serm.* 82, 2, "Cum paene omnibus dominaretur (sc. Roma) gentibus, omnium gentium serviebat erroribus et magnam sibi videbatur suscepisse religionem, quia nullam respuerat falsitatem, unde quantum erat per diabolum tenacius illigata, tantum per Christum est mirabilius absoluta." Cf. Steeger, *Die Klauseltechnik Leos d. Gr.,* Hassfurta, M. (1908).

[70] *Serm.* 40, 1. *P.L.* 54, 268.

[71] *Serm.* 39, 3. *P.L.* 54, 264. "accedentes . . . ad quadragesimae initium"; cf. *Serm.* 44, 2; *P.L.* 54, 286, "ut apostolica institutio quadraginta dierum ieiuniis impleatur." This statement appears to be at variance with the evidence of Socrates, *H.E.,* 5, 22, regarding the practice of the Church of Rome in the earlier half of the fifth century: "*οἱ μὲν γὰρ ἐν Ῥωμῇ, τρεῖς πρὸ τοῦ Πάσχα ἑβδομάδας, πλὴν σαββάτου καὶ Κυριακῆς, συνημμένας νηστεύουσιν.*" For an explanation of the apparent discrepancy cf. Duchesne, *Origines* (1889), p. 233, n. 1.

[72] *Serm.* 49, 6. *P.L.* 54, 305. "peccata quae aut baptismi aquis, aut poenitentiae lachrymis abluuntur, etiam eleemosynis deleantur."

[73] *Serm.* 45, 1. *P.L.* 54, 288. "Sive enim illam partem populi cogitemus quae dudum certamina evangelici agonis ingressa, per spiritalis stadii cursum indesinenter tendit ad palmam: sive illam quam lethalium conscia peccatorum, per reconciliationis auxilium festinat ad veniam: sive illam quae sancti spiritus regeneranda baptismate . . . et Christi cupit novitate vestiri." Notice that in *Serm.* 48, 1, *P.L.* 54, 298, Leo makes it clear that he regards the obligation as embracing also the clergy.

already baptized ought to treat it as a spiritual preparation for the observance of Easter.[74] In one passage at least it should be noticed that he emphasizes the ethical aspect of fasting and almsgiving and suggests that the Lenten season should be specially marked by efforts to lay aside malice and hatred and to practise fairness and justice at home.[75]

The sermons on the Passion[76] are for the most part in pairs, one belonging to the Sunday and one to the Wednesday in Holy Week.[77] They are remarkable for their frequent allusions to the liturgical recitation of the record of the Passion, which is thus shown to have been a normal feature of the Roman liturgy of the fifth century.[78]

Of the two sermons which belong to Easter itself, one was evidently preached during the initiatory rites of Holy Saturday, while the other occurred in the course of the liturgy of Easter day.[79]

It should be noticed that each of the sermons delivered in connexion with the feast of Pentecost concludes with a notice of the forthcoming Ember fast, that is to say the Wednesday, Friday and Saturday of the current week.[80] It is interesting to note that Leo ascribes the origin of the custom to Apostolic institution, and suggests that their special purpose is to make good the harm done by sins committed during the Paschal season.[81] Similar notices in regard to the observance of the

[74] *Ibid.*, and *Serm.* 41, 1. *P.L.* 54, 272.

[75] *Serm.* 40, 5. *P.L.* 54, 271. "dominorum atque servorum tam ordinati sint mores, ut et illorum potestas mitior, et istorum sit disciplina devotior." In the same connexion Leo alludes to the custom of reprieving criminals at the Paschal feast, adopted by the Christian Emperors. *Serm.* 51 shows that already in his time to the liturgical Gospel of Ember Saturday in Lent was the record of the Transfiguration.

[76] *Serm.* 52–70. *P.L.* 54, 313.

[77] Five, however, *Serm.* 60, 61, 66, 69, 70 appear to be unattached to any particular day of the week. Wednesday enjoyed special importance liturgically as the occasion of the *Redditio Symboli.*

[78] e.g. in *Serm.* 70, 1. *P.L.* 54, 380.

[79] *Serm.* 71 and 72. *P.L.* 54, 385.

[80] *Serm.* 75–7. *P.L.* 54, 400. It should be noticed that in the second of these he alludes to the recent baptism, presumably on the Vigil of Pentecost, of some of his hearers.

[81] *Serm.* 78, 3. *P.L.* 54, 417. "ut si quid forte inter ipsa festivitatum gaudia negligens libertas et licentia inordinata praesumpsit, hoc religiosae abstinentiae censura castiget."

Ember seasons occur in the sermons on the subject preached respectively in September and December.[82]

In the course of one of the sermons on the anniversary known as the "Collecta," [83] the preacher specially mentions its apostolic origin and mentions his view that it was a Christian substitute for a pagan celebration. It is clear that an important feature of the observance was an act of corporate almsgiving.[84]

One sermon, the eighty-fourth,[85] deserves special consideration. It is concerned with a commemoration of the deliverance of Rome from the evils of barbarian invasion, and evidently belongs to a date some years after the actual event commemorated, since the preacher deplores the present neglect of the observance.[86] With scathing irony he invites his hearers to say whether it was the "games" or the intercession of the saints which had saved the city from its enemies. Its deliverance, he affirms, was due not to the influence of the stars but to the intervention of God.[87]

The allusion here to belief in the influence of the stars indicates the persistence of oriental pagan ideas in Roman society of Leo's time, and finds a parallel in the mention which he makes elsewhere of the practice observed by some Chris-

[82] *Serm.* 86–94. *P.L.* 54, 437. *Serm.* 12–20. *P.L.* 54, 168. Notice that in *Serm.* 15, 2; *P.L.* 54, 175 the origin of the December fast is ascribed to the Mosaic law, and that in *Serm.* 19, 2; *P.L.* 54, 185 four seasons of fasting are enumerated.

[83] *Serm.* 6–11. *P.L.* 54, 157.

[84] *Serm.* 9, 3. *P.L.* 54, 162. "Ad horum ergo operum (sc. charitatis) . . . piam curam dies nos apostolicae institutionis invitat, in quo sanctarum collationum prima collectio est prudenter a Patribus et utiliter ordinata: ut quia in hoc tempore gentilis quondam populus superstitiosius daemonibus serviebat contra, profanas hostias impiorum sacratissima nostrarum eleemosynarum celebraretur oblatio." The Ballerini, *P.L.* 54, 155–7, argue from the fact that this group in a number of collections follows those sermons which belong to the feast of St. Peter that the date of the observance of the "Collecta" is July 6th, on which the *ludi apollinares* were accustomed to begin.

[85] *P.L.* 54, 433–4.

[86] The Ballerini associate this anniversary with the invasion of Italy by the Vandals under Genseric in A.D. 455 on June 16th. Notice Leo's comment, "devotionem . . . pene ab omnibus proxime fuisse neglectam ipsa paucorum qui adfuerunt raritas demonstravit."

[87] *Ibid.*, 2. "liberationem nostram, non, sicut opinantur impii, stellarum effectibus, sed ineffabili omnipotentis Dei misericordiae deputantes, qui corda furentium barbarorum mitigare dignatus est." Attention may be drawn to the allusion in this sermon to the survival of pagan games at this date. Cf. Salvian, *De gubernatione Dei*, 6, 3–17.

tian worshippers of turning towards the rising sun on the top of the steps of the basilica of St. Peter and of paying worship to the heavenly bodies.[88] Yet unlike his predecessor, Innocent I, who in a time of national emergency was alleged to have permitted the revival of pagan sacrifice,[89] Leo has nothing but condemnation for such superstitious survivals.[90]

For the most part, however, Leo treats the doctrines which he presents for the consideration of his audience in a purely objective fashion, and only rarely introduces an application of his teaching to contemporary events. A notable example of such an application is to be found in his publication of the facts regarding the practices of the Manichees, which had been revealed in the course of an investigation held under his personal supervision.[91] Similarly in a later sermon he delivers a solemn warning against the monophysite propaganda which had been introduced into Rome by certain Egyptians.[92]

Doubtless to modern ears many of Leo's sermons would sound austere and aloof, yet there is every reason to believe that they were well suited to the audiences which listened to them for the first time. The average Roman citizen of the fifth century had little use for speculative theology nor for rhetorical display such as delighted the ears of the Greeks. He only wished to be told in simple and ungarnished language just what he was expected to believe and to do. Plainly the sermons of Leo satisfied such a demand. Nevertheless, judged from a literary standpoint alone, they can claim little merit.

[88] *Serm.* 27, 4. *P.L.* 54, 218. "nonnulli etiam Christiani adeo se religiose facere putant, ut priusquam ad B. Petri apostoli basilicam . . . perveniant, superatis gradibus quibus ad suggestum areae superioris ascenditur, converso corpore ad nascentem se solem reflectant, et curvatis cervicibus in honorem se splendidi orbis inclinent." Notice that Leo's description of this custom presupposes the "orientation" of the basilica towards the west. For other references to the worship of the heavenly bodies cf. *Serm.* 22, 6 (where Leo alludes to the view held by some in his time that the festival of December 25th originated as a celebration in honour of the rebirth of the sun); *Serm.* 27, 3; 43, 2; 57, 5; *Ep.* 15. *Praef.*, and 10, JK 412.

[89] Zosimus, *Historia nova*, 5, 41.

[90] e.g. *Serm.* 22, 6, etc.

[91] Cf. Chap. III, pp. 43ff.

[92] *Serm.* 96, 1. "Quosdam Aegyptios . . . ad Urbem venisse, eaque quae Alexandriae sceleste ab haereticis sunt admissa, defendere, asserentes solam deitatis in Christo fuisse naturam, nec carnis humanae quam sumpsit ex beata Maria virgine, habuisse penitus veritatem."

Frequent repetitions and straightforward platitudes are, however, the making of a good instruction, and we have no right to demand of compositions intended to instruct and edify the simplest of the faithful the character of a polished treatise.

Leo differs from some of the best known preachers of antiquity, such as John Chrysostom or Cyril of Alexandria, in the use which he makes of Holy Scripture. His sermons abound in Scriptural quotation and in Scriptural appeal, but he does not comment successively on a continuous passage as they do. As we have already seen, the basis of his sermon course is not the text of a Gospel or of an Epistle, but the succession of fast and festival in the Christian year. Nor is the difference to be seen only here.

" (Leo's) sermons singularly contrast with the florid, desultory and often imaginative and impassioned style of Greek preachers. They are brief, simple, severe; without fancy, without metaphysic subtlety, without passion; it is the Roman censor animadverting on the vices of the people: the Roman praetor dictating the law, and delivering with authority the doctrine of the faith." [93]

His latinity displays a terseness and brevity of expression which, in spite of his frequent use of abstractions and of inverted constructions in conformity with the taste of the period, justifies his being assigned a place of distinction among post classical authors.

"Leo's exhortations revolve in a narrow circle; there are certain things which he is bent on bringing home to his flock; he is quite indifferent as to repeating himself, if thereby he can deepen the impression." [94]

We are bound to recognize that his words bear the impress of a majestic personality, which while supremely conscious of the solemn dignity of his office was bent on working out the spiritual and moral salvation of the people committed to his charge. It is a personality the force of which still persists in the spirit and outlook of the Roman Church to-day, and as we stand in the pillared nave and aisles of some great basilica we can perhaps still recapture in our imagination the sound of the great Pope's sonorous voice ringing through its walls.

[93] Milman, *History of Latin Christianity,* Vol. I, p. 233.
[94] Bright, *Sermons of St. Leo, praef.*

CHAPTER XVIII

LAST YEARS—LEO THE GREAT

THE year A.D. 452 was a crucial one not only in Leo's career but in the life of the Empire. Attila the Hun had passed over into north-eastern Italy. In his path lay the smouldering ruins of Aquileia and many another centre of Roman culture. Rome herself, it seemed, was already within his grasp. It was a time of tense anxiety for all those who valued the heritage of the past, and the secular glories of the Empire. Nor was it less so for Leo himself. Admittedly he had won a spectacular triumph at the recent Council of Chalcedon in the all but unanimous adoption of his "Tome" by the eastern bishops as a test of orthodoxy and a standard of belief. Yet it had proved in a sense a "Pyrrhic" victory. Much that the Roman see had gained in respect of prestige in the sphere of doctrine it seemed likely to lose in the sphere of jurisdiction. Once the Roman legates had returned and had unfolded the full story of the decisions made by the council, it was only too clear that the very thing which the Papacy had foreseen and feared for the past eighty years or more was now more or less an accomplished fact. The council had turned the *de facto* primacy of the see of Constantinople into one which for the future was to exist *de iure*.

We have already followed the course of events which followed the council, and watched with interest and sympathy the strenuous rearguard action fought by Leo against unequal odds in defence of orthodox doctrine and canonical principle, and in the interests of ecclesiastical unity. We have now to see him once more in the role of an ambassador, almost of a suppliant, for the security of the Empire.

When news reached Rome that Attila was pressing on southwards,[1] and that Aetius appeared to ignore or be unaware of the danger threatening the capital, Valentinian and the Senate resolved to have recourse to diplomacy as a means of saving the city. An embassy was hastily nominated consisting

[1] Leo himself probably alludes to this invasion in *Ep.* 113, 1, JK 489, dated March 10th, A.D. 453.

of two leading senators, Gennadius Avienus, who had been consul two years previously,[2] Trigetius,[3] and Leo himself.[4] It was a distinguished company, not least because it included the august figure of the Roman bishop. Leo's spiritual potency might well be expected to strike fear into the heart of an infidel, whose barbarian mind was probably a prey to superstitious terror. The accredited representatives of the Senate and the Roman people encountered Attila and his hordes in the neighbourhood of Mantua, near the south shores of Lake Garda. It must have been an impressive scene and one which more than any other incident in Leo's career has appealed to the imagination of posterity.[5] Most important of all, the

[2] Sidonius Apoll., *Ep.* 1, 9; Seeck, *Regesten,* p. 385.

[3] Bury, *Later Roman Empire,* Vol. I, p. 295, points out that Trigetius had already successfully negotiated a treaty with Genseric the Vandal in A.D. 435.

[4] The chief sources for this event are Prosper, *Chronicon,* sub ann. 452, *M.G.H.,* Auct. antiqu., Vol. IX, *Chron. min.,* Vol. I, p. 482; *Chronicon,* sub ann. 452, *M.G.H.,* Auct. antiqu., Vol. XI, *Chron. min.,* Vol. II, p. 154. It is sometimes thought that the account of an embassy which omits the name of Leo supplied by Cassiodorus, *Variae,* 1, 4, *M.G.H.,* Vol. XII, p. 13, represents a variant tradition. Yet it is always possible that there was more than one embassy of this kind. The opposite extreme is represented by the record provided by the *Liber pontificalis,* ed. Duchesne, Vol. I, p. 239, which assigns the initiative in this diplomatic step to Leo himself. There was actually nothing new in the employment of a distinguished ecclesiastic on a diplomatic mission. Ambrose was so used twice, once as an emissary to the usurper Maximus to sue for peace (*De obitu Valent.* 28: *Ep.* 24), and again later to urge Valentinian II to come to the defence of Italy (*De obitu Valent.* 2, 4, 22–5); and on a similar occasion to the one just described in the text Innocent I was chosen to petition Honorius to accept the terms of Alaric rather than subject the imperial city to the humiliation of a sack at the hands of the Goths (Zosimus, *Hist.* 5, 41). Cf. Chap. I, p. 7.

[5] The earliest mention of supernatural intervention on this occasion is to be found in Paulus Diaconus, *Hist. Rom.,* 14, 12, 2. *M.G.H.,* Auct. antiqu., Vol. II, p. 205; Kirch, *Fontes,* No. 1110, composed A.D. 740–50. "Fertur itaque post discessum pontificis interrogatum esse Attilam a suis, cur ultra solitum morem tantam reverentia Romano papae exhibuerit, quando paene ad omnia, quae ille imperasset, obtemperavit, tum regem respondisse, non se eius qui advenerat personam reveritum esse, sed alium se virum iuxta eum in habitu sacerdotali adstantem vidisse, forma augustiore, canitie venerabilem, illumque evaginato gladio sibi terribiliter mortem minitantem, nisi cuncta quae ille expetebat, explesset." The identification of this mysterious visitant with the person of St. Peter was, of course, too obvious to be missed, and was supplied in due course by an editor of Landulphus Sagax, *Historia miscella* (ed. Muratori), *Script. rer. Ital.,* Vol. I, 1, p. 98. It only remained for Raphael to paint the scene, with the proper addition of the figure of St. Paul, an idea which he probably owed to Leo's own inspiration, *Serm.* 84, 1, for the saga to be complete. His painting may still be seen on the walls of the Camera della Segnatura in the Vatican.

embassy met with success. Attila withdrew and for the time being Italy was freed from the menace of hostile invasion. Yet in spite of the fact that ecclesiastical tradition has been unanimous in assigning the credit of this achievement to Leo there appears some reason to wonder whether there was not some cause other than the impression created by the unarmed dignity of the Roman Pontiff which was actually responsible for this dramatic change of plan on the part of the Hun.[6]

Attila himself died in the following year. But the process of destruction and spoliation, which he had meditated, continued; less swiftly, no doubt, yet not less surely, by reason of the total loss of cohesion within the borders of Italy itself. Aetius, to whose protection, since the fall of Stilicho in the early years of the century, the western provinces had been so much indebted for their security, had acquired a position which invited competition. Once the danger of invasion was removed a self-chosen competitor made his appearance, in the person of Petronius Maximus. A wealthy senator, who had held office at the court of Honorius, Petronius was deficient in any of the qualities which are to be sought in those to whom serious responsibility is assigned. Yet in a circle such as that with which an Emperor like Valentinian chose to surround himself, his word counted for much. He found little difficulty in persuading his suspicious Sovereign that with the arrival of Aetius in Rome the imperial person was in danger. Valentinian decided to take no risks and used the opportunity of an imperial private audience treacherously to despatch Aetius

[6] Jordanes, *Hist. Get.*, 42, 6. *M.G.H.*, Auct. antiqu., Vol. V, pp. 114f.; Kirch, *Fontes*, No. 1039, quotes Priscus as saying that Attila's withdrawal was due to the receipt of unfavourable news from his native kingdom, and attributes his retirement chiefly to the advice of his counsellors, who reminded him that Alaric had not long survived the capture of Rome by the Visigoths. Bury, *op. cit.*, Vol. I, p. 295, n. 3, comments, "There may be something in this." Attila's advisers were doubtless open to bribes. Two other factors may also be taken into account, namely, a famine in Italy in the previous year (cf. Valent. III, *Novell.* 33 dated January 31st, A.D. 451) and the arrival of troops sent by Marcian from Constantinople. It is thought by some that Leo himself refers to this deliverance in *Serm.* 84, 1, and such was doubtless the belief in Raphael's time; the usual view to-day, however, is that he has in mind the invasion by Genseric some years later. See above, Chap. XVII, p. 408.

with his own hand.[7] It was the act of a coward and a fool. However real the danger may have been which he thus sought to avert it was not removed by the elimination of a figure who on more than one occasion, whether by diplomacy or military skill, had proved himself the saviour of the Roman people. A far more real danger lay in his own character, which by reason of his own lack of true ability caused him to distrust even those who wished to be his friends. It was to this lack of trust that he owed his own life. Petronius, defrauded of his ambition to succeed to the place of the murdered Aetius, sought the realization of his hopes by planning the Emperor's death himself. The deed was accomplished by an assassin's hand when Valentinian was holding a military review on the Campus Martius.[8] Few but the most worthless in the State had any cause to regret his death, and with his passing the direct male line of the Theodosian imperial house came to an end. A brief experiment had been made in hereditary monarchy which showed little reason to commend its repetition.

Petronius now found his opportunity for acquiring the supreme power. By judicious bribery he procured his nomination to the principate and at once proceeded to legitimize his position as successor to the heirs of Theodosius I by persuading or compelling Valentinian's widow, Licinia, to become his consort.[9] His reign, however, was brief. Within ten weeks of his accession news arrived in Rome that the Vandals under Gaiseric (or Genseric), their king, had landed in Italy and were marching on the capital.[10] The city fell into his hands

[7] Since A.D. 440 Aetius had enjoyed the title and prestige of the "Emperor's Patrician" while also holding the office of supreme *Magister utriusque militiae* in the West. Cf. Valentinian III, *Novell.*, 9. His position had been made even more imposing by his marriage with Valentinian's own daughter, Placidia, in A.D. 454. *Consularia Italica*, 572, *M.G.H.*, Auct. antiqu, Vol. IX, *Chron. min.*, Vol. I, p. 303. He was assassinated on September 21st, A.D. 454.

[8] Prosper, *Chronicon, Addit.*, 2, 2, sub ann. 455. *M.G.H.*, Auct. antiqu., Vol. IX, *Chron. min.*, Vol. I, p. 490.

[9] *M.G.H., op. cit.*, Vol. IX, pp. 303, 484 and 492.

[10] There was a rumour current at the time that Gaiseric had been invited by Licinia herself to free her from the unwelcome embraces of Petronius. See Idatius, *Chronicon*, 167. Gibbon, *Decline*, Vol. IV, p. 4 (1929), who always shows a marked inclination to accept scandal of this kind, evidently believed the story. Bury, *op. cit.*, Vol. I, p. 324, observes, "The story . . . is credible, though it is not certainly true."

without a blow having been struck in its defence and the upstart Emperor, who thought only of saving himself by an ignominious flight, met a coward's death at the hands of a disillusioned and indignant populace.

Without an Emperor, without an army, without defences, Rome lay prostrate at the conqueror's feet. Only one man remained who might succeed by his influence and personality in saving the city from the worst evils of a sack by the Vandals. When Petronius was vainly fleeing for his life, it was the bishop of Rome who had the courage to meet the invader face to face. The meeting took place, it appears, outside the city walls on the eve of the barbarian occupation.[11] Gaiseric consented with somewhat grudging generosity to spare the capital from fire, massacre and torture. Even so the entry of the Vandals marked the beginning of a period of spoliation, which lasted fourteen days. All the most valuable works of art were removed, and an abundance of treasure, including the sacred vessels and seven-branched candlestick which Titus had brought to Rome after the destruction of the Jewish Temple nearly four centuries before.[12] Among those taken captive were some of the most distinguished members of Roman society including the Empress Licinia and her daughter, Placidia. Many important buildings suffered severe damage including the imperial palaces and the vast temple of Jupiter Capitolinus. The larger basilicas were spared, probably in deference to Leo's own request, but the lesser churches were plundered without scruple.[13] How thoroughly the Vandals did their work may be seen from the steps taken by Leo him-

[11] Prosper, *Chronicon*, sub ann. 455, *M.G.H.*, Auct. antiqu., Vol. IX, *Chron. min.*, Vol. I, p. 484. Mirbt, *Quellen*, No. 177, supplies the following: "Post hunc Maximi exitum confestim secuta est multis digna lacrimis romana captivitas, et urbem omni praesidio vacuam Gisiricus obtinuit, occurrente sibi extra portas sancto Leone episcopo, cuius supplicatio ita cum Deo agente lenivit, ut, cum omnia potestati ipsius essent tradita, ab igni tamen et caede atque suppliciis abstinerentur. Per quattuordecim igitur dies secura et libera scrutatione opibus suis Roma vacuata est, multaque milia captivorum, prout quique aut aetali aut arte placuerunt, cum regina et filiabus eius Carthaginem abducta sunt." Cf. Procopius, *Bell. Vand.*, 1, 5, ed. Teubner, p. 332.

[12] Procopius, *op. cit.*, 2, 9. *Ibid.*, p. 455.

[13] Possibly the Vandals got out of hand here and there for it seems that at least one church, dedicated to St. Hippolytus and situated near the mouth of the Tiber, was reduced to ashes. See Cantarelli, *Di uno frammento Bullett. arch. comm.*, 1896, Nos. 67, 76.

self to make good the losses of these churches, after the Vandals had withdrawn.[14]

As soon as the news of the sack of Rome reached Gaul the Goths at Tolosa (Toulouse) proclaimed as Augustus Avitus, a person of little distinction who had fought with the armies of Aetius, and had been appointed to succeed him as *Magister utriusque militiae* by Petronius. Shortly afterwards he was invested with the imperial insignia at Arles,[15] and towards the end of the same year (A.D. 455) crossed the Alps, intending to assume the consulship at Rome.[16] As the nominee of the Goths his candidature for the Principate met with a hostile reception in Italy and in spite of Marcian's acknowledgment of him as his colleague his tenure was anything but secure. Nevertheless he showed some courage in facing the difficulties of his position, and even ventured to despatch a legation to Carthage, bidding Gaiseric observe the terms of the treaty drawn up in A.D. 442, and to refrain from molesting the remnant of the imperial provinces in Africa. Gaiseric's reply took the form of a naval raid on the Italian coast.

It is as commander of the Roman fleet which defeated the Vandal raiders off the coast of Corsica that Ricimer, the future *de facto* ruler of Italy, first makes his appearance. He had recently been appointed by Avitus to the office of *Magister Militum*[17] and, as the unpopularity of the Emperor increased, Ricimer gradually assumed the reigns of power, until in the end Avitus found it expedient to withdraw from the city altogether.[18] He was on his way back to Gaul when he was intercepted by the all powerful *Magister militum,* who was accompanied by his favourite Majorian, and at Placentia compelled to lay aside the imperial purple.[19]

Ricimer, but for his Arian religion and his Gothic birth,

[14] *Liber pontificalis,* ed. Duchesne, Vol. I, pp. 239, 240, n. 5. Cf. pp. 28, 51f. above.

[15] *Consularia Ital. M.G.H.*, Vol. IX, *Chron. min.*, Vol. I, p. 304.

[16] *Ibid.* See also Apoll. Sidon., *Carm.* 7, 6ff.

[17] Apoll. Sidon., *op. cit.*, 2, 361ff.

[18] Joannes Antioch, *Fragm.* 86, *De Ins. Fragm. Hist. Graec.*, Vol. IV, p. 573, suggests that Avitus had incensed the Roman people by the removal of precious metals, presumably fragments overlooked by the Vandals, in order to discharge debts incurred by the urban administration.

[19] *Cons. Ital., ibid.* Theophanes, *Chronographia,* 5948, *P.G.* 108, 278.

himself might have assumed the imperial diadem. Instead he asserted the right to nominate his friend Majorian to the vacant throne, and a compliant Senate addressed a petition to Leo I, the new Emperor in the East, inviting him to confirm the nomination. As soon as a favourable reply was received from Constantinople Majorian was proclaimed Augustus.[20] But it was only too evident that the effective master of Rome was Ricimer, whose prestige had been increased by his recent acquisition of the title of Patrician.

The new reign opened with some show of promise. A vigorous campaign was launched in order to check the centrifugal tendencies already evident in the Gaulish provinces.[21] After this effort had been rewarded with considerable success Majorian turned his attention to the problem of grappling with the ever present Vandal menace. A formidable naval expedition was prepared and was mustered off the coast of Spain.[22]

Hitherto a strange fate had dogged the expeditions against Vandal Africa.[23] The present undertaking proved no exception. The Roman fleet under the personal command of the Emperor was defeated by a surprise attack and suffered serious losses.[24] After a second force had met with similar misfortune[25] it became clear to Majorian that further effort was useless. Africa must be treated as finally and irretrievably lost. His failure proved his ruin, and on his return to Italy the unhappy Emperor was put to death by Ricimer's orders.[26]

Leo survived Majorian by about three months. During that period his namesake ruled in Constantinople as sole emperor, while Ricimer controlled the destinies of Italy.

Valentinian III was the last Emperor of the West with whom, so far as is known, Leo had any direct relations. After his death at the hands of the avenger of Aetius in A.D. 455 none of his successors has left any record of any intervention

[20] *Ibid.* *M.G.H., ibid.*, p. 305.
[21] Apoll. Sidon., *Carm.* 5, 510. 576: 13, 24.
[22] *M.G.H.*, Vol. XI, *Chron. min.*, Vol. II, pp. 31, 200.
[23] Such as the expeditions despatched from Constantinople under Aspar and Ardaburius.
[24] *M.G.H., ibid.*
[25] *M.G.H., ibid.*
[26] *Cons. Ital.*, 588; *Chron. Gall.*, 635. *M.G.H.*, Vol. IX, *Chron. min.*, Vol. I, pp. 305, 604.

in the affairs of the Church,[27] nor do our sources throw any light on the internal life of the Roman see during the last six years of Leo's pontificate. Not that he was idle during this period, as the considerable mass of correspondence with the East still serves to testify.[28] His last surviving letter bears the date of August 18th, A.D. 460 [29] and was addressed to the consecrators of Timothy Salofaciol, the orthodox successor of the murdered Proterius in the see of Alexandria.

It was, so far as we can tell, Leo's final word. The end came not long after, on November 10th of the following year,[30] and seven days or so later Hilary, the hero of the dramatic escape from the tumultuous scenes which marked the conclusion of the *Latrocinium*,[31] who as legate of the Roman see to that council and subsequently as archdeacon of Rome had been Leo's right-hand man, was elected in accordance with the tradition usually prevailing in Rome at this time to fill the vacant see.[32] Leo's remains were interred on the left-hand side of the entrance leading into the *secretarium* of St. Peter's basilica.[33] The original epitaph which marked the site has perished, although from the mention of it in the

[27] The single exception to this is the *Leg. nov. Maioriani,* 11.

[28] JK 519–50 excepting JK 536, 543, 544, 545.

[29] JK 550.

[30] The evidence as to the exact date, however, is somewhat conflicting. The *Liber pontificalis,* ed. Duchesne, Vol. I, p. 247, mentions an interval of seven days between Leo's death and the consecration of his successor, Hilary I. Thiel, *Epp. Rom. Pont.,* Vol. I, p. 126, quotes a late authority in support of November 12th as the date of the latter event. This would give us November 4th. On the other hand the duration of Leo's pontificate mentioned by the *Liber pontificalis,* namely twenty-one years, one month and thirteen days, gives us November 11th as possible. The date suggested in the text, which is probably to be preferred to the notoriously inaccurate chronological data of the *Liber pontificalis,* is the one supplied by the *Martyrologium hieronymianum, P.L.* 30, 481, where the entry "Romae depositio sancti Leonis episcopi" appears. On the accuracy of this date see Kirch, *Die Stadtrömische Christliche Festkalender im Altertum* (1924), pp. 116f. The Berne MS. of the *Martyrologium hieron.,* actually gives "Romae Leonis papae" under April 11th, a date which has found its way into the latest recension of the *Liber pontificalis,* ed. Duchesne, Vol. I, p. 250, cf. p. 508, and also into the later liturgical kalendar. It probably commemorates the translation of Leo's remains in A.D. 688.

[31] See above Chap. X, p. 241.

[32] The elections of Zosimus and of Felix III are the only examples during the fifth century of the choice of a candidate from outside the diaconate of the Roman Church.

[33] Joannes Diacon, *Vita Gregorii,* 4, 68, "in extrema porticu basilicae beati Petri Apostoli ante secretarium tunc antiquissimum."

life of Gregory I, composed by John the Deacon,[34] it is known still to have been in existence as late as the ninth century. On June 28th, A.D. 688, during the pontificate of Sergius I, his body was translated from its first resting place to a more honourable position within the church itself.[35] The remains of Leo II (A.D. 681–3) and subsequently those of Leo III (A.D. 795–816) and Leo IV (A.D. 847–55) were laid to rest close to those of their illustrious predecessor.[36] To mark this translation a new epitaph was composed as follows:

Testantur missi pro recto dogmate libri
Quos pia corda colunt, quos prava turba timet.
Rugiit, et pavida stupuerunt corda ferarum,
Pastorisque sui iussa sequuntur oves.[37]

A third and final translation of the relics took place when the Constantinian basilica was ruthlessly destroyed to make way for the new and pretentious church erected to the designs of Bramante and Michaelangelo. The rebuilding of St. Peter's involved the destruction of the resting place provided by Sergius I, and a new site was formed in the south-western chapel of the present structure. His body now rests beneath the altar of this chapel, and above the altar is a marble bas-relief depicting the memorable scene on the shores of Lake Garda.

It was formerly supposed that the destructive hand of time had spared yet another memorial of this strange event in the gigantic statue of the Apostle, which is still the cynosure of multitudes of pilgrims. Tradition related that the metal from which the statue had been cast was the product of the colossal image of Jupiter, for centuries the sole denizen of the vast Capitoline Temple, and that it had been made to the orders of Leo himself, in memory of the Apostle's aid. Like many a legend[38] it enshrines the truth that few accomplished so much as he to ensure the final and complete victory of Chris-

[34] Id. *ibid.* "suis hactenus epitaphiis praedicantur."
[35] *Liber pontificalis,* ed. Duchesne, Vol. I, p. 375.
[36] *D.T.C.,* Art. *Leo I,* Vol. IX, col. 278.
[37] Cf. *Liber pontificalis,* Vol. I, p. 379.
[38] Grisar, *History of Rome and the Popes,* E.T., Vol. II, p. 62 says, "Neither the date, nor the maker, nor the source of the material as accounted for in this story, can, however, be said to be probable."

tianity over the decaying forces of paganism in the Roman world.

It is now time to evaluate the personal character and historical significance of this great Pope, whose career has been our study in these pages.

(a) So far as his personal character is concerned, four marks particularly arrest our notice—his indomitable energy, his magnanimity, his consistency and his devotion to simple duty.

The most conspicuous element in his personality is his indomitable energy. Though, so far as we are told, he was seldom absent from the capital, and then after his election to the Papacy never travelled beyond the confines of Italy, he seemed to be able to keep his finger on the pulse of the Church's life from one end of the Mediterranean to the other. Whether it was irregularities within the Roman province, or the organization of the Church in Gaul, or a question of preferment in the Church of Constantinople, each problem as it arose was dealt with in a manner which showed clearly his capacity for making himself master, not only of points of detail, but of the broader issues. But possibly the best testimony to this side of his character is the mass of his correspondence which has survived. This makes it evident that Leo belonged to that type of men who can throw themselves completely and without reserve into the immediate business of the moment. Though from time to time he suffered disappointment, nothing could deter him from carrying out to the utmost of his power the task which had been committed to his care.

Many of his predecessors had displayed similar energy, yet few succeeded in upholding to the same extent the fine tradition of Roman dignity. Leo's character set side by side with theirs, or compared with the personalities of many of his contemporaries, whether ecclesiastical or secular, exhibits a moral grandeur which raises him head and shoulders above them all. Leo was no heresy hunter. In his eastern correspondence letter after letter reiterates the same theme and expresses the hope that every possible step may be taken to procure from those guilty of misbelief a penitent renunciation of their error before proceeding to the extreme course of excommunication. Unlike Celestine I in his relations with

Nestorius, or Zosimus in his conduct towards the African bishops, Leo insisted always on having first-hand evidence before allowing himself to form a decisive opinion. In dealing with Eutyches he continued to put the best possible construction on the views expressed by the old archimandrite until he had received unmistakable proof of his error. His treatment of Hilary has rendered him the target of severe criticism; yet a strictly impartial and objective study of the whole affair only serves to show that every possible allowance was made for Hilary's idiosyncrasies and that it was he, far more than Leo himself, who precipitated the final rupture. Similarly, in his conduct towards the two eastern Emperors, Theodosius II and Leo I, Pope Leo was large-minded enough to appreciate the difficulties with which he was faced, and unlike Felix III and Gelasius I never made the mistake of straining delicate relations with the eastern Sovereigns to breaking point. Yet, while observing the conventions of contemporary courtesy, he did not shrink from addressing stern admonitions even to the rulers of half the Empire.

Never allowing himself to lose sight of the wider issues, in spite of much preoccupation with the details of administration, his character displays a remarkable consistency. Leo was essentially a man of principle, and it is this characteristic perhaps more than any other which helps to explain the admiration or resentment shown towards him, not only by his contemporaries but by posterity. In doctrine he upheld the standards of Holy Scripture and the tradition of the Roman Church as represented by the Apostles' Creed. If Holy Scripture was the word of God and the Creed the voice of His Church what need of " any further witness "? Equally in the sphere of discipline he started with the principle that because he believed the Nicene Canons to be divinely inspired they were therefore unalterable and irreformable. We are not, of course, bound to defend his premises, but we cannot with honesty refrain from applauding the imperturbable steadfastness with which he upheld their logical conclusions.

Logicality and thoroughness are not less prominent in Leo's performance of the commonplace duties of his episcopal office. It is the duty of a bishop not only " to banish and drive away all erroneous and strange doctrine," but also " to instruct the people committed to his charge." Whether or not his predecessors were assiduous in the performance of the latter obligation, the copious collection of his surviving sermons is sufficient to testify to his devoted attention to the spiritual needs of the humblest of his flock. His exhortations, as we have seen, bear the mark of directness and unmistakable sincerity. Some of them actually remind one of the addresses of a parish priest instructing a simple congregation.

These four qualities go to make up a character of exceptional nobility. Like Ambrose in the preceding century he may be described as "the outstanding figure of his time." It is true that he occupied the most important see in Christendom, towards which Roman and barbarian looked with affection or respect. But it is also true that his personal merits reflected an added glory to his position, and made of the Papacy in his day not only the rallying point of all that was best and truest in the Christian world, but the bulwark of orthodoxy and the custodian of unity and order. The reverence shown for him by friend and foe was born of either a spontaneous or a grudging recognition of a majestic and forceful personality.

(b) Leo has been called "the real founder of the medieval papacy." However far this may be true, it by no means constitutes his sole claim to historical importance.

He took a leading part in the defence of Catholic doctrine against the menace of "monophysitism." He strengthened the ecclesiastical ties of the western churches with the Roman see. He put up a vigorous resistance to the encroachments of "Caesaro-papism" on the independent spiritual authority of the Church; finally, he did much to promote the development of Canon Law.

Doubtless it is chiefly for the part which he played in exercising the power of the chief see in Christendom that he is best known. Yet it is not always that sufficient credit is assigned to the achievements of his predecessors in making good the claims of the Roman see, not only to a primacy within the Church, but also to a jurisdiction superior to all other diocesan and regional jurisdictions. Sufficient has already been said to render further emphasis on this point unnecessary, but it needs to be borne in mind in estimating the place of Leo in history. "Creator of the medieval papacy" he certainly was not, for the Church, the Emperors and the prestige of the Apostolic founders, not to mention the reflected glory of the imperial capital, had already supplied all the material needful for the purpose. We may, however, allow the description of him as its "founder," if by "founder" we mean one who gave added strength to the "material," as well as supplying to it cohesiveness and, best of all, a Scriptural *apologia,* which it had previously lacked.

As to his part in the defence of Catholic doctrine it is from this that Leo derives a claim to be almost unique amid the long line of occupants of the Roman see. Neither before nor after him was there any Pope who actually took the initiative *motu proprio* in a controversy in which a purely doctrinal issue was at stake. And even if it is true, as must be admitted, that his personal contributions contained little that was strictly original, or seriously constructive, yet the fact that they bore the impress of the Roman see was sufficient to win for them not merely respectful attention but even a heartfelt welcome as a refuge from the intricate thought and expression of more accomplished theologians. The "Tome," as we have seen, was essentially "the plain man's guide to the doctrine of the Incarnation." But Leo, by the sheer force of his personality added to the prestige of his see, after procuring its adoption as a document of oecumenical rank, made of it a touchstone of orthodoxy, the acceptance or refusal of which became the decisive factor in the retention or otherwise of their sees by the most influential bishops in Christendom.

Yet whatever the prestige of the Roman see at this time in the East, it was certainly immeasurably greater in the West. Since the earliest time the western churches had without question recognized it as their natural centre, from which guidance and advice was to be sought as a matter of course. But it was easy for the giving of advice to be phrased in language appropriate to the issue of commands in the form of decretals, and for the position of counsellor to be exchanged for the role of supreme arbiter. If Leo did not find the Papacy precisely enjoying this role he undoubtedly did much to bring about its realization. As a result, the Papal fiat became as effective in southern Gaul and in northern Africa as it was in Sicily and

Campania. It was now no longer necessary to insist, as some of Leo's predecessors had done on the Petrine origin of Western Christianity. For many a century after Leo's death Western Christendom accepted, for the most part without question, the voice of the Papacy as the voice of Peter, and that voice as the expression of the mind of God.

The chief opposition to the "Petrine" idea of Church organization and discipline came from the East. There since the foundation of Constantinople as new Rome a rival conception of the Church, especially of the Church in its relation to the State, had established itself to the exclusion of any other. In the West in spite of the efforts of "Erastianizing" Emperors, such as Constantius II, the Church's independence of the State had never been wholly lost, and had been vigorously reasserted by Ambrose of Milan. In Leo's time State interference with the Church was inconceivable; on the contrary there is good reason to believe that the State showed itself highly amenable to the Church's influence. In the East, however, the Emperor Constantine I, whose policy of imperial unity embraced every department of life, not excluding religion, was astute enough to use for his own purposes the current usages of synodical government. By summoning councils of an oecumenical character, in which the Emperor and the Emperor's ecclesiastical policy enjoyed a preponderating influence, Constantine, Theodosius I and his fifth century successors in the East made of the Church and its hierarchy something analogous to a department of the State.

Consequently it was the policy supported by the Emperor which had won the day at Nicaea, at Constantinople, at Ephesus both in A.D. 431 and in A.D. 449. So long as the same policy was equally favoured by the Papacy no awkward questions had arisen. But the time came when, as with Theodosius II and Leo, Emperor and Pope found themselves in opposing camps. Yet in spite of all Leo could do to restrain the growth of this conception, in particular by seeking to prevent the creation of a second "Papacy" at Constantinople, the development followed its logical course, leading to the "Caesaro-papism" of Justinian I. The subsequent history of Eastern Christianity serves to show how far-sighted Leo had been. In the West alone the spiritual independence preserved by the Papacy ensured the Church's ability to speak with a "living voice." In the East that voice silenced by the State became but an echo of imperial edicts, or a mute appeal to the doctrinal and disciplinary decisions of the first eight centuries.

This independence of the Western Church manifested itself particularly in the development of a code of Canon Law, supported by the arm of the State, yet without owing to the State its origin. As we have seen again and again, Leo unhesitatingly appealed to the authority of Canon Law, in particular to the real or supposed Canons of Nicaea, as the final and unalterable word in matters of discipline. And from time to time he cited decisions of his predecessors in a way which shows that he regarded them as possessing an authority not inferior to that of Canons enjoying oecumenical status. The subsequent fusion of this twofold strand of law, Synodical canons and Papal decretals, which was finally completed by the great canonist, Dionysius Exiguus, was undoubtedly fostered by Leo more than by any of his predecessors. In this way he gave impetus to a movement which had an enduring influence on the life of the medieval and post-reformation Church, and led to the creation of a code, often at variance with its secular rival, which claimed to be possessed of superior validity simply in virtue of its spiritual origin.

Among all Leo's achievements, however, there was none greater than the success with which he vindicated the claim of the Roman see to a Primacy in the sphere of doctrine. It was a claim which in spite of all the vicissitudes of the new few hundred years was destined to prevail, and of which even the "theologizing" Emperors of the East, like Justinian I, found themselves obliged to take account.

CHAPTER XIX

LEO AS A TEACHER OF ETHICS

UNLIKE Ambrose [1] Leo left behind him no formal treatise dealing exhaustively with the whole subject of Christian ethics. Fortunately, however, we can find in his letters, and to an even greater extent in his sermons, abundant material with which to form a comprehensive picture of his ethical teaching. Such a picture may begin with a statement of certain fundamental principles, as they are exhibited in his writings.

I. BASIC IDEAS: GOD, MAN AND THE WORLD

Leo's ethic embraces definite opinions regarding God, man and the world, which are here summarized.

(a) *God.* Nothing less than belief in God as a Person satisfies the Christian moralist. It is moreover belief in a Person who is essentially good,[2] and who for this reason expects and demands goodness of all His creatures. In consequence of this demand rewards and punishments attach to the actions of those creatures capable of moral distinctions in proportion to the goodness or absence of goodness shown in such actions.[3] Herein lies a strong incentive to moral behaviour. Hence in two passages Leo stresses the obligation to acts of a humanitarian nature, on the ground that they will be taken into account at the last judgment at which rewards and punishments will be finally assigned.[4] Equally he emphasizes with constant reiteration the need of right faith thereby revealing his conviction that faith in God is an indispensable requisite of the moral life.[5]

[1] For the ethical teaching of Ambrose, to which that of Leo bears a very close resemblance, see esp. his *De Officiis Ministrorum, P.L.* 16, 23–184. On the whole subject of ethical teaching in this period, see Scullard, *Early Christian Ethics in the West,* London, 1907; and more generally Kirk, *Vision of God,* London, 1931.

[2] *Serm.* 22, 1. "Deus . . . cuius natura bonitas."

[3] Cf. e.g. *Serm.* 43, 3.

[4] *Serm.* 9, 2; 45, 3, alluding to Matt. xxv. 31–46.

[5] *Serm.* 24, 6. "nihil sine illa (sc. fide) sanctum, nihil castum est."

The principle source from which the Christian moral law is derived is, of course, Holy Scripture, as containing the direct revelation of God's will. Nevertheless Leo allows that it may be known, at least so far as natural law is concerned, by simple reflection on racial experience or on natural phenomena. Thus he writes of "The things which considerations of piety have instituted for moral rules," [6] and points out that something may be learnt from nature itself as to the character of the divine commandments.[7] On the other hand, philosophical argument and speculation is treated with an impatient disdain,[8] such as is to be met with frequently in other Western writers.[9]

Virtue is only attained by acquiring a right relation with God, and in so thinking Leo is only consistent with his view that the *Summum Bonum* is God Himself.[10] Like Ambrose, Leo distinguishes between three degrees of virtue—fear of God, love of God and resemblance to God. Christian progress starts from the *fear of God,* derived not from terror of punishment but from the love which is in God Himself.[11] Next after this comes the *love of God*. Since it belongs to every rational mind to feel affection, such a mind must love either God or the world.[12] To achieve the former the mind must be detached from the pursuit of earthly desires and objects. "The love of the world accords not with the love of God, nor can that man attain to the fellowship of the sons of God who does not separate himself from a materialistic society." [13] It is to be defined as a love of righteousness [14] and is the counterpart of the love of our neighbour.[15] It is independent of good or bad fortune; [16] its claims are perpetual.[17] The final stage is

[6] *Serm.* 17, 1. "ea quae vel ad regulas morum vel ad simplicem Dei cultum ratio pietatis instituit."

[7] *Serm.* 18, 2.

[8] *Serm.* 25, 4; 46, 3.

[9] e.g. Ambrose, *De Officiis,* 2, 8.

[10] *Serm.* 93, 2.

[11] *Serm.* 89, 3.

[12] *Serm.* 90, 3. *Serm.* 27, 6.

[13] *Serm.* 95, 9. "Amor mundi cum Dei amore non congruit, nec ad societatem filiorum Dei pervenit, qui se a carnali generatione non dividit."

[14] *Serm.* 95, 6.

[15] *Serm.* 90, 3.

[16] *Serm.* 12, 3. "amor directus in Deum nec inter secunda superbiat, nec inter adversa deficiat."

[17] *Serm.* 90, 3. "in nullo nos vult (sc. Deus) ab amoris sui vinculis relaxari."

resemblance to God. This is the chief end and perfection of virtue. "Rightly God demands imitation of Himself from those whom He has made after His own image and likeness."[18] This is further explained as involving conformity with the moral qualities to be found in God Himself. "Mercy wills thee to be merciful, Righteousness to be righteous, that the Creator may be seen in His creature, and that the image of God described in lines of resemblance may shine forth in the mirror of the human heart."[19]

Clearly Leo can only think of religion in terms of morality. For as morals derive their sanction from religion, so real religion understood as a right relationship with God is inconceivable apart from moral progress.

(b) *Man.* An indispensable part of moral development is the recognition by man himself of his true nature. "Awake, O man," he writes, "and recognize the dignity of thy nature. Remember that thou hast been made in the image of God."[20] As to his constitution, Leo like other Western writers adopts formally the Trichotomist or Platonic view. Man consists of spirit, soul and body. The two former are not distinct, but two principles within man's spiritual nature. The first of them called the *mens* or *animus* is the highest or dominating principle. This is the rational or thinking principle,[21] and is the seat of God's indwelling presence.[22] As the "interior homo" it is meant to be the master of the bodily or visible part of man.[23] The second principle, namely the *anima,* is the seat of feelings and desires.[24] Its special task is to refrain the outward nature from what is unfitting.[25] Yet these two principles are not always clearly distinguished, as they are by

[18] *Serm.* 45, 2. "merito Deus imitationem sui ab eis exigit quos ad imaginem et similitudinem suam fecit." Cf. *Serm.* 24, 2.

[19] *Serm.* 95, 7.

[20] *Serm.* 27, 6.

[21] *Serm.* 81, 2. "agnoscat rationalis animus maiores delicias menti datas esse quam carni."

[22] *Serm.* 27, 6. "plus est quod fidelis quisque in suo habet animo, quam quod miratur in coelo."

[23] *Serm.* 87, 1. "Agnoscat interior homo exterioris sui se esse rectorem, ut meus divino gubernata dominatu terrenam substantiam in bonae voluntatis cogat obsequium."

[24] *Serm.* 19, 1. "sine anima nihil caro desideret."

[25] *Ibid.*

Ambrose,[26] and in one passage at least Leo speaks of the *anima rationalis*.[27] The body, described as *caro*, is the lower of the two elements. Leo frequently insists on the necessity of its being subject to the soul,[28] while acknowledging that in fallen humanity the body is the means by which the soul is corrupted.[29] Hence arises the familiar interior conflict, and the constant duty of care lest the flesh be productive of "thorns and briers." [30] Although it is asserted that the body and the soul are created together,[31] yet the prior importance and worth of the soul is not left in doubt.[32] Nothing is said as to the immortality of the soul, though it is clear that this is among those Christian beliefs, the truth of which Leo assumes without discussion. This is shown by the view which he holds as to the meaning of blessedness. Unlike the conception held by the Stoics, and followed at least in part by Ambrose,[33] which identified blessedness with the life of virtue, Leo teaches that true blessedness is only to be attained in the future State,[34] and treats it as synonymous with the "kingdom of heaven." [35] It is the certainty of this future blessedness which serves to reconcile a man to present misfortune.[36]

Free Will. In contrast to the Stoic and Pelagian view that man is by nature capable of virtue, Leo lays much emphasis on the unhappy effects of sin on humanity, so that apart from the operations of Divine Grace all possibility of moral action is excluded. At every moment of his life man is beset by temptations,[37] nor is anyone without sin.[38] On all sides he

[26] Cf. Homes Dudden, *St. Ambrose*, Vol. II, p. 506.
[27] *Serm.* 78, 1, where he stresses the importance of purging it by means of mortification of the body.
[28] e.g. *Serm.* 81, 2. "ut et caro mentis iudicio . . . regatur."
[29] *Serm.* 90, 1.
[30] *Serm.* 81, 3.
[31] *Ep.* 15, 9, 10. On the authenticity of this letter see above, p. 154, n. 155. In *Ep.* 35, 3, Leo excludes the doctrine of Origen that the soul is prior to the body. Cf. Origen, *De princ.*, 3, 22. *Philocalia,* ed. Robinson, p. 176.
[32] *Serm.* 51, 2, with allusion to Matt. xvi. 25.
[33] Homes Dudden, *op. cit.*, Vol. II, p. 508.
[34] *Serm.* 15, 1; 23, 3; 49, 2.
[35] *Serm.* 35, 3.
[36] *Serm.* 51, 2. "pro spe aeternorum levissimum ducerent temporalium detrimentum."
[37] *Serm.* 15, 1. "non possunt istos dies sine tentatione transire."
[38] *Serm.* 37, 3; 49, 1. "quis enim in huius vitae constitutus incerto, aut immunis a tentatione, aut liber inveniatur a culpa?"

is attacked by the inveterate enemies of mankind.[39] Yet the devil could not have subdued Adam, apart from the free co-operation of the latter's will.[40] As it is, however, the human race is corrupt through the fall of its first parent.[41] If Adam had remained in his primal innocence, death would not have supervened.[42] Now there is hope only in restoration. This restoration is effected through the Incarnation.[43] Justification is therefore the outcome of supernatural intervention, and can be accomplished only by the bestowal of Grace.[44] It is for man to co-operate to the utmost of his power with this Grace.[45] Hence all human moral achievement is to be referred to the power of God.[46]

(c) *The World.* Leo shares to some extent the pessimistic outlook not infrequently found in other Western writers,[47] yet he constantly urges that the good things of the world are to be used and used aright,[48] while the duty remains of seeking detachment from earthly pleasures and attractions.[49] The " flesh " is to be continually restrained by self-control,[50] and it is the effort so demanded which gives rise to that inner conflict of which every Christian must be aware. Nevertheless it is clear that Leo's pessimism is due chiefly to his deeply-rooted sense of human sin, and is tempered by his unshakable conviction that all created things are good by nature.[51]

[39] *Serm.* 49, 4.
[40] *Serm.* 28, 3.
[41] *Serm.* 93, 1. "peccante humani generis patre non dubitant in propagine vitiatum esse, quod est in radice corruptum." Cf. *Ep.* 139, 3, and *Serm.* 25, 5.
[42] *Serm.* 24, 2.
[43] *Serm.* 21, 3. Cf. *Ep.* 167, *praef.*
[44] *Serm.* 49, 3. "iustificatio non meritis retribuitur, sed sola gratiae largitate donatur." Cf. *Serm.* 67, 3; 90, 2.
[45] *Serm.* 43, 1.
[46] *Serm.* 79, 3. "omni se merito laude dispoliat qui de studiis industriae suae in se magis quam in Domino gloriatur." Cf. 1 Cor. i. 31. Cf. *Serm.* 5, 4; 38, 4.
[47] e.g. in Ambrose. Cf. Homes Dudden, *op. cit.*, Vol. II, p. 511.
[48] *Serm.* 27, 6. Cf. *Serm.* 74, 5.
[49] *Serm.* 71, 5. "non ergo nos rerum temporalium occupent species, nec ad se contemplationem nostram a coelestibus terrena deflectant."
[50] *Serm.* 81, 2.
[51] *Ep.* 15, 6–8.

2. THE DOCTRINE OF VIRTUE

(i) THE CARDINAL VIRTUES AND OTHERS

Although we do not find in Leo's surviving works any systematic treatment of this subject, it is possible to build up a comprehensive view of his ideas. In the first place though like Ambrose [52] he appears to imply that all the several virtues are interdependent, in such a way that "the real possession of one virtue involves possession of the rest," [53] yet it might be said that from his standpoint the virtue of *Charity* is absolutely indispensable.[54] Of the Cardinal Virtues he has most to say on the subject of *Justice* and chiefly on its humanitarian aspect. Thus he identifies love of Justice with love for God and adds in the same sentence that "as the love of one's neighbour is added to the love of God so the virtue of Mercy is linked with this desire for Justice." [55] Elsewhere he uses Justice as denoting a state of moral perfection as for example when he writes, "This is the true Justice (Righteousness) of the perfect, that they should never presume themselves to be perfect, lest by abandoning their project of a journey not yet completed they may run the risk of failing in the very thing in which they have abandoned the desire for progress." [56] In view of what has just been said it is natural to find frequent reference to the duty of *Almsgiving*. It is a duty which is imposed on all alike, on the poor no less than the rich. "Let no man," he writes, "beloved, excuse himself of a good work, let no man plead his poverty, as if one who scarcely has enough for himself cannot help another as well." [57] It is owed to all, Christian and heathen alike, though naturally to Chris-

[52] Homes Dudden, *op. cit.*, Vol. II, p. 522.

[53] *Ibid.*

[54] *Serm.* 10, 2. "Haec virtus (sc. charitas) omnes facit utiles esse virtutes." Cf. *Serm.* 48, 3, "nudae sunt tamen omnes sine charitate virtutes."

[55] *Serm.* 95, 4.

[56] *Serm.* 40, 1. "Haec est perfectorum vera iustitia, ut numquam praesumant se esse perfectos, ne ab itineris nondum finiti intentione cessantes, ibi incidant deficiendi periculum, ubi proficiendi deposuerint appetitum."

[57] *Serm.* 20, 3; 44, 2. Even without discrimination of rank or sex, *Serm.* 88, 4.

tians first of all; [58] among Christians care should be taken that those who hesitate on grounds of self-respect to ask for what they need are not overlooked.[59] To neglect one's duty to the poor is a serious sin [60] and deprives virtue of all its value,[61] for it is of little merit to refrain from stealing if liberality is absent.[62] On the other hand Almsgiving is an act of generosity to Christ Himself,[63] while the giver himself is in very deed a minister of God's mercy.[64] Leo emphasizes the need of regulating generosity by consideration of obligations to the home,[65] and in so doing shows a practical common sense which was not lacking also in Ambrose.[66] Finally he reminds his hearers that consideration for the needs of others is one of the points which differentiates man from the animals.[67]

Courage is a virtue which Leo mentions only once. He writes that "few have sufficient courage not to be disturbed by the shocks of adversity." [68] It is therefore closely akin to patience.

Temperance with him is equivalent to self-control. "Since we ought not to satisfy all desires, nor to perform all that the flesh lusts after, we realize that we have been enjoined to apply the restraint of self-control with a view to refusing to the flesh, which has been placed under the authority of the mind, all that is excessive, while not denying to it what is necessary." [69]

Leo gives most attention of all to the virtue of *Charity*. He uses the word both of love owed to God and of love owed to man. "Lest self-examination which consists of a painstaking

[58] *Serm.* 41, 3. "Quamvis ergo fidelium praecipue sit adiuvanda paupertas, etiam illi tamen, qui nondum Evangelium receperunt, in suo labore miserandi sunt." These injunctions shed some light on the economic and social conditions prevailing in Rome at this time. Cf. *Serm.* 8.

[59] *Serm.* 9, 3. For Leo's definition of "neighbour" see *Serm.* 12, 2.

[60] *Serm.* 10, 2.

[61] *Ibid.*

[62] *Serm.* 86, 2.

[63] *Serm.* 6; 11, 2. With reference to Matt. xxv. 40.

[64] *Serm.* 49, 6.

[65] *Serm.* 88, 5.

[66] *De Officiis,* 2, 109.

[67] *Serm.* 20, 2. Cf. also *Serm.* 48, 5; 95, 7.

[68] *Serm.* 43, 2. "paucorum est tam solida fortitudo, ut nulla inaequalitatum perturbatione quatiantur." Ambrose has a similar passage in *De Officiis,* 1, 180.

[69] *Serm.* 71, 5.

discrimination be burdened with many matters, let him (sc. the Christian man) search in the secret places of his mind for charity, the very mother of all virtues, and whether he has found it devoted heartily to the love of God and of neighbour, so that he desires the same to be granted to his enemies that he would wish to be allotted to himself."[70] Charity is God's own nature and brings its own reward,[71] is due first to God and then to one's neighbour; "all a man's affections are to be guided by this principle that he remain faithful to the worship of God and to the service of his fellow-servant."[72] Without Charity other virtues are devoid of value;[73] charity and faith are interdependent; together they are the way of approach to God.[74] He who is a stranger to the truth is not merciful; nor is he capable of righteousness who is devoid of sympathy. He exhibits neither virtue who is not endowed with both. "Charity is the strength of faith, faith the courage of charity. Only then do they truly deserve the name and show real fruit, when the connexion between them is indissoluble. For when they are not side by side they are alike deficient . . . without faith no love, without love no faith. . . . For this is a kind of very effective two-winged flight, by which the purity of the mind rises both in displaying and in beholding God."[75] This twofold love is the power and the wisdom of the Christian faith.[76] At the same time in his eagerness to emphasize the manward aspect of Charity, Leo often runs the risk of overlooking Charity in its Godward aspect, for though he has much to say on the subject of the former he nowhere defines the nature of Godward Charity apart from its manward manifestation, so much so that Charity with him is almost a synonym for Almsgiving. Love

[70] *Serm.* 38, 4. "ipsam matrem virtutum omnium charitatem."
[71] *Serm.* 92, 3.
[72] *Serm.* 19, 2.
[73] *Serm.* 48, 3; 74, 5; 79, 3, with allusion to 1 Cor. xiii. 1.
[74] *Serm.* 45, 2.
[75] *Serm.* 45, 2. "Hic est enim quidam efficacissimus geminarum alarum volatus, quo ad promerendum et videndum Deum puritas mentis attollitur." Leo uses the same metaphor of the relation between charity and chastity in *Serm.* 55, 5. "Charitatis opere ac nitore pudicitiae, tamquam duabus elevati alis, de terrenis mercamur esse coelestes."
[76] *Ibid.*, 1. Yet the two are clearly distinguished in *Serm.* 9, 1, where charity is reduced to a fruit of faith.

of one's neighbour is a copy of God's love towards ourselves.[77] It is a sign of the presence of God within the soul.[78] It is characterized by devotion to the things which God Himself loves.[79] It is a mark of a "son of God." [80] It has no limits because God Himself is without limit.[81]

Closely connected with Charity in this sense is the virtue of *Kindness,* which because it is in accordance with the will of God [82] is specially pleasing to Him.[83] An exterior sign of the possession of these virtues is the performance of *Good Works.* Such works are not only desirable [84] but actually necessary [85] in a Christian; their performance inflicts loss on the evil one [86] while it benefits the whole Church.[87] They bring salvation in their train.[88] The good man is to be known by his single-minded love of goodness.[89] He is an object of hatred to the wicked.[90]

Apart from the passages in which the virtue of *Faith* is associated with Charity Leo has a good deal to say on this virtue. Its merit lies in belief in things not seen.[91] Nothing less than real Faith linked with dispassionate humility can comprehend the "mystery of human salvation." [92] Yet it is indispensable that Faith should be manifested in works.[93] Usually Leo equates Faith with orthodox belief. Of faith in this sense he writes frequently. It is the means of justification.[94] It is derived from the mercy of God,[95] proclaimed in

[77] *Serm.* 20, 2. Love of enemies is specially mentioned in *Serm.* 12, 2; 20, 3; 39, 5.
[78] *Serm.* 48, 3.
[79] *Serm.* 12, 1; 26, 3.
[80] *Serm.* 49, 6.
[81] *Serm.* 48, 3. Cf. *ibid.,* 1.
[82] *Serm.* 95, 7.
[83] *Serm.* 48, 5.
[84] *Ep.* 169, 2.
[85] *Serm.* 15, 1.
[86] *Serm.* 8.
[87] *Serm.* 3, 4.
[88] *Serm.* 9, 2.
[89] *Serm.* 89, 4; 85, 1.
[90] *Serm.* 47, 1. Elsewhere, *Serm.* 74, 5, he points out the efficacy of charity against the devil.
[91] *Serm.* 69, 2, with allusion to Hebrews xi. 1. "virtus fidei in iis quae visui non subiacent constituta sit." Cf. *Serm.* 5, 2.
[92] *Ep.* 102, 2.
[93] *Serm.* 10, 2.
[94] *Ep.* 71. "vos qui iustificamini per fidem."
[95] *Ep.* 102, 2.

the teaching of the Gospels and the Apostles.[96] Perfectly unsullied[97] and self-consistent,[98] it admits of no diversity,[99] nor can be added to nor diminished.[100] Once defined it can no longer be discussed or form a topic of argument.[101] It belongs to every man specially to safeguard it,[102] and its defence is always worthy of praise.[103]

Compared with its sister virtues Leo has little to say on the subject of *Hope*. It is a gift of God.[104] The same hope which is given to Christians now was shared by the Jews of old.[105]

In three passages the relation of one theological virtue to another is described. Thus Leo writes in the last of his "anniversary" sermons, "'He gave gifts unto men,' that is to say Faith, Hope and Charity, which are great, powerful and valuable for this reason that the thing to which the eyes of the flesh cannot attain, by a wondrous devotion of the mind is believed and hoped for and loved." [106] So too in a later sermon on the Ascension, "As to those things which are inaccessible to human sight . . . Faith doubts not, Hope wavers not, Charity does not grow cold." [107] Finally he writes in a sermon on the Ember fast, "We refer to the progress of the whole Church, of which the seed is in Faith, growth in Hope, and maturity in Charity." [108]

Elsewhere he calls attention to the virtues of *Humility* and *Obedience*. Humility is not merely an essential virtue in a

[96] *Ep.* 94. Cf. *Ep.* 89.
[97] *Serm.* 65, 1.
[98] *Ep.* 29; *Serm.* 70, 3.
[99] *Ep.* 161, 1.
[100] *Epp.* 124, 1; 145, 1.
[101] This is a favourite idea of Leo's, doubtless arising from his view that his "Tome" embodied the "Catholic Faith." Cf. *Epp.* 23, 2; 90, 2; 94; 145, 2; 146, 2; 147, 2; 149, 2; 156, 1; 160, 2; 161, 2; 162, 1; 164, 1, 2.
[102] *Ep.* 129, 1.
[103] *Ep.* 38.
[104] *Serm.* 5, 2, with allusion to Ps. lxvii. (lxviii.) 19.
[105] *Serm.* 63, 2; 66, 2.
[106] *Serm.* 5, 2.
[107] *Serm.* 74, 1. "remotis a conspectu hominum . . . fides non diffideret, spes non fluctuaret, charitas non tepesceret."
[108] *Serm.* 18, 3. "ad totius ecclesiae profectus esse referendum, quorum in fide germen est, in spe incremendum, in charitate maturitas."

Christian,[109] it is a characteristic of God Himself.[110] It is taught by Christ.[111] To the obedient and the humble no duty is arduous.[112]

It will have been noticed that Leo is chiefly concerned to emphasize the social aspect of virtue. For him Altruism is an integral part of the Christian profession. In this respect his ethical teaching closely resembles that of Ambrose and shows a marked divergence from the view, so prevalent in the East, that Christian virtue is impossible of attainment by one living in the midst of worldly society. Though he nowhere discusses such a problem as the relation between the virtuous and the useful, it is clear that he regards the virtuous course of seeking the good of all as itself the true expediency. "Be assured, brethren," he says, "that the effort with which you resist vice, and spurn carnal desires is pleasing in the sight of God, and profitable in obtaining the mercy of God not only for yourselves but also for me; since the dutifulness of the shepherd is appraised in proportion to the progress of the Lord's flock." [113]

3. POLITICAL AND SOCIAL ETHICS

THE STATE. The idea of obedience owed to the State is implied rather than expressed in Leo's writings. Nevertheless it is clear that to him the Roman State was the work of Divine Providence.[114]

[109] *Serm.* 37, 3. "Christianae sapientiae disciplina . . . in vera et voluntaria humilitate . . . amat Christus infantiam, humilitatis magistram."

[110] *Serm.* 52, 2. Cf. *Serm.* 37, 1.

[111] *Serm.* 31, 3.

[112] *Serm.* 35, 3. "Nihil ergo . . . arduum est humilibus, nihil asperum mitibus, . . . quando . . . obedientia mollit imperium."

[113] *Serm.* 3, 4. "Certi autem estote, dilectissimi, quod labor vester, quo vitiis resistitis, et carnalibus desideriis repugnatis, placens in conspectu Dei est atque pretiosus, nec solum vobis, sed etiam mihi apud Dei misericordiam profuturus: quia de profectu Dominici gregis gloriatur cura pastoris."

[114] *Serm.* 82, 2. "Ut autem huius inerrabilis gratiae per totum mundum diffunderetur effectus, Romanum regnum divina providentia praeparavit; cuius ad eos limites incrementa perducta sunt, quibus cunctarum undique gentium vicina et contigua esset universitas. Disposito namque divinitus operi maxime congruebat, ut multa regna uno confoederarentur imperio, et cito pervios haberet populos praedicatio generalis, quos unius teneret regimen civitatis."

The purpose of the Roman Empire in the Divine scheme of history was to provide a suitable sphere for the spread of the Christian Gospel, so that as all nations formed part of a single political unity so they might together enjoy the benefits of the Christian religion. In the social aspect of the Empire Leo has no special interest. This was no doubt due to his assumption that its society was equally a matter of Divine ordering, and that in consequence it neither needed nor was capable of improvement.

Nevertheless he sharply contrasts the achievements of the secular State with those of the Christian Church. Apostrophizing Rome he says: "Though thou hast extended the rule of thine empire by land and sea by means of many successes, all that warlike struggle has subjected to thee is far less than the conquests of Christian peace." [115]

Those outside the empire are simply "raging barbarians," who are unworthy of being mentioned more than once.[116]

Leo has a good deal to say as to the relation of the State to the Church and particularly of the part which the Monarch has to play in regard to the latter. He frequently urges that the welfare of humanity depends wholly on the co-operation of the State with the Church.[117]

Later on he shows his belief that the security of the Empire against barbarian inroads depends on the integrity of the orthodox faith.[118] Since Leo was largely preoccupied with the ecclesiastical policy of the Emperor, he had no cause to express his views on constitutional questions. Yet it is clear that absolutist ideas go far to account for a number of his statements regarding the ecclesiastical status of the Sovereign. Thus he writes of Marcian as one "in whom for the salvation of the whole world there flourishes both royal power and priestly zeal." [119]

[115] *Ibid.*, 1. "Quamvis enim multis aucta victoriis ius imperii tui terra marique protuleris, minus tamen est quod tibi bellicus labor subdidit quam quod pax Christiana subiecit."

[116] *Serm.* 84, 2.

[117] *Ep.* 60. But he does not attempt to argue that the State is subordinate to the Church.

[118] *Ep.* 82, 1. "profectus charitatis et fidei utrorumque armorum potentiam insuperabilem facit ut . . . simul et haeretica falsitas et barbara destruitur hostilitas." Cf. *Ep.* 83, 1.

[119] *Ep.* 115, 1. Cf. *Ep.* 116, 1. "sacerdotalis . . . industria."

Similarly he writes that God has accorded to the Emperor "in addition to a royal crown, priestly honour." [120]

Speaking of Marcian's successor, Leo I, he makes use of like expressions,[121] and equally in addressing the new Emperor himself.[122] In spite of attempts which have been made to explain language of this sort as merely complimentary,[123] it is difficult to reconcile such an explanation with the evident acknowledgment of the Emperor's authority in relation to ecclesiastical matters, at least *de facto* if not *de iure,* which we find elsewhere. Thus he writes: "It is praiseworthy for you to concede this to the universal Church at my request." [124]

So too he reminds the Emperor "you ought to remember constantly that royal authority has been conferred on you, not only for the government of the whole world, but specially for the protection of the Church." [125] He even goes so far as to assert that the Emperor's faith is more trustworthy than the sense of duty shown by bishops.[126]

It is difficult to avoid the impression that provided the Emperor's faith accorded with that of the Roman see, Leo was prepared to concede to him an authority in the Church which was limited only by Canon Law, just as strictly speaking civil law was the sole limit of imperial authority in the State.

SLAVERY. Leo evidently assumes the rightfulness of slavery, though he regards a slave or a person of servile status as permanently incapable of consecration to the episcopate.[127]

[120] *Ep.* 111, 3. "sacerdotalem palmam." Cf. *Ep.* 117, 2. "sacerdotalis sanctitatis." *Ep.* 134, 1. "sacerdotalem . . . affectum."

[121] *Ep.* 155, 2. "sacerdotalem mentem."

[122] *Ep.* 156, 6. "sacerdotalem . . . et apostolicum tuae pietatis animum."

[123] e.g. by the Ballerini in *P.L.* 54, 1441 CD.

[124] *Ep.* 145, 2. Cf. *Epp.* 146, 1; 147, 1. In the following letter *Ep.* 148, he actually speaks of the Emperor as "the guardian of the Chalcedonian council."

[125] *Ep.* 156, 3. So too in c. 5. "Diademati vestro de manu Domini etiam fidei addatur corona, et de hostibus Ecclesiae triumphetis." Cf. *Ep.* 164, 1.

[126] *Ep.* 157, 1. Cf. *Ep.* 162, 1. "excellentissimam fidem . . . animi sacerdotalis." Even if such expressions belong to the language of courtesy, they were at least fraught with danger, if the Emperor chose to take them *au sérieux*. Even Batiffol, Art. "Leo I," *D.T.C.,* Vol. IX, col. 300, admits "le pape se prêtait à un jeu singulièrement dangereux!"

[127] *Ep.* 4, 1. This is clearly the point of the passage, not merely that slaves were being consecrated without the permission of their masters. "sacrum ministerium talis consortii vilitate polluitur." Cf. *Ep.* 167, 4, where he takes for granted the justice of Roman civil law declaring a slave incapable of marrying a free woman.

Nevertheless he insists that slaves are to be treated with humanity, especially at such times as Lent.[128]

PROPERTY. Leo nowhere denies the right to hold private property. At the same time he insists that Christians are trustees rather than absolute owners of property[129] and that it is to be used primarily for spiritual ends,[130] that is to say for relieving the needs of others.[131] Hence its excessive increase is strongly deprecated.[132] God permits the rich to enjoy abundance of wealth, but solely in order that they may have the opportunity of performing charitable acts.[133] Hence a rich man is a minister of God and a steward of the poor.[134] To neglect duty to the poor is as bad as stealing the property of another.[135] To engage in trade or commerce is to invite occasions of sin.[136] Traders are reminded that in times of plenty no one has a right to complain of small profits.[137]

There is little that is either new or original in Leo's ethical teaching. Most of his points can be found already in the writings of others; of Ambrose, for example. Yet it is noteworthy that one who was so much preoccupied with questions of doctrine and discipline did not lose sight of the trivialities of everyday Christian life, and that the same pen which set down the doctrine of the Roman see on the Incarnation or denounced violations of Canon Law, also described the common duty of every Christian to his peers as well as to humbler brethren.

[128] *Serm.* 40, 5; 41, 3; 45, 4; 47, 3.
[129] *Serm.* 10, 1. "rationem eorum quaesiturus sit, quae non magis possidenda tradidit (sc. Deus) quam dispensanda commisit."
[130] *Serm.* 90, 3.
[131] *Serm.* 19, 3.
[132] *Serm.* 41, 1.
[133] *Serm.* 6; 16, 1; 20, 2.
[134] *Serm.* 49, 6.
[135] *Serm.* 86, 2.
[136] *Ep.* 167, 11.
[137] *Serm.* 12, 3.

CHAPTER XX

LEO AS A THEOLOGIAN

It is undeniable that Leo owed his reputation as a theologian, both during his lifetime and in succeeding centuries,† largely to the supposed merits of his celebrated letter to Flavian, generally known as the "Tome." Yet apart from the adequacy or otherwise of this document as a contribution to the solution of the problems inherent in the doctrine of the Incarnation, it must be acknowledged that the enthusiastic welcome accorded to it by the fathers of the council of Chalcedon, and equally by others, was due more to its evident simplicity of language and directness of statement than to any other consideration. As a straightforward exposition of belief it offered to the harassed eastern bishops, as we have seen, a convenient way of escape from the subtleties and intricate arguments of their own theologians. Yet as a serious contribution to the unravelling of the Christological tangle, or even as an explanation of the manner in which the Divine and human natures in the Incarnate Lord were united, without loss to either, while maintaining a permanent abiding unity, it was plainly deficient. In fact it might be said that its author had never intended to make such a contribution, and that his primary aim was to state in plain and unequivocal language the traditional faith of the Roman see. Hence if this was his purpose it is vain for us to seek in such a statement either originality of thought or inventiveness of idea.

For the most part it may be said that what is true of Leo's doctrine of the Incarnation applies also to his treatment of other Christian dogmas. Generally speaking this treatment is confined to the straightforward statement of a principle to meet some particular case.[1] It is not his habit, as a rule, to discuss a problem in detail nor to devote space to the working out of an argument. In this respect his method is consistent with that of western writers generally, and in particular with

† Cassiodorus, *Exp. in Ps.* 65, *P.L.* 70, 452 calls him "doctor apostolicus."

[1] e.g. in *Ep.* 1, 3, JK 398, on the Doctrine of Grace.

that of his predecessors and successors in the Roman see. Systematic treatment of doctrinal subjects among such writers of this period is to be found only in the writings of Augustine. Apart from him the Popes generally were content to leave precise definition to more subtle minds in the East.

The main points of Leo's doctrine will be reviewed under the following subjects:

1. The Sources of Belief.
2. The Doctrine of God.
3. The Doctrine of the Holy Trinity.
4. The Doctrine of Creation.
5. The Doctrine of Angels and Demons.
6. The Doctrine of the Incarnation.
7. The Doctrine of Salvation.
8. The Doctrine of the Fall and its Results.
9. The Doctrine of Man's Restoration.
10. The Doctrine of the Church and the Sacraments.
11. The Doctrine of the Last Things.
12. The Doctrine of the Saints.
13. Summary.

1. THE SOURCES OF BELIEF

The Holy Scriptures are the chief source of religious knowledge. No enumeration of the contents of the Bible is to be found in Leo's writings, but we can infer from quotations that his view on the point did not differ from that which had prevailed in the West since the time of Jerome.[2] We can also gather that he regarded the books of the "Apocrypha" as possessing the same canonical authority as those of the Old and New Testaments.[3] He assumes the authority of Scripture in the sphere of religion without making any attempt to explain or to justify it.[4] So to understand it in the sense of

[2] If the so-called *Decretum Gelasianum, De libris recipiendis, P.L.* 59, 157–80 be rightly assigned to the Roman synod of A.D. 382 under Damasus I (see above, p. 76, n. 41), the Roman Church had already determined its Canon of Scripture before Leo's time.

[3] *Serm.* 10, 2. *P.L.* 54, 165f. shows that he regarded such books as *Ecclesiasticus* and *Tobit* as possessing canonical status.

[4] *Serm.* 52, 1. "indubitabilem obtineat auctoritatem sacra narratio." Cf. *Ep.* 82, 1, JK 462. At the same time he firmly repudiates the authority of Christian "pseudepigrapha," such as those treasured by the Priscillianists. Cf. *Ep.* 15, 15, JK 412.

penetrating its inner meaning is of less importance in his view than to believe that it is wholly devoid of error, although he is confident that those who are possessed of a sincere faith may count on the aid of the Holy Ghost in interpreting its true sense.[5] He frequently directs attention to the essential concord between the Old and New Testaments [6] while explaining the difference between them.[7] The Old Testament is the type, the New Testament its fulfilment.[8]

What has just been said as to his view on the interpretation of Scripture needs, however, to be qualified in the light of what he has to say elsewhere as to the knowledge on this subject to be derived from the living voice of the Church,[9] sometimes identified by him with the Catholic Faith.[10] That faith is one, true, unique, unsusceptible of either addition or subtraction.[11] It is victorious over all heresies, because God is its author and its guardian.[12] Heretical attacks only serve to bring it out into a clearer light.[13] It is epitomized in the Roman baptismal creed, " which was approved by all the votes of the Twelve Apostles," [14] and " has been so accorded heavenly protection, that like a single sword it suffices to decapitate all the opinions of heretics." [15]

Elsewhere he exhorts his hearers " to cast aside the arguments of worldly wisdom, hateful to God, by means of which none was able to reach a knowledge of the truth, and keep those words fixed in your minds, which you repeat in the Creed." [16] After which he cites the first two paragraphs of the baptismal symbol in a slightly expanded form. A similar

[5] *Serm.* 64, 1.
[6] *Serm.* 54, 1 ; 60, 1 ; 63, 2.
[7] *Serm.* 95, 1.
[8] *Serm.* 60, 3 ; 66, 2 ; 69, 2. For references to the liturgical use of Scripture in worship see *Serm.* 31, 3 ; 40, 3 ; 42, 1 ; 52, 1 ; 55, 1 ; 77, 5.
[9] *Ep.* 82, 1.
[10] *Ep.* 102, 2.
[11] *Ep.* 124, 2.
[12] *Serm.* 30, 3.
[13] *Epp.* 102, 1 ; 104, 1 ; 120, 1.
[14] *Ep.* 31, 4. Notice that here Leo alludes to the tradition, which first appears in Cassian, *De Incarn.*, 6, 3, that the local Roman creed was actually drawn up by the Twelve Apostles. Cf. *Serm.* 24, 6 ; 62, 2 ; 96, 1 ; 102, 2.
[15] Cf. *Serm.* 96, 1 ; *Ep.* 45, 2 ; 124, 8.
[16] *Serm.* 25, 4 ; 46, 3.

notion occurs in the "Tome," where he says, "He (sc. Eutyches) at least should have listened patiently to that universally accepted confession, by which the whole body of the faithful acknowledge their belief 'in God the Father Almighty, and in Jesus Christ His only Son our Lord, who was born of the Holy Ghost and the Virgin Mary,' by which three statements the devices of wellnigh every heretic are overthrown." [17] In a later sermon, when alluding to Monophysitism, he repeats a similar view.[18] Special mention should be made in this connexion of the authority in the doctrinal sphere which he attaches to the definitions of councils, and above all to those of Nicaea, or to the statements believed by him to be Nicene in origin.[19] It is clear from his references to the subject that he holds them to possess an authority not less than that of Holy Scripture itself. An equal authority also belongs in his view to the decisions of his predecessors in the Roman see.[20]

In keeping with his oft-repeated emphasis on the sufficiency of the Catholic Faith for providing men with a knowledge of the truth, Leo is unmistakably contemptuous when he refers to worldly philosophy.[21] In fact he sometimes goes so far as to suggest that human reasoning tends rather in the direction of error,[22] as when he writes:

"If there is always freedom to wrangle with man-made arguments there will always be people who do not hesitate to violate the truth and to put their trust in the verbosity of worldly wisdom; and that in spite of the fact that our Lord Jesus Christ's own method teaches them how wide a berth Christian faith and wisdom ought to give to this most dangerous nonsense; who, when He was about to call all nations to the light of Faith, did not choose from philosophers or orators the men who were to be His companions in preaching the Gospel, but took from men of low estate and fishermen those through whom He could make Himself known,

[17] *Ep.* 28, 2. Cf. *Epp.* 59, 2; 123, 2.
[18] *Serm.* 72, 7.
[19] *Epp.* 12, 4; 106, 4; 107, 1. He cites the Nicene Creed itself in *Ep.* 165, 3.
[20] *Epp.* 12, 5; 1, 1; 13, 3.
[21] *Serm.* 46, 3.
[22] *Serm.* 69, 5.

lest the heavenly doctrine, which was full of power, might seem to be in need of the help supplied by eloquence." [23]

Thus it is clear that for Leo the chief sources of religious knowledge are Holy Scripture and Catholic tradition. His general teaching on this subject may be summed up as follows; it is the duty of every Christian not to reason out his belief, but to accept whole-heartedly whatever is presented to him by legitimate authority.

2. THE DOCTRINE OF GOD

As is usual in Western authors, Leo makes no attempt to prove the existence of God in any systematic fashion. He is content to draw the attention of his hearers to inferences which may reasonably be drawn from natural phenomena, in particular from the beauty in nature, as when he writes: "To each of the faithful Nature herself teaches that God is to be worshipped, while heaven and earth, the sea and all that in them is proclaim the goodness and omnipotence of their Creator, and the wonderful beauty of the revolving spheres call forth thanksgiving from an intelligent being." [24]

Apart from this there are allusions in isolated passages to the attributes of God, such as His Justice and Mercy,[25] to His Prescience,[26] to His Omniscience,[27] to His Patience,[28] to His Changelessness.[29] His providence sustains life.[30] His love is shown by the interest which He has always displayed in the welfare of the human race; [31] in fact it is the inward conviction of the fact of this love and of His indwelling Presence, which is by far the most persuasive argument in favour of His Existence.[32] "God is omnipotent and kindly, His nature is goodness, His will is power, His work is mercy." [33]

[23] *Ep.* 164, 2. A similar attitude prevails in other Western authors, e.g. Ambrose, *De Spiritu.*, 3, 164; *Hexaem.*, 2, 3. *Peter Chrysol.*, *Serm.* 16. *P.L.* 52, 240; 44. *P.L.* 52, 325.

[24] *Serm.* 44, 1. "famulantium elementorum" appears to refer generally to the whole system of heavenly bodies. Cf. *Serm.* 19, 2.

[25] *Serm.* 12, 2, 3.

[26] *Serm.* 67, 1.

[27] *Serm.* 43, 3.

[28] *Serm.* 43, 4; 50, 1.

[29] *Serm.* 5, 3.

[30] *Serm.* 16, 1.

[31] *Serm.* 12, 1; 23, 1.

[32] *Serm.* 27, 6.

[33] *Serm.* 22, 1.

When we remember that, if we except his letters dealing with the doctrine of the Incarnation, Leo wrote no formal treatises on the cardinal points of the Christian Faith, and that his chief interest lay more in soteriology than in cosmology, it will not surprise us to find how meagre and limited is his treatment of the basic idea of Theism. It is necessary also to recall that the main sources for his doctrine on this idea are his sermons, and that we should not expect a preacher to engage in lengthy and detailed discussion of the problems which it involves.

3. THE DOCTRINE OF THE HOLY TRINITY

Numerous references to this doctrine are to be found in Leo's sermons and letters dealing with the subject of the Incarnation,[34] and also in those on the feast of Pentecost,[35] in which he is specially concerned to emphasize the truth of the Godhead of the Holy Ghost. In the following passage he lays particular stress on the unity in the Trinity.

" Godhead, which is one in the Trinity of the Father and of the Son and of the Holy Ghost, rules out any idea of inequality. For eternity in that respect has nothing that is temporal, nothing that is dissimilar in nature: therein there is one will, the same substance, equal power, and there are not three gods but one God." [36] Similarly he emphasizes the unity when he says that in the Godhead there can be no thought of temporal succession, but that the same eternity belongs to the Son as to the Father,[37] and when he comments upon Matt. xvii. 5, " when the Father says, 'This is my beloved Son, in whom I am well pleased; hear ye him,' do we not clearly hear, 'This is My Son, with whom I am one in Godhead, united in power, identical in eternity'? " [38] Though the senses may perceive distinctions in the Godhead, the understanding does not allow separation.[39] How distinctions are to be described is suggested in various ways. A notable passage is one in which he writes " those things which are enlightened

[34] *Serm.* 21–30.
[35] *Serm.* 75–7.
[36] *Serm.* 23, 2.
[37] *Serm.* 25, 2.
[38] *Serm.* 41, 6.
[39] *Serm.* 76, 2.

by the Father are enlightened also by the Son and by the Holy Ghost: and there is one Person of Him who is sent, and another of Him who sends, and another of Him who promises; the unity of the Trinity is shown to us at the same time." [40] Special attention is called to the co-operation of the Three Persons in the work of redemption. "For we know and confess with the whole heart that the Godhead of the Father, and of the Son and of the Holy Ghost is one, and that the being of the eternal Trinity is consubstantial, divided from Itself in nothing, diverse in nothing, since It is at once beyond time, at once unchangeable, at once abiding as It is. Yet in this unity of the Trinity which is beyond description, whose works and judgments are common in all respects, the Person of the Son Himself undertook the restoration of the human race." [41] In a later sermon he adds "the mercy of the Trinity divided among Itself the work of our redemption, so that the Father should be propitiated, the Son propitiate, and the Holy Ghost enflame." [42] Elsewhere, censuring the doctrine of Sabellius, he calls attention to the truth that in the Trinity three Persons, not merely names, are to be distinguished.

"Sabellius," he writes, "confused in the obscurity of error, while recognising the inseparable unity of substance in the Father, and the Son and the Holy Ghost, assigned to singularity what he ought to have attributed to equality. And since he was incapable of understanding a real Trinity, he believed It was one and the same Person under a threefold name." [43]

His teaching on this point is sufficiently summed up in the following passage: "In the Divine Trinity nothing is dissimilar, nothing unequal: and all things which can be thought of concerning that substance are identical both in power and glory and eternity. For though in respect of the properties of Persons the Father is one, the Son other, and the Holy Ghost other, yet there is not another Godhead nor a different nature." [44]

[40] *Serm.* 77, 1.
[41] *Serm.* 64, 2.
[42] *Serm.* 77, 2.
[43] *Serm.* 24, 5. Cf. *Ep.* 15, 1. "singularis unitas in tribus quidem vocabulis, sed non in tribus sit accipienda personis."
[44] *Serm.* 75, 2.

The sermon from which these words are taken is specially concerned with the Godhead of the Holy Ghost. In the words which follow Leo insists that the Holy Ghost is not a creature, but " lives and rules and exists eternally in virtue of that which is the Father and the Son." [45] Hence he repudiates the doctrine of Macedonius, who because he denied the equality of nature of the Holy Ghost with the Father and the Son incurred the guilt of the sin referred to in Matt. xii. 32. For the Holy Ghost is our intercessor, and the giver of true penitence.[46] It eternally belongs to the Holy Ghost to be the spirit of the Father and of the Son,[47] and it was He who sanctified the patriarchs, prophets and priests of the Old Testament.[48] It is to be noticed that in one place He is described as " proceeding from both " (the Father and the Son).[49] He came upon the Apostles particularly on the day of Pentecost, though He had been given to them before.[50] Of His work in the Church He is spoken of as the source of sacerdotal grace,[51] and as One who " by a single action in the hearts of the faithful drives away darkness and burns up sins." [52]

It is to be noticed that Leo uses the technical expressions of Christian theology, " essentia," " substantia," " persona," " natura," without in any way defining their meaning. He does not discuss the problems involved in a belief in a Triune God, still less does he offer any reason, apart from revelation, which might demonstrate, after the manner of Augustine's famous analogy of love, the necessity for belief in a Trinity. As usual Leo assumes the truth of the scriptural data and argues from them alone.

A number of passages are found in his works in refutation of anti-Trinitarian teaching ; as, for example, those in which mention is made of Arian doctrines, such as the generation of

[45] *Serm.* 75, ibid.
[46] *Serm.* 75, 4. It should be noticed that Leo regards 1 Cor. xii. 4–6 as indicative of the doctrine of the Holy Trinity.
[47] *Serm.* 76, 2.
[48] *Ibid.*, 3.
[49] *Ep.* 15, 1, but see p. 154, n. 155.
[50] *Serm.* 76, 4.
[51] *Serm.* 3, 1.
[52] *Serm.* 50, 2.

the Son in time,[53] or the "lesser" Godhead of the Son,[54] or the Son as a creature of the Father, or the Holy Ghost as created by the Son, though upholding the eternity and unchangeability of the Father; [55] or of the error of Photinus, which denied that "the same Christ was God of God begotten before all worlds," [56] but taught that he was "merely a man"; [57] or finally of the extreme Arianism of Eunomius.[58]

4. THE DOCTRINE OF CREATION

In accordance with the view to be expected of a Christian writer Leo affirms the doctrine of creation *ex nihilo,* as, for example, when he speaks of "the majesty which made the universe out of nothing, and fashioned and measured earthly and heavenly substance, as He willed, by omnipotent causation." [59] Although he does not assert that the three Persons of the Holy Trinity co-operated in this work, it may be inferred from references to their co-operative activity [60] that this was his belief. Creation was not only essentially good,[61] it was also beautiful, and by its very beauty proclaims itself to be the handiwork of God.[62] Yet, in being subject to change, it differs in essence from Him who made it.[63] Although the kindly governance of the Creator underlies the manifold and beneficent changes of the natural order,[64] yet His kindliness has been shown pre-eminently towards the human race.[65]

[53] *Ep.* 15, 2. "Dicentium quod Pater Filio prior sit, quia fuerit aliquando sine Filio."
[54] *Serm.* 23, 2. Cf. *Serm.* 25, 3; 75, 4.
[55] *Serm.* 24, 5. Mention is also made of Arius' condemnation at Nicaea. *Ep.* 106, 4.
[56] *Ibid.*
[57] *Ep.* 59, 5. "hominem tantum."
[58] *Serm.* 16, 3, where he and other heresiarchs are spoken of as agents of the devil.
[59] *Serm.* 22, 6. Cf. Ambrose, *Hexaem.*, 1, 16.
[60] Cf. *Serm.* 77, 1. "quidquid in dispositione omnium rerum agit divina moderatio, ex totius venit providentia Trinitatis" . . . "nec aliquid est in actione divisum, ubi nihil est in voluntate diversum."
[61] *Ep.* 15, 6. It should be remembered that there is some doubt as to the genuineness of this letter. See above, p. 154, n. 155. Yet even if its authenticity is rejected, there can be no doubt that this passage represents Leo's own view.
[62] *Serm.* 19, 2, with allusion to Rom. i. 20.
[63] *Serm.* 15, 13.
[64] *Serm.* 16, 1. It is noteworthy that in one passage, *Serm.* 60, 3 Leo draws attention to the analogy between Redemption and Creation, in that, as he says, both events began on the first day of the week. It may be inferred that Leo, like many of his contemporaries, accepted the literal truth of the record in Gen. i.
[65] *Serm.* 24, 1.

5. THE DOCTRINE OF ANGELS AND DEMONS

(a) *Angels* are but rarely mentioned in Leo's writings. He does not discuss their origin nor explain their function. Once he mentions the value of their example to Christians, as exhibiting the virtue of perfect obedience.[66] Otherwise he alludes to them only in connexion with reference to incidents described in Holy Scripture, such as the ministry of angels to our Lord after His temptation,[67] our Lord's own saying as to the possibility of summoning them to His aid at the time of His arrest,[68] their appearance at the Ascension,[69] and their coming at the Last Judgment.[70]

(b) *The Devil and Demons.* As against the Priscillianists Leo insists that the devil is a created being.[71] Like other evil spirits, the existence of which is assumed rather than demonstrated, it is implied that he belonged in respect of origin to the angelic order of creation, the privileges of which he lost as a consequence of his own sin. "The enemy of innocence . . . filled with pride lost all the glory of his nature." [72] The demons collectively are the inveterate enemies of mankind. Their hostility, like that of the devil himself, arises from their jealousy when they see men gaining by the grace of God those very blessings which they by their own sin had forfeited.[73]

Leo never tires of describing the devil's "ingenuity." He transforms himself into an "angel of light," and spreads abroad everywhere the snares of his deceit. He knows just how to probe the weaknesses in every individual Christian. He uses those whom he has entrapped by his wiles to entice others, and thrives on the growth of superstitious antidotes

[66] *Serm.* 22, 5.
[67] *Serm.* 40, 3.
[68] *Serm.* 54, 4. "cui ad exterminationem persequentium poterat plusquam duodecim millia angelicarum servire legionum," with allusion to Matt. xxvi. 53. The reading "millia" is to be found also in *Vers. lat. vet., b* and *f,* as well as in Hilary, *in Ps.* liii. 1 ; liv. 6 ; *De Trin.,* 10, 42 ; Augustine, *De Spir. et lit.,* 1 and 35.
[69] *Serm.* 74, 4.
[70] *Serm.* 9, 2, with allusion to Matt. xxv. 31.
[71] *Ep.* 15, 6. "Unde et diabolus bonus esset, si in eo quod factus est permaneret."
[72] *Serm.* 48, 2. Cf. *Serm.* 9, 1. In both passages the devil's fall is attributed to his pride. Cf. Ambrose, *Expos. ps. cxviii,* 7, 8, where the nature of this sin is discussed.
[73] *Serm.* 39, 4, with allusion to Eph. vi. 12. Cf. *Serm.* 48, 2.

against his power.[74] All that is contrary to the Christian faith, or subversive of God's commands arises from his deceits, "who strives to turn you aside from eternal life by countless devices, seizing upon certain occasions of human weakness through which he ensnares in his own ruin incautious and negligent souls."[75]

His favourite mode of attack is by means of our bodily nature, always susceptible to his allurements,[76] which are the more attractive because they have the appearance of conferring benefits. Such "benefits," however, prove in the end to be more harmful than the wounds which he inflicts.[77] It was with such deceit that he tricked "the man," and so caused him to be deprived of divine gifts.[78] By this means he infected the human race with a deadly poison.[79] Elsewhere Leo speaks of the devil's success as having obtained for him a *ius* over mankind, a cruel tyranny, from which none but the Son of Man Himself could justly deliver us.[80] Now his attacks are directed chiefly against Christians,[81] and those whom he cannot tempt to sin he corrupts with erroneous beliefs.[82] Hence all heretics are his instruments, especially those who deny the truth of the Incarnation.[83] For he himself was deceived by the birth of Christ.[84] The means by which the devil and his minions may be attacked and defeated is by the armour of God.[85] Every good deed is an onslaught on the demons,[86]

[74] *Serm.* 27, 3, with allusion to 2 Cor. xi. 14. The passage contains a warning against the futility of astrology. "Unde commentum impium sua ratione destruitur, quia si praedicta non permanent, non sunt fata metuenda; si permanent, non sunt astra veneranda." A curious *petitio principii!*

[75] *Serm.* 57, 5. Cf. *Serm.* 70, 4.

[76] *Serm.* 89, 3.

[77] *Serm.* 70, 5.

[78] *Ep.* 28, 3 = *Serm.* 22, 1.

[79] *Serm.* 22, 4.

[80] *Serm.* 22, 3. "Nam superbia hostis antiqui non immerito sibi in omnes homines ius tyrannicum vindicabat, nec indebito dominatu premebat, quos a mandato Dei spontaneos in obsequium suae voluntatis illexerat. Non itaque iuste amitteret originalem humani generis servitutem, nisi de eo quod subegerat vinceretur." Cf. *Serm.* 69, 3.

[81] *Serm.* 41, 2. Cf. *Serm.* 36, 3.

[82] *Serm.* 69, 5.

[83] *Serm.* 36, 2; 40, 2; 47, 2.

[84] *Serm.* 22, 3.

[85] *Serm.* 39, 4, with allusion to Eph. vi. 14.

[86] *Serm.* 14, 2.

who are tormented by the sanctification of Christians.[87] "For he (sc. the devil) sees that from among the whole human race new peoples are adopted to be sons of God, and that by the virginal fertility of the Church births of regeneration are increased. He sees himself deprived of the right of his own lordship, and expelled from the hearts of those whom he possessed; that there are snatched away from him thousands from both sexes, old, young and children alike . . . that those who had fallen and been deceived by the guile of his subtleties are washed by the tears of penitence, and by means of the apostolic key opening wide the gates of mercy are admitted to the remedy of reconciliation." [88]

For Leo the earnest of the devil's ultimate defeat and destruction is the sight of crowds of neophytes and penitents welcomed to the fellowship of the Church in the solemn rites of initiation.

6. THE DOCTRINE OF THE INCARNATION

Leo is scarcely less well known for his teaching on the Incarnation than for his work in defending and developing the authoritarian conception of the Roman see in its relation to the Universal Church. This is due, no doubt, not only to the part played in Christological controversy by his famous letter to Flavian of Constantinople, generally known as the "Tome," but to the fact that of his surviving letters and sermons, a considerable number contain direct allusions to or explanations of this doctrine. Indeed so extensive is the material at our disposal that we must be content to make only a summary of the more important points of his teaching on this subject.

Our principal sources, in addition to the "Tome," [89] are fifty-four sermons on the Incarnate Life,[90] and a number of important letters.[91] Here he maintains against the Arians that our Lord is truly God, against the Apollinarians and Eutychians (and incidentally the Manichaeans) that He is

[87] *Serm.* 16, 3; 40, 2.
[88] *Serm.* 49, 3.
[89] *Ep.* 28, JK 423.
[90] *Serm.* 21–38, 52–77.
[91] e.g. *Epp.* 31, 59, 124, 165.

perfectly Man, against the Nestorians that while possessing two distinct Natures—the Divine and the Human—He is still one Person. Leo is primarily concerned to show the necessity of the " Two Nature " or " dyophysite " doctrine for a right belief in the Incarnation, and the insufficiency and falsity of monophysitism, though he also says much that is illuminating and a few things which are permanently valuable on the general subject of the experience of the Incarnate Word.

(a) *The Deity of our Lord.* Leo nowhere mentions the view of those who while ascribing " divinity " to Christ distinguish Him from other holy men by assigning to Him a higher degree of " divinity." [92] On the other hand he describes, only to reject, the Arian view which spoke of " the lesser Godhead of the Son." [93] In another passage he repudiates the characteristic Arian doctrine of the temporal generation of the Son.[94] Christ is therefore to be identified with the Second Person of the Holy Trinity—" God the Son of God, equal and of the same nature from the Father and with the Father, the Maker and Lord of the universe, everywhere wholly present, and wholly exceeding all things." [95] He is " the Almighty Son of God, filling all things and sustaining all things, equal in all respects to the Father, and co-eternal in one being from Him and with Him." [96] " For the Son of God is God, only begotten of the eternal and unbegotten Father, abiding eternally in the form of God, and unchangeably and without time possessing that being which is the Father." [97] Only one who was, in fact, true God could have redeemed mankind.[98] Leo repeatedly emphasizes his conviction that the Incarnation involved no change or diminution in Christ's Godhead.[99]

[92] Cf. e.g. Theod. Mops., *De Incarn.* 7, ed. Swete, pp. 293–6.
[93] *Serm.* 23, 2. " caecitas Ariana . . . quae Unigenitum Dei eiusdem cum Patre gloriae atque substantiae esse non credens minorem dixit Filii deitatem." Cf. *Serm.* 24, 5 ; *Serm.* 75, 3.
[94] *Serm.* 25, 3, where he shows that Arianism makes the Father Himself subject to change. Cf. *Ep.* 15, 2.
[95] *Serm.* 23, 1.
[96] *Serm.* 24, 3. Cf. *Serm.* 25, 3 ; 27, 2.
[97] *Serm.* 28, 1.
[98] *Serm.* 21, 2. " Nisi enim esset Deus verus, non afferret remedium." Cf. also *Serm.* 30, 2, 3 ; 46, 1, 2, 3 ; 47, 2 ; 51, 2 ; 54, 1 ; 64, 4. *Epp.* 28 ; 31, 1 ; 32, 1 ; 35, 2 ; 59, 2 ; 74 ; 88, 1 ; 102, 3 ; 124, 2, 3 ; 139, 2 ; 165.
[99] *Serm.* 21, 2. " ita se ad susceptionem humilitatis nostrae sine diminutione suae maiestatis inclinans."

"He remained what He was, and assumed what He was not." [100] The *kenosis* or *exaninitio* mentioned by St. Paul in Phil. ii. 6 is therefore interpreted to mean that, though He accepted human infirmities, yet He abandoned nothing of His Power.[101] It was the condescension of God's pity for man.[102]

"Yet for the sake of our weakness He condescended to things within which He was incomprehensible, and concealed with the veil of the body the splendour of His majesty, the sight of which was unbearable to men. So He is said to have "emptied Himself," as though He stripped Himself of His own power, when in that lowliness, with which He came to aid us, He was made inferior not only to the Father but even to Himself." [103]

(b) *The Manhood of our Lord.* Leo takes as much pains to assert the reality and completeness of our Lord's humanity as he does to uphold the truth of His Godhead.

(i) Against Docetists of all kinds, including especially Manichaeans, who in denying the fact of Christ's birth of the Virgin Mary, deny also the historicity of His whole Incarnate Life,[104] and "to destroy the souls of those who are misled weave a beastly fabrication of abominable doctrine from blasphemies and lying fairy tales, . . . so that they fashion for themselves a Christ of a false body, who presented in Himself nothing solid nor true to the eyes and touch of men: but showed the empty semblance of simulated flesh," [105] Leo affirms "He who is true God is also true Man; and there is no deceit in either substance." [106] Hence His body, as a real human body, was subject to human infirmities and necessities and even the common law of death.

[100] *Ibid.*
[101] *Serm.* 23, 2. "ex inanitio enim illa qua se invisibilis visibilem praebuit, inclinatis fuit miserationis, non defectio potestatis."
[102] *Ep.* 28, 3.
[103] *Serm.* 25, 2. This passage taken by itself might suggest an almost Docetic view of our Lord's humanity.
[104] *Serm.* 24, 4. Cf. *Serm.* 47, 2.
[105] *Serm.* 34, 4 (reading "tactibus" for "actionibus"). Cf. *Ep.* 124, 2, where he attributes without justice the same view to Apollinarius "hominem Jesum Christum simulatorie omnia credit egisse, nec humanum in ipso corpus, sed phantasticam corporis speciem oculis apparuisse cernentium." Cf. *Ep.* 165, 2.
[106] *Serm.* 24, 3.

"So when the time was come, beloved, which had been provided for the redemption of men, Jesus Christ the Son of God entered the lowliness of this world, descending from His heavenly throne, though not withdrawing from the Father's glory, being born in a new order by a new Birth. In a new order because, though invisible in His own Being, He became visible in our Being: the Incomprehensible willed to be comprehended; abiding before all time He began a temporal existence; the Lord of the universe, the dignity of His Majesty overshadowed took the form of a slave; the impassible God did not spurn to be passible man and the Immortal One to be subject to the laws of death." [107]

Yet in certain respects our Lord's humanity was dissimilar to our own, in manner of His birth, for example, by being born of a Virgin.[108] His Mother the blessed Virgin Mary was purely human, and it was from her that He derived all that He possessed which was human; yet the human nature which she gave Him was given without the co-operation of a human father, and though she may be described as "the Mother of God," [109] yet she is not the Mother of the Godhead.[110]

"For He was born by a new Birth, conceived of a Virgin, born of a Virgin, without the concupiscence of a father's body, without injury to a mother's maidenhood." [111]

From this it follows that, though as against Eutyches, Leo strongly affirms that our Lord's human nature was consubstantial with our own,[112] yet he insists that in consequence of the Virgin Birth, He was immune from the contagion of human sin.[113] Indeed on his premises that the Incarnation would not have taken place if man had not sinned,[114] and that its primary purpose was to redeem man from its unhappy con-

[107] *Serm.* 22, 2.
[108] *Ibid.* "Origo dissimilis, sed natura consimilis."
[109] *Serm.* 21, 1. "Dei genetrix."
[110] *Serm.* 28, 2. "sine matre Deitas et sine patre esset humanitas."
[111] *Serm.* 22, 2.
[112] *Serm.* 30, 6.
[113] *Serm.* 22, 2. "In se haberet humanae substantiae naturam, et humanae carnis inquinamenta nesciret."
[114] *Serm.* 77, 2. "Si enim homo . . . nec . . . per concupiscentiam deviasset, Creator mundi creatura non fieret, neque . . . aut aequalis Deo Patri Filius Deus formam servi et similitudinem carnis peccati assumeret."

sequences, it was inevitable that he should hold that the human nature assumed by our Lord was itself altogether sinless.[115]

(ii) Against Apollinarians and others who denied the integrity of our Lord's human nature,[116] Leo upholds its completeness. " In an entire and perfect nature of true man True God was born, complete in all things appertaining to Him, complete in all things appertaining to us." [117] " The mystery of our redemption is rendered void, if Christ is not believed to have taken the real and complete nature of true man." [118]

(c) *The Union of Two Natures in One Person.* The relation between the Godhead and the Manhood in Christ only became a matter of acute controversy in the fifth century. Yet in insisting that the ascription of human experiences to the Word by the Arians must be repudiated, on the ground that it impugned the impassibility of the Godhead, the orthodox were bound to find an answer sooner or later to the question as to how the Divine and human were to be reconciled, without

[115] *Ep.* 28, 3. " Assumpsit formam servi sine sorde peccati " ; *ibid.*, 4. " Assumpta est de matre Domini natura, non culpa." Evidently Leo did not feel it necessary, as it was felt in later ages, to postulate the Immaculate Conception of the blessed Virgin herself, in order to safeguard our Lord's immunity from sin.

[116] *Ep.* 59, 5. " aliquid ei desit quod ad humanam certum est pertinere naturam, sive animam, sive mentem rationalem."

[117] *Ep.* 28, 3.

[118] *Ep.* 35, 1. *Serm.* 28, 4, contains a characteristic passage summarizing doctrinal errors as to the Incarnation. " Alii etenim Domino solam humanitatem, alii solam ascripsere Deitatem. Alii veram quidem in ipso Divinitatem, sed carnem dixerunt fuisse simulatam. Alii professi sunt veram eum suscepisse carnem, sed Dei Patris non habuisse naturam ; et Deitati eius, quae erant humanae substantiae deputantes, maiorem sibi Deum minoremque finxerunt, cum gradus in vera Divinitate esse non possit : quoniam quidquid Deo minus est, Deus non est. Alii cognoscentes Patris et Filii nullam esse distantiam, quia non poterant unitatem Deitatis intelligere nisi in unitate personae, eumdem asseruerunt esse Patrem quem Filium : ut nasci et nutriri, pati et mori, sepeliri et resurgere, ad eumdem pertineret, qui per omnia et hominis personam impleret et Verbi. Quidam putaverunt Dominum Jesum Christum non nostrae substantiae corpus habuisse, sed ab elementis superioribus ac subtilioribus sumptum. Quidam autem aestimaverunt in carne Christi humanam animam non fuisse, sed partes animae ipsam Verbi implesse Deitatem. Quorum imprudentiam in hoc transiit, ut animam quidem fuisse in Domino faterentur, sed eamdem dicerent mente caruisse, quia sufficeret homini sola Deitas ad omnia rationis officia. Postremo iidem asserere praesumpserunt partem quamdam Verbi in carnem fuisse conversam, ut in unius dogmatis varietate multiplici, non carnis tantum animaeque natura, sed etiam ipsius Verbi solveretur essentia."

either impairing the integrity of one or the other, or abandoning any real unity between them.

The Nestorian controversy had been formally closed by the council of Ephesus of A.D. 431. Yet resistance to the Alexandrine Christology which had prevailed at that council continued and, as a consequence, those who emphasized the distinctness of the Divine and human in our Lord found themselves compelled to meet the charge of Nestorianism. As we have seen, this was the very charge which was levelled by the objectors to Leo's "Tome" at the council of Chalcedon and after, and for this reason his anti-Nestorian arguments have special interest.

"He who was made in the form of a slave, did not cease to be the form of God, neither is He one (person) and another, but a single (Person) in both, . . . whether in the miracles of power, or in the insults of suffering we believe that both He who is Man is God, and He who is God is Man."[119] "Let Nestorius therefore be condemned, who believed that the blessed Virgin Mary was only the mother of a man, so that he made one person of the flesh and another of the Godhead, and did not suppose that there was one Christ in the Word of God and the flesh, but taught that there was one Son of God and one Son of Man, separately and apart from one another."[120] In the first place therefore Leo insists that the Incarnate Christ is a single Person. Yet he does not attempt to explain, as Cyril did, that this unity of Person existed because the humanity taken by our Lord was actually "impersonal." He contents himself with the bare assertion of its unity.[121]

[119] *Serm.* 91, 2. "Qui enim factus est forma servi, forma Dei esse non destitit, nec alter cum altero, sed unus in utroque est . . . sive in miraculis virtutum, sive in contumeliis passionum, et Deum qui homo est, et hominem credamus esse qui Deus est." Cf. *Serm.* 28, 6.

[120] *Ep.* 124, 2.

[121] When he does attempt an explanation he ventures on a statement which almost certainly in later ages would have been rejected as heretical. Thus in *Serm.* 23, 1, we read, "Hic enim mirabilis sacrae Virginis partus, vere humanam vereque divinam unam edidit prole personam, quia non ita proprietates suas tenuit utraque substantia, ut personarum in eis possit esse discretio; nec sic creatura in societatem sui Creatoris est assumpta, ut ille habitator, et illa esset habitaculum; sed ita ut naturae alteri altera *misceretur*."

Leo had become familiar with the defects of Nestorian teaching in the period of his diaconate, and it was not till after his election to the Roman see that he came into contact with the opposite error, later known as "monophysitism."

The greater part of his Christological writings is concerned with demonstrating the falsity of monophysite teaching, and in particular with exposing the errors of opinions held by or attributed to Eutyches. Of those writings the best known as well as the most characteristic is the celebrated letter to Flavian, known as the "Tome." [122] In that letter, after asserting the belief that our Lord is one Person, he points out that in Him there are two natures, Godhead and Manhood, united yet distinct. "For what was proper to each nature and substance remained unimpaired, and was united in one Person; thus humility was assumed by Majesty, weakness by Power, mortality by Eternity. . . . Each nature retains without loss its own proper character." [123] "For although in the Lord Jesus Christ God and Man are one Person, nevertheless it is not the same thing to say that an insult is common to both (natures), as to say that the glory is common." [124]

Each of the two natures has its own peculiar properties, and its own proper scope of operation, which it performs not independently of the other, but in virtue of its unalterable unity with the other. "Each nature *in communion with the other* performs the function proper to itself, that is to say, the Word carries out that which is proper to the Word, and the flesh that which is proper to the flesh." [125] Leo expands this point at some length, and indicates what he means by what is "proper to the Word," and what, on the other hand, is "proper to the flesh." Thus he argues that it is not proper to the same nature "to bemoan with pitying affection a dead

[122] *Ep.* 28.

[123] *Ibid.*, 3.

[124] *Ibid.*, 4. "Quamvis enim in Domino Jesu Christo Dei et hominis una persona sit; aliud tamen est unde in utroque communis est contumelia, aliud unde communis est gloria." This appears to mean that while the sufferings attributable to the one Person are attributable to the Godhead only by divine permission, the honour attributable to the Manhood is only to be regarded as a consequence of the unity of Person.

[125] *Ibid.* "Agit enim utraque forma cum alterius communione quod proprium est, Verbo scilicet operante quod Verbi est, et carne exsequente quod carnis est." Cf. *Serm.* 46, 2.

friend, and with a word of command to raise the same man to life again," . . . "or to say 'I and the Father are one,' and to say 'The Father is greater than I.'"[126] Thus as God, Christ performed actions which exceed the limitations of human nature; as Man He underwent human experiences.[127]

Lest however such a view might appear to endanger the unity of Christ's Person, Leo points out that though the Divine acts belong properly to the Divine nature, and the human acts to the human nature, yet the Divine and human nature alike may equally be predicated of the one Divine Person. Thus he writes, "Invisible in His own nature, He became visible in ours, and though incomprehensible He chose to be comprehended: abiding before time He began to exist in time";[128] and "By reason therefore of this unity of Person recognized in each nature, even the Son of Man is stated to have come down from heaven, when the Son of God took flesh of the Virgin, of whom He was born." And further, "The Son of God is said to have been crucified and buried, though He suffered these things not in the Godhead itself, wherein the only begotten is coeternal and consubstantial with the Father. Wherefore we all confess in the Creed that the only begotten Son of God was crucified and buried."[129]

[126] *Ep.* 28, 4. It is sometimes urged that the phrase which occurs in this chapter, namely, "nullum est in hac unitate mendacium, dum *invicem* sunt et humilitas hominis et altitudo Deitatis," is blatantly Nestorian since it attributes to our Lord a dual Personality, in virtue of which He acts by turns as God and as Man. Yet this is not what Leo actually says. Viewed objectively his assertions in this chapter only amount to saying that it is proper to God to act above the laws of nature and to man to conform with them. Nor is it necessary or even correct to render "invicem" as "by turns." The word occurs in two other passages in his works; *Serm.* 28, 5. "post diversas impietates, quae sibi *invicem* sunt multiformium blasphemiarum cognatione connexae," and in *Serm.* 54, 1, "Nihil ab *invicem* vacat, tota est in maiestate humilitas, tota in humilitate maiestas." In the first case it is used as a predicate; in the second as an adverb; in the third as a noun. In the second it must mean "mutually"; in the third "one or the other," so that it may be inferred that for the first "reciprocal . . ." is a fitting translation. This is in conformity with the late Latin use of the expression. Cf. Lewis and Short, s.v. *invicem* II.

[127] An identical view is to be found in the works of St. Ambrose. Cf. Homes Dudden, *op. cit.*, Vol. II, p. 597.

[128] *Ep.* 28, 4.

[129] *Ibid.*, 5. "Propter hanc ergo unitatem personae in utraque natura intelligendam, et filius hominis legitur descendisse de caelo, cum filius Dei carnem de ea Virgine, de qua est natus, assumpserit. Et rursus filius Dei crucifixus dicitur ac sepultus, cum haec non in divinitate ipse, qua Unigenitus consempiternus et consubstiantialis est Patri, sed in naturae

(d) *The Experience of the Incarnate Lord. The Virgin Birth.* We have already seen that Leo emphasized repeatedly his conviction that our Lord was born of the Virgin Mary without the co-operation of a human father. " For when the Holy Ghost came upon her and the Power of the Highest overshadowed her, the changeless Word of God took to Himself from a stainless body a habitation of human flesh: which derived no contagion from the concupiscence of the flesh, yet possessed all things which belong to the nature of soul and body." [130] Yet she retained her virginity. " Sustained by Divine power, she conceived as a virgin, brought forth as a virgin and remained a virgin." [131]

It follows that the Birth of Christ was a miracle. Other exceptional births such as those of Isaac, Samuel and John the Baptist had taken place but, " the Birth of our Lord Jesus Christ surpasses our understanding and exceeds all examples; nor can it be compared to any other, being unique among them all." [132]

The pre-eminent reason for such a Birth was in order that human nature might have a new beginning, by being freed *ab initio* from the hereditary contamination of evil.[133] " For when our Lord Jesus Christ was born as true man, He who never ceased to be true God, He made unto Himself the beginning of a new creation, and in the character of His Birth gave to the human race a spiritual origin, so that for the sake of removing the contagion of carnal generation, there might be for those who were to be reborn a beginning without the seed of sin." [134]

humanae sit infirmitate perpessus. Unde unigenitum filium Dei crucifixum et sepultum omnes etiam in symbolo confitemur." It should not be supposed that Leo himself originated this idea, generally known as the " *communicatio idiomatum.*" It had already been described by Ambrose in *De fide.*, 2, 58. Cf. Homes Dudden, *op. cit.*, Vol. II, p. 598.

[130] *Serm.* 30, 4.

[131] *Serm.* 22, 2. " divina potestate subnixum est, quod virgo conceperit, quod virgo pepererit, et virgo permanserit." The view of Helvidius that Mary had other children after giving birth to Christ was evidently no longer a matter of controversy at Rome. Cf. *Serm.* 23, 1; 24, 1, 3; 27, 2; 30, 4; *Ep.* 28, 4; 35, 3.

[132] *Serm.* 30, 4. Cf. *Serm.* 33, 3.

[133] *Serm.* 22, 2. Cf. *Ep.* 124, 3.

[134] *Serm.* 27, 2. The same theme constantly recurs. Cf. e.g. *Serm.* 21, 1; 22, 3; 24, 3; 25, 4, 5; 26, 3; 28, 2; 59, 1; 63, 4; 64, 2; 77, 2. *Epp.* 28, 3, 4. With further reference to our Lord's Birth and

(e) *The Sinlessness of our Lord.* Leo yields to none in his insistence on the reality and completeness of our Lord's human nature and on its utter identity with our own. Yet he always qualifies his assertions by remarking that Christ was altogether without sin.[135] In fact, as we shall see, it is this sinlessness which plays an important part in his theory of the "devil's blunder." [136]

Yet he does not deny the fact that our Lord was subject to temptation. "The Lord allowed Himself to be tempted by the tempter, so that we might be edified by His example, by whose help we are defended." [137] He urges that the whole record of the Temptation proves the truth of the Incarnation,[138] and points out that Christ preferred to attack the devil with the righteousness of true man rather than show forth the power of His Godhead.[139] The value of His temptation is to give us power that we might be able to conquer.[140]

(f) *Christ's Passion, Death and Resurrection.* Leo devotes a considerable amount of attention to the details of Christ's Passion. He points out with reference to John xviii. 4, 5 that even in the moment of His betrayal, He showed forth His Godhead.[141] Special attention is devoted to the significance of His prayer in the garden as proving the co-existence in Him of two wills,[142] though elsewhere it is interpreted as a prayer not for Himself but on our behalf.[143] In various passages Leo describes our Lord's arrest,[144] His trial and accusation,[145] His carrying of the Cross and the incidents along the Via

Infancy see *Serm.* 29, 3; 31, 2, 3; 34, 1; 37, 3. *Ep.* 16, 6; 139, 2. Leo never grows tired of affirming that the Infant Saviour was Himself True God, e.g. *Serm.* 32, 4. "quem magi infantem venerati sunt in cunabulis, nos omnipotentem adoremus in coelis."

[135] *Serm.* 23, 2. "nec quia communionem humanarum subiit infirmitatum, ideo nostrorum fuit particeps delictorum."

[136] See below, pp. 464ff.

[137] *Serm.* 39, 3. Yet in so saying, there was a danger of suggesting that the temptation was unreal.

[138] *Serm.* 40, 3.

[139] *Ibid.* Cf. *Serm.* 42, 3.

[140] *Serm.* 39, 3. "vicit ille, ut et nos similiter vinceremus." It is noticeable that Leo fails to meet the difficulty as to how One who had no experience of evil could Himself know the force of Temptation.

[141] *Serm.* 52, 3.

[142] *Serm.* 56, 2. Cf. *Serm.* 59, 1.

[143] *Serm.* 58, 5. Once again a dangerous idea.

[144] *Serm.* 52, 3.

[145] *Serm.* 57, 3; 59, 2, 3; 61, 1.

Dolorosa.[146] Of special interest is his explanation of the cries from the Cross,[147] particularly of "Quare me dereliquisti?" This cry, he says, was not a complaint but a doctrine, for it was "a showing forth of the great mystery that the power of the Redeemer would confer nothing on the human race, if our weakness were to obtain whatever it sought."[148] In another place he explains it as showing that "the delivering of the Lord to His Passion was the result as much of His own will as of His Father's: so that not only His Father abandoned Him, but that He even in some fashion forsook Himself, not by a retreat in fear but by a voluntary withdrawal."[149]

In His Death His Godhead did not abandon His human body and soul,[150] while the Passion itself was inflicted on His humanity alone.[151] His Burial was actual,[152] though the length of it was shortened for the sake of His disciples.[153] His Descent into Hell, too, was for our sakes.[154] As to His Resurrection, Leo draws attention to the abundant proof existing in support of it.[155] After the Resurrection the properties of Christ's flesh were changed, but not its nature. "What could be crucified was made impassible; what could be slain was made immortal: what could be wounded was made incorruptible."[156] He explains the reason why the disciples were permitted to doubt by saying that it was in order to strengthen our faith,[157] and that the scars of the nails and lance remained for the same cause.[158] He answers the question as to why the Ascension was delayed for forty days, by replying that it was to give us a further opportunity of apprehending the fact of the Resurrection.[159] Its effect was to imbue the Apostles with

[146] *Serm.* 59, 4, 5; 61, 3.
[147] *Serm.* 67, 7; 68, 2; 55, 4.
[148] *Serm.* 67, 7. Leo appears to mean that the cry showed the dependence of human nature on God.
[149] *Serm.* 68, 2. This explanation, which sounds somewhat artificial, was probably intended to mean that the power of His Godhead was held in temporary suspense.
[150] *Serm.* 71, 2.
[151] *Serm.* 65, 3.
[152] *Ep.* 15, 17.
[153] *Serm.* 71, 2.
[154] *Serm.* 25, 5.
[155] *Serm.* 71, 3.
[156] *Ibid.*, 4.
[157] *Serm.* 73, 1.
[158] *Ibid.*, 3.
[159] *Serm.* 73, 1.

the spiritual strength necessary to carry out their mission.[160]

(g) *The Purpose of the Incarnation.* The Incarnation was accomplished for the sake of mankind. " He was made man of our race, that we might be partners of the Divine nature."[161] Elsewhere Leo speaks of it as intended to provide humanity with a new birth[162] or to restore to mortal men their lost immortality.[163]

The particular reasons for it, mentioned by him, may be summarized under two main headings. (a) The Son of God became incarnate in order that He might provide us with an example of human virtue.[164] He has shown us how temptation may be overcome and fear abolished.[165] (b) The Son of God became incarnate in order that by taking on Himself our flesh and sharing the penalty of sin in His Death and Passion, though Himself wholly without sin, He might free mankind from the bondage of the devil,[166] and restore the human race to true freedom,[167] since in so doing He offered Himself as a sufficient victim for man's transgression.[168] We shall find Leo's teaching on this point set forth in fuller detail in the following section.

7. THE DOCTRINE OF SALVATION

The theme that through Christ and Him alone is salvation possible for the human race is one which recurs repeatedly throughout Leo's sermons on the Incarnation and the Passion.[169] Thus in the first of his sermons on the Passion he says:

[160] *Serm.* 74, 2.
[161] *Serm.* 25, 5.
[162] *Serm.* 27, 2.
[163] *Serm.* 70, 3.
[164] *Serm.* 25, 6. " Haec Domini nostra opera . . . non solum sacramento nobis utilia sunt, sed etiam imitationis exempla. . . . Frustra enim appellamur Christiani, si imitatores non simus Christi."
[165] See above.
[166] *Serm.* 24, 2; 28, 3; 52, 1; 77, 2. *Epp.* 28, 2; 59, 4; 124, 7, etc.
[167] *Serm.* 37, 1.
[168] *Serm.* 23, 3.
[169] *Serm.* 30, 7. " eum (sc. Christum) in quo uno erat salus omnium," in a passage in which he shows that the purpose of the Matthaean genealogy was to demonstrate that the promise to Abraham was fulfilled in Christ, while the Lucan genealogy aimed at showing the applicability of His merits even to those who preceded the Flood. Cf. *Ep.* 31, 2.

"Every single worshipper of the true God in old time, the whole company of saints in former ages lived in this faith and pleased (God); yet neither for patriarchs nor prophets nor anyone whatsoever of the saints was there salvation and justification save in the redemption of Jesus Christ our Lord." [170]

The doctrine of the universal applicability of the saving merits of Christ occurs elsewhere.[171] If the value of His redemption had only been universally appreciated all would have been freed from the bondage of the devil.[172]

As to the means by which the salvation of mankind was effected Leo makes frequent mention of the Passion and Death of the Cross and the Blood of Christ.[173]

One of the finest passages in his sermons deals with this idea: "O the wonderful power of the Cross! O the unspeakable glory of the Passion! in which is seen at once the Lord's judgment seat, the trial of the world and the power of the Crucified. For thou, O Lord, didst draw all things unto Thee, and when Thou hadst spread forth Thine hands all day to a faithless and gainsaying people, the whole world took knowledge of undeniable Majesty. Thou didst draw all things unto Thee, when in condemnation of the wickedness of the Jews the entire elements uttered a single verdict when, as the heavenly luminaries were darkened, and day was turned into night, the earth was shaken with unwonted movement, and the whole creation refused its service to the ungodly. . . . For Thy Cross is the source of all blessings, cause of all the gifts of Grace: through It to them that believe is given strength out of weakness, glory out of shame, life out of death." [174]

Similarly in other sermons: "What else has the Cross of Christ effected and effects even now than that, with the abolition of enmity, the universe is reconciled to God and all

[170] *Serm.* 52, 1. The use of the military term "numerus" here is noteworthy.

[171] *Serm.* 69, 2. "salus quae in Christo est, nullis saeculis sub eadem iustificatione defuerit." Cf. *Serm.* 66, 2.

[172] *Ep.* 165, 4. In *Serm.* 54, 2, he includes those who slew Christ, and in *Serm.* 62, 4 Judas himself within its scope, if only they had believed.

[173] e.g. *Serm.* 52, 1; 55, 1; 56, 1; 60, 1.

[174] *Serm.* 59, 7. Cf. *Serm.* 55, 2, quoting Ps. xcv. 10 (vulg.), "Dominus regnavit a ligno."

things are restored to true peace by the sacrifice of the immaculate Lamb?"[175] "There (sc. on the Cross) the Blood of the immaculate Lamb broke the bonds of the ancient transgression: there the whole malignity of the devil's tyranny was destroyed and victorious humility triumphed over the boastfulness of pride."[176]

"The Blood of Christ is shed for all sinners."[177] The Blood of Christ is the "price" of every Christian,[178] "for there was offered to God a unique victim for the salvation of the universe, and the slaying of Christ the true Lamb, foretold throughout so many centuries, adopted the sons of promise into the freedom of faith. The new covenant was confirmed and heirs of the eternal kingdom were enrolled by the Blood of Christ."[179] "The Cross of Christ, which is granted for the salvation of mortals, is both a mystery and an example: a mystery by which the power of God is shown forth; an example, by which man's devotion is aroused."[180] "The Cross of Christ is the true ground and chief cause of Christian hope."[181]

In order to explain the reason for the efficacy of the Death of Christ, Leo advances three theories.

(a) *The Theory of the Devil's Deception.* More subtle than the "Ransom" theory sponsored by Ambrose[182] and derived by him from Origen,[183] is the view preferred by Leo, itself borrowed from Augustine.[184] According to this view Adam's sin rendered him a subject or slave of the devil, in a state of bondage in which all his descendants have been involved. The devil thus became the governor or tyrant of the human race. Since, however, man had become the devil's subject by a free act of his own will he could not in justice be made free.[185]

[175] *Serm.* 66, 3.
[176] *Serm.* 55, 3. Cf. *Ep.* 165, 4.
[177] *Serm.* 54, 3.
[178] *Serm.* 21, 3.
[179] *Serm.* 68, 3.
[180] *Serm.* 72, 1.
[181] *Serm.* 56, 1.
[182] e.g. in *Ep.* 72, 8. On this theory see further Homes Dudden, *Ambrose,* Vol. II, pp. 607ff.
[183] e.g. in *Hom. in Matth.* xvi. 8. *P.G.* 13, 1397.
[184] *De Trinitate,* 13, 16, 18.
[185] *Serm.* 64, 2. Cf. *Serm.* 22, 3.

Hence it was necessary to outwit the devil.[186] Such a task was possible to God alone, and was achieved by the assumption of our human nature by God the Son Himself, who by being born of a Virgin broke the entail of sin which hitherto had fettered fallen humanity.[187] The devil in bringing about the death of Christ inflicted the punishment due to one guilty of sin whereas Christ was wholly innocent.

Thus while Leo does not hesitate to say: "The omnipotence of the Son of God, in which through the same being He is equal to the Father, might have delivered the human race from the domination of the devil by the mere fiat of His will, if it had not been more in accord with the operations of God, that the enmity of the adversary's wickedness should be overcome by that which he had overcome, and the freedom of our nature should be restored by that nature, by which universal bondage had been induced." [188]

Elsewhere we read: "For the trustworthy mercy of God, though many things mysteriously served it for the restoration of the human race, chose this particular mode of action so as to use for the destruction of the devil's work not the might of force but the method of justice. For the pride of the ancient enemy deservedly claimed for himself a tyrannical right over all men, and oppressed with a well-merited domination those whom with their own assent he had enticed from God's commandment to the obedience of his own will. So he would only with justice lose his original lordship over the human race, if he were conquered by that which he had overcome." [189]

Later in the same sermon he describes the "pious deceit" practised on the devil, who, being misled by the human infirmities of the Incarnate Word, exceeded his just limitations and thus lost his rights. In this way the devil was outwitted and mankind was set free.

This strange idea appears in a number of passages, of

[186] It will be seen that this theory bears a close resemblance to the "heavenly snare" invented by Gregory the Great. *Moral.* 33, 31.

[187] On the special importance of the Virgin Birth in this connexion see above, p. 459.

[188] *Serm.* 63, 1.

[189] *Serm.* 22, 3.

which the following are typical: "He (sc. Christ), to deliver the human race from the bonds of a deadly transgression, concealed from the raging devil the power of His majesty and cast in his way the weakness of our humility. For if the cruel proud enemy had been able to realize the plan of God's mercy, he would have rather hastened to restrain the wills of the Jews with kindness than to inflame them with unjust hatred; lest he should lose the service of all his prisoners, by attacking the freedom of One who owed nothing to him. So his own malice deceived him; he inflicted suffering on the Son of God, which turned to the healing of all the sons of men. He shed innocent Blood, which was to be the price and the cup for the reconciliation of the universe."[190]

And again: "He (sc. the devil) went beyond the handwriting, on which he relied, by exacting the penalty of sin from Him, in whom was found no fault. So the unhappy covenant with its death inflicting clauses was made void, and through the injustice of too much being demanded the account was cleared of the whole debt."[191]

It is noteworthy, however, that Leo appears at times to be inconsistent. He describes the devil's right as a *ius tyrannicum*. Yet if it may be called *tyrannicum* in the strict sense of "unconstitutional," it could not properly be a *ius*. For if, as he says, "man deserved what he got," then it was, from the standpoint of his theory, a *ius* pure and simple. Evidently the author himself was conscious of a certain weakness in a theory which was too ingenious to be true.

(b) *The Theory of Expiatory Sacrifice.* This view which often acquires so much prominence in Western treatment of the idea of Atonement is suggested rather than expounded by Leo. Once, however, he writes explicitly of the sacrifice of Himself offered by Christ to the Father:

"Who offering Himself as a new and true sacrifice of reconciliation to the Father, not in the Temple . . . but outside and without the court, He was crucified that, with the end of the mystery of former victims, a new victim should be

[190] *Serm.* 62, 3.
[191] *Serm.* 22, 4. Cf. *Serm.* 64, 2; 69, 3, 4; and with special reference to the Temptation, *Serm.* 42, 3.

set upon a new altar, and the Cross of Christ should be the the altar, not of the temple, but of the universe." [192]

So later he asks, " What sacrifice was ever more holy than that which the true and eternal High priest by the immolation of His flesh laid upon the altar of the Cross? For though the death of many saints was dear in the sight of the Lord, the slaying of an innocent person (in itself) was not the redemption of the universe." [193]

It is for this reason that he stresses the necessity of Christ's Death. " Who if He willed to resist, . . . the redemption of the universe would be delayed, and He who was to die for the salvation of all men would save no man if He were not stricken." [194]

In one passage he appears to speak of the perpetuation of Christ's offering of Himself in the Eucharist. " For He is our true and eternal High priest, whose governance can have neither change nor end, He whose type was shown by the priest Melchizedek, not offering Jewish victims to God, but offering the sacrifice of that mystery, which our Redeemer consecrated in His own Body and Blood." [195]

(c) *The Theory of the Mystical Incorporation of Humanity in Christ.* According to this view Christ is not so much the Substitute for the human race as its Representative. Thus Leo writes of the ideal union of the whole race with Christ, " in whom all were crucified, all died, all were buried, all were raised again." [196] Moreover, as in the first Adam, the whole of humanity is conceived of as having sinned and consequently having suffered death, so in the second Adam the whole of humanity is conceived as having risen again. " For the first Adam and the second Adam were one in flesh, though not in action: and in the former all die, in the latter all shall be made alive. The former through lust springing from pride

[192] *Serm.* 59, 3, with allusion to Heb. xiii. 11. Cf. *ibid.*, 5, and *Serm.* 56, 3; 68, 3.
[193] *Serm.* 64, 3 = *Ep.* 165, 5, JK 542.
[194] *Serm.* 59, 1. Cf. *Serm.* 23, 3; 63, 4.
[195] *Serm.* 5, 3. It is remarkable that Leo nowhere appears to associate Christ's self-oblation with His heavenly High-priesthood.
[196] *Ep.* 165, 5. Cf. *Serm.* 72, 3.

built the road to misfortune, the latter through the courage of humility prepared the way to glory." [197]

8. THE DOCTRINE OF THE FALL AND ITS RESULTS

Leo's teaching as to the constitution of man has already been examined. We have now to consider his doctrine concerning the Original State of Man, the Fall and its Results.

The Image of God. Leo simply asserts without explanation that " man was made in the image of God," [198] and proceeds to say at once that " there is nothing so appropriate to his own nature as to imitate the generosity of his Maker." [199] It was this image which was lost in the first Adam and is restored in the second Adam.[200] The following passage is no doubt typical of Leo's standpoint:

" For the first man received the substance of flesh from the earth and was animated with a rational spirit by the inspiration of the Creator, so that by living after the image and likeness of his Maker he might preserve the form of the goodness and justice of God in the brightness of imitation as if in the reflexion of a mirror." [201]

The Original State of Man. As contrasted with Ambrose,[202] for example, Leo has but little to tell us on this subject. In a well-known passage in the " Tome " he implies that man possessed originally special divine gifts including the endowment of immortality: [203]

" If he (sc. man) cherished with constancy the glorious dignity of his nature by observance of the Law given, an incorrupt mind would lead that very nature of an earthly body to heavenly glory." [204] He evidently believed that the first man was perfectly free to choose between good and evil,[205] and, as we have just seen, supposed that had he chosen

[197] *Serm.* 69, 3.
[198] *Serm.* 12, 1; 20, 2.
[199] *Ibid.*
[200] *Ibid.*
[201] *Serm.* 24, 2.
[202] Homes Dudden, *op. cit.*, Vol. II, pp. 613f.
[203] *Ep.* 28, 3.
[204] *Serm.* 24, 2.
[205] *Serm.* 28, 3. " quia non ita in primum hominem diabolus violentus exstiterat, ut eum in partes suas sine liberi arbitrii consensione transferret."

aright man would have passed easily and naturally from a state of innocence to one of indefectible perfection.[206]

The Fall. This happy condition enjoyed by Adam was abruptly terminated by his " transgression " or " Fall." [207] As to the exact nature of this sin, Leo offers various opinions. In one place he points to ambition,[208] in others to gluttony,[209] in another to concupiscence,[210] and in yet another to feminine credulity.[211]

Thus it was through the lower part of human nature that the devil attacked our humanity as a whole, and in consequence man's nature has in itself a defect, not implanted by the Creator, but contracted from the transgressor and conveyed by the principle of generation to his descendants, so that there arises from the corruptible body that which can corrupt even the soul." [212] Thus both the higher and the lower parts of our humanity combined to produce sin.

The Consequences of the Fall. As a result of the first sin Man was driven forth from Paradise.[213] Disharmony in his nature ensued. The image of God in him was corrupted.[214] The inner conflict of flesh and spirit began.[215] More than this, Adam himself became subject to the penalty of death,[216] and so " the sentence together with the sin passing from one to all abode, and nature being corrupted by a deadly wound found no remedy." [217] Leo does not discuss the character of this " death," nor distinguish clearly between the " death of the body " and the " death of the soul."

[206] *Serm.* 66, 1.
[207] It is noteworthy that Leo consistently uses " praevaricatio," with the occasional variant of " originale peccatum," but never " lapsus." On the use of these terms see N.P. Williams, *Ideas of the Fall,* p. 303.
[208] *Serm.* 25, 5. Cf. *Serm.* 44, 3; *Ep.* 106, 1. In *Serm.* 24, 2, Man is said " repositum honoris augmentum occupare maluit quam mereri."
[209] *Serm.* 81, 1. " illecebram cibi "; 87, 1. " per illecebram edendi omnium concupiscentiam virus infudit."
[210] *Serm.* 79, 1. " concupiscentia initium peccatorum."
[211] *Serm.* 16, 5 " (diabolus) perque femineam credulitatem omnes homines a paradisi felicitate deiecerit."
[212] *Serm.* 90, 1.
[213] *Serm.* 22, 5.
[214] *Serm.* 27, 6.
[215] *Serm.* 90, 1.
[216] *Serm.* 72, 2. Cf. *Serm.* 22, 1, 5; 25, 5, with allusion to Rom. v. 14.
[217] *Serm.* 24, 2.

The most serious effect of the Fall, however, was the infection of man's nature with an inclination to evil. "Since the father of the human race sinned, they (sc. men) do not doubt that that which was corrupted in the root was infected in his descendants."[218] This defect is variously described. It is a "captivity" or "slavery" to the devil,[219] a "contagion,"[220] which corrupts successive generations of the human race or a "poison"[221] instilled into humanity.

The effect of this transmitted weakness is to make the lower part of Man's nature more powerful than the higher.[222] Even so, Man's will is capable of responding to divine Grace.[223]

The Mode of Transmission. Like Ambrose Leo offers two main answers to the question as to how the contagion is handed down from Adam to his posterity.

(a) By the sin of concupiscence. Leo asserts roundly that the normal process of conception necessarily involves sinful pollution.[224] Elsewhere he writes of the "contagion of carnal generation,"[225] and of the defect transmitted to posterity by the principle of generation.[226] Christ alone was conceived without the "pollution of carnal concupiscence."[227]

(b) By "seminal identity." Leo quotes Rom. v. 12 in the Western version current in the fifth century (in which the phrase "for that all sinned" is incorrectly translated "in whom all sinned," with reference to Adam) and adds "no one could escape the awful mastery of the devil, none escape the bonds of dread captivity . . . unless . . . the Son of God . . . deigned to be the Son of Man."[228] Yet it must be admitted that Leo nowhere elaborates or expands this idea, so as to hold

[218] *Serm.* 93, 1.
[219] *Serm.* 22, 3; 23, 3; 24, 2; 69, 3.
[220] *Serm.* 90, 1.
[221] *Serm.* 22, 4.
[222] *Serm.* 18, 1.
[223] *Serm.* 88, 4.
[224] *Serm.* 22, 3. "in omnibus matribus non fiat sine peccati sorde conceptio."
[225] *Serm.* 27, 2.
[226] *Serm.* 90, 1.
[227] *Serm.* 25, 5. "solus (sc. Christus) sine carnalis concupiscentiae pollutione conceptus." The same idea is common to other Western writers. Cf. Williams, *op. cit.*, pp. 364–8.
[228] *Serm.* 52, 1. Cf. *Serm.* 25, 5. "Ille (sc. Adam) diabolo obtemperans usque ad praevaricationem meruit ut in ipso omnes morerentur," see Sanday and Headlam, *Romans, ad loc.*

as Ambrose and others did that "all mankind participated in Adam's fall, because all mankind existed in germ in Adam's loins." [229]

In consequence of this transmission of "original sin" (Leo nowhere suggests the idea of original guilt), every human individual is to a greater or less extent a sinner.[230] It was man's sin which caused the wonder of the Incarnation.[231]

9. THE DOCTRINE OF MAN'S RESTORATION

It is important to realize that Leo's conception of the effect of the Saviour's Atoning word is strictly potential. For its effect to become applicable to any individual, it is indispensable that the individual should himself receive and make his own the redeeming Grace of which that work is the only source.

Leo occasionally mentions the idea of mystical union with Christ. Thus he urges every Christian to be "mindful of what Body he is a member, and to what Head he is attached," [232] and speaks of the whole body of the faithful, risen in the fount of Baptism, "as they are crucified with Christ in His Passion, raised again in His Resurrection, placed together at the right hand of the Father in His Ascension, so they are born together with Him in His Birth." [233] A similar thought appears in other passages, such as:

"It is certain, beloved, that human nature was taken into such an association by the Son of God, that, not only in that Man who is 'the first begotten of all creation,' but also in His Saints, Christ is one and the same: and as the Head cannot be parted from His members, so neither can the members be parted from their Head." [234]

If we ask the question, how is this mystical union effected, we receive an answer which is at first sight highly confusing in

[229] Homes Dudden, *op. cit.*, Vol. II, p. 621.

[230] *Serm.* 49, 1. "Quis enim in huius vitae constitutus incerto . . . liber inveniatur a culpa?" It is possible that Leo's omission of any reference to the idea of "original guilt" is due to the absence of any need to justify the growing practice of infant baptism. As there is no indication of its prevalence at Rome among contemporary writers at this period, it is unlikely that the practice was more than exceptional.

[231] *Serm.* 77, 2.

[232] *Serm.* 23, 5.

[233] *Serm.* 26, 2. Cf. *Serm.* 69, 5.

[234] *Serm.* 63, 3.

its multiplicity. We must therefore analyse the main ideas which appear in Leo's writings on this subject.

Faith is the indispensable first step in the direction of apprehending the benefits of salvation, "without it nothing is holy, nothing is pure." [235] Yet to him Faith is simply the acceptance of orthodox belief and is practically synonymous with the "Catholic Faith." At the same time he constantly reminds us that Faith must be informed by Charity,[236] and Charity in the sense of charitable acts.[237]

Leo has much to say of the necessity and importance of *Prayer*. He speaks of its necessity against the power of Temptation,[238] describes it as a natural consequence of the relation between God and Man,[239] and emphasizes its value.[240] He treats in detail successive clauses of the Lord's Prayer,[241] and stresses the profit of Common Prayer.[242]

The connexion between Prayer and Almsgiving and Fasting which is emphasized in a number of passages,[243] leads naturally to the frequent recommendation of these practices. *Fasting* was instituted by the authority of the Holy Ghost,[244] is commanded by the Apostles,[245] and enjoined by their example and tradition.[246] It is in fact part of Christian practice no less than Jewish.[247] It is to be observed both in Lent,[248] at the Ember seasons,[249] and at the "Collecta." [250] Christian Fasting, he tells us, must be full of joy.[251] It is a fast from sin,

[235] *Serm*. 24, 6.
[236] *Serm*. 45, 2.
[237] *Serm*. 37, 1.
[238] *Serm*. 56, 2.
[239] *Serm*. 46, 4.
[240] *Serm*. 12, 4.
[241] *Serm*. 90, 3; 93, 1; 46, 4; 49, 5; 50, 2.
[242] *Serm*. 18, 2; 88, 2.
[243] With Almsgiving *Serm*. 16, 2; 17, 1. With Fasting *Serm*. 12, 4; 14, 1; 16, 2.
[244] *Serm*. 78, 1.
[245] *Serm*. 20, 1.
[246] *Serm*. 78, 2; 44, 2; 81, 1.
[247] *Serm*. 15, 2; 17, 1; 90, 1.
[248] *Serm*. 44, 2; 50, 1.
[249] *Serm*. 19, 2; 12, 4; 13, 1; 16, 2; 17, 1; 20, 2; 78, 3; 81, 3; 94, 3. The purpose of fasting after Pentecost as a remedy for sins committed during Eastertide is mentioned in Serm. 78, 2. Cf. *Sacram. Leon.*, 10, 2. *P.L.* 55, 41.
[250] *Serm*. 8; 9, 3.
[251] *Serm*. 87, 5.

a fast of the soul as well as of the body.[252] It is marked both by a difference of food,[253] and a reduction of its quantity.[254] It is commended for its power against the wiles of the devil.[255] It is associated with the exclusion of vices of all kinds.[256] All are under obligation to fast,[257] not excluding catechumens,[258] but its provisions are to be modified in the case of the sick.[259] It is specially profitable when performed in common with the rest of the Church.[260] United with Penance,[261] or with Almsgiving,[262] it is effective in extinguishing the effects of sin.[263]

Freewill and Grace. In speaking of God's commandments, Leo tells us that their purpose is to stimulate us to pray for aid to keep them, from Him who commands.[264] The usual term used by him to describe this divine help is Grace, a concept which plays an important part in his doctrine on the subject of Man's Restoration.

Some treatment of the subject of the relation between Freedom and Grace, to be found in the *Syllabus,* is often attributed to Leo. Its author formally denies Man's capacity to form good desires apart from Grace, or to begin without divine aid the work of his salvation, or even to respond on his own initiative to God's call.[265]

Yet he avoids any reference to the efficacy of Grace by itself, to predestination, to the question whether God intends to save

[252] *Serm.* 91, 2; 94, 2; 19, 2; 46, 1; 50, 2.
[253] *Serm.* 42, 5.
[254] *Serm.* 42, 4.
[255] *Serm.* 18, 1.
[256] *Serm.* 87, 2, with allusion to Matt. xvii. 20.
[257] *Serm.* 49, 1.
[258] *Serm.* 43, 3.
[259] *Serm.* 44, 2.
[260] *Serm.* 88, 2; 89, 2.
[261] *Serm.* 90, 1.
[262] *Serm.* 94, 3.
[263] Other passages in which fasting is commended in connexion with Almsgiving are the following: *Serm.* 13, 1; 15, 2; 20, 3; 39, 6; 40, 4; 44, 2; 48, 5 and 87, 3, in which the duty of Almsgiving is urged on those who are unable to fast Mention is also made of *Abstinence* apparently in the sense of self-control in *Serm.* 19, 1; 78, 2; 91, 1, and of *Continence* in *Serm.* 50, 2, 3; 69, 2; 91, 1; 94, 1. Other references to ascetic practices such as *Retreat* and *Meditation* are *Serm.* 19, 1 and *Serm.* 88, 3. In one place, *Serm.* 56, 2, Leo examines the difficulty of unanswered Prayer. For Leo's teaching on Almsgiving see pp. 433ff., 483.
[264] *Serm.* 43, 1; 94, 2.
[265] On this document see above, pp. 41f.

all or only a part of mankind; in fact he excludes it. That is not because, as he says, we should despise such questions, but rather because to have a right faith regarding Grace, all that is needed is to accept the decisions of the Roman see, which he appends.[266]

In the undoubted writings of Leo we find: "He who grants the will, will give also the power." [267] Hence he constantly urges the need of asking for Grace.[268] Yet in spite of the fact that he has so little to say on the subject of human freedom, he insists that Grace remains inoperative without human co-operation.[269] He warns his hearers that in spite of its power it does not deprive those who receive it of the necessity for effort,[270] and that as a result all need to be on their guard against undue confidence.[271] Man is in fact confronted with a perpetual struggle against evil, and needs to exercise such power as he possesses, "for whoever does not advance, recedes; and he who gains nothing, loses something." [272] Yet Grace is altogether independent of merit, "which if it is not given *gratis,* is not grace at all." [273]

Summarizing Leo's teaching on this subject, it is clear that he not only repudiates Pelagianism in any form, but even goes far in the direction of Augustinianism.[274] If he finds room for human freedom, he does so only with marked qualification.

10. THE DOCTRINE OF THE CHURCH AND THE SACRAMENTS

(i) *The Church.* The Church, "being the Body of Christ, rejoices in the mysteries of His salvation." [275] She derives her origin from the Saviour's Birth,[276] her progress is assured by

[266] *Syllabus,* 15.

[267] *Serm.* 26, 4. "Ipse qui dedit velle, donabit et posse." Cf. *Serm.* 38, 3; 94, 2.

[268] *Serm.* 43, 1; 49, 4.

[269] *Serm.* 18, 1; 43, 1.

[270] *Serm.* 78, 2.

[271] *Serm.* 38, 3.

[272] *Serm.* 59, 8.

[273] *Ep.* 1, 3, JK 398. "Quae (sc. gratia) utique nisi gratis detur, non est gratia." Contrast however *Serm.* 8, "neminem fraudat (sc. Deus) mercede meritorum."

[274] e.g. *Serm.* 67, 2. "Cum enim et qualitates actionum nostrarum, et effectus omnium voluntatum scientia divina praeveniat, quanto magis nota Deo sunt opera sua."

[275] *Serm.* 25, 5. Cf. *Serm.* 46, 3; 82, 7, in which the place of SS. Peter and Paul in the Church is specially mentioned: *Ep.* 80, 2.

[276] *Serm.* 26, 2.

practices of asceticism: [277] she is increased by the attacks of persecution.[278] She is pre-eminently the "household of freedom." [279] But above all she is one, undivided and indivisible. "With the same Spirit are we sanctified, in the same faith we live; we resort to the same mysteries." [280] As an outward demonstration of this inner unity, Leo attaches the highest importance to the concord of bishops in matters of faith and discipline,[281] and urges the need of its due safeguarding by secular authority.[282] Though there is diversity of rank among her members [283] and diversity of place, all share the same life.[284] Her customs rest on the authority of apostolic or rather divine appointment.[285] She is the favoured recipient of sanctification by the Holy Ghost,[286] whose presence is denied to heretics.[287] These by separating themselves from her faith are outside her fold,[288] beyond which "nothing is whole, nothing is pure." [289]

Though the sins of individuals, even of bishops, do not vitiate her essential perfection,[290] yet she has both the power and the duty to exclude unworthy members,[291] only however after every effort has been made to win them to true repentance and renunciation of their errors.[292] Once such a sinner has been excluded from communion he must be banished from the society of the faithful.[293]

The relation of the Roman see to the Catholic Church. To

[277] *Serm.* 18, 3.
[278] *Serm.* 36, 3.
[279] *Serm.* 53, 3. "familia libertatis."
[280] *Serm.* 42, 3.
[281] *Ep.* 14, 11.
[282] *Ep.* 95, 2; 118, 2. Cf. *Ep.* 60.
[283] *Serm.* 4, 1.
[284] *Serm.* 89, 5.
[285] *Serm.* 79, 1; 81, 1.
[286] *Serm.* 75, 5. "Sancti Spiritus, per quem omnis ecclesia catholica sanctificatur."
[287] *Serm.* 76, 7.
[288] *Ep.* 102, 2, with special reference to the followers of Nestorius or Eutyches.
[289] *Serm.* 79, 2, with allusion to Rom. xiv. 23. Cf. *Ep.* 80, 1.
[290] *Ep.* 105, 3.
[291] e.g. *Ep.* 102, 3 and 4; *Ep.* 155, 2; 15, 15.
[292] *Ep.* 48, 2; 109, 3. See esp. *Ep.* 31, 1, on the professed moderation of the Roman see in the exercise of such discipline. Other references to the power of excommunication are *Epp.* 10, 8; 32.
[293] *Serm.* 96, 3.

Leo there is but a single touchstone of membership of the Catholic Church, namely, visible communion with the Roman see. To him any idea of claiming to be described as Catholic, while repudiating the need of unity with that see, is inconceivable.

We may briefly summarize here the evidence already set forth in an earlier chapter.[294]

First of all the Roman see is the see of St. Peter.[295] In it abides St. Peter's authority and influence.[296] It has been divinely appointed to preside over all other sees,[297] and in it God " set originally the highest rank among the Apostles and teachers." [298] It enjoys this status in virtue of the privileges assigned in the first instance by our Lord to St. Peter, whose heir and partner is the Roman bishop,[299] and who still governs the Church in the person of his successors.[300]

The privileges of St. Peter. St. Peter is the " primate of all bishops," [301] the " beginning of the whole Church [302] and of the Apostolic order." [303] To him " is entrusted besides the keys of the kingdom the care of the Lord's flock beyond all others." [304] He is " preferred before the calling of all nations

[294] *Serm.* 2, 2.
[295] *Serm.* 3, 3.
[296] *Ibid.*, 4.
[297] *Ep.* 120, 1. " eam (sc. sedem) quam caeteris omnium Dominus statuit praesidere." This view as to the primacy of the Roman see is supported by the bishops of southern Gaul e.g. *Inter Leon. Epp.*, No. 65, 2, " per beatissimum Petrum apostolorum principem sacrosancta ecclesia Romana teneret supra omnes totius mundi ecclesias principatum " ; No. 68, 1, " merito illic (sc. Romae) principatum sedis apostolicae constitutum, unde adhuc apostolici spiritus oracula reserantur " (with allusion to the " Tome "). Notice also titles used of the Papacy, *ibid.*, 1, " Domino sancto, beatissimo patri et apostolica sede dignissimo papae ") and perhaps by the Emperors, *Inter Leon. Epp.*, No. 55, " τὴν ἱερωσύνην κατὰ πάντων," cf. No. 58 ; No. 73, " τήν τε σὴν ἁγιωσύνην ἐπισκοπεύουσαν καὶ ἄρχουσαν τῆς θείας πίστεως." Cf. No. 55, and the dictum of the Chalcedonian bishops, *Inter Leon. Epp.*, No. 98, 1. " κεφαλὴ μελῶν."
[298] *Ibid.*, 2. " ubi culmen summum in apostolis et doctoribus principaliter collocavit." There is good reason to believe that " principaliter " and its cognates have a temporal rather than a " hierarchical " sense. See Lewis and Short, *s.v. princeps.* Mention of the see of Antioch occurs in *Serm.* 82, 5 ; *Epp.* 106, 5 ; 119, 2. Of his arrival in Rome, *Serm.* 82, 4.
[299] *Serm.* 2, 2 ; 3, 3 and 4 ; 5, 4.
[300] *Serm.* 3, 3 ; 5, 4. Cf. Peter Chrys., *Inter Leon. Epp.*, No. 25, 2.
[301] *Serm.* 3, 4. Cf. *Inter Leon. Epp.*, No. 11.
[302] *Serm.* 4, 4.
[303] *Serm.* 82, 3. Cf. *Serm.* 3, 2 ; 82, 5.
[304] *Serm.* 73, 2.

and all the Apostles with all the Fathers of the Church,"[305] "The first in the confession of the Lord, who is the first in Apostolic dignity."[306] "For Christ assigned to Peter the primacy of Apostolic dignity, as a reward of his faith, establishing the universal Church on the firmness of that foundation."[307]

The passage just quoted is among those in which Leo interprets the well-known Dominical saying, Matthew xvi. 16, not of St. Peter's person, but of his faith.[308] Elsewhere he writes of the "Rock of the Catholic Faith, the surname of which Peter received from the Lord."[309] In the majority of passages, however, the foundation of the Church is identified with St. Peter himself. "He (sc. St. Peter) received the stability of a rock, which would not be shaken by any onslaughts."[310] Hence St. Peter enjoys participation in the rights of Christ Himself,[311] and through him, not only the rest of the Apostles, but the whole hierarchy derives its authority.[312] Nor can any structure which does not rest on him as a foundation enjoy any stability.[313]

Of the inferences which Leo draws from these ideas as to the rights and privileges of his see enough has been said elsewhere to render further treatment here unnecessary. They may be summed up by saying that he claims for himself and his see, not only supreme jurisdiction over the whole Church, and holds himself to be the final and sovereign interpreter of the laws of ecclesiastical discipline. The view taken by his contemporaries of those claims has occupied our attention throughout the greater part of this work and has already been sufficiently examined.

(ii) *The Sacraments.* The gift of God's Grace is imparted

[305] *Serm.* 4, 2.
[306] *Ibid.*
[307] *Ep.* 5, 2.
[308] This interpretation is not unknown elsewhere, e.g. Ambrose, *Expos. ev. Luc.*, 6; 97, 98. Cf. Homes Dudden, *op. cit.*, Vol. II, pp. 639f.
[309] *Ep.* 119, 2, cf. *Serm.* 3, 2.
[310] *Serm.* 3, 3. Cf. *Serm.* 51, 1; *Ep.* 104, 3.
[311] *Serm.* 4, 2.
[312] *Ep.* 10, 1; *Serm.* 4, 3.
[313] *Ep.* 104, 3. Other passages bearing on this important text are *Epp.* 28, 5; 33, 1. *Serm.* 49, 1, in which Leo alludes to the power of the keys with reference to Absolution.

chiefly through the "mysteries" or sacraments of the Church.[314] The character and effect of the two great rites of Baptism and the Eucharist is set forth by Leo in considerable detail, as well as of other rites "commonly called sacraments."

(a) *Baptism and Confirmation.* The matter of Baptism is water;[315] the form is nowhere explicitly mentioned;[316] equally it is taken for granted that the normal minister of the sacrament is the bishop.[317] The power operating in Baptism which endows it with efficacy, absent from the rite administered by St. John Baptist[318] or by the heretics,[319] is the action of the Holy Ghost.[320] The manner in which the regeneration thus effected is brought about is to be compared to the operation of the same Holy Ghost in the womb of the blessed Virgin Mary. "Every man," he writes, "attains in regeneration His (sc. Christ's) spiritual Birth; and the water of Baptism for every one who is reborn is like the Virgin's womb, since the same Holy Spirit fills the font, who also filled the Virgin; so that here the mystical washing takes away the sin which the holy Conception removed there."[321] Baptism received its sacramental efficacy through the shedding of blood and water from the side of Christ.[322]

As to its effect, Leo clearly teaches the doctrine of baptismal regeneration. "Whosoever in whatever part of the world

[314] The term "sacramentum" is used in a wide sense by Leo of any "mystery" in the purpose of God. *Serm.* 22, 1, *et alit.*

[315] *Serm.* 24, 6; 25, 5; 57, 5. The letter of Turibius appended to *Ep.* 15, c. 5, mentions that Baptism was conferred with oil by the Priscillianists. This is to be compared with *Acts of St. Thomas,* in *Apocryphal New Testament*, ed. James, p. 433.

[316] Mention of threefold immersion, *Serm.* 70, 4; *Ep.* 16, 3, seems to imply the use of the Trinitarian formula.

[317] Administration by the bishop is implied; administration by a priest is mentioned only once in connexion with the Church of Melitene in Sicily, *Ep.* 3, 3.

[318] *Ep.* 16, 6. "illus baptismi (sc. Ioannis) aliam gratiam, aliam fuisse rationem; nec ad eamdem pertinuisse virtutem, qua per Spiritum sanctum renascuntur."

[319] *Ep.* 159, 7. "hi qui baptismum ab haereticis acceperunt, . . . formam tantum baptismi sine sanctificatione virtute sumpserunt."

[320] *Serm.* 57, 5. "per aquam et Spiritum sanctum renati." Cf. *Serm.* 25, 5. "virtus . . . Spiritus sancti, quae fecit ut Maria pareret Salvatorem, eadem facit ut regeneret unda credentem."

[321] *Serm.* 24, 3.

[322] *Ep.* 16, 6. Cf. *Ep.* 28, 5, where the same event is regarded as the source from which the Grace both of Baptism and of Eucharist is derived. "sanguis et aqua fluxerit, ut ecclesia Dei et lavacro rigaretur et poculo."

who as a believer is reborn in Christ . . . by being reborn becomes a new man." [323] By the power of the Holy Ghost life is restored and sin taken away.[324] Baptism makes the Christian the temple of the Holy Ghost.[325] By this sacrament a countless multitude of "sons of God" is begotten.[326] The body of the regenerate person becomes the flesh of the Crucified.[327] The mystical union of the baptized with the Passion, Death and Resurrection of Christ has already begun in the actual mystery of regeneration, "where there is the death of sin and the life of the reborn, and the threefold immersion imitates the three days' death of the Lord." [328]

Those who receive the sacrament are persons of both sexes, of all ages and every race.[329] Even infants are suitable subjects for its administration.[330] It is the first of all the "means of grace" administered by the Church.[331] For its due reception admission to the catechumenate is normally indispensable.[332] The period of preparation includes exorcism, fasting and instruction.[333] The normal times appropriate for Baptism are the feasts of Easter and Pentecost only.[334] In its administration sin is renounced and the faith of the Church confessed; [335] in addition the candidate receives the token of the Cross.[336]

[323] *Serm.* 26, 2.
[324] *Ep.* 16, 6.
[325] *Serm.* 21, 3. "Per baptismatis sacramentum Spiritus sancti factus es templum."
[326] *Serm.* 63, 6. "innumerabilis filiorum Dei multitudo."
[327] *Ibid.*
[328] *Serm.* 70, 4. Note in *Ep.* 6, 3 he denies that Baptism can dissolve a pre-existing marriage.
[329] *Serm.* 49, 3. Cf. *Ep.* 15, 10.
[330] *Serm.* 32, 3, referring to the SS. Innocents, "nova gloria coronabat infantes . . . ut disceretur neminem hominum divini incapacem esse sacramenti, quando etiam illa aetas gloriae esset apta martyrii." Leo's half-apologetic tone here suggests that infant Baptism was by no means normal at Rome in the mid-fifth century.
[331] *Ep.* 16, 1 and 5. The use of the term "principalis" in a temporal sense should be noted.
[332] *Ep.* 16, 6.
[333] *Ibid.* For the use of exorcism cf. *Serm.* 87, 2.
[334] *Ep.* 3, 3; 16, 3 and 4. In this letter and in *Ep.* 168 the use of such occasions as the Epiphany and feasts of martyrs is forbidden.
[335] *Serm.* 66, 3. Cf. *Ep.* 124, 8; *Serm.* 24, 6.
[336] *Serm.* 24, 6. "signaculum vitae eternae." Cf. *Ep.* 124, 8. In *Serm.* 4, 1, Leo appears to contrast the effect of the Sign of the Cross in Baptism with that of the Unction of the Holy Ghost by saying that the former makes us "kings," the latter "priests" (cf. Rev. i. 6). It is clear that he is here referring to the two first "stages" of Christian

Leo insists more than once that in no circumstances may the sacrament be repeated,[337] though those who are uncertain whether they have received it are to be baptized.[338] Those certainly baptized by heretics are to receive simply the " laying on of the hand." [339] Mention is made of Chrism in close connexion with Baptism in a number of passages,[340] but there is nothing to show what view he held, if any, as to the essential " form " or " matter " of Confirmation.

(b) *The Eucharist.* " Jesus, informed of his (sc. Judas') plan, and fearless in the performance of His Father's purpose, completed the Old Covenant and founded the new Passover. For as His disciples were lying down with Him to eat the mystical Supper . . . He instituting the sacrament of His Body and Blood, taught us what sort of victim ought to be offered to God, though not even the traitor was absent from this mystery." [341] It is important to notice, not only the emphasis which Leo lays on the sacrificial character of our Lord's action at the Last Supper [342] (" the offering of Thy Body and Blood replaces all different sorts of victims "),[343] of which the offering of Melchizedek was a type,[344] but also the fact that he evidently identifies the sacramental elements with the actual Body and Blood of Christ. Thus after quoting John vi. 54 he says, " You ought so to communicate at the holy table, that you have no doubt henceforth as to the truth of the Body and Blood of Christ." [345] Easter is pre-eminently the occasion of general Communion,[346] which is administered

initiation, of which First Communion forms the third and last. It should be remembered that at this period the two rites would not normally be regarded as distinct, and it is only when the question of admission to the Church of those baptized by heretics is discussed that they are at all clearly differentiated.

[337] *Epp.* 159, 7; 166, 1. Cf. *Ep.* 18.

[338] *Epp.* 166, 1; 167, 16.

[339] *Epp.* 159, 7; 166, 2. See above, pp. 171f.

[340] *Serm.* 24, 6; 66, 2; cf. *Ep.* 156, 5.

[341] *Serm.* 58, 3. In c. 4 he associates the sacrament with Christ's Passion and Death.

[342] *Epp.* 9, 2 and 156, 5, both describe the Eucharist as " sacrificii oblatio " ; the former also uses the term " missa."

[343] *Serm.* 59, 7.

[344] *Serm.* 5, 2. " Melchizedek . . . illius sacramenti immolans sacrificium, quod Redempta noster in suo corpore et sanguine consecravit."

[345] *Serm.* 91, 3. Cf. *Ep.* 59, 2.

[346] *Serm.* 50, 1, where the need of penitential preparation is mentioned.

to penitents,[347] and is given under both kinds.[348] As to the effect of a right reception of the sacrament on the faithful communicant he says, " The participation in the Body and Blood of Christ actually effects our transformation into that which we receive," [349] and in another passage, " receiving the strength of the heavenly food, we may be transformed into the Flesh of Him who was made our flesh." [350]

(c) *Penance*. Although Leo admits that all sins committed after Baptism are by no means of the same gravity,[351] yet he urges all Christians alike to avail themselves of the benefits of the Paschal Sacraments. " For not only those who through the mystery of the Death and Resurrection of Christ by the regeneration of Baptism are about to enter a new life, but also all those who are reborn receive for themselves profitably and of necessity the protection of this sanctification: the former that they may receive that which they do not yet possess, the latter that they preserve that which they have received." [352] At the same time he shows that for certain sins special remedies are necessary and speaks of " wounds to which a more severe mode of healing is to be applied," [353] as well as of " that part of the people . . . which conscious of deadly sins hastens to receive pardon by the aid of reconciliation." [354] He repeatedly urges that great danger lies in postponing the day of seeking such pardon. " Let not the sinner be falsely confident by reason of his impunity, since if he misses the time of penitence, will have no opportunity for forgiveness." [355]

[347] *Ep.* 108, 2.
[348] *Serm.* 42, 5.
[349] *Serm.* 63, 7.
[350] *Ep.* 59, 2.
[351] *Serm.* 50, 1. " multis modis multisque mensuris et peccatum a peccato, et crimen distat a crimine."
[352] *Serm.* 43, 3.
[353] *Serm.* 44, 1.
[354] *Serm.* 45, 1. " lethalium conscia peccatorum, per reconciliationis auxilium festinat ad veniam." He does not define the nature of the sins which are so described, but probably the usual grave sins are meant.
[355] *Serm.* 36, 4; 50, 1. Cf. *Ep.* 108, 5. It should be noted that in the first passage Leo adds " Qui autem sibi correctionis reparationem experitur esse difficilem, confugiat ad auxiliantis Dei clementiam, et vincula malae consuetudinis ab illo poscat abrumpi. . . . Non erit vacua confitentis oratio . . . et dabit (sc. Deus) quod petitur, qui dedit unde peteretur." Here he evidently contemplates the remission of certain sins by prayer alone.

"For by the healing of Penance hope of eternal life is restored." [356] The method by which this "reconciliation" is to be obtained is clearly set forth in a number of passages. Of primary importance is the part played by the intercession of others, of the saints,[357] and of the Church generally,[358] particularly of the bishops.[359]

Through the ministry of the Church, that is through the episcopate, which has been divinely entrusted with the power of binding and loosing,[360] the gravest sins can be remitted.[361] Yet it is necessary for the sinner to do his part and to subject himself to the onerous and painful procedure of public Penance.

It is clear from Leo's treatment of the subject that he contemplated three essential stages in Penance of any sort, whether public or private.

(a) *Penitence.* Frequent emphasis is laid on the fact that no human individual can claim to be without sin.[362] Yet there can be no forgiveness without penitence.[363] "Happy, O holy Apostle, were thy tears, which for the remission of the guilt of denial had the virtue of holy Baptism." [364] Penitence, how-

[356] *Ep.* 108, 2. "per poenitentiae medicinam spes vitae reparetur aeternae."

[357] Of SS. Peter and Paul in particular, *Serm.* 82, 7. Cf. *Serm.* 85, 3, of St. Lawrence; 88, 5.

[358] *Serm.* 88, 3. "Plenissima autem peccatorum obtinetur abolitio, quando totius ecclesiae una est oratio et una confessio." With allusion to Matt. xviii. 20. Cf. *Ep.* 171, 1.

[359] *Ep.* 108, 2. "indulgentia Dei nisi supplicationibus sacerdotum nequeat obtineri." The precise meaning of this phrase is considered elsewhere. See pp. 141ff., 484.

[360] *Serm.* 49, 3. "Lapsos quoque et insidiarum suarum (sc. diaboli) fraude deceptos, poenitentiae lacrymis ablui, et portas misericordiae apostolica clave reserante, ad remedia reconciliationis admitti." It should be noted that Leo nowhere attributes this power to the priesthood as distinct from the episcopate. Cf. *Serm.* 5, 5, and *Serm.* 58, 5, "aderit precantibus vobis gratia Dei, quae mihi solvendi debiti tribuat facultatem."

[361] This is to be inferred from the fact that Leo nowhere excludes any sin from the scope of forgiveness. Cf. *Serm.* 88, 3 and 92, 1.

[362] *Serm.* 5, 1; 37, 3; 49, 1.

[363] Some difficulty arises from the fact that "poenitentia" may be rendered either "Penance" or "penitence."

[364] *Serm.* 60, 4. Cf. Ambrose, *Expos. ev. Luc.*, 10, 89, 90.

ever, must include real sorrow for sin.[365] The penitence of despair only brings ruin.[366]

(b) *Confession* or the acknowledgment of sins committed delivered the penitent from condemnation.[367] It must be full and sincere, for an untrue confession cannot obtain remission;[368] even the most intimate secrets of the heart are known to God.[369] Such confession is to be made normally in private to the bishop.[370]

(c) *Satisfaction* is a normally indispensable part of the whole process. It is often spoken of as "penance" and is assigned by the bishop to the penitent, who is said to request "penance."[371] Satisfaction includes the performance of such exercises as prayer, fasting and almsgiving. In fact an outstanding importance is assigned to the latter as a means to obtaining forgiveness.[372]

On the negative side the penitent is required to undergo a number of serious privations.[373] He may not undertake any

[365] *Ep.* 159, 5 "(poenitentia) cordis compunctione pensanda." Cf. *Serm.* 49, 3.

[366] *Serm.* 52, 5; 56, 3; 62, 4, with reference to Judas.

[367] *Serm.* 50, 1. "nec remanet iudicio condemnandum, quod fuerit confessione purgatum."

[368] *Ep.* 89. It is possible, however, that Leo here refers to a confession of orthodox belief.

[369] *Serm.* 43, 3. *Serm.* 41, 1, contains some advice for the examination of conscience.

[370] *Ep.* 168, 2. "reatus conscientiarum sufficiat solis sacerdotibus indicari confessione secreta." It is sometimes supposed that in prohibiting detailed acknowledgment of sins in public, Leo was actually modifying existing practice. Yet if this were so it is scarcely conceivable that he could have referred to the practice as "Illam etiam contra apostolicam regulam praesumptionem, quam nuper agnovi a quibusdam illicita usurpatione committi." The phrase "apostolicam regulam" is sufficient in itself to suggest that secret confession was traditional at Rome. Cf. *ibid.* "sufficit enim illa confessio quae primum Deo offertur, tum etiam sacerdoti."

[371] *Ibid.* "poenitentiam poscunt." Cf. *Ep.* 108, 2, "ut et confitentibus actionem poenitentiae darent, et eosdem salubri satisfactione purgatos ad communionem . . . admitterent."

[372] *Serm.* 49, 6, where the efficacy of Almsgiving is compared with that of Baptism. Both here and in *Serm.* 10, 2 he quotes Ecclus. iii. 33 (vulg.) [iii. 30, R.V.]. Cf. *Serm.* 7; 16, 2; 20, 2, 3; 78, 4; 87, 3, where Luke xi. 41 is quoted "Date eleemosynam et ecce omnia munda sunt vobis." *Serm.* 93, 3. This view as to the efficacy of "works" in obtaining forgiveness is shared by Ambrose, *Expos. ps.* 118, 8, 41, and Augustine, *Serm.* 9, 17; *Serm. ad cat.*, 7, 8, 15.

[373] Cf. *Conc. Nic.*, Can. 12.

part in the civil service nor any litigation nor trading for profit, nor may he engage in marriage.[374]

(d) *Absolution* or Reconciliation is the final stage. This is accorded by the bishop,[375] normally only after the penitential exercises have been performed. Those who accept a penance in sickness are required to perform it, should they recover, as a condition of absolution.[376] Yet while those who die before their penance is accomplished are to be left to the judgment of God,[377] should a penitent on his deathbed desire absolution it should not be refused to him, although the requisite penance has not been performed.[378] Equally in the case of one at the point of death, who is physically unable to express himself, the testimony of others as to his sincerity is to be accepted.[379] The following passage contains much that is illuminating as to Leo's doctrine on this subject:

"The manifold mercy of God so assists human falls that the hope of eternal life is restored not only by the Grace of Baptism, but also by the medicine of penitence, so that those who have done violence to the gifts of regeneration, condemning themselves by their own judgment, may attain to the remission of sins; since the protection of divine goodness has been so provided that the pardon of God cannot be obtained save by the prayers of bishops. For the Mediator of God and man, the Man Christ Jesus, had granted this power to the leaders of His Church, that they should not only grant the performance of Penance to those who confess and, when they have been cleansed by saving satisfaction, should admit them to communion of the sacraments by the door of reconciliation. Moreover, in this work the Saviour Himself ceaselessly intervenes and shares in those things with the per-

[374] *Ep.* 167, 12, 10, 11, 13. Leo seems prepared to allow special licence to the young penitent to marry. Cf. *Conc. Tolet.*, Canon 8. Mansi, *Concilia*, Vol. IX, 666.

[375] *Ep.* 108, 2. "indulgentia Dei nisi supplicationibus sacerdotum nequeat obtineri." Cf. *Ep.* 168, 2, "qui (sc. sacerdos) pro delictis poenitentium precator accedit." Galtier, *L'église et la rémission des péchés*, pp. 70–9, shows that these passages cannot be dismissed as merely alluding to sacerdotal intercession. Absolution appears to be dependent on the intercession of the Holy Ghost. Cf. *Serm.* 76, 4.

[376] *Ep.* 167, 7.

[377] *Ep.* 108, 3.

[378] *Ibid.*, 4.

[379] *Ibid.*, 5.

formance of which He has entrusted His ministers . . .; so that whatever is fulfilled by our ministry with regularity and happy result, we do not doubt that it has been granted by the Holy Ghost." [380]

(e) *Holy Matrimony* is declared to be strictly indissoluble.[381] At the same time a clear distinction is drawn between legitimate marriage and liaison with a concubine.[382]

(f) *Holy Orders*. Leo recognizes the three Scriptural grades in the Christian ministry.[383] In one passage he mentions in addition the subdiaconate,[384] and in another the order of lectors.[385] Apart from the last he insists that the obligation of continence is binding on all those who belong to the major orders, including also subdeacons.[386] In answer to the question as to whether priests and deacons are to be subjected to public Penance he replies that suspension from office in their case is to take its place.[387]

From the passages already cited we may infer that the diaconate at this time had already acquired certain important liturgical functions, though it still retained its original connexion with the administration of ecclesiastical property.[388]

[380] *Ibid.*, 2.

[381] *Ep.* 159, 1–4 treats of various problems connected with marriage in relation to the barbarian invasions.

[382] *Ep.* 167, 4–6. For detailed examination of these passages see above, pp. 146f. In *Ep.* 12, 3, he describes marriage as a "sacramentum."

[383] *Serm.* 59, 7. "Nunc etenim et ordo clarior levitarum, et dignitas amplior seniorum, et sacratior est unctio sacerdotum." It should be remembered that at this date "sacerdos" normally denotes a bishop. For a priest "presbyter" or rarely as here "senior" is used. *Serm.* 48, 1, describes the three orders thus, "summos . . . antistites, aut secundi ordinis sacerdotes nec solos sacramentorum ministros."

[384] *Ep.* 14, 4. "Quod si in hoc ordine (sc. subdiaconatu), qui quartus a capite est, dignum est custodiri, quanto magis in primo aut secundo vel tertio servandum est, ne aut levitico aut presbyterali honore aut episcopali excellentia quisquam idoneus aestimetur. . . ." Cf. *Ep.* 167, 3, "Lex continentiae eadem est ministris altaris quae episcopis atque presbyteris, qui cum essent laici sive lectores, licito et uxores ducere et filios procreare potuerunt."

[385] See passage just cited.

[386] *Epp.* 14, 4; 167, 3. The question of the marriage of the subdiaconate was a source of some difficulty in Sicily in the following century. Cf. Greg. Magn., *Reg.* 1, *Ep.* 42. See also Epiphanius, *Haer.*, 2, 39 (59); *Exp. fid. cath.*, 3, 21; *Conc. Chal.*, Canon 14.

[387] *Ep.* 167, 2. It is probable, however, that at this date the clergy in Gaul were subjected to public Penance. Cf. *Conc. Araus.*, Canon 4. Mansi, *op. cit.*, Vol. VI, 437.

[388] *Serm.* 85, 2.

He mentions nothing, however, as to the special functions of the presbyterate [389] or of the other orders except the episcopate.

Nor does he supply any details as to the manner of making deacons or ordaining priests, except that he specifies that, while bishops may be consecrated only on Sundays, priests and deacons may be ordained on any day.[390] At the same time he insists that candidates for the two inferior orders, no less than for the episcopate, shall have passed through all the orders of the clerical status.[391]

Leo has a great deal to tell us on the subject of the episcopate. In the first place he lays down with great precision the qualifications to be required of a suitable candidate. He is not to be a neophyte,[392] nor a slave.[393] He must be one who is but once married, and, if married, the husband of a virgin.[394] He is to be possessed of a good moral reputation, and have been trained in ecclesiastical discipline from early years.[395] He must have passed through the successive grades of the ministry,[396] and should be elected from among the priests or deacons of the Church over which he is to preside.[397] As to the election of a bishop Leo urges that the proceeding should take place as soon as possible on the avoidance of the see.[398] At the election the consent of both clergy and laity is to be sought,[399] and in the event of a dispute the decision is to rest with the bishop of the "metropolis" of the province in which the church is situated.[400] But in no case is a candidate

[389] It is to be inferred from *Inter Leon. Epp.*, No. 3, 3, that in Sicily presbyters were authorized to baptize; and possibly from *Epp.* 119, 6; 120, 6 that they were permitted, though this is by no means certain. Seniority among presbyters is to be carefully observed. Cf. *Ep.* 19, 1.

[390] *Ep.* 6, 6. Notice that he says of priests and deacons "circa quos par consecratio fieri debet." Yet in *Ep.* 9, 1, he appears to restrict these ordinations also to Saturday evening or Sunday.

[391] *Ibid.*

[392] *Ep.* 12, 4, 6; 14, 3.

[393] *Ep.* 4, 1.

[394] *Ep.* 4, 2; 5, 3; 6, 3; 10, 3; 12, 3.

[395] *Ep.* 12, 2, 4. Probably in Rome only those who had been accepted in childhood or soon after Baptism were considered qualified for an ecclesiastical office. See *P.L.* 54, 649, note l.

[396] *Ep.* 6, 6.

[397] *Ep.* 14, 6.

[398] *Ibid.*

[399] *Epp.* 10, 4, 6; 13, 3; 14, 5; 167, 1.

[400] *Ep.* 14, 5. Notice use of "diocese" in modern sense in *Ep.* 157, 2.

to be forced on a church against its will.[401] When the election has taken place, the candidate is to be consecrated by his comprovincials with the assent of the metropolitan bishop.[402]

The episcopate is the *fastigium sacerdotii*.[403] It is set over all other ranks[404] and has the primary duty of preserving unity of faith.[405] The bishop alone has the prerogative of preaching.[406] Yet orthodoxy by itself is not a sufficient qualification for the holder of the office.[407] Negligence of duty and ignorance of Canon Law are inexcusable.[408] Unremitting constancy and watchfulness for errors of conduct are of paramount importance.[409] Bishops should not forsake their churches even in time of war,[410] and may not be translated for trivial reasons to other sees.[411] They have the duty of giving "letters dimissory" for the ordination of their clergy by other bishops.[412]

All bishops are not of the same rank, though of common dignity. In each province there is one who has the "first vote" among his comprovincials, and in greater cities one of wider authority,[413] while the centre of episcopal unity is the successor of St. Peter himself.[414] Metropolitan bishops are called "primates."[415] They are to be consulted by bishops subordinate to them,[416] and to have the right to consecrate other bishops.[417] Special care is to be taken in regard to their election,[418] and the privileges assigned to their sees are to be care-

[401] *Epp.* 13, 3; 14, 5.
[402] *Ep.* 167, 1. It is probable that the allusions to "unction of bishops" in *Serm.* 3, 1; 59, 6 are metaphorical. Consecrations are to take place on Saturday evening or Sunday. *Ep.* 9, 1; 10, 6.
[403] *Ep.* 4, 1.
[404] *Ep.* 12, 2.
[405] *Ep.* 129, 1. Cf. *Ep.* 15, 15.
[406] *Epp.* 33, 1; 38, 1; 58, 1; 62, 1; 72, 1; 118, 2; 119, 6; 120, 6; 139, 1.
[407] *Ep.* 169, 2.
[408] *Ep.* 16, *praef.*; *Epp.* 4, 2; 16, 1; 59, 1; 139, 1.
[409] *Epp.* 140; 152; 155, 2.
[410] *Ep.* 83, 2.
[411] *Ep.* 14, 8.
[412] *Ep.* 13, 4.
[413] These bishops were later known as "patriarchs."
[414] *Ep.* 14, 11.
[415] *Epp.* 105, 2; 106, 5.
[416] *Ep.* 108, 1.
[417] *Ep.* 6, 4.
[418] *Ibid.*

fully safeguarded.[419] An inferior rank of bishops, known as *chorepiscopi,* is mentioned in connexion with the Church of Africa.[420]

As to maintenance of discipline among bishops special mention must be made of numerous provisions as to reports to be transmitted to the Roman see regarding such matters.[421] He also insists on the traditional custom of sending notifications of elections to important sees among the "greater churches." [422]

It is clear from the evidence just reviewed that Leo regarded the security and progress of the Church, as well as the maintenance of its faith and discipline, as strictly dependent on the preservation of a high standard of qualification and of conduct in the episcopal office. Of particular interest, too, is the emphasis which he lays on the propriety of due observance of the "democratic" constitution of the Church. It is not perhaps too much to say that if his ideals had been more fully realized in practice, the Church of later ages might have had less cause to deplore loss of spirituality and failure in her mission.

II. THE DOCTRINE OF THE LAST THINGS

Leo is but seldom a pictorial writer. This is sufficient perhaps to explain the paucity of references to the Last Things in his works. In one passage, however, he goes so far as to suggest that the end of the world is near at hand.[423] At the same time he expresses his view that the *Last Judgment* will not come until the number of the sons of the Church is complete.[424] The event itself he describes with a considerable amount of detail.[425] In it will be shown forth the power of Christ.[426] He as Supreme Judge will examine each man as to his merciful conduct towards the poor.[427]

Hell finds a place in a number of Leo's sermons. He affirms

[419] *Ep.* 106, 5.
[420] *Ep.* 12, 10. Cf. *Ep.* 52, 7 with reference to the Church of the East.
[421] *Epp.* 5, 6; 6, 5; 13, 1; 14, 1, 7, 11; 166, 1; 167. *Praef.*
[422] *Ep.* 149, 1.
[423] *Serm.* 19, 1.
[424] *Serm.* 74, 2. Cf. *Serm.* 35, 3.
[425] *Serm.* 9, 2; 45, 3, mainly with reference to Matt. xxv. 31–46.
[426] *Serm.* 52, 3.
[427] *Serm.* 10, 2; 11, 1.

that its gates cannot prevail against the faith of St. Peter.[428] It is a place not only of eternal fire,[429] but also of eternal death.[430] Equally he describes it as a place of eternal punishment.[431] In it no opportunity is given for amendment.[432]

In one passage only is any reference to the Beatific Vision to be found in which Leo says that it is unattainable for those who are still "in the flesh."[433]

The limitations of his doctrine on these subjects (for he has nothing to tell us about the General Resurrection or about Purgatory) will not seem surprising when it is remembered that Leo was a teacher of a predominantly practical outlook who was unwilling to be led down the bypaths of speculative imagination.

12. THE DOCTRINE OF THE SAINTS

We have already noticed the emphasis with which Leo affirms the virginity of Mary as necessary in order that the entail of sin might be broken.[434] She conceived as a virgin, gave birth as a virgin and remained a virgin.[435] Thus human nature for the first time brought forth by Mary a blessed fruit.[436] He repeatedly stresses her virginity, as unimpaired by giving birth;[437] and calls attention to the fact that He who was born of her was God Himself.[438]

He frequently alludes to the intimate concern of St. Peter in the well-being of Roman Christians and to the help supplied by his intercession.[439] They should be eager to invoke the aid of the Saints, among whom are numbered the patri-

[428] *Serm.* 3, 3.
[429] *Serm.* 10, 2.
[430] *Serm.* 21, 2.
[431] *Serm.* 9, 2; 43, 3. *Ep.* 155, 2, with allusion to Matt. xviii. 8.
[432] *Serm.* 35, 4. "in inferno nulla est correctio, nec datur remedium satisfactionis."
[433] *Serm.* 51, 2.
[434] See above, p. 459.
[435] *Serm.* 22, 2. *P.L.* 54, 195. "divina potestate subnixum est, quod virgo conceperit, quod virgo perpererit, et virgo permanserit."
[436] *Serm.* 24, 3. *P.L.* 54, 206.
[437] *Serm.* 23, 1. *P.L.* 54, 200. Cf. *Serm.* 30, 4. *P.L.* 54, 232. *Ep.* 35, 3, JK 429.
[438] *Serm.* 26, 1. *P.L.* 54, 212. "Deus Dei Filius, genitus de Patre coaeterno, idem etiam partu est natus humano." Cf. *Serm.* 27, 2; *Serm.* 28, 5. *P.L.* 54, 224, "ipse esset filius Virginis, qui creator est matris"; *Serm.* 35, 1; *Ep.* 59, 5, JK 447.
[439] e.g. *Serm.* 15, 2. *P.L.* 54, 176. "eius orationibus adiuti."

archs, prophets, apostles and martyrs.[440] God has given us in them an example and protection.[441] Nevertheless we are not to regard the effect of the death of martyrs, as comparable to that of the Saviour, " from the courage of faithful people there spring examples of patience, not gifts of righteousness." [442] In the honour which we pay to them we must have in mind the honour and love thereby offered to God.[443] It is worth while to call attention to the restraint of Leo's treatment of this subject in contrast to the exuberance of later Latin writers.

13. SUMMARY

While it must be acknowledged that there is comparatively little that is new or original in the whole corpus of Leo's teaching, yet there remain a few points to which it is worth while to call particular attention.

(a) In his treatment of the doctrine of the Incarnation, Leo set himself primarily to expound what he believed to be the true content of scriptural and credal statements on this subject. It was not his chief aim to elaborate any new theory, and in insisting on the indispensability of a truly "dyophysite" doctrine, he did little more than follow in the path already indicated by such Western writers as Ambrose.

Leo's Christology has been attacked from two different angles. It has been criticized by those who show a general impatience and dissatisfaction with the products of orthodox Chalcedonian theology, on the ground that it fails to do more than state the facts, without succeeding in providing any constructive solution of the real problem to which the facts give rise. Criticism of this sort is probably met by underlining what has already been said more than once, namely, that it is altogether beside the point to compare Leo's work with that of a Theodore or a Cyril. His aim was not to theorize, but to state traditional established doctrine in simple and unequivocal language, such as was capable of being understood, not only by eastern controversialists, but by the simple members of his Roman congregations. On the other hand, there have been some liberal Anglican and Protestant critics who have

[440] *Serm.* 35, 4. *P.L.* 54, 253.
[441] *Serm.* 85, 4. *P.L.* 54, 437.
[442] *Serm.* 64, 3. *P.L.* 54, 359.
[443] *Serm.* 70, 5. *P.L.* 54, 383.

raised objections to Leo's Christology on the very serious ground that, though intended to exclude Nestorianism no less than the Monophysitism of his opponents, it failed to do so, and laid itself open to the charge of so distinguishing between the Divine and human in Christ as to destroy the unity of His Person. Mere perusal of the *Acta* of Chalcedon is sufficient to show that criticism of this sort is not new, and it appears at first sight to be not without some measure of justification. Readers of the gospel do not naturally spend their time assigning this saying or action to the Godhead and that saying or action to the Manhood. Yet it has to be remembered that Leo was writing with a particular end in view. The tendency all along of Alexandrine theology (and in a certain measure of orthodox theology as well) was to ignore "the Jesus of history," and to exaggerate the wonder of His Godhead at the expense of the reality of His Manhood. All theological writing suffers from the limitations of the period and setting in which it is written; a limitation to which Leo's works are no exception. Hence we do him an injustice if we lay too much stress on a feature of his teaching which rightly regarded may be seen to be no more than a somewhat developed *argumentum ad hominem*. Yet side by side with his dichotomist phrases, we should place his superb epigrams in which the identity of the Eternal Son with the Man of Sorrows is proclaimed, and to remember that whatever else he did, or failed to do, he never evolved a theory of the union which afterwards had to be discarded as insufficient. The mere fact that some success has recently been achieved in the direction of absolving even Nestorius himself of Nestorianism should suggest caution on the part of any who feel impelled to label this great Pope with a stigma so little deserved.[444]

(b) Leo's treatment of the Atonement is less easy to justify. Yet we have to remember that the juridical turn given to western theology by the jurist Tertullian left a lasting impression, and the concern felt by Leo for the devil's "rights" was only in keeping with the legalist standpoint which dominated western thought for so many centuries. In any case Leo may be absolved of the charge of ever having

[444] See Additional Note, *Recent Criticism of Leo's Christology*.

ventured to assert, as others did, that some ransom was due to the devil for the deliverance of humanity from his power.

(c) The element in his teaching which later ages have recognized as having the most lasting influence on the subsequent history and development of the Church is that which concerns the origin and authority of the Roman see. It is unnecessary to add anything here on this subject to that which has already been written. Leo believed that St. Peter had received the plenitude of power in the Church, that the Roman bishops were his successors, and that as a result he himself had not only the privilege but the duty of exercising the authority divinely committed to him. His claim to be personally entrusted with "the care of all the Churches" sprang not from an ambitious lust for power, but from the inner conviction that neglect of the responsibilities of the Roman see was equivalent to a denial of his Master.

Additional Note

RECENT CRITICISM OF LEO'S CHRISTOLOGY

Leo's Christology has been examined and rejected as unsound by two different groups of critics.

(a) Those who repudiate generally the "dyophysite" Christology of the fifth century. Thus Mackintosh writes, "The doctrine of the two natures, in its traditional form, imports into the life of Christ an incredible and thoroughgoing dualism. In place of that perfect unity which is felt in every impression of Him, the whole is bisected sharply by the fissure of distinction. No longer one, He is divided against Himself. . . . The simplicity and coherence of all that Christ was and did vanishes, for God is not after all living a human life. On the contrary, He is still holding Himself at a distance from its experiences and conditions. There has been no saving descent. Christ executed this as God, it is said, and suffered that as man." [445]

Yet it may be said that Mackintosh has only allowed us to see one aspect of dyophysite Christology. He has permitted himself to exaggerate the dualistic impression conveyed by

[445] *The Person of Jesus Christ*, p. 294.

some methods of employing the doctrine of the Two Natures, and has not allowed for the effect of the doctrine of the impersonal manhood. This doctrine, however, has also been impugned on the ground that it leaves us with an impaired humanity in Christ. But as Mozley observes, "Catholic theology never meant that, in the concrete, the human nature of Christ lacked its *persona*. . . . But regarded in abstraction the human nature of Christ is rightly spoken of as impersonal, since in this case and this alone discrimination can be made between human experiences and a human subject of the experiences."[446] On the other hand, if Mackintosh's line of thought is followed, we may run the risk of obliterating any distinction whatever between Godhead and manhood, and by mingling the Natures find ourselves unconscious Pantheists. The value of Leo's doctrine is that it serves, not only to safeguard the reality of our Lord's humanity, but to warn us against so confusing Godhead and manhood as to make God in man's image.

(b) Those who while accepting on the whole the "findings" of orthodox Christology reject Leo's doctrine as falling short of its "standards." Among this group of critics we include Westcott, *Hebrews,* Add. Note on ii, 10, p. 67 (3rd edn.), where he says, "It is unscriptural, though the practice is supported by strong patristic authority, to regard the Lord during His historic life as acting now by His human and now by His Divine Nature only." There can be no doubt that, as Hall, "Incarnation" in *Dogmatic Theology,* Vol. VI, pp. 56f., points out, Westcott had in mind Leo's "Tome," in referring to "an alleged view . . . that the Godhead and Manhood operated *by turns.*" The same criticism, doubtless equally intended to apply to Leo, reappears in Mason, *The Conditions of our Lord's Life on Earth,* pp. 84f., when he writes of the opinion that our Lord was "alternately acting in two capacities." Raven, *Jesus and the Gospel of Love,* pp. 340f., makes a direct and unambiguous attack. He says, "Rome frankly divided the unity of the Incarnate." Then, after quoting in support of his statement, Tertullian, *Adv. Praxeam* 27 and "*The Tome,*" 4 (where incidentally he renders *invicem* as "alternate"), he concludes, "Thus the antithesis between God

[446] Art. *The Incarnation,* in *Essays Catholic and Critical,* p. 192.

and man is carried down into the life of Jesus: and even in Him no reconciliation is achieved." After this, he goes on to maintain that Leo's doctrine is inferior to that of the Antiochenes who were "at once more intelligent and more religious." It should be noticed that among the "Antiochenes" he expressly includes Nestorius. This extreme view is also shared by MacGregor in *Asking Them Questions,* ed. Wright, O.U.P., where he frankly declares Leo's theology to be "wrongheaded," pp. 84f.

Thus Leo is not only "also among the Nestorians" but is regarded as even less sound than they. Yet it is possible after all that a closer study of Leo's Latinity might have led these critics to treat Leo with greater fairness, and to refrain from imputing to him views which he did not actually hold. As we have shown in the foregoing chapter "*Invicem*" in Leo's usage never means "alternate" but rather "reciprocal" or "mutual." Nor is it correct to speak of an antithesis between God and man in his theology. None is more concerned than to stress the "antithesis" between God and fallen humanity, but that is not the same thing as to teach an "antithesis" between God and perfect human nature as assumed by the Incarnate Word. Reference to the section above,[447] "The Purpose of the Incarnation," will be sufficient to remove any suspicion that Leo interposed between God and man an impassable gulf. "Distinction in being" but "unity in spirit" has always been the standpoint of Catholic theology regarding the mutual relations of God and ideal humanity. It is not Leo's fault if his critics are too impatient to examine and allow for the distinction between the actual and the ideal, between fallen and perfected humanity, which Leo himself so evidently taught.

[447] See above, p. 462.

CHAPTER XXI

MANUSCRIPTS AND EDITIONS

A. MANUSCRIPTS OF THE SERMONS

THE manuscript sources for Leo's sermons are:

(1) Church Lectionaries.

(2) Collections comprising Leonine sermons with others or Leonine sermons only.

That Leo himself carefully preserved the autographs of his sermons is shown by the fact that from time to time he quotes from them in his letters,[1] and it is likely that they were deposited with other documents of papal origin in the official archives of the Roman see. Within a comparatively short time of the author's death selections from the collection began to be included in the Lectionaries of the Roman Church, whence they passed into the service books of other Western churches. But for many centuries there is no trace of any attempt having been made to issue a specifically Leonine collection.

The most ancient sources are therefore the fragments of these primitive lectionaries which survive in quotations made by early medieval authors of the eighth and ninth centuries, such as Paul the Deacon,[2] Hincmar of Rheims[3] and Prudentius of Troyes.[4]

(1) *Lectionaries of the Roman Church*

(i) *Lectionary of SS. Philip and James* in two MSS. *Codd. Vaticani* 3835 and 3836, *saec. viii.* The former contains *Serm.* 52–61, 73, 74, 75–77, 82, 83, i.e. on the Passion, Ascension, Pentecost and the *natale* of St. Peter. The latter contains *Serm.* 12, 18, 19, 1 + 2, 3, 4, 86–94, 85.

[1] e.g. in *Ep.* 28, 3, JK 423, cf. *Serm.* 21, 2.
[2] *Homiliarius, P.L.* 95, 1159ff.
[3] *De Praedestinatione,* 2, 25, *P.L.* 125, 261ff.
[4] *De Praedestinatione,* 1, *P.L.* 115, 1014ff.

(ii) *Lectionary of the basilica of St. Peter,* MSS. 105 and 107. Both copied from a more ancient lectionary, itself probably derived from the archetype. They contain the whole of the surviving sermons from December Embertide to Passiontide inclusive, except *Serm.* 20, 51, 56 and 60, to which they add *Serm. in festo Machab., P.L.* 54, 517 and *Ep.* 28, JK 423. MS. 105, however, is defective as to the conclusions of some festal sermons. Unhappily the part, i.e. that containing the sermons from Passiontide to Advent, has not been preserved.

(iii) *Lectionarium Vallicellanum* A 6, containing four sermons "de Collectis," *Serm.* 6–9 and *Serm.* 84.

(iv) *Lectionarium Vallicellanum* A 7, containing *Serm.* 1–4.

(v) *Codex Thuanaeus,* Paris; the sole authority for *Serm.* 5, 11 and 20, but attributing them mistakenly to Prosper. (*Serm.* 96 does not appear in any of the Lectionaries.)

(2) *Collection of Sermons*

(i) *First Collection,* extant in a single MS., *Codex Casinensis* 126, *saec. xi,* containing in all ninety-one sermons, of which seventy-nine are of significance. These are as follows: on December Embertide, *Serm.* 12, 18, 19, 16, 17, 13, 14 + 15; on Christmas, *Serm.* 22, 27, 30, 29, 28, 25, 24, 26, 21, 23; on the Epiphany, *Serm.* 31, 32, 33, 34, 38, 35, 37, 36; on Lent, *Serm.* 41, 39, 43, 40, 42, 44, 50, 45, 46, 47, 48, 49; 38 (*bis*); on Passiontide, *Serm.* 64, 66, 69, 58, 70, 56, 54, 57, 59, 61, 55, 67; on the Resurrection, *Serm.* 68, 71, 70, 52, 65, 63, 62, 72, *spur.*; on the Ascension, *Serm.* 73, 74, *spur.*; on Pentecost, *Serm.* 75, 78, 76, 79, 80, 81; on "his ordination," *Serm.* 2, 3, 4, 1; on the feast of SS. Peter and Paul (three sermons belonging to Maximus of Turin), *Serm.* 72, 83; on the feast of St. Lawrence (two sermons belonging to Maximus of Turin); on September Embertide, *Serm.* 86, 87, 92, 93, 94; on the Beatitudes, *Serm.* 95; on Pentecost, *Serm.* 77; on the Ascension, a sermon ascribed to Augustine, *App. Serm.* 179.

Two points are to be noticed in regard to this collection; first that it resembles *Lectionarium S. Petri* 107, in joining *Serm.* 14 and 15, and in the order of the sermons on Christmas, as well as in adding after *Serm.* 49 *prim.* two sermons, the former of which is in Isidore of Seville, *De eccl. officiis*, 37–40. Secondly that the same order of the sermons on " his ordination " is found in *Vallicellanum* A 7, which similarly places them before the sermons on the feast of St. Peter.

(ii) *Second Collection,* extant in *Codd. Casanatensis G.* III 7, *Basilicae S. Petri* 210, *saec. xii, Barberinus,* 88. The first of these is deficient in a number of leaves and shows a number of variant readings entered from later collections. The collection contains in all one hundred sermons and prefaces them with *Ep.* 28. It includes seven sermons on the December Embertide in the same order as *Collectio 1;* ten sermons on the Nativity and eight on the Epiphany, but in a different order. Between *Serm.* 26 and 21 is introduced *Serm.* " de Absalon," *P.L.* 56, 11, 51, which in other later collections is added at the end. It omits the sermon, now identified as by Maximus of Turin, *Hom. 2 de Nativ.*, which in *Collect. 1* followed *Serm.* 23. It contains the same sermons on Lent and Passiontide, with the two unauthentic ones following *Serm.* 49. But in the place of the repetition of *Serm.* 49 it gives *Serm.* 53 which is absent from *Collect. 1*. It includes the spurious sermon on the Resurrection, *Serm.* 73 and 74, omitting the spurious one which follows them in *Collect. 1*. It gives the seven sermons on Pentecost in a different order. From this point onwards the resemblance becomes less close, as will be seen from the following list: on the September Embertide, *Serm.* 91, 86, 92, 87, 93, 94. Apart from *Serm.* 91 all these appear in almost the same order in *Collect. 1*, but follow the two unauthentic sermons on the feast of St. Lawrence. Next come two sermons on " his ordination," *Serm.* 3, 1 with three sermons of Maximus as in *Collect. 1* on SS. Peter and Paul; *Serm.* 83; another spurious sermon; on the day of the " Collecta," *Serm.* 9, 10, 6 and 8; on the neglected festival, *Serm.* 84. The six preceding sermons appear in the same order in *Vallicellanum* A 6, though the last five are omitted in *Collect. 1*. Then on the anniversary of SS. Peter and Paul, *Serm.* 82; on the anniversary of blessed Peter, *Serm.* 4; two spurious sermons on St. Lawrence the Martyr as in *Collect. 1* followed by the genuine *Serm.* 85; on the feast of All Saints (the Beatitudes), *Serm.* 95; on the "Saturday of the first month," *Serm.* 51: the spurious sermon "on the Maccabees," *P.L.* 54, 517; lastly on the September Embertide, *Serm.* 88, 89, 90. These last five sermons which do not appear in *Collect. 1* are clearly out of place. *Serm.* 51 evidently belongs to the Lenten group, in which it frequently appears in the Lectionaries and also in later collections. The sermon "on the Maccabees" should precede those on St. Lawrence, and the last three on the September Embertide should be included with the other six on the same subject, namely, *Serm.* 86–94. It seems therefore that the collection was compiled from Lectionaries which lacked these sermons and that they were subsequently added from other sources. The only sermon which appears in *Collect. 1* and is missing here is *Serm.* 2, though twelve new ones are included.

The *Cod. Basilicae S. Petri* 210 also contains certain works of Cyprian. *Vallicellanus* 26 includes beside the Leonine sermons his *Ep.* 165 and fourteen other sermons of spurious origin. These latter also appear in *Barberin.* 88, but the fact that they are absent from *Casanatensis G.* III 7 shows that they are not part of the collection in its original form.

This collection was known by Peter Mallius (12th c.). Cf. *Historia S. Petri basilicae* in *Acta SS. Bolland,* Vol. VI, pt. ii, 7, 131. He alludes to Ps. Leo, *Serm.* 16, i, *P.L.* 54, 511 (one of the spurious fourteen) and mentions (*ibid.,* 3, 37) that the collection was prefaced by *Ep.* 28.

(iii) *Third Collection,* extant in *Cod. Vatican.* 545 (sermons only) and in the variants derived from *Cod. Bononiensis* given in *Cod. Barberin.* 3520. It embraces ninety-three Leonine sermons, all genuine with the exception of the one "on the Maccabees." The fact that the sermons on the Nativity in this collection are prefaced by *Ep.* 28 appears to show that it too is derived from the Lectionaries. Only three of the genuine sermons, *Serm.* 5, 11 and 20 are missing and these, as we have seen, only appear in the *Cod. Thuanaeus* (1 (v) above). The order of the sermons is the same as in the later collections which equally lack these three, except that here *Serm.* 51 is included among the Lenten group. Compared with the foregoing it contains two new sermons, namely, *Serm.*

7 and 96. The titles are sufficient to indicate that its sources differ from those of *Collect. 1* and *2*. It was on this collection that the first printed edition of 1470 was based.

(iv) *Fourth Collection.* Extant in *Codd. Vatican.* 541, 546, 547; *Vatican. Urbinas* 65; *Angelicae Erem. S. Aug.; Venetus S. Marci* 79; *Faesulanus can. Lateran.;* which contain a group of letters as well as the sermons. The following, however, contain besides the sermons only *Ep.* 28; *Codd. Justinae Patav. Casin.; Venetus Georgianus.* This collection gives the sermons in the same order as the preceding, but no MS. is earlier than *saec. xiv.* It is less trustworthy than the preceding, though it was used by later editors who were unaware of the edition of 1470 (see p. 511 below).

(v) *Fifth Collection.* Contains only genuine sermons. Extant in *Codd. Vatican.* 544, *saec. xii.*; *Vat. Reginae Sueciae* 139, *saec. xiii.–xiv.*; *Caesenas Minor. Com. S. Franc., saec. xv.*; *Victorinus.* All MSS. of this collection include a group of letters, while differences in text both of letters and sermons point to derivation from sources differing from those of the foregoing collections. Apart from the omission of *Serm.* 83 on St. Peter and the sermon "on the Maccabees," and the placing of *Serm.* 84 before *Serm.* 82 as in *Collect. 2*, the arrangement of the matter is the same as in *Collect. 3* and *4*.

(vi) *Sixth Collection.* Extant only in *Cod. Orielensis* xlii *saec. xi.–xii.* This MS. was the one used by Quesnel in his edition of the *Cod. Canonum, P.L.* 56, 359. It contains in addition to a group of sermons and letters the edicts of Valentinian III against the Manichaeans, *Ep.* [8], and Hilary of Arles, *Ep.* [11], and to the sermons are added *Epp.* [133] and [3], together with some other matter relative to Leo's life. Quesnel, however, was mistaken in supposing that it represented a contemporary collection.

(vii) The *Homilarius* of Paul the Deacon compiled *saec. viii, P.L.* 95, 1159–1566, at the request of Charlemagne. Paul's object was to draw up a choice of patristic selections for reading at Matins, and he included twenty Leonine sermons derived from MSS. then in existence at Rome. They are identical as to order and titles with the Petrine Lectionary (see p. 496 (ii)).

B. MANUSCRIPTS OF THE LETTERS [7]

There are three principal kinds of codices in which the letters of Leo are found:

(1) Collections of conciliar canons and papal decretals.
(2) Collections made by individual churches embracing letters of Leonine authorship or of Leo's letters only, which, compiled from ancient copies or even original autographs, are of very early origin.
(3) Collections of Leonine letters of more recent date, but derived for the most part from the first group.

As in the case of the sermons, no contemporary collection was made of all the letters,[8] and so there is no likelihood of any complete codex being found. What happened was that the letters as they were written were deposited in the papal archives alongside of those decretals and letters of Leo's predecessors which were there preserved.[9] But as collections of conciliar canons and papal decretals came into general use, the popes themselves began to cite letters of their predecessors, not from the archetypes but from some convenient collection. Hence the original autographs were neglected and allowed to perish, and for this reason the primitive collections are the most ancient sources which we still possess for the letters of the early popes. In fact, generally speaking, only those papal letters which were included in the Collections have survived.

(1) Collections of Conciliar Canons and Papal Decretals

(i) *First Collection* extant in *Cod. Vatican. Reginae Sueciae* 1997. Containing eight letters: *Epp.* 167, 12, 28, 15, 16, 159, 1 and 2.

(ii) *Second Collection* extant in *Cod. Corbeiensis* (Paris lat. 12097) containing fourteen letters: *Epp.* 4, 7, 10, 14, 15, [22], 28, 29, 31, 35, 59, 103, 139 and 165.[10]

[7] See Additional Note A, *Early "testimonia" to the letters of Leo.*
[8] The first of the early popes whose letters were collected into a registrum is Gregory I.
[9] See Additional Note B, *The Papal Archives.*
[10] The order given here is that of the Ballerini, *P.L.* 54, 555.

(iii) *Third Collection* extant in *Codd. Barberin.* 2888 and *Vatican.* 1342 containing sixteen letters in the following order: *Epp.* 14, 167, 16, 1, 12, 159, 9, 139, 145, 119, 23, [22], 20, 28, 165, 80.

(iv) *Fourth Collection* extant in *Codd. Lucensis* and *Colbertin.* 784 containing four letters: *Epp.* 167, 12, 1, 2.

(v) *Fifth Collection* (Quesnel's Collection; Cf. *Cod. Canonum, P.L.* 56, 359) extant in *Cod. Thuanaeus* (*Colbertin.* 932): *Cod. Pithou.* (Paris lat. 1564): *Codd. Vindebonensis* 39 and 42 (the latter with some additions from the *Collectio Hispana, v. infra*): *Cod. Orielensis* xlii (but containing a different series of Leonine letters). The contents of this collection are as follows: *Epp.* 165, 139, 28, 108, 15, 167, 14, 159, 18, 4, 7, 16, 31, 59, 124, 1, 2, 12, 33, 44, 45, 25, 29, 104, 106, 114, 155, 162, 163, 135, 93, 19. In several codices the following precede the Leonine letters [97], [99] and [68].[11]

The *Oriel Codex* contains the following letters: *Epp.* 28 [68], [99], [97], 29, 31, 33, 45, 69, 70, 93, 114, 104, 106, 79, 80, 135, 163, 155, 59, 162, 165, 124, 139, 35, 108, 15, 7, 8, 167, 159, 18, 1, 2, 166, 19, 14, 9, (*spurious* JK † 551), 138, 168, 4, 16, 12, to which after a series of sermons are added the Paschal letters [133] and [3].

It should be observed that those four of the above collections which contain *Ep.* 167 include the queries of Rusticus himself, which shows that they are to be preferred to the collection of Dionysius, who substituted titles for the queries.

(vi) *Sixth Collection* (Dionysius Exiguus), *Codd. Vatican.* 5845 and *Regius Parisiensis.*, incorporating seven letters: *Epp.* 4, 7, 16, 18, 167, 14, 159. *Ep.* 12 was added among later additions.

The MSS. of the unadulterated *Dionysiana* were used by Cresconius Africanus, who inserted the whole collection of Dionysius arranged under headings. Hence MSS. of Cresconius supply evidence of the Dionysian archetype. MSS.

[11] Numbers in square brackets [ ] are those which, though not of Leonine authorship, appear in the Leonine *corpus*.

are *Codd. Vallicell.* XVIII, *Vatican.* 1347, *Vatican. Reginae* 849, *Vatican. Palatin.* 579 and *Veronensis* 60, *saec. viii.*

(vii) *Seventh Collection* (*Hadriana*). Compiled by Hadrian I and sent by him to Charlemagne. Principal MSS. *saec. ix.–x.,* are *Codd. Vatican.* 4969, *Vatican. Palat.* 578, *Vatican. Reginae* 1021 and 1043, *Vatican.* 1337 (described by the Roman editors in an edition of Gratian as the *Cod. Canonum*) and *Vallicell. A.S.* and *XVIII.* The only additional letter here, as compared with the *Dionysiana,* is *Ep.* 12.

(viii) *Eighth Collection* (the enlarged *Hadriana*), *Codd. Vallicell. A.S., Vatican.* 1353 and *Vercellensis,* containing fifteen letters: *Epp.* 9, 15, 1, 2, 108, 17, 20, 23, [22], 28, 139, 119, 80, 145 and 165.

(ix) *Ninth Collection* (*Hispana*) compiled in the first half of the seventh century in the time of Isidore of Seville, and extant in *Codd. Vatican.* 1341 and *Vindebonensis* 41, *saec. ix,* the former being derived from Gallican, the latter from purer Spanish copies. From the former the collection known as the "Isidorian" was derived, but in view of the corruptions in the Gallican original its readings are of little value when they differ from those of the *Cod. Vindebonensis.*

The author of the *Hispana* included the seven letters given by Dionysius with the same titles, except that in *Ep.* 167 he adds the titles and headings which Dionysius omitted. Besides these seven he adds thirty others, with the letter of Peter Chrysologus to Eutyches and another of Flavian to Leo. His list reads: *Epp.* 20, 23, [22], 28, [25], 33, 44, 45, 60, 61, 69, 70, 71, 79, 80, 82, 83, 85, 90, 93, 104, 106, 115, 130, 134, 165, 15, 7, 16, 4, 18, 167, 14, 159, 12, 108, 166, 9, 168.

Three points are to be observed. First, that the "dogmatic" letters with the exception of [22] and [25] are roughly in chronological order. Secondly, that although the forty letters of Leo in all, mentioned in the index prefixed to this collection of papal decretals, include three addressed to Marcian, the actual collection contains at this point only two, viz., *Epp.* 82, 83. Thirdly, the form of *Ep.* 12 is shorter and differs from that which is given in the *Hadriana,* showing that it was absent from the pure Dionysian codex which he used.

(x) *Tenth Collection* (Isidorian) compiled in the ninth century by Isidorus Mercator. Pure Isidorian codices e.g. *Codd. Vatican.* 630, *saec. ix.* and *Vatican.* 631, *saec. xiii.* contain same number of letters and similar errors to the *Hispana.* Others, however, contain additions to the Leonine matter and hence must be reckoned as representing a different collection.

(xi) *Eleventh Collection* derived from the Isidorian. Extant in *Vatican. Ottob.* 93, *saec. ix.–x.*, mutilated at the conclusion, and in *Cod. Vatican.* 3791. Besides the thirty-nine letters copied from the *Hispana,* with slight changes of order, eighteen other letters are added, making fifty-seven letters in all including two distinct texts of *Ep.* 28. The following letters precede the Isidorian: *Epp.* 120, [97], [99], 139, 28 (derived from the text of the ancient Homilaries and differing from the text derived from the *Hispana,* which is given in its place among the letters copied from that source), 31, 59, 124, 1, 35, 29, 114, 155, 162, 135. The Isidorian letters follow (thirty-nine in all), among which is inserted *Ep.* 19, absent from that collection. The text of *Ep.* 12 is not that given in the *Isidoriana* but is derived from the *Hadriana,* to which is appended the additional matter from the text of the *Isidoriana.* Finally there is the spurious letter of Leo, " ad episcopos Germaniae et Galliae," JK † 551, " de chorepiscopis," believed to have been composed by Ps. Isidore himself. This collection is referred to by Hincmar of Rheims, I, 5, p. 23 (Paris), who mentions the cases considered by Leo in *Ep.* 12. Two other MSS. appear to belong to this collection, namely, *Cod. Barberinn.* 57, *saec. xii. mutilus,* and *Vatican.* 4902 of a much later date. It is likely that the additional letters contained here, except *Epp.* 120, [97] and [99] were derived from *Collect.* 5 (*v. supra*).

(xii) *Twelfth Collection* (of North Gallic origin since it includes the *Acta* of a council held at Rheims in A.D. 1148). Extant in *Codd. Vatican.* 1340 and *Venetus S. Marci* 169. The largest collection except *Collect. 18* (*v. infra*) since it contains ninety-nine letters, including some which do not appear elsewhere. It comprises the thirty-nine letters of the *Hispana,* and sixteen others letters from *Collect. 11,* though omitting

Ep. [97] and without the repetition of *Ep.* 28. The forty-four additional letters are the following: *Epp.* 24, 102, 121, 122, 2, 10, 41, 95, 94, 105, 113, 111, 112, 118, 123, 125, 127, [68] (*spur.* App. *Ep.* 3), 103, 138, 54, 34, 36, 37, 38, 39, 50, 47, 49, 48, 51, 74, 78, 81, 84, 87, 89, 116, 119, 145, 148, 156, 30.

It will be seen that the order of the letters from *Ep.* 54 onwards corresponds to that of the *Cod. Grimani* (*v. infra*) and it may therefore be inferred that they are derived from a common source. Many of these letters appear in no earlier collection, and even if some are subsequently found in some rare MSS. and others in the MSS. of *Collect. 24,* five are given in no other collection, namely, *Epp.* 39, 47, 48, 74 and 138. The same collector also included "Tanta seculi," which belongs not to Leo the Great, but to Leo, bishop of Biturica, (*P.L.* 54, 1239). This collection was published by Merlin, *Collect. concil. . . . et decret. pont.* (Paris) 1524 from *Cod. Vatican.* 1340, but with the omission of *Epp.* [25] and [68], and some slight changes of order. It may be added that *Codd. Remensis S. Remigii* and *Isidorianus,* mentioned by Quesnel belong to this collection. The latter was used by Sichard in his edition of papal letters (Basel), 1536.

(xiii) *Thirteenth Collection.* Extant in a single MS. *Cod. Florentinus S. Marci* 182, *saec. xii.* It contains only papal letters, and from the contents which include both genuine and unauthentic letters up to the pontificate of Xystus III, it may be inferred that the source was Isidorian, i.e. Collect. 10, 11. But the Leonine letters show considerable discrepancies from the Isidorian text both in respect of order and character, and differ from any other collection. From the fact that *Ep.* 12 is given intact in this codex alone it may be inferred that the collection is of African origin. It contains twenty-four letters, the last mutilated, showing that there may have been others. These are: *Epp.* 4, 7, 16, 18, 167, 14, 159, 12, 124, 59, 33, 44, 45, 29, 35, 31, 1, 2, 163, 135, 95, 19, 28, 165. The seven first letters follow *Collect. 6,* but the form of *Ep.* 12 as given here is derived neither from *Collect.* 7 nor *11*.

(2) *Collections made for individual churches and special purposes*

(i) *The Collection belonging to the Roman Church*, known as the *Collectio Avellana*, compiled in the time of Pope Vigilius and containing a number of letters belonging to the months of June and August, A.D. 460, which are absent from any other collection. The principal MS. in which this collection is extant is *Cod. Vatican.* 4961, *saec. xi*, formerly belonging to the monastery of St. Crux of the Fons Avellana in Umbria. There are also *Codd. Vatican.* 3786, 4903, *saec. xvi, Corsini*, n. 817, *saec. xvi, Angelica*, n. 292, *saec. xvi*. Three others, *Cod. Vatican.* 3787 and *Codd. Veneti Marciani Iur. Can.* 13 and 14, *saec. xv.–xvi*, are independent of the *Avellana* MS. This collection must have been derived directly from the papal archives and contains the following letters: *Epp.* 169, 170, 171, 172, 173, i.e. Nos. 51–55 of the whole *Collectio*.

(ii) *The Collection belonging to the Church of Arles*, known as the *Collectio Arelatensis*. Embracing letters addressed by the Roman see to the see of Arles or vice versa, in proof of the rights and privileges enjoyed or claimed by the latter. Extant in *Codd. Regius, Colbertinus* and *Vallicellanus* G. 99, which is derived from a most ancient Arelatine MS. This collection contains four letters which are not found elsewhere, namely *Epp.* 40, 42, [65], 66.

(iii) *The Collection belonging to the Church of Thessalonica*. The collection was produced by Theodosius of Echinus at the Roman synod held in A.D. 531 under Pope Boniface II and incorporated in the *Acta* of that synod. (Mansi, *Concilia*, Vol. VII, 748.) It is extant in *Cod. Barberinus* 3386. Leo Allatius in his *Concordia Eccl. Orient. cum Occident.*, pp. 1370f. quoted from a very ancient Vatican MS. now lost. The *Cod. Barberinus* is later and is derived from two older Vatican MSS. It was used by Holsten for his edition *Collectio bipartita*, pp. 103–63 (Rome) 1662. Unfortunately it does not contain the whole of the document cited at the synod of A.D. 531 and stops short at the letter mistakenly attributed to Leo as addressed to Anastasius of Thessalonica, which is actually a letter from Boniface I to Rufus, *Ep.* 5, JK 351.

Whether or not it originally contained other Leonine letters we have as yet no means of knowing, since the MS. concludes with the phrase *Item recitata est.* It contains the following nine letters: *Epp.* [100], 104, 106, 136, [132], 135, 6, 5, 13. Of these *Epp.* [100], 136, [132], 6, 5, 13 were unknown previous to their appearance in Holsten's edition of the *Cod. Barberinus.* But *Ep.* 136 appears both in the *Cod. Grimani* and in the *Cod. Monacensis* MS. lat. 14 540 (*v. infra*) and *Ep.* [100] in *Cod. Blodeianus* and *Vatican. Graecus* 1455.

(iv) *Collections bearing on the Council of Chalcedon.*

(a) A Greek collection evidently made between the year A.D. 453, the death of Pulcheria, and A.D. 455, the death of Valentinian III, since in the titles of certain letters it refers to the latter as *dominus,* and not, as in the case of Pulcheria, *divae memoriae,* and was evidently compiled at Constantinople. Moreover, it omits *Ep.* 165 which, had it been written, must certainly have been included. Extant in *Cod. Venetus* 555, *saec. xi,* and *Cod. Vindebonensis hist. gr.* 27, *saec. xii.* It is divided into three parts; the first containing the documents which preceded the council, *ante gesta* and including twenty-seven letters, namely, *Epp.* 20, [25], 23, [22], 72, 26, 35, 32, 29, 30, 33, 43, 44, 45, [46], [58], [55], [56], [57], [62], [63], [64], 50, 51, [73], [76], [77]. One is inserted in the *Acta,* namely, *Ep.* 28 and two are added subsequently, namely, *Epp.* [98] and 114. The Greek *Codd.* omit *Ep.* 114 and include among the *ante gesta Ep.* 93.

(b) A Latin version of the *Acta* of Chalcedon, probably the one made by Julian of Cios at Leo's request. See *Ep.* 113, 4, JK 489. Extant in *Codd. Parisinus,* lat. 16832; *Vatican. Reginae* 1045 and *Barberin.* xiv. 53. Unhappily these only contain *Epp.* 28 and [98].

(c) The Latin version of the *Acta* made by Rusticus in connexion with the "Three Chapters" controversy containing thirty-five letters among the *ante gesta* including the following: *Epp.* 20, [25], 23, [22], 72, 28, [62], 35, 32, 29, 30, 33, 43, 44, 45, [46], [58, 55, 56, 57, 62, 63, 64], 50, 51, [73, 76, 77], and among the *gesta, Ep.* 114. Rusticus used throughout Latin originals where they were obtainable except possibly in the case of *Ep.* 72. It is extant in *Codd. Corbeiensis, Divionensis, Colbertinus, Chigianus* 483, *Vatican.* 1323 and 4166, *Veronensis* 57, *saec. vii.*

(d) *Codex encyclius,* Mansi, *Concilia,* Vol. VII, 785. Translated into Latin by order of Cassiodorus, saec. vi., cf. *De inst. div. litt.* 11. Extant so far as is known in one MS. only. *Paris, lat.* 12098, *saec. ix.* Among the letters included is *Ep.* 165.

(3) Collections of Leonine Letters only of more recent date

(i) *Codex Grimani, saec. xii.* Paris, *Biblioth. Mazarin.* 1645. This codex was discovered by Quesnel and is held by Constant, *Epp. Rom. pont., praef.* 166, to be derived from the papal archives. It contains one hundred and eight letters and is thought by Turner, *Miscellanea Ceriani,* p. 727 to have originated in Udine in the sixth century. It is for the most part chronologically arranged. The following twenty-eight letters appear in this collection for the first time: *Epp.* 27, 75, 86, 92, 117, 131, 140, 141, 147, 152, 88, 91, 143, 146, 157, 126, 128, 137, 142, 129, 153, 149, 150, 154, 158, 160, 161 and 164.

(ii) *Codex Monacensis* (Ratisbon), *saec. viii.* Clm 14 540. This MS. contains seventy-two letters divided into two groups of thirty-six in each, the earlier group comprising those written before the council of Chalcedon, the later those written after the council. It was first used by the Ballerini in producing their edition and is held by them to have been compiled previous to the correspondence between pope Pelagius II and the bishops of Istria, JK 1054, *c.* A.D. 585.[12]

It contains the following letters: *Epp.* 24, 23, 29, 30, 28, 35, 34, 33, 32, 37, 38, 44, 45, 51, 50, 54, 60, 61, 69, 70, 75, 78, 79, 80, 81, 83, 84, 85, 86, 88, 90, 91, 92, 93, 94, 95, 104, 105, 106, 107, 114, 119, 109, 102, 115, 116, 117, 121, 122, 123, 126, 127, 139, 130, 129, 131, 136, 142, 143, 144,

[12] Pelagius II mentions *Ep.* 28 in *Ep.* 3, JK 1054, and quotes *Epp.* 114, 1 and 119, 5 in *Ep.* 4, JK 1055. Cf. also *Ep.* 5, 3, JK 1056. *M.G.H. Epp.*, Vol. II, p. 449, No. 3. Turner, *op. cit.,* considers that the Istrian bishops employed and cited this collection, as against the Ballerini who hold that it was used by Pelagius II himself.

145, 146, 147, 148, 149, 150, 151, 152, 153, 164, 165, 162. There are two important dogmatic letters which are found in the *Cod. Grimani* and not here, namely, *Epp.* 59 and 124. The contractions which are reproduced here, as well as the use of *papa* in titles to the letters, point to a sixth century date for its compilation. Hence Turner suggests that it represents the collection made by pope Vigilius in A.D. 540. The Ballerini regard this collection as more important than the *Cod. Grimani* and it holds a high place for purity and accuracy. Cf. Nostiss-Reineck in *Hist. Jahrbuch,* Vol. XVIII (1897), p. 133, and Bardenhewer, *Geschichte der altkirch. lit.,* Vol. IV, p. 621. But Turner, *Miscellanea Ceriani,* p. 734 points out that in the citation of the Nicene Creed contained in *Ep.* 165, the *Cod. Grimani* agrees with the older MSS., while *Cod. Monacensis* stands alone, and infers that while *Cod. Grimani* and the older canonical collections have copied their source, *Cod. Monacensis* has edited it. The fact that there are signs of chronological and methodical arrangement in both these codices suggests that, as contrasted with the smaller and more haphazard collections, which obtained their material more or less at random, the ultimate source of both were the archives of the Roman see.

(iii) *Other Collections.* The Ballerini, *P.L.* 54, 574 mention the following:

(1) A Roman collection represented by *Cod. S. Crucis in Jerusalem* 237, *saec. xi,* containing *Epp.* 28, 35, 31, 59, 124, 1, 163, 165, and including *Epp.* 12, JK †551 and 19.

(2) A collection resembling *Collect. 11*, and containing the same fifty-six letters, but in a different order and with divergent readings. It begins with *Ep.* 20 and ends with *Ep.* 168. Codices including letters only are *Venetus Marcianus* 170, *saec. xii, Vatican.* 542 and 543, *saec. xiv.*: those also including the sermons of *Collect. 4* are *Vatican.* 546, 547; *Vatican. Urbinas* 65; *Angelica* 5, 10; *Florentin. Medic.* 11, 23; *Faesulanus can. Lateran.* 7; *Vatican.* 541. The latter contains twelve additional letters, eleven of which appear in *Collect.* (iii) (5) (*v. infra*), the supplementary one being *Ep.* 119. Two further MSS. appear to belong to this collection, namely, *Vatican.* 3137 and *Vatican. Ottob.* 332. In these

MSS. eleven of the additional letters are inserted between No. 26 and No. 27.

(3) A collection resembling the above and the *Coll. Chalcedonensis* represented by *Cod. Venet. Marcianus* 79. It includes besides the sermons of *Collect. 4* twenty-six letters as in (iii) (2), then all the letters of *Collect. 17* in the same order, omitting two which have already been entered. Finally the rest of the letters in (4) (ii) are given but omitting *Epp.* [97], [99] and 168 with some changes of order and differences of readings.

(4) A collection resembling the enlarged *Hadriana* extant in *Cod. Vatican. Ottob.* 297, *saec. xii.* It contains the first fifteen letters of the enlarged *Hadriana* up to *Ep.* 165. At this point four papal documents are inserted of pre-Leonine origin. Then the compiler adds the *Testimonia patrum* belonging to *Ep.* 165. Next fifty-six letters of (iii) (2) but omitting those which have already appeared and with some changes of order. Finally he adds *Epp.* 107, 50, 49, 51.

(5) A collection resembling (iii) (2) and extant in *Codd. Vatican.* 544, *saec. xii.*; *Vatican. Regius* 139, *saec. xiii.*; *Caesenas patr. min. Conv. S. Franc; Laurentian. Florent.* 14 but lacking *Epp.* 119 and 145; *Victorinus; Regniacensis; S. Martin Antissiod; Faesulanus* containing twenty-five letters only and with the shorter form of *Ep.* 12. It contains besides the sermons of *Collect. 5* seventy-one letters. Of these fifty-four are the same as those in (iii) (2) but omitting *Ep.* [25] and [97]. The remaining seventeen are among the more rarely found and appear in *Collect. 12,* namely, *Epp.* 2, 10, 24, 41, 94, 95, 102, 105, 111, 112, 113, 118, 121, 122, 123, 125 and 127. *Ep.* 12 is given in the shortened form. Hence the collection must be in some way independent of *Collect. 12* and (iii) (2). In any case it shows considerable differences of order and divergencies of reading.

(iv) *Other Codices.* A MS. of the New Testament including Leonine matter, e.g. *Cod. Veronensis* 8 which gives *Ep.* 28 after the Catholic Epistles; *Cod. Veronensis* 58 embracing a number of documents relating to the councils of Ephesus and Chalcedon, and including *Epp.* 28 and 167; *Vaticanus* 1322 which gives *Epp.* 87, 89, 93, 94 and 144. This is described by

Turner, *Miscellanea Ceriani,* p. 716 as "a small but very ancient collection." It also appears in *Cod. Novarensis* 30 (66) which was printed for the first time by Amelli, in *Spicilegium Casinense,* I, pp. 33–62, and included the appeals of Flavian and Eusebius of Dorylaeum, then rediscovered. (Cf. Mommsen in *Neues Archiv.,* Vol. XI (1886), pp. 364–7.) Further there are *Cod. Vatican. Reginae* 293, *saec. xii,* which gives *Epp.* 31, 35, 139 and 165; *Cod. Thuanaeus; Cod. Vallicell.* 18, *saec. xi,* op. 73 includes *Epp.* 106, 93; *Cod. Vatican.* 1343, *saec. x,* with *Epp.* 9, 17, 20 and 108; *Codd. Vatican.* 1347, *saec. x, Vatican Palat.* 579, *Vatican. Reginae* 849 with *Ep.* 14; *Cod. Barberin.* 77 with *Ep.* 12 in the shortened form.

(v) *The Greek Manuscripts.* The existing corpus of Leonine documents has already been found to include a number of documents of Eastern origin. Naturally the originals of these were for the most part written in Greek. Besides this it should be remembered that the increasing tendency, already apparent in the fourth century, for the eastern and western provinces to drift apart both culturally and linguistically meant that by the middle of the fifth century Latin was probably as little understood in the East as Greek in the West.[13] Hence there is evidence that within three years of the council of Chalcedon a Greek version of a number of Leo's letters was made with a view to their circulation among the eastern churches; later in the time of Pope Hormisdas after the reconciliation of the eastern churches with the see of Rome, assent to the dogmatic letters including *Ep.* 28 was required as a proof of orthodoxy. In fact so important are these early Greek versions that in some cases the earliest MS. evidence for certain letters of which the Latin original has perished is the existing Greek rendering. Such letters are *Epp.* 43 and 72, both Leonine, [46], the latter part of [25] and the four imperial letters [55, 56, 57 and 58].

[13] Augustine himself was unfamiliar with Greek. Cf. Kidd, *History,* Vol. III, p. 122, n. 4. Evidence of the ignorance of Greek in the West is to be found in Celestine I, *Ep.* 13, 3, JK 374; Cyril, *Ep.* 8 to Celestine; Leo, *Ep.* 113, 4, JK 489. Similarly ignorance of Latin in the East is shown in Proterius, *Ep. ad Leonem,* 9. *Inter Leon. Epp.,* No. 133, *P.L.* 54, 1093; Leo, *Epp.* 130, 3, JK 506; 131, 1, JK 507, with reference to the provision of a more accurate Greek rendering of the "Tome."

The Ballerini have edited in all forty-one letters in a Greek version including *Epp.* [22], [52], [55], [56], [57], [62], [63], [64], [73], [77], [98], [26], [53], [100], [110], [101], 104, 106, 114, 115, 139 and 165 (the best of all the Greek versions). The MSS. used by them were *Codd. Veneti Marciani* 555, *saec., xi–xii;* 164, of later date; 165, including *Epp.* [26] and 28; *Romanus Pat. Basil.* 19.

(C) EDITIONS OF SERMONS AND LETTERS

A summary of all the editions of Leo's works is given in Schoenemann, *Bibliotheca,* Leipzig 1792–4, an extract from which is printed in Migne, *P.L.* 54, 50–114. The first edition containing twelve sermons and five letters was published at Rome in 1470 by Joannes Andreas Aleriensis (ep.). Twelve successive editions appeared in the fifteenth century, thirty-two in the sixteenth, and nineteen in the seventeenth, up to the appearance of the edition of P. Quesnel, Paris 1675. To the latter part of the seventeenth century belong four further editions, and to the eighteenth fourteen up to the edition of P. and H. Ballerini, Venice 1755–7. This edition is reprinted by Migne, *P.L.* 54–56, Paris 1865. The importance of Quesnel's edition was due to the corrections made by him in the text, and to the notes and dissertations which were published with it. But his commentary was marked by strong Gallican partiality, for which it was placed on the Index by a decree of June 22nd, 1676. The Ballerini brothers, who had already made their name by the publication in 1736 of the Leonine Sermons, were invited by Benedict XIV to undertake the task of correcting Quesnel's edition. This involved a revision of the whole text, and the refutation of his tendentious notes and dissertations. They also included a supplement containing the "Leonine Sacramentary" and Collections of Canons issued previous to Gratian.

Since then A. Haberda has undertaken on behalf of the *Corpus Scriptorum Ecclesiasticorum Latinorum,* Vienna, a critical edition of the Sermons, which in spite of long delay has not yet (1940) appeared. (In addition to the twenty apocryphal sermons included in their edition by the Ballerini, Caillau has published eight others, reproduced in *P.L.* 54, 1131–54.) An inventory of Leo's letters is given in Jaffe-Kaltenbrunner,

Regesta Pont. Rom., Leipzig 1885. Krusch, *Studien z. christl. mittelalt. Chron.*, Leipzig 1880, has published the Letters on the Paschal Question, i.e. *Epp.* 88, 121, 122, 127, 131, 137, 142. The edition of the *Collectio Avellana* in *C.S.E.L.* Vol. XXXV, Vienna 1895, includes *Epp.* 169–173 (Nos. 51–55). The Letters relative to the see of Arles, *Epp.* 40–42, 65–67, appear in the edition of the *Collectio Arelatensis* published by Gundlach in *M.G.H. Epp.* Vol. III, pp. 15–22, Berlin 1892. Hurter in his *SS. Patrum opuscula,* Innsbruck 1868f., Nos. 14, 25, 26, gives a selection of sermons and letters. Finally mention must be made of the edition of the *Acta Conciliorum Oecumenicorum,* Tom. II, Berlin 1932, produced by E. Schwartz, which in Vol. III, pp. 3ff. includes the Letters contained in the *Collectio Grimanica* (see p. 507 above), in the *Collectio Casinensis,* pp. 143ff. (see p. 509 (iv)), in the *Collectio Corbeiensis,* pp. 156ff. (see p. 500 (ii)), with Letters from the *Collectio Quesneliana*, pp. 159f. (see p. 501 above), and from the *Collectio Thessalonicensis*, pp. 167f. (see p. 505 above), together with the *Collectiones* belonging to the Council of Chalcedon, *ibid.,* Vol. I, pp. 3ff.; Vol. II, pp. 24ff.; Vol. III, pp. 5ff. (see p. 505 above).

Additional Note A

THE PAPAL ARCHIVES

The earliest references to the existence of an official register of papal letters and documents are the following:

(i) Damasus, epigram in the porch of St. Lawrence *in Damaso*. Cf. De Rossi, *Inscript. Christ,* Vol. II, p. 134, and Grisar, *History of Rome and the Popes,* E.T., Vol. I, pp. 204f., and n. 1.

(ii) Roman synod of A.D. 369. Cf. Mansi, *op. cit.*, Vol. III, 459; Basil, *Ep.* 244.

(iii) Jerome, *adv. Rufin.*, 3, 20, who shows that at least from the time of Anastasius I, A.D. 398–402, copies of all official letters were preserved in the *chartarium* of the Roman see.

(iv) Innocent I, *Ep.* 13 ad Rufum, JK 300.

(v) Zosimus (and later popes). In the title of Zosimus, *Ep.* 4 the expression *a pari* is used. This is an imitation of secular practice and refers to the filing of one copy of a letter sent to different destinations.

(vi) Boniface I, *Ep.* 4 ad Rufum, JK 350.

(vii) Roman synod of A.D. 495 under Gelasius I. Cf. Mansi, *op. cit.,* Vol. VIII, 184.

(viii) Dionysius Exiguus, *Ep. ad. Joann. I papam,* dated A.D. 526, referring to a letter of Paschasinus to Leo, *Ep.* 4, then rediscovered in the archives, thus showing that the actual originals of Leo's pontificate were still in existence seventy years after his death.

(ix) Roman synod of A.D. 531 under Boniface II with reference to the dependence of the see of Thessalonica on the Roman see. Cf. Mansi, *op. cit.,* Vol. VIII, 748. Unhappily all the texts preserved in the archives are not quoted to which Boniface refers.

Additional Note B

EARLY "TESTIMONIA" TO THE LETTERS OF LEO

(i) Prosper, *Chronicon,* ad ann. 455. *M.G.H.,* Auct. antiqu., Vol. IX, *Chron. min.,* Vol. XI, p. 484, where he quotes "studio unitatis et pacis" from *Ep.* 142 and "haec persuasio" from *Ep.* 122.

(ii) Simplicius, *Ep.* 3, 4. 5., *ad Basiliscum,* JK 573; *Ep. ad presbyteros CP.,* JK 574.

(iii) Gennadius, *De vir. illustr.* 71 (ed. *Texte u. Unters.,* XIV, 1, p. 85), with reference to the "Tome": *ibid.,* 85, p. 90 (cf. Bardenhewer, *Geschichte,* Vol. IV, p. 620).

(iv) Gelasius, *Ep. ad episc. Dardan.,* JK 623, in which he alludes to *Epp.* [100], [110], [132], 104–6.

(v) *Liber Pontificalis* (Felician abridgement; ed. Duchesne, Vol. I, p. 90), referring to Leonine letters as preserved in the archives of the Roman see. Cf. *ibid.,* p. 238, "ad Marcianum epistolas xii, ad Leonem Augustum epistolas xiii, ad Flavianum episcopum epistolas ix, episcopis per Orientem epistolas xviii," showing that a number of letters then in existence have now perished.

(vi) Vigilius. (a) *Ep. ad Justinianum imp.,* JK 910, in

which it is mentioned that *Epp.* 28 and 165 together with the decrees of the first four councils are recognized as the doctrinal standard of the Roman Church.

(b) *Ep. ad Mennam CP,* JK 911, which shows that in A.D. 540 a collection of Leonine letters were preserved at CP.

(c) *In connexion with the "Three Chapters."*

(1) *Ep. ad Rusticum,* JK 927, referring to Leo's practice of sending copies of the same letter to more than one place, e.g. *Epp.* 149, 150.

(2) *Constitutum I* (Mansi, *Concilia,* Vol. IX, 102–4), in which Vigilius cites *Epp.* 93, 3; 98, 4; 79, 2; 162, 1 and 3; 164, 1–3, and possibly *Ep.* 149 from a copy addressed to Anatolius (cf. *Ep.* 151 which may omit all that is common to it and *Ep.* 149).

(3) *Constitutum II.* (Mansi, *op. cit.,* Vol. IX, 460, 487), citing *Ep.* 28, and possibly referring to *Ep.* 120.

(vii) Facundus of Hermiane. *Pro defensione trium capit.,* (*P.L.* 67, 527ff), ii. 3 = *Ep.* 106, 4; ii. 5, 6 = *Ep.* 162, 2 (cf. v. 5 and xii. 2); ii. 6 = *Epp.* 164, 1, 114, 1 (cf. v. 4), *Ep.* 28, 6 (cf. v. 3); iii. 3 = *Ep.* 139, 2; v. 3 = *Ep.* 28, 4; v. 4 = *Epp.* 114, 1, 106, 2, 114, 2, 119, 5 and 6 [104 and 105]; v. 5 = *Ep.* 162, 3, 4; xii. 2 = *Epp.* 164, 1, 156, 1, 162, 1, 160, 2, 161, 2.

(viii) Pelagius II.

(1) *Ep. ad Eliam,* JK 1054, quoting *Ep.* 28.

(2) *Ep. ad Eliam,* JK 1055 mentioning quotations read from the archives esp. *Epp.* 114, 1, and 119, 5.

(3) *Ep. ad Eliam,* JK 1056. Here Pelagius cites a letter of the Istrian bishops in which they quote *Ep.* 162, 3 and 2 ("epistola ultima"); the *Codex encyclius* (cf. Mansi, *op. cit.,* Vol. VII, 540, 538); *Epp.* 164, 1, 2; 162, 1; 149, 2; 164, 3; 162, 2, and a letter to Aetius now lost. Pelagius II himself quotes *Epp.* 162, 1; 106, 2, 3; 114, 1; 163, 1; the *Codex encyclius* (cf. Mansi, *op. cit.,* Vol. VII, 538, 540); *Epp.* 149, 1; 115, 1, 2; *Ep. ad Aetium* (perd.); 115, 2; 116, 2; 117, 1; 112, 2; 119; *Cod. encycl.* (cf. Mansi, *op. cit.,* Vol. VII, 596).

BIBLIOGRAPHY

ABBREVIATIONS USED IN FOOTNOTES AND BIBLIOGRAPHY

A. SS. = *Acta Sanctorum Bollandiana. Brussels.* 1643–1894. 60 vols.
C.Q.R. = *Church Quarterly Review.* London.
C.S.C.O. = *Corpus scriptorum christianorum orientalium.* Chabot, J. B., and others. Paris, etc. 1903ff.
C.S.E.L. = *Corpus scriptorum ecclesiasticorum latinorum.* Vienna. 1866, in progress.
C.S.H.B. = *Corpus scriptorum historiae Byzantinae.* Niebuhr, B. G., and others. Bonn. 1828–97. 49 vols.
D.A.C. = *Dictionnaire de l'Archéologie chrétienne et de la Liturgie.* Cabrol, F. Paris. 2nd edn. 1907, in progress.
D.C.B. = *Dictionary of Christian Biography.* Smith, W., and Wace, H. London. 1877–87. 4 vols.
D.C.A. = *Dictionary of Christian Antiquities.* Smith, W., and Cheetham, S. London. 1875–80. 2 vols.
D.T.C. = *Dictionnaire de Théologie catholique.* Vacant, A., and others. 1923, in progress.
E.R.E. = *Encyclopaedia of Religion and Ethics.* Hastings, Jas. Edinburgh. 1908–26. 12 vols. with Index.
G.C.S. = *Die Griechischen christlichen Schriftsteller der ersten drei Jahrhunderte.* Leipzig. 1897, in progress.
J.E. / J.K. = *Regesta pontificum Romanorum.* Jaffé, P., and others. 2nd edn. Berlin. 1885. 2 vols.
J.T.S. = *Journal of Theological Studies.* London and Oxford.
L.P. = *Liber Pontificalis.* Duchesne, L. Paris. 1886. 2 vols.
M.G.H. = *Monumenta Germaniae Historica.* Pertz, G. H., and others. Berlin and Hanover. 1826, in progress.
P.G. = *Patrologiae cursus completus.* Series graeca. Migne, J. P. Paris. 1857–66. 161 vols. in 166.
P.L. = *Patrologiae cursus completus.* Series latina. Migne, J. P. Paris. 1844–55. 221 vols.
R.E. = *Real-Enkyklopädie der klassischen Alterthumswissenschaft.* Pauly, A. F. von, and Wissowa, G. Stuttgart. New edn. 1904, in progress.

I. Dictionaries and General Works of Reference

Cabrol, F. *Dictionnaire de l'Archéologie chrétienne et de la Liturgie.* Paris. 1901. 2nd edn., 1907, in progress. *(D.A.C.)*

Hastings, Jas. *Encyclopaedia of Religion and Ethics.* 12 vols. Edinburgh. 1908–21. Index, Edinburgh. 1926. *(E.R.E.)*

Pauly, A. F. von. *Real-Enkyklopädie der klassischen Alterthumswissenschaft.* Ed. Wissowa, G. Stuttgart. New edn., 1904, in progress. *(Pauly-Wissowa.) (R.E.)*

Smith, Wm., and Cheetham, S. *Dictionary of Christian Antiquities.* 2 vols. London. 1875–80. *(D.C.A.)*

Smith, Wm., and Wace, Hy. *Dictionary of Christian Biography, Literature, Sects and Doctrines.* 4 vols. London. 1877–87. *(D.C.B.)*

Vacant, A., Mangenot, E., and Amann, É. *Dictionnaire de Théologie catholique.* Paris. 1923, in progress. *(D.T.C.)*

II. Atlases and Geography

Heussi, K., and Mulert, H. *Atlas zur Kirchengeschichte.* Tübingen. 2nd edn. 1919.
Poole, R. L. (ed.). *Historical Altas of Modern Europe.* Oxford. 1902.

III. Collections of Sources

A. Collections of Complete Works

Acta Apostolorum Apocrypha. Edd. Lipsius, K. A. and Bonnet, M. 2 vols. Leipzig. 1891–1903.
Acta Conciliorum Oecumenicorum. Ed. Schwartz, E. Tom. I, *Concilium universale Ephesenum.* 5 vols. Berlin and Leipzig. 1922–30. Tom. II, *Concilium universale Chalcedonense.* 6 vols. Berlin and Leipzig. 1932–38.
Acta Sanctorum Bollandiana. Brussels. 1643–1894. 60 vols. *(A. SS.)*
Codex Gregorianus. Ed. Haenel, G. *(Corpus juris Romani antejustiniani,* Fasc. 2.) Bonn. 1837.
Codex Justinianus. See *Corpus Juris civilis.*
Codex Theodosianus. Edd. Mommsen, Th., and Meyer, P. M. 2 vols. Berlin, 1905.
Corpus Juris civilis. Edd. Krüger, P., and others. 3rd edn. Berlin. 1872–80. (Vol. II. *Codex Justinianus.* 1877.)
Corpus scriptorum christianorum orientalium. Edd. Chabot, J. B., and others. Paris, Rome and Leipzig. 1903ff. *(C.S.C.O.)*
Corpus scriptorum ecclesiasticorum latinorum. Vienna. 1866, in progress. *(C.S.E.L.)*
Corpus scriptorum historiae Byzantinae. Edd. Niebuhr and others. Bonn. 1828–97. *(C.S.H.B.)*
Duchesne, L. *Fastes épiscopaux de l'ancienne Gaule.* 3 vols. Paris. 1894–1915. Vol. I. 2nd edn. Paris. 1907.
Grumel, V. *Le Patriarchat Byzantin.* Séries I. *Les Regestes des Actes du Patriarchat de Constantinople.* Vol. I. *Les Actes des Patriarches.* Fasc. I. *Les Regestes de 381 à 715.* Constantinople. 1932, in progress. *(Regestes.)*
Jaffé, Phil. *Regesta pontificum Romanorum ab condita ecclesia ad annum post Christum natum 1198.* Berlin. 2nd edn. Wattenbach, W. Löwenfeld, S. Kaltenbrunner, F. Ewald, P. 2 vols. *Leipzig.* 1885–88. *(J.E., J.K.)*
Liber Pontificalis. Ed. Duchesne, L. 2 vols. Paris. *(Bibl. des écoles d'Athènes et de Rome.)* 1886–92. *(L.P.)* Vol. I. to 795. Ed. Mommsen, Th., in *M.G.H.* 1898.
Mansi, J. D. *Sacrorum conciliorum collectio.* Florence and Venice. 1759–98. 31 vols. Reprint Martin, J. B., and Petit, L. Paris. 1901, in progress.
Migne, J. P. *Patrologiae cursus completus.* Series graeca. Paris. 1857–66. 161 vols. in 166. *(P.G.)*
Series latina. 221 vols. Paris. 1844–55. Index, 4 vols. 1862–64. *(P.L.)*
Monumenta Germaniae Historica. Edd. Pertz, G. H., Mommsen, Th., and others. Hanover. 1826ff. New edd. in prog., Hanover and Berlin. *(M.G.H.)* Index, 1890.
Auctores Antiquissimi. 14 vols. In many pts. 1876ff. (Auct. ant.) Vols. IX, XI, XIII form *Chronica minora (saec.* IV, V. VI). Ed. Mommsen, Th. 1892–98.
Epistolae. Vol. III.
Gesta pontificum Romanorum. I. 1898.

Libelli de lite imperatorum et pontificum (saec. XI–XII). I–III. 1891ff.
Scriptores rerum Merovingicarum. I–IV. 1885–96.
Monumenta Historica Britannica. Edd. Petri, H., and Sharpe, T. London. 1848. *(Hist. Briton.)*
Müller, C. *Fragmenta Historicorum Graecorum.* 5 vols. Paris. 1841–83 (Vol. V, ii, ed. Langlois, V.). *(F.H.G.)*
Seeck, O. *Regesten der Kaiser und Päpste fur die Jahre 311 bis 476 n. Chr.* Stuttgart. 1919. *(Regesten.)*
Thiel, A. *Epistolae Romanorum pontificum.* One vol. alone publ. Brunsberg. 1868.
Turner, C. H. *Ecclesiae Occidentalis monumenta juris antiq. Canonum et conciliorum Graecorum interpret. Latinae.* Fasc. I, 1, 2; II, 1–4. Oxford. 1899–1939.

Inscriptions

Corpus Inscriptionum Graecarum. Edd. Böckh, A., and others. Berlin. 1828–77. (For Christian inscriptions cf. Vol. IV, part 2, ed. Kirchhoff.)
Diehl, E. *Inscriptiones latinae veteres.* Bonn, etc. 1912.
Margarini, —. *Inscriptiones Sancti Pauli.* Rome. 1654.
Rossi, G. B. de. *Inscriptiones Christianae urbis Romae, VII saeculo antiquiores.* Rome. 1857–88. (2 vols. only publ.)

B. Collections of extracts from Patristic and other authors

Cavallera, F. *Thesaurus doctrinae catholicae ex documentis magisterii ecclesiastici.* Paris. 1920.
Denzinger, H., and Bannwart, C. *Enchiridion symbolorum, definitionum et declarationum de rebus fidei et morum.* 14th and 15th edn. Umberg, J. B. Freiburg im B. 1922. *(Enchiridion.)*
Kirch, C. *Enchiridion fontium historiae ecclesiasticae antiquae.* 4th edn. Freiburg im B. 1923. *(Fontes.)*
Mirbt, C. *Quellen zur Geschichte des Papsttums und des römischen Katholizismus.* 5th edn. Tübingen. 1934. *(Quellen.)*
Rouët de Journel, M. J. *Enchiridion Patristicum, loci SS. patrum, doctorum, scriptorum ecclesiasticorum.* 4th and 5th edn. Freiburg im B. 1922.

IV. Original Authorities

A. Greek and Latin writers

Ambrose. Opera, *P.L.* 14–17. The works are being re-edited by Schenkl, K., in *C.S.E.L.,* Vol. XXXII, etc.
Athanasius. Opera, *P.G.* 25–28.
Augustine. Opera. Ed. Gaume. 11 vols. Paris. 1836. *P.L.* 32–46.
Anti-manichaean writings, ed. Zycha, J. *C.S.E.L.* Vol. XXV, pts. 1 and 2. 1891–92.
Confessions, ed. Knöll, P. *C.S.E.L.,* Vol. XXXIII. 1896.
Epistles, ed. Goldbacher, Al. *C.S.E.L.,* Vols. XXXIV, XLIV, LVII. 1895–1911.
Ausonius. Opera. Edd. Schenkl, C., in *M.G.H.* 1883. Peiper, R. Leipzig. 1886. *P.L.* 19.
Beda. *Historia ecclesiastica gentis anglorum.* Ed. Plummer, C. 2 vols. Oxford. 1896. *P.L.* 90–95.

Boniface I. Epistles. *P.L.* 20.
Canones Apostolorum see *Didaschalia et Constitutiones Apostolorum.*
Cassian. Opera. Ed. Petschenig, M. *C.S.E.L.* Vols. XIII and XVII. 1886–88. *P.L.* 50.
Cassiodorus. *Variarum libri XII.* Ed. Mommsen, Th. *M.G.H.*, Auct. ant., Vol. XII. 1894. *P.L.* 69, 70.
Catalogus Liberianus. Ed. Mommsen, Th. *M.G.H.*, Auct. ant., Vol. IX. Berlin. 1892.
Celestine I. Epistles. *P.L.* 50.
Chronica Gallica a. 452 et 511. *M.G.H.*, Auct. ant., Vol. IX. 1892.
Chronicon pascale. Ed. Dindorf, L. *C.S.H.B.* 2 vols. 1838–39. *P.L.* 92.
Chrysostom, John. *Hom. in Matth.* Ed. Field. Cambridge. 1839. Opera. *P.G.* 47–64.
Claudian. Carmina. Ed. Birt, Th. *M.G.H.* 1892. Rec. Koch, J. Leipzig. 1893.
Clement. Epistle to the Corinthians. Ed. Lightfoot, J. B. London. 1890.
Collectio Arelatensis. Ed. Gundlach, W. *M.G.H.*, *Epp.*, Vol. III.
Collectio Avellana. Epistolae Imperatorum pontificum aliorum, inde ab a. CCCLXVII usque ad DLIII datae, Avellana quae dicitur collectio. Ed. Günther, O. *C.S.E.L.*, Vol. XXXV. 2 pts. 1895–98.
Consularia Constantinopolitana. Ed. Mommsen, Th. *M.G.H.*, Auct. ant., Vol. IX. 1892.
Italica. Ibid.
Cyprian. Opera. Ed. Hartel, G. *C.S.E.L.*, Vol. III. 3 pts. 1868–71.
Cyril of Alexandria. Opera. *P.G.* 68–77. Epistles. *P.G.* 77.
Damasus I. Epistles. *P.L.* 13.
Decretum Gelasianum. See Dobschütz, E. von, in *Bibl.*, V. *P.L.* 59.
Didaschalia et Constitutiones Apostolorum. Ed. Funk, F. X. 2 vols. Paderborn. 1905.
Dionysius Exiguus. Opera. *P.L.* 67.
Epiphanius. Opera. Ed. Holl, K. *G.C.S.* 3 vols. Leipzig. 1915. *P.G.* 41–43.
Eusebius. Opera. Edd. Heikel, I. A., Schwartz, E., and Mommsen, Th. *G.C.S.* Leipzig. 1902–9. *P.G.* 19–24.
Evagrius. *Historia ecclesiastica.* Edd. Bidez, J., and Parmentier, L. London. 1899. *P.G.* 86.
Facundus of Hermia. Opera. *P.L.* 67.
Gennadius of Marseilles. Ed. Richardson, E. C., in *Texte und Untersuchungen.* Vol. XIV. Leipzig. 1896. *P.L.* 58.
Gratian. *Corpus juris canonici.* Ed. Friedberg, Ae. Leipzig. 1879. *P.L.* 187.
Gregory I. *Registrum.* Edd. Ewald, P., and Hartmann, L. M. *M.G.H.*, *Epp.*, Vol. II. Berlin. 1887–99. Opera. *P.L.* 75–79.
Gregory of Nazianzus. Opera. *P.G.* 35–38.
—of Tours. Opera. Edd. Arndt, W., Bonnet, M., Krusch, Br. *M.G.H.*, *Script. rer merov.*, Vol. I. 1885. *P.L.* 71.
Hegemonius. *Acta Archelai.* Ed. Beeson, C. H. *G.C.S.* Leipzig. 1906.
Hieronymus see Jerome.
Hilary, Pope. Epistles. Ed. A. Thiel. Brunsberg. 1868. *P.L.* 58.
Hincmar of Rheims. *De Praedestinatione.* *P.L.* 125.
Humbert, Cardinal. *Adversus Simoniacos.* Ed. Thaner, F. *M.G.H.*, *Libelli de lite*, Vol. I, pp. 95ff. Hanover. 1891.
Idatius (Hydatius). *Chronicon.* Ed. Mommsen, Th. *M.G.H.*, Auct. ant., Vol. XI. 1894.
Ignatius. Epistles. Ed. Lightfoot, J. B. London. 1889.

Innocent I. Epistles. *P.L.* 20
Irenaeus. Opera. Ed. Harvey, W. 2 vols. Cambridge. 1857. *P.G.* 7.
Isidore of Seville. *De officiis ecclesiasticis*. *P.L.* 83.
Jerome. Epistles. Ed. Hilberg, I. *C.S.E.L.*, Vols. LIV–LVI. 1910–12. Opera. *P.L.* 22–30.
Joannes Antiochenus. *Fragmenta*. Ed. Müller, C. *F.H.G.*, Vol. IV, p. 355; Vol. V, p. 27. Paris. 1851–70.
Joannes Diaconus. *Vita Gregorii*. *P.L.* 75.
Joannes Malala. *Chronicon*. Ed. Bekker, I. *C.S.H.B.* Bonn. 1831.
Jordanes. Opera. Ed. Mommsen, Th. *M.G.H.*, Auct. ant., Vol. V, pt. 1. 1882.
Landulphus Sagax. *Historia miscella*. Ed. Muratori, L. A. *Scriptores rer. Ital.*, Vol. I, pt. 1, p. 98. Città di castello. 1900.
Leo I, Pope. Sermons and Epistles. *P.L.* 54. (For modern editions see pp. 511f. above.)
Libellus Precum. See *Collectio Avellana*.
Liberatus. *Breviarium*. *P.L.* 68.
Marcellinus, Comes. *Chronicon*. Ed. Mommsen, Th. *M.G.H.*, Auct. ant., Vol. XI. Berlin. 1894.
Martyrologium Hieronymianum. Edd. Rossi, G. B. de, and Duchesne, L., in *A. SS. (Boll.)*, November, Vol. II. Paris. 1894.
Notitia Dignitatum. Ed. Seeck, O. Berlin. 1876.
Novellae Valentiniani III, Majoriani, etc., see *Codex Theodosianus*.
Optatus Milevitanus. Opera. Ed. Ziwsa, C. *C.S.E.L.*, Vol. XXVI. 1893.
Origen. Opera. Edd. Koetschau, P., Klostermann, E., and others. *G.C.S.* Leipzig. 1899–1930.
Philocalia. Ed. Robinson, J. A. Cambridge. 1893. *P.G.* 11–17.
Orosius, Paulus. *Historiae adversus paganos libri septem*. Ed. Zangemeister, C. *C.S.E.L.*, Vol. V. 1882. *Commonitorium*. Ed. Schepss, G. *C.S.E.L.*, Vol. XVIII. 1889.
Palladius. *Dialogus de vita s. Ioannis Chrysostomi*. *P.G.* 47.
Paulus Diaconus. *Historia Romana*. Ed. Droysen, H. *M.G.H.*, Auct. ant., Vol. II. *Homiliarius*. *P.L.* 95.
Philocalian Kalendar. Ed. Mommsen, Th. *M.G.H.*, Auct. ant., Vol. IX. 1892.
Philostorgius. *Historia ecclesiastica*. Ed. Bidez, J. *G.C.S.* Leipzig. 1913. *P.G.* 65.
Photius. Opera. *P.G.* 102. *(Contra Manichaeos.)*
Pontificale Romanum. Malines. 1895.
Priscillian. Opera. Ed. Schepss, G. *C.S.E.L.*, Vol. XVIII. 1889.
Priscus. *Fragmenta*. Ed. Müller, C. *F.H.G.*, Vol. IV.
Procopius. *De Bello Vandalico*, etc. Ed. Haury, J. 2 vols. Leipzig. 1906. *(C.S.H.B.)*
Prosper Tiro. *Chronicon*. Ed. Mommsen, Th. *M.G.H.*, Auct. ant., Vol. IX. 1892. *P.L.* 51.
Prudentius. *Carmina*, etc. Ed. Dressel, A. Leipzig. 1860. *P.L.* 59, 60.
Prudentius of Troyes. *De Praedestinatione*. *P.L.* 115.
Sacramentarium Gelasianum. Ed. Wilson, H. A. Oxford. 1894.
Sacramentarium Leonianum. Ed. Feltoe, C. L. Cambridge. 1896. *P.L.* 55.
Salvian. *De Gubernatione Dei*. Ed. Pauly, F. *C.S.E.L.*, Vol. VIII. 1883. Ed. Halm, C. *M.G.H.*, Auct. ant., Vol. I. 1878. *P.L.* 53.
Sidonius Apollinaris. Opera. Ed. Krusch, B. *M.G.H.*, Auct. ant., Vol. VIII. Berlin. 1887.
Simplicius. Epistles. See Thiel, A. *Bibl.* III.
Siricius. Epistles. *P.L.* 13.

Socrates. *Historia ecclesiastica.* Ed. Bright, W. Oxford. 1872. *P.G.* 67.
Sozomen. *Historia ecclesiastica.* Ed. Hussey, R. Oxford. 1860. *P.G.* 67.
Statuta ecclesiastica antiqua. P.L. 56, 889ff.
Sulpicius Severus. Opera. Ed. Halm, C. *C.S.E.L.,* Vol. I. 1866.
Synesius. *De Providentia. P.G.* 66
Tertullian. Opera. Edd. Reifferscheid, A., and Wissowa, G. *C.S.E.L.,* Vol. XX. 1890. Ed. Kroymann, E. *C.S.E.L.,* Vol. XLVII. 1906.
Theodore Lector. *Historia ecclesiastica. Fragmenta. P.G.* 86, pt. 1.
Theodore of Mopsuestia. Opera. *P.G.* 66.
Theodoret. *Historia ecclesiastica.* Ed. Parmentier, L. *G.C.S.* Leipzig. 1911. Opera. *P.G.* 80–84.
Theophanes. *Chronographia.* Ed. Classen, J. 2 vols. *C.S.H.B.* 1839–41. Ed. de Boor, C. 2 vols. Leipzig. 1883–35. *P.G.* 108.
Victor Vitensis. *Historia persecutionis (De persecutione vandalica).* Ed. Halm, C. *M.G.H.,* Auct. ant., Vol. VII, pt. 1. Ed. Petschenig, M. *C.S.E.L.,* Vol. VII. 1881.
Victorius (Victorinus). *Canon pascalis.* Ed. Mommsen, Th. *M.G.H.,* Auct. ant., Vol. IX. 1892.
Vigilius. Epistles. See Thiel, A. *Bibl.* III.
Vigilius of Thapsus. *Contra Eutycheten. P.L.* 62.
Zacharias of Mitylene. *Chronicon. P.G.* 85.
Zeitz. Paschal Table. Ed. Mommsen, Th. *M.G.H.,* Auct. ant., Vol. IX. 1892.
Zosimus. *Historia nova.* Ed. Mendelssohn, L. Leipzig. 1887.

B. Oriental writers and documents

Chronicon Edessae. Ed. Hallier, L., in *Texte und Untersuchungen.* Vol. IX, pt. 1. Leipzig. 1892.
Cureton, W. *Kitab almil al* (Manichaean). London. 1842.
Driver, G. R., and Hodgson, L. *The Bazaar of Heracleides* (Nestorius). Eng. Transl. Oxford. 1925.
Ephrem Syrus. Opera. 6 vols. Ed. Assemani, P. Rome. 1732.
Flemming, J. *Die syrische Akten der Raübersynode* in *Abhandlungen der Gött. Gesellschaft der Wissens.* Vol. XV. Berlin. 1917.
Michael the Syrian. *Chronicon* (Syr.). Ed. and transl. French. Chabot, J. B. 3 vols. *C.S.C.O.* Paris. 1899–1910.
Raabe, R. *Vita Petri Iberiae.* Leipzig. 1895.
Theopistus. *Histoire de Dioscore.* Ed. Nau, M. F. *Journal asiatique.* Ser. X, pt. 1. Paris. 1903.

V. Modern Works

A. Works on the History of the Church and Papacy

Babut, E. C. *Le Concile de Turin.* Paris. 1904.
Bardenhewer, O. *Geschichte der altkirchlichen Literatur.* Freiburg in B. Vol. I. 2nd edn. 1913. Vol. II. 2nd edn. 1914. Vol. III. 2nd edn. 1923. Vol. IV. 1st and 2nd edn. 1924. Vol. V. 1932.
Batiffol, P. *Le Catholicisme des origines à S. Léon.* 4 vols. Vol. IV. *Le Siège apostolique.* Paris. 1919–24.
Bright, W. *Age of the Fathers.* 2 vols. London, etc. 1903.
Notes on the Canons of the first four General Councils. 2nd edn. Oxford. 1892.

Bury, J. B. *History of the Later Roman Empire.* 2nd edn. Repr. 2 vols. London. 1931.
The Life of St. Patrick and his place in history. London. 1905.
Butler, Dom C. *The Vatican Council.* 2 vols. London. 1930.
Caspar, E. *Geschichte des Papsttums.* 2 vols alone publ. Tübingen. 1930–33.
Die älteste römische Bischofsliste. Berlin. 1926.
Dill, S. *Roman Society in the last century of the Western Empire.* London. 1898.
Dobschütz, E. von. *Decretum Gelasianum* in *Texte und Untersuchungen.* Vol. XXXVIII, pt. 4. Leipzig. 1912.
Duchesne, L. *Histoire ancienne de l'Église.* Paris. Vol. I. 6th edn. 1911. Vol. II. 4th edn. 1910. Vol. III. 5th edn. 1911.
Dudden, F. H. *The life and times of St. Ambrose.* 2 vols. Oxford. 1935.
Gibbon, E. *The History of the Decline and Fall of the Roman Empire.* 7 vols. Ed. Bury, J. B. London. 1926–29.
Gougaud, Dom L. *Les chrétientés celtiques.* Paris. 1911.
Grisar, H. *History of Rome and the Popes in the Middle Ages.* Eng. transl. ed. Cappadelta, L. 3 vols. London. 1911–12.
Gwatkin, H. M., and Whitney, J. P., edd., and others. *The Cambridge Mediaeval History.* 8 vols. with Atlas. Cambridge. 1911–36. (Vol. I, *The Christian Roman Empire.* Cambridge. 1911.)
Harnack, A. *Geschichte der altchristlichen Litteratur bis Eusebius.* 2 pts. 3 vols. (Pt. 2, Vol. I, *Die Chronologie der Litteratur bis Irenäus.)* Leipzig. 1837.
Hefele, C. J., contin. Hergenröther, J. A. G. *Conciliengeschichte.* New Fr. transl. Leclercq, H. Paris. 1907ff., in progress.
Kidd, B. J. *A History of the Church to* A.D. *461.* 3 vols. Oxford. 1922.
The Roman Primacy to A.D. *461.* London. 1936.
Langen, J. *Geschichte der römischen Kirche.* 4 vols. Vol. I. *Bis zum Pontifikate Leos I.* Bonn. 1881–93.
Le Nain de Tillemont, L. S. de. *Mémoires pour servir à l'histoire ecclésiastique des six premiers siècles.* 15 vols. Brussels. 1693–1707. 2nd edn. 16 vols. Paris. 1701–12. 3rd edn. Venice. 1732.
Leclercq, H. *L'Espagne chrétienne.* Paris. 1906.
Lietzmann, H. *Apollinaris von Laodicaea und seine Schule.* 1 vol. alone publ. Tübingen. 1904.
Petrus und Paulus in Rom. 2nd edn. Berlin-Leipzig. 1927.
Maassen, F. *Geschichte der Quellen und der Litteratur des kanonischen Rechts im Abendlande bis zum Ausgang des Mittelalters.* 1 vol. alone publ. Gratz. 1870.
Martin, P. *Actes du Brigandage d'Ephèse.* Amiens. 1874.
Le pseudosynode connu sous le nom du brigandage d'Ephèse. Paris. 1875.
Milman, H. H. *History of Latin Christianity.* 4th edn. 9 vols. London. 1867.
Puller, F. W. *The Primitive Saints and the See of Rome.* 3rd edn. London, etc. 1900.
Quentin, H. (ed.). *Les Martyrologes historiques du moyen âge.* Paris. 1908.
Rauschen, G. R., and Wittig, J. *Grundriss der Patrologie.* 6th and 7th edn. Freiburg im B. 1921.
Seeck, O. *Geschichte des Untergangs der antiken Welt.* 2nd edn. 6 vols. Berlin. 1898–1921.

Swete, H. B. (ed.). *Essays on the early history of the Church and the Ministry* by various writers. London. 1918.
Tillemont see Le Nain de Tillemont.
Turmel, J. *Histoire du Dogme de la Papauté*. Paris. 1908.
Zeiller, J. *Les Origines chrétiennes dans les provinces danubiennes de l'Empire romain*. Paris. 1918.

B. Works on Christian Doctrine

Galtier, P. *L'Église et la rémission des péchés aux premiers siècles*. Paris. 1932.
Hall, F. J. *Dogmatic Theology*. 10 vols. Vol. VI. *The Incarnation*. 2nd edn. 1921. New York, etc. 1907–22.
Mackintosh, H. R. *The Doctrine of the Person of Jesus Christ*. Edinburgh. 1913.
Mason, A. J. *The Conditions of our Lord's life on earth*. London. 1897.
Mozley, J. K. *The Incarnation* in *Essays Catholic and Critical*. London. 1926.
Raven, C. E. *Jesus and the Gospel of Love*. London. 1931.
Stone, D. *Holy Baptism*. London. 1899.
Tixeront, J. *Histoire des Dogmes*. 3 vols. Paris. Vol. I. 8th edn. 1915. Vol. II. 5th edn. 1912. Vol. III. 4th edn. 1919.
Williams, N. P. *The Ideas of the Fall and of Original Sin*. (Bampton Lectures, 1924.) London. 1927.

C. Works on St. Leo, his pontificate, doctrine, etc.

Amelli, G. *S. Leone magno e l'Oriente*. Montecassino. 1882.
Batiffol, P., in *D.T.C. Léon Ier (Saint) pape*.
Bright, W. *Select Sermons of St. Leo the Great*. Text and Transl. with notes. London. 1886.
Canisius, P. *De vita et rebus gestis S. Leonis*. *P.L.* 55, 183.
Gore, C. *Leo the Great*. London. 1880.
in *D.C.B.* Leo I, Pope.
Kuhn, P. *Die Christologie Leos I d. G. in systematischer Darstellung*. Wurzburg. 1894.
Lietzmann, H., in *Pauly-Wissowa, R.E.* 2nd edn. *Leo I, papst*.
Pschmadt, J. *Leo der Grosse als Prediger*. Elberfeld. 1912.
Saltet. *Le recueil patristique de St. Léon* in *Revue d'histoire ecclésiastique*. Vol. VI. Paris. 1905.
Steeger. *Die Klauseltechnik Leos des G.* 1908.
Turner, C. H. *The collection of the Dogmatic letters of St. Leo* in *Miscellanea Ceriani*. Milan. 1910.

D. Works on Liturgy

Batiffol, P. *History of the Roman Breviary*. Transl. Baylay, A.M.Y. London. 1912.
Baümer, Dom S. *Histoire du Bréviare*. French transl. Biron, Dom R. 2 vols. Paris. 1905.
Clarke, W. K. L., and Harris, C. (edd.). *Liturgy and Worship*. London. 1933.
Duchesne, L. *Origines du culte chrétien*. 1889. Later edns. incl. 4th edn. Paris. 1910.
Freestone, W. H. *The Sacrament Reserved*. (Alcuin Club Collections, XXI.) London, etc. 1917.
Frere, W. H. *Studies in early Roman liturgy*. 2 vols. (Alcuin Club Collections, XXVIII.) London. 1930.

E. Works on Christian heresies, sects, etc.

Alfaric, P. *L'évolution intellectuelle de Saint Augustin.* Paris. 1918.
Les écritures manichéens. Paris. 1918.
Babut, E. C. *Priscillien et le Priscillianisme.* Paris. 1909.
Burkitt, F. C. *The Religion of the Manichees.* Cambridge. 1925.
Cumont, F. *Recherches sur le manichéisme.* 2 fasc. Brussels. 1908–12.
Flügel, G. *Mani, seine Lehre und seine Schriften.* Leipzig. 1862.
Künstle, K. *Antipriscilliana.* Freiburg im B., etc. 1905.
Sachau, C. E. *The Chronology of ancient nations.* London. 1879.

F. Works on Architecture and Topography

Kirsch, J. P. *Die römische Titelkirchen* in *Studien zur Geschichte und Kultur des Altertums.* Vol. IX. Paderborn. 1918.
Lanciani, R. *L'Itinerario.* (Wanderings through ancient Roman churches.) Illustrated. London, etc. 1925.
Pagan and Christian Rome. London. 1892.
Leclercq, H., in *D.A.C. Chalcédoine.*
Mallius, P. *Historia S. Petri basilicae* in *A. SS. (Boll.)* Vol. VI, pt. ii.
Murray, J. *Handbook to Constantinople.* London. 1883.
Richter, O. *Topographie der Stadt Rom.* Munich. 1901.
Rossi, G. B. de. *La Roma sotterranea.* Vol. I. Rome. 1864. Vol. II. 1867. Vol. III. 1877.
Tyrrell-Green, E. *French Church Architecture.* London. 1928.

G. Miscellaneous Monographs and Articles in Periodicals

Bishop, E. *Liturgical Comments and Memoranda* in *J.T.S.* Vol. XI. 1909.
Burn, A. E. *Priscillian and Priscillianism* in *C.Q.R.* Vol. LXXIV. 1912.
Cantarelli, L. *Di un frammento* in *Bullettino della commissione archeologica comunale di Roma.* Ser. IV. Ann. XXIV. Rome. 1896.
Chavannes, E., et Pelliot, P. *Un Traité manichéen* in *Journal asiatique,* Nov.–Dec. Paris. 1911.
Duchesne, L. *Notes sur la topographie de Rome au moyen âge,* pt. 2. *Les titres presbytéraux et les diaconies* in *Mélanges d'archéologie et d'histoire.* Vol. VII. Paris. 1887.
La question de la Pâque au concile de Nicée in *Revue des questions historiques.* Vol. XXVIII, pp. 1–42. Paris. 1880.
Concile de Turin, etc., in *Comptes rendus de l'Academie des inscriptions.* Ser. IV. Vol. XIX, pp. 369ff. Paris. 1891.
Fabricius, C. *Litterae formatae* in *Archiv für Urkundenforschung.* Vol. IX. Leipzig. 1924.
Grisar, H., in *Analecta Romana.* Vol. I. Diss. 14. Cracow. 1894.
Die alte Peterskirche in *Römische Quartalschrift.* Vol. IX, pp. 237ff. Rome. 1895.
Gundlach, W. *Der Streit der Bistümer Arles und Vienne um den Primatus Galliarum* in *Neues Archiv der Gesellschaft für ältere deutsche Geschichtskunde.* Vol. XIV, pp. 251ff.; and Vol. XV, pp. 9ff.; pp. 233ff. Hanover. 1889–90.
Kirsch, J. P. *Die stadtrömische Festkalender im Altertum.* Münster i. W. 1924.
Kissling, W. *Das Verhältnis zwischen Sacerdotium und Imperium.* Paderborn. 1921.
Krusch, B. *Studien zur christlich-mittelalterlich. Chronologie.* Leipzig. 1880.

Mommsen, Th. *Actenstücke zur Kirchengeschichte aus dem Cod. Cap. Novar. 30* in *Neues Archiv. f. alt. deut. Geschichtskunde.* Vol. XI, pp. 364ff. Hanover. 1886.

Morin, Dom G. *Études, textes, découvertes.* Marédsous, etc. (Tamines). 1913.

Nostiss-Reineck. *Die Briefe Papst Leos I im Cod. Mon. 14, 540* in *Historisches Jahrbuch.* Vol. XVIII, pp. 117ff. Munich. 1897.

Rossi, G. B. de, in *Bullettino di archaeologia cristiana.* Vol. XX. Rome. 1882.

Schmid, J. *Die Osterfestberechnung in der abendländischen Kirche.* Freiburg im B. 1908.

Schwartz, E. *Christliche und jüdische Ostertafeln* in *Abhandlungen der Gött. Gesells. d. Wiss. Philolog. historische Klasse. Neue Folge.* Vol. VIII, pt. 6. Berlin. 1905.

Das Nicaenum u. das Constantinopolitanum auf d. Synode von Chalkedon in *Zeitschrift für neutestamentliche Wissenschaft.* Vol. XXV, pp. 38ff. Giessen. 1926.

Vorst, C. van de. *La vie grecque de saint Léon le grand* in *Analecta Bollandiana.* Vol. XXIX, pp. 400–8. 1910.

Willie, A. *Bischof Julian von Kios. Diss. Würzburg.* Kempten. 1909.

Zernov, N. *Eusebius and the Paschal Controversy at the end of the second century* in *C.Q.R.* Vol. CXVI. London. 1933.

INDEX OF SCRIPTURAL PASSAGES QUOTED OR MENTIONED

INDEX OF PAPAL LETTERS QUOTED OR MENTIONED

No references are given in the above Index to letters mentioned by number only in Chap. XXI.

INDEX

PRINTED IN GREAT BRITAIN BY THE FAITH PRESS, LTD., LEIGHTON BUZZARD